PROGRESS IN PSYCHOBIOLOGY

Readings from
**SCIENTIFIC
AMERICAN**

PROGRESS IN PSYCHOBIOLOGY

With Introductions by
Richard F. Thompson
University of California, Irvine

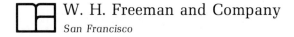 W. H. Freeman and Company
San Francisco

All of the SCIENTIFIC AMERICAN articles in *Progress in Psychobiology* are available as separate Offprints. For a complete list of more than 950 articles now available as Offprints, write to W. H. Freeman and Company, 660 Market Street, San Francisco, California 94104.

Library of Congress Cataloging in Publication Data

Main entry under title:

Progress in psychobiology.

  Bibliography: p.
  Includes index.
  1. Psychobiology—Addresses, essays, lectures.
I. Thompson, Richard Frederick, 1930–   II. Scientific American. [DNLM: 1. Behavior—Collected works. 2. Psychophysiology—Collected works. WL102 P964]
QP360.P758   612′.8   75–42362
ISBN 0–7167–0532–X
ISBN 0–7167–0531–1 pbk.

CONTENTS

PREFACE

This collection of readings from *Scientific American* focuses on new and intriguing developments in the study of brain and behavior. The field of psychobiology, or physiological psychology, is an enormously exciting subject at the very frontier of our understanding of the biological bases of psychology. There is no topic of greater interest to people than themselves and other human beings. The great advances in our understanding of ourselves in recent years have come largely from biological approaches to behavior and experience. Application of the techniques and knowledge of the physical and biological sciences to the study of the nervous system has led us to a much more profound understanding of that most complex of all structures in the known universe: the human brain. We are approaching a much better understanding of many of the basic questions in psychology—the nature of perception, how language is organized, the physical basis of consciousness—through the study of the brain.

This book of readings deliberately emphasizes recent and current topics. Most of the articles have been published in the past five years. A few classic articles are also included, partly because they have not been superseded, but also because they provide excellent introductions and overviews of topics. The articles, prepared by outstanding scientists in many fields ranging from chemistry to psychology, share the important features of clarity and accessibility; they are understandable to an interested reader who may have no special background or training. Characteristic of *Scientific American* is the almost unique way in which work on the forefronts of scientific knowledge is presented with accuracy and, at the same time, in a highly readable and interesting manner.

Psychobiology, or physiological psychology, represents the common ground of psychology and biology. As such, it is incorporated in courses and programs both in biology and in psychology. This reader is designed to meet the needs of students and teachers in both disciplines. It is divided into ten sections, which treat the most important topics in the field. It has been planned to serve either as a text on its own or as a reader to accompany current texts in physiological psychology and psychobiology (see, for example, R. F. Thompson, *Introduction to Physiological Psychology*, Harper & Row, 1975).

The first section presents man in an evolutionary context, dealing specifically with evolution and human behavior, including the critically important issue of current human evolution. Section II focuses on the genetic and developmental roots of behavior. Analysis of the behaviors of simple organisms—insects, for example—has led to genuine breakthroughs in our understanding of the genetic mechanisms of behavior. In the behavior of more complex animals—birds and mammals—the roles of genetics and experience are intertwined in much more complex ways. Study of the development of behavior, both in the field and in the laboratory, helps us to understand these factors and to clarify the process of development itself.

Section III reviews the basic processes of information conduction and transfer in nerve cells—processes that depend on the axon and the synapse. These are the basic mechanisms underlying integration and plasticity in the brain. The activity of the brain as a whole can be studied by recording the EEG. Basic processes of the EEG and the changes in brain activity that occur in the states of waking and sleep are also reviewed in Section III.

The chemistry of the brain is a field of rapid progress today. Section IV reviews our current knowledge of synaptic transmitters—the chemical messengers that convey information from one nerve cell to the next. Hormones, another critical component of the chemistry of brain and behavior are also treated, as are the action of psychologically active drugs—the hallucinogens.

The biological basis of sensory processes is treated in Section V. We have limited the topic to processes of vision, partly because progress has been so rapid here and also because it would require too much space to deal adequately with all the sensory systems. Movement-control systems are reviewed in Section VI. Much recent progress has been made in our understanding of brain systems controlling the actual movements that constitute our behavior. Section VII treats perception, the higher integration of sensory and motor processes in the brain that results in our sensing the world as we do.

The key problem of brain substrates of learning and memory is treated in Section VIII. There are four major approaches to the psychobiology of learning: use of simplified model neuronal systems, chemical studies, anatomical studies, and analysis of electrophysiological processes. All approaches are represented here. Perhaps the most important and the most complex learning is that required for human language. Communication and brain substrates of language are treated in Section IX. Finally, Section X deals with the most complex human brain processes: attention, consciousness, and thought.

A brief bibliography is provided at the end of the book that should be of help to those desiring to pursue a topic further. Cross-references within the articles are consistent with the following conventions: A reference to an article included in this book is noted by the title of the article and the page on which it begins; a reference to an article that is available as a *Scientific American* Offprint, but is not included here, is noted by the article's title and Offprint number; and a reference to an article published by *Scientific American*, but not available as an Offprint, is noted by the title of the article and the month and year of its publication.

June 1975   *Richard F. Thompson*

PROGRESS IN PSYCHOBIOLOGY

EVOLUTION AND HUMAN BEHAVIOR

I   EVOLUTION AND HUMAN BEHAVIOR

INTRODUCTION

Human beings are biological organisms that have striking similarities in structure, function, and even behavioral patterns to other animals, particularly to other primates. Indeed, *Homo sapiens*, the modern form of human being, is very recent. We appeared in our present form only about 50,000 years ago. This is not such a very long time. If you were to trace your ancestral tree back more than one or two thousand generations, your ancestors would begin to look distinctly nonhuman. Our ancestors began to diverge from other primate lines several million years ago. During most of the vast period of time from then up until the emergence of civilization as we know it today, perhaps 10,000 years ago, the overwhelmingly powerful forces of natural selection shaped man as a food-gathering and hunting primate. Indeed, man is the most awesomely successful species, some would even say carnivorous hunter, ever to appear on the face of the earth. Our evolutionary past has shaped our present behavior. Of this there can be no dispute. However, which aspects of evolutionary pressure resulted in present human behavior and brain structure is a much more complicated question. A successful hunter may be successful not simply because he is big and powerful, but rather because he belongs to a well-organized society that has and uses an excellent communication system—a kind of system whose model *par excellence* may be human language.

An old debate in evolution concerned the development of the human brain. One extreme view, now clearly known to be untrue, was that an apelike creature somehow developed a very large brain, then stood up and started making tools. This was not the case. In the first article, written by Sherwood L. Washburn ("Tools and Human Evolution"), the evolution of *Homo sapiens* is considered in the light of the development of tool use. It is clear that the earliest manlike apes with upright posture still had very small apelike brains and their use of tools was limited. From this point on, the development of tools and the rapid enlargement of the brain seemed to go hand in hand. Thus, the *Australopithecus*, whose remains were discovered by L. S. B. and Mary Leakey in Africa, used very crude pebble tools more than a million years ago. As Washburn emphasizes, the development of the human brain was gradual and the result of interaction with the development of certain human traits—the increased use of hands, particularly the thumb, and the increased mental powers associated with social organization, and, perhaps most important, with language. The human aspects of human nature did not develop by accident, they developed because they possessed survival value.

Washburn's article, written in 1960, is a classic in the field; relatively little has changed in our understanding of the broad picture of human evolution since that time. However, more recent discoveries of fossil hominid skulls have pushed the time-span back somewhat. In the next article ("The Casts of Fossil Hominid Brains"), Ralph L. Holloway reviews this very recent evidence on the development of the human brain in the course of human evolution. He notes that even the *Australopithecus* brain was not simply an ape brain; it had begun to show some hint of the enlargements of certain areas that would later form the speech areas in a modern human brain. In agreement with Washburn, Holloway emphasizes the fact that the development of social behavior and language are among the most critical elements of human evolution.

This section closes with the classic article by Theodosius Dobzhansky entitled "The Present Evolution of Man." We tend to forget the fact that human evolution did not stop with the development of the first human civilization. It is still proceeding. However, the forces currently acting in human evolution are quite different from the forces that must have acted in the environment of early primitive man. As Dobzhansky emphasizes, a key concept in considerations of human evolution is "fitness," which means reproductive success. A primitive *Homo sapien* who is large and powerful enough—perhaps because of a mutation—to kill a sabertoothed tiger with his bare hands might be considered very fit to survive. However, if he has no offspring and cannot transmit this important mutation to others of the species, he has no biological fitness whatever. Fitness is what influences the development of the species and is measured by the number of offspring. Consequently, to view possible current trends in evolution we must examine those forces or influences that lead to a greater or lesser number of offspring. A particularly striking example of current human evolution in America relates to sickle-cell anemia. Many American blacks whose ancestors came from the malaria belts of Africa have sickle-cell genes. These genes are adaptive where malaria is endemic because the person carrying a sickle-cell gene has some resistance to malaria. However, the gene clearly confers no adaptive value in the United States today. Possessing the genes leads to a decrease in the number of viable offspring. As a consequence, the incidence of sickle-cell anemia among American blacks is decreasing. Dobzhansky discusses the issues relating to the present evolution of man and indicates some of the directions in which mankind is still evolving.

Tools and Human Evolution

by Sherwood L. Washburn
September 1960

*Presenting a series of articles on the human species,
with special reference to its origins. It is now clear
that tools antedate man, and that their use
by prehuman primates gave rise to Homo sapiens*

A series of recent discoveries has linked prehuman primates of half a million years ago with stone tools. For some years investigators had been uncovering tools of the simplest kind from ancient deposits in Africa. At first they assumed that these tools constituted evidence of the existence of large-brained, fully bipedal men. Now the tools have been found in association with much more primitive creatures, the not-fully bipedal, small-brained near-men, or man-apes. Prior to these finds the prevailing view held that man evolved nearly to his present structural state and then discovered tools and the new ways of life that they made possible. Now it appears that man-apes—creatures able to run but not yet walk on two legs, and with brains no larger than those of apes now living—had already learned to make and to use tools. It follows that the structure of modern man must be the result of the change in the terms of natural selection that came with the tool-using way of life.

The earliest stone tools are chips or simple pebbles, usually from river gravels. Many of them have not been shaped at all, and they can be identified as tools only because they appear in concentrations, along with a few worked pieces, in caves or other locations where no such stones naturally occur. The huge advantage that a stone tool gives to its user must be tried to be appreciated. Held in the hand, it can be used for pounding, digging or scraping. Flesh and bone can be cut with a flaked chip, and what would be a mild blow with the fist becomes lethal with a rock in the hand. Stone tools can be employed, moreover, to make tools of other materials. Naturally occurring sticks are nearly all rotten, too large, or of inconvenient shape; some tool for fabrication is essential for the efficient use of wood. The utility of a mere pebble seems so limited to the user of modern tools that it is not easy to comprehend the vast difference that separates the tool-user from the ape which relies on hands and teeth alone. Ground-living monkeys dig out roots for food, and if they could use a stone or a stick, they might easily double their food supply. It was the success of the simplest tools that started the whole trend of human evolution and led to the civilizations of today.

From the short-term point of view, human structure makes human behavior possible. From the evolutionary point of view, behavior and structure form an interacting complex, with each change in one affecting the other. Man began when populations of apes, about a million years ago, started the bipedal, tool-using way of life that gave rise to the man-apes of the genus *Australopithecus*. Most of the obvious differences that distinguish man from ape came after the use of tools.

The primary evidence for the new view of human evolution is teeth, bones and tools. But our ancestors were not fossils; they were striving creatures, full of rage, dominance and the will to live. What evolved was the pattern of life of intelligent, exploratory, playful, vigorous primates; the evolving reality was a succession of social systems based upon the motor abilities, emotions and intelligence of their members. Selection produced new systems of child care, maturation and sex, just as it did alterations in the skull and the teeth. Tools, hunting, fire, complex social life, speech, the human way and the brain evolved together to produce ancient man of the genus *Homo* about half a million years ago. Then the brain evolved under the pressures of more complex social life until the species *Homo sapiens* appeared perhaps as recently as 50,000 years ago.

With the advent of *Homo sapiens* the tempo of technical-social evolution quickened. Some of the early types of tool had lasted for hundreds of thousands of years and were essentially the same throughout vast areas of the African and Eurasian land masses. Now the tool forms multiplied and became regionally diversified. Man invented the

STENCILED HANDS in the cave of Gargas in the Pyrenees date back to the Upper Paleolithic of perhaps 30,000 years ago. Aurignacian man made the images by placing hand against wall and spattering it with paint. Hands stenciled in black (*top*) are more distinct and apparently more recent than those done in other colors (*center*).

6

OLDUVAI GORGE in Tanganyika is the site where the skull of the largest known man-ape was discovered in 1959 by L. S. B. Leakey and his wife Mary. Stratigraphic evidence indicates that skull dates back to Lower Pleistocene, more than 500,000 years ago.

bow, boats, clothing; conquered the Arctic; invaded the New World; domesticated plants and animals; discovered metals, writing and civilization. Today, in the midst of the latest tool-making revolution, man has achieved the capacity to adapt his environment to his need and impulse, and his numbers have begun to crowd the planet.

The later events in the evolution of the human species are treated in other articles in the September 1960 issue of SCIENTIFIC AMERICAN. This article is concerned with the beginnings of the process by which, as Theodosius Dobzhansky says in "The Present Evolution of Man" [*page 29*], biological evolution has transcended itself. From the rapidly accumulating evidence it is now possible to speculate with some confidence on the manner in which the way of life made possible by tools changed the pressures of natural selection and so changed the structure of man.

Tools have been found, along with the bones of their makers, at Sterkfontein, Swartkrans and Kromdraai in South Africa and at Olduvai in Tanganyika. Many of the tools from Sterkfontein are merely unworked river pebbles, but someone had to carry them from the graveis some miles away and bring them to the deposit in which they are found. Nothing like them occurs naturally in the local limestone caves. Of course the association of the stone tools with man-ape bones in one or two localities does not prove that these animals made the tools. It has been argued that a more advanced form of man, already present, was the toolmaker. This argument has a familiar ring to students of human evolution. Peking man was thought too primitive to be a toolmaker; when the first manlike pelvis was found with man-ape bones, some argued that it must have fallen into the deposit because it was too human to be associated with the skull. In every case, however, the repeated discovery of the same unanticipated association has ultimately settled the controversy.

This is why the discovery by L. S. B. and Mary Leakey in the summer of 1959 is so important. In Olduvai Gorge in Tanganyika they came upon traces of an old living site, and found stone tools in clear association with the largest man-ape skull known. With the stone tools were a hammer stone and waste flakes from the manufacture of the tools. The deposit also contained the bones of rats, mice, frogs and some bones of juvenile pig and antelope, showing that even the largest and latest of the

SKULL IS EXAMINED *in situ* by Mary Leakey, who first noticed fragments of it protruding from the cliff face at left. Pebble tools were found at the same level as the skull.

SKULL IS EXCAVATED from surrounding rock with dental picks. Although skull was badly fragmented, almost all of it was recovered. Fragment visible here is part of upper jaw.

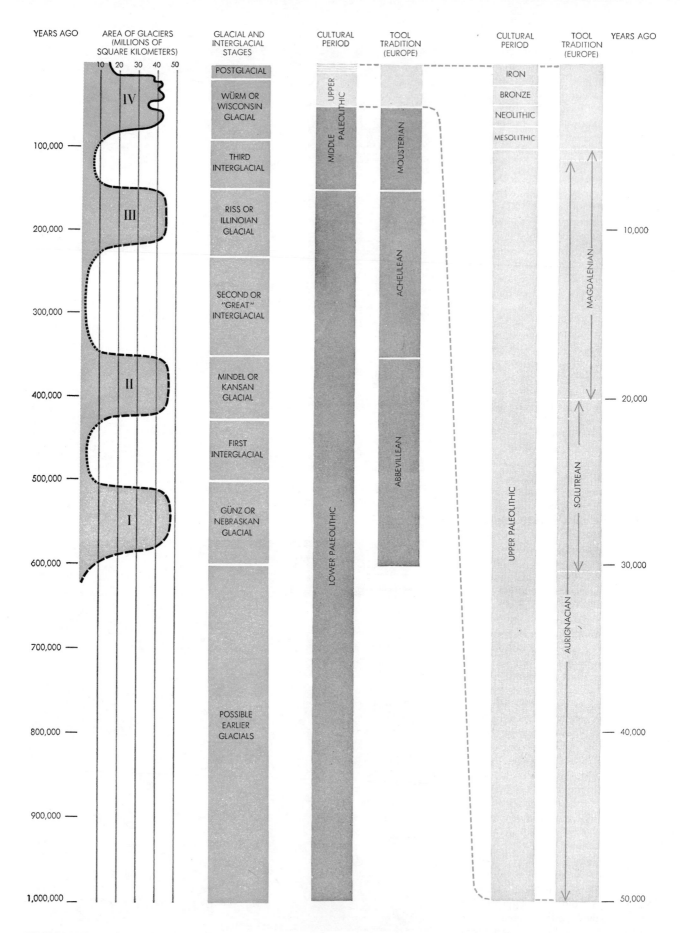

YEARS AGO	AREA OF GLACIERS (MILLIONS OF SQUARE KILOMETERS)	GLACIAL AND INTERGLACIAL STAGES	CULTURAL PERIOD	TOOL TRADITION (EUROPE)	CULTURAL PERIOD	TOOL TRADITION (EUROPE)	YEARS AGO

TIME-SCALE correlates cultural periods and tool traditions with the four great glaciations of the Pleistocene epoch. Glacial advances and retreats shown by solid black curve are accurately known; those shown by broken curve are less certain; those shown by dotted curve are uncertain. Light gray bars at far right show an expanded view of last 50,000 years on two darker bars at center. Scale was prepared with the assistance of William R. Farrand of the Lamont Geological Observatory of Columbia University.

man-apes could kill only the smallest animals and must have been largely vegetarian. The Leakeys' discovery confirms the association of the man-ape with pebble tools, and adds the evidence of manufacture to that of mere association. Moreover, the stratigraphic evidence at Olduvai now for the first time securely dates the man-apes, placing them in the lower Pleistocene, earlier than 500,000 years ago and earlier than the first skeletal and cultural evidence for the existence of the genus Homo [see illustration on next two pages]. Before the discovery at Olduvai these points had been in doubt.

The man-apes themselves are known from several skulls and a large number of teeth and jaws, but only fragments of the rest of the skeleton have been preserved. There were two kinds of man-ape, a small early one that may have weighed 50 or 60 pounds and a later and larger one that weighed at least twice as much. The differences in size and form between the two types are quite comparable to the differences between the contemporary pygmy chimpanzee and the common chimpanzee.

Pelvic remains from both forms of man-ape show that these animals were bipedal. From a comparison of the pelvis of ape, man-ape and man it can be seen that the upper part of the pelvis is much wider and shorter in man than in the ape, and that the pelvis of the man-ape corresponds closely, though not precisely, to that of modern man [see top illustration on page 13]. The long upper pelvis of the ape is characteristic of most mammals, and it is the highly specialized, short, wide bone in man that makes possible the human kind of bipedal locomotion. Although the man-ape pelvis is apelike in its lower part, it approaches that of man in just those features that distinguish man from all other animals. More work must be done before this combination of features is fully understood. My belief is that bipedal running, made possible by the changes in the upper pelvis, came before efficient bipedal walking, made possible by the changes in the lower pelvis. In the man-ape, therefore, the adaptation to bipedal locomotion is not yet complete. Here, then, is a phase of human evolution characterized by forms that are mostly bipedal, small-brained, plains-living, tool-making hunters of small animals.

The capacity for bipedal walking is primarily an adaptation for covering long distances. Even the arboreal chimpanzee can run faster than a man, and any monkey can easily outdistance him.

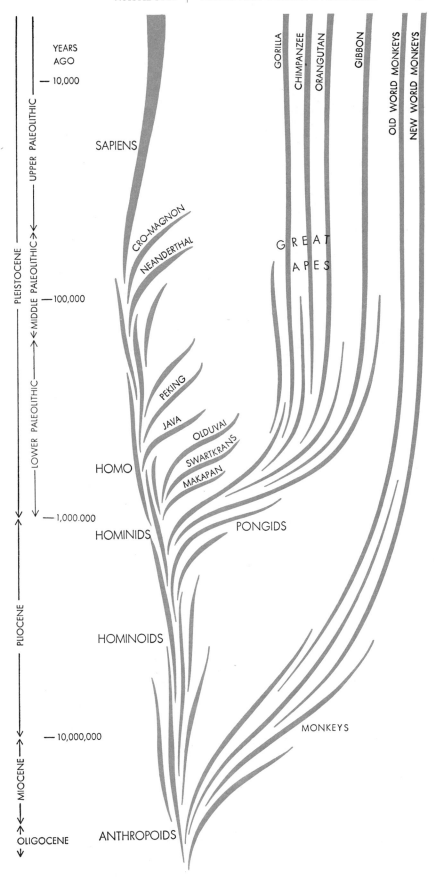

LINES OF DESCENT that lead to man and his closer living relatives are charted. The hominoid superfamily diverged from the anthropoid line in the Miocene period some 20 million years ago. From the hominoid line came the tool-using hominids at the beginning of the Pleistocene. The genus *Homo* appeared in the hominid line during the first interglacial (*see chart on opposite page*); the species *Homo sapiens*, around 50,000 years ago.

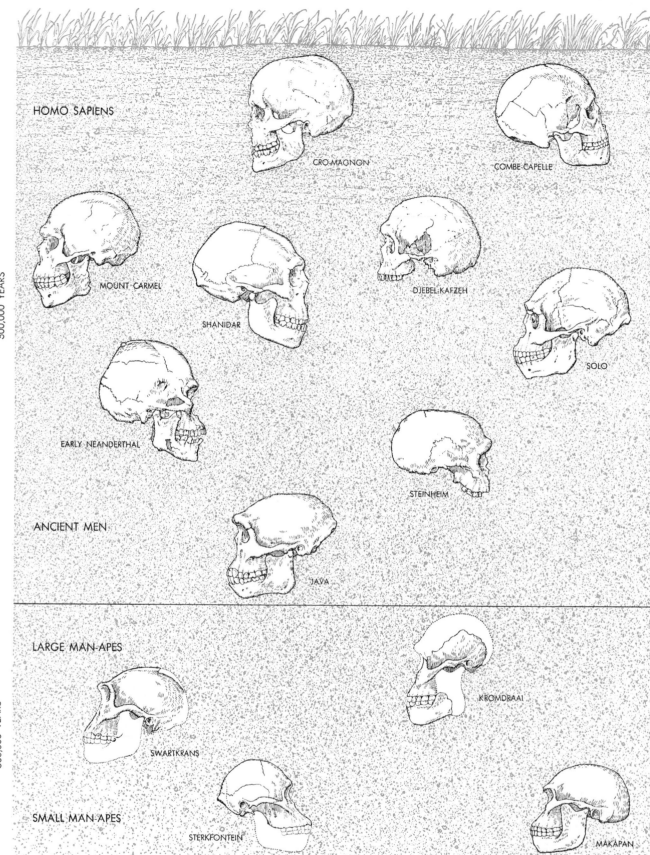

HOMO SAPIENS

CRO-MAGNON

COMBE-CAPELLE

MIDDLE AND UPPER PLEISTOCENE
500,000 YEARS

MOUNT CARMEL

SHANIDAR

DJEBEL-KAFZEH

SOLO

EARLY NEANDERTHAL

STEINHEIM

ANCIENT MEN

JAVA

LOWER PLEISTOCENE
500,000 YEARS

LARGE MAN-APES

KROMDRAAI

SWARTKRANS

SMALL MAN-APES

STERKFONTEIN

MAKAPAN

FOSSIL SKULLS of Pleistocene epoch reflect transition from man-apes (*below black line*) to *Homo sapiens* (*top*). Relative age of intermediate specimens is indicated schematically by their posi-

tion on page. Java man (*middle left*) and Solo man (*upper center*) are members of the genus *Pithecanthropus*, and are related to Peking man (*middle right*). The Shanidar skull (*upper left*) be-

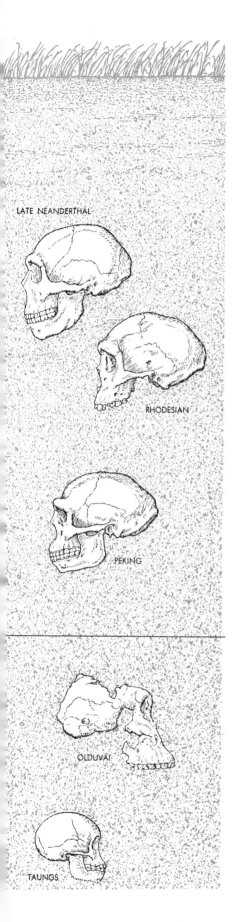

LATE NEANDERTHAL

RHODESIAN

PEKING

OLDUVAI

TAUNGS

longs to the Neanderthal family, while Mount Carmel skull shows characteristics of Neanderthal and modern man.

A man, on the other hand, can walk for many miles, and this is essential for efficient hunting. According to skeletal evidence, fully developed walkers first appeared in the ancient men who inhabited the Old World from 500,000 years ago to the middle of the last glaciation. These men were competent hunters, as is shown by the bones of the large animals they killed. But they also used fire and made complicated tools according to clearly defined traditions. Along with the change in the structure of the pelvis, the brain had doubled in size since the time of the man-apes.

The fossil record thus substantiates the suggestion, first made by Charles Darwin, that tool use is both the cause and the effect of bipedal locomotion. Some very limited bipedalism left the hands sufficiently free from locomotor functions so that stones or sticks could be carried, played with and used. The advantage that these objects gave to their users led both to more bipedalism and to more efficient tool use. English lacks any neat expression for this sort of situation, forcing us to speak of cause and effect as if they were separated, whereas in natural selection cause and effect are interrelated. Selection is based on successful behavior, and in the man-apes the beginnings of the human way of life depended on both inherited locomotor capacity and on the learned skills of tool-using. The success of the new way of life based on the use of tools changed the selection pressures on many parts of the body, notably the teeth, hands and brain, as well as on the pelvis. But it must be remembered that selection was for the whole way of life.

In all the apes and monkeys the males have large canine teeth. The long upper canine cuts against the first lower premolar, and the lower canine passes in front of the upper canine. This is an efficient fighting mechanism, backed by very large jaw muscles. I have seen male baboons drive off cheetahs and dogs, and according to reliable reports male baboons have even put leopards to flight. The females have small canines, and they hurry away with the young under the very conditions in which the males turn to fight. All the evidence from living monkeys and apes suggests that the male's large canines are of the greatest importance to the survival of the group, and that they are particularly important in ground-living forms that may not be able to climb to safety in the trees. The small, early man-apes lived in open plains country, and yet none of them had large canine teeth. It would appear that the protection of the group must have shifted from teeth to tools early in the evolution of the man-apes, and long before the appearance of the forms that have been found in association with stone tools. The tools of Sterkfontein and Olduvai represent not the beginnings of tool use, but a choice of material and knowledge in manufacture which, as is shown by the small canines of the man-apes that deposited them there, derived from a long history of tool use.

Reduction in the canine teeth is not a simple matter, but involves changes in the muscles, face, jaws and other parts of the skull. Selection builds powerful neck muscles in animals that fight with their canines, and adapts the skull to the action of these muscles. Fighting is not a matter of teeth alone, but also of seizing, shaking and hurling an enemy's body with the jaws, head and neck. Reduction in the canines is therefore accompanied by a shortening in the jaws, reduction in the ridges of bone over the eyes and a decrease in the shelf of bone in the neck area [see illustration on page 14]. The reason that the skulls of the females and young of the apes look more like man-apes than those of adult males is that, along with small canines, they have smaller muscles and all the numerous structural features that go along with them. The skull of the man-ape is that of an ape that has lost the structure for effective fighting with its teeth. Moreover, the man-ape has transferred to its hands the functions of seizing and pulling, and this has been attended by reduction of its incisors. Small canines and incisors are biological symbols of a changed way of life; their primitive functions are replaced by hand and tool.

The history of the grinding teeth— the molars—is different from that of the seizing and fighting teeth. Large size in any anatomical structure must be maintained by positive selection; the selection pressure changed first on the canine teeth and, much later, on the molars. In the man-apes the molars were very large, larger than in either ape or man. They were heavily worn, possibly because food dug from the ground with the aid of tools was very abrasive. With the men of the Middle Pleistocene, molars of human size appear along with complicated tools, hunting and fire.

The disappearance of brow ridges and the refinement of the human face may involve still another factor. One of the essential conditions for the organi-

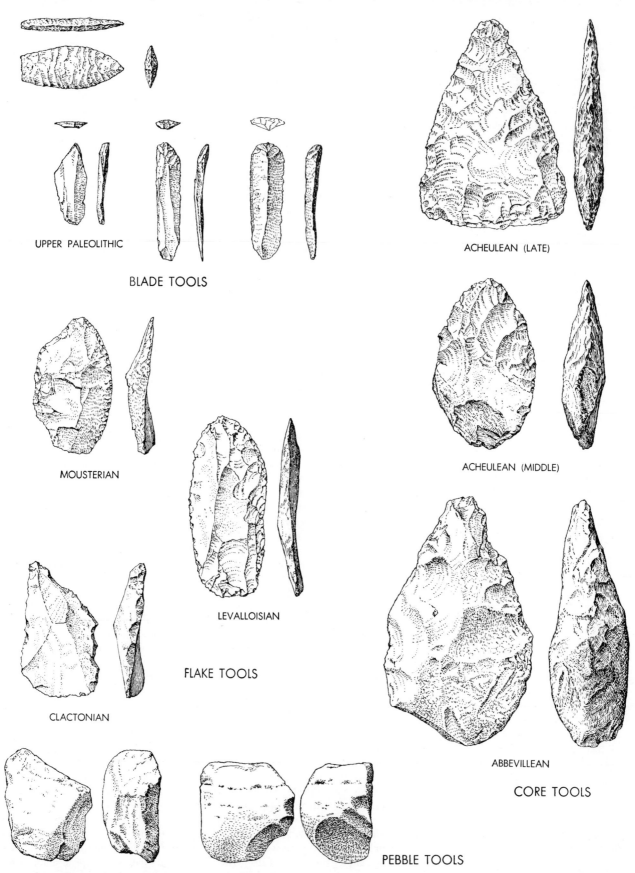

UPPER PALEOLITHIC

BLADE TOOLS

ACHEULEAN (LATE)

MOUSTERIAN

LEVALLOISIAN

FLAKE TOOLS

ACHEULEAN (MIDDLE)

CLACTONIAN

ABBEVILLEAN

CORE TOOLS

PEBBLE TOOLS

TOOL TRADITIONS of Europe are the main basis for classifying Paleolithic cultures. The earliest tools are shown at bottom of page; later ones, at top. The tools are shown from both the side and the edge, except for blade tools, which are shown in three views. Tools consisting of a piece of stone from which a few flakes have been chipped are called core tools (*right*). Other types of tool were made from flakes (*center and left*); blade tools were made from flakes with almost parallel sides. Tool traditions are named for site where tools of a given type were discovered; Acheulean tools, for example, are named for St. Acheul in France.

zation of men in co-operative societies was the suppression of rage and of the uncontrolled drive to first place in the hierarchy of dominance. Curt P. Richter of Johns Hopkins University has shown that domestic animals, chosen over the generations for willingness to adjust and for lack of rage, have relatively small adrenal glands. But the breeders who selected for this hormonal, physiological, temperamental type also picked, without realizing it, animals with small brow ridges and small faces. The skull structure of the wild rat bears the same relation to that of the tame rat as does the skull of Neanderthal man to that of *Homo sapiens*. The same is true for the cat, dog, pig, horse and cow; in each case the wild form has the larger face and muscular ridges. In the later stages of human evolution, it appears, the self-domestication of man has been exerting the same effects upon temperament, glands and skull that are seen in the domestic animals.

Of course from man-ape to man the brain-containing part of the skull has also increased greatly in size. This change is directly due to the increase in the size of the brain: as the brain grows, so grow the bones that cover it. Since there is this close correlation between brain size and bony brain-case, the brain size of the fossils can be estimated. On the scale of brain size the man-apes are scarcely distinguishable from the living apes, although their brains may have been larger with respect to body size. The brain seems to have evolved rapidly, doubling in size between man-ape and man. It then appears to have increased much more slowly; there is no substantial change in gross size during the last 100,000 years. One must remember, however, that size alone is a very crude indicator, and that brains of equal size may vary greatly in function. My belief is that although the brain of *Homo sapiens* is no larger than that of Neanderthal man, the indirect evidence strongly suggests that the first *Homo sapiens* was a much more intelligent creature.

The great increase in brain size is important because many functions of the brain seem to depend on the number of cells, and the number increases with volume. But certain parts of the brain have increased in size much more than others. As functional maps of the cortex of the brain show, the human sensory-motor cortex is not just an enlargement of that of an ape [see illustrations on last three pages of this article]. The areas

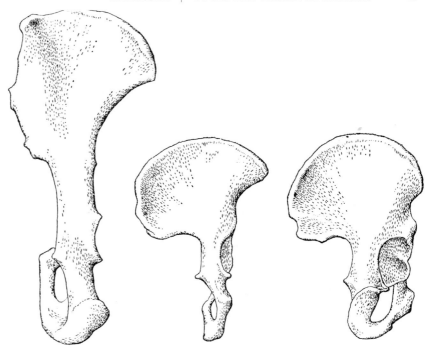

HIP BONES of ape (*left*), man-ape (*center*) and man (*right*) reflect differences between quadruped and biped. Upper part of human pelvis is wider and shorter than that of apes. Lower part of man-ape pelvis resembles that of ape; upper part resembles that of man.

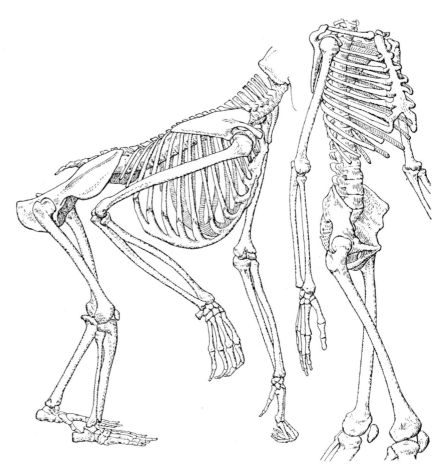

POSTURE of gorilla (*left*) and man (*right*) is related to size, shape and orientation of pelvis. Long, straight pelvis of ape provides support for quadrupedal locomotion; short, broad pelvis of man curves backward, carrying spine and torso in bipedal position.

14

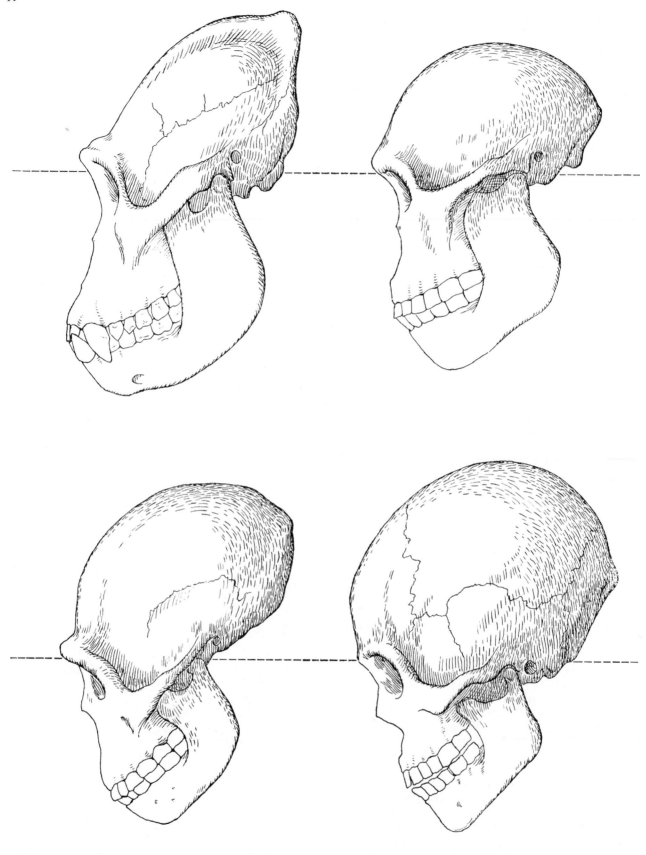

EVOLUTION OF SKULL from ape (*upper left*) to man-ape (*upper right*) to ancient man (*lower left*) to modern man (*lower right*) involves an increase in size of brain case (*part of skull above broken lines*) and a corresponding decrease in size of face (*part of skull below broken lines*). Apes also possess canine teeth that are much larger than those found in either man-apes or man.

for the hand, especially the thumb, in man are tremendously enlarged, and this is an integral part of the structural base that makes the skillful use of the hand possible. The selection pressures that favored a large thumb also favored a large cortical area to receive sensations from the thumb and to control its motor activity. Evolution favored the development of a sensitive, powerful, skillful thumb, and in all these ways —as well as in structure—a human thumb differs from that of an ape.

The same is true for other cortical areas. Much of the cortex in a monkey is still engaged in the motor and sensory functions. In man it is the areas adjacent to the primary centers that are most expanded. These areas are concerned with skills, memory, foresight and language; that is, with the mental faculties that make human social life possible. This is easiest to illustrate in the field of language. Many apes and monkeys can make a wide variety of sounds. These sounds do not, however, develop into language [see "The Origin of Speech," by Charles F. Hockett; SCIENTIFIC AMERICAN Offprint 603]. Some workers have devoted great efforts, with minimum results, to trying to teach chimpanzees to talk. The reason is that there is little in the brain to teach. A human child learns to speak with the greatest ease, but the storage of thousands of words takes a great deal of cortex. Even the simplest language must have given great advantage to those first men who had it. One is tempted to think that language may have appeared together with the fine tools, fire and complex hunting of the large-brained men of the Middle Pleistocene, but there is no direct proof of this.

The main point is that the kind of animal that can learn to adjust to complex, human, technical society is a very different creature from a tree-living ape, and the differences between the two are rooted in the evolutionary process. The reason that the human brain makes the human way of life possible is that it is the result of that way of life. Great masses of the tissue in the human brain are devoted to memory, planning, language and skills, because these are the abilities favored by the human way of life.

The emergence of man's large brain occasioned a profound change in the plan of human reproduction. The human mother-child relationship is unique among the primates as is the use of tools. In all the apes and monkeys the baby clings to the mother; to be able to do so,

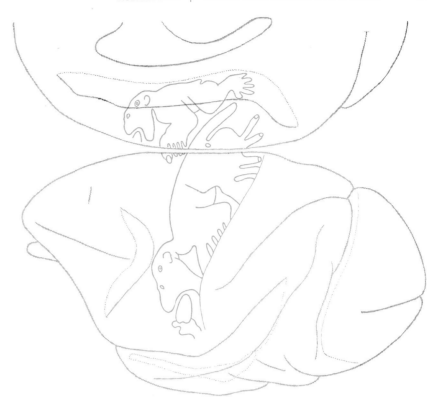

MOTOR CORTEX OF MONKEY controls the movements of the body parts outlined by the superimposed drawing of the animal (*color*). Gray lines trace the surface features of the left half of the brain (*bottom*) and part of the right half (*top*). Colored drawing is distorted in proportion to amount of cortex associated with functions of various parts of the body. Smaller animal in right half of brain indicates location of secondary motor cortex.

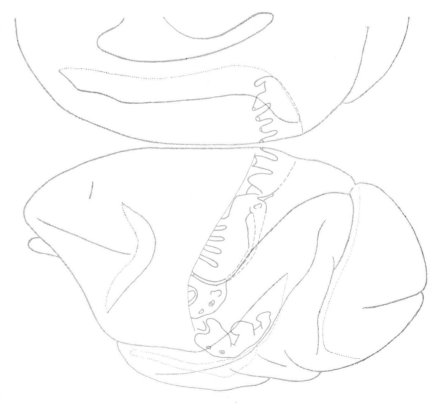

SENSORY CORTEX OF MONKEY is mapped in same way as motor cortex (*above*). As in motor cortex, a large area is associated with hands and feet. Smaller animal at bottom of left half of brain indicates location of secondary sensory cortex. Drawings are based on work of Clinton N. Woolsey and his colleagues at the University of Wisconsin Medical School.

the baby must be born with its central nervous system in an advanced state of development. But the brain of the fetus must be small enough so that birth may take place. In man adaptation to bipedal locomotion decreased the size of the bony birth-canal at the same time that the exigencies of tool use selected for larger brains. This obstetrical dilemma was solved by delivery of the fetus at a much earlier stage of development. But this was possible only because the mother, already bipedal and with hands free of locomotor necessities, could hold the helpless, immature in-

fant. The small-brained man-ape probably developed in the uterus as much as the ape does; the human type of mother-child relation must have evolved by the time of the large-brained, fully bipedal humans of the Middle Pleistocene. Bipedalism, tool use and selection for large brains thus slowed human development and invoked far greater maternal responsibility. The slow-moving mother, carrying the baby, could not hunt, and the combination of the woman's obligation to care for slow-developing babies and the man's occupation of hunting imposed a fundamental pat-

tern on the social organization of the human species.

As Marshall D. Sahlins suggests ["The Origin of Society," SCIENTIFIC AMERICAN Offprint 602], human society was heavily conditioned at the outset by other significant aspects of man's sexual adaptation. In monkeys and apes year-round sexual activity supplies the social bond that unites the primate horde. But sex in these species is still subject to physiological—especially glandular—controls. In man these controls are gone, and are replaced by a bewildering variety of social customs. In no other primate does

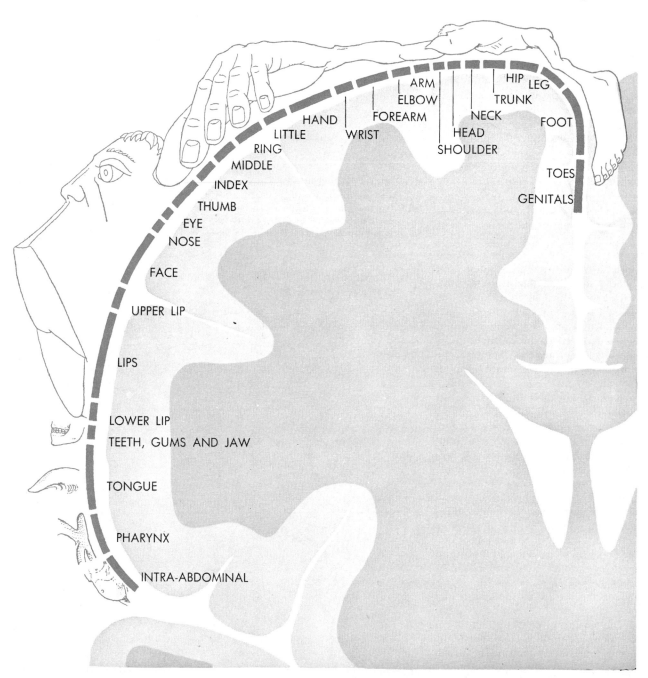

SENSORY HOMUNCULUS is a functional map of the sensory cortex of the human brain worked out by Wilder Penfield and his associates at the Montreal Neurological Institute. As in the map of the sensory cortex of the monkey that appears on the preceding page, the distorted anatomical drawing (*color*) indicates the areas of the sensory cortex associated with the various parts of the body.

a family exist that controls sexual activity by custom, that takes care of slow-growing young, and in which—as in the case of primitive human societies—the male and female provide different foods for the family members.

All these family functions are ultimately related to tools, hunting and the enlargement of the brain. Complex and technical society evolved from the sporadic tool-using of an ape, through the simple pebble tools of the man-ape and the complex toolmaking traditions of ancient men to the hugely complicated culture of modern man. Each behavioral

stage was both cause and effect of biological change in bones and brain. These concomitant changes can be seen in the scanty fossil record and can be inferred from the study of the living forms.

Surely as more fossils are found these ideas will be tested. New techniques of investigation, from planned experiments in the behavior of lower primates to more refined methods of dating, will extract wholly new information from the past. It is my belief that, as these events come to pass, tool use will be found to have been a major factor, beginning with

the initial differentiation of man and ape. In ourselves we see a structure, physiology and behavior that is the result of the fact that some populations of apes started to use tools a million years ago. The pebble tools constituted man's principal technical adaptation for a period at least 50 times as long as recorded history. As we contemplate man's present eminence, it is well to remember that, from the point of view of evolution, the events of the last 50,000 years occupy but a moment in time. Ancient man endured at least 10 times as long and the man-apes for an even longer time.

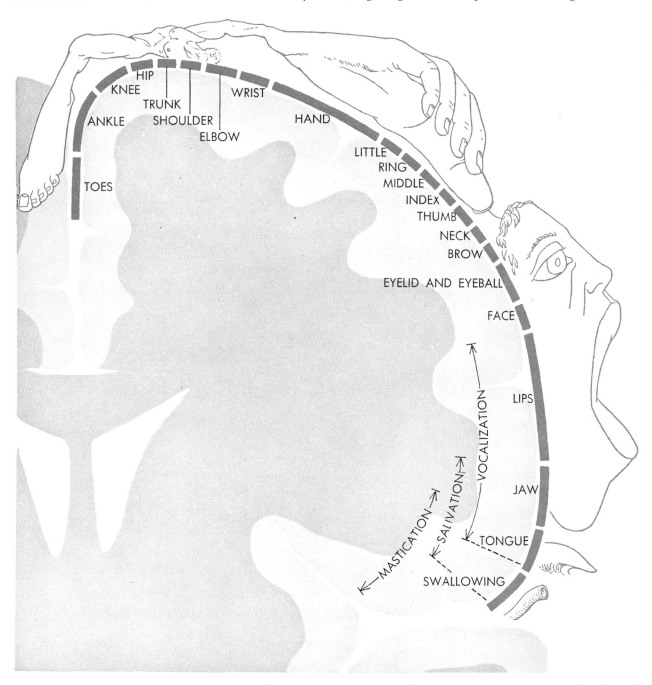

MOTOR HOMUNCULUS depicts parts of body and areas of motor cortex that control their functions. Human brain is shown here in coronal (ear-to-ear) cross section. Speech and hand areas of both motor and sensory cortex in man are proportionately much larger than corresponding areas in apes and monkeys, as can be seen by comparing homunculi with diagram of monkey cortex.

2

The Casts of Fossil Hominid Brains

by Ralph L. Holloway
July 1974

The skulls of man and his precursors can be used as molds to make replicas of the brain. These casts indicate that man's brain began to differ from that of other primates some three million years ago

Man is not the largest of the primates (the gorilla is larger), but he has the largest brain. How did this come about? The question is hardly a new one, but a considerable amount of new evidence is now available to those in search of the answer. In brief the evidence suggests that, contrary to what is widely believed, the human brain was not among the last human organs to evolve but among the first. Neurologically speaking, brains whose organization was essentially human were already in existence some three million years ago.

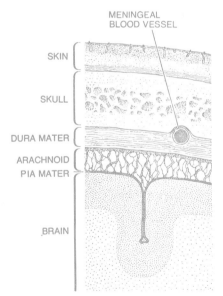

MENINGEAL
BLOOD VESSEL

SKIN

SKULL

DURA MATER

ARACHNOID
PIA MATER

BRAIN

LAYERS OF TISSUE lie between the surface of the brain and the cranium. They include the pia mater, the arachnoid tissue that contains the cerebrospinal fluid, and the thick dura mater. Meningeal blood vessels (*color*) often leave a clear imprint on the inner surface of the cranium. The sutures of the cranial bones may also show, but among higher primates the convolutions of the cerebral cortex are not often apparent.

The brain is the most complex organ in the primate body or, if one prefers, the most complex set of interacting organs. It consists of a very large number of interconnected nuclei and fiber systems, and its cells number in the billions. With certain exceptions, however, the cortex, or upper layer, of one primate brain exhibits much the same gross morphology as the cortex of another, regardless of the animals' relative taxonomic status. Whether the animal is a prosimian (for example a lemur), a monkey, a pongid (an ape) or a hominid (a member of the family that includes the genus *Homo*), what varies from one primate brain to another is not so much the appearance of the cortex as the fraction of its total area that is devoted to each of the major cortical subdivisions. For instance, whereas the chimpanzee is taxonomically man's closest living primate relative and the brains of both look much alike superficially, the chimpanzee brain is significantly different from the human brain in the relative size and shape of its frontal, temporal, parietal and occipital lobes. The differences are reflected in the different position of the sulci, or furrows, that mark the boundaries between lobes, and in the differently shaped gyri, or convolutions, of the lobes themselves.

The comparative neurology of living primates can of course cast only the most indirect light on human brain evolution. After all, the living representatives of each primate line have reached their own separate evolutionary pinnacle; their brains do not "recapitulate" the evolutionary pathway that man has followed. The neurological evidence is nonetheless invaluable in another respect. It is the only source of information linking aspects of gross brain morphology with aspects of behavior. The results of a great many primate studies allow some valid generalizations on this subject. For example, it is well established that the occipital lobe of the cortex, at the back of the brain, is involved in vision. The parietal lobe is involved in sensory integration and association, the frontal lobe in motor behavior and the more complex aspects of adaptive behavior, and the temporal lobe in memory. It is the interactions among these gross cortical divisions, and also among the subcortical nuclei and fiber tracts, that organize coordinated behavior.

It is also a valid generalization to say that a gross brain morphology which emphasizes relatively small temporal and parietal lobes and a relatively large area of occipital cortex is neurologically organized in the pongid mode and is thus representative of the apes' line of evolutionary advance. Conversely, a gross morphology that emphasizes a reduced area of occipital cortex, particularly toward the sides of the brain, and an enlarged parietal and temporal cortex is hominid in its neurological organization. It follows that any evidence on the neurological organization of early primates, including hominids and putative hominids, is of much importance in tracing the evolution of the human brain.

Such evidence is of three kinds: direct, indirect and inferential. The only direct evidence comes from the study of endocranial casts, that is, either a chance impression of a skull interior that is preserved in fossil form or a contemporary man-made replica of the interior of a fossil skull. The indirect evidence is of two kinds. The first is a by-product of endocranial studies; it consists of the conclusions that can be drawn from a comparison of brain sizes. To draw conclusions of this kind, however, can involve some degree of acceptance of the

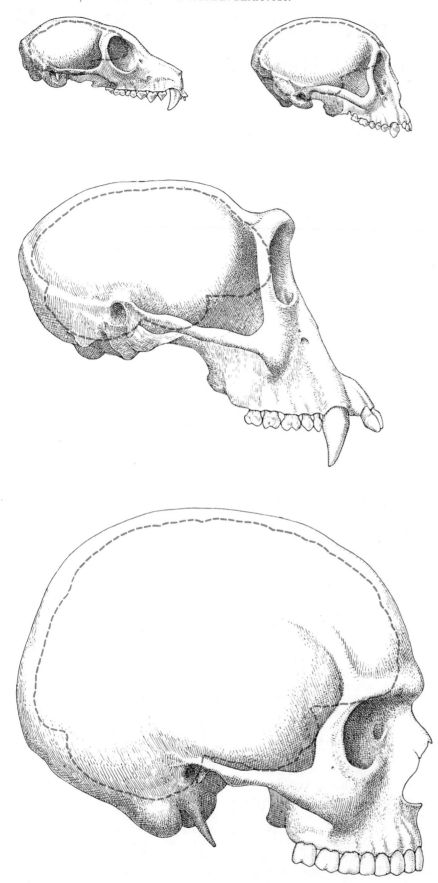

INCREASE IN BRAIN SIZE among primates is apparent in the different dimensions of the skull of a prosimian (*top left*), a New World monkey (*top right*), a great ape (*second from bottom*) and modern man (*bottom*). The brains (*color*) of the latter three are illustrated on the opposite page; skulls are reproduced at approximately half actual size.

questionable premise that there is a correlation between brain size and behavioral capacity. The second kind of indirect evidence comes from the study of other fossil remains: primate hand and foot bones, limb bones, pelvises, vertebral components, jaws and teeth. From these noncranial parts conclusions can be drawn about body size and behavioral capabilities such as bipedal locomotion, upright posture, manual dexterity and even mastication. Various patterns of musculoskeletal organization, of course, reflect matching variations in neurological organization.

Finally there is inferential evidence, particularly with respect to early hominid evolution. This can be described as fossilized behavior. The inferential evidence includes stone tools that exhibit various degrees of standardization (suggesting "cultural norms") and bone debris that reveals what animals the hominids selected as their prey. Any evidence of activity provides some grounds for inference about the general state of the individuals' neurological organization. Our concern here, however, will be with the direct endocranial evidence and with a part of the indirect evidence.

The convolutions of the cerebral cortex and its boundary furrows are kept from leaving precise impressions on the internal bony table of the skull by the brain's surrounding bath of cerebrospinal fluid and by such protective tissues as the pia mater, the arachnoid tissue and the dura mater, or outer envelope. In mammals the extent of masking varies from species to species and with the size and age of the individual. The skull interiors of apes and men, both living and fossil, are notable for bearing only a minimal impression of the brain surface. In virtually all cases the only detailed features that can be traced on the endocranial cast of a higher primate are the paths of the meningeal blood vessels. Depending on the fossil's state of preservation, however, even a relatively featureless cast will reveal at least the general proportions and shape of the brain. This kind of information can be indicative of a pongid neurological organization or a hominid one.

Just how far back in time can the distinction between pongid and hominid brains be pursued? There is a barrier represented by the key Miocene primate fossil *Ramapithecus*: no skull of the animal has been discovered. *Ramapithecus* flourished some 12 million to 15 million years ago both in Africa and in Asia. Elwyn L. Simons and David Pilbeam of Yale University have proposed that it is a hominid, but its only known remains are teeth and fragments of jaws. For the present we must make do with more numerous, although still rare, primate skulls that are many millions of years more recent.

The first of these skulls became known in 1925, when Raymond A. Dart of the University of Witwatersrand described the fossilized remains of a subadult primate that had been discovered in a limestone quarry at Taung in South Africa. The find consisted of a broken lower jaw, an upper jaw, facial bones, a partial cranium and a natural endocranial cast [see illustrations on page 25]. In the half-century since Dart named the specimen Australopithecus, or "southern ape," seven other skulls of Australopithecus (six of them internally measurable) have been found in South Africa and from three to six more in East Africa.

"Three to six" refers not to any uncertainty about how many skulls have been found but to how they are to be assigned to one or another genus or species of hominid. For example, the genus Australopithecus consists of two species: A. africanus, the "gracile," or lightly built, form to which the Taung fossils belong, and A. robustus, a larger, more heavily built species [see illustration on page 26]. Of the eight South African skulls, six are gracile, one is robust and the eighth (a specimen from Makapansgat designated MLD 1) is not definitely assigned to either species. In the same way three of the East African skulls are unanimously assigned to the robust species of Australopithecus. The other three, designated Homo habilis by their discoverers, Louis and Mary Leakey, are classed with the gracile species by some students of the subject, but they are still generally known by the name the Leakeys gave them. As will become apparent, there are grounds for preserving the distinction.

Fortunately, no matter what controversy may surround the question of how these early African hominids are related to one another, it has very little bearing on the question of their neurological development. The reason is that in each instance where an endocast is available, whether the skull is less than a million years old or more than two million years old, the brain shows the distinctive pattern of hominid neurological organization. Let us review the cortical landmarks that distinguish between the pongids and the hominids. Starting with the frontal lobe, the Australopithecus endocasts show a more hominid pattern in the third inferior frontal gyrus, being larger and more convoluted than endo-

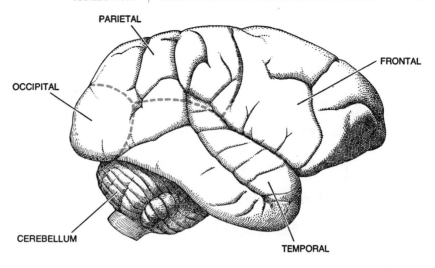

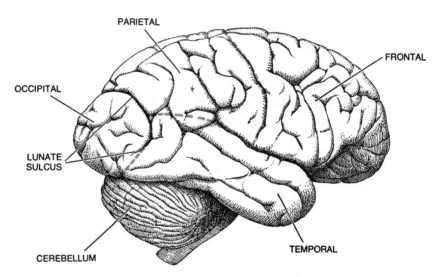

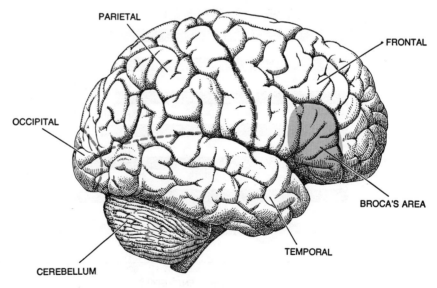

GROSS DIFFERENCES in the neurological organization of three primate brains are apparent in the size of the cerebral components of a ceboid monkey (*top*), a chimpanzee (*middle*) and modern man (*bottom*). The small occipital lobe and the large parietal and temporal lobes in man, compared with the other primates, typify the hominid pattern. Lunate sulcus, or furrow (*color*), on the chimpanzee's brain bounds its large occipital lobe.

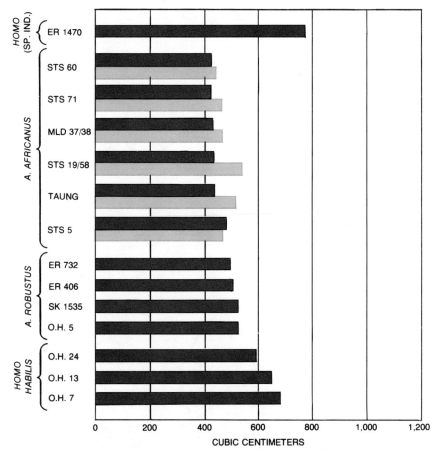

ABSOLUTE BRAIN SIZES varied both among and between the four earliest African hominid species. The 14 specimens are shown here in order of increasing brain volume, except for the earliest of all: the three-million-year-old specimen from East Rudolf, ER 1470, at the head of the list. The other abbreviations stand for Sterkfontein (STS), Makapansgat (MLD), Olduvai hominid (O.H.) and Swartkrans (SK). Double bars show former (*color*) and present calculated brain sizes of six specimens; the Taung volumes are adult values.

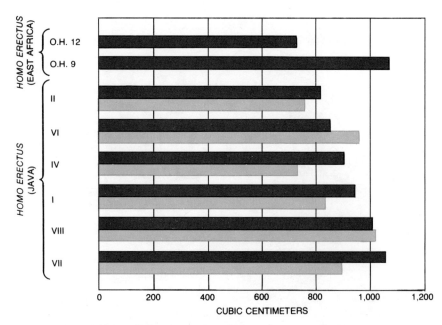

LATER HOMINID'S BRAINS were larger both on the average and absolutely, with the exception of one doubtful specimen from Olduvai Gorge. Shown here are the brain volumes for the seven certain specimens and one doubtful specimen of *Homo erectus*; two are from East Africa and six are from Java. Double bars show former (*color*) and present calculated brain sizes of the Java specimens. Casts of other *H. erectus* brains are not available.

casts of pongid brains of the same size. The orbital surface of their frontal lobes displays a typically human morphology rather than being marked by the slender, forward-pointing olfactory rostrum of the pongid. The height of the brain, from the anterior tips of the temporal lobes to the summit of the cerebral cortex, is proportionately greater than it is in pongids, suggesting an expansion of the parietal and temporal lobes and a more "flexed" cranium. Moreover, the temporal lobes and particularly their anterior tips show the hominid configuration and not the pongid one.

Another landmark of neurological organization provides further evidence, in part negative. This is the lunate sulcus, the furrow that defines the boundary between the occipital cortex and the adjacent parietal cortex. In all ape brains the lunate sulcus lies relatively far forward on the ascending curve of the back of the brain. The position is indicative of an enlarged occipital lobe. In modern man, when the lunate sulcus appears at all (which is in fewer than 10 percent of cases), it lies much closer to the far end of the occipital pole. On those *Australopithecus* endocasts where the feature can be located, the lunate sulcus is found in the human position, which indicates that the (perhaps associative) parietal lobes of the *Australopithecus* brain were enlarged far beyond what is the pongid norm.

It may seem surprising that *Australopithecus*, a genus that has only in recent years been granted hominid status on other anatomical grounds, should have an essentially human brain. It has certainly been a surprise to those who view the human brain as a comparatively recent product of evolution. The finding is not, however, the only surprise of this kind. The most remarkable new fossil primate discovery in Africa is the skull known formally as ER 1470, found by Richard Leakey and his colleagues in the region east of Lake Rudolf in Kenya in 1972. The fossil is nearly three million years old.

Through the courtesy of its discoverer I recently made an endocranial cast of ER 1470. Two facts were immediately apparent. Not only had the skull contained a brain substantially larger than the brain of either the gracile or the robust species of *Australopithecus* (and that of *Homo habilis* too) but also this very ancient and relatively large brain was essentially human in neurological organization. Leakey's find pushes the history of hominid brain evolution back in time at least as far as the shadowy

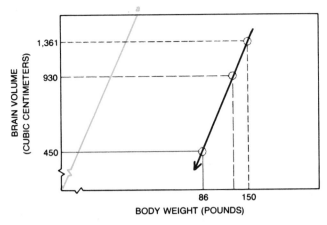

ALLOMETRIC GROWTH EQUATIONS with different exponential slopes are tested against known data in this group of graphs. A known average body weight of 150 pounds for modern man, combined with a known average brain volume of 1,361 cubic centimeters, is tested against a slope of 1.9 (*a, color*); the slope appears as a straight line on the double-log plot. At a brain volume of 450 c.c., the *Australopithecus* average, a projected body weight of 86 pounds is heavier than estimates of *Australopithecus* weight allow.

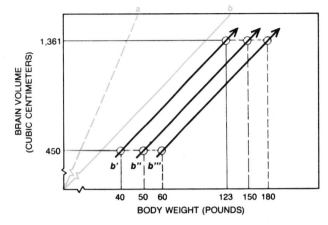

LESS RADICAL SLOPE, 1.0 (*b, color*), is tested in this graph against three different estimates of the average body weight of *Australopithecus:* 40 pounds, 50 pounds and 60 pounds. Where the parallel exponential slopes intersect the average cranial capacity for modern man (*b', b'', b'''*) only the 50-pound body weight estimated for *Australopithecus* yields a projected body weight for man that agrees with the known average. An *Australopithecus* body weight much above or below 50 pounds thus appears improbable.

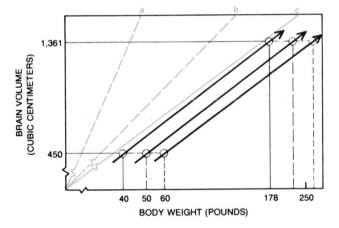

STILL A THIRD SLOPE, .66 (*c, color*), which is usually the most favorable allometric rate for mammals, is tested against the same three *Australopithecus* body-weight estimates. The .66 slope proves clearly unsuited to hominids. When even the minimum weight for *Australopithecus* is projected, the predicted weight for modern man is excessive; added weight yields even more grotesque results.

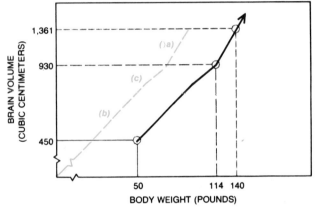

COMBINATION OF SLOPES tests the assumption that hominid rates of growth differed at different times. The zigzag predicts a plausible 114-pound body weight for *Homo erectus* with an average-size brain (930 c.c.) and a body weight for modern man not far below average. The implication is that rates of growth probably did vary, thereby varying selection pressures for changes in brain size.

boundary between the Pliocene and Pleistocene eras.

To summarize the direct evidence of the endocasts, it is now clear that primates with essentially human brains existed some three million years ago. Let us go on to see what details, if any, the indirect evidence of brain size can add to this finding. Here it is necessary, however, to state an important qualification. So far as modern man is concerned, at least, no discernible association between brain size and behavior can be demonstrated. On the average, to be sure, *Homo sapiens* is a big-brained primate. What is sometimes forgotten, however, is that the human average embraces

some remarkable extremes. The "normal" sapient range is from 1,200 cubic centimeters to 1,800, but nonpathological brains that measure below 1,000 c.c. and above 2,000 are not uncommon. Moreover, this range of more than 1,000 c.c. is in itself greater than the average difference in brain size between *Australopithecus* and *H. sapiens*.

As to how such variations may affect behavior, it is probably sufficient to note that the brains of Jonathan Swift and Ivan Turgenev exceeded 2,000 c.c. in volume, whereas Anatole France made do with 1,000 c.c. Clearly the size of the human brain is of less importance than its neurological organization. This con-

clusion is supported by studies of pathology. For example, microcephaly is a disease characterized by the association of a body of normal size with an abnormally small brain. The brain may have a volume of 600 c.c., which is smaller than some gorilla brains. (The gorilla average is 498 c.c., and brains almost 200 c.c. larger have been measured.) Humans with microcephaly are quite subnormal in intelligence, but they still show specifically human behavioral patterns, including the capacity to learn language symbols and to utilize them.

I have recently made complete or partial endocasts of 15 early fossil hominids from South and East Africa. These

SQUIRREL MONKEY	1:12
PORPOISE	1:38
HOUSE MOUSE	1:40
TREE SHREW	1:40
MODERN MAN	1:45
MACAQUE	1:170
GORILLA	1:200
ELEPHANT	1:600
BLUE WHALE	1:10,000

WEIGHT OF THE BRAIN, expressed as a proportion of the total body weight, varies widely among mammals. In spite of his large brain modern man is far from showing the highest proportional brain weight. The proportional weight for man, however, is greater than that of other higher primates. So too, it appears, was the proportional weight for the hominid predecessors of modern man.

endocasts, together with natural ones, have allowed me to calculate the specimens' brain size [see top illustration on page 22]. Leaving aside for the moment two specimens from Olduvai Gorge (one of them certainly *Homo erectus* and the other possibly so), my findings are as follows. First, the brains of most of the South African specimens were substantially smaller than had previously been calculated. Of the six gracile specimens of *Australopithecus* from South Africa none had brains that exceeded 500 c.c. in volume, and most were well below 450 c.c. In contrast, none of the four specimens of the robust *Australopithecus* species had a brain volume of less than 500 c.c. Moreover, two of the four, the one from South Africa and one from East Africa, had brains measuring 530 c.c. Of the three representatives of *Homo habilis*, all from Olduvai, the one with the smallest brain was hominid No. 24, with a possibly overestimated cranial capacity of 590 c.c. The brains of the other two respectively measured 650 c.c. and 687 c.c.

Now, one reason—perhaps the main reason—students of human evolution were so slow to accept *Australopithecus africanus* as a hominid, even though Dart had emphasized the manlike appearance of the Taung endocast from the first, was that its estimated cranial capacities were so small. The brains of some apes, particularly the brains of gorillas, were known to be larger. In fact, as we now know, the brains of the gracile species of *Australopithecus* are even smaller than was originally thought. Since it is now also evident that the *Australopithecus* brains were essentially human in neurological organization, what are we to make of their surprisingly small size? The answer, it seems to me, is that in all likelihood the size of *Australopithecus'* brain bore the same proportional relation to the size of its body that modern man's brain does to his body.

This contention cannot be proved beyond doubt on the basis of the *Australopithecus* fossils known today. One can estimate body weight on the basis of known height, but the height of both the gracile and the robust species must also be estimated, on the basis of an imperfect sample of limb bones. Even though guesswork is involved, however, it is still possible to estimate various body weights and relate each of these guesses to the species' known brain size. One can then see how the results compare with the known brain-to-body ratio among the other mammals, particularly the primates.

The exponential relation between variations in overall body size and in the size of a specific organ, known technically as allometry, has been studied for nearly a century, so that the brain-to-body ratio is well known for a number of animals [see illustration on this page]. The brain-to-body ratio of modern man is not first among mammals; various marine mammals, led by the porpoise *Tursiops*, rank higher than man. So does one small primate, the ceboid squirrel monkey. However, among the hominoids, that is, the subdivision of primates that includes both the apes and man, modern man's brain-to-body ratio does rank first. Depending to some extent on what weight estimate one accepts for *Australopithecus*, this early hominid appears to have enjoyed a position similar to modern man's.

Thanks to Heinz Stephan and his colleagues at the Max Planck Institute for Brain Research in Frankfurt, an assessment of the relation between brain size and body size has become available that is subtler than simple allometry. Stephan's group has been collecting quantitative data with respect to animal brains for many years. The size and weight of various parts of the brain are measured, and these measurements are related to similar measurements of the animals' entire brain and body. One outcome of the work has been the development of what Stephan calls a progression index. It is the ratio between an animal's brain weight and what the brain weight would have been if the animal had belonged to another species with the same body dimensions. As their standard in this comparison Stephan and his colleagues use the brain-to-body ratio of "basal insectivores" such as the tree shrew, which are representative of the original stock from which all the primates evolved.

When the progression index is calculated for modern man, assuming an average body weight of 150 pounds and an average cranial capacity of 1,361 c.c., the resulting index value is 28.8. If different body weights are used with the same average cranial capacity and vice versa, the range of progression indexes for modern man extends from a minimum of 19.0 to a maximum of 53.0. It is interesting to compare the range of the human progression indexes with the indexes of other primates, including those based on estimated brain-to-body ratios for the two species of *Australopithecus*. For example, the maximum progression index for chimpanzees is 12.0. If one works the formula backward and assumes a chimpanzeelike progression index for the gracile species of *Australopithecus*, using an average cranial capacity of 442 c.c., the required body weight turns out to be about 100 pounds. That is nearly twice the maximum estimated weight for the species.

If one uses the same average cranial capacity and assumes that the body weight of the gracile species was only 40 pounds, the progression index is 21.4, which is well within the human range and comfortably close to the human average. When the body weight of the gracile species is estimated at 50 and 60 pounds and the body weight of the robust species is estimated at 60 and 75 pounds, the resulting progression indexes also fall close to or within the human range.

To recapitulate, both the direct evidence of neurological organization and the indirect evidence of comparative brain size appear to indicate that *Australopithecus* and at least one other African primate of the period from three million to one million years ago had brains that were essentially human in organization and that *Australopithecus* was also probably within the human range of sizes with respect to the proportion of the brain to the body. That the brain was small in absolute size, particularly in the gracile species of *Australopithecus*, therefore seems to be without significance. The ratio of brain size to body was appropriate. So far as the subsequent absolute cranial enlargement is concerned, the major mechanism involved, although surely not the only one, appears to have been that as hominids grew larger in body their brains enlarged proportionally. Quite possibly this ex-

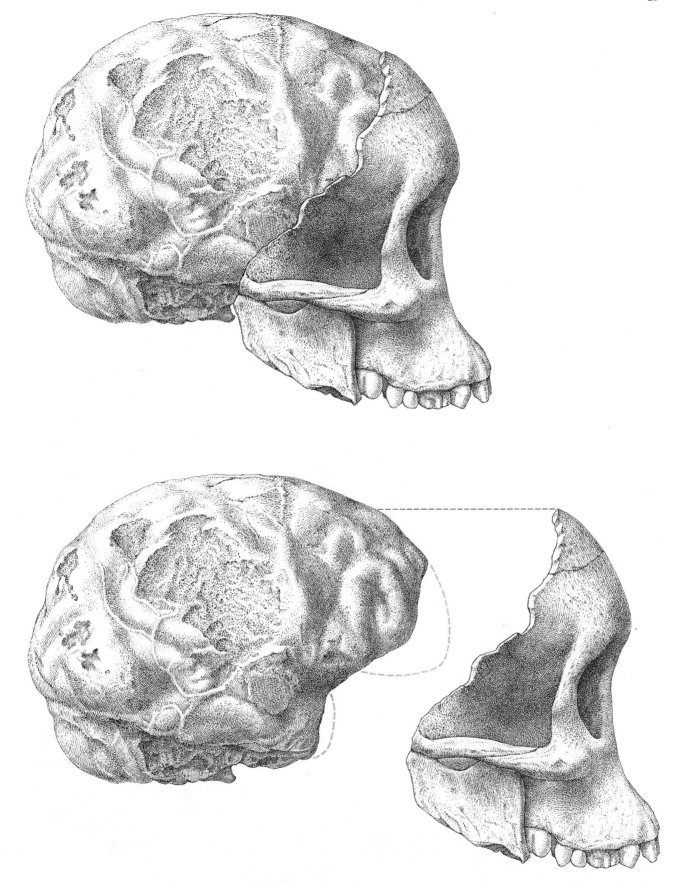

TAUNG JUVENILE, the first specimen of *Australopithecus* to be unearthed, is shown in the top drawing with a portion of the fossilized skull (including the facial bones, the upper jaw and a part of the lower jaw) in place on the natural cast of its brain. The cast is seen separately in the bottom drawing; parts of the frontal and temporal lobes that were not preserved are indicated. The estimated brain volume of an adult of this lineage, once calculated at about 525 cubic centimeters, has now been scaled down to 440 c.c.

pansion progressed at different rates at
different times [*see illustrations on page
23*]. In any event, for at least the past
three million years there has been no
kind of cranial Rubicon waiting to be
crossed.

Considering the gaps in the primate
fossil record, it is remarkable that so
many specimens of a hominid intermediate between the earliest African fossil
forms and modern man have been unearthed. The intermediate form is *Homo
erectus*. The skulls and fragmentary
postcranial remains of that species have
been found at various sites in China and
in Java, and more fossils are steadily being turned up in both areas. There is also
one specimen (and possibly a second)
from Olduvai and, depending on one's
choice of authorities, one from southern
Africa, one from eastern Europe and
perhaps two from northern Africa. With
the possible exception of the Olduvai
and Java fossils, no *H. erectus* specimen
is much more than 500,000 years old,
and one or more may be a great deal
younger.

I have made endocasts of five of the
six available *H. erectus* specimens from
Java and of both the certain Olduvai
specimen and the doubtful one. The
erectus fossil with the largest cranial capacity is Olduvai hominid No. 9; its
brain measures 1,067 c.c. Omitting the
doubtful Olduvai specimen, the *erectus*
fossil with the smallest brain is one of
those from Java. Its cranial capacity is
815 c.c., only 40 c.c. larger than the capacity of the three-million-year-old East
Rudolf skull. The average *erectus* cranial capacity, based on the endocasts I
have made, is 930 c.c.

Working with this average brain size
and estimating the body weight of *H.
erectus* to have been 92 pounds, one
finds that the Stephan progression index
for the species is 26.6. That is remark-

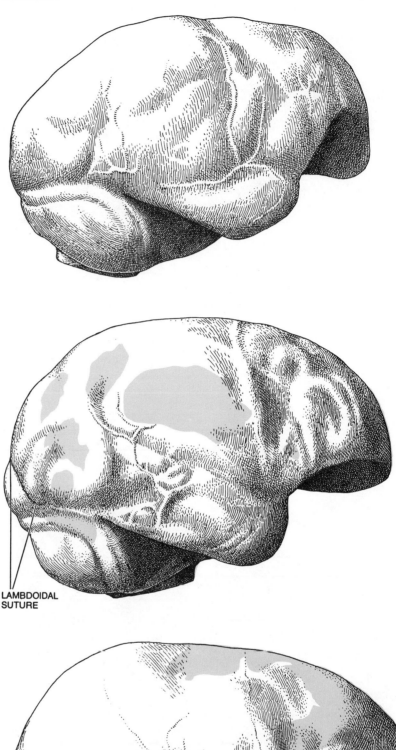

LAMBDOIDAL
SUTURE

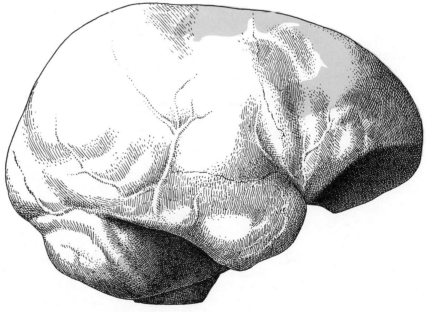

ENDOCRANIAL CASTS are those of (*top*)
a chimpanzee, *Pan troglodytes*, (*middle*)
a gracile *Australopithecus africanus*, and
(*bottom*) the other species, *A. robustus* (col-
or indicates restored areas). In all three casts
details of the gyral and sulcal markings of
the cerebral cortex are minimal. A differing
neurological organization, however, ·can be
seen. Both of the hominid brains are higher,
particularly in the parietal region. Orbital
surface of their frontal lobes is displaced
downward in contrast to chimpanzee's for-
ward-thrusting olfactory rostrum. The location of the hominids lunate sulcus, indicated (*middle*) by suture markings, implies
a far smaller occipital lobe than the ape's.

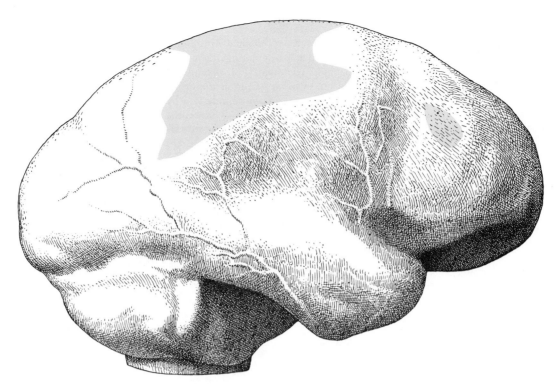

BRAIN CAST OF HOMO ERECTUS shows similar evidence of human neurological organization. As is true of most human cranial casts, the position of the lunate sulcus cannot be determined but the expansion of the temporal lobe and the human shape of the frontal lobe are evident. This is a cast of Java specimen VIII (1969); it reflects the flat-topped skull conformation typical of the fossil forms of *H. erectus* found in Indonesia. Like endocranial casts on preceding page and below it is shown 90 percent actual size.

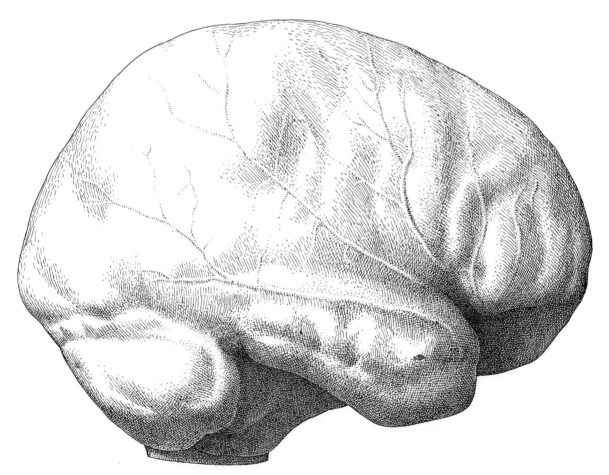

BRAIN CAST OF HOMO SAPIENS was made from a cranium in the collection at Columbia University. The height of the cerebral cortex, measured from its summit to the tip of the temporal lobe, and the fully rounded, expanded frontal lobe, showing a strong development of Broca's area (*see illustration on page 21*), typify the characteristic *H. sapiens* pattern of neurological organization.

ably close to modern man's average of 28.8. Even if the body-weight estimate is raised by some 30 pounds, the progression index falls only to 22.0. This being the case, it is difficult to escape the conclusion that, like *Australopithecus, H. erectus* possessed a brain that had become enlarged in proportion to the enlargement of the body. Although the average *erectus* brain is smaller than the average brain of modern man, it nonetheless conforms in gross morphology to the species' status as a recognized member of the genus *Homo* [*see top illustration on preceding page*].

I am not suggesting that any simple, straight-line progression connects the earliest African hominids, by way of *Homo erectus*, to modern man. As others have noted, it is the investigator's mind, and not the evidence, that tends to follow straight lines. The data are still far too scanty to trace the detailed progress of the human brain during the course of hominid evolution. For example, it would not even be safe to assume that, after attaining the stage represented by the earliest-known hominid endocasts, the brain thereafter consistently increased in size. Perhaps there were times when on the average brain sizes decreased simply because body sizes also decreased. One might even go so far as to speculate, and it would be pure speculation, that we are seeing something like this when we observe that the specimens of *Homo habilis* at Olduvai had substantially smaller brains than the far older East Rudolf hominid did.

Some generalizations are nonetheless possible. First, both the direct evidence of the endocasts and the indirect evidence of comparative cranial capacities indicate that the human brain appeared very much earlier than the time when *H. erectus* emerged, perhaps 500,-000 years ago. Second, it can be inferred that the emergence of the human brain was paralleled by the initiation of human social behavior. It is not appropriate here to review the evidence of relations between nutrition and behavioral development or of those between the endocrine system and brain growth. Still, it is obvious that brains do **not operate in** a vacuum and that a part of the nourishment the brain requires is social as well as dietary. Much of the humanness of man's brain is the result of social evolution. The weight of the inferential evidence today suggests that the genesis has been long in the making. It may well predate such elements of fossil behavior as the systematic use of stone tools and the large-scale practice of hunting.

3

The Present Evolution of Man

by Theodosius Dobzhansky
September 1960

*Man still evolves by natural selection for his
environment, but it is now an environment largely
of his own making. Moreover, he may be changing
the environment faster than he can change biologically*

Any discussion of the evolution of the human species deals with a natural process that has transcended itself. Only once before, when life originated out of inorganic matter, has there occurred a comparable event.

After that first momentous step, living forms evolved by adapting to their environments. Adaptation—the maintenance or advancement of conformity between an organism and its surroundings —takes place through natural selection. The raw materials with which natural selection works are supplied by mutation and sexual recombination of hereditary units: the genes.

Mutation, sexual recombination and natural selection led to the emergence of *Homo sapiens*. The creatures that preceded him had already developed the rudiments of tool-using, toolmaking and cultural transmission. But the next evolutionary step was so great as to constitute a difference in kind from those before it. There now appeared an organism whose mastery of technology and of symbolic communication enabled it to create a supraorganic culture. Other organisms adapt to their environments by changing their genes in accordance with the demands of the surroundings. Man and man alone can also adapt by changing his environments to fit his genes. His genes enable him to invent new tools, to alter his opinions, his aims and his conduct, to acquire new knowledge and new wisdom.

Numerous authors of numerous studies have shown how the possession of these faculties brought the human species to its present biological eminence. Man has spread to every section of the earth, bringing high culture to much of it. He is now the most numerous of the mammals. By these or any other reasonable standards, he is by far the most successful product of biological evolution.

For better or worse, biological evolution did not stop when culture appeared. In this short article we address ourselves to the question of where evolution is now taking man. The literature of this subject has not lacked for prophets who wish to divine man's eventual fate. In our age of anxiety, prediction of final extinction has become the fashionable view, replacing the hopes for emergence of a race of demigods that more optimistic authorities used to foresee. Our purpose is less ambitious. What biological evolutionary processes are now at work is a problem both serious and complex enough to occupy us here.

The impact of human works on the environment is so strong that it has become very hard to make out the forces to which the human species is now adjusting. It has even been argued that *Homo sapiens* has already emancipated himself from the operation of natural selection. At the other extreme are those who still assume that man is nothing but an animal. The second fallacy is the more pernicious, leading as it does to theories of biological racism and the justification of race and class prejudice which are bringing suffering to millions of people from South Africa to Arkansas. Assuming that man's genetic endowment can be ignored is the converse falsehood, perhaps less disastrous in its immediate effects, but more insidious in the long run.

Like all other animals, man remains the product of his biological inheritance. The first, and basic, feature of his present evolution is that his genes continue to mutate, as they have since he first appeared. Every one of the tens of thousands of genes inherited by an individual has a tiny probability of changing in some way during his generation. Among the small, and probably atypical, sample of human genes for which very rough estimates of the mutation frequencies are available, the rates of mutation vary from one in 10,000 to one in about 250,000. For example, it has been calculated that approximately one sex cell in every 50,000 produced by a normal person carries a new mutant gene causing retinoblastoma, a cancer of the eye affecting children.

These figures are "spontaneous" frequencies in people not exposed to any special agents that can induce mutation. As is now widely known, the existence of such agents, including ionizing radiation and certain chemicals, has been demonstrated with organisms other than man. New mutagens are constantly being discovered. It can hardly be doubted that at least some of them affect human genes. As a consequence the members of an industrial civilization have increased genetic variability through rising mutation rates.

There is no question that many mutations produce hereditary diseases, malformations and constitutional weaknesses of various kinds. Some few must also be useful, at least in certain environments; otherwise there would be no evolution. (Useful mutants have actually been observed in experiments on lower organisms.) But what about minor variations that produce a little more or a little less hair, a slightly longer or a slightly shorter nose, blood of type O or type A? These traits seem neither useful nor harmful. Here, however, we must proceed with the greatest caution. Beneficial or damaging effects of ostensibly neutral traits may eventually be discovered. For example, recent evidence indicates that people with blood of type O have a slightly higher rate of duodenal ulcer than does the general population. Does it follow that O blood is bad? Not necessarily; it is the most frequent type in many populations, and it may conceivably confer some advantages yet undiscovered.

Still other mutants that are detrimental when present in double dose (the so-called homozygous condition, where the same type of gene has been inherited from both parents) lead to hybrid vigor in single dose (the heterozygous condition). How frequently this happens is uncertain. The effect surely operates in the breeding of domestic animals and plants, and it has been detected among X-ray-induced mutations in fruit flies. Only one case is thus far known in man. Anthony C. Allison of the University of Oxford has found that the gene causing sickle-cell anemia in the homozygous condition makes its heterozygous carriers relatively resistant to certain forms of malaria. This gene is very frequent in the native population of the central African lowlands, where malaria has long been endemic, and relatively rare in the inhabitants of the more salubrious highlands. Certainly there are other such adaptively ambivalent genes in human populations, but we do not know how many.

Despite these uncertainties, which cannot be glossed over, it is generally agreed among geneticists that the effects of mutation are on the average detrimental. Any increase of mutation rate, no matter how small, can only augment the mass of human misery due to defective heredity. The matter has rightly attracted wide attention in connection with ionizing radiation from military and industrial operations and medical X-rays. Yet these form only a part of a larger and more portentous issue.

Of the almost countless mutant genes that have arisen since life on earth began, only a minute fraction were preserved. They were preserved because they were useful, or at least not very harmful, to their possessors. A great majority of gene changes were eliminated. The agency that preserved useful mutants and eliminated injurious ones was natural selection. Is natural selection still operating in mankind, and can it be trusted to keep man fit to live in environments created by his civilization?

One must beware of words taken from everyday language to construct scientific terminology. "Natural" in "natural selection" does not mean the state of affairs preceding or excluding man-made changes. Artificially or not, man's environment has altered. Would it now be natural to try to make your living as a Stone Age hunter?

Then there are phrases like "the struggle for life" and "survival of the fittest." Now "struggle" was to Darwin a metaphor. Animals struggle against cold by growing warm fur, and plants against dryness by reducing the evaporating leaf surface. It was the school of so-called social Darwinists (to which Darwin did not belong) who equated "struggle" with violence, warfare and competition

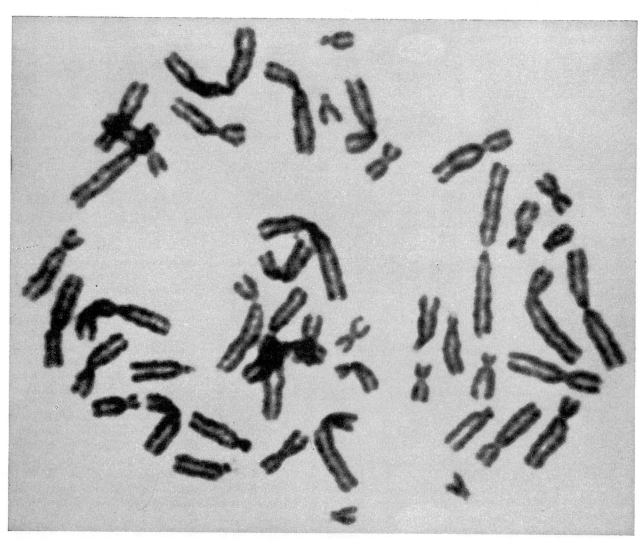

HUMAN CHROMOSOMES are enlarged some 5,000 times in this photomicrograph made by J. H. Tjio and Theodore T. Puck at the University of Colorado Medical Center. The photomicrograph shows all of the 23 pairs of chromosomes in a dividing body cell.

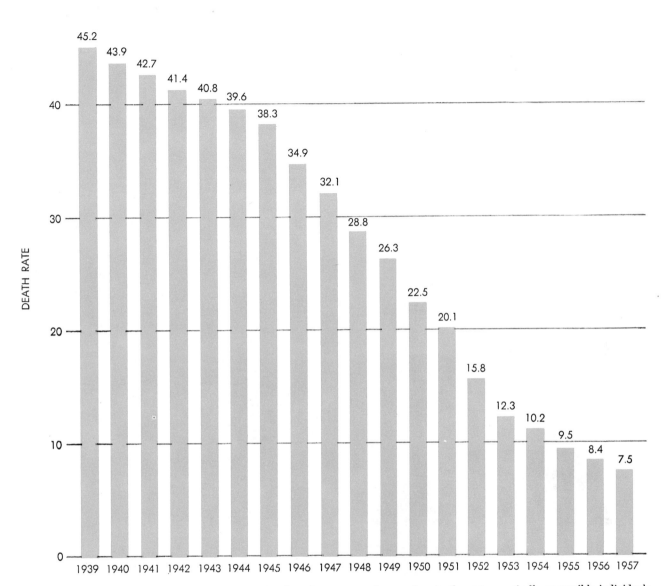

GENERAL DISTRIBUTION OF PENICILLIN
INTRODUCTION OF STREPTOMYCIN IN HOSPITALS
INTRODUCTION OF PENICILLIN IN HOSPITALS

GENERAL DISTRIBUTION OF STREPTOMYCIN
INTRODUCTION OF ISONIAZID

DEATH RATE

45.2 43.9 42.7 41.4 40.8 39.6 38.3 34.9 32.1 28.8 26.3 22.5 20.1 15.8 12.3 10.2 9.5 8.4 7.5

1939 1940 1941 1942 1943 1944 1945 1946 1947 1948 1949 1950 1951 1952 1953 1954 1955 1956 1957

TUBERCULOSIS DEATH RATE per 100,000 people showed a dramatic decline with the introduction of antibiotics and later of the antituberculosis drug isoniazid. As tuberculosis becomes less prevalent, so does its threat to genetically susceptible individuals, who are enabled to survive and reproduce. The chart is based upon information from the U. S. National Office of Vital Statistics.

without quarter. The idea has long been discredited.

We do not deny the reality of competition and combat in nature, but suggest that they do not tell the whole story. Struggle for existence may be won not only by strife but also by mutual help. The surviving fit in human societies may in some circumstances be those with the strongest fists and the greatest readiness to use them. In others they may be those who live in peace with their neighbors and assist them in hour of need. Indeed, co-operation has a long and honorable record. The first human societies, the hunters of the Old Stone Age, depended on co-operation to kill big game.

Moreover, modern genetics shows that "fitness" has a quite special meaning in connection with evolution. Biologists now speak of Darwinian fitness, or adaptive value, or selective value in a reproductive sense. Consider the condition known as achondroplastic dwarfism, caused by a gene mutation that produces people with normal heads and trunks, but short arms and legs. As adults they may enjoy good health. Nevertheless, E. T. Mørch in Denmark has discovered that achondroplastic dwarfs produce, on the average, only some 20 surviving children for every 100 children produced by their normal brothers and sisters. In technical terms we say that the Darwinian fitness of achondroplasts is .2 or, alternatively that achondroplastic dwarfism is opposed by a selection-coefficient of .8.

This is a very strong selection, and the reasons for it are only partly understood. What matters from an evolutionary point of view is that achondroplasts are much less efficient in transmitting their genes to the following generations than are nondwarfs. Darwinian fitness is reproductive fitness. Genetically the surviving fittest is neither superman nor conquering hero; he is merely the parent of the largest surviving progeny.

With these definitions in mind, we can answer the question whether natural selection is still active in mankind by considering how such selection might be set aside. If all adults married, and each couple produced exactly the same number of children, all of whom survived to get married in turn and so on, there would be no selection at all. Alternatively, the number of children, if any, that each person produced might be determined by himself or some outside authority on the basis of the desirability of his hereditary endowment. This would be replacing natural selection by artificial selection. Some day it may come to pass. Meantime natural selection is going on.

It goes on, however, always within the context of environment. As that changes, the Darwinian fitness of various traits changes with it. Thus by his own efforts man is continually altering the selective pressure for or against certain genes.

The most obvious example, and one with disturbing overtones, is to be found in the advance of medicine and public health. Retinoblastoma, the eye cancer of children, is almost always fatal if it is not treated. Here is "natural" selection at its most rigorous, weeding out virtually all of the harmful mutant genes

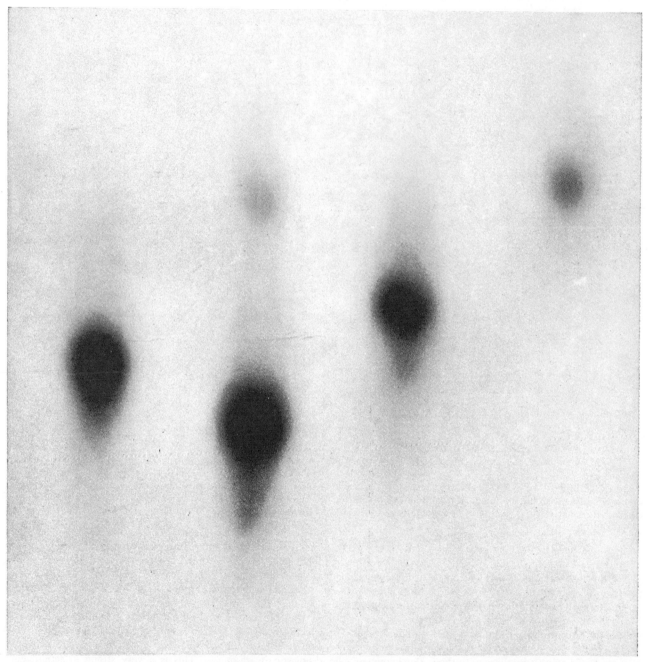

CHEMICAL STRUCTURE OF HEMOGLOBIN in an individual's blood is determined by his genes. Normal and abnormal hemoglobins move at different speeds in an electric field. This photograph, made by Henry G. Kunkel of the Rockefeller Institute, shows surface of a slab of moist starch on which samples of four kinds of human hemoglobin were lined up at top, between a negative electrode at top and a positive electrode at bottom (electrodes are not shown). When current was turned on, the samples migrated toward positive electrode. At right hemoglobin C, the cause of a rare hereditary anemia, has moved down only a short way. Second from right is hemoglobin S, the cause of sickle-cell anemia, which has moved farther in same length of time. Normal hemoglobin, third from right, has separated into its A and A_2 constituents. At left is normal fetal hemoglobin F, obtained from an umbilical cord.

before they can be passed on even once. With proper treatment, however, almost 70 per cent of the carriers of the gene for retinoblastoma survive, become able to reproduce and therefore to transmit the defect to half their children.

More dramatic, if genetically less clear-cut, instances are afforded by advances in the control of tuberculosis and malaria. A century ago the annual death rate from tuberculosis in industrially advanced countries was close to 500 per 100,000. Improvement in living conditions and, more recently, the advent of antibiotic drugs have reduced the death rate to 7.5 per 100,000 in the U. S. today. A similarly steep decline is under way in the mortality from malaria, which used to afflict a seventh of the earth's population.

Being infectious, tuberculosis and malaria are hazards of the environment. There is good evidence, however, that individual susceptibility, both as to contracting the infection and as to the severity of the disease, is genetically conditioned. (We have already mentioned the protective effect of the gene for sickle-cell anemia. This is probably only one of several forms of genetic resistance to malaria.) As the prevalence of these diseases decreases, so does the threat to susceptible individuals. In other words, the Darwinian fitness of such individuals has increased.

It was pointed out earlier that one effect of civilization is to increase mutation rates and hence the supply of harmful genes. A second effect is to decrease the rate of discrimination against such genes, and consequently the rate of their elimination from human populations by natural selection. In thus disturbing the former genetic equilibrium of inflow and outflow, is man not frustrating natural selection and polluting his genetic pool?

The danger exists and cannot be ignored. But in the present state of knowledge the problem is tremendously complex. If our culture has an ideal, it is the sacredness of human life. A society that refused, on eugenic grounds, to cure children of retinoblastoma would, in our eyes, lose more by moral degradation than it gained genetically. Not so easy, however, is the question whether a person who knows he carries the gene for retinoblastoma, or a similarly deleterious gene, has a right to have children.

Even here the genetic issue is clear, although the moral issue may not be. This is no longer true when we come to genes that are harmful in double dose,

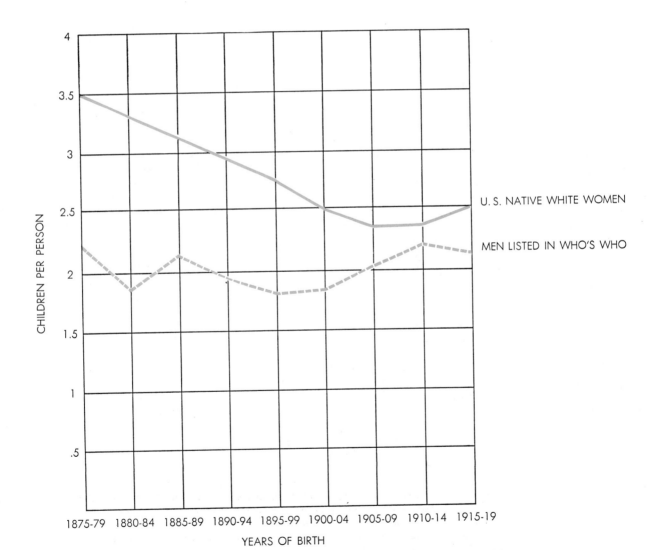

FERTILITY RATE among relatively intelligent people, as represented by a random sample of men listed in *Who's Who in America* for 1956 and 1957, is lower than fertility rate of the U. S. population as a whole, as represented by all native white women. The two fertility rates have recently been moving toward each other. Vertical scale shows average number of children per person; horizontal scale shows approximate birth date of parents. Chart is based upon information collected by Dudley Kirk of the Population Council.

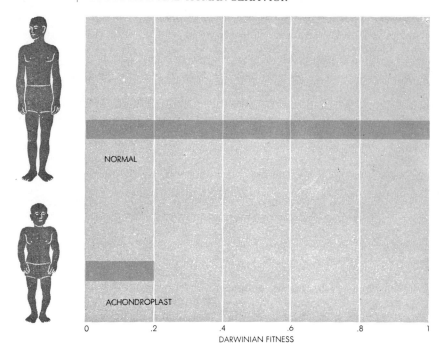

NORMAL

ACHONDROPLAST

0   .2   .4   .6   .8   1
DARWINIAN FITNESS

DARWINIAN FITNESS of achondroplastic dwarfs is low. Dwarfs may be healthy, but they have only 20 surviving children to every 100 surviving children of normal parents.

but beneficial in single. If the central African peoples had decided some time ago to breed out the sickle-cell gene, they might have succumbed in much larger numbers to malaria. Fortunately this particular dilemma has been resolved by successful methods of mosquito control. How many other hereditary diseases and malformations are maintained by the advantages their genes confer in heterozygous carriers, we simply do not know.

Conversely, we cannot yet predict the genetic effect of relaxing selection pressure. If, for example, susceptibility to tuberculosis is maintained by recurrent mutations, then the conquest of the disease should increase the concentration of mutant genes as time goes on. On the other hand, if resistance arises from a single dose of genes that make for susceptibility in the double dose, the effects of eradication become much less clear. Other selective forces might then determine the fate of these genes in the population.

In any case, although we cannot see all the consequences, we can be sure that ancient genetic patterns will continue to shift under the shelter of modern medicine. We would not wish it otherwise. It may well be, however, that the social cost of maintaining some genetic variants will be so great that artificial selection against them is ethically, as well as economically, the most acceptable and wisest solution.

If the evolutionary impact of such biological tools as antibiotics and vaccines is still unclear, then computers and rockets, to say nothing of social organizations as a whole, present an even deeper puzzle. There is no doubt that human survival will continue to depend more and more on human intellect and technology. It is idle to argue whether this is good or bad. The point of no return was passed long ago, before anyone knew it was happening.

But to grant that the situation is inevitable is not to ignore the problems it raises. Selection in modern societies does not always encourage characteristics that we regard as desirable. Let us consider one example. Much has been written about the differential fertility that in advanced human societies favors less intelligent over more intelligent people. Studies in several countries have shown that school children from large families tend to score lower on so-called intelligence tests than their classmates with few or no brothers and sisters. Moreover, parents who score lower on these tests have more children on the average than those who get higher marks.

We cannot put our finger on the forces responsible for this presumed selection against intelligence. As a matter of fact, there is some evidence that matters are changing, in the U. S. at least. People included in *Who's Who in America* (assuming that people listed in this directory are on the average more intelligent

than people not listed there) had fewer children than the general population during the period from 1875 to 1904. In the next two decades, however, the difference seemed to be disappearing. L. S. Penrose of University College London, one of the outstanding human geneticists, has pointed out that a negative correlation between intelligence and family size may in part be corrected by the relative infertility of low-grade mental defectives. He suggests that selection may thus be working toward maintaining a constant level of genetic conditioning for intelligence in human populations. The evidence presently available is insufficient either to prove or to contradict this hypothesis.

It must also be recognized that in man and other social animals qualities making for successful individuals are not necessarily those most useful to the society as a whole. If there were a gene for altruism, natural selection might well discriminate against it on the individual level, but favor it on the population level. In that case the fate of the gene would be hard to predict.

If this article has asked many more questions than it has answered, the purpose is to suggest that answers be sought with all possible speed. Natural selection is a very remarkable phenomenon. But it does not even guarantee the survival of a species. Most living forms have become extinct without the "softening" influence of civilization, simply by becoming too narrowly specialized. Natural selection is opportunistic; in shaping an organism to fit its surroundings it may leave the organism unable to cope with a change in environment. In this light, man's explosive ability to change his environment may offer as much threat as promise. Technological evolution may have outstripped biological evolution.

Yet man is the only product of biological evolution who knows that he has evolved and is evolving further. He should be able to replace the blind force of natural selection by conscious direction, based on his knowledge of nature and on his values. It is as certain that such direction will be needed as it is questionable whether man is ready to provide it. He is unready because his knowledge of his own nature and its evolution is insufficient; because a vast majority of people are unaware of the necessity of facing the problem; and because there is so wide a gap between the way people actually live and the values and ideals to which they pay lip service.

II

GENETIC AND DEVELOPMENTAL ROOTS OF BEHAVIOR

II GENETIC AND DEVELOPMENTAL ROOTS OF BEHAVIOR

INTRODUCTION

That there is genetic determination of bodily structure has been known and accepted for some time. However, it is only recently that genetic factors in the development of behavior have become appreciated. Indeed, the modern and exciting field of behavior genetics has a very short history. Genes, of course, do not act directly on behavior. In fact, they act only to regulate the production of proteins responsible for the structure and enzymatic activities of an organism. In most cases we are ignorant of the immediate structural bases of behavior. An example often used concerns breeding race horses. Breeders do not breed for any particular characteristic, such as long legs; instead they mate horses that have the best track records. Being a good race horse combines many kinds of behavioral properties—strength, stamina, coordination, and temperament. It is important to emphasize that the study of behavior genetics does not disregard environmental effects on behavior. On the contrary, the interactions of genes and environment are critical in the development of behavior. All behavior is *phenotypic*—that is, it is always the result of interactions between genetic influences and environment. Further, the vast majority of behavioral characteristics in higher animals are *polygenetic;* they are the result of the actions of many different genes, each contributing some aspect or some small cumulative effect to the net behavioral outcome.

Great progress is now being made by the use of simple animals, such as insects, to study the genetic bases of behavior. It is possible with insects, and even simpler organisms such as bacteria, to relate gene actions directly to behaviors. A specific example of a behavior that has been studied may be mentioned: Fruit flies of a certain mutant strain collapse when the temperature goes above 82° Fahrenheit, although the behavior of normal flies is not affected. When the temperature is subsequently lowered, the mutant flies promptly stand up and move about normally. The temperature effect is specific to certain motor nerves; when the temperature rises above 82° the nerves in these mutant flies are blocked, and as soon as the temperature falls below that level they become functional again. Here is a simple and dramatic example of genetic determination of behavior. In a brilliant article entitled "Genetic Dissection of Behavior," Seymour Benzer describes the work that he and his colleagues have been doing at the California Institute of Technology in recent years with fruit flies. In order to trace the path from gene to behavior, Benzer's group generates mosaic flies and studies their developing structural properties from the fertilized egg through the blastoderm, a stage at which the different structures of the organism have not yet formed, to the final behaving organism.

Study of the genetic and developmental roots of behavior always goes hand in hand, as Benzer indicates in his article. It is much easier to see the influences of genetic predispositions during the development of an organism than at any other period in its life cycle. In higher organisms, such as birds and mammals, the interactions between genes and environment are complex and continual. However, it is quite clear that there are genetic predispositions for certain forms and outcomes of behavior-environment interaction. The ethologists—zoologists who have specialized in the study of the natural behavior of animals—have made particularly important contributions in this area. Imprinting, described by Eckhard H. Hess in the next article ("'Imprinting' in a Natural Laboratory'"), is a particularly good example. Imprinting was discovered by the Austrian zoologist Konrad Lorenz in the 1930's. He made the now famous observation that newly hatched goslings would follow him rather than their mother if they saw him immediately after hatching before they saw their mother. Imprinting takes place only at a very early period in a bird's life. The animal is predisposed to imprint on the first mother-like object encountered. Hess, a professor of psychology at the University of Chicago, has done a comprehensive series of experiments, both in nature and in the laboratory, analyzing the factors most important in the development of imprinting. It is very tempting to relate the imprinting phenomenon to developmental processes in young children.

It cannot be emphasized too strongly that genetic and environmental factors constantly interplay in the development of behavior in higher animals. Among the most important analyses of this process is the now classical work of Daniel S. Lehrman. His article, "The Reproductive Behavior of Ring Doves," is a brilliant analysis of both the innate and experimental factors that interact to produce a relatively stereotyped, although very complex, behavior sequence—reproductive behavior. It is impossible to state whether the behavior is entirely genetically determined or entirely environmentally determined. It is in fact a continual interplay and interaction. External stimuli and hormonal factors are involved in courtship, which in turn establishes hormonal and brain changes that lead to nest building, which provides stimuli for further internal changes associated with egg laying and incubation. This complex sequence of behaviors depends on the existence of appropriate external stimuli and internal hormonal events and brain mechanisms at every step. The total sequence begins with external stimuli, which lead to hormonal secretions that are the result of genetic factors, which result in brain changes, which lead back to changes in behavior that produce further external stimuli, which in turn lead back to the brain and hormones.

Finally, in the last article in this section, Jay S. Rosenblatt examines learning in newborn kittens. Earlier studies of learning in young mammals often seemed to indicate that they were relatively incapable of learning. However, Rosenblatt has found that in fact they learn very well indeed, but only certain kinds of things. What they learn is what they must learn to survive. They have structural and genetic predispositions to learn certain kinds of behaviors. In particular they very quickly learn to find their way to the favorite nipple of the mother and they come to know their home territories. Rosenblatt's studies are reminiscent of the brilliant earlier studies by Harry Harlow at Wisconsin showing how infant monkeys quickly formed an attachment to cloth surrogate mothers and treated the cloth mother as the center of security and comfort. Newborn infant mammals are predisposed to learn those things that will maximize their chances of survival.

4

Genetic Dissection of Behavior

by Seymour Benzer
December 1973

By working with fruit flies that are mosaics of normal and mutant parts it is possible to identify the genetic components of behavior, retrace their development and locate the sites where they operate

When the individual organism develops from a fertilized egg, the one-dimensional information arrayed in the linear sequence of the genes on the chromosomes controls the formation of a two-dimensional cell layer that folds to give rise to a precise three-dimensional arrangement of sense organs, central nervous system and muscles. Those elements interact to produce the organism's behavior, a phenomenon whose description requires four dimensions at least. Surely the genes, which so largely determine anatomical and biochemical characteristics, must also interact with the environment to determine behavior. But how? For two decades molecular biologists were engaged in tracking down the structure and coding of the gene, a task that was pursued to ever lower levels of organization [see "The Fine Structure of the Gene," by Seymour Benzer; Scientific American Offprint 120]. Some of us have since turned in the opposite direction, to higher integrative levels, to explore development, the nervous system and behavior. In our laboratory at the California Institute of Technology we have been applying tools of genetic analysis in an attempt to trace the emergence of multidimensional behavior from the one-dimensional gene.

Our objectives are to discern the genetic component of a behavior, to identify it with a particular gene and then to determine the actual site at which the gene influences behavior and learn how it does so. In brief, we keep the environment constant, change the genes and see what happens to behavior. Our choice of an experimental organism was constrained by the fact that the simpler an organism is, the less likely it is to exhibit interesting behavioral patterns that are relevant to man; the more complex it is, the more difficult it may be to analyze

and the longer it takes. The fruit fly *Drosophila melanogaster* represents a compromise. In mass, in number of nerve cells, in amount of DNA and in generation time it stands roughly halfway on a logarithmic scale between the colon bacillus *Escherichia coli* (which can be regarded as having a one-neuron nervous system) and man. Although the fly's nervous system is very different from the human system, both consist of neurons and synapses and utilize transmitter molecules, and the development of both is dictated by genes. A fly has highly developed senses of sight, hearing, taste, smell, gravity and time. It cannot do everything we do, but it does some things we cannot do, such as fly and stand on the ceiling. Its visual system can detect the movement of the minute hand on a clock. One must not underestimate the little creature, which is not an evolutionary antecedent of man but is itself high up on the invertebrate branch of the phylogenetic tree. Its nervous system is a miracle of microminiaturization, and some of its independently evolved behavior patterns are not unlike our own.

Jerry Hirsch, Theodosius Dobzhansky and many others have demonstrated that if one begins with a genetically heterogeneous population of fruit flies, various behavioral characters can be enhanced by selective breeding pursued over many generations. This kind of experiment demonstrates that behavior can be genetically modified, but it depends on the reassortment of many different genes, so that it is very difficult to distinguish the effect of each one. Also, unless the selective procedure is constantly maintained, the genes may reassort, causing loss of the special behavior. For analyzing the relation of specific genes to behavior, it is more effective to begin

with a highly inbred, genetically uniform strain of flies and change the genes one at a time. This is done by inducing a mutation: an abrupt gene change that is transmitted to all subsequent generations.

A population of flies exposed to a mutagen (radiation or certain chemicals) yields some progeny with anatomical anomalies such as white eyes or forked bristles, and it also yields progeny with behavioral abnormalities. Workers in many laboratories (including ours) have compiled a long list of such mutants, each of which can be produced by the alteration of a single gene. Some mutants are perturbed in sexual behavior, which in normal *Drosophila* involves an elaborate sequence of fixed action patterns. Margaret Bastock showed years ago that some mutant males do not court with normal vigor. Kulbir Gill discovered a mutant in which the males pursue one another as persistently as they do females. The mutant *stuck*, found by Carolyn Beckman, suffers from inability to disengage after the normal 20-minute copulation period. A converse example is *coitus interruptus*, a mutant Jeffrey C. Hall has been studying in our laboratory; mutant males disengage in about half the normal time and no offspring are produced. Obviously most such mutants would not stand a chance in the competitive natural environment, but they can be maintained and studied in the laboratory.

As for general locomotor activity, some mutants are *sluggish* and others, such as one found by William D. Kaplan at the City of Hope Medical Center, are *hyperkinetic*, consuming oxygen at an exaggerated rate and dying much earlier than normal flies. Whereas normal flies show strong negative geotaxis (a tendency to move upward against the force of gravity), *nonclimbing* mutants do not.

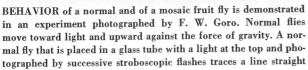

BEHAVIOR of a normal and of a mosaic fruit fly is demonstrated in an experiment photographed by F. W. Goro. Normal flies move toward light and upward against the force of gravity. A normal fly that is placed in a glass tube with a light at the top and photographed by successive stroboscopic flashes traces a line straight up the tube (*left*). A mosaic fly, with one good eye and one blind eye, also climbs straight up if there is no light, guided by its sense of gravity. If there is a light at the top of the tube, however, the mosaic fly traces a helical path (*right*), turning its bad eye toward the light in a vain effort to balance the light input to both eyes.

"WINGS-UP" FLIES are mutants that keep their wings straight up and cannot fly. Such behavior could be the result of flaws in wing structure, in musculature or in nerve function. Mosaic experiments in the author's laboratory have traced the defect to the muscle.

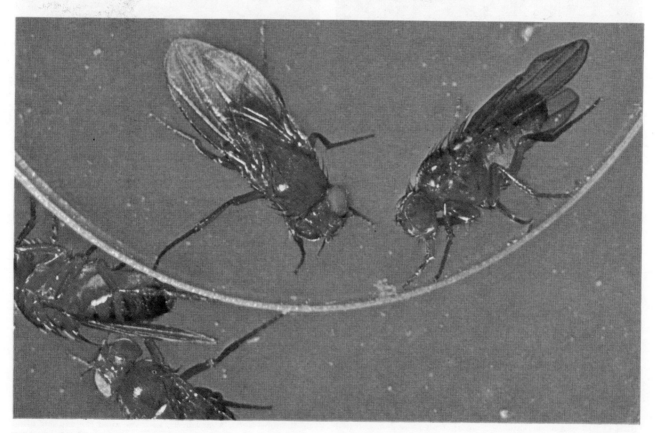

MOSAIC FLIES used for investigating behavior are gynandromorphs: partly male and partly female. The female parts are normal, the male parts mutant in one physical or behavioral trait or more. These flies have one normal red eye and one mutant white eye, and the male side of each fly also has the shorter wing that is normal for a male fly. The flies are about three millimeters long.

Flightless flies do not fly even though they may have perfectly well-developed wings and the male can raise his wing and vibrate it in approved fashion during courtship. Some individuals that appear to be quite normal may harbor hereditary idiosyncrasies that show up only under stress. Take the *easily shocked* mutants we have isolated, or the one called *tko*, found by Burke H. Judd and his collaborators at the University of Texas at Austin. When the mutant fly is subjected to a mechanical jolt, it has what looks like an epileptic seizure: it falls on its back, flails its legs and wings, coils its abdomen under and goes into a coma; after a few minutes it recovers and goes about its business as if nothing had happened. John R. Merriam and others working in our laboratory have found several different genes on the *X* chromosome that can produce this syndrome if they are mutated.

In many organisms mutations have been discovered that are temperature-sensitive, that is, the abnormal trait is displayed only above or below a certain temperature. David Suzuki and his associates at the University of British Columbia discovered a behavioral *Drosophila* mutant of this type called *paralyzed*: when the temperature goes above 28 degrees Celsius (82 degrees Fahrenheit), it collapses, although normal flies are unaffected; when the temperature is lowered, the mutant promptly stands up and moves about normally. We have found other mutants, involving different genes, that become similarly paralyzed at other specific temperatures. In one of these, *comatose*, recovery is not instantaneous but may take many minutes or hours, depending on how long the mutant was exposed to high temperatures. Recent experiments by Obaid Siddiqi in our laboratory have shown that action potentials in some of the motor nerves are blocked until the fly recovers.

An important feature of behavior in a wide range of organisms is an endogenous 24-hour cycle of activity. The fruit fly displays this "circadian" rhythm, and one can demonstrate the role of the genes in establishing it. A fly does well to emerge from the pupal stage around dawn, when the air is moist and cool and the creature has time to unfold its wings and harden its cuticle, or outer shell, before there is much risk of desiccation or from predators. (The name *Drosophila*, incidentally, means "lover of dew.") Eclosion from the pupa at the proper time is controlled by the circadian rhythm: most flies emerge during a few hours around dawn and those missing that interval tend to wait until dawn on the following day or on later days. This rhythm, which has been much studied by Colin S. Pittendrigh of Stanford University, persists even in constant darkness provided that the pupae have once been exposed to light; having been set, the internal clock keeps running. The clock continues to control the activity of the individual fly after eclosion, even if the fly is kept in the dark. By monitoring the fly's movement with a photocell sensitive to infrared radiation (which is invisible to the fly) one can observe that it begins to walk about at a certain time and does so for some 12 hours; then it becomes quiescent, as if it were asleep on its feet, for half a day. After that, at the same time as the first day's arousing or within an hour or so of it, activity begins anew. Ronald Konopka demonstrated the genetic control of this internal clock as a graduate student in our laboratory. By exposing normal flies to a mutagen he obtained mutants with abnormal rhythms or no rhythm at all. The *arrhythmic* flies may eclose at any time of day; if they are maintained in the dark

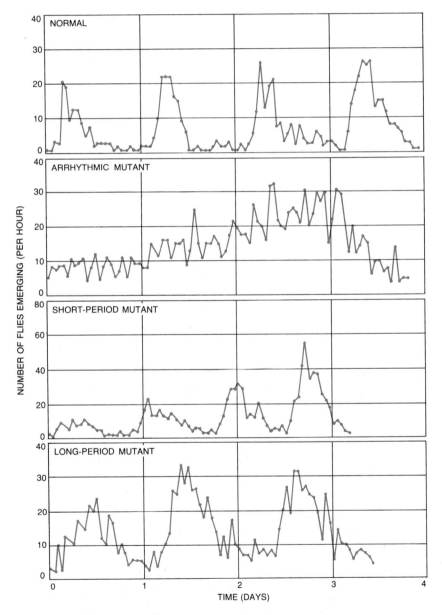

"BIOLOGICAL CLOCK" is an example of a behavioral mechanism that is genetically determined. It governs the periodicity of the time flies eclose from the pupa and also their daily cycle of activity as adults. The curves are for the eclosion of flies kept in total darkness. Normal flies emerge from the pupa at a time corresponding to dawn; those that miss dawn on one day emerge 24 hours later (*top*). Mutants include arrhythmic flies, which emerge at arbitrary times in the course of the day, and flies with 19-hour and 28-hour cycles.

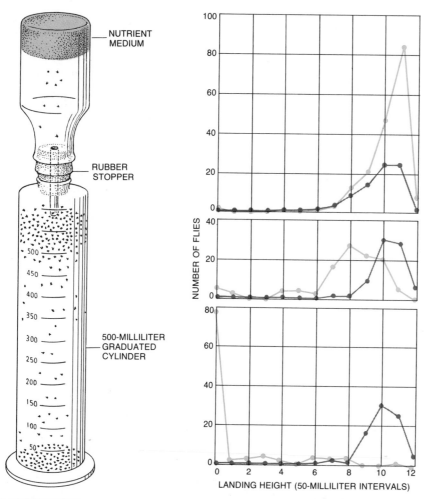

FLIGHT TESTER is a simple device for measuring the flying ability of normal and mutant flies. It is a 500-milliliter graduated cylinder, its inside wall coated with paraffin oil. Flies are dumped in at the top. They strike out horizontally as best they can, and so the level at which they hit the wall and become stuck in the oil film reflects their flying ability. The curves compare the performance of female control flies (*gray*) with that of males (*color*) that fly normally (*top*) or poorly (*middle*) and with male *flightless* mutants (*bottom*).

the dark, which suggests that they are blind.

My colleague Yoshiki Hotta, who is now at the University of Tokyo, and I studied the electrical response of the nonphototactic flies' eyes. Similar mutant isolation and electrical studies have also been carried out by William L. Pak and his associates at Purdue University and by Martin Heisenberg at the Max Planck Institute for Biology at Tübingen, so that many mutants are now available, involving a series of different genes. The stimulus of a flash of light causes the photoreceptor cells of a normal fly's eye to emit a negative wave, which in turn triggers a positive spike from the next cells in the visual pathway; an electroretinogram, a record of this response, can be made rather easily with a simple wick electrode placed on the surface of the eye. In some nonphototactic mutants the photoreceptor cells respond but fail to trigger the second-order neurons; in other cases the primary receptor cells are affected so that there is no detectable signal from them even though they are anatomically largely normal. These mutants may be useful in understanding the primary transduction mechanism in the photoreceptor cells. Mutant material provides perturbations, in other words, that enable one to analyze normal function. When Hotta and I examined the eyes of some of the nonphototactic mutants, we found that the photoreceptor cells are normal in the young adult but that they degenerate with age. There are genetic conditions that produce this result in humans, and it may be that the fly's eye can provide a model system for studying certain kinds of blindness.

Now, if one knows that a certain behavior (nonphototactic, say) is produced by a single-gene mutation and that it seems to be explained by an anatomical fault (the degenerated receptors), one still cannot say with certainty what is the primary "focus" of that genetic alteration, that is, the site in the body at which the mutant gene exerts its primary effect. The site may be far from the affected organ. Certain cases of retinal degeneration in man, for example, are due not to any defect in the eye but to ineffective absorption of vitamin A from food in the intestine, as Peter Gouras of the National Institute of Neurological Diseases and Blindness has demonstrated. In order to trace the path from gene to behavior one must find the true focus at which the gene acts in the developing organism. How? A good way to troubleshoot in an electronic system—a stereophonic set with two identical

after emergence, they are insomniacs, moving about during random periods throughout the day. The *short-period* mutant runs on a 19-hour cycle and the *long-period* mutant on a 28-hour cycle. (May there not be some analogy between such flies and humans who are either cheerful early birds or slow-to-awaken night owls?)

Let me now use a defect in visual behavior to illustrate in some detail how we analyze behavior. The first problem is to quantitate behavior and to detect and isolate behavioral mutants. It is possible to handle large populations of flies, treating each individual much as a molecule of behavior and fractionating the group into normal and abnormal types. We begin, using the technique devised by Edward B. Lewis at Cal Tech, by feeding male flies sugar water to which has been added the mutagen ethyl methane sulfonate, an alkylating agent that induces mutations in the chromosomes

of sperm cells. The progeny of mutagenized males are then fractionated by means of a kind of countercurrent distribution procedure [*see illustration on opposite page*], somewhat as one separates molecules into two liquid phases. Here the phases are light and darkness and the population is "chromatographed" in two dimensions on the basis of multiple trials for movement toward or away from light. Normal flies—and most of the progeny in our experiment—are phototactic, moving toward light but not away from it. Some mutants, however, do not move quickly in either direction; they are *sluggish* mutants. There are *runners*, which move vigorously both toward and away from light. A *negatively phototactic* mutant moves preferentially away from light. Finally, there are the *nonphototactic* mutants, which show a normal tendency to walk but no preference for light or darkness. They behave in light as normal flies behave in

channels, for example—is to interchange corresponding parts. That is in effect what we do with *Drosophila*. Rather than surgically transplanting organs from one fly to another, however, we use a genetic technique: we make mosaic flies, composite individuals in which

some tissues are mutant and some have a normal genotype. Then we look to see just which part has to be mutant in order to account for the abnormal behavior.

One method of generating mosaics depends on a strain of flies in which there is an unstable ring-shaped X chromo-

some. Flies, like humans, have X and Y sex chromosomes; if a fertilized egg has two X chromosomes in its nucleus, it will normally develop into a female fly; an XY egg yields a male. In *Drosophila* it is the presence of two X chromosomes that makes a fly female; if there is only one X,

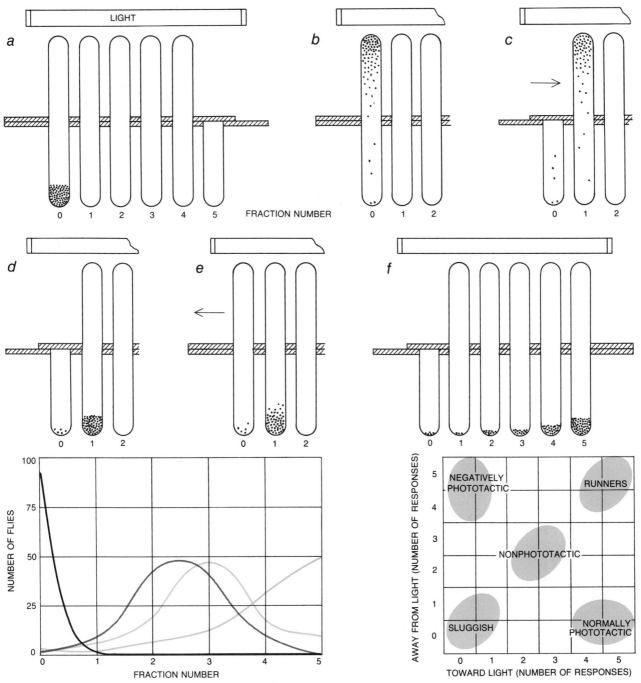

COUNTERCURRENT APPARATUS developed by the author can "fractionate" a population of flies as if they were molecules of behavior. The device consists of two sets of plastic tubes arranged in a plastic frame. Flies are put in Tube *0*; the device is held vertically and tapped to knock the flies to the bottom of the tube, and then the frame is laid flat and placed before a light at the far end of the tubes (*a*). Flies showing the phototactic response move toward the light, whereas others stay behind (*b*). After 15 seconds the top row of tubes is shifted to the right (*c*) and the responders are tapped down again (*d*), falling into Tube *1*. The upper frame is returned to the left (*e*), the frame is laid flat and again the responders move

toward the light. The procedure is repeated five times in all. By then the best responders are in Tube *5*, the next best in Tube *4* and so on (*f*). The curves (*bottom left*) show typical results. Phototactic flies show two very distinct peaks depending on whether the light was at the opposite end of the tubes from the starting point (*color*) or at the starting end (*black*). Nonphototactic flies, however, yield about the same curve (*light color or gray*) regardless of the position of the light. In order to distinguish variation in motor activity from phototaxis, the separation is carried out first toward light and then, processing the flies in each tube again, away from light, yielding a two-dimensional "chromatogram" (*bottom right*).

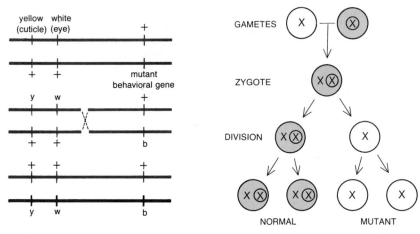

PREPARATION OF MOSAIC FLIES depends on the recombination on one *X* chromosome of genes for mutant "marker" traits and for a behavioral mutation. Recombination occurs through the crossing-over of segments of two homologous chromosomes, as shown at left. Males with an *X* chromosome carrying the desired recombination (*black*) are mated with females carrying an unstable ring-shaped *X* chromosome (*top row at right*). Among the resulting zygotes, or fertilized eggs, will be some carrying the mutation-loaded *X* and a ring *X*. In the course of nuclear division the ring *X* is sometimes lost. Tissues that stem from that nucleus are male, and mutant. In tissues that retain the ring *X*, however, the mutant genes are masked by the genes on the ring *X*, and these tissues are female and normal.

the fly will be male. The ring *X* chromosome has the property that it may get lost during nuclear division in the developing egg. If we start with female eggs that have one normal *X* and one ring *X*, in a certain fraction of the embryos some of the nuclei formed on division lose the ring *X* and therefore have only one *X* chromosome left, and will therefore produce male tissues. This loss of the ring *X*, when it occurs, tends to happen at a very early stage in such a way as to produce about equal numbers of *XX* and *X* nuclei. The nuclei divide a

few times in a cluster and then migrate to the surface of the egg to form the early embryonic stage called a blastula: a single layer of cells surrounding the yolk [*see bottom illustration on this page*]. The nuclei tend to retain their proximity to their neighbors in the cluster, so that the female (*XX*) cells populate one part of the blastoderm (the surface of the blastula) and the male cells cover the rest. It is a feature of *Drosophila* that the axis of the crucial first nuclear division is oriented arbitrarily with respect to the axes of the egg. The dividing line between the *XX* and *X* cells can therefore cut the blastoderm in different ways. Once the blastoderm is formed the site occupied by a cell largely determines its fate in the developing embryo, and so the adult gynandromorph, a male-female mosaic, can have a wide variety of arrangements of male and female parts depending on how the dividing line falls in each particular embryo. The division of parts often follows the intersegmental boundaries and the longitudinal midline of the fly's exoskeleton. The reason is that the exoskeleton is an assembly of many parts, each of which was formed independently during metamorphosis from an imaginal disk in the larva that was in turn derived from a specific area of the blastoderm [*see illustrations on opposite page*].

The reader will perceive that a mosaic fly is a system in which the effects of normal and of mutant genes can be distinguished in one animal. We use this system by arranging things so that both a behavioral gene and "marker" genes that produce anatomical anomalies are combined on the same *X* chromosome. This is done through the random workings of the phenomenon of recombination, in which segments of two chromosomes (in this case the *X*) "cross over" and exchange places with each other during cell division in the formation of the egg. In this way we can, for example, produce a strain of flies that are *nonphototactic* and also have white eyes (instead of the normal red) and a yellow body color. Then we breed males of this strain with females of the ring *X* strain. Some of the resulting embryos will have one ring *X* chromosome and one mutation-loaded *X* chromosome. In a fraction of these embryos the ring *X* (carrying normal genes) will be lost at an early nuclear division. The *XX* body parts of the resulting adult fly will have one *X* chromosome with normal genes and one with mutations; because both the behavioral and the anatomical genes in question are recessive (their effect is masked by the presence of a single nor-

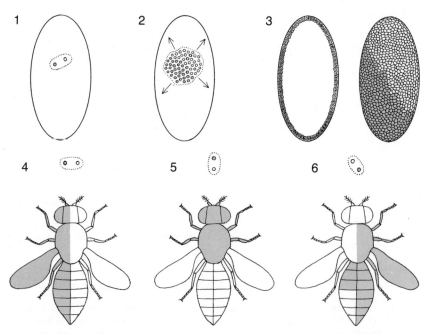

DEVELOPMENT OF A MOSAIC FLY proceeds from nuclear division (*shown in the illustration at top of page*), in which loss of the ring *X* occurs, producing an *XX* (*color*) nucleus and an *X* (*white*) nucleus (*1*). The nuclei divide a few times (*2*), then migrate to the surface of the egg and form a blastula: a single layer of cells, shown here in section and surface views (*3*). Note that female (*XX*) cells cover part of the surface and male (*X*) cells the other part. The arrangement of male (*white*) and female (*color*) parts in the adult fly depends on the way the boundary between the *XX* and *X* cells happened to cut the blastula, and that in turn depends on the orientation of the axis along which the original nucleus divides (*4–6*).

mal gene) the mutations will not be expressed in those parts. In the body parts having lost the ring X, however, the single X chromosome will be the one carrying the mutations. And because it is all alone the mutations will be expressed. Examination of the fly identifies the parts that have normal color and those in which the mutant genes have been uncovered. We can select from among the randomly divided gynandromorphs individuals in which the dividing line falls in various ways: a normal head on a mutant body, a mutant head on a normal body, a mutant eye and a normal one and so on. And then we can pose the question we originally had in mind: What parts must be mutant for the mutant behavior to be expressed?

When Hotta and I did that with certain visually defective mutants, for instance ones that produce no receptor potential, we found that the electroretinogram of the mutant eye was always completely abnormal, whereas the normal eye functioned properly. Even in gynandromorphs in which everything was normal except for one eye, that eye showed a defective electroretinogram. This makes it clear that the defects in those mutants are not of the vitamin A type I mentioned above; the defect must be autonomous within the eye itself.

The behavior of flies with one good eye and one bad eye is quite striking. A normal fly placed in a vertical tube in the dark climbs more or less straight up, with gravity as its cue. If there is a light at the top of the tube, the fly still climbs straight up because phototaxis (which the fly achieves by moving so as to keep the light intensities on both eyes equal) is consistent in direction with the negative geotaxis. A mosaic fly with one good eye also climbs straight up in the dark, since its sense of gravity is unimpaired. If a light is turned on at the top, however, the fly tends to trace a helical path, turning its defective eye toward the light in a futile attempt to balance input signals. If the right eye is the bad one, the fly traces a right-handed helix; if the left eye is bad, the helix is left-handed. (Sometimes it is difficult to resist the temptation, out of nostalgia for the old molecular-biology days, to put in two flies and let them generate a double helix.)

In these mutants the primary focus of the *phototactic* defect is in the affected organ itself. More frequently, however, the focus is elsewhere. A good way to see how this situation is dealt with is to consider a *hyperkinetic* mutant that

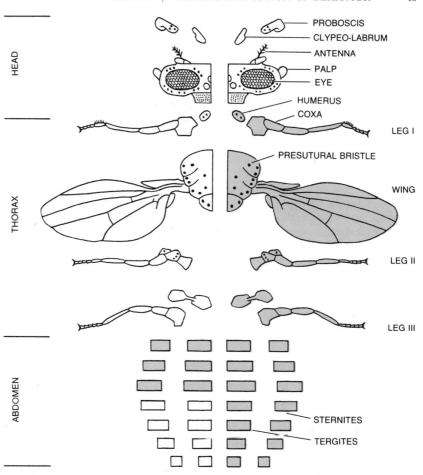

ADULT FLY is an assembly of a large number of external body parts, each of which was formed independently from a primordial group of cells of the blastula. In a mosaic fly the boundary between male and female tissues tends to follow lines of division between discrete body parts. Here the main external parts are named; black dots are the major bristles.

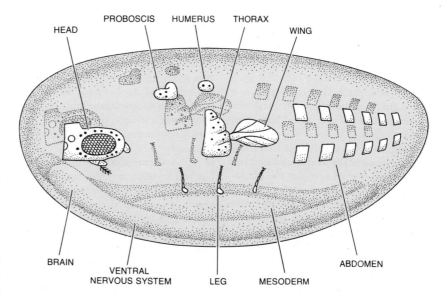

FANCIFUL DRAWING of the blastula shows how each adult body part came from a specific site on the blastula: left-side and right-side parts (or left and right halves of parts such as the head) from the left and right sides of the blastula respectively. The nervous system and the mesoderm (which gives rise to the muscles) have also been shown by embryologists to originate in specified regions of the blastula. It is clear that the probability that any two parts will have a different genotype (that is, that they will be on different sides of the mosaic boundary that cuts across the blastula) will depend on how far they are from each other on the blastoderm, the blastula surface. Conversely, the probability that two parts are of different genotypes should be a measure of their distance apart on the blastoderm.

was studied by Kaplan and Kazuo Ikeda. When such a fly is anesthetized with ether, it does not lie still but rather shakes all six of its legs vigorously. Kaplan and Ikeda found that flies that are mosaics for the gene shake some of their legs but not others and that the shaking usually correlates well with the leg's surface genotype as revealed by markers—but not always. (Suzuki and his colleagues found the same to be true of flies mosaic for the *paralyzed* mutation.) The point is that the markers are on the outside of the fly. The genotype of the surface is not necessarily the same as that of the underlying tissues, which arise from different regions of the embryo. And one might well expect that leg function would be controlled by nervous elements somewhere inside the fly's body that could have a different genotype from the leg surface. The problem is to find a way of relating internal behavioral foci to external landmarks. Hotta and I developed a method of mapping this relation by extending to behavior the idea of a "fate map," which was originally conceived by A. H. Sturtevant of Cal Tech.

Sturtevant was the genius who had earlier shown how to map the sequence of genes on the chromosome by measuring the frequency of recombination among genes. He had seen that the probability of crossing over would be greater the farther apart the genes were on the chromosome. In 1929 he proposed that one might map the blastoderm in an analogous way: the frequency with which any two parts of adult mosaics turned out to be of different genotypes could be related to the distance apart on the blastoderm of the sites that gave rise to those parts. One could look at a large group of mosaics, score structure *A* and structure *B* and record how often one was normal whereas the other was mutant, and vice versa. That frequency would represent the relative distance between their sites of origin on the blastoderm, and with enough such measurements one could in principle construct a two-dimensional map of the blastoderm. Sturtevant scored 379 mosaics of *Drosophila simulans*, put his data in a drawer and went on to something else. At Cal Tech 40 years later Merriam and Antonio Garcia-Bellido inherited those 379 yellowed sheets of paper, computed the information and found they could indeed make a self-consistent map.

When Hotta and I undertook to map behavior in *D. melanogaster*, we began by preparing our own fate map of the adult external body parts based on the scores for 703 mosaic flies [see *upper il-*

lustration on these two pages]. Distances on the map are in "sturts," a unit Merriam, Hotta and I have proposed in memory of Sturtevant. One sturt is equivalent to a probability of 1 percent that the two structures will be of different genotypes.

Now back to *hyperkinetic*. We produced 300 mosaic flies and scored each for a number of surface landmarks and for the coincidence of marker mutations at those landmarks with the shaking of each leg. We confirmed the observations of Ikeda and Kaplan that the behavior of each leg (whether it shakes or not) is independent of the behavior of the other legs and that the shaking behavior and the external genotype of a leg are frequently the same—but not always. The independent behavior of the legs indicated that each had a separate focus. For each leg we calculated the distance from the shaking focus to the leg itself and to a number of other landmarks [see *lower illustration on these two pages*] and thus determined a map location for each focus. They are near the corresponding legs but below them, in the region of the blastoderm that Donald F. Poulson of Yale University years ago identified by embryological studies as the origin of the ventral nervous system. This is consistent with electrophysiological evidence, obtained by Ikeda and Kaplan, that neurons in the thoracic ganglion of the ventral nervous system behave abnormally in these mutants.

Another degree of complexity is represented by a mutant we call *drop-dead*. These flies develop, walk, fly and otherwise behave normally for a day or two after eclosion. Suddenly, however, an individual fly becomes less active, walks in an uncoordinated manner, falls on its back and dies; the transition from apparently normal behavior to death takes only a few hours. The time of onset of the syndrome among a group of flies hatched together is quite variable; after the first two days the number of survivors in the group drops exponentially, with a half-life of about two days. It is as if some random event triggers a cataclysm. The gene has been identified as a recessive one on the *X* chromosome. Symptoms such as these could result from malfunction almost anywhere in the body of the fly, for example from a blockage of the gut, a general biochemical disturbance or a nerve disorder. In order to localize the focus we did an analysis of 403 mosaics in which the *XX* parts were normal and the *X* body parts expressed the *drop-dead* gene and surface-marker mutations, and we scored

for *drop-dead* behavior and various landmarks.

Drop-dead behavior, unlike shaking behavior, which could be scored separately for each leg, is an all-or-none property of the entire fly. First we did a rough analysis to determine whether the behavior was most closely related to the head, thorax or abdomen, considering only flies in which the surface of each of these structures was either completely mutant or completely normal. Among mosaics in which the entire head surface was normal almost all behaved

		ANTENNA	
		NORMAL	MUTANT
COXA OF LEG I	NORMAL	35	12
	MUTANT	13	40

$$\frac{12 + 13}{100} = 25 \text{ PERCENT} = 25 \text{ STURTS FROM ANTENNA TO COXA I}$$

		COXA OF LEG I	
		NORMAL	MUTANT
PRESUTURAL BRISTLE	NORMAL	45	8
	MUTANT	6	41

$$\frac{8 + 6}{100} = 14 \text{ PERCENT} = 14 \text{ STURTS FROM COXA I TO PRESUTURAL BRISTLE}$$

FATE MAP, a two-dimensional map of the blastoderm, is constructed by calculating the distances between the sites that gave rise to various parts. This is done by observing a large number of adult flies and recording the number of times each of two parts is mu-

		COXA OF LEG I	
		NORMAL	MUTANT
SHAKING OF LEG I	NORMAL	277	51
	MUTANT	33	224

$$\frac{84}{600} = 14 \text{ STURTS FROM COXA I TO SHAKING FOCUS}$$

		ANTENNA	
		NORMAL	MUTANT
SHAKING OF LEG I	NORMAL	253	82
	MUTANT	85	180

$$\frac{167}{600} = 28 \text{ STURTS FROM ANTENNA TO SHAKING FOCUS}$$

BEHAVIORAL FOCI, the sites at which a mutant gene exerts its effect on behavior, are plotted in the same way. The behavior in this example (*left*) is abnormal shaking of

normally, but six flies out of 97 died in the *drop-dead* manner; in the reciprocal class eight flies of 80 with mutant head surfaces lived. In other words, the focus was shown to be close to, but distinct from, the blastoderm site of origin of the head surface. Comparable analysis showed that the focus was substantially farther away from the thorax and farther still from the abdomen. Next we considered individuals with mosaic heads. The reader will recall that in certain visual mutants the visual defect was always observed in the eye on the mutant

side of the head; flies with half-normal heads had normal vision in one eye. For *drop-dead*, on the other hand, of mosaics in which half of the head surface was mutant only about 17 percent dropped dead. All the rest survived.

Now, a given internal part should occur in normal or mutant form with equal probability, as the external parts in these mosaics did. On that reasoning, if there were a single focus inside the head of the fly, half of the bilateral-mosaic flies should have dropped dead. We formed the hypothesis, therefore, that there

must be two foci, one on each side, and that they must interact. Both of them must be mutant for the syndrome to appear. In other words, a mutant focus must be "submissive" to a normal one. In that case, if an individual exhibits *drop-dead* behavior, both foci must be mutant, and if a fly survives, one focus may be normal or both of them may be.

Mapping a bilateral pair of interacting foci calls for special analysis. By considering the various ways a mosaic dividing line could fall in relation to a pair of visible external landmarks (one on

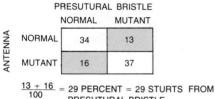

$$\frac{13 + 16}{100} = 29 \text{ PERCENT} = 29 \text{ STURTS FROM}$$
PRESUTURAL BRISTLE
TO ANTENNA

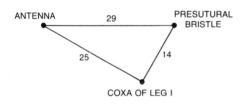

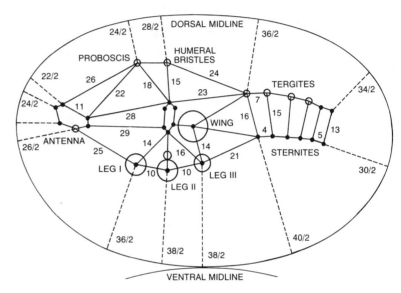

tant or normal. The numbers are entered in a matrix, as shown (*left*) for three pairs of parts. Instances in which one part is normal whereas the other part is mutant on the same fly (*colored boxes*) are totaled. That figure, divided by the total number of instances, gives the probability that the two parts are of different genotypes. And that probability is proportional to the distance between them,

indicated in "sturts." Plotting the three distances triangulates the relative locations of the three sites. By thus scoring 703 mosaic flies for body parts, Yoshiki Hotta in the author's laboratory built up the fate map of external body parts (*right*). Broken lines represent distances to the blastula midlines, obtained by dividing by two the distances between homologous parts on opposite sides of the fly.

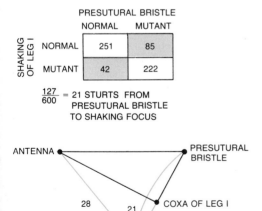

$$\frac{127}{600} = 21 \text{ STURTS FROM}$$
PRESUTURAL BRISTLE
TO SHAKING FOCUS

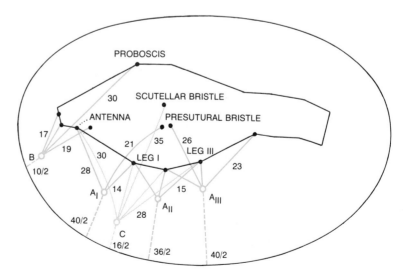

the legs under ether. The shaking is independent for each leg and here leg *I* has been scored for 300 flies—or 600 instances, since the data can be doubled to represent both sides of the fly. (The total of instances can be less than 600 because cases in which both the body

part and the behavior are mosaic are eliminated.) Distances calculated (*colored lines*) triangulate the focus. In this way the foci for shaking behavior for each leg (*A*) are added to the map (*right*). Foci for *drop-dead* (*B*) and *wings-up* (*C*) behavior are also found.

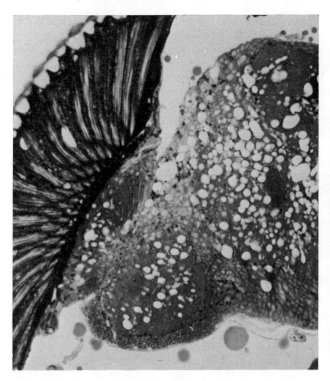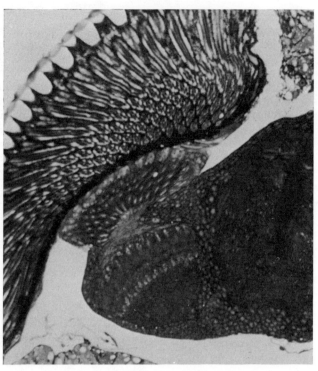

BRAINS OF DROP-DEAD MUTANTS that have reached the symptomatic stage show striking degeneration, as shown by photomicrograph (*left*) of a section of such a fly's head enlarged 300 diameters. The brain and the optic ganglia are full of holes. Sections fixed before a mutant has shown any symptoms, on the other hand, show no more degeneration than a section of a normal brain does (*right*).

each side of the body) and a symmetrical pair of internal foci, one can set up equations based on the probability of each possible configuration. Using the observed data on how many mosaic flies showed the various combinations of mutant and normal external landmarks and mutant or normal behavior, it is possible to solve these equations for the map distance from each landmark to the corresponding focus and from one focus to the homologous focus on the other side of the embryo. The *drop-dead* foci turn out to be below the head-surface area of the blastoderm, in the area embryologists have assigned to the brain. Sure enough, when we examined the brain tissue of flies that had begun to exhibit the initial stages of *drop-dead* behavior, it showed striking signs of degeneration, whereas brain tissue fixed before the onset of symptoms appeared normal. As for mosaics whose head surfaces are half-normal, those that die show degeneration of the brain on both sides; the survivors' brains show no degeneration on either side, a finding consistent with the bilateral-submissive-focus hypothesis. It appears that the normal side of the brain supplies some factor that prevents the deterioration of the side with the mutant focus.

There is another kind of bilateral focus, "domineering" rather than submissive. An example is the mutant we call

wings-up. There are two different genes, *wup A* and *wup B*, which produce very similar overt behavior: shortly after emergence each of these flies raises its wings straight up and keeps them there. It cannot fly, but otherwise it behaves normally. Is *wings-up* the result of a defect in the wing itself, in its articulation or in the muscles or neuromuscular junctions that control the wing, or of some "psychological quirk" in the central nervous system? The study of mosaic flies shows that the behavior is more often associated with a mutant thorax than with a mutant head or abdomen. The focus cannot be in the wings themselves or anywhere on the surface of the thorax, however, because in some mosaics the wings and the thorax surface are normal and yet the wings are held up and in other mosaics the wings and thorax display all the mutant markers and yet the fly flies. These observations suggest that some structure inside the thorax could be responsible.

Once again we look at the bilateral mosaics, those with one side of the thorax carrying mutant markers and the other side appearing normal. Unlike the *drop-dead* bilateral mosaics, most of which were normal, these bilaterals are primarily mutant; well over half of them hold both wings up. Both wings seem to act together; either both are held up or both are in the normal position. This sug-

gests two interacting foci, one on each side, with the mutant focus domineering with respect to the normal one, that is, if either of the foci is mutant, or both are, then both wings will be up. Again we can set up equations based on the probability of the various mosaic configurations and solve to find the pertinent map distances. The focus comes out to be close to the ventral midline of the blastula. That is a region known to produce the mesoderm, the part of the developing embryo from which muscle tissue is derived, which suggested that a defect in the fly's thoracic muscle tissue could be responsible for *wings-up* behavior.

The abnormality became obvious when we dissected the thorax. In the fly the raising and lowering of the wings in normal flight is accomplished by changes in the shape of the thorax, changes brought about by the alternate action of sets of vertical and horizontal muscles. Under the phase-contrast microscope these indirect flight muscles are seen to be highly abnormal in both *wings-up* mutants. Developmental studies show that in *wup A* the muscles form properly at first, then degenerate after the fly emerges. In the *wup B* mutant, on the other hand, the myoblasts that normally produce the muscles fuse properly but the muscle fibrils fail to appear. In both mutants the other muscles, such as those of the leg, appear to be quite normal,

FLIGHT MUSCLE OF WINGS-UP MUTANTS shows degeneration that seems to account for their behavior. Normal flight muscle, enlarged 30,000 diameters in an electron micrograph, has bundles of filaments crossed by straight, dense bands: the Z lines (*left*). In the muscle of flies heterozygous for the gene *wup B*, which hold their wings normally but cannot fly, the Z lines are irregular (*right*).

and the flies walk and climb perfectly well. In flies that are heterozygous for *wup A* (nonmosaic flies with one mutated and one normal gene) the muscles and flight behavior are normal, that is, the gene is completely recessive. In *wup B* heterozygotes, on the other hand, the wings are held in the normal position but the flies cannot fly. Electron microscopy shows that even in these heterozygotes the indirect flight muscles are defective: the microscopic filaments that constitute each muscle fibril are arranged correctly, but the Z line, a dense region that should run straight across the fibril, is often crooked and forked. Examination of the muscles in bilateral mosaics confirmed the impression that the *wup* foci are domineering. In every mosaic that had shown *wings-up* behavior one or more muscle fibers were degenerated or missing; no fibers were seriously deficient in any flies that had displayed normal behavior. The natural shape of the thorax apparently corresponds to the *wings-up* position, and the presence of defective muscles on either side is enough to make it impossible to change the shape of the thorax, locking the wings in the vertical position.

The mutants so far mapped provide examples involving the main components of behavior: sensory receptors, the nervous system and the muscles. For some of the mutants microscopic examination has revealed a conspicuous lesion of some kind in tissue. The obvious question is whether or not fate mapping is necessary; why do we not just look directly for abnormal tissue? One answer is that for many mutants we do not know where to begin to look, and it is helpful to narrow down the relevant region. Furthermore, in many cases no lesion may be visible, even in the electron microscope. More important, and worth reiterating, is the fact that the site of a lesion is not necessarily the primary focus. For example, an anomaly of muscle tissue may result from a defect in the function of nerves supplying the muscle. This possibility has been a lively issue in the study of diseases such as muscular dystrophy. Recently, by taking nerve and muscle tissues from a dystrophic mutant of the mouse and from its normal counterpart and growing them in tissue culture in all four combinations, the British workers Belinda Gallup and V. Dubowitz were able to show that the nerves are indeed at fault.

The mosaic technique in effect does the same kind of experiment in the intact animal. In the case of the *wings-up* mutant the primary focus cannot be in the nerves, since if that were so the focus would map to the area of the blastoderm destined to produce the nervous system, not to the mesoderm, where muscle tissue is formed. The *wings-up* mutants clearly have defects that originate in the muscles themselves.

Another application of mosaics is in tagging cells with genetic labels to follow their development. The compound eye of *Drosophila* is a remarkable structure consisting of about 800 ommatidia: unit eyes containing eight receptor cells each. The arrangement of cells in an ommatidium is precise and repetitive; the eye is in effect a neurological crystal in which the unit cell contains eight neurons. Thomas E. Hanson, Donald F. Ready and I have been interested in how this structure is formed. Are the eight photoreceptor cells derived from one cell that undergoes three divisions to produce eight, or do cells come together to form the group irrespective of their lineage? This can be tested by examining the eyes of flies, mosaic for the *white* gene, in which the mosaic dividing line passes through the eye. By sectioning the eye and examining ommatidia near the border between white and red areas microscopically, it is possible to score the tiny pigment granules that are present in normal photoreceptor cells but absent in *white* mutant cells. The result is clear: A single ommatidium can contain a mixture of receptor cells of both genotypes. This proves that the eight cells cannot be derived from a single ancestral cell but have become associated in their special group of eight irrespective of lineage. The same conclusion applies to the other cells in each ommatidium, such as the normally heavily pigmented cells that surround the receptors.

Not all cells have such convenient pigment markers. It would obviously be valuable to have a way of labeling all the internal tissues as being either mutant or normal, much as yellow color labels a landmark on the surface. This can now be done for many tissues by utilizing mutants that lack a specific enzyme. If a recessive enzyme-deficient mutant gene is recombined on the X chromosome along with the *yellow, white* and behavioral genes and mosaics are produced in the usual way, the male tissues of the mosaic will lack the enzyme. By making a frozen section of the fly and staining it for enzyme activity one can identify normal and mutant cells.

In order to apply this method in the nervous system one needs to have an enzyme that is normally present there in a large enough concentration to show up in the staining procedure and a mutant that lacks the enzyme, and the lack should have a negligible effect on the behavior under study. Finally, the gene in question should be on the X chromosome. Douglas R. Kankel and Jeffrey Hall in our laboratory have developed several such mutants, including one with an acid-phosphatase-deficient gene found by Ross J. MacIntyre of Cornell University. By scoring the internal tissues they have constructed a fate map of the internal organs of the kind made earlier for surface structures. We are now adapting the staining method for electron microscopy in order to work at the level of the individual cell.

The staining procedure has demon-

strated graphically that the photoreceptor cells of the eye come from a different area of the blastoderm than do the neurons of the lamina, to which they project. In the adult fly the two groups of cells are in close apposition, but the former arise in the eye whereas the latter come from the brain. The distance between them on the fate map, determined by Kankel, is about 12 sturts, so that a considerable number of mosaic flies have a normal retina and a mutant lamina or vice versa. This makes it possible to distinguish between presynaptic and postsynaptic defects in mutants with blocks in the visual pathway. In the nonphototactic mutants Hotta and I analyzed in mosaics, the defect in the electroretinogram was always associated with the eye. In contrast, a mutant with a similar electroretinogram abnormality that was studied by Linda Hall and Suzuki

MOSAIC EYE contains a patch of cells that carry the *white* gene and therefore lack the normal red pigment. The fly's compound eye is an array of hexagonal ommatidia, each containing eight photoreceptor cells (*circles*) and two primary pigment cells (*crescents*) and surrounded by six shared secondary pigment cells (*ovals*). The fact that a single ommatidium can have *white* and normal genotypes shows its cells are not necessarily descended from a common ancestral cell. Nor is the mirror-image symmetry about the equator (*heavy line*) the result of two cell lines: mutant cells appear on both sides. Drawing is based on observations by Donald Ready.

showed, in some mosaics, a normal trace for a mutant eye—and vice versa. Fate mapping placed the focus in precisely the region corresponding to the lamina. What appeared to be similar malfunctions in two mutants were thus shown to be different, due in one case to a presynaptic block and in the other case to a postsynaptic one.

Much of what has been done so far involves relatively simple aspects of behavior chosen to establish the general methodology of mutants and mosaic analysis. Can the methodology be applied to more elaborate and interesting behavior such as circadian rhythm, sexual courtship and learning? Some beginnings have been made on all of these. By making flies that are mutant for normal and mutant rhythms, Konopka has shown that the internal clock is most closely associated with the head. Looking at flies with mosaic heads, he found that some exhibited the normal rhythm and others the mutant rhythm but that a few flies exhibited a peculiar rhythm that appears to be a sum of the two, as if each side of the brain were producing its rhythm independently and the fly responded to both of them. By applying the available cell-staining techniques it may be possible to identify the cells that control the clock.

Sexual courtship is a higher form of behavior, since it consists of a series of fixed action patterns, each step of which makes the next step more likely. The sex mosaics we have generated lend themselves beautifully to the analysis of sexual behavior. A mosaic fly can be put with normal females and its ability to perform the typical male courtship steps can be observed. Hotta, Hall and I found that the first steps (orientation toward the female and vibrating of the wings) map to the brain. This is of particular interest because the wings are vibrated by motor-nerve impulses from the thoracic ganglion; even a female ganglion will produce the vibration "song" typical of the male if directed to do so by a male brain. It would appear that the thoracic ganglion in a female must "know" the male courtship song even though she does not normally emit it. This is consistent with recent experiments by Ronald Hoy and Robert Paul at the State University of New York at Stony Brook, in which they showed that hybrid cricket females responded better to the songs of hybrid males than to males of either of the two parental species.

Sexual behavior in *Drosophila*, although complex, is a stereotyped series of instinctive actions that are performed

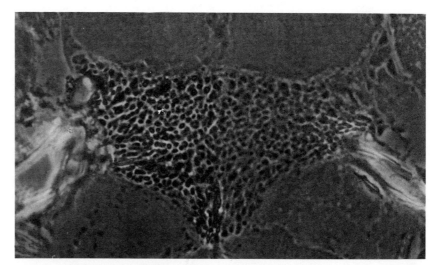

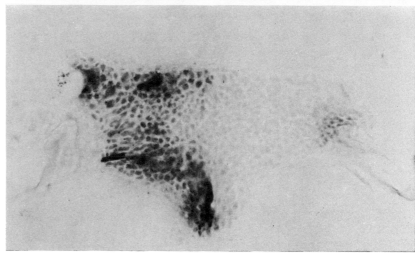

DIRECT SCORING OF NORMAL AND MUTANT CELLS within the nervous system is possible with a staining method developed by Douglas Kankel and Jeffrey Hall in the author's laboratory. Mosaics are produced in which mutant cells are deficient in the enzyme acid phosphatase. When the proper stain is applied to a section of nerve tissue, normal cells stain brown and mutant cells are unstained. Here a section of the thoracic ganglion, thus stained, is shown in phase-contrast (*top*) and bright-field (*bottom*) photomicrographs. In the bottom picture normal cells are marked by the stain, delineating the mosaic boundary.

correctly by a fly raised in isolation and without previous sexual experience. Other forms of behavior such as phototaxis also appear to be already programmed into the fly when it ecloses. Whether a fruit fly can learn has long been debated; various claims have been made and later shown to be incorrect. Recently William G. Quinn, Jr., and William A. Harris in our laboratory have shown in carefully controlled experiments that the fly can learn to avoid specific odors or colors of light that are associated with a negative reinforcement such as electric shock. This opens the door to genetic analysis of learning behavior through mutations that block it.

In tackling the complex problems of behavior the gene provides, in effect, a microsurgical tool with which to produce very specific blocks in a behavioral pathway. With temperature-dependent mutations the blocks can be turned on and off at will. Individual cells of the nervous system can be labeled genetically and their lineage can be followed during development. Genetic mosaics offer the equivalent of exquisitely fine grafting of normal and mutant parts, with the entire structure remaining intact. What we are doing in mosaic mapping is in effect "unrolling" the fantastically complex adult fly, in which sense organs, nerve cells and muscles are completely interwoven, backward in development, back in time to the blastoderm, a stage at which the different structures have not yet come together. Filling the gaps between the one-dimensional gene, the two-dimensional blastoderm, the three-dimensional organism and its multidimensional behavior is a challenge for the future.

5

"Imprinting" in a Natural Laboratory

by Eckhard H. Hess
August 1972

*A synthesis of laboratory and field techniques has
led to some interesting discoveries about imprinting,
the process by which newly hatched birds rapidly
form a permanent bond to the parent*

In a marsh on the Eastern Shore of Maryland, a few hundred feet from my laboratory building, a female wild mallard sits on a dozen infertile eggs. She has been incubating the eggs for almost four weeks. Periodically she hears the faint peeping sounds that are emitted by hatching mallard eggs, and she clucks softly in response. Since these eggs are infertile, however, they are not about to hatch and they do not emit peeping sounds. The sounds come from a small loudspeaker hidden in the nest under the eggs. The loudspeaker is connected to a microphone next to some hatching mallard eggs inside an incubator in my laboratory. The female mallard can hear any sounds coming from the laboratory eggs, and a microphone beside her relays the sounds she makes to a loudspeaker next to those eggs.

The reason for complicating the life of an expectant duck in such a way is to further our understanding of the phenomenon known as imprinting. It was through the work of the Austrian zoologist Konrad Z. Lorenz that imprinting became widely known. In the 1930's Lorenz observed that newly hatched goslings would follow him rather than their mother if the goslings saw him before they saw her. Since naturally reared geese show a strong attachment for their parent, Lorenz concluded that some animals have the capacity to learn rapidly and permanently at a very early age, and in particular to learn the characteristics of the parent. He called this process of acquiring an attachment to the parent *Prägung*, which in German means "stamping" or "coinage" but in English has been rendered as "imprinting." Lorenz regarded the phenomenon as being different from the usual kind of learning because of its rapidity and apparent permanence. In fact, he was hesitant at first to regard imprinting as a form of learn-

ing at all. Some child psychologists and some psychiatrists nevertheless perceived a similarity between the evidence of imprinting in animals and the early behavior of the human infant, and it is not surprising that interest in imprinting spread quickly.

From about the beginning of the 1950's many investigators have intensively studied imprinting in the laboratory. Unlike Lorenz, the majority of them have regarded imprinting as a form

of learning and have used methods much the same as those followed in the study of associative learning processes. In every case efforts were made to manipulate or stringently control the imprinting process. Usually the subjects are incubator-hatched birds that are reared in the laboratory. The birds are typically kept isolated until the time of the laboratory imprinting experience to prevent interaction of early social experience and the imprinting experience. Various objects

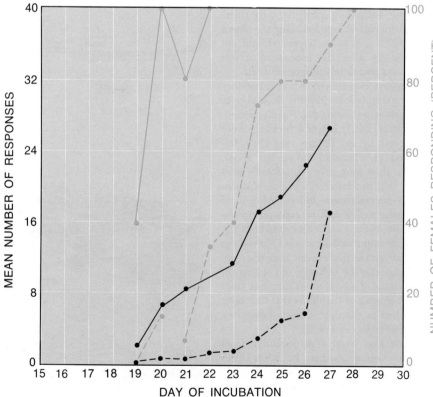

VOCAL RESPONSES to hatching-duckling sounds of 15 female wild mallards (*broken curves*) and five human-imprinted mallards (*solid curves*), which were later released to the wild, followed the same pattern, although the human-imprinted mallards began responding sooner and more frequently. A tape recording of the sounds of a hatching duckling was played daily throughout the incubation period to each female mallard while she was on her nest. Responses began on the 19th day of incubation and rose steadily until hatching.

have been used as artificial parents: duck decoys, stuffed hens, dolls, milk bottles, toilet floats, boxes, balls, flashing lights and rotating disks. Several investigators have constructed an automatic imprinting apparatus into which the newly hatched bird can be put. In this kind of work the investigator does not observe the young bird directly; all the bird's movements with respect to the imprinting object are recorded automatically.

Much of my own research during the past two decades has not differed substantially from this approach. The birds I have used for laboratory imprinting studies have all been incubated, hatched and reared without the normal social and environmental conditions and have then been tested in an artificial situation. It is therefore possible that the behavior observed under such conditions is not relevant to what actually happens in nature.

It is perhaps not surprising that studies of "unnatural" imprinting have produced conflicting results. Lorenz' original statements on the permanence of natural imprinting have been disputed. In many instances laboratory imprinting experiences do not produce permanent and exclusive attachment to the object selected as an artificial parent. For example, a duckling can spend a considerable amount of time following the object to which it is to be imprinted, and immediately after the experience it will follow a completely different object.

In one experiment in our laboratory we attempted to imprint ducklings to ourselves, as Lorenz did. For 20 continuous hours newly hatched ducklings were exposed to us. Before long they followed us whenever we moved about. Then they were given to a female mallard that had hatched a clutch of ducklings several hours before. After only an hour and a half of exposure to the female mallard and other ducklings the human-imprinted ducklings followed the female on the first exodus from the nest. Weeks later the behavior of the human-imprinted ducks was no different from the behavior of the ducks that had been hatched in the nest. Clearly laboratory imprinting is reversible.

We also took wild ducklings from their natural mother 16 hours after hatching and tried to imprint them to humans. On the first day we spent many hours with the ducklings, and during the next two months we made lengthy attempts every day to overcome the ducklings' fear of us. We finally gave up. From the beginning to the end the ducks

remained wild and afraid. They were released, and when they had matured, they were observed to be as wary of humans as normal wild ducks are. This result suggests that natural imprinting, unlike artificial laboratory imprinting, is permanent and irreversible. I have had to conclude that the usual laboratory imprinting has only a limited resemblance to natural imprinting.

It seems obvious that if the effects of natural imprinting are to be understood, the phenomenon must be studied as it operates in nature. The value of such studies was stressed as long ago as 1914 by the pioneer American psychologist John B. Watson. He emphasized that field observations must always be made to test whether or not conclusions drawn from laboratory studies conform to what actually happens in nature. The disparity between laboratory results and what happens in nature often arises from the failure of the investigator to really look at the animal's behavior. For years I have cautioned my students against shutting their experimental animals in "black boxes" with automatic recording

devices and never directly observing how the animals behave.

This does not mean that objective laboratory methods for studying the behavior of animals must be abandoned. With laboratory investigations large strides have been made in the development of instruments for the recording of behavior. In the study of imprinting it is not necessary to revert to imprecise naturalistic observations in the field. We can now go far beyond the limitations of traditional field studies. It is possible to set up modern laboratory equipment in actual field conditions and in ways that do not disturb or interact with the behavior being studied, in other words, to achieve a synthesis of laboratory and field techniques.

The first step in the field-laboratory method is to observe and record the undisturbed natural behavior of the animal in the situation being studied. In our work on imprinting we photographed the behavior of the female mallard during incubation and hatching. We photographed the behavior of the ducklings during and after hatching. We recorded

CLUCKS emitted by a female wild mallard in the fourth week of incubating eggs are shown in the sound spectrogram (*upper illustration*). Each cluck lasts for about 150 milliseconds

all sounds from the nest before and after hatching. Other factors, such as air temperature and nest temperature, were also recorded.

A detailed inventory of the actual events in natural imprinting is essential for providing a reference point in the assessment of experimental manipulations of the imprinting process. That is, the undisturbed natural imprinting events form the control situation for assessing the effects of the experimental manipulations. This is quite different from the "controlled" laboratory setting, in which the ducklings are reared in isolation and then tested in unnatural conditions. The controlled laboratory study not only introduces new variables (environmental and social deprivation) into the imprinting situation but also it can prevent the investigator from observing factors that are relevant in wild conditions.

My Maryland research station is well suited for the study of natural imprinting in ducks. The station, near a national game refuge, has 250 acres of marsh and forest on a peninsula on which there are many wild and semiwild mallards. Through the sharp eyes of my technical assistant Elihu Abbott, a native of the Eastern Shore, I have learned to see much I might otherwise have missed. Initially we looked at and listened to the undisturbed parent-offspring interaction of female mallards that hatched their own eggs both in nests on the ground and in specially constructed nest boxes. From our records we noticed that the incubation time required for different clutches of eggs decreased progressively between March and June. Both the average air temperature and the number of daylight hours increase during those months; both are correlated with the incubation time of mallard eggs. It is likely, however, that temperature rather than photoperiod directly influences the duration of incubation. In one experiment mallard eggs from an incubator were slowly cooled for two hours a day in a room with a temperature of seven degrees Celsius, and another set of eggs was cooled in a room at 27 degrees C. These temperatures re-spectively correspond to the mean noon temperatures at the research station in March and in June. The eggs that were placed in the cooler room took longer to hatch, indicating that temperature affects the incubation time directly. Factors such as humidity and barometric pressure may also play a role.

We noticed that all the eggs in a wild nest usually hatch between three and eight hours of one another. As a result all the ducklings in the same clutch are approximately the same age in terms of the number of hours since hatching. Yet when mallard eggs are placed in a mechanical incubator, they will hatch over a two- or three-day period even when precautions are taken to ensure that all the eggs begin developing simultaneously. The synchronous hatching observed in nature obviously has some survival value. At the time of the exodus from the nest, which usually takes place between 16 and 32 hours after hatching, all the ducklings would be of a similar age and thus would have equal motor capabilities and similar social experiences.

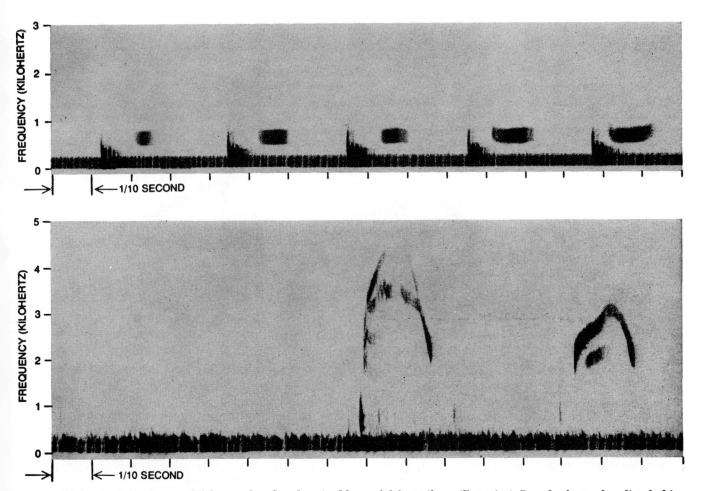

and is low in pitch: about one kilohertz or less. Sounds emitted by ducklings inside the eggs are high-pitched, rising to about four kilohertz (*lower illustration*). Records of natural, undisturbed imprinting events in the nest provide a control for later experiments.

Over the years our laboratory studies and actual observations of how a female mallard interacts with her offspring have pointed to the conclusion that imprinting is related to the age after hatching rather than the age from the beginning of incubation. Many other workers, however, have accepted the claim that age from the beginning of incubation determines the critical period for maximum effectiveness of imprinting. They base their belief on the findings of Gilbert Gottlieb of the Dorothea Dix Hospital in Raleigh, N.C., who in a 1961 paper described experiments that apparently showed that maximum imprinting in ducklings occurs in the period between 27 and 27½ days after the beginning of incubation. To make sure that all the eggs he was working with started incubation at the same time he first chilled the eggs so that any partially developed embryos would be killed. Yet the 27th day after the beginning of incubation can hardly be the period of maximum imprinting for wild ducklings that hatch in March under natural conditions, because such ducklings take on the average 28 days to hatch. Moreover, if the age of a duckling is measured from the beginning of incubation, it is hard to explain why eggs laid at different times in a hot month in the same nest will hatch within six to eight hours of one another under natural conditions.

Periodic cooling of the eggs seems to affect the synchronization of hatching. The mallard eggs from an incubator that were placed in a room at seven degrees C. hatched over a period of a day and a half, whereas eggs placed in the room at 27 degrees hatched over a period of two

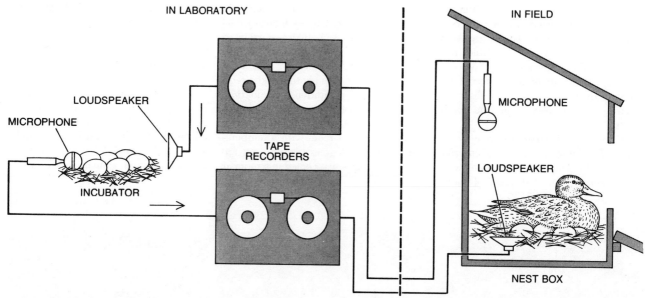

FEMALE MALLARD sitting on infertile eggs hears sounds transmitted from mallard eggs in a laboratory incubator. Any sounds she makes are transmitted to a loudspeaker beside the eggs in the laboratory. Such a combination of field and laboratory techniques permits recording of events without disturbing the nesting mallard and provides the hatching eggs with nearly natural conditions.

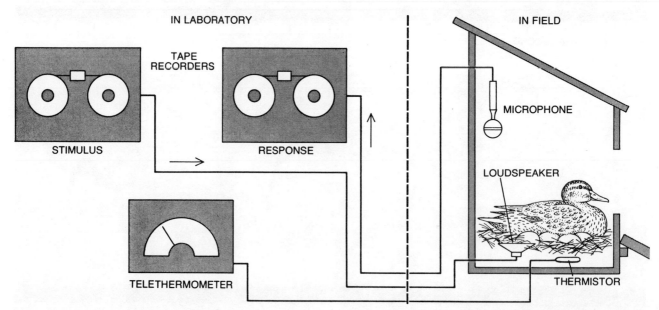

REMOTE MANIPULATION of prehatching sounds is accomplished by placing a sensitive microphone and a loudspeaker in the nest of a female wild mallard who is sitting on her own eggs. Prerecorded hatching-duckling sounds are played at specified times through the loudspeaker and the female mallard's responses to this stimulus are recorded. A thermistor probe transmits the temperature in the nest to a telethermometer and chart recorder. The thermistor records provide data about when females are on nest.

and a half days (which is about normal for artificially incubated eggs). Cooling cannot, however, play a major role. In June the temperature in the outdoor nest boxes averages close to the normal brooding temperature while the female mallard is absent. Therefore an egg laid on June 1 has a head start in incubation over those laid a week later. Yet we have observed that all the eggs in clutches laid in June hatch in a period lasting between six and eight hours.

We found another clue to how the synchronization of hatching may be achieved in the vocalization pattern of the brooding female mallard. As many others have noted, the female mallard vocalizes regularly as she sits on her eggs during the latter part of the incubation period. It seemed possible that she was vocalizing to the eggs, perhaps in response to sounds from the eggs themselves. Other workers had observed that ducklings make sounds before they hatch, and the prehatching behavior of ducklings in response to maternal calls has been extensively reported by Gottlieb.

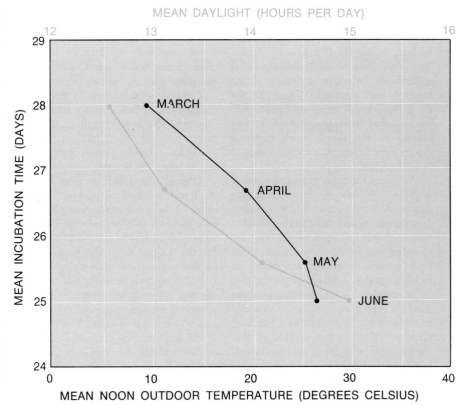

INCUBATION TIME of mallard eggs hatched naturally in a feral setting at Lake Cove, Md., decreased steadily from March to June. The incubation period correlated with both the outdoor temperature (*black curve*) and the daily photoperiod (*colored curve*).

We placed a highly sensitive microphone next to some mallard eggs that were nearly ready to hatch. We found that the ducklings indeed make sounds while they are still inside the egg. We made a one-minute tape recording of the sounds emitted by a duckling that had pipped its shell and was going to hatch within the next few hours. Then we made a seven-minute recording that would enable us to play the duckling sounds three times for one minute interspersed with one-minute silences. We played the recording once each to 37 female mallards at various stages of

NEST EXODUS takes place about 16 to 32 hours after hatching. The female mallard begins to make about 40 to 65 calls per minute and continues while the ducklings leave the nest to follow her. The ducklings are capable of walking and swimming from hatching.

incubation. There were no positive responses from the female mallards during the first and second week of incubation. In fact, during the first days of incubation some female mallards responded with threat behavior: a fluffing of the feathers and a panting sound. In the third week some females responded to the recorded duckling sounds with a few clucks. In the fourth week maternal clucks were frequent and were observed in all ducks tested.

We found the same general pattern of response whether the female mallards were tested once or, as in a subsequent experiment, tested daily during incubation. Mallards sitting on infertile eggs responded just as much to the recorded duckling sounds as mallards sitting on fertile eggs did. Apparently after sitting on a clutch of eggs for two or three weeks a female mallard becomes ready to respond to the sounds of a hatching duckling. There is some evidence that the parental behavior of the female mallard is primed by certain neuroendocrine mechanisms. We have begun a study of the neuroendocrine changes that might accompany imprinting and filial behavior in mallards.

To what extent do unhatched ducklings respond to the vocalization of the female mallard? In order to find out we played a recording of a female mallard's vocalizations to ducklings in eggs that had just been pipped and were scheduled to hatch within the next 24 hours. As before, the sounds were interspersed with periods of silence. We then recorded all the sounds made by the ducklings during the recorded female mallard vocalizations and also during the silent periods on the tape. Twenty-four hours before the scheduled hatching the ducklings emitted 34 percent of their sounds during the silent periods, which suggests that at this stage they initiate most of the auditory interaction. As hatching time approaches the ducklings emit fewer and fewer sounds during the silent periods. The total number of sounds they make, however, increases steadily. At the time of hatching only 9 percent of the sounds they make are emitted during the silent periods. One hour after hatching, in response to the same type of recording, the ducklings gave 37 percent of their vocalizations during the silent periods, a level similar to the level at 24 hours before hatching.

During the hatching period, which lasts about an hour, the female mallard generally vocalizes at the rate of from zero to four calls per one-minute inter-

val. Occasionally there is an interval in which she emits as many as 10 calls. When the duckling actually hatches, the female mallard's vocalization increases dramatically to between 45 and 68 calls per minute for one or two minutes.

Thus the sounds made by the female mallard and by her offspring are complementary. The female mallard vocalizes most when a duckling has just hatched. A hatching duckling emits its cries primarily when the female is vocalizing.

After all the ducklings have hatched the female mallard tends to be relatively quiet for long intervals, giving between zero and four calls per minute. This continues for 16 to 32 hours until it is time for the exodus from the nest. As the exodus begins the female mallard quickly builds up to a crescendo of between 40 and 65 calls per minute; on rare occasions we have observed between 70 and 95 calls per minute. The duration of the high-calling-rate period depends on how quickly the ducklings leave the nest to follow her. There is now a change in the sounds made by the female mal-

lard. Up to this point she has been making clucking sounds. By the time the exodus from the nest takes place some of her sounds are more like quacks.

The auditory interaction of the female mallard and the duckling can begin well before the hatching period. As I have indicated, the female mallard responds to unhatched-duckling sounds during the third and fourth week of incubation. Normally ducklings penetrate a membrane to reach an air space inside the eggshell two days before hatching. We have not found any female mallard that vocalized to her clutch before the duckling in the egg reached the air space. We have found that as soon as the duckling penetrates the air space the female begins to cluck at a rate of between zero and four times per minute. Typically she continues to vocalize at this rate until the ducklings begin to pip their eggs (which is about 24 hours after they have entered the air space). As the eggs are being pipped the female clucks at the rate of between 10 and 15 times per minute. When the pipping is completed, she

SOUND SPECTROGRAM of the calls of newly hatched ducklings in the nest and the mother's responses is shown at right. The high-pitched peeps of the ducklings are in the

DISTRESS CALLS of ducklings in the nest evoke a quacklike response from the female mallard. The cessation of the distress calls and the onset of normal duckling peeping sounds

drops back to between zero and four calls per minute. In the next 24 hours there is a great deal of auditory interaction between the female and her unhatched offspring; this intense interaction may facilitate the rapid formation of the filial bond after hatching, although it is quite possible that synchrony of hatching is the main effect. Already we have found that a combination of cooling the eggs daily, placing them together so that they touch one another and transmitting parent-young vocal responses through the microphone-loudspeaker hookup between the female's nest and the laboratory incubator causes the eggs in the incubator to hatch as synchronously as eggs in nature do. In fact, the two times we did this we found that all the eggs in the clutches hatched within four hours of one another. It has been shown in many studies of imprinting, including laboratory studies, that auditory stimuli have an important effect on the development of filial attachment. Auditory stimulation, before and after hatching, together with tactile

stimulation in the nest after hatching results in ducklings that are thoroughly imprinted to the female mallard that is present.

Furthermore, it appears that auditory interaction before hatching may play an important role in promoting the synchronization of hatching. As our experiments showed, not only does the female mallard respond to sounds from her eggs but also the ducklings respond to her clucks. Perhaps the daily cooling of the eggs when the female mallard leaves the nest to feed serves to broadly synchronize embryonic and behavioral development, whereas the auditory interaction of the mother with the ducklings and of one duckling with another serves to provide finer synchronization. Margaret Vince of the University of Cambridge has shown that the synchronization of hatching in quail is promoted by the mutual auditory interaction of the young birds in the eggs.

Listening to the female mallards vocalize to their eggs or to their newly hatched offspring, we were struck by the

fact that we could tell which mallard was vocalizing, even when we could not see her. Some female mallards regularly emit single clucks at one-second intervals, some cluck in triple or quadruple clusters and others cluck in clusters of different lengths. The individual differences in the vocalization styles of female mallards may enable young ducklings to identify their mother. We can also speculate that the characteristics of a female mallard's voice are learned by her female offspring, which may then adopt a similar style when they are hatching eggs of their own.

The female mallards not only differ from one another in vocalization styles but also emit different calls in different situations. We have recorded variations in pitch and duration from the same mallard in various nesting situations. It seems likely that such variations in the female mallard call are an important factor in the imprinting process.

Studies of imprinting in the laboratory have shown that the more effort a duckling has to expend in following the im-

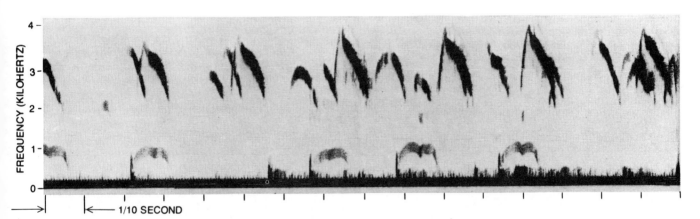

two-to-four-kilohertz range. They normally have the shape of an inverted *V*. The female mallard's clucks are about one kilohertz and last about 130 milliseconds. After the eggs hatch the vocalization of the female changes both in quantity and in quality of sound.

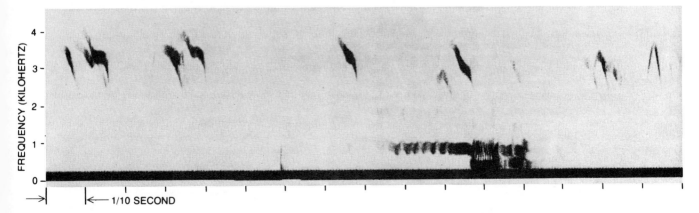

is almost immediate, as can be seen in this sound spectrogram. The female mallard's quacklike call is about one kilohertz in pitch and has a duration of approximately 450 milliseconds. The call is emitted about once every two seconds in response to distress cries.

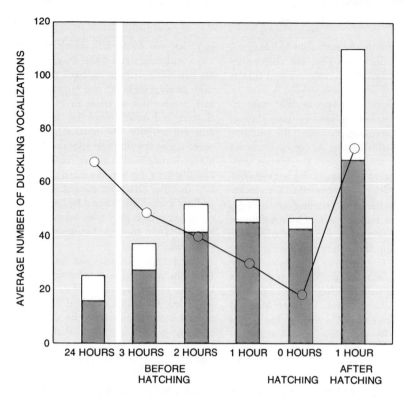

NUMBER OF SOUNDS from ducklings before and after hatching are shown. The ducklings heard a recording consisting of five one-minute segments of a female mallard's clucking sounds interspersed with five one-minute segments of silence. The recording was played to six mallard eggs and the number of vocal responses by the ducklings to the clucking segments (*gray bars*) and to the silent segments (*white bars*) were counted. Twenty-four hours before hatching 34 percent of the duckling sounds were made during the silent interval, indicating the ducklings initiated a substantial portion of the early auditory interaction. As hatching time approached the ducklings initiated fewer and fewer of the sounds and at hatching vocalized most in response to the clucks of the female mallard.

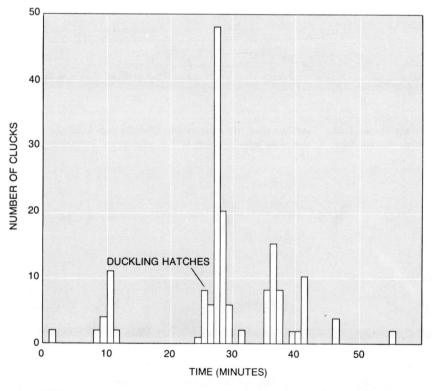

CLUCKING RATE of a wild, ground-nesting female mallard rose dramatically for about two minutes while a duckling hatched and then slowly declined to the prehatching rate. Each bar depicts the number of clucks emitted by the female during a one-minute period.

printing object, the more strongly it prefers that object in later testing. At first it would seem that this is not the case in natural imprinting; young ducklings raised by their mother have little difficulty following her during the exodus from the nest. Closer observation of many nests over several seasons showed, however, that ducklings make a considerable effort to be near their parent. They may suffer for such efforts, since they can be accidentally stepped on, squeezed or scratched by the female adult. The combination of effort and punishment may actually strengthen imprinting. Work in my laboratory showed that chicks given an electric shock while they were following the imprinting object later showed stronger attachment to the object than unshocked chicks did. It is reasonable to expect similar results with ducklings.

Slobodan Petrovich of the University of Maryland (Baltimore County) and I have begun a study to determine the relative contributions of prehatching and posthatching auditory experience on imprinting and filial attachment. The auditory stimuli consist of either natural mallard maternal clucks or a human voice saying "Come, come, come." Our results indicate that prehatching stimulation by natural maternal clucks may to a degree facilitate the later recognition of the characteristic call of the mallard. Ducklings lacking any experience with a maternal call imprint as well to a duck decoy that utters "Come, come, come" as to a decoy that emits normal mallard clucks. Ducklings that had been exposed to a maternal call before hatching imprinted better to decoys that emitted the mallard clucks. We found, however, that the immediate posthatching experiences, in this case with a female mallard on the nest, can highly determine the degree of filial attachment and make imprinting to a human sound virtually impossible.

It is important to recognize that almost all laboratory imprinting experiments, including my own, have been deprivation experiments. The justification for such experiments has been the ostensible need for controlling the variables of the phenomenon, but the deprivation may have interfered with the normal behavioral development of the young ducklings. Whatever imprinting experiences the experimenter allows therefore do not produce the maximum effect.

Although our findings are far from complete, we have already determined enough to demonstrate the great value of studying imprinting under natural conditions. The natural laboratory can be profitably used to study questions about imprinting that have been raised but not answered by traditional laboratory experiments. We must move away from the in vitro, or test-tube, approach to the study of behavior and move toward the in vivo method that allows interaction with normal environmental factors. Some of the questions are: What is the optimal age for imprinting? How long must the imprinting experience last for it to have the maximum effect? Which has the greater effect on behavior: first experience or the most recent experience? Whatever kind of behavior is being studied, the most fruitful approach may well be to study the behavior in its natural context.

6 The Reproductive Behavior of Ring Doves

by Daniel S. Lehrman
November 1964

An account of experiments showing that the changes in activity that constitute the behavior cycle are governed by interactions of outside stimuli, the hormones and the behavior of each mate

In recent years the study of animal behavior has proceeded along two different lines, with two groups of investigators formulating problems in different ways and indeed approaching the problems from different points of view. The comparative psychologist traditionally tends first to ask a question and then to attack it by way of animal experimentation. The ethologist, on the other hand, usually begins by observing the normal activity of an animal and then seeks to identify and analyze specific behavior patterns characteristic of the species.

The two attitudes can be combined. The psychologist can begin, like the ethologist, by watching an animal do what it does naturally, and only then ask questions that flow from his observations. He can go on to manipulate experimental conditions in an effort to discover the psychological and biological events that give rise to the behavior under study and perhaps to that of other animals as well. At the Institute of Animal Behavior at Rutgers University we have taken this approach to study in detail the reproductive-behavior cycle of the ring dove (*Streptopelia risoria*). The highly specific changes in behavior that occur in the course of the cycle, we find, are governed by complex psycho-

REPRODUCTIVE-BEHAVIOR CYCLE begins soon after a male and a female ring dove are introduced into a cage containing nesting material (hay in this case) and an empty glass nest bowl (*1*). Courtship activity, on the first day, is characterized by the "bowing

  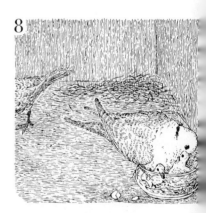

CYCLE CONTINUES as the adult birds take turns incubating the eggs (*6*), which hatch after about 14 days (*7*). The newly hatched squabs are fed "crop-milk," a liquid secreted in the gullets of the adults (*8*). The parents continue to feed them, albeit reluctantly,

biological interactions of the birds' inner and outer environments.

The ring dove, a small relative of the domestic pigeon, has a light gray back, creamy underparts and a black semicircle (the "ring") around the back of its neck. The male and female look alike and can only be distinguished by surgical exploration. If we place a male and a female ring dove with previous breeding experience in a cage containing an empty glass bowl and a supply of nesting material, the birds invariably enter on their normal behavioral cycle, which follows a predictable course and a fairly regular time schedule. During the first day the principal activity is courtship: the male struts around, bowing and cooing at the female. After several hours the birds announce their selection of a nest site (which in nature would be a concave place and in our cages is the glass bowl) by crouching in it and uttering a distinctive coo. Both birds participate in building the nest, the male usually gathering material and carrying it to the female, who stands in the bowl and constructs the nest. After a week or more of nest-building, in the course of which the birds copulate, the female be-

comes noticeably more attached to the nest and difficult to dislodge; if one attempts to lift her off the nest, she may grasp it with her claws and take it along. This behavior usually indicates that the female is about to lay her eggs. Between seven and 11 days after the beginning of the courtship she produces her first egg, usually at about five o'clock in the afternoon. The female dove sits on the egg and then lays a second one, usually at about nine o'clock in the morning two days later. Sometime that day the male takes a turn sitting; thereafter the two birds alternate, the male sitting for about six hours in the middle of each day, the female for the remaining 18 hours a day.

In about 14 days the eggs hatch and the parents begin to feed their young "crop-milk," a liquid secreted at this stage of the cycle by the lining of the adult dove's crop, a pouch in the bird's gullet. When they are 10 or 12 days old, the squabs leave the cage, but they continue to beg for and to receive food from the parents. This continues until the squabs are about two weeks old, when the parents become less and less willing to feed them as the young birds

gradually develop the ability to peck for grain on the floor of the cage. When the young are about 15 to 25 days old, the adult male begins once again to bow and coo; nest-building is resumed, a new clutch of eggs is laid and the cycle is repeated. The entire cycle lasts about six or seven weeks and—at least in our laboratory, where it is always spring because of controlled light and temperature conditions—it can continue throughout the year.

The variations in behavior that constitute the cycle are not merely casual or superficial changes in the birds' preoccupations; they represent striking changes in the overall pattern of activity and in the atmosphere of the breeding cage. At its appropriate stage each of the kinds of behavior I have described represents the predominant activity of the animals at the time. Furthermore, these changes in behavior are not just responses to changes in the external situation. The birds do not build the nest merely because the nesting material is available; even if nesting material is in the cage throughout the cycle, nest-building behavior is concentrated,

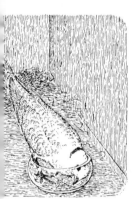  

coo" of the male (2). The male and then the female utter a distinctive "nest call" to indicate their selection of a nesting site (3).

There follows a week or more of cooperation in nest-building (4), culminating in the laying of two eggs at precise times of day (5).

as the young birds learn to peck for grain themselves (9). When the squabs are between two and three weeks old, the adults ignore

them and start to court once again, and a new cycle begins (10). Physical changes during the cycle are shown on the next page.

as described, at one stage. Similarly, the birds react to the eggs and to the young only at appropriate stages in the cycle.

These cyclic changes in behavior therefore represent, at least in part, changes in the internal condition of the animals rather than merely changes in their external situation. Furthermore, the changes in behavior are associated with equally striking and equally pervasive changes in the anatomy and the physiological state of the birds. For example, when the female dove is first introduced into the cage, her oviduct weighs some 800 milligrams. Eight or nine days later, when she lays her first egg, the oviduct may weigh 4,000 milligrams. The crops of both the male and the female weigh some 900 milligrams when the birds are placed in the cage, and when they start to sit on the eggs some 10 days later they still weigh about the same. But two weeks afterward, when the eggs hatch, the parents' crops may weigh as much as 3,000 milligrams. Equally striking changes in the condition of the ovary, the weight of the testes, the length of the gut, the weight of the liver, the microscopic structure of the pituitary gland and other physiological indices are correlated with the behavioral cycle.

Now, if a male or a female dove is placed alone in a cage with nesting material, no such cycle of behavioral or anatomical changes takes place. Far from producing two eggs every six or seven weeks, a female alone in a cage lays no eggs at all. A male alone shows no interest when we offer it nesting material, eggs or young. The cycle of psychobiological changes I have described is, then, one that occurs more or less synchronously in each member of a pair of doves living together but that will not occur independently in either of the pair living alone.

In a normal breeding cycle both the male and the female sit on the eggs almost immediately after they are laid. The first question we asked ourselves was whether this is because the birds are always ready to sit on eggs or because they come into some special condition of readiness to incubate at about the time the eggs are produced.

We kept male and female doves in isolation for several weeks and then placed male-female pairs in test cages, each supplied with a nest bowl containing a normal dove nest with two eggs. The birds did not sit; they acted almost as if the eggs were not there. They courted, then built their own nest (usually on top of the planted nest and its eggs, which we had to keep fishing out to keep the stimulus situation constant!), then finally sat on the eggs—five to seven days after they had first encountered each other.

This clearly indicated that the doves are not always ready to sit on eggs; under the experimental conditions they changed from birds that did not want to incubate to birds that did want to incubate in five to seven days. What had induced this change? It could not have been merely the passage of time since their last breeding experience, because this had varied from four to six or more weeks in different pairs, whereas the variation in time spent in the test cage before sitting was only a couple of days.

Could the delay of five to seven days represent the time required for the birds to get over the stress of being handled and become accustomed to the strange cage? To test this possibility we placed pairs of doves in cages without any nest bowls or nesting material and separated each male and female by an opaque partition. After seven days we removed the partition and introduced nesting material and a formed nest with eggs. If the birds had merely needed time to recover from being handled and become acclimated to the cage, they should now have sat on the eggs immediately. They did not do so; they sat only after five to seven days, just as if they had been introduced into the cage only when the opaque partition was removed.

The next possibility we considered was that in this artificial situation stimulation from the eggs might induce the change from a nonsitting to a sitting "mood" but that this effect required five to seven days to reach a threshold value at which the behavior would change.

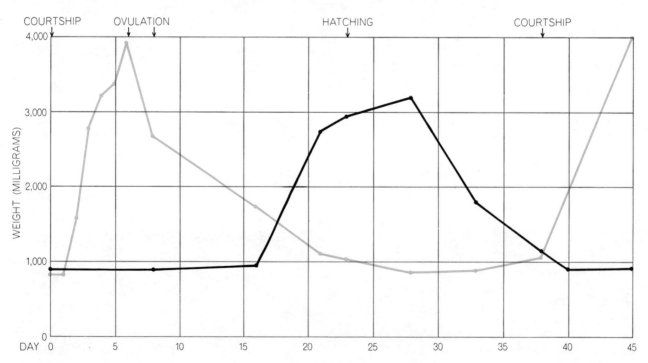

ANATOMICAL AND PHYSIOLOGICAL changes are associated with the behavioral changes of the cycle. The chart gives average weights of the crop (*black curve*) and the female oviduct (*color*) at various stages measured in days after the beginning of courtship.

We therefore placed pairs of birds in test cages with empty nest bowls and a supply of nesting material but no eggs. The birds courted and built nests. After seven days we removed the nest bowl and its nest and replaced it with a fresh bowl containing a nest and eggs. All these birds sat within two hours.

It was now apparent that some combination of influences arising from the presence of the mate and the availability of the nest bowl and nesting material induced the change from nonreadiness to incubate to readiness. In order to distinguish between these influences we put a new group of pairs of doves in test cages without any nest bowl or nesting material. When, seven days later, we offered these birds nesting material and nests with eggs, most of them did not sit immediately. Nor did they wait the full five to seven days to do so; they sat after one day, during which they engaged in intensive nest-building. A final group, placed singly in cages with nests and eggs, failed to incubate at all, even after weeks in the cages.

In summary, the doves do not build nests as soon as they are introduced into a cage containing nesting material, but they will do so immediately if the nesting material is introduced for the first time after they have spent a while together; they will not sit immediately on eggs offered after the birds have been in a bare cage together for some days, but they will do so if they were able to do some nest-building during the end of their period together. From these experiments it is apparent that there are two kinds of change induced in these birds: first, they are changed from birds primarily interested in courtship to birds primarily interested in nest-building, and this change is brought about by stimulation arising from association with a mate; second, under these conditions they are further changed from birds primarily interested in nest-building to birds interested in sitting on eggs, and this change is encouraged by participation in nest-building.

The course of development of readiness to incubate is shown graphically by the results of another experiment, which Philip N. Brody, Rochelle Wortis and I undertook shortly after the ones just described. We placed pairs of birds in test cages for varying numbers of days, in some cases with and in others without a nest bowl and nesting material. Then we introduced a nest and eggs into the cage. If neither bird sat within three hours, the test was scored as nega-

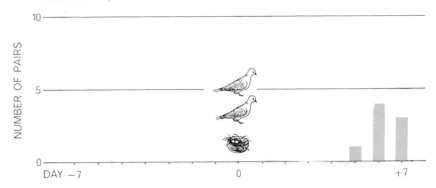

READINESS TO INCUBATE was tested with four groups of eight pairs of doves. Birds of the first group were placed in a cage containing a nest and eggs. They went through courtship and nest-building behavior before finally sitting after between five and seven days.

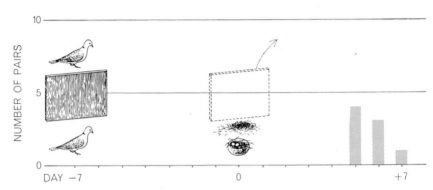

EFFECT OF HABITUATION was tested by keeping two birds separated for seven days in the cage before introducing nest and eggs. They still sat only after five to seven days.

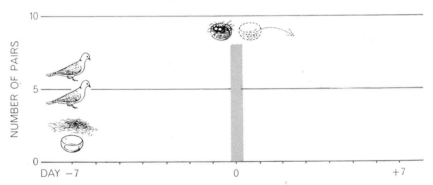

MATE AND NESTING MATERIAL had a dramatic effect on incubation-readiness. Pairs that had spent seven days in courtship and nest-building sat as soon as eggs were offered.

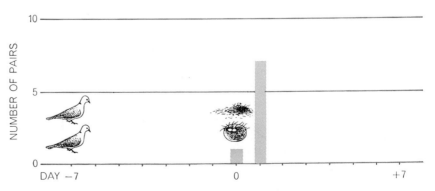

PRESENCE OF MATE without nesting activity had less effect. Birds that spent a week in cages with no nest bowls or hay took a day to sit after nests with eggs were introduced.

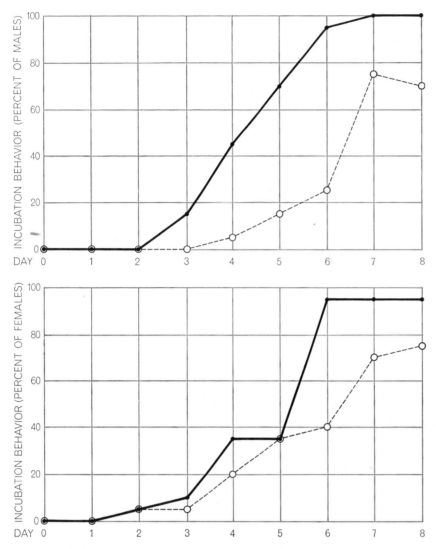

DURATION OF ASSOCIATION with mate and nesting material affects incubation behavior. The abscissas give the length of the association for different groups of birds. The plotted points show what percentage of each group sat within three hours of being offered eggs. The percentage increases for males (*top*) and females (*bottom*) as a function of time previously spent with mate (*open circles*) or with mate and nesting material (*solid dots*).

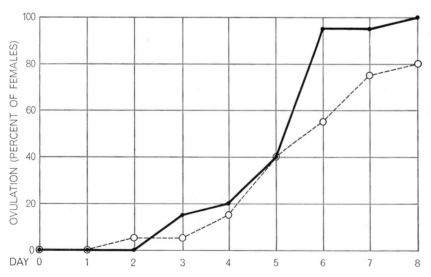

OVULATION is similarly affected. These curves, coinciding closely with those of the bottom chart above, show the occurrence of ovulation in the same birds represented there.

tive and both birds were removed for autopsy. If either bird sat within three hours, that bird was removed and the other bird was given an additional three hours to sit. The experiment therefore tested—independently for the male and the female—the development of readiness to incubate as a function of the number of days spent with the mate, with or without the opportunity to build a nest.

It is apparent [*see top illustration at left*] that association with the mate gradually brings the birds into a condition of readiness to incubate and that this effect is greatly enhanced by the presence of nesting material. Exposure to the nesting situation does not stimulate the onset of readiness to incubate in an all-or-nothing way; rather, its effect is additive with the effect of stimulation provided by the mate. Other experiments show, moreover, that the stimulation from the mate and nesting material is sustained. If either is removed, the incidence of incubation behavior decreases.

The experiments described so far made it clear that external stimuli normally associated with the breeding situation play an important role in inducing a state of readiness to incubate. We next asked what this state consists of physiologically. As a first approach to this problem we attempted to induce incubation behavior by injecting hormones into the birds instead of by manipulating the external stimulation. We treated birds just as we had in the first experiment but injected some of the birds with hormones while they were in isolation, starting one week before they were due to be placed in pairs in the test cages. When both members of the pair had been injected with the ovarian hormone progesterone, more than 90 percent of the eggs were covered by one of the birds within three hours after their introduction into the cage instead of five to seven days later. When the injected substance was another ovarian hormone—estrogen—the effect on most birds was to make them incubate after a latent period of one to three days, during which they engaged in nest-building behavior. The male hormone testosterone had no effect on incubation behavior.

During the 14 days when the doves are sitting on the eggs, their crops increase enormously in weight. Crop growth is a reliable indicator of the secretion of the hormone prolactin by the birds' pituitary glands. Since this growth coincides with the development of incubation behavior and culminates in the secretion of the crop-milk the birds feed to their young after the eggs hatch, Brody and I have recently examined the effect of injected prolactin on incubation behavior. We find that prolactin is not so effective as progesterone in inducing incubation behavior, even at dosage levels that induce full development of the crop. For example, a total prolactin dose of 400 international units induced only 40 percent of the birds to sit on eggs early, even though their average crop weight was about 3,000 milligrams, or more than three times the normal weight. Injection of 10 units of the hormone induced significant increases in crop weight (to 1,200 milligrams) but no increase in the frequency of incubation behavior. These results, together with the fact that in a normal breeding cycle the crop begins to increase in weight only after incubation begins, make it unlikely that prolactin plays an important role in the initiation of normal incubation behavior in this species. It does, however, seem to help to maintain such behavior until the eggs hatch.

Prolactin is much more effective in inducing ring doves to show regurgitation-feeding responses to squabs. When 12 adult doves with previous breeding experience were each injected with 450 units of prolactin over a seven-day period and placed, one bird at a time, in cages with squabs, 10 of the 12 fed the squabs from their engorged crops, whereas none of 12 uninjected controls did so or even made any parental approaches to the squabs.

This experiment showed that prolactin, which is normally present in considerable quantities in the parents when the eggs hatch, does contribute to the doves' ability to show parental feeding behavior. I originally interpreted it to mean that the prolactin-induced engorgement of the crop was necessary in order for any regurgitation feeding to take place, but E. Klinghammer and E. H. Hess of the University of Chicago have correctly pointed out that this was an error, that ring doves are capable of feeding young if presented with them rather early in the incubation period. They do so even though they have no crop-milk, feeding a mixture of regurgitated seeds and a liquid. We are now studying the question of how early the birds can do this and how this ability is related to the onset of prolactin secretion.

The work with gonad-stimulating hormones and prolactin demonstrates that the various hormones successively produced by the birds' glands during their reproductive cycle are capable of inducing the successive behavioral changes that characterize the cycle.

Up to this point I have described two main groups of experiments. One group demonstrates that external stimuli induce changes in behavioral status of a kind normally associated with the progress of the reproductive cycle; the second shows that these behavioral changes can also be induced by hormone administration, provided that the choice of hormones is guided by knowledge of the succession of hormone secretions during a normal reproductive cycle. An obvious—and challenging—implication of these results is that external stimuli may induce changes in hormone secretion, and that environment-induced hormone secretion may constitute an integral part of the mechanism of the reproductive behavior cycle. We have attacked the problem of the environmental stimulation of hormone secretion in a series of experiments in which, in addition to examining the effects of external stimuli on the birds' behavioral status, we have examined their effects on well-established anatomical indicators of the presence of various hormones.

Background for this work was provided by two classic experiments with the domestic pigeon, published during the 1930's, which we have verified in the ring dove. At the London Zoo, L. H. Matthews found that a female pigeon would lay eggs as a result of being placed in a cage with a male from whom she was separated by a glass plate. This was an unequivocal demonstration that visual and/or auditory stimulation provided by the male induces ovarian development in the female. (Birds are quite insensitive to olfactory stimulation.) And M. D. Patel of the University of Wisconsin found that the crops of breeding pigeons, which develop strikingly during the incubation period, would regress to their resting state if the incubating birds were removed from their nests and would fail to develop at all if the birds were removed before crop growth had begun. If, however, a male pigeon, after being removed from his nest, was placed in an adjacent cage from which he could see his mate still sitting on the eggs, his crop would develop just as if he were himself incubating! Clearly stimuli arising from participation in in-

cubation, including visual stimuli, cause the doves' pituitary glands to secrete prolactin.

Our autopsies showed that the incidence of ovulation in females that had associated with males for various periods coincided closely with the incidence of incubation behavior [see bottom illustration on opposite page]; statistical analysis reveals a very high degree of association. The process by which the dove's ovary develops to the point of ovulation includes a period of estrogen secretion followed by one of progesterone secretion, both induced by appropriate ovary-stimulating hormones from the pituitary gland. We therefore conclude that stimuli provided by the male, augmented by the presence of the nest bowl and nesting material, induce the secretion of gonad-stimulating hormones by the female's pituitary, and that the onset of readiness to incubate is a result of this process.

As I have indicated, ovarian development, culminating in ovulation and egg-laying, can be induced in a female dove merely as a result of her seeing a male through a glass plate. Is this the result of the mere presence of another bird or of something the male does because he is a male? Carl Erickson and I have begun to deal with this question. We placed 40 female doves in separate cages, each separated from a male by a glass plate. Twenty of the stimulus animals were normal, intact males, whereas the remaining 20 had been castrated several weeks before. The intact males all exhibited vigorous bow-cooing immediately on being placed in the cage, whereas none of the castrates did so. Thirteen of the 20 females with intact males ovulated during the next seven days, whereas only two of those with the castrates did so. Clearly ovarian development in the female is not induced merely by seeing another bird but by seeing or hearing it act like a male as the result of the effects of its own male hormone on its nervous system.

Although crop growth, which begins early in the incubation period, is apparently stimulated by participation in incubation, the crop continues to be large and actively secreting for quite some time after the hatching of the eggs. This suggests that stimuli provided by the squabs may also stimulate prolactin secretion. In our laboratory Ernst Hansen substituted three-day-old squabs for eggs in various stages of incubation and after four days compared the adults' crop weights with those of birds that had continued to sit on their eggs dur-

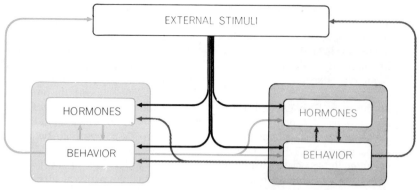

INTERACTIONS that appear to govern the reproductive-behavior cycle are suggested here. Hormones regulate behavior and are themselves affected by behavioral and other stimuli. And the behavior of each bird affects the hormones and the behavior of its mate.

ing the four days. He found that the crops grow even faster when squabs are in the nest than when the adults are under the influence of the eggs; the presence of squabs can stimulate a dove's pituitary glands to secrete more prolactin even before the stage in the cycle when the squabs normally appear.

This does not mean, however, that any of the stimuli we have used can induce hormone secretion at *any* time, regardless of the bird's physiological condition. If we place a pair of ring doves in a cage and allow them to go through the normal cycle until they have been sitting on eggs for, say, six days and we then place a glass partition in the cage to separate the male from the female and the nest, the female will continue to sit on the eggs and the male's crop will continue to develop just as if he were himself incubating. This is a simple replication of one of Patel's experiments. Miriam Friedman and I have found, however, that if the male and female are separated from the beginning, so that the female must build the nest by herself and sit alone from the beginning, the crop of the male does

not grow. By inserting the glass plate at various times during the cycle in different groups of birds, we have found that the crop of the male develops fully only if he is not separated from the female until 72 hours or more after the second egg is laid. This means that the sight of the female incubating induces prolactin secretion in the male only if he is in the physiological condition to which participation in nest-building brings him. External stimuli associated with the breeding situation do indeed induce changes in hormone secretion.

The experiments summarized here point to the conclusion that changes in the activity of the endocrine system are induced or facilitated by stimuli coming from various aspects of the environment at different stages of the breeding cycle, and that these changes in hormone secretion induce changes in behavior that may themselves be a source of further stimulation.

The regulation of the reproductive cycle of the ring dove appears to depend, at least in part, on a double set of reciprocal interrelations. First, there

is an interaction of the effects of hormones on behavior and the effects of external stimuli—including those that arise from the behavior of the animal and its mate—on the secretion of hormones. Second, there is a complicated reciprocal relation between the effects of the presence and behavior of one mate on the endocrine system of the other and the effects of the presence and behavior of the second bird (including those aspects of its behavior induced by these endocrine effects) back on the endocrine system of the first. The occurrence in each member of the pair of a cycle found in neither bird in isolation, and the synchronization of the cycles in the two mates, can now readily be understood as consequences of this interaction of the inner and outer environments.

The physiological explanation of these phenomena lies partly in the fact that the activity of the pituitary gland, which secretes prolactin and the gonad-stimulating hormones, is largely controlled by the nervous system through the hypothalamus. The precise neural mechanisms for any complex response are still deeply mysterious, but physiological knowledge of the brain-pituitary link is sufficiently detailed and definite so that the occurrence of a specific hormonal response to a specific external stimulus is at least no more mysterious than any other stimulus-response relation. We are currently exploring these responses in more detail, seeking to learn, among other things, the precise sites at which the various hormones act. And we have begun to investigate another aspect of the problem: the effect of previous experience on a bird's reproductive behavior and the interactions between these experiential influences and the hormonal effects.

7

Learning in Newborn Kittens

by Jay S. Rosenblatt
December 1972

A series of experiments demonstrates that, although kittens seem virtually helpless at birth, they quickly learn to find their way to their favorite nipple and their home territory

The young of many species of mammals appear to be almost totally helpless at birth. Indeed, a well-known hypothesis of mammalian development is that such newborn mammals are not even capable of learning until they enter a critical period when they have attained a certain level of sensory and motor development. At the Rutgers University Institute of Animal Behavior we have been looking into suckling and homing behavior of newborn kittens. We find that these particular newborn mammals are quite capable of learning immediately after birth. Moreover, such learning plays an important role in the animal's growth and development.

During its first weeks of life a kitten develops a rich repertory of behavior, which makes it a favorable subject for investigating early development. In collaboration with the late T. C. Schneirla of the American Museum of Natural History, Gerald Turkewitz and I began an experimental study of behavioral development in kittens. Our first objective was to observe and describe the normal course of social development in kittens in our particular laboratory conditions. The kittens lived with their mothers in cubical cages that were three feet on a side. We observed the activities of the kittens and mothers for a three-hour period each day during the eight-week nursing period.

After we had observed a large number of mothers and their litters, certain regular features in the behavioral development of kittens became apparent. Suckling begins within a few minutes of birth and is initiated by the mother: she lies on her side and guides the kittens to the nipple region. The mother continues to initiate nursing for the next three weeks. During this period nursing takes place only in a part of the cage we call the home area. The mother approaches the kittens, which are huddled together in the home corner, arouses them by nuzzling and licking them and then lies down on her side so that her nipples face them. Her body and outstretched hind limbs and forelimbs encircle the kittens.

The kittens' eyes open at the end of the first week after birth, but they do not make any use of the visual sense until the end of the second week. After the third week the kittens begin to wander from the home area. They also begin to approach the mother when they want to nurse. She stands still until the kittens begin to suckle, and then she lies down. After the fifth week the mother becomes less willing to nurse, but now the kittens are able to pursue her around the cage until they can get hold of a nipple, after which the mother allows them to nurse.

The play activities of the kittens—mouthing, pawing, hugging, rolling and licking—are primarily directed at other kittens, but the mother often is an unwilling subject. The kittens paw and climb over her face or leap on her back when she is lying down. When they paw at the mother's face, she often moves her tail to divert their attention. Simple forms of play among kittens appear as early as the third week. The more active forms of play—chasing, rolling and hugging—appear in about the fourth week when the kittens begin to move out of the home area.

We noted a definite relation between the behavior of the kittens and the behavior of the mother as the kittens matured. The behavior of both changed, and the changes gave us a hint of how kittens are weaned, or in other words why mother cats gradually act in a less maternal way toward their young. There was a shelf in the cage that the mother could jump onto to escape her kittens. Except for a brief period during the first week after the birth of the litter, the mother did not spend any time on the shelf until after the third week. The mother was always on the floor of the cage near her litter. As the play activity of the kittens increased the mother spent an increasing amount of time on the shelf beyond the reach of the kittens. Nursing periods became less frequent and of shorter duration, and at about the fifth week the kittens began to eat and drink from dishes that had been placed in the cage. Once the process of weaning had begun, it progressed rapidly, even though suckling did not stop entirely. By the end of the eighth week the kittens were virtually weaned, but they continued to suckle on occasions when they could grasp a nipple. When there was only a single kitten in the litter, weaning tended to take longer because there was less play activity to disturb the mother.

After we had established the normal course of kitten development in the cages, we began to remove individual kittens from litters at birth and to place each kitten alone in a brooder with an artificial mother consisting of a soft cloth and a small rubber nipple. At the end of a week each kitten was returned to its natural mother. At first the kittens were disoriented and could not find the mother; they huddled in a far corner of the cage. Eventually they made contact with the mother, and then they remained near her. It took several hours for them to find a nipple to suckle. After they had learned to nurse they also were able to learn to find the home area when they had been placed outside it.

At the time these studies were done the prevailing view was that newborn mammals cannot learn until they reach a critical age that can be anywhere from a few days to several weeks, depending on the species. That view was based on studies where attempts to form conditioned reflexes in newborn puppies were unsuccessful until the puppies had reached an age of two or three weeks. In those studies the conditioned reflex was lifting the foreleg in response to an auditory, visual or olfactory stimulus. Working with the more natural behavior of newborn animals, such as suckling and home orientation, we found that one could come to quite another conclusion.

With normal litters we had observed that the kittens line up at the mother's nipples in an orderly way to suckle and that each kitten has a preferred nipple position. Kittens tend to develop a preference for the nipple on which they suckle during the first and second day. At the end of the third day more than 80 percent of the kittens we observed suckled from a single nipple position at

NURSING IS INITIATED by the mother cat shortly after the kittens are born. She lies on her side to expose her nipples and licks the blind kittens, which orients them to her body. They crawl to her, nuzzle in her fur and while maintaining constant contact with the fur move along her body to the nipple region. There nuzzling changes into gentle nose-tapping until a nipple is touched. The touch of the nipple stimulates the kitten to make mouthing movements that change into sucking when the nipple is grasped.

NIPPLE PREFERENCE is developed by the kittens within a few days. They show rapid improvement in the speed with which they find the preferred nipple. When a kitten accidentally takes another kitten's nipple, it readily abandons that nipple when the rightful owner nuzzles it. When a kitten is sucking from its preferred nipple, it will hold on tenaciously when another kitten tries to take it.

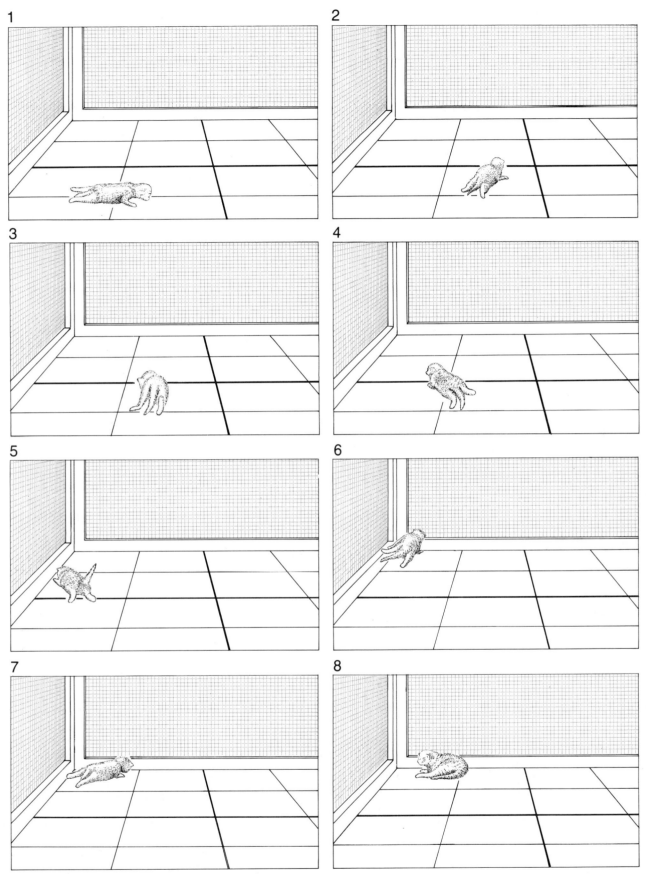

HOME-FINDING BEHAVIOR of a blind five-day-old kitten is depicted in these drawings based on photographs. The kitten is placed in the adjacent corner of the home cage. It begins to crawl and moves its head from side to side sniffing the floor. At first the crawling is random, but the kitten soon heads in the right direction. Often the kitten's tail goes up after it enters the home quadrant, perhaps because it senses a strong home odor. The kitten continues to crawl to the home corner. In home area it relaxes and falls asleep.

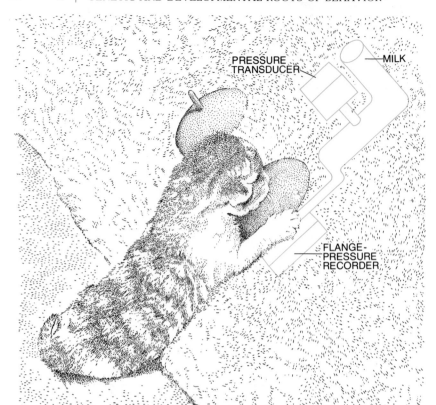

ARTIFICIAL MOTHER consisted of a carpeted board with two nipples, each surrounded by a rubber flange. Pressure-sensitive devices recorded how much the kitten touched each flange and sucked on each nipple. Only one nipple provided milk; the other was sealed.

each feeding. The rate at which nipple preference is established is independent of the size of the litter. When a kitten takes the wrong nipple, it may suckle on it until the rightful owner nuzzles at it. A kitten readily abandons a wrong nipple, but when it is at its own nipple, it holds on tenaciously when an intruder tries to nuzzle in.

How do kittens identify the preferred nipple out of the array of four pairs of nipples that are available to them? To find out Robert J. Woll and Natalie Freeman, graduate students at the Institute of Animal Behavior, have been conducting experiments with kittens exposed to an artificial mother and to natural mothers whose nipple region has been washed or shaved. Here the artificial mother consists of two rubber nipples mounted on a carpeted board. Around each nipple is a two-inch rubber flange. One nipple provides milk; the other is sealed but is filled with water. Each nipple and its flange are linked to pressure sensors that record how much the kitten nuzzles at the flange and sucks at the nipple.

Kittens are removed from the litter at birth and are fed by syringe for the first day and a half. They suck on a small nipple at the tip of the syringe, and behind the nipple is a rubber flange corresponding to the milk nipple they will encounter later on the artificial mother. Some of the flanges are textured either with raised dots or raised concentric rings; others are smooth and are scented with men's cologne or oil of wintergreen. Thus when the kittens are fed, they are exposed to a particular tactile or olfactory stimulus. They associate the stimulus with feeding from the first day, and when they are placed in a cage with the artificial mother, they tend to nuzzle the flange and nipple with the associated tactile or olfactory stimulus much more than a control flange and nipple. They suckle almost exclusively at the correct nipple.

After the kittens have learned to identify the milk nipple they begin to make a path to the nipple along the carpeted surface of the artificial mother. The path consists of an area that is matted by the kitten's repeatedly crawling over it. Very likely it also has a distinct odor left by the kitten itself. An effort was made to study the path's texture and its odor independently, but the kittens always managed to introduce the other stimulus. It was possible, however, to show that the kittens could identify the milk nipple by texture alone. The entire area surrounding both nipples was washed, and in a series of tests the position of the milk nipple was shifted from one side to the other.

Nipple-preference experiments were much more difficult to perform with a natural mother. Not only were the odors and textures of the mammary surface subtler but also there were differences in the temperature gradients around the nipples to which the kittens could be sensitive. When the mammary surface, including the fur, of a mother cat was washed to remove odors, the kittens began to suckle at random nipples, but within a day or two they returned to their preferred nipple position. When we shaved portions of the mother's mammary region, the kittens were much less confused and continued

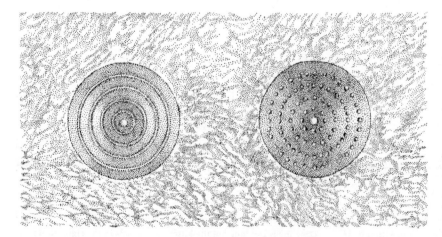

TEXTURED FLANGES, one with a raised-dot pattern and the other with raised concentric circles, were used in a study to determine the learning ability of newborn kittens. To obtain food a kitten had to learn to associate the milk-filled nipple with one of the two textures.

to suckle from their preferred position. It seems that texture may not play an important role when odors are present. As the kittens matured, particularly after the third week, visual cues began to play a part in the initiation of suckling.

In our observations of normal laboratory litters we noted that kittens appeared to be able to recognize their home cage even before they made contact with their mother or their littermates in the home area. Kittens removed from their cage for weighing began to cry immediately, and the crying stopped abruptly when they were returned to the same cage. We also found that the kittens seemed to know whether they were in the home area of the cage or in some other area. A kitten placed in the corner adjacent to the home area would crawl to the home area and not stop until it had reached it, whereupon it usually fell asleep.

Even before a kitten is able to see it is able to divide its home cage into identifiable regions. When the kitten is placed in an area of the cage other than the home corner, it is able to find its way back to the home corner. When the kitten is put into a strange cage that is physically identical with the home cage, it immediately begins to cry and often backs into a corner.

In order to trace the development of home orientation in kittens we tested a large number of animals daily from birth to 22 days of age. The test kitten was placed in a strange cage, which we called a field, for two minutes and its reactions were observed. Then the kitten was placed alone in the home cage, either in the home corner or the adjacent corner or the diagonal corner, and its behavior for three minutes was recorded. During the various tests the kittens cried to a greater or lesser extent. As the kitten crawled about the floor of the cage, the intensity of its crying was scored on a scale of from one to four.

For the first few days after birth the crawling behavior of the kittens remains the same regardless of where they are placed. They tend to crawl in a circular path around the starting point. As they grow older their pattern of movement begins to change depending on where they are placed. In the home corner they crawl in circles and then fall asleep. In the corner adjacent to the home corner they crawl randomly at first but after a short time head for the home corner. Once they enter the home area the kittens sniff the floor and soon fall asleep.

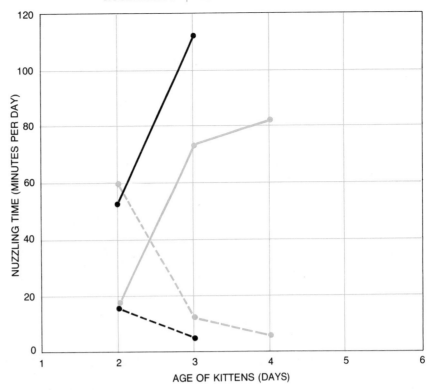

IDENTIFICATION OF A MILK-FILLED NIPPLE by the texture or odor of the surrounding flange is rapidly learned by newborn kittens. The kitten nuzzles the textured flange around the milk-filled nipple (*solid black curve*) much more than the textured flange around a sealed nipple (*broken black curve*) and learns to feed itself independently at the age of three days. It needs more time to learn to discriminate the odor of the milk-filled nipple (*solid colored curve*) from the odor of the sealed nipple (*broken colored curve*).

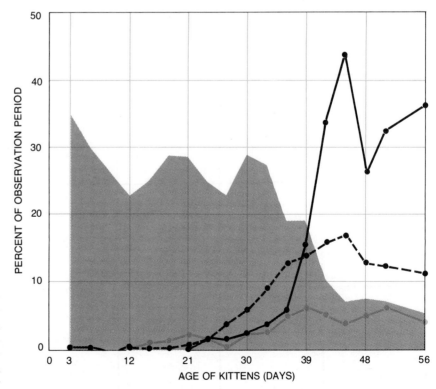

PLAY ACTIVITIES of kittens directed toward the mother (*colored curve*) and toward each other (*broken curve*) increase from about 30 days after birth, and at the same time the mother begins to spend more time on a shelf out of reach of the kittens (*black curve*). The amount of nursing during the daily observation period is shown by the shaded area.

By the age of five to seven days nearly three-quarters of the kittens find their way home from the adjacent corner. Kittens usually do not learn the way home from the diagonal corner until they are from 14 to 16 days of age. Instead of crawling directly to the home corner from the diagonal corner, the kittens first crawl to the adjacent corner and then turn homeward. There is little change in the animals' behavior in a strange cage until they are 19 days old.

The kitten has a distinct response, which we call the settling reaction, when it reaches the home area. The same response is seen in newborn kittens when they regain contact with the mother after having been separated from her. The kitten's movements slow down and its vocalization becomes softer and gradually stops. The kitten relaxes and soon lowers its head to the floor and falls asleep.

Kittens are able to distinguish between a strange cage and their home cage from the first day after birth. When they are placed in a strange cage, their crying becomes more intense; when they are placed anywhere in the home

cage, the crying immediately becomes less intense. The rate at which the crying declines in intensity and the final level that is reached are different for each of the home-cage corners. The initial decline in the intensity of crying when the kitten is placed in the home cage indicates that the kittens recognize the home cage. By the time the kitten is five days old it is able to distinguish what area of the cage it is in. After an initial decline in crying the kittens react to the specific region they are in. In the home area crying remains at a low level throughout the test. In the other corners, however, after the initial decline in crying the kittens begin to vocalize louder. The farther the corner is from the home area, the louder are the kittens' cries.

Was the home orientation of the kittens possibly the result not of normal development but of the kittens' daily experience in the tests? To examine this possibility a number of kittens from various litters were not tested daily with their littermates. Some kittens were tested for the first time at about one week of age and others at about two weeks. In

both cases the naïve kittens showed the same patterns of movement and vocalization as their littermates that had been tested every day from birth. Therefore the daily testing of kittens was not the crucial factor in the development of home orientation.

To determine whether or not a kitten had to grow up in the home cage in order to orient itself to its home area, we raised newborn kittens away from the home cage and prevented them from developing home-orientation behavior. After one week several of the isolated kittens were tested in the home cage of their littermates. None of the naïve kittens was able to distinguish the home corner from the other corners. For these kittens the home cage was only slightly different from the isolation cage. A kitten kept in isolation for two weeks also failed to orient itself to the home area when it was placed in its mother's cage. The isolated kittens were returned to their mother and after several days began to develop the typical pattern of home orientation. In other words, they had learned how to orient themselves to the home area.

In the home cage kittens are able to reach the home area from the adjacent corner when they are from five to seven days old and their eyes have not yet opened. This behavior indicates that nonvisual cues enable them to find their way. It seemed likely to us that the cues that enable the kittens to locate and identify their home area are odors. Presumably the odors are continuously deposited by the mother and kittens. The cages had removable floor panels, and in one study we took out the floor of the home corner and washed it to remove odors. We then tested kittens ranging in age from four to 18 days that already had proved they could return to the home corner from an adjacent corner. These kittens came to an abrupt halt when they reached the freshly washed home-corner floor. They backed away from the home quadrant and came to rest in the adjacent quadrant, where the odor was now most heavily concentrated [see bottom illustration on next page]. When the kittens were placed on the freshly washed home-corner floor, they tended to crawl out of it to the adjacent quadrant.

In the same study the home-quadrant floor was washed and then put back in place so that olfactory deposits from the mother and the kittens could accumulate again. When the kittens were tested the next day, they found the home area

CAGE FLOOR PLAN shows the three major quadrants: home, adjacent and diagonal. The remaining quadrant contained litter material and was not used in the testing. Each 18-inch-square quadrant consisted of four smaller panels that could be individually removed.

almost as acceptable as the normal unwashed home area. The results confirmed our belief that the kittens follow odors deposited on the floor to find their way home. Removal of the home-area odors by washing does not prevent the kittens from crawling toward the home area when they are placed in the adjacent corner. This result suggests that they follow an odor trail that lies within the adjacent quadrant in order to reach the home quadrant. If the home quadrant lacks odors, the kittens return to the area with the strongest odor and remain there.

The use of olfactory cues gradually gives way to the use of visual cues when the kittens reach their third and fourth week. We tried several methods for determining the importance of visual cues in home orientation. In one method we put blinds on the inside walls of the cage to mask any visual cues the wall might have provided. In tests with kittens from 13 to 21 days of age there was a 30 percent increase in the failure of the kittens to orient themselves to the home from the adjacent and diagonal corners. When all the olfactory cues are removed, leaving only visual cues, successful orientation drops from 92 to 50 percent when the kittens begin in the adjacent corner, and it goes down from 83 to 25 percent when the kittens are put in the diagonal corner.

When the home area is made visually prominent by putting a black-and-white checkerboard pattern on the floor, three-week-old kittens are able to successfully orient themselves to the home area by means of the visual cue alone. In one test the home checkerboard floor was left in place but all the other floor panels were removed and replaced with freshly washed panels. Even in the absence of odor trails the kittens were able to find the home corner. They were equally successful when the home floor was replaced with a freshly washed panel that had the checkerboard pattern.

The growth in the relative importance of visually based orientation eventually leads to a change in the behavior of the kittens. Beginning at about 16 days of age kittens will voluntarily leave the home area, although they return quickly. At the age of 22 days most of the kittens will leave the home area and will stay away for several minutes. Incidentally, we found that one reason kittens left the home area at this age was to investigate the investigator who was standing in front of the cage.

There is also a change in suckling at about this time. The kittens begin

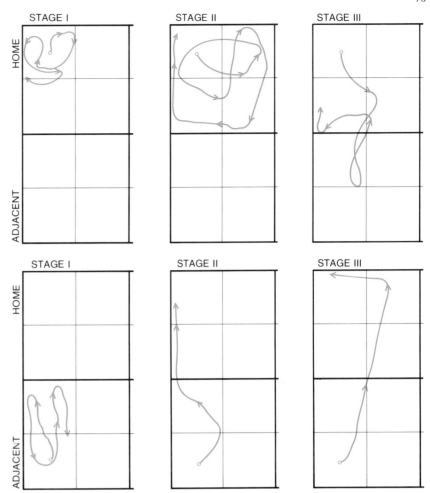

EXPLORATORY BEHAVIOR from its home corner of a kitten during its first 22 days develops in three stages (*top illustration*). In the first stage the kitten tends to crawl in circles within the home corner. In the second stage it crawls along the border of the home quadrant but seldom leaves it. In the third stage the kitten makes exploratory forays outside the home quadrant. When the kitten is placed in the adjacent corner, its crawling is increasingly directed toward the home corner as it becomes older (*bottom illustration*). The arrows mark position and direction of a kitten at successive 15-second intervals.

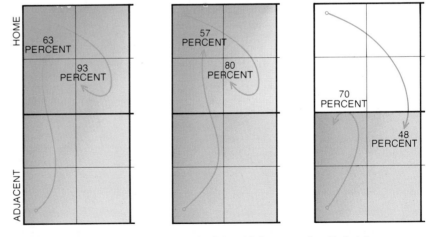

ODORS DEPOSITED ON THE CAGE FLOOR enable kittens to identify their home corner. The gradient of odors is indicated by the intensity of the color. In the undisturbed home cage (*left*) 93 percent of the kittens remained in the home quadrant, and when placed in the adjacent corner, 63 percent crawled home. Later the home-area floor was washed and replaced so that odors could again accumulate. Kittens tested the next day (*middle*) found the home corner almost as readily as before. When kittens were tested on a freshly washed home floor (*right*), the lack of accumulated odors caused them to avoid the home quadrant.

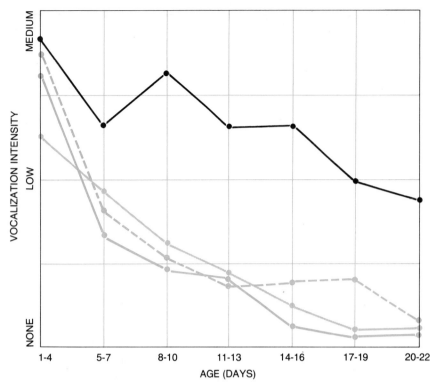

INTENSITY OF VOCALIZATION in kittens was rated at the start of the tests as a measure of their distress. Within a week the kittens cried much less when they were put anywhere in the home cage (*colored curves*) than when they were placed in a strange cage (*black curve*). Crying decreased equally in the home (*solid color*), adjacent (*light color*) and diagonal (*broken curve*) corners, indicating that the kittens recognized the home cage.

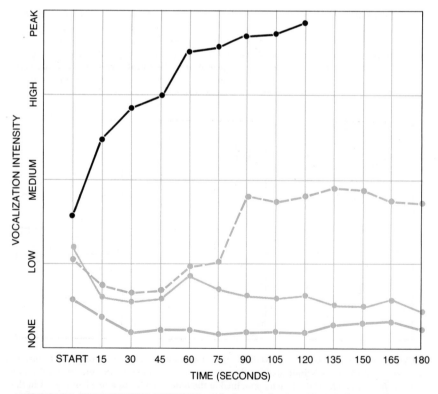

ABILITY TO DISTINGUISH REGIONS of the home cage is evident in kittens that were tested at five to seven days of age. Crying is lowest when kittens are placed in the home corner (*solid colored curve*). It takes the kittens about a minute to distinguish between the adjacent corner (*light color*) and the diagonal corner (*broken*). When the kittens are placed in a strange cage, the intensity of their crying steadily increases (*black curve*).

to pursue the mother to initiate feeding. The kittens shift their orientation from the home area to the mother and to some extent to their littermates. The presence of littermates in a strange environment tends to calm the kittens. If the kitten is outside the home area and becomes distressed during the period when it is dependent on odors to identify the home area, it is not calmed until it has returned to the home area. When the kitten can use vision to identify the home, it can take the most direct route home and later can remain outside the home area and still retain the emotional security provided by the home area.

Our studies thus show that learning plays an important role in the behavioral development of newborn kittens. Such learning, however, is closely related to the maturation of sensory and motor processes and cannot be studied apart from such processes. Specific behavior patterns arise from a fusion of experience and maturation. Therefore behavior patterns will vary according to the circumstances in the life situation of the newborn animal.

The similarity of behavioral development in the young of many animals indicates that there may be a general pattern of infantile development. Young rats show signs of recognizing nest odors by the ninth day after birth and strong home-orientation behavior appears when they are from 12 to 16 days of age and before their eyes have opened. In several species of herbivores (such as sheep, deer and cows) the young can see and walk shortly after birth and rapidly develop a strong orientation toward the mother. The importance of bodily contact in the emotional development of infant monkeys has been well established by the experiments of Harry F. Harlow at the University of Wisconsin. Studies with human infants show that the infant can orient itself toward its mother at a very early age.

With kittens the learning of home orientation has the function of keeping the kitten in the home area while the mother is away. In other species comparable forms of early orientation learning serve to keep the young in the safety of the nest or close to the mother. The infant builds a zone of emotional security within which it develops its capacities first to cope with nearby features in its environment and then to deal with more distant features. By maintaining contact with its home base the growing infant lessens the emotional impact of the new and strange environment it must enter as it becomes independent of its mother and its original home.

III

NEURON, SYNAPSE, AND BRAIN ACTIVITY

III

NEURON, SYNAPSE, AND BRAIN ACTIVITY

INTRODUCTION

In all higher organisms behavior is a reflection of the activity of the brain. In a sense each of us is simply a brain together with a few minor input and output appendages. The brain itself is essentially a set of interconnecting elements—the neurons, or nerve cells. Each neuron receives information from other neurons or from sensory receptors and transmits information to still other neurons or to muscles to produce behavior. All stimuli impinging upon us, all sensations, thoughts, actions, and feelings, must be coded into the language of the neuron. Every neuron transmits information in two quite different modes: A message is either continuous or all-or-none. A particular neuron is activated in a continuous fashion by other neurons: this is the graded-decision process, the process of *synaptic transmission*. Once the nerve cell is activated to transmit this information along its fiber to another neuron, it converts the graded-decision language into an all-or-none spike or *action potential*, the digital language of the nerve fiber. The two basic processes of neuronal activity thus depend on the action potential and synaptic transmission.

This section begins with a description of how a nerve fiber—the axon—conducts the all-or-none action potential from its cell body out to its terminals to influence other nerve cells. Peter F. Baker ("The Nerve Axon") describes the classical studies that were done using a large simplified nerve axon, the giant axon of the squid. It is a very large structure about the size of a thread, which can be studied in an isolated experimental chamber. The interior contents of the axon, the axoplasm, can actually be squeezed out like toothpaste and analyzed, and the axon can be refilled with experimental solutions. By a series of such studies, Hodgkin, Huxley, Keynes, Baker, and others analyzed the basic mechanism of the nerve action potential.

The other basic mode of communication in the nervous system is synaptic transmission, effected by interactions between nerve cells. These functional interconnections between neurons are described by Sir John Eccles in his article "The Synapse." When an action potential arrives at the end of an axon, it meets the synapse. This term refers to the space between the end of the axon and the adjacent region of the next nerve cell, together with the specialized portions of the axon terminal and the adjacent nerve cell membrane. Instead of simply inducing electrical activity across the synaptic space, as was thought earlier, the axon terminal releases a small amount of chemical transmitter substance that activates the adjacent nerve cell. Excitation and inhibition of nerve-cell activity are both accomplished in this manner by the release of chemical substances. We should note that in many invertebrate and some vertebrate synapses electrical transmission does seem to occur. However, the predominant synaptic interaction in the mammalian brain seems to be by way of chemical transmitter substances.

In the next article, "The Analysis of Brain Waves," Mary A. B. Brazier presents a comprehensive account of brain waves, their characteristics, and meaning. Waves in the human brain and, of course, in the brains of all higher organisms, are the net result of the activity of thousands and millions of individual nerve cells acting sometimes in a synchronized and coordinated manner and at other times in a seemingly uncoordinated way. The basic mechanism that generates brain waves seems to be synaptic transmission. Brain waves represent the summed electrical activity of many synapses acting together. Perhaps the most surprising thing about brain waves is that they exist. The existence of such regular rhythmic activity as alpha waves suggests that many millions of neurons must somehow be acting synchronously. In Brazier's article the modern techniques used to record and analyze brain waves in humans are described and the various types of waves and their possible meanings are discussed.

The state of an organism has a profound effect on the kinds of brain waves that can be recorded from its brain. In particular, sleep is one of the most powerful determiners of brain waves. As a higher organism falls asleep, its EEG shows a regular sequence of changes from the rapid, low-voltage, irregular activity of aroused and alert mentation, through the alpha activity of quiet restful waking, through spindling as sleep develops, to the very slow delta waves of slow-wave sleep. One of the most important discoveries in recent years regarding the patterns of brain waves concerns *paradoxical sleep*, often termed deep sleep or rapid-eye-movement (REM) sleep. Periodically during uninterrupted sleep, the EEG of a sleeper shifts from the slow-wave pattern to the fast, or arousal, pattern of the alert waking brain. However, the organism remains fast asleep. At the time when the fast pattern is being recorded, rapid, jerky eye movements occur. There is at present much argument in the field regarding the correlation between the deep-sleep state and the occurrence of dreaming. This argument has yet not been resolved. However, there is no question that paradoxical sleep does occur. Michel Jouvet summarizes our current knowledge of the different EEG states of sleep and of the possible brain mechanisms that may underlie them in his article, "The States of Sleep."

8

The Nerve Axon

by Peter F. Baker
March 1966

*The fiber that conducts the nerve impulse is a tubelike
structure. Its operation can be studied by squeezing
the contents out of the giant axon of the squid and
replacing them with various solutions*

Axons are the communication lines of the nervous system, and along them message-bearing electrical impulses travel from one part of the body to another. They are sometimes compared to electric cables, but they do not carry an electric current the way a wire does. Whereas in a copper wire electricity travels at a speed approaching the velocity of light, in an axon an impulse moves at only about 100 meters per second at best. The interior of an axon is about 100 million times more resistant to the flow of electricity than a copper wire is. Moreover, the membrane sheathing the axon is about a million times leakier to electric current than the sheath of a good cable. If the propagation of electricity in an axon depended on conduction alone, a current fed into it would die out within a few millimeters. The fact is that the axon propagates a current not by simple conduction but by means of a built-in amplifying and relay system.

How does the system work? This is a central question in the investigation of the nervous system, and it has long intrigued physiologists. This article is primarily an account of one of the new techniques developed for investigating the process of nerve-impulse conduction. The technique can be described briefly as experimenting with perfused axons.

The electrical activity of an axon is based on the interaction of three elements: (1) the fluid contents of the axon, called the axoplasm, (2) the membrane that encloses these contents and (3) the outside fluid that bathes the axon. The key to the axon's propagation of an impulse lies in the membrane. Essentially our technique consists in emptying the axon of its contents and perfusing the emptied tube with various experimental solutions, the ob-

ject being to determine just what factors are required to make an electric current travel along the axon.

These studies, like many others that have been done on the transmission of nerve impulses, are made possible by that remarkably convenient gift of nature: the giant axon of the squid. This axon measures up to a millimeter in diameter. The axons of human nerve cells, in contrast, are only about a hundredth of a millimeter in diameter. For the squid the giant axon represents an adaptation to a vital need in its particular way of life. For the physiologist this axon provides an ideal experimental preparation. All the available evidence suggests that experimental results obtained with squid axons are applicable to all other nerve fibers.

Why some animals and not others have evolved giant axons is not fully understood, but such axons appear to be involved in escape responses. The giant axon of the squid is part of the mechanism by which the animal flees its enemies in the water. In order to dart away rapidly the squid uses a jet-propulsion system, squirting water out of a tube at one end of its body. This calls for the synchronous contraction of muscles located throughout its body mantle, and therefore all those muscles must receive the message from the brain simultaneously. The device that takes care of this timing is a variation in the size of the axons radiating from the brain to the various muscles. The farther the muscle is from the brain, the thicker is the axon leading to it, and experiments have shown that the thicker the axon, the faster it conducts impulses. Hence the diameter of the axon is adjusted to the length of the route to be covered, and this ensures that the

signal will reach all the muscles at the same time.

The giant axon is easily dissected out of the squid. It is by probing the isolated axon with microelectrodes and by other means that Kenneth S. Cole in the U.S., A. L. Hodgkin, A. F. Huxley and Bernhard Katz in Britain and other investigators have since 1939 developed an outline of the main events that take place when an electrical impulse passes along a nerve fiber. Much of this story has already been related in *Scientific American*. I shall only briefly review the principal features of the picture.

Between the axoplasm inside the axon and the fluid bathing the axon on the outside there are distinct chemical and electrical differences. Chemically the axoplasm is distinguished by the presence of various organic molecules and a comparatively high content of potassium. The outside fluid, on the other hand, is quite similar to seawater: it principally contains sodium ions and chloride ions. The concentration of potassium is about 30 times higher inside the axon than outside; the concentration of sodium is about 10 times higher outside than inside. Because of these differences potassium ions tend to leak out of the axon (by diffusion) and sodium ions to leak in, to the extent that the membrane will allow the ions to pass. (We can disregard the axoplasm's organic molecules and the outside fluid's chloride in this connection, because the membrane is highly impermeable to them.)

The electric-charge situation complicates the picture. Inside the axon we have a high concentration of positively charged potassium ions; outside, a high concentration of positively charged so-

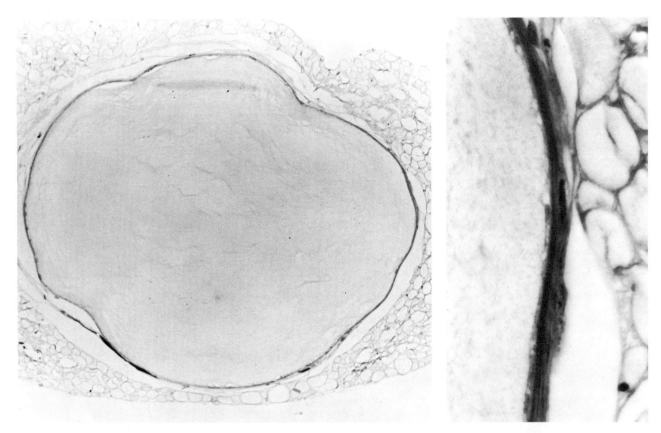

INTACT SQUID AXON is seen in transverse section in these photomicrographs made by J. S. Alexandrowicz of the Plymouth Marine Laboratory. The section is enlarged 140 diameters (*left*). A segment of the axon's perimeter is enlarged 1,150 diameters (*right*). The gray material inside the axon is the axoplasm. The dark boundary of the axon is composed primarily of a layer of Schwann cells.

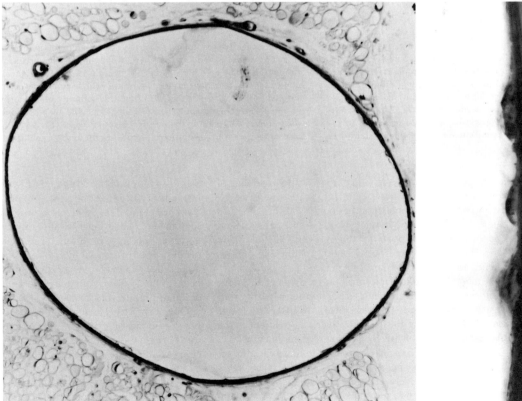

PERFUSED AXON (*left*) and part of its perimeter (*right*) are enlarged as in the top micrographs. The axoplasm has been replaced with a potassium sulfate solution. The small amount of grayish residual axoplasm is thickest near a nucleus of a Schwann cell (*right*).

82

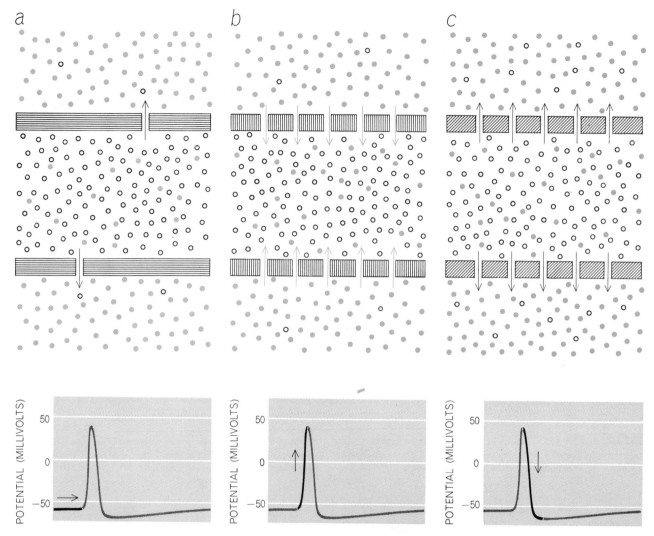

INTERNAL POTENTIAL of an axon is established by the concentration gradients of potassium and sodium ions and by the axon membrane's changing permeability to these two positive ions. Because it is more concentrated inside the axon than outside, potassium (*open circles*) tends to diffuse out; sodium (*colored dots*), more concentrated outside than inside, diffuses in. A normal resting axon membrane is more permeable to potassium than to sodium. The resulting net outward diffusion of potassium establishes the inside-negative resting potential (*a*). An action potential occurs when the nerve is depolarized (by a nerve impulse or artificial stimulation). The action potential has two phases. First the membrane becomes very permeable to sodium, which enters the axon and makes the inside positive (*b*). Then the sodium "gates" close; the membrane thereupon becomes very permeable to potassium, which moves out, making the interior negative again (*c*). A reduction in potassium permeability reestablishes the resting condition.

dium ions. When the membrane is in its unstimulated resting condition, it is highly permeable to potassium but only slightly permeable to sodium. Because of potassium's relative freedom to pass through the membrane and its steep concentration gradient, it tends to leak out of the axon at a high rate. The result is that the inside of the axon becomes electrically negative with respect to the outside. There is a limit to this process; an equilibrium is reached when the tendency for potassium to diffuse out is balanced by the electric field that has been set up. At this point the interior of the axon is about 60 millivolts (thousandths of a volt) negative in relation to the external fluid. That difference—a negative potential of 60 milli-

volts—is called the resting potential of the nerve cell. It is created, in effect, by a potassium battery.

It is relevant to inquire what would happen to the potential if the membrane were highly permeable not to potassium but to one of the other ions. The concentration gradient of the positively charged sodium ions is from outside to inside, acting to make the inside of the axon positive. The gradient of the negatively charged organic molecules is from inside to outside and will also act to make the inside positive. The negatively charged chloride ions are more concentrated outside the axon than inside and will act to make the inside negative. Altering the permeability of the membrane to these ions can estab-

lish a wide range of potentials, the inside being negative (because of potassium or chloride) or positive (because of sodium or organic ions) or anything in between (because of a mixture). The possibilities this variability offers for the control of membrane potential have been thoroughly exploited by the cells of the central nervous system.

Obviously any change in the membrane's permeability to one of the ions can change the potential. This is precisely what happens when an electrical impulse passes along the axon. The current reduces the potential at the point of its arrival, and the resting potential there drops toward zero; the membrane is said to be depolarized. In response to the drop in potential the membrane's permeability to sodium suddenly increases; this further reduces the potential, which in turn makes the membrane still more permeable to sodium. As if a door were suddenly opened wide, sodium ions from the surrounding fluid rush into the axon. The result is that within a small fraction of a second the interior of the axon switches from a *negative* potential of about 60 millivolts to a *positive* potential of about 50 millivolts. The new condition is the first phase of what is called an action potential.

The local region within the axon is now positive, whereas the next adjacent section, which still has a normal resting potential, is negative. Consequently a current flows from the positive to the negative region, completing the circuit by returning to the positive region through the conducting solution outside the axon. The current arriving in the region of normal resting potential opens the membrane door to sodium and thus triggers the generation of an action potential like that in the region it has just left. In this manner the impulse is regenerated from point to point along the axon and flows from one end of it to the other. In each region, shortly after an action potential has been generated, the membrane's permeability to sodium is switched off and its permeability to potassium increases, and as a result that section of the axon returns to the resting potential. The entire local action potential lasts only about a millisecond.

For many years physiologists have been looking into this process experimentally. What would happen if the concentration of ions on one side of the membrane or the other was changed artificially? Isolated axons remain functional for many hours when they are immersed in a simple salt solution containing the major ions present in seawater. It is an easy matter to vary the concentration of these ions in order to study their influence on the process of impulse conduction. Experimenters found that when they added potassium to the medium, thereby reducing the potassium gradient between the inside of the axon and the outside, the resting potential dropped. When they removed sodium from the medium (replacing it with an osmotically equivalent amount of sugar or the positive organic molecule choline), the axon became incapable of propagating an electrical impulse. These results supported the general view of the critical roles normally played by the sodium and potassium

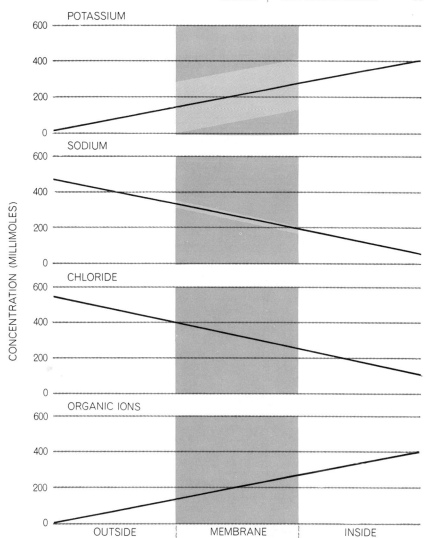

CONCENTRATION GRADIENTS for the major nerve-axon ions are shown. The concentration of each ion on the outside (*left*) and inside (*right*) of the membrane (*color*) is given; the slope shows the direction of the concentration gradient, down which the ions have a tendency to diffuse. This diffusion is blocked by the membrane, which resists mixing of internal and external ions except as it is permeable to one or another of them. The permeability of the membrane during the normal resting phase is suggested here: it is 10 times as permeable to sodium as to organic ions or chloride, 10 times as permeable to potassium as to sodium. Sodium and potassium ions are positive, chloride and organic ions negative.

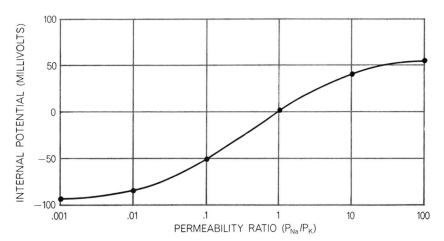

MEMBRANE PERMEABILITY to potassium and sodium ions can be varied. The curve shows, for the concentrations given in the chart at the top of the page, the effect on the internal potential of changes in the membrane's relative permeability to sodium and potassium.

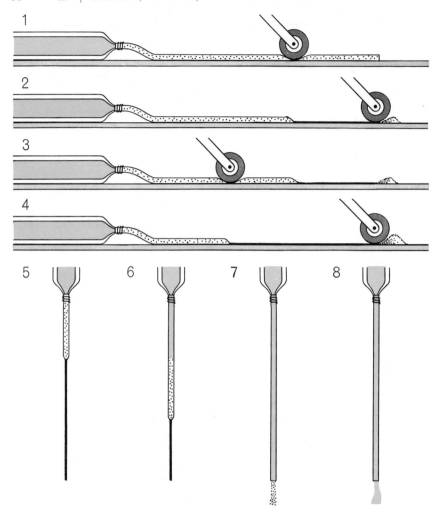

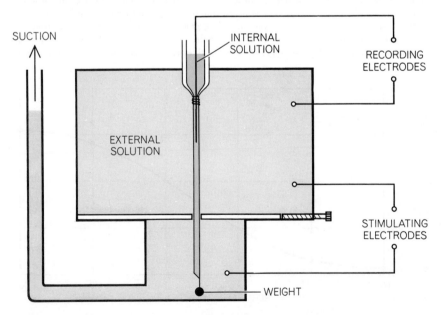

AXOPLASM is removed from a piece of squid axon and replaced with an experimental solution. A piece of axon with a cannula fixed to its smaller end is placed on a rubber pad and axoplasm is squeezed out of it by successive passes with a rubber roller (*1–4*). Then the nearly empty sheath is suspended vertically in seawater (*5*) and the perfusion fluid is forced through it, removing the remaining plug of axoplasm and refilling the axon (*6–8*).

PERFUSED AXON is mounted so as to allow solutions to be changed with an internal electrode in position. To fill it with a new solution, suction is applied to the external fluid.

gradients in the generation of the action potential and the resting potential.

Experiments were also performed in changing the composition of the axoplasm within the axon. To inject extra sodium or potassium into the intact fiber a special microsyringe was used by Harry Grundfest, C. Y. Kao and M. Altamirano at the Columbia University College of Physicians and Surgeons, and also by Hodgkin and Richard D. Keynes at the University of Cambridge. It is not possible to change the inside-outside gradients of ions by any great amount in this way, but when extra sodium was injected into the axon, raising its concentration closer to the level of the sodium outside, the action potential produced by an electrical impulse was smaller than normal, presumably because the usual inrush of sodium ions was checked.

Could one find a way to remove the core of the axon and substitute a strictly experimental solution inside the fiber? Recently two different techniques for doing this were developed almost simultaneously, one by Ichiji Tasaki and his co-workers at the Marine Biological Laboratory in Woods Hole, Mass., and the other by T. I. Shaw and the author at the Plymouth Marine Laboratory in Britain. In Tasaki's method a fine capillary tube is used to ream out some of the axoplasm, and then a fluid is run through the tube to wash out as much of the remaining material as possible. It is an extremely tricky operation, particularly on the comparatively small "giant" axons of the squid found in North American waters, and a considerable amount of axoplasm is left in the fiber.

Our technique is crude by comparison, but we have found that it effectively removes most of the axoplasm. It is based on an old stratagem: in 1937 Richard S. Bear, Francis O. Schmitt and J. Z. Young, working at the Marine Biological Laboratory in Woods Hole, discovered that if an end of an axon was cut, they could squeeze the axoplasm out of it much as one squeezes toothpaste out of a tube. We were led to wonder about the casing left by this operation. Did the squeezing spoil the membrane's properties or could it still conduct an electrical impulse? We undertook an experiment to answer the question. We laid a section of axon about eight centimeters long (a little more than three inches) on a rubber pad and squeezed axoplasm out of the wider end by a series of fairly firm strokes with a rubber-covered roller. When the axoplasm had been extruded from half of the axon's length, leaving that part a flattened sheath, we rolled the other half to push some of its axoplasm into the emptied section. To our surprise we found that the roughly handled membrane could still conduct and boost electrical impulses. This experiment showed that the excitable properties of the membrane are not destroyed by extrusion and encouraged us to try to replace the axoplasm with artificial solutions.

Our procedure was to insert a small glass cannula into the narrower end of the axon and squeeze out as much of the axoplasm as possible; then, attaching the cannula to a motor-driven syringe, we suspended the nerve in sea-water and forced "artificial axoplasm" through the flattened sheath. When the nerve was refilled, its excitability was tested, and in about 75 percent of the experiments the preparation was found to function like a normal nerve. With this method about 95 percent of the axoplasm is extruded and a long length of axon can be perfused. Once perfused, the axon can be tied off at both ends and handled like a normal axon. It is more convenient, however, to mount it in such a way that a microelectrode can be inserted into the axon and, with the electrode in place, the perfusion fluid can be changed repeatedly [*see illustrations on opposite page*]. It is also possible to change the external solution.

W e now undertook a series of perfusion experiments in collaboration with Hodgkin. The first question we asked was: What substances must the axoplasm contain in order to generate a resting potential and an action potential? The requirements turned out to be simple indeed. The only essentials are that the solution be rich in potassium ions and poor in sodium ions, and that it have about the same osmotic pressure and concentration of hydrogen ions as normal axoplasm. As for the negatively charged ions (which normally are ionized organic molecules), their nature is not critical; we have used a wide variety of negative ions successfully. A particularly convenient solution is buffered potassium sulfate. When axons are perfused with this solution, they produce resting and action potentials that are almost identical with those generated by intact fibers [*see top illustration at right*].

It appears, then, that the bulk of the natural axoplasm is not necessary for the propagation of impulses. Are crucial remnants of the original material left in our axons—substances that could not be dispensed with and that make conduction possible? It is not easy to answer categorically; all that can be said is that the axons are still fully functional and can conduct up to half a million impulses, even after they have been washed by a flow of artificial solution amounting to 100 times the volume of the original fluid. If essential molecules were diffusing from the remaining axoplasm to the membrane, they should have been completely washed out by such a massive flow. There remains the possibility that something essential for impulse conduction is supplied by a layer of cells that surrounds the giant axon. The function of these cells, called Schwann cells, is obscure. Various kinds of evidence suggest, however, that they are not directly involved in electrical conduction. For instance, when the Venezuelan workers R. Villegas, Maximo Gimenez and L. Villegas inserted two microelectrodes into a squid nerve—one into a Schwann cell and the other into the axon—they were unable to detect any electrical change in the Schwann cell when an action potential passed along the axon.

Perhaps the most remarkable finding is the fact that apparently no source of energy other than the difference in ion concentrations on the two sides of the membrane is needed to amplify an electical impulse and propagate it along the axon. Our artificial axoplasm contained no sugar, adenosine triphosphate (ATP) or other chemical source of energy, and it is unlikely that any ATP was produced by the traces of original axoplasm left in the sheath. Yet the axon could generate both resting and action potentials whenever the inside and outside solutions had the right concentrations of potassium ions and sodium ions.

To produce the resting potential we need only make sure that the fluid perfusing the experimental axon is primed with a sufficiently high concentration of potassium. If we substitute sodium for potassium in the potassium sulfate perfusion fluid, the resting potential drops, and the amount of this drop depends on the extent of the substitution; when the concentration of potassium inside the axon is reduced to the same level as that outside, the potential drops to zero. If we make the potassium concentration outside much higher than that inside, the inside of the axon becomes positive,

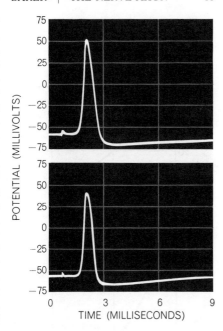

ACTION POTENTIALS from an axon perfused with potassium sulfate (*top*) and from an intact axon (*bottom*) are quite similar.

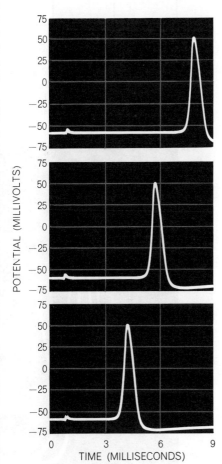

DEGREE OF INFLATION with perfusion fluid does not change the action potential but does increase the conduction velocity. These potentials were recorded from an empty axon (*top*), a partly inflated one (*middle*) and a fully inflated one (*bottom*).

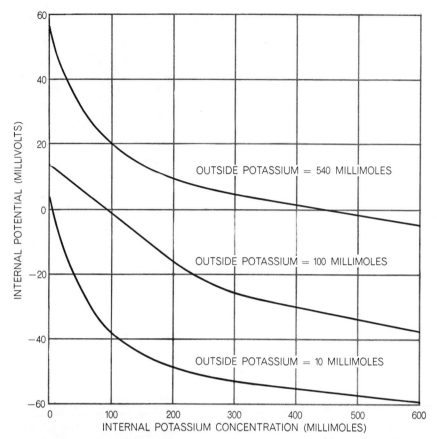

RESTING POTENTIALS of perfused axons depend on the potassium concentration gradient. The internal potassium content was changed by substituting sodium chloride for potassium chloride inside the axons. The lower the potassium gradient, the less negative the internal potential became. With the gradient reversed the internal potential became positive.

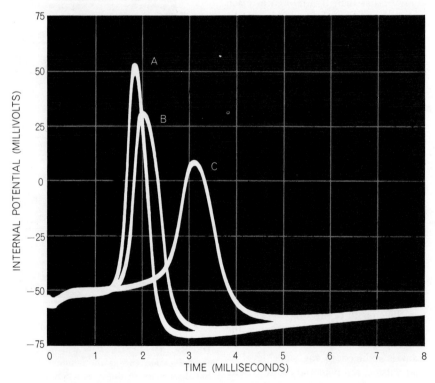

"OVERSHOOT," the amount by which the action potential rises above zero, decreases as the sodium gradient is reduced. These potentials are from a normally perfused axon (A) and axons in which a quarter (B) and half (C) of the potassium was replaced with sodium.

that is, the sign of the resting potential is plus instead of minus. These observations are what would be expected if the resting nerve membrane is freely permeable to potassium ions but not to other ions. The magnitude and the sign of the potential generated are dependent on the steepness and the direction of the potassium concentration gradient.

These experiments also show that the inward diffusion of the negatively charged chloride ions contributes very little to the resting potential. When there is no potassium concentration gradient, there is still a steep gradient for chloride, and yet the measured resting potential is close to zero. This type of experiment suggests that the resting membrane is highly impermeable to negative ions but freely permeable to potassium. A similar argument applied to sodium indicates that the resting membrane is also impermeable to this ion.

During the action potential, on the other hand, the permeability to sodium ions is markedly increased, but the amount by which the action potential overshoots zero and becomes positive is dependent on the sodium concentration gradient. The progressive replacement of potassium inside the axon by sodium reduces the overshoot and finally abolishes the axon's ability to conduct impulses; the ability is restored as the sodium is washed out and replaced with potassium. A rather interesting corollary is the change in action potential that occurs when most of the potassium sulfate in the perfusion fluid is replaced by an osmotically equivalent amount of sugar. Under these conditions the overshoot of the action potential is increased, only to fall again when the axon is refilled with potassium sulfate. This suggests that when potassium is present within the axon, it acts to some extent as a barrier to the inflow of sodium. That is to say, the potassium ions serve in some degree as if they were sodium ions, and when they are absent, the sodium gradient from outside to inside is steepened.

In performing these experiments we noticed that, although the substitution of sugar for potassium sulfate enhanced the action potential, it slowed the axon's conduction of impulses. Presumably this could be attributed to the low electrical conductivity of sugar, which would shorten the range of each stage of propagation (that is, each local circuit) and thereby slow the overall rate of travel. Indeed, we found by experiment that the higher the electrical conductivity of the material we used for perfusing the axon, the faster the speed of impulse propagation.

Recent experiments on perfused axons have been directed toward a detailed analysis of the properties of the action-potential mechanism. These investigations have depended to a large extent on the device known as the voltage clamp. This technique was devised almost 20 years ago by Cole and his co-workers and by Hodgkin, Huxley and Katz, and in their hands it provided almost all the detailed evidence for the sequence of changes in membrane permeability that occurs during the action potential.

The technique is simple in principle but often very difficult in practice. The idea is to produce a sudden displacement of the membrane potential from its resting value and to hold the potential at this new fixed level by means of a feedback amplifier. The current that flows through a definite area of membrane under the influence of the impressed voltage is measured with a separate amplifier [see illustration at right].

When the membrane of an intact axon is depolarized and the potential is held at some value close to zero, the current that flows is at first directed inward, but it rapidly reverses its direction and continues to flow outward as long as the membrane is kept depolarized. There is every indication that the initial inward current is carried by a rapid inflow of sodium ions resulting from a transient increase in the membrane's permeability to sodium, and that the delayed outward current results from a prolonged increase in its permeability to potassium. For one thing, experiments with the same technique show that if sodium is absent from the outside medium, so that the downward gradient of sodium concentration is from inside to outside instead of the other way around, there is a small initial outward flow of current instead of an inward one. Sodium ions now move from inside to outside through the door of increased permeability opened by depolarization of the membrane. The same result can be obtained, even when the axon is bathed on the outside by seawater, by reversing the resting potential, that is, by making the inside of the axon positive instead of negative and holding the potential at the positive value. The potential difference then drives sodium ions out of the axon against the chemi-

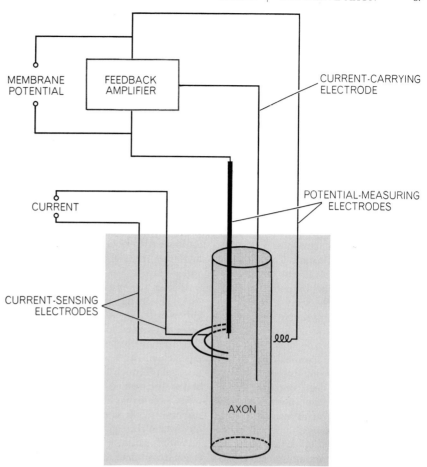

"VOLTAGE CLAMP" is set up as shown in this schematic diagram. A change in membrane potential is produced by the current-carrying electrode. Sensed by two other electrodes, the potential is thereafter maintained by a small current regulated by feedback. The current that flows through a known area of membrane at this fixed potential is then measured.

cal gradient, and a current flows outward. At some intermediate value the applied potential just balances the tendency of sodium ions to enter the axon and there is no detectable early current. This potential is called the sodium equilibrium potential.

The technique of perfusing axons allows the voltage clamp to be applied to situations in which the interior of the axon, as well as the external environment, can be varied. What will happen if sodium is completely absent both outside and inside the axon? In such a case we might expect that, if the axon contains only potassium, depolarization of the membrane should simply bring about a lasting outward current, carried by potassium ions diffusing out of the axon. When Knox Chandler and Hans Meves of our laboratory applied the voltage clamp, they found that depolarization always resulted promptly in a small outward current that was identical in its prop-

erties with the one normally carried by sodium ions. Were potassium ions in the axon acting like sodium ions in this case, passing out through the same membrane channel that opened up for sodium ions during depolarization?

Chandler and Meves tested this surmise by adding sodium to the formerly sodium-free outside medium. If the potassium ions within the axon did not behave like sodium, the downward gradient of sodium concentration from outside to inside would be very steep; hence a large inside-positive potential should be required to prevent a flow of current across the membrane. Actually the experiments showed that the equilibrium potential (the potential required to abolish the early inward current) had the value that would be expected if the potassium inside the axon acted like a small amount of sodium. These results indicate that the channel by which sodium ions enter the axon during an action potential is not completely specific for sodium ions. Chandler and

Meves were able to calculate from their measurements that the "sodium channel" enables sodium ions to pass about 12 times more easily than potassium ions.

This conclusion has recently been strengthened by a different approach. The fish known as the puffer manufactures a potent nerve poison called tetrodotoxin; analysis by means of the voltage clamp of how this poison acts has shown that it very specifically blocks the increase in permeability to sodium that occurs immediately following depolarization. It has no effect on the delayed increase in permeability to potassium. When tetrodotoxin was applied to perfused axons, Chandler and Meves found that it also blocks the early current carried by potassium ions, thus confirming the view that the potassium is passing through the "sodium channel."

The axon membrane loses its capacity for increasing its permeability to sodium when its resting potential is kept at progressively less negative levels. Hence as the resting potential is reduced toward zero (for instance by the replacement of potassium ions inside the axon with sodium or choline) the mechanism for admitting sodium is progressively inactivated, and therefore the axon's capacity for producing an action potential becomes progressively smaller. If, however, the potassium in the perfusion fluid is replaced by sugar instead of another ion, this loss is not so sharp; the membrane maintains its activity, or ability to increase its permeability to sodium, at much lower levels of resting potential. Chandler, Hodgkin and Meves have proposed a possible explanation

for this puzzling result. They suggest that the reduction or elimination of ions in the perfusion fluid uncovers negatively charged groups of atoms on the inner face of the membrane. This process would increase the electric field within the membrane without altering the total potential difference between the internal and external solutions. Accordingly a charged molecule within the membrane will experience an imposed electric field identical with that which it experiences in an intact axon at the resting potential.

Experiments with perfused axons have yielded results that would have been impossible to obtain with intact axons and thus represent a considerable advance, but in general they have not produced any revolutionary changes in ideas about the mechanism of propagation of the nerve impulse. They have, however, served to define more sharply the questions to be answered about the basic chemistry of the process. How do ions pass through the membrane? What makes the resting membrane so much more permeable to potassium than to sodium? What specific change in the membrane (brought about by a drop in potential) causes it suddenly to open its doors to sodium?

There are many hypotheses on these questions but so far no convincing items of evidence. The difficulties facing those who are trying to solve such problems in chemical terms are immense. Many of the unique properties of living membranes are dependent on the potential that normally exists across them. The application of the routine biochemical technique of homogenizing cells in order to isolate the cell membrane would

break up the membrane and destroy the potential across it; this might so alter the architecture of the molecular groups involved in nerve activity that they would be unrecognizable. Moreover, the relevant groups are probably quite thinly scattered through the membrane material and hence much diluted by less interesting molecules. Perhaps artificial membranes, synthesized from substances extracted from natural ones, will yield some clues, but a complete explanation of the behavior of the nerve membrane in molecular terms is probably still a long way off.

Further experiments with perfused axons may tell us something about the process of recovery from nerve activity. During the passage of an impulse in an intact nerve there is a small net gain of sodium and a small net loss of potassium. If this were to continue unchecked, the nerve would lose potassium and gain sodium, and the concentration gradients on which nerve activity depends would be destroyed. The tendency is counteracted by the mechanism known as the "sodium pump," which uses metabolic energy in the form of ATP to extrude sodium ions from the axon in exchange for potassium ions. Although an intact nerve can function for some time without an operating sodium pump, the pump is essential for the long-term maintenance of nerve activity. In perfused axons this is not the case, since fresh fluid can be constantly passed through the axon. There is evidence, however, that the pump mechanism survives perfusion and that it can be activated by adding ATP and small amounts of magnesium and sodium to the perfusion fluid.

The Synapse

9

by Sir John Eccles
January 1965

*How does one nerve cell transmit the nerve impulse to
another cell? Electron microscopy and other methods
show that it does so by means of special extensions
that deliver a squirt of transmitter substance*

The human brain is the most highly organized form of matter known, and in complexity the brains of the other higher animals are not greatly inferior. For certain purposes it is expedient to regard the brain as being analogous to a machine. Even if it is so regarded, however, it is a machine of a totally different kind from those made by man. In trying to understand the workings of his own brain man meets his highest challenge. Nothing is given; there are no operating diagrams, no maker's instructions.

The first step in trying to understand the brain is to examine its structure in order to discover the components from which it is built and how they are related to one another. After that one can attempt to understand the mode of operation of the simplest components. These two modes of investigation—the morphological and the physiological—have now become complementary. In studying the nervous system with today's sensitive electrical devices, however, it is all too easy to find physiological events that cannot be correlated with any known anatomical structure. Con-

versely, the electron microscope reveals many structural details whose physiological significance is obscure or unknown.

At the close of the past century the Spanish anatomist Santiago Ramón y Cajal showed how all parts of the nervous system are built up of individual nerve cells of many different shapes and sizes. Like other cells, each nerve cell has a nucleus and a surrounding cytoplasm. Its outer surface consists of numerous fine branches—the dendrites—that receive nerve impulses from other nerve cells, and one relatively long branch—the axon—that transmits nerve impulses. Near its end the axon divides into branches that terminate at the dendrites or bodies of other nerve cells. The axon can be as short as a fraction of a millimeter or as long as a meter, depending on its place and function. It has many of the properties of an electric cable and is uniquely specialized to conduct the brief electrical waves called nerve impulses [see "How Cells Communicate," by Bernhard Katz; SCIENTIFIC AMERICAN Offprint 98]. In very thin axons these impulses travel at less than

one meter per second; in others, for example in the large axons of the nerve cells that activate muscles, they travel as fast as 100 meters per second.

The electrical impulse that travels along the axon ceases abruptly when it comes to the point where the axon's terminal fibers make contact with another nerve cell. These junction points were given the name "synapses" by Sir Charles Sherrington, who laid the foundations of what is sometimes called synaptology. If the nerve impulse is to continue beyond the synapse, it must be regenerated afresh on the other side. As recently as 15 years ago some physiologists held that transmission at the synapse was predominantly, if not exclusively, an electrical phenomenon. Now, however, there is abundant evidence that transmission is effectuated by the release of specific chemical substances that trigger a regeneration of the impulse. In fact, the first strong evidence showing that a transmitter substance acts across the synapse was provided more than 40 years ago by Sir Henry Dale and Otto Loewi.

It has been estimated that the hu-

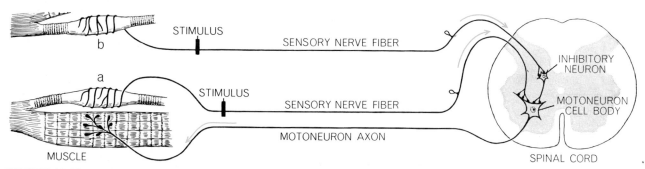

REFLEX ARCS provide simple pathways for studying the transmission of nerve impulses from one nerve cell to another. This transmission is effectuated at the junction points called synapses. In the illustration the sensory fiber from one muscle stretch receptor (*a*) makes direct synaptic contact with a motoneuron in the spinal cord. Nerve impulses generated by the moto-neuron activate the muscle to which the stretch receptor is attached. Stretch receptor *b* responds to the tension in a neighboring antagonistic muscle and sends impulses to a nerve cell that can inhibit the firing of the motoneuron. By electrically stimulating the appropriate stretch-receptor fibers one can study the effect of excitatory and inhibitory impulses on motoneurons.

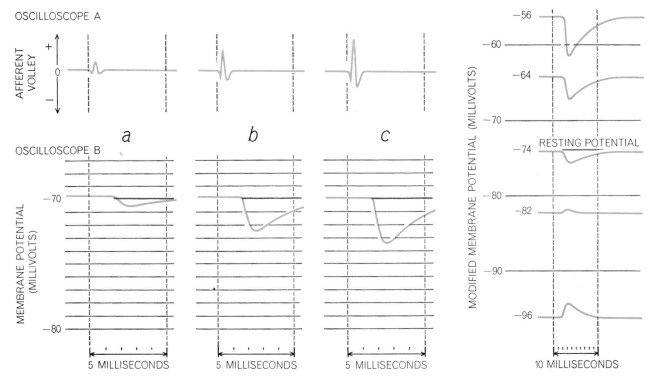

OSCILLOSCOPE A

AFFERENT VOLLEY

a   b   c

OSCILLOSCOPE B

MEMBRANE POTENTIAL (MILLIVOLTS)

−70

−80

5 MILLISECONDS   5 MILLISECONDS   5 MILLISECONDS

MODIFIED MEMBRANE POTENTIAL (MILLIVOLTS)

−56
−60
−64
−70
−74 RESTING POTENTIAL
−80
−82
−90
−96

10 MILLISECONDS

INHIBITION OF A MOTONEURON is investigated by methods like those used for studying the EPSP. The inhibitory counterpart of the EPSP is the IPSP: the inhibitory postsynaptic potential. Oscilloscope A records an afferent volley that travels to a number of inhibitory nerve cells whose axons form synapses on a nearby motoneuron (*see illustration on page 89*). A microelec-

trode in the motoneuron is connected to oscilloscope B. The sequence a, b and c shows how successively larger afferent volleys produce successively deeper IPSP's. Curves at right show how the IPSP is modified when a background current is used to change the motoneuron's resting potential. The equilibrium potential where the IPSP reverses direction is about minus 80 millivolts.

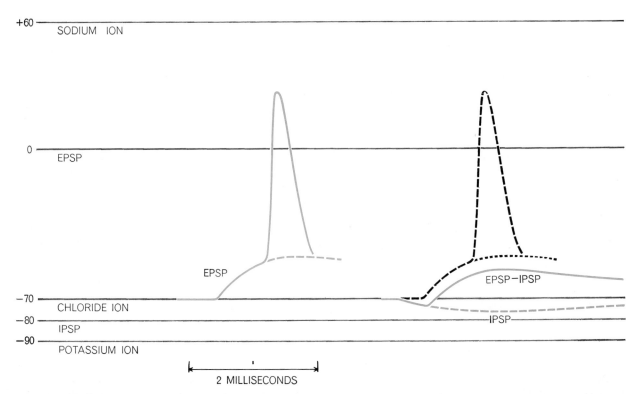

+60   SODIUM ION

0   EPSP

EPSP

EPSP−IPSP

−70   CHLORIDE ION
−80   IPSP
−90   POTASSIUM ION

IPSP

2 MILLISECONDS

INHIBITION OF A SPIKE DISCHARGE is an electrical subtraction process. When a normal EPSP reaches a threshold (*left*), it will ordinarily produce a spike. An IPSP widens the gap between the cell's internal potential and the firing threshold. Thus if

a cell is simultaneously subjected to both excitatory and inhibitory stimulation, the IPSP is subtracted from the EPSP (*right*) and no spike occurs. The five horizontal lines show equilibrium potentials for the three principal ions as well as for the EPSP and IPSP.

man central nervous system, which of course includes the spinal cord as well as the brain itself, consists of about 10 billion (10^{10}) nerve cells. With rare exceptions each nerve cell receives information directly in the form of impulses from many other nerve cells—often hundreds—and transmits information to a like number. Depending on its threshold of response, a given nerve cell may fire an impulse when stimulated by only a few incoming fibers or it may not fire until stimulated by many incoming fibers. It has long been known that this threshold can be raised or lowered by various factors. Moreover, it was conjectured some 60 years ago that some of the incoming fibers must inhibit the firing of the receiving cell rather than excite it [*see illustration at right*]. The conjecture was subsequently confirmed, and the mechanism of the inhibitory effect has now been clarified. This mechanism and its equally fundamental counterpart—nerve-cell excitation—are the subject of this article.

Probing the Nerve Cell

At the level of anatomy there are some clues to indicate how the fine axon terminals impinging on a nerve cell can make the cell regenerate a nerve impulse of its own. The top illustration on the next page shows how a nerve cell and its dendrites are covered by fine branches of nerve fibers that terminate in knoblike structures. These structures are the synapses.

The electron microscope has revealed structural details of synapses that fit in nicely with the view that a chemical transmitter is involved in nerve transmission [*see lower two illustrations on next page*]. Enclosed in the synaptic knob are many vesicles, or tiny sacs, which appear to contain the transmitter substances that induce synaptic transmission. Between the synaptic knob and the synaptic membrane of the adjoining nerve cell is a remarkably uniform space of about 20 millimicrons that is termed the synaptic cleft. Many of the synaptic vesicles are concentrated adjacent to this cleft; it seems plausible that the transmitter substance is discharged from the nearest vesicles into the cleft, where it can act on the adjacent cell membrane. This hypothesis is supported by the discovery that the transmitter is released in packets of a few thousand molecules.

The study of synaptic transmission was revolutionized in 1951 by the introduction of delicate techniques for recording electrically from the interior

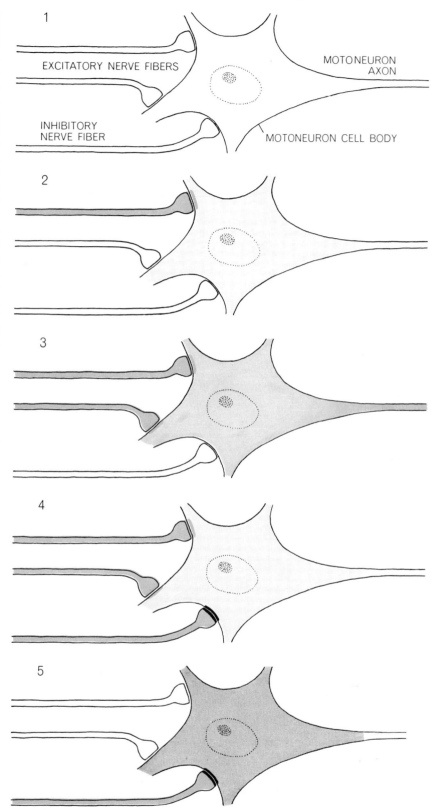

EXCITATION AND INHIBITION of a nerve cell are accomplished by the nerve fibers that form synapses on its surface. Diagram *1* shows a motoneuron in the resting state. In *2* impulses received from one excitatory fiber are inadequate to cause the motoneuron to fire. In *3* impulses from a second excitatory fiber raise the motoneuron to firing threshold. In *4* impulses carried by an inhibitory fiber restore the subthreshold condition. In *5* the inhibitory fiber alone is carrying impulses. There is no difference in the electrical impulses carried by excitatory and inhibitory nerve fibers. They achieve opposite effects because they release different chemical transmitter substances at their synaptic endings.

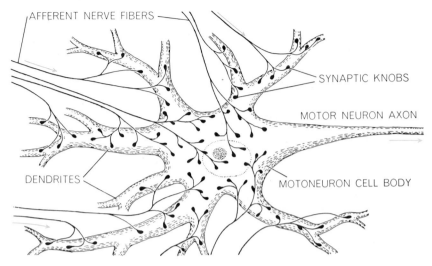

MOTONEURON CELL BODY and branches called dendrites are covered with synaptic knobs, which represent the terminals of axons, or impulse-carrying fibers, from other nerve cells. The axon of each motoneuron, in turn, terminates at a muscle fiber.

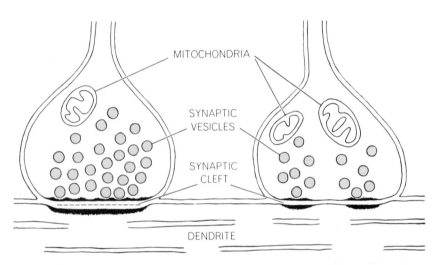

SYNAPTIC KNOBS are designed to deliver short bursts of a chemical transmitter substance into the synaptic cleft, where it can act on the surface of the nerve-cell membrane below. Before release, molecules of the chemical transmitter are stored in numerous vesicles, or sacs. Mitochondria are specialized structures that help to supply the cell with energy.

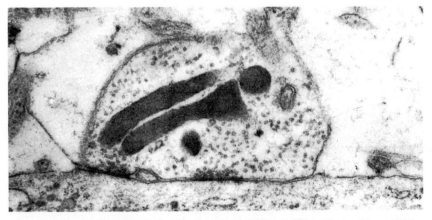

ASSUMED INHIBITORY SYNAPSE on a nerve cell is magnified 28,000 diameters in this electron micrograph by the late L. H. Hamlyn of University College London. Synaptic vesicles, believed to contain the transmitter substance, are bunched in two regions along the synaptic cleft. The darkening of the cleft in these regions is so far unexplained.

of single nerve cells. This is done by inserting into the nerve cell an extremely fine glass pipette with a diameter of .5 micron—about a fifty-thousandth of an inch. The pipette is filled with an electrically conducting salt solution such as concentrated potassium chloride. If the pipette is carefully inserted and held rigidly in place, the cell membrane appears to seal quickly around the glass, thus preventing the flow of a short-circuiting current through the puncture in the cell membrane. Impaled in this fashion, nerve cells can function normally for hours. Although there is no way of observing the cells during the insertion of the pipette, the insertion can be guided by using as clues the electric signals that the pipette picks up when close to active nerve cells.

When my colleagues and I in New Zealand and later at the John Curtin School of Medical Research in Canberra first employed this technique, we chose to study the large nerve cells called motoneurons, which lie in the spinal cord and whose function is to activate muscles. This was a fortunate choice: intracellular investigations with motoneurons have proved to be easier and more rewarding than those with any other kind of mammalian nerve cell.

We soon found that when the nerve cell responds to the chemical synaptic transmitter, the response depends in part on characteristic features of ionic composition that are also concerned with the transmission of impulses in the cell and along its axon. When the nerve cell is at rest, its physiological makeup resembles that of most other cells in that the water solution inside the cell is quite different in composition from the solution in which the cell is bathed. The nerve cell is able to exploit this difference between external and internal composition and use it in quite different ways for generating an electrical impulse and for synaptic transmission.

The composition of the external solution is well established because the solution is essentially the same as blood from which cells and proteins have been removed. The composition of the internal solution is known only approximately. Indirect evidence indicates that the concentrations of sodium and chloride ions outside the cell are respectively some 10 and 14 times higher than the concentrations inside the cell. In contrast, the concentration of potassium ions inside the cell is about 30 times higher than the concentration outside.

How can one account for this remarkable state of affairs? Part of the explanation is that the inside of the cell is negatively charged with respect to the outside of the cell by about 70 millivolts. Since like charges repel each other, this internal negative charge tends to drive chloride ions (Cl⁻) outward through the cell membrane and, at the same time, to impede their inward movement. In fact, a potential difference of 70 millivolts is just sufficient to maintain the observed disparity in the concentration of chloride ions inside the cell and outside it; chloride ions diffuse inward and outward at equal rates. A drop of 70 millivolts across the membrane therefore defines the "equilibrium potential" for chloride ions.

To obtain a concentration of potassium ions (K⁺) that is 30 times higher inside the cell than outside would require that the interior of the cell membrane be about 90 millivolts negative with respect to the exterior. Since the

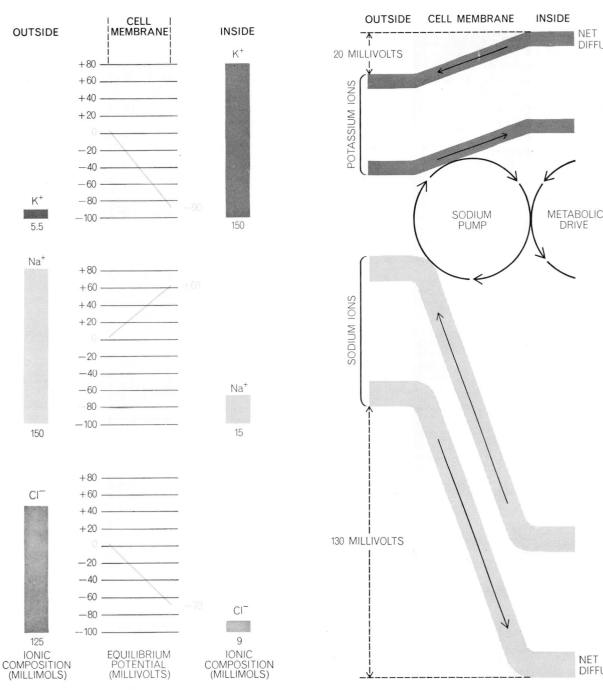

IONIC COMPOSITION outside and inside the nerve cell is markedly different. The "equilibrium potential" is the voltage drop that would have to exist across the membrane of the nerve cell to produce the observed difference in concentration for each type of ion. The actual voltage drop is about 70 millivolts, with the inside being negative. Given this drop, chloride ions diffuse inward and outward at equal rates, but the concentration of sodium and potassium must be maintained by some auxiliary mechanism (*right*).

METABOLIC PUMP must be postulated to account for the observed concentrations of potassium and sodium ions on opposite sides of the nerve-cell membrane. The negative potential inside is 20 millivolts short of the equilibrium potential for potassium ions. Thus there is a net outward diffusion of potassium ions that must be balanced by the pump. For sodium ions the potential across the membrane is 130 millivolts in the wrong direction, so very energetic pumping is needed. Chloride ions are in equilibrium.

actual interior is only 70 millivolts negative, it falls short of the equilibrium potential for potassium ions by 20 millivolts. Evidently the thirtyfold concentration can be achieved and maintained only if there is some auxiliary mechanism for "pumping" potassium ions into the cell at a rate equal to their spontaneous net outward diffusion.

The pumping mechanism has the still more difficult task of pumping sodium ions (Na$^+$) out of the cell against a potential gradient of 130 millivolts. This figure is obtained by adding the 70 millivolts of internal negative charge to the equilibrium potential for sodium ions, which is 60 millivolts of internal *positive* charge [*see illustrations on preceding page*]. If it were not for this postulated pump, the concentration of sodium ions inside and outside the cell would be almost the reverse of what is observed.

In their classic studies of nerve-impulse transmission in the giant axon of

the squid, A. L. Hodgkin, A. F. Huxley and Bernhard Katz of Britain demonstrated that the propagation of the impulse coincides with abrupt changes in the permeability of the axon membrane. When a nerve impulse has been triggered in some way, what can be described as a gate opens and lets sodium ions pour into the axon during the advance of the impulse, making the interior of the axon locally positive. The process is self-reinforcing in that the flow of some sodium ions through the membrane opens the gate further and makes it easier for others to follow. The sharp reversal of the internal polarity of the membrane constitutes the nerve impulse, which moves like a wave until it has traveled the length of the axon. In the wake of the impulse the sodium gate closes and a potassium gate opens, thereby restoring the normal polarity of the membrane within a millisecond or less.

With this understanding of the nerve

impulse in hand, one is ready to follow the electrical events at the excitatory synapse. One might guess that if the nerve impulse results from an abrupt inflow of sodium ions and a rapid change in the electrical polarity of the axon's interior, something similar must happen at the body and dendrites of the nerve cell in order to generate the impulse in the first place. Indeed, the function of the excitatory synaptic terminals on the cell body and its dendrites is to depolarize the interior of the cell membrane essentially by permitting an inflow of sodium ions. When the depolarization reaches a threshold value, a nerve impulse is triggered.

As a simple instance of this phenomenon we have recorded the depolarization that occurs in a single motoneuron activated directly by the large nerve fibers that enter the spinal cord from special stretch-receptors known as annulospiral endings. These receptors in turn are located in the same muscle that

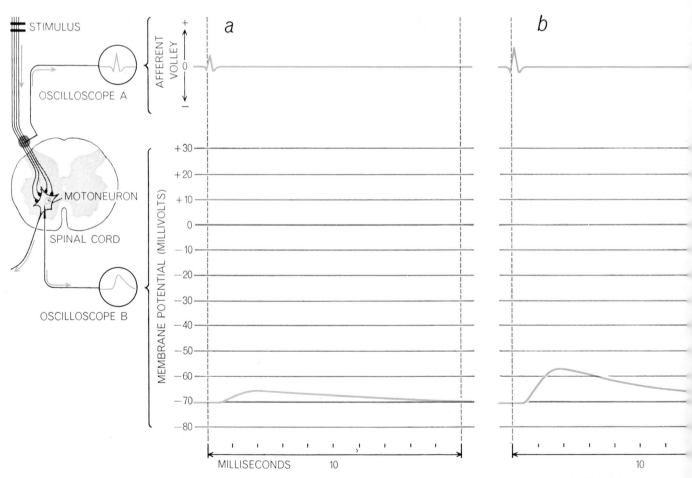

EXCITATION OF A MOTONEURON is studied by stimulating the sensory fibers that send impulses to it. The size of the "afferent volleys" reaching the motoneuron is displayed on oscilloscope *A*. A microelectrode implanted in the motoneuron measures the changes in the cell's internal electric potential. These changes, called excitatory postsynaptic potentials (EPSP's), appear on os-

cilloscope *B*. The size of the afferent volley is proportional to the number of fibers stimulated to fire. It is assumed here that one to four fibers can be activated. When only one fiber is activated (*a*), the potential inside the motoneuron shifts only slightly. When two fibers are activated (*b*), the shift is somewhat greater. When three fibers are activated (*c*), the potential reaches the threshold

is activated by the motoneuron under study. Thus the whole system forms a typical reflex arc, such as the arc responsible for the patellar reflex, or "knee jerk" [*see illustration on page 89*].

To conduct the experiment we anesthetize an animal (most often a cat) and free by dissection a muscle nerve that contains these large nerve fibers. By applying a mild electric shock to the exposed nerve one can produce a single impulse in each of the fibers; since the impulses travel to the spinal cord almost synchronously they are referred to collectively as a volley. The number of impulses contained in the volley can be reduced by reducing the stimulation applied to the nerve. The volley strength is measured at a point just outside the spinal cord and is displayed on an oscilloscope. About half a millisecond after detection of a volley there is a wavelike change in the voltage inside the motoneuron that has received the volley. The change is detected by a microelectrode

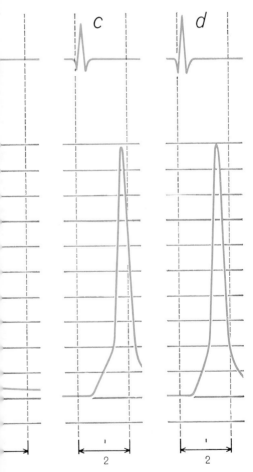

at which depolarization proceeds swiftly and a spike appears on oscilloscope *B*. The spike signifies that the motoneuron has generated a nerve impulse of its own. When four or more fibers are activated (*d*), the motoneuron reaches the threshold more quickly.

inserted in the motoneuron and is displayed on another oscilloscope.

What we find is that the negative voltage inside the cell becomes progressively less negative as more of the fibers impinging on the cell are stimulated to fire. This observed depolarization is in fact a simple summation of the depolarizations produced by each individual synapse. When the depolarization of the interior of the motoneuron reaches a critical point, a "spike" suddenly appears on the second oscilloscope, showing that a nerve impulse has been generated. During the spike the voltage inside the cell changes from about 70 millivolts negative to as much as 30 millivolts positive. The spike regularly appears when the depolarization, or reduction of membrane potential, reaches a critical level, which is usually between 10 and 18 millivolts. The only effect of a further strengthening of the synaptic stimulus is to shorten the time needed for the motoneuron to reach the firing threshold [*see illustration at left*]. The depolarizing potentials produced in the cell membrane by excitatory synapses are called excitatory postsynaptic potentials, or EPSP's.

Through one barrel of a double-barreled microelectrode one can apply a background current to change the resting potential of the interior of the cell membrane, either increasing it or decreasing it. When the potential is made more negative, the EPSP rises more steeply to an earlier peak. When the potential is made less negative, the EPSP rises more slowly to a lower peak. Finally, when the charge inside the cell is reversed so as to be positive with respect to the exterior, the excitatory synapses give rise to an EPSP that is actually the reverse of the normal one [*see illustration at right*].

These observations support the hypothesis that excitatory synapses produce what amounts virtually to a short circuit in the synaptic membrane potential. When this occurs, the membrane no longer acts as a barrier to the passage of ions but lets them flow through in response to the differing electric potential on the two sides of the membrane. In other words, the ions are momentarily allowed to travel freely down their electrochemical gradients, which means that sodium ions flow into the cell and, to a lesser degree, potassium ions flow out. It is this net flow of positive ions that creates the excitatory postsynaptic potential. The flow of negative ions, such as the chloride ion, is apparently not involved. By artificially

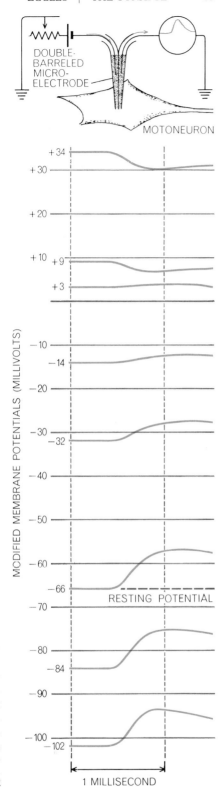

MANIPULATION of the resting potential of a motoneuron clarifies the nature of the EPSP. A steady background current applied through the left barrel of a microelectrode (*top*) shifts the membrane potential away from its normal resting level (minus 66 millivolts in this particular cell). The other barrel records the EPSP. The equilibrium potential, the potential at which the EPSP reverses direction, is about zero millivolts.

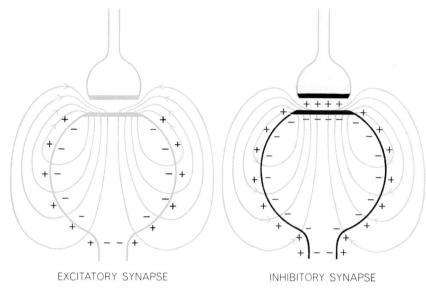

EXCITATORY SYNAPSE   INHIBITORY SYNAPSE

CURRENT FLOWS induced by excitatory and inhibitory synapses are respectively shown at left and right. When the nerve cell is at rest, the interior of the cell membrane is uniformly negative with respect to the exterior. The excitatory synapse releases a chemical substance that depolarizes the cell membrane below the synaptic cleft, thus letting current flow into the cell at that point. At an inhibitory synapse the current flow is reversed.

altering the potential inside the cell one can establish that there is no flow of ions, and therefore no EPSP, when the voltage drop across the membrane is zero.

How is the synaptic membrane converted from a strong ionic barrier into an ion-permeable state? It is currently accepted that the agency of conversion is the chemical transmitter substance contained in the vesicles inside the synaptic knob. When a nerve impulse reaches the synaptic knob, some of the vesicles are caused to eject the transmitter substance into the synaptic cleft [see illustration below]. The molecules of the substance would take only a few microseconds to diffuse across the cleft and become attached to specific receptor sites on the surface membrane of the adjacent nerve cell.

Presumably the receptor sites are as-

sociated with fine channels in the membrane that are opened in some way by the attachment of the transmitter-substance molecules to the receptor sites. With the channels thus opened, sodium and potassium ions flow through the membrane thousands of times more readily than they normally do, thereby producing the intense ionic flux that depolarizes the cell membrane and produces the EPSP. In many synapses the current flows strongly for only about a millisecond before the transmitter substance is eliminated from the synaptic cleft, either by diffusion into the surrounding regions or as a result of being destroyed by enzymes. The latter process is known to occur when the transmitter substance is acetylcholine, which is destroyed by the enzyme acetylcholinesterase.

The substantiation of this general picture of synaptic transmission requires the solution of many fundamental problems. Since we do not know the specific transmitter substance for the vast majority of synapses in the nervous system we do not know if there are many different substances or only a few. The only one identified with reasonable certainty in the mammalian central nervous system is acetylcholine. We know practically nothing about the mechanism by which a presynaptic nerve impulse causes the transmitter substance to be injected into the synaptic cleft. Nor do we know how the synaptic vesicles not immediately adjacent to the synaptic cleft are moved up to the firing line to replace the emptied vesicles. It is conjectured that the vesicles contain the enzyme systems needed to recharge themselves. The entire process must be swift and efficient: the total amount of transmitter substance in synaptic terminals is enough for only a few minutes of synaptic activity at normal operating rates. There are also knotty problems to be solved on the other side of the synaptic cleft. What, for example, is the nature of the receptor sites? How are the ionic channels in the membrane opened up?

The Inhibitory Synapse

Let us turn now to the second type of synapse that has been identified in the nervous system. These are the synapses that can inhibit the firing of a nerve cell even though it may be receiving a volley of excitatory impulses. When inhibitory synapses are examined in the electron microscope, they look very much like excitatory synapses.

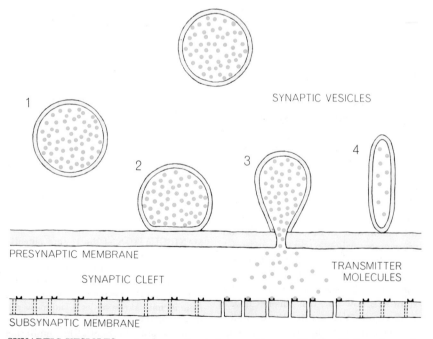

SYNAPTIC VESICLES

1

2

3

4

PRESYNAPTIC MEMBRANE

SYNAPTIC CLEFT

TRANSMITTER MOLECULES

SUBSYNAPTIC MEMBRANE

SYNAPTIC VESICLES containing a chemical transmitter are distributed throughout the synaptic knob. They are arranged here in a probable sequence, showing how they move up to the synaptic cleft, discharge their contents and return to the interior for recharging.

(There are probably some subtle differences, but they need not concern us here.) Microelectrode recordings of the activity of single motoneurons and other nerve cells have now shown that the inhibitory postsynaptic potential (IPSP) is virtually a mirror image of the EPSP [*see top illustration on page 90*]. Moreover, individual inhibitory synapses, like excitatory synapses, have a cumulative effect. The chief difference is simply that the IPSP makes the cell's internal voltage more negative than it is normally, which is in a direction opposite to that needed for generating a spike discharge.

By driving the internal voltage of a nerve cell in the negative direction inhibitory synapses oppose the action of excitatory synapses, which of course drive it in the positive direction. Hence if the potential inside a resting cell is 70 millivolts negative, a strong volley of inhibitory impulses can drive the potential to 75 or 80 millivolts negative. One can easily see that if the potential is made more negative in this way the excitatory synapses find it more difficult to raise the internal voltage to the threshold point for the generation of a spike. Thus the nerve cell responds to the algebraic sum of the internal voltage changes produced by excitatory and inhibitory synapses [*see bottom illustration on page 90*].

If, as in the experiment described earlier, the internal membrane potential is altered by the flow of an electric current through one barrel of a double-barreled microelectrode, one can observe the effect of such changes on the inhibitory postsynaptic potential. When the internal potential is made less negative, the inhibitory postsynaptic potential is deepened. Conversely, when the potential is made more negative, the IPSP diminishes; it finally reverses when the internal potential is driven below minus 80 millivolts.

One can therefore conclude that inhibitory synapses share with excitatory synapses the ability to change the ionic permeability of the synaptic membrane. The difference is that inhibitory synapses enable ions to flow freely down an electrochemical gradient that has an equilibrium point at minus 80 millivolts rather than at zero, as is the case for excitatory synapses. This effect could be achieved by the outward flow of positively charged ions such as potassium or the inward flow of negatively charged ions such as chloride, or by a combination of negative and positive ionic flows such that the interior reaches equilibrium at minus 80 millivolts.

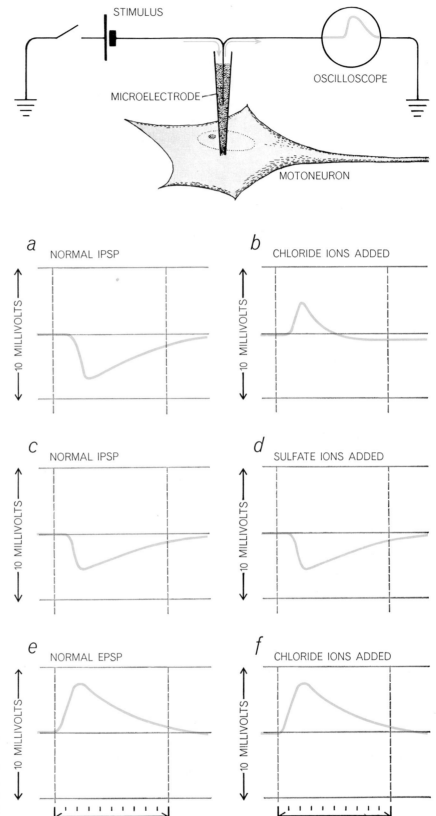

MODIFICATION OF ION CONCENTRATION within the nerve cell gives information about the permeability of the cell membrane. The internal ionic composition is altered by injecting selected ions through a microelectrode a minute or so before applying an afferent volley and recording the EPSP or IPSP. In the first experiment a normal IPSP (*a*) is changed to a pseudo-EPSP (*b*) by an injection of chloride ions. When sulfate ions are similarly injected, the IPSP is practically unchanged (*b, c*). The third experiment shows that an injection of chloride ions has no significant effect on the EPSP (*e, f*).

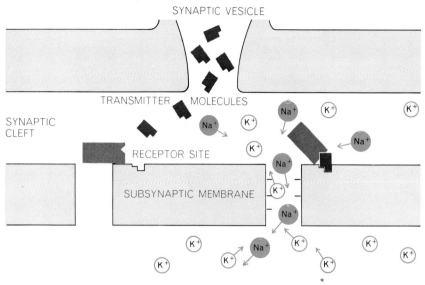

SYNAPTIC VESICLE

TRANSMITTER MOLECULES

SYNAPTIC CLEFT

RECEPTOR SITE

SUBSYNAPTIC MEMBRANE

EXCITATORY SYNAPSE may employ transmitter molecules that open large channels in the nerve-cell membrane. This would permit sodium ions, which are plentiful outside the cell, to pour through the membrane freely. The outward flow of potassium ions, driven by a smaller potential gradient, would be at a much slower rate. Chloride ions (*not shown*) may be prevented from flowing by negative charges on the channel walls.

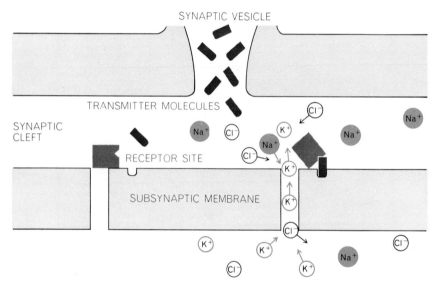

SYNAPTIC VESICLE

TRANSMITTER MOLECULES

SYNAPTIC CLEFT

RECEPTOR SITE

SUBSYNAPTIC MEMBRANE

INHIBITORY SYNAPSE may employ another type of transmitter molecule that opens channels too small to pass sodium ions. The net outflow of potassium ions and inflow of chloride ions would account for the hyperpolarization that is observed as an IPSP.

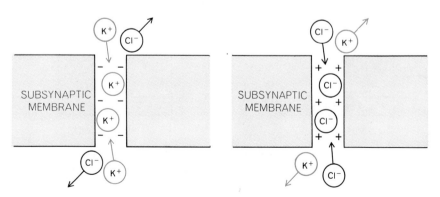

SUBSYNAPTIC MEMBRANE

SUBSYNAPTIC MEMBRANE

MODIFICATIONS OF INHIBITORY SYNAPSE may involve channels that carry either negative or positive charges on their walls. Negative charges (*left*) would permit only potassium ions to pass. Positive charges (*right*) would permit only chloride ions to pass.

In an effort to discover the permeability changes associated with the inhibitory potential my colleagues and I have altered the concentration of ions normally found in motoneurons and have introduced a variety of other ions that are not normally present. This can be done by impaling nerve cells with micropipettes that are filled with a salt solution containing the ion to be injected. The actual injection is achieved by passing a brief current through the micropipette.

If the concentration of chloride ions within the cell is in this way increased as much as three times, the inhibitory postsynaptic potential reverses and acts as a depolarizing current; that is, it resembles an excitatory potential. On the other hand, if the cell is heavily injected with sulfate ions, which are also negatively charged, there is no such reversal [*see illustration on preceding page*]. This simple test shows that under the influence of the inhibitory transmitter substance, which is still unidentified, the subsynaptic membrane becomes permeable momentarily to chloride ions but not to sulfate ions. During the generation of the IPSP the outflow of chloride ions is so rapid that it more than outweighs the flow of other ions that generate the normal inhibitory potential.

My colleagues have now tested the effect of injecting motoneurons with more than 30 kinds of negatively charged ion. With one exception the hydrated ions (ions bound to water) to which the cell membrane is permeable under the influence of the inhibitory transmitter substance are smaller than the hydrated ions to which the membrane is impermeable. The exception is the formate ion (HCO_2^-), which may have an ellipsoidal shape and so be able to pass through membrane pores that block smaller spherical ions.

Apart from the formate ion all the ions to which the membrane is permeable have a diameter not greater than 1.14 times the diameter of the potassium ion; that is, they are less than 2.9 angstrom units in diameter. Comparable investigations in other laboratories have found the same permeability effects, including the exceptional behavior of the formate ion, in fishes, toads and snails. It may well be that the ionic mechanism responsible for synaptic inhibition is the same throughout the animal kingdom.

The significance of these and other studies is that they strongly indicate that the inhibitory transmitter substance opens the membrane to the flow of potassium ions but not to sodium ions. It is known that the sodium ion is somewhat larger than any of the negatively charged ions, including the formate ion, that are able to pass through the membrane during synaptic inhibition. It is not possible, however, to test the effectiveness of potassium ions by injecting excess amounts into the cell because the excess is immediately diluted by an osmotic flow of water into the cell.

As I have indicated, the concentration of potassium ions inside the nerve cell is about 30 times greater than the concentration outside, and to maintain this large difference in concentration without the help of a metabolic pump the inside of the membrane would have to be charged 90 millivolts negative with respect to the exterior. This implies that if the membrane were suddenly made porous to potassium ions, the resulting outflow of ions would make the inside potential of the membrane even more negative than it is in the resting state, and that is just what happens during synaptic inhibition. The membrane must not simultaneously become porous to sodium ions, because they exist in much higher concentration outside the cell than inside and their rapid inflow would more than compensate for the potassium outflow. In fact, the fundamental difference between synaptic excitation and synaptic inhibition is that the membrane freely passes sodium ions in response to the former and largely excludes the passage of sodium ions in response to the latter.

Channels in the Membrane

This fine discrimination between ions that are not very different in size must be explained by any hypothesis of synaptic action. It is most unlikely that the channels through the membrane are created afresh and accurately maintained for a thousandth of a second every time a burst of transmitter substance is released into the synaptic cleft. It is more likely that channels of at least two different sizes are built directly into the membrane structure. In some way the excitatory transmitter substance would selectively unplug the larger channels and permit the free inflow of sodium ions. Potassium ions would simultaneously flow out and thus would tend to counteract the large potential change that would be produced by the massive sodium inflow. The inhibitory transmitter substance would selectively unplug the smaller channels that are large enough to pass potassium and chloride ions but not sodium ions [see upper two illustrations on opposite page].

To explain certain types of inhibition other features must be added to this hypothesis of synaptic transmission. In the simple hypothesis chloride and potassium ions can flow freely through pores of all inhibitory synapses. It has been shown, however, that the inhibition of the contraction of heart muscle by the vagus nerve is due almost exclusively to potassium-ion flow. On the other hand, in the muscles of crustaceans and in nerve cells in the snail's brain synaptic inhibition is due largely to the flow of chloride ions. This selective permeability could be explained if there were fixed charges along the walls of the channels. If such charges were negative, they would repel negatively charged ions and prevent their passage; if they were positive, they would similarly prevent the passage of positively charged ions. One can now suggest that the channels opened by the excitatory transmitter are negatively charged and so do not permit the passage of the negatively charged chloride ion, even though it is small enough to move through the channel freely.

One might wonder if a given nerve cell can have excitatory synaptic action at some of its axon terminals and inhibitory action at others. The answer is no. Two different kinds of nerve cell are needed, one for each type of transmission and synaptic transmitter substance. This can readily be demonstrated by the effect of strychnine and tetanus toxin in the spinal cord; they specifically prevent inhibitory synaptic action and leave excitatory action unaltered. As a result the synaptic excitation of nerve cells is uncontrolled and convulsions result. The special types of cell responsible for inhibitory synaptic action are now being recognized in many parts of the central nervous system.

This account of communication between nerve cells is necessarily oversimplified, yet it shows that some significant advances are being made at the level of individual components of the nervous system. By selecting the most favorable situations we have been able to throw light on some details of nerve-cell behavior. We can be encouraged by these limited successes. But the task of understanding in a comprehensive way how the human brain operates staggers its own imagination.

The Analysis
of Brain Waves

by Mary A. B. Brazier
June 1962

*By rapid averaging and other procedures,
electronic computers are helping investigators
to extract much new information from the complex
recordings of the electrical activity of the brain*

The electrical activity that can be recorded from the surface of the human head is probably the most baffling cryptogram to be found in nature. It is therefore not surprising that electrophysiologists have turned to electronic computers for help. First observed in animals by the English physiologist Richard Caton in 1875, the surface waves reflect the rich and constantly changing electrical activity of the brain. The first recordings from the human brain were made in 1924 by Hans Berger, a German psychiatrist who, because of his oddly secretive nature, withheld publication of his "electroencephalograms" until 1929. The reception was at first skeptical, but the electroencephalogram, or EEG, soon demonstrated its value in the diagnosis of epilepsy and other brain damage. Now, within the past 20 years, physiologists have made a start at decoding the EEG and have begun to show how it is related to the functioning of the nervous system.

For analyzing the electrical activity of the brain the electronic computer has emerged as an instrument of great power and versatility. One of the principal uses of the computer is to extract meaningful signals from the background electrical noise generated by the brain, which normally makes any single recording undecipherable. Although analyses of this sort are usually performed with magnetic-tape records of the brain's activity, the computer becomes even more useful when it is designed to make its analyses in "real" time, while the subject is still connected to the recording apparatus and while the investigator is still able to manipulate the experimental variables. Employed in this way, the computer becomes a subtle new tool for the studies of neurophysiology.

In man the fluctuating potential dif-ference between leads on the unshaved scalp is commonly between 50 and 100 millionths of a volt, or about a tenth the magnitude of electrocardiographic potentials. These waves are most prominent at the back of the head over the visual-association areas of the brain; waves recorded there are called alpha waves. The alpha rhythm, which has a frequency of between eight and 13 per second in adult subjects, is most conspicuous when the eyes are closed. The alpha waves disappear momentarily when the eyes are opened.

Because of the regularity of the alpha rhythm, its frequency characteristics received most of the attention in the early days of electroencephalography. Physi-

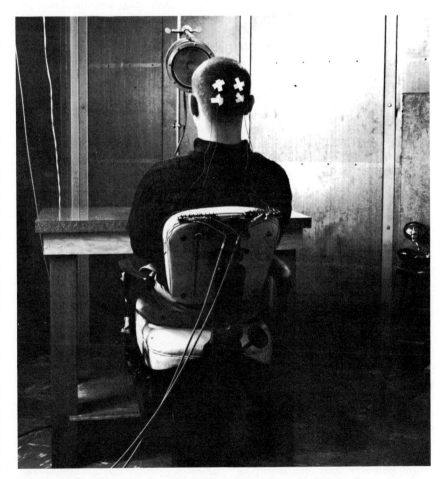

ELECTRODES ON SCALP detect brain waves. This subject, in an isolated room, is viewing brief flashes of light at regular intervals. A special computer simultaneously analyzes the brain waves from the visual region in back of head, producing the record seen in illustration on page 10. The photograph was made at the Massachusetts Institute of Technology.

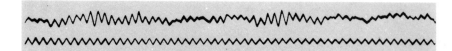

FIRST PUBLISHED ELECTROENCEPHALOGRAM (EEG) of man appeared in 1929. The recording was made by the German psychiatrist Hans Berger from the scalp of his young son. Upper channel is the EEG, lower one an artificial sine wave used as a marker.

ologists reasoned that if these waves were analyzed mathematically, using the technique known as Fourier analysis, components might be uncovered that were hidden to the unaided eye. The principle behind Fourier analysis is that any periodic wave form, however complex, can be resolved into elementary sine-wave components. Unfortunately the brain emits so many irregular and nonperiodic potential changes that the usefulness of this well-known principle is open to challenge.

During World War II W. Grey Walter of the Burden Neurological Institute in England spearheaded the development of the first practical instrument for making an automatic frequency analysis of consecutive short segments—each arbitrarily limited to 10 seconds—of an EEG trace. The Walter analyzer reports the mean relative amplitude at each frequency over the whole period being integrated but cannot indicate the time sequence in which the frequencies occur. A short wave train of high amplitude has the same effect on the integrating device as a long train of low amplitude. Also lost is all information about phase relations between trains of waves.

This type of analysis proved especially valuable when coupled with the finding that the frequency characteristics of the human EEG can often be controlled by having the subject look at a flashing light; the technique, called photic driving, was discovered in the early 1940's. Subsequently it was found that flashes of specific frequency will induce epileptic seizures in some epileptic patients. This is an example of a physiological finding reaching over into medicine to become a clinical diagnostic test. The Walter analyzer, which can be regarded as an early form of computer, still provides the simplest and most practical method for obtaining the average frequency spectrum of an EEG trace.

The rapid development of high-speed general-purpose and special-purpose computers in the past decade has opened up many new ways of analyzing the brain's electrical activity. At the same time techniques have been perfected for recording from electrodes implanted within the unanesthetized brain and left in place for weeks or months. Although used primarily with animals, the technique has been extended to man for diagnostic and therapeutic purposes.

It is therefore now possible to study the relation of the brain's electrical activity to behavioral performance and, in the case of man, to subjective experience. After a long period of concentrating on the rhythm observable when the subject was at rest with the eyes closed, electroencephalographers began to divert their attention from "the engine when idling" to the "engine at work," thereby examining how the brain responds to various stimuli.

Many types of stimulation can be used —sounds, odors, flashes of light, touch and so on—and their effect can be traced in brain recordings made both at the surface and deep within the brain. When such studies were first attempted in unanesthetized animals and man, it was soon discovered that the specific responses were largely masked, in the unanalyzed trace, by the ongoing EEG activity of the normal brain, activity that had been conveniently depressed by the anesthetic agents in the earlier studies. Since the electrodes used must be small enough to discriminate between neuronal structures less than a millimeter apart, appropriate computer techniques are essential for detecting the faint signals that are all but lost in the roar of biological noise that is the normal milieu of the active brain.

The principal means for increasing the signal-to-noise ratio is simply to have the computer add up a large number of responses—anywhere from a few dozen to a few hundred—and calculate an average response. One can then regard this average response, or certain features of it, as the characteristic "signal" elicited by a given stimulus. In applying this technique the neurophysiologist must necessarily make certain assumptions about the character of the biological phenomena he regards as signal and that which he chooses to call noise.

In the usual averaging procedure the brain's potential changes, as picked up by several electrodes, are recorded on multichannel magnetic tape, in which one channel carries a pulse coincident with delivery of the stimulus. Since the stimulus may be presented at irregular intervals, a pulse is needed as a time marker from which the responses are "lined up" for averaging. In the averaging process only those potential changes that occur with a constant time relation to the pulse are preserved and emphasized. Those unrelated in time cancel out in the averaging process, even though in any single record they may be of higher amplitude. In this way responses never before detectable at the surface of the human skull not only can be found but also can be correlated with the subject's report of his sensations.

For example, the lightest of taps on the back of the hand is found to evoke a clear-cut response in one special area on the opposite side of the head [see illustrations on page 107]. Other computer analyses show that a click in the ear gives a decipherable response in another location on the scalp. A flash of light not only evokes an immediate sharp response in the visual area at the back of the head but also gives rise to a long-lasting train of waves, all time-locked to the flash [see illustration on page 109]. It has been shown, moreover, that clinical patients who report a disturbance in their subjective sensation of touch, hearing or sight produce EEG traces that reveal distortions when analyzed by computer.

The long-lasting train of waves evoked by a flash of light raises a number of

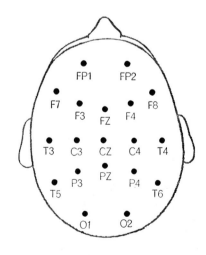

TYPICAL MODERN EEG shows that different regions of cortex give rhythms that differ widely. Berger thought the whole brain

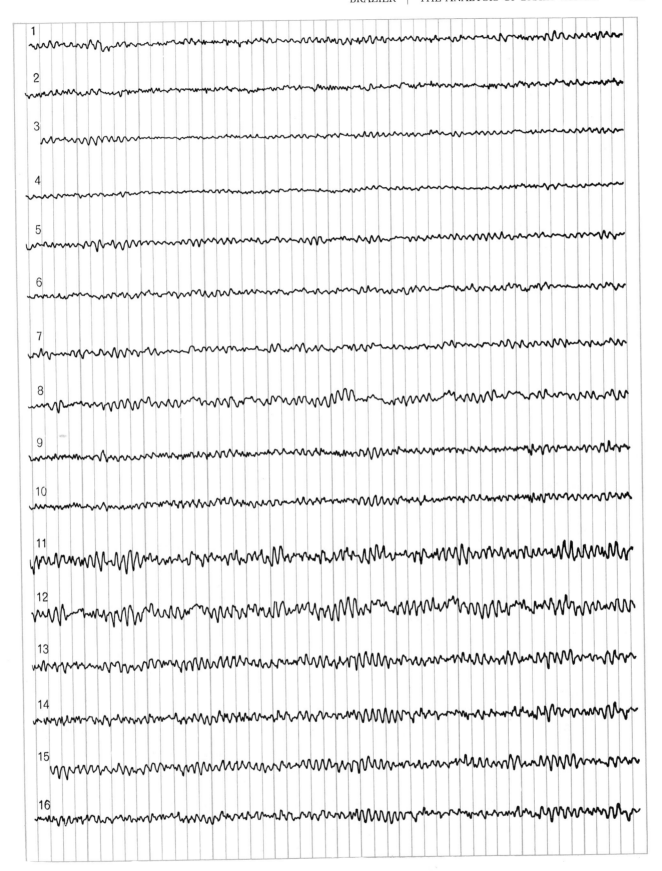

emitted only one rhythm. Today as many as 16, 24 and even 32 channels can be used. The great complexity obviously makes computer analysis desirable. Each EEG trace records changes in electric potential between two electrodes. Thus line 1 came from electrodes FP1 and F7 on head as diagramed at left, while line 10 came from FP2 and C4. This data has not been processed by a computer.

questions. Is this the electrical sign of further processing of the initial message received by the eye? Is it the sign that the experience is being passed into storage, initiating in its passage the cellular changes that underlie memory? There is already evidence that under conditions that retain the initial sharp response but obliterate the subsequent wave train all memory of the experience is expunged. Two such conditions, which support this suggestion in human experiments, are anesthesia and hypnotically induced blindness.

Valuable though computers can be for averaging taped EEG records, they still leave the investigator feeling somewhat frustrated. Hours, and sometimes days, may elapse between the experiment and the completed analysis of the recordings. When he sees the results, the investigator often wishes he could have changed the experimental conditions slightly, perhaps to accentuate a trend of some sort that seemed to be developing, but it is too late. The experimental material of the biologist, and

particularly of the electrophysiologist studying the brain, is living, changing material from which he must seize the opportunity to extract all possible information before the passage of time introduces new variables. The computers familiar to business and industry have not been designed with this problem in mind.

To meet the needs of the neurophysiologist a few computers have now been built that process brain recordings virtually as fast as data is fed in from the electrodes. The investigator can observe the results of his manipulations on the face of a cathode-ray tube or other display device and can modify his experiment at will. One of the first machines built to operate in this way is the Average Response Computer (ARC), designed by W. A. Clark, Jr., of the Lincoln Laboratory of the Massachusetts Institute of Technology [see illustration on this page]. ARC is a simple-to-operate, special-purpose digital computer that requires no programmer as a middleman between the biologist and the machine.

When searching for an evoked response, Clark's computer samples the EEG at a prescribed interval after the stimulus, converts it into a seven-digit binary number proportional to the amplitude and sends the number into one of the many memory registers. This particular register receives and adds all further numbers obtained at the same interval after each stimulus. ARC is equipped to sample the EEG at 254 different time intervals and to store thousands of samples at each interval. Only rarely, however, is the full capacity of the register required. The cumulative sums in each register are displayed on an oscilloscope after each stimulus [see illustration on page 105]. The investigator watches the cumulative display and stops the stimulation when he sees that he has enough signal-to-noise discrimination to satisfy the needs of the experiment. He can then photograph the face of the oscilloscope or have the cumulative wave form printed out graphically by a plotter.

What might one see if one were to watch the build-up of summed re-

AVERAGE RESPONSE COMPUTER (ARC) was designed by W. A. Clark, Jr., of the Lincoln Laboratory of M.I.T. It samples the brain waves for a prescribed interval after each stimulus, adding and averaging the samples. Oscilloscope face on computer (left) displays trace of average as the experiment proceeds. Reels of magnetic tape (center, rear) permanently record all the raw data. In the foreground, beside the laboratory technician, is an "X-Y plotter," which makes pen tracings of the averaged data.

sponses? If the man or animal being studied were anesthetized, the response would be markedly stereotyped; the averaged sum of 100 responses would look very much like the average of 50 responses. This is not so if the subject is unanesthetized. Responses to a series of clicks or flashes of light may show great variation, both in wave shape and in amplitude, and may require many samples before the characteristic signal emerges clearly from the background noise.

Operating in another of its modes, ARC can give an amplitude histogram, or profile, at any chosen interval after the stimulus. Such histograms indicate the degree of fluctuation of the response and its complexity. They supply the investigator with important clues to the behavioral state of the subject, to his level of wakefulness, to the degree of attention he is paying to the stimulus and to the feelings the stimulus arouses.

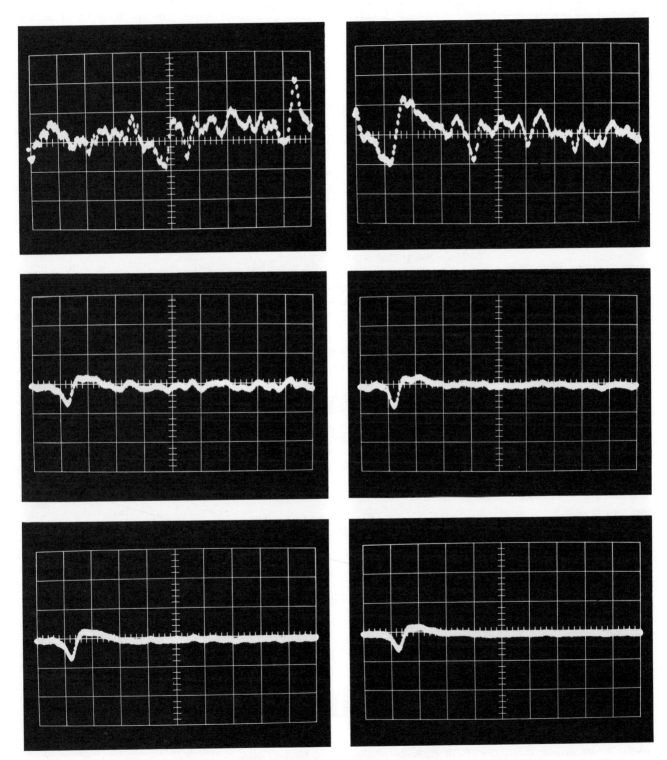

OSCILLOSCOPE TRACES of responses as averaged by computer appear while experiment is in progress, enabling experimenter to observe in "real time." As a result he can change conditions and stop when he has enough data. The traces (*left to right, top to bottom*) are averages of 1, 2, 32, 64, 128 and 512 responses. These traces appeared during an experiment by Nelson Kiang of the Eaton-Peabody Laboratory of the Massachusetts Eye and Ear Infirmary in Boston. The subject was responding to a long series of clicks.

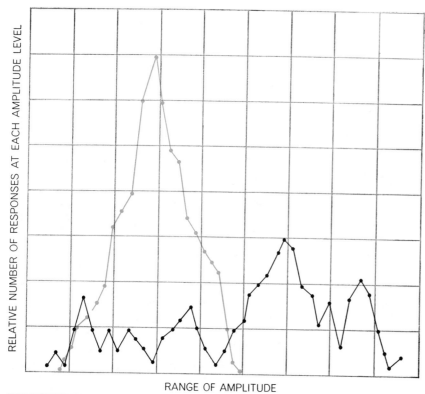

RELATIVE NUMBER OF RESPONSES AT EACH AMPLITUDE LEVEL

RANGE OF AMPLITUDE

STEREOTYPED RESPONSE of brain of anesthetized animal to flash of light (*colored curve*) shows plainly when computer is programed to give information on amplitude variation. Unanesthetized animal gives widely fluctuating response (*black curve*). In each case the computer analyzed point in time at which response reached its maximum amplitude.

When ARC is operated in the histogram mode, the memory registers are set to count the number of times the amplitude, or voltage, of the EEG falls within a certain preset range. Each register is set for a different range and the results are finally written out as a histogram for the chosen interval [*see top illustration on this page*]. By analyzing other intervals similarly one can put together a composite survey.

The study of such records may reveal little dispersion of amplitude at some particular interval after the stimulus and a much greater dispersion at some other interval. This may be a clue that the neuronal message in the first case

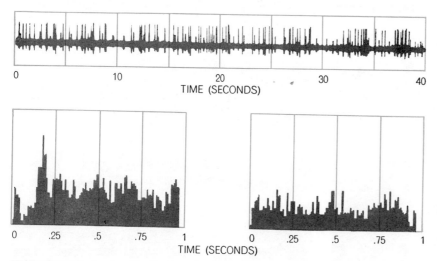

TIME (SECONDS)

TIME (SECONDS)

HISTOGRAMS showing distribution of cell discharges relative to stimulus were made by George L. Gerstein at M.I.T. Upper line shows a short section of raw data consisting of cell discharges in the auditory part of a cat's brain in response to one-per-second clicks. The histogram at left shows number of cell discharges at fractional-second intervals after clicks. The histogram at right shows same analysis of cell discharges when no click occurred.

has traveled over a nerve pathway containing few synapses, or relays, and thus has been subject to little dispersion, whereas in the second case the message has reached the recording site after traveling through multiple paths that finally converge. The complex wave train evoked by a single flash of light is susceptible to this interpretation. The initial deflection is caused by impulses that have traveled through a few synapses only and by means of the large, rapidly conducting fibers of the specific visual system. The subsequent shallower waves—so clearly revealed by the computer—reach the cortex through the more slowly conducting, indirect, nonspecific system with its many relay stations. The histogram of the earlier event, being more stereotyped, shows less dispersion around the median than does the histogram of the later events. Still more elaborate processing of histograms can show whether the amplitudes follow a normal, bell-shaped distribution pattern or are skewed in some manner.

If a physicist were to analyze the results of a series of complex experiments in his field, he would normally expect to find the results to be invariant. The biologist, working with an unanesthetized animal or man, can search in vain for an invariant response. It is precisely this subtlety of variation that electrophysiologists have recently identified as the concomitant of behavioral change. One such change is known as habituation. Early workers in electrophysiology could perceive, in their unanalyzed records, subtle changes in the shape of an EEG trace when the subject had been repeatedly exposed to the same stimulus. Computer analyses have now revealed clearly that under such conditions significant changes take place not only in the EEG as recorded.outside the skull but even more markedly in recordings made deep within the brain.

For example, the Average Response Computer has been used to analyze the electrical activity recorded from a particular relay station in a nucleus located deep in the mid-line region of an animal's brain. The nucleus, in turn, lies within the portion of the brain called the thalamus. Until a dozen years ago little except its anatomy was known about this mid-line region of the thalamus and its inflow from the portion of the brain stem called the reticular formation. The thalamic region and the reticular formation together constitute the nonspecific sensory system mentioned earlier.

In 1949 H. W. Magoun (now at the

University of California in Los Angeles) and G. Moruzzi (now at the University of Pisa) jointly discovered that the reticular system is crucially concerned with the organism's state of alertness and with the behavioral nuances that lie in the continuum between vigilant attention and the oblivion of sleep. Later work has revealed further nuances that can be discerned in the electrical record only with the fine-grained analyses that a computer can provide.

Computer analyses of records from one of the mid-line nuclei of this nonspecific sensory system in an unanesthetized animal have detected many unsuspected details. For example, when a light, flashing at a constant rate, is directed into the animal's eye, the ARC oscilloscope reveals that the averaged response is not at all simple but contains

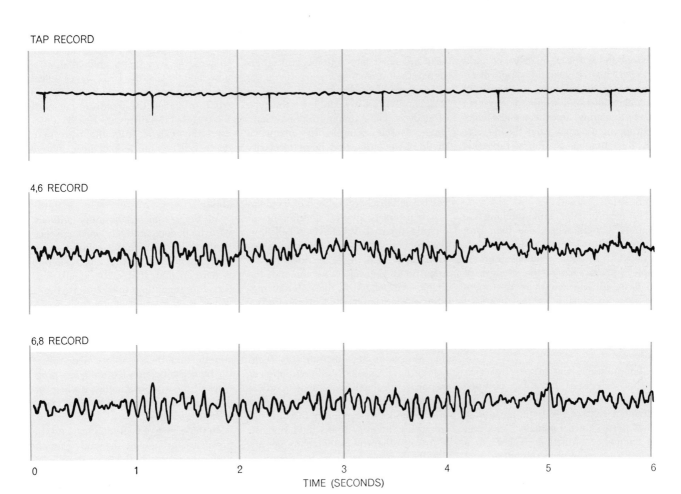

TAP RECORD

4,6 RECORD

6,8 RECORD

0   1   2   3   4   5   6

TIME (SECONDS)

REGULAR TAPS ON LEFT HAND, indicated by top trace, do not show up in standard EEG *(next two traces)*. Ongoing activity of brain drowns signal even though electrode 4 *(see diagram of head on next page)* is over area that receives nerve inflow from hand.

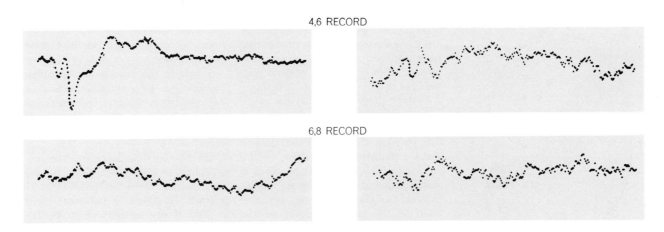

4,6 RECORD

6,8 RECORD

AVERAGED RESPONSE after 90 taps, however, tells a different story. Upper trace at left, from electrodes 4 and 6, shows that the brain definitely reacts to the taps. The computer also detects a faint response when the right hand, which is on the same side of the body as the electrodes, is tapped. (Nerves on the left side of the body are connected with the right side of the brain and vice versa.)

three distinct components and that, as time passes, one of these components gradually fades out. If the computer's mode of operation is then changed so as to produce amplitude histograms, the third component is found to have a greater dispersion than the other two and a skewed distribution.

A hypothesis suggests itself. One of the relatively constant components may pass on to the visual cortex, thereby signifying to the animal that the stimulus is visual and not, say, olfactory or auditory. Perhaps the second component indicates that the stimulus is a recurrent one. The third and waning component may be signaling "unexpectedness" and, by dropping out, may carry the message that the stimulus is simply repeating over and over without change. It may be saying, in effect, that the stimulus is devoid of novelty (or information) and can be safely ignored.

The experimenter, still watching the computer's oscilloscope, can then proceed to test this hypothesis by introducing novelty into the stimulus. For example, he can change the strength of the flash, its wavelength or its repetition rate, and watch for the reappearance of the third component. In this way the three-way interlocution between investigator, subject and machine proceeds.

The questions the investigator asks are not exhausted by those outlined above. He may want to know what the individual cells of the brain are doing. It has been known for many years that the frequency of action "spikes" in a nerve fiber is related to the intensity of the stimulus. As a rule the more intense the stimulus, the higher the firing rate. But how wasteful of "channel capacity"

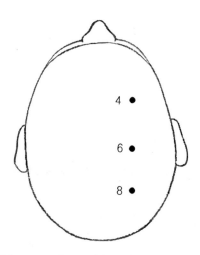

The averaged record from electrodes 6 and 8, which are not over the "hand area" of the brain, shows no response to the taps.

(to use the language of information theory) it would be if the only information conveyed by the action spikes were limited to stimulus intensity.

This has led investigators to consider the fluctuations in the groupings of these unit discharges. The unanalyzed record is bewildering, because different kinds of cell give different patterns of response to a given stimulus. Some that were busily active stop firing when the stimulus is given; others wake from idleness and burst into activity; still others signal their response by a change in the pattern of discharge.

Computers are invaluable for this type of analysis. The Average Response Computer, as one example, has a special mode of operation that helps to clarify this patterning of activity in individual brain cells. It does this by giving a histogram of the time intervals between successive cell discharges. Each of its memory registers is allotted a different interspike interval. Whenever a cell fires, the interval since the last firing is established and a digit is added to the appropriate register. On command, the digits accumulated in the different registers are written out as a histogram [see *bottom illustration on page 106*]. Analyses of this kind, pioneered by George L. Gerstein with the TX-O computer at the Massachusetts Institute of Technology, have revealed a differentiation of response mechanisms among cortical cells that indicates a far greater degree of discriminatory capability than the old frequency-intensity rule would suggest.

Among other computer techniques under development are those for identification of temporal patterns in the EEG. These techniques should relieve the electroencephalographer of the tedium of searching many yards of records for meaningful changes. For example, Belmont Farley of the Lincoln Laboratory of M.I.T. has worked out programs for analyzing the trains of alpha rhythm that come and go in the EEG of man and provide clues to his level of consciousness and to the normality of his brain.

Farley's program specifies the range of amplitude, frequency and duration of the pattern known as an alpha burst. The program allows the investigator to make a statistical examination of the EEG of the same individual, as recorded under different experimental circumstances. The investigator may be interested in the effect of drugs or the changes brought about by conditioning of behavior. The degree of variation in the EEG can be accurately and objectively assessed, removing the hazards of subjective judgment. It is obvious that

such objective methods of appraisal can be of great value in the clinical use of the EEG.

The rhythmicity of the EEG, as exemplified in the alpha rhythm, continues to be a mystery. It was first thought that brain waves were merely the envelopes of the spike discharges of the underlying neurons. But this view had to be abandoned when microelectrodes, reporting from inside the brain, showed the hypothesis untenable. It is now thought that the EEG waves reflect the waxing and waning of excitability in what are called the dendritic layers of the cortex. (Dendrites are hairlike processes that extend from the body of a nerve cell.) Quite unlike the explosive discharge of the nerve cell itself, the finely graded changes in dendritic activity seem to modulate cortical excitability.

In the common laboratory animals, with their comparatively small association cortexes, the simple, almost sinusoidal oscillation of the alpha rhythm is hard to find, if it exists at all. It is therefore tempting to relate rhythmic waves to the large volume of association cortex possessed by man. These rhythmic waves usually signify that the brain is not under bombardment by stimuli, and their stability may reflect the homeostatic, or self-stabilizing, processes of the association cortex when undisturbed by the processing of transmitted messages.

In the course of evolution homeostatic processes throughout the body, largely under the control of the brain stem, have provided the higher animals with a remarkably constant internal environment. The constancy of this *milieu intérieur*, as the French physiologist Claude Bernard pointed out, is "la condition de la vie libre." Conceivably it is the stabilizing effect of the brain stem that frees the cortex of man for its highest achievements.

Whatever the case, it has been discovered by the statistical method of autocorrelation analysis that EEG recordings from man often show a long-persisting phase constancy that has not been found in lower animals. There are also individual differences. In some people phase-locking of oscillations is, for long periods, nearly as predictable as a clock. In others (a minority) there is little, if any, stability of phase. Are the people who lack a stable phase-locked oscillation unable to clear their association cortex of interfering activity? Have they not yet attained the "free life" of Claude Bernard?

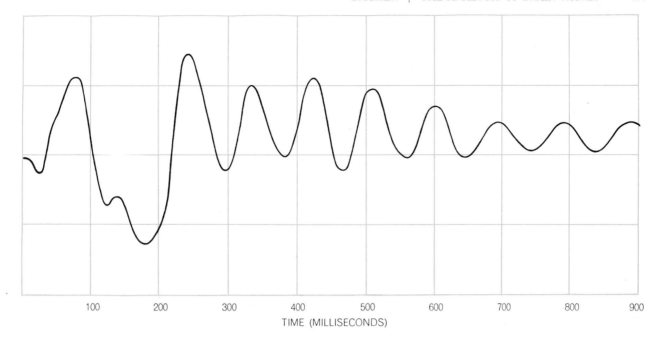

TIME (MILLISECONDS)

LONG-LASTING TRAIN OF WAVES can be recorded from scalp following flash of light. This, of course, is an averaged record of many responses to many flashes. It emphasizes only the changes in electric potential time-locked to the flash and washes out the "noisy" background activity, which is actually of much higher amplitude. The flashes were all synchronized with beginning of trace.

One of the earliest workers to encourage electroencephalographers to explore this approach was the M.I.T. mathematician Norbert Wiener. His strong influence lies behind much of the computer work in this area, and especially that which has come from the laboratory of Walter A. Rosenblith of M.I.T.'s Research Laboratory for Electronics.

No account of the electroencephalographer's use of computers should omit their recent use in seeking information about the correlations between deep and superficial activity in various parts of the brain. What is the correlation between the waves recorded from the outside of man's skull and activity in the depths? With what confidence can one say that an EEG is "normal" when only scalp recordings can be made?

The first answers to these and many other questions are just emerging as computer analyses of electrical potentials from inside man's head are being correlated with those simultaneously recorded from his scalp. As more and more clinical investigators adopt computer techniques it should be possible to build up for the electroencephalographer, who can record only from the surface of the unopened scalp, a reference library of correlations to use in assessing the probability of events in the hidden depths of the brain.

Nearly all the applications of the computer described here have involved averaging. This is not only because the average is an empirically useful statistic but also because many brain investigators suspect that the brain may work on a probabilistic basis rather than a deterministic one. To analyze the myriad complexities of the brain's function by nonstatistical description is too gigantic a task to be conceived, but exploration in terms of probability theory is both practical and rational. In characterizing nervous activity one would not therefore attempt the precise definition that arithmetic demands but would seek the statistical characteristics of the phenomena that appear to be relevant.

The margin of safety that the brain has for acting appropriately on a probabilistic basis would be much greater than that which would be imposed by a deterministic, arithmetically precise operation. Chaos would result from the least slip-up of the latter, whereas only a major divergence from the mean would disturb a system working on a probability basis. The rigidity of arithmetic is not for the brain, and a search for a deterministic code based on arithmetical precision is surely doomed to disappointment.

One can speculate how a brain might work on statistical principles. Incoming sensory messages would be compared with the statistical distribution of nerve cell characteristics that have developed as functions of the past activities of these cells. Significance of the message would then be evaluated and, according to the odds, its message could be appropriately acted on or ignored. The brain, with its wealth of interconnections, has an enormous capacity for storage, and one can observe the development of appropriate responses by watching the limited capacity of the child grow to the superior capacity of the man.

One might ask why it is the brain investigator, among biological scientists, who has reached out most eagerly to the computer for help. A likely answer is that within man's skull—a not very large, rigidly limited space—a greater number of transactions are taking place simultaneously than in any other known system of its size. The multiplicity of signals that these transactions emit and the truly formidable complexity of codes that they may use have proved beyond the capabilities of analysis by the methods of an earlier age.

The neurophysiologist cannot hope to study a single variable in isolation. The living brain will not still its busy activity so that the investigator can control whatever he wishes; neither will it forget its past. Every stimulus, however "constant" the experimenter may succeed in making it, enters a nervous system that is in an ever changing state. The "stimulus-response" experiment of an earlier day is no longer adequate. Experiment has to enter a phase of greater sophistication that may well prove out of reach without the help of the computer.

11   The States of Sleep

by Michel Jouvet
February 1967

*Light and deep sleep differ physiologically,
deep sleep having much in common with being awake.
Studies with cats now suggest that the two states
of sleep are induced by different biochemical secretions*

Early philosophers recognized that there are two distinctly different levels of sleep. An ancient Hindu tale described three states of mind in man: (1) wakefulness (*vaiswanara*), in which a person "is conscious only of external objects [and] is the enjoyer of the pleasures of sense"; (2) dreaming sleep (*taijasa*), in which one "is conscious only of his dreams [and] is the enjoyer of the subtle impressions in the mind of the deeds he has done in the past," and (3) dreamless sleep (*prajna*), a "blissful" state in which "the veil of unconsciousness envelops his thought and knowledge, and the subtle impressions of his mind apparently vanish."

States 2 and 3 obviously are rather difficult to investigate objectively, and until very recently the phases of sleep remained a subject of vague speculation. Within the past few years, however,

studies with the aid of the electroencephalograph have begun to lift the veil. By recording brain waves, eye movements and other activities of the nervous system during the different sleep states neurophysiologists are beginning to identify the specific nervous-system structures involved, and we are now in a position to analyze some of the mechanisms responsible.

Brain Activities in Sleep

Lucretius, that remarkably inquisitive and shrewd observer of nature, surmised that the fidgetings of animals during sleep were linked to dreaming. Some 30 years ago a German investigator, R. Klaue, made a significant discovery with the electroencephalograph. He found that sleep progressed in a characteristic sequence: a period of light sleep, during

which the brain cortex produced slow brain waves, followed by a period of deep sleep, in which the cortical activity speeded up. Klaue's report was completely overlooked at the time. In the 1950's, however, Nathaniel Kleitman and his students at the University of Chicago took up this line of investigation. Kleitman and Eugene Aserinsky found (in studies of infants) that periods of "active" sleep, alternating with quiescent periods, were marked by rapid eye movements under the closed lids. Later Kleitman and William C. Dement, in studies of adults, correlated the eye movements with certain brain-wave patterns and definitely linked these activities and patterns to periods of dreaming [see the article "Patterns of Dreaming," by Nathaniel Kleitman; SCIENTIFIC AMERICAN Offprint 460]. In 1958 Dement showed that cats may have periods of sleep similarly marked by rapid eye movement and fast cortical activity. He called such periods "activated sleep."

Meanwhile at the University of Lyons, François Michel and I had been conducting a series of experiments with cats. In the cat, which spends about two-thirds of its time sleeping, the process of falling asleep follows a characteristic course, signaled by easily observable external signs. Typically the animal curls up in a ball with its neck bent. The flexing of the nape of its neck is a clear sign that the muscles there retain some tonus, that is, they are not completely relaxed. In this position the cat lapses into a light sleep from which it is easily awakened.

After about 10 to 20 minutes there comes a constellation of changes that mark passage over the brink into deep sleep. The cat's neck and back relax their curvature, showing that the muscles have completely lost tonus: they are now altogether slack. At the same time there

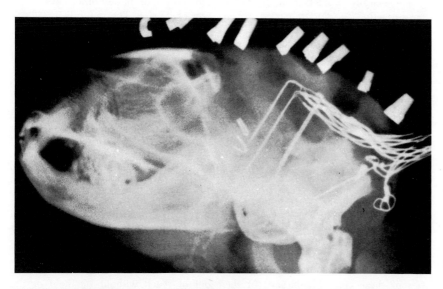

X RAY OF CAT'S HEAD shows a cluster of electrodes with which the author obtained a record of the electrical signals from various parts of the cat's brain. The cat's mouth is at the left; one electrode at far right measures the changes in the animal's neck-muscle tension.

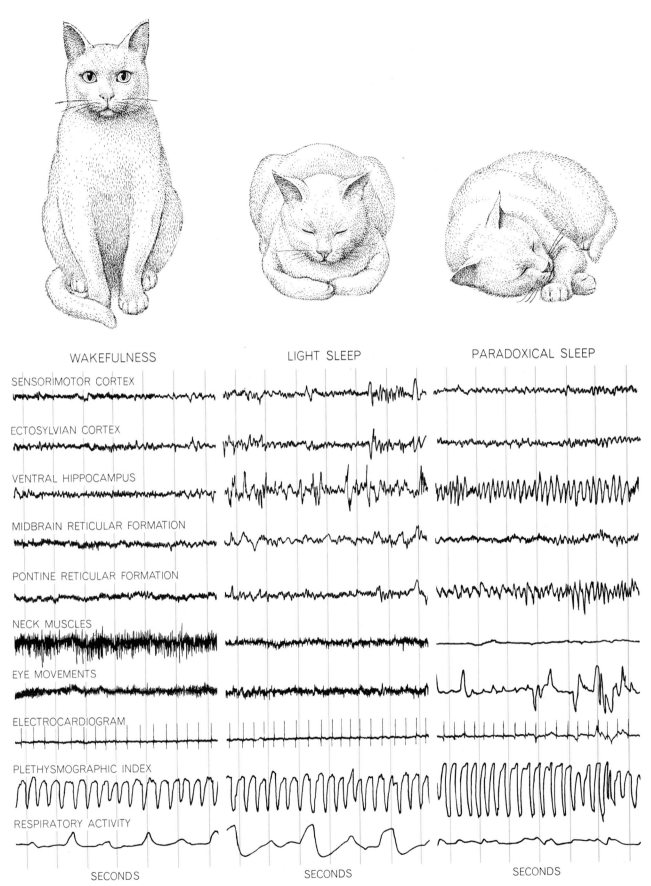

WAKEFULNESS   LIGHT SLEEP   PARADOXICAL SLEEP

SENSORIMOTOR CORTEX

ECTOSYLVIAN CORTEX

VENTRAL HIPPOCAMPUS

MIDBRAIN RETICULAR FORMATION

PONTINE RETICULAR FORMATION

NECK MUSCLES

EYE MOVEMENTS

ELECTROCARDIOGRAM

PLETHYSMOGRAPHIC INDEX

RESPIRATORY ACTIVITY

SECONDS   SECONDS   SECONDS

CHARACTERISTIC RHYTHMS associated with deep sleep in a cat (*group of traces at right*) are so much like those of wakefulness (*left group*) and so different from those of light sleep (*middle group*) that the author has applied the term "paradoxical" to deep sleep. Normal cats spend about two-thirds of the time sleeping. They usually begin each sleep period with 25 minutes of light sleep, followed by six or seven minutes of paradoxical sleep. In the latter state they are hard to wake and their muscles are relaxed.

CAT'S BRAIN, seen in front-to-back section, has a number of segments. Some of the principal ones are identified in the illustration at the top of the opposite page. Many segments of the cat's brain, such as the cerebellum (*top right*), have no role to play in sleep.

are bursts of rapid eye movements (eight to 30 movements in each burst) in either the side-to-side or the up-and-down direction, like the movements in visual use of the eyes. Occasionally these eyeball movements behind the closed eyelids are accompanied by a sudden dilation of the pupils, which in the main are tightly constricted during sleep. Along with the eye movements go events involving many other parts of the body: small tremors of muscles at the ends of the extremities, causing rapid flexing of the digits and now and then small scratching motions; very rapid movements of the ears, the whiskers, the tail and the tongue, and an episode of fast and irregular breathing.

It is somewhat startling to realize that all this activity goes on during a period in which the animal's muscular system is totally atonic (lacking in tension). The activities are also the accompaniment of deep sleep, as is indicated by the fact that it takes an unusually high level of sound or electrical stimulation to arouse the cat during this phase. The state of deep sleep lasts about six or seven minutes and alternates with periods of lighter sleep that last for an average of about 25 minutes.

To obtain more objective and specific information about events in the brain during sleep we implanted electrodes in the muscles of the neck and in the midbrain of cats. We used animals that were deprived of the brain cortex, since we wished to study the subcortical activities. In the course of extended recordings of the electrical events we were surprised to find that the electrical activity of the neck muscles disappeared completely for regular periods (six minutes long), and the condition persisted when sharp spikes of high voltage showed up now and then in the pontine reticular formation, situated just behind the "arousal center" of the midbrain. These electrical signs were correlated with eye movements of the sleeping animal. Further, we noted that in cats with intact brains both the abolition of muscle tonus and the sharp high-voltage spikes were strikingly correlated with the rapid eye

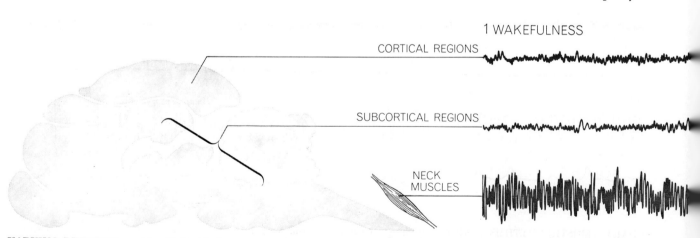

VARYING RHYTHMS are identified with the various states of sleep. From left to right, a wakeful cat (1) shows high-speed alternations in electric potential in both cortical and subcortical regions of the brain, as well as neck-muscle tension. In light sleep (2) the cat shows a slower rhythm in the traces from the cortical and subcortical regions, but neck-muscle tension continues. The phasic, or

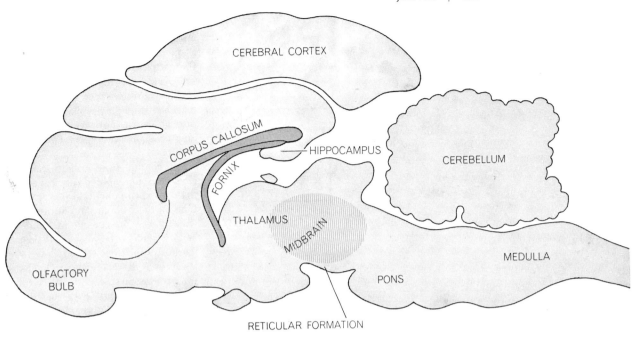

BRAIN SEGMENTS associated with sleep include the reticular formation, which controls wakefulness. This region is under the control of an area in the lower brain. When the control is blocked by making a cut through the pons, a normal cat becomes insomniac.

movement and fast cortical activity Dement had described. These findings presented a paradox. It was surely strange to find fast cortical activity (generally a sign of wakefulness) coupled with complete muscular atony (invariably a sign of deep sleep)!

The Two Sleep States

We named this strange state "paradoxical sleep." It is also called deep sleep, fast-wave sleep, rapid-eye-movement (REM) sleep and dreaming sleep, whereas the lighter sleep that precedes it is often called slow-wave sleep. We consider paradoxical sleep a qualitatively distinct state, not simply a deepened version of the first stage of sleep. Very schematically (for the cat) we can describe the three states—wakefulness, light sleep and paradoxical sleep—in the following physiological terms. Wakefulness is accompanied by fast, low-voltage electrical activity in the cortex and the subcortical structures of the brain and by a significant amount of tonus in the muscular system. The first stage of sleep, or light sleep, is characterized by a slackening of electrical activity in the cortex and subcortical structures, by the occurrence of "spindles," or groups of sharp jumps, in the brain waves and by retention of the muscular tension. Paradoxical sleep presents a more complex picture that we must consider in some detail.

We can classify the phenomena in paradoxical sleep under two heads: tonic (those having to do with continuous phenomena) and phasic (those of a periodic character). The principal tonic phenomena observed in the cat are fast electrical waves (almost like those of wakefulness) in the cortex and subcortical structures, very regular "theta" waves at the level of the hippocampus (a structure running from the front to the rear of the brain) and total disappearance of electrical activity in the muscles of the neck. The principal phasic phenomena are high-voltage spikes, isolated or grouped in volleys, that appear at the level of the pons and the rear part of the cortex (which is associated with the visual sys-

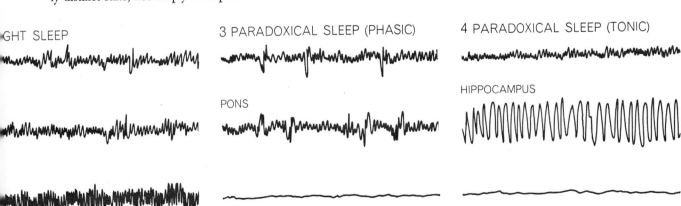

GHT SLEEP

3 PARADOXICAL SLEEP (PHASIC)

PONS

4 PARADOXICAL SLEEP (TONIC)

HIPPOCAMPUS

periodic, aspects of paradoxical sleep (3) are marked by isolated spike discharges from the rear of the cortex and the pons, as well as by rapid eye movement and limb movements. Loss of neck-muscle tension is a tonic (4) rather than a phasic phenomenon. Other tonic, or continuous, aspects of paradoxical sleep are high-speed cortical rhythms and regular "theta" waves from hippocampus.

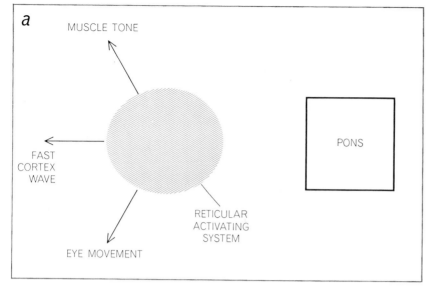

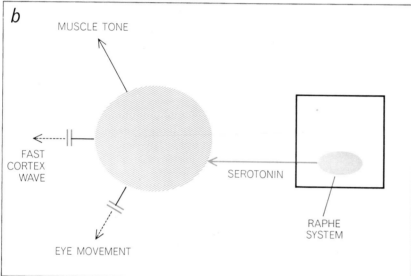

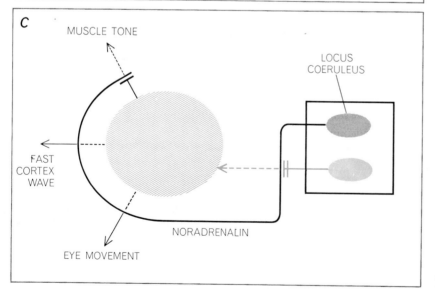

WORKING HYPOTHESIS, proposed by the author to provide a bridge between the neuro-physiology and the biochemistry of sleep, suggests that the normal state of wakefulness (*a*) is transformed into light sleep (*b*) when a secretion produced by the nuclei of raphe modifies many effects of the reticular activating system. Paradoxical sleep follows (*c*) when a second secretion, produced by the locus coeruleus, supplants the raphe secretion and produces effects that resemble normal wakefulness except for the loss of muscle tension.

tem). These spikes make their appearance about a minute before the tonic phenomena. Just as the latter show up, the peripheral phasic phenomena come into evidence: rapid eye movements, clawing movements of the paws and so on. The high-voltage spikes during paradoxical sleep in the cat come at a remarkably constant rate: about 60 to 70 per minute.

Our continuous recordings around the clock in a soundproofed cage have shown that cats spend about 35 percent of the time (in the 24-hour day) in the state of wakefulness, 50 percent in light sleep and 15 percent in paradoxical sleep. In most cases the three states follow a regular cycle from wakefulness to light sleep to paradoxical sleep to wakefulness again. An adult cat never goes directly from wakefulness into paradoxical sleep.

Thus we find that the two states of sleep have well-defined and clearly distinct electrical signatures. Equipped with this information, we are better prepared to search for the nervous structures and mechanisms that are responsible for sleep and dreaming.

The Suppression of Wakefulness

The first and most important question we must answer is this: Does the nervous system possess a specific sleep-producing mechanism? In other words, should we not rather confine our research to the operations of the mechanism that keeps us awake? Kleitman has put the issue very clearly; he observes that to say one falls asleep or is put to sleep is not the same as saying one ceases to stay awake. The first statement implies that an active mechanism suppresses the state of wakefulness—a mechanism analogous to applying the brakes in an automobile. The second statement implies that the wakefulness-producing mechanism simply stops operating—a situation analogous to removing the foot from the accelerator. Thus the mechanism responsible for sleep would be negative or passive, not active.

Now, it has been known for nearly two decades that the brain contains a center specifically responsible for maintaining wakefulness. This was discovered by H. W. Magoun of the U.S. and Giuseppe Moruzzi of Italy, working together at Northwestern University [see "The Reticular Formation," by J. D. French; SCIENTIFIC AMERICAN Offprint 66]. They named this center, located in the midbrain, the reticular activating system (RAS). Stimulation of the RAS center in a slumbering animal arouses the animal; conversely, destruction of the center causes the animal to go into a permanent coma. To explain normal sleep, then, we must find out what process or mechanism brings about a deactivation of the RAS for the period of sleep.

On the basis of the known facts about the RAS there seemed at first no need to invoke the idea of a braking mechanism to account for deactivation of the system. The Belgian neurophysiologist Frédéric Bremer suggested that the RAS could simply lapse into quiescence as a result of a decline of stimuli (such as disturbing noise) from the surroundings [see "Sleep," by Nathaniel Kleitman; SCIENTIFIC AMERICAN Offprint 431].

Several years ago, however, explorations of the brain by the Swiss neurophysiologist W. R. Hess and others began to produce indications that the brain might contain centers that could suppress the activity of the RAS. In these experiments, conducted with cats, the cats fell asleep after electrical stimulation of various regions in the thalamus and elsewhere or after the injection of chemicals into the cerebrum. Interesting as these findings were, they were not very convincing on the question at issue. After all, since a cat normally sleeps about two-thirds of the time anyway, how could one be sure that the applied treatments acted through specific sleep-inducing centers? Moreover, the experiments seemed to implicate nearly all the nerve structures surrounding the RAS, from the cerebral cortex all the way down to the spinal cord, as being capable of inducing sleep. It was implausible that a sleep-inducing system could be so diffuse. Nevertheless, in spite of all these doubts, the experiments at least pointed to the possibility that the RAS might be influenced by other brain centers.

Moruzzi and his group in Italy proceeded to more definitive experiments. Seeking to pin down the location of a center capable of opposing the action of the RAS, they focused their search on the lower part of the brainstem. They chose a site at the middle of the pons in front of the trigeminal nerve, and with cats as subjects they cut completely through the brainstem at that point. The outcome of this operation was that the cats became insomniac: they slept only 20 percent of the time instead of 65 percent! The brain cortex showed the characteristic electrical activity of wakefulness (fast, low-voltage activity), and the eye movements also were those of a wakeful animal pursuing moving objects. The experiments left no doubt that the cut had disconnected the RAS from some structure in the lower part of the brainstem that normally exercised con-

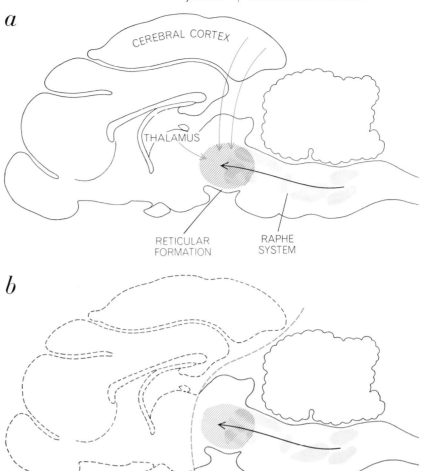

BRAIN STRUCTURES involved in light sleep include the raphe system, which, by producing the monoamine serotonin, serves to counteract the alerting effects of the brain's reticular formation ("*a*," *color at left*). The author suggests that raphe system structures act to modulate the fast wave pattern of the alert cortex into the slower pattern typical of light sleep. Such slow activity, however, depends on higher as well as lower brain structures (*b*); when a cat is deprived of its cerebral cortex and thalamus, the brain stem wave pattern characteristic of light sleep disappears. The reason for this is not yet understood.

trol over the waking center. It was as if a brake had been removed, so that the RAS was essentially unrestricted and kept the animal awake most of the time.

The new evidence leads, therefore, to the conclusion that sleeping is subject to both active and passive controls. The active type of control consists in the application of a brake on the RAS by some other brain structure or structures; the passive type corresponds to a letup on the accelerator in the RAS itself.

Sleep Centers

What, and where, are the sleep-inducing centers that act on the RAS? Our suspicions are now focused on a collection of nerve cells at the midline of the brainstem that are known as the "nuclei of raphe" (from a Greek word meaning "seam" and signifying the juncture of the two halves of the brain). In Sweden, Annica Dahlström and Kzell Fuxe have

shown that under ultraviolet light these cells emit a yellow fluorescence that shows they are rich in the hormone-like substance serotonin, which is known to have a wide spectrum of powerful effects on the brain and other organs of the body [see "Serotonin," by Irvine H. Page; SCIENTIFIC AMERICAN, December, 1957]. Suspecting from various preliminary pharmacological experiments that serotonin might play a role in sleep, we decided to test the effects of destroying the raphe cells, which are the principal source of the serotonin supply in the brain. We found that when we destroyed 80 percent of these cells at the level of the medulla in cats (the animals could not have survived destruction of a larger percentage), the cats became even more sleepless than those on which Moruzzi had performed his operation. In more than 100 hours of continuous observation with electrical recording instruments, our animals slept less than 10 percent of the time. Our results were closely related to those of Moruzzi's. His operation dividing the brainstem cut through the raphe system. We found that when we destroyed only the raphe cells on one side or the other of the site of his cut, our animals were reduced to the same amount of sleep (20 percent) as those on which he had performed his experiment. This gives us further reason to believe the raphe system may indeed be the main center responsible for bringing on sleep in cats.

These new developments bring serotonin into a prominent place in the research picture and offer an avenue for biochemical attack on the mysteries of sleep. The fact that the raphe cells are chiefly notable for their production of serotonin seems to nominate this substance for an important role in producing the onset of sleep. We have recently been able to demonstrate a significant correlation between the extent of the lesion of the raphe system, the decrease

in sleep and the decrease in the amount of serotonin in the brain as measured by means of spectrofluorescent techniques.

In physiological terms we can begin to see the outlines of the system of brain structures involved in initiating the onset of sleep and maintaining the first stage of light slumber. At the level of the brainstem, probably within the raphe system, there are structures that apparently counteract the RAS and by their braking action cause the animal to fall asleep. Associated with these structures there presumably are nearby structures that account for the modulations of electrical activity (notably the slow brain waves) that have been observed to accompany light sleep. This slow activity seems to depend primarily, however, on the higher brain structures, particularly the cortex and the thalamus; in a decorticated animal the pattern characteristic of light sleep does not make its appearance. We must therefore conclude that the set of mechanisms brought into

play during the process of falling asleep is a complicated one and that a number of steps in the process still remain to be discovered.

Paradoxical Sleep

In searching for the structures involved in paradoxical, or deep, sleep we are in a somewhat better position. When an animal is in that state, we have as clues to guide us not only the electrical activities in the brain but also conclusive and readily observable signs such as the disappearance of tonus in the muscles of the neck. This is the single most reliable mark of paradoxical sleep. Furthermore, it enables us to study animals that have been subjected to drastic operations we cannot use in the study of light sleep because they obliterate the electrical activities that identify the falling-asleep stage.

A cat whose brainstem has been cut through at the level of the pons, so that essentially all the upper part of the brain has been removed, still exhibits the cycle of waking and deep sleep. Such an animal can be kept alive for several months, and with the regularity of a biological clock it oscillates between wakefulness and the state of paradoxical sleep, in which it spends only about 10 percent of the time. This state is signaled, as in normal animals, by the typical slackness of the neck muscles, by the electroencephalographic spikes denoting electrical activity in the pons structures and by lateral movements of the eyeballs.

When, however, we sever the brainstem at a lower level, in the lower part of the pons just ahead of the medulla, the animal no longer falls into paradoxical sleep. The sign that marks this cyclical state—periodic loss of muscle tonus—disappears. It seems, therefore, that the onset of paradoxical sleep must be triggered by the action of structures somewhere in the middle portion of the pons. Further experiments have made it possible for us to locate these structures rather precisely. We have found that paradoxical sleep can be abolished by destroying certain nerve cells in a dorsal area of the pons known as the locus coeruleus. Dahlström and Fuxe have shown that these cells have a green fluorescence under ultraviolet light and that they contain noradrenalin. Hence it seems that noradrenalin may play a role in producing paradoxical sleep similar to the one serotonin apparently plays in bringing about light sleep.

What mechanism is responsible for the elimination of muscular tonus that accompanies paradoxical sleep? It seems

a

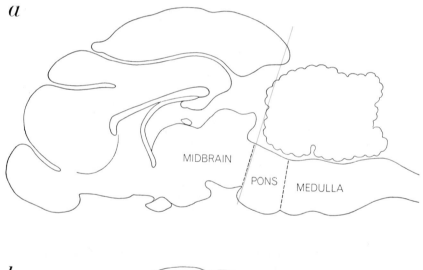

b

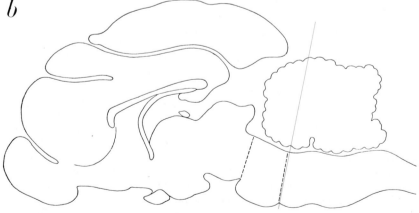

MIDBRAIN

PONS MEDULLA

PARADOXICAL-SLEEP STRUCTURES evidently lie far back along the brainstem. A cat deprived of all its higher brain function by means of a cut through the pons (*a*) will live for months, alternately awake and in paradoxical sleep. If a cut is made lower (*b*) along the brainstem, however, the cat will no longer fall into paradoxical sleep, because the cut destroys some brain cells in that region, which produce another monoamine, noradrenalin.

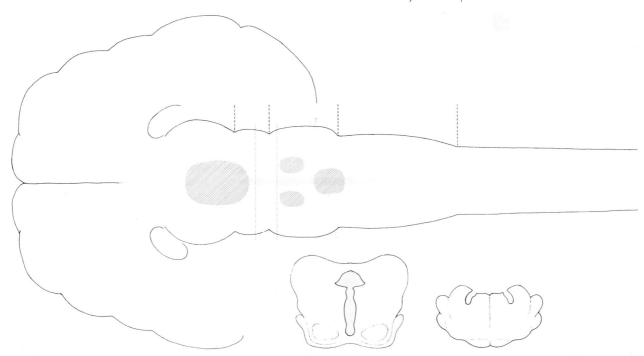

CAT'S BRAINSTEM is the site of the two groups of cells that produce the substances affecting light and paradoxical sleep. The nuclei of raphe (*color*) secrete serotonin; another cell group in the pons, known as the locus coeruleus (*gray*), secretes noradrenalin.

most likely that the source of this inhibition lies in the spinal cord, and Moruzzi and his colleague Ottavio Pompeiano are making a detailed investigation of this hypothesis.

The objective information about paradoxical sleep developed so far gives us some suggestions about the mechanisms involved in dreaming. The controlling structures apparently are located in the dorsal part of the pons. They give rise to spontaneous excitations that travel mainly to the brain's visual tracts, and it seems possible that this excitation is related to the formation of the images that one "sees" in dreams. Regardless of how strongly the brain is stimulated by these spontaneous impulses (as Edward V. Evarts of the National Institute of Mental Health and others have shown by means of microelectrode recordings of the visual system), during sleep the body's motor system remains inactive because a potent braking mechanism blocks electrical excitation of the motor nerves. This inhibitory mechanism seems to be controlled by the hormone-secreting nerves of the locus coeruleus structure. If this structure is destroyed, the animal may periodically exhibit a spasm of active behavior, which looks very much as if it is generated by the hallucinations of a dream. In such episodes the cat, although it evinces the unmistakable signs of deep sleep and does not respond to external stimuli, will sometimes perform bodily movements of rage,

fear or pursuit for a minute or two. The sleeping animal's behavior may even be so fierce as to make the experimenter recoil.

All in all the experimental evidence from mammals obliges us to conclude that sleep has a fundamental duality; deep sleep is distinctly different from light sleep, and the duality is founded on physiological mechanisms and probably on biochemical ones as well. Can we shed further light on the subject by examining animal evolution?

The Evolution of Sleep

Looking into this question systematically in our laboratory, we failed to find any evidence of paradoxical sleep in the tortoise and concluded that probably reptiles in general were capable only of light sleep. Among birds, however, we start to see a beginning of paradoxical sleep, albeit very brief. In our subjects—pigeons, chicks and other fowl—this state of sleep lasts no longer than 15 seconds at a time and makes up only .5 percent of the total sleeping time, contrasted with the higher mammals' 20 to 30 percent. In the mammalian order all the animals that have been studied, from the mouse to the chimpanzee, spend a substantial portion of their sleeping time in paradoxical sleep. We find a fairly strong indication that the hunting species (man, the cat, the dog) enjoy more deep sleep than the hunted (rabbits, ruminants). In

our tests the former average 20 percent of total sleep time in paradoxical sleep, whereas the latter average only 5 to 10 percent. Further studies are needed, however, to determine if what we found in our caged animals is also true of their sleep in their natural environments.

The evolutionary evidence shows, then, that the early vertebrates slept only lightly and deep sleep came as a rather late development in animal evolution. Curiously, however, it turns out that the opposite is true in the development of a young individual; in this case ontogeny does not follow phylogeny. In the mammals (cat or man) light sleep does not occur until the nervous system has acquired a certain amount of maturity. A newborn kitten in its first days of life spends half of its time in the waking state and half in paradoxical sleep, going directly from one state into the other, whereas in the adult cat there is almost invariably a transitional period of light sleep. By the end of the first month the kitten's time is divided equally among wakefulness, light sleep and paradoxical sleep (that is, a third in each); thereafter both wakefulness and light sleep increase until adulthood stabilizes the proportions of the three states at 35, 50 and 15 percent respectively.

Considering these facts of evolution and development, we are confronted with the question: What function does paradoxical sleep serve after all? As Kleitman reported in his article "Patterns

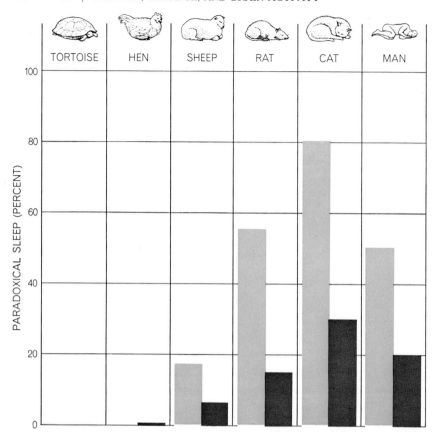

PARADOXICAL SLEEP among three vertebrate classes of increasing evolutionary complexity is shown as a percentage of each animal's time spent in light sleep. None is known in the case of the reptile, a tortoise; in the case of the hen it is only two-tenths of 1 percent of the total. In the case of each of the four mammal species shown, the newborn spend at least twice as much time in paradoxical sleep (*color*) as do their adult counterparts (*black*).

of Dreaming," Dement found that when he repeatedly interrupted people's dreams by waking them, this had the effect of making them dream more during their subsequent sleep periods. These results indicated that dreaming fulfills some genuine need. What that need may be remains a mystery. Dement's subjects showed no detectable disturbances of any importance—emotional or physiological—as a result of their deprivation of dreaming.

We have found much the same thing to be true of the deprivation of paradoxical sleep in cats. For such a test we place a cat on a small pedestal in a pool of water with the pedestal barely topping the water surface. Each time the cat drops off into paradoxical sleep the relaxation of its neck muscles causes its head to droop into the water and this wakes the animal up. Cats that have been deprived of paradoxical sleep in this way for several weeks show no profound disturbances, aside from a modest speeding up of the heart rate. They do, however, have a characteristic pattern of aftereffects with respect to paradoxical sleep. For several days following their removal from the pedestal they spend

much more than the usual amount of time (up to 60 percent) in paradoxical sleep, as if to catch up. After this rebound they gradually recover the normal rhythm (15 percent in deep sleep), and only then does the heart slow to the normal rate. The recovery period depends on the length of the deprivation period: a cat that has gone without paradoxical sleep for 20 days takes about 10 days to return to normal.

The Chemistry of Sleep

All of this suggests that some chemical process takes place during the recovery period. Let us suppose that the deprivation of paradoxical sleep causes a certain substance related to the nervous system to accumulate. The excess of paradoxical sleep during the recovery period will then be occupied with elimination of this "substance," presumably through the agency of "enzymatic" factors that act only during paradoxical sleep.

There is reason to believe that certain enzymes called monoamine oxidases, which oxidize substances having a single amine group, play a crucial role in bringing about the transition from light sleep

to paradoxical sleep. We have found that drugs capable of inhibiting these enzymes can suppress paradoxical sleep in cats without affecting either light sleep or wakefulness. A single injection of the drug nialamide, for example, will eliminate paradoxical sleep from the cycle for a period of hundreds of hours. We have also found that this potent drug can suppress paradoxical sleep in cats that have first been deprived of such sleep for a long period in the pool experiment.

The findings concerning the probable importance of the monoamine oxidases in the sleep mechanism raise the hope that it may soon be possible to build a bridge between neurophysiology and biochemistry in the investigation of sleep. If it is indeed a fact that these enzymes play an important role in sleep, this tends to strengthen the hypothesis that serotonin and noradrenalin, which are monoamines, are involved in the two states of sleep—serotonin in light sleep and noradrenalin in paradoxical sleep. There are other bits of chemical evidence that support the same view. For example, the drug reserpine, which is known to prevent the accumulation of monoamines at places where these compounds are usually deposited, has been found to be capable of producing some specific electrical signs of paradoxical sleep in experimental animals. Further, the injection of certain precursors involved in the synthesis of serotonin in the brain can produce a state resembling light sleep, whereas drugs that selectively depress the serotonin level in the brain produce a state of permanent wakefulness.

We can put together a tentative working hypothesis about the brain mechanisms that control sleep. It seems that the raphe system is the seat responsible for the onset of light sleep, and that it operates through the secretion of serotonin. Similarly, the locus coeruleus harbors the system responsible for producing deep sleep, and this uses noradrenalin as its agent. In cyclic fashion these two systems apply brakes to the reticular activating system responsible for wakefulness and also influence all the other nerve systems in the brain, notably those involved in dreaming.

Dreaming itself, particularly the question of its evolutionary origin and what function it serves, is still one of the great mysteries of biology. With the discovery of its objective accompaniments and the intriguing phenomenon of paradoxical sleep, however, it seems that we have set foot on a new continent that holds promise of exciting explorations.

CHEMISTRY OF BEHAVIOR AND AWARENESS: Transmitters, Hormones, and Drugs

IV

IV CHEMISTRY OF BEHAVIOR AND AWARENESS:
Transmitters, Hormones, and Drugs

INTRODUCTION

The study of the chemical basis of behavior, awareness, and experience has undergone a major revolution in the past few years. One unfortunate facet of this is the widespread use of psychedelic and other mind-altering drugs. In some ways we have become a drugged society. We are just now beginning to understand how these mind-altering drugs may work. Indeed, one of the major advances in recent years has been a much increased understanding of the chemical transmitters that act at synapses in the brain. These are the chemical substances that are released from a nerve terminal and cross the synaptic space to influence other nerve cells, the so-called *neurotransmitters*. In the first article, entitled "Neurotransmitters," Julius Axelrod provides a comprehensive and exciting review of our current knowledge of synaptic transmitter substances. The best known neurotransmitter is acetylcholine, which has been known for some time to act at the junctions between motor nerve fibers and striated muscle fibers. In recent years we have gained much understanding of other substances, particularly the biogenic amines—dopamine, epinephrine and norepinephrine, and serotonin. There are striking relationships between the effects of certain kinds of drugs on behavior and awareness and the actions of these drugs on particular neurotransmitter systems in the brain.

The hormones are another very important set of chemical transmitter substances that work in a somewhat different manner. The hormones of the endocrine system are released by the hypothalamus and the pituitary gland to act on various peripheral target endocrine glands—such as the adrenal gland, the ovaries, or the testes—which in turn release factors that in turn regulate the activity of the hypothalamus and pituitary gland. In the next article, "Hormones of the Hypothalamus," these critically important hormonal systems are reviewed by Roger Guillemin and Roger Burgus in the light of current knowledge. The hypothalamus itself is a brain structure, although in many ways it acts as an endocrine gland. It is intimately associated with the anterior and posterior pituitary glands, which are the actual sites from which hormones are released into the circulating bloodstream to act on various target organs. Hormones can be thought of as long-distance chemical transmitters acting on target organs rather than target neurons. It is becoming increasingly clear that hypothalamic hormones themselves exert powerful influences on synaptic transmission in the brain. The converse, of course, is also true. Synaptic activities in the brain lead to regulation and alteration of the release of hormones from the hypothalamus and pituitary. These substances, the hormones, have enormously powerful influences on the growth of bodily structures and the regulation of behavior.

Hormones play a particularly important role in stress. Seymour Levine, in his article "Stress and Behavior," describes important new findings about these functions of hormones. Behavioral and physical stresses initiate a chain of events that mobilizes an organism for responses. The mechanism involves unknown brain actions in response to stress that lead to hypothalamic release of certain substances, particularly the corticotropin-releasing factor (CRF). CRF acts on the anterior pituitary gland, causing it to release ACTH (adrenocorticotropic hormone), which acts on the cortex of the adrenal gland, causing it to release the cortico-steroid hormones, particularly hydrocortisone in man. These are the so-called stress hormones. They provide feedback to the brain and in this way regulate the CRF and hence ACTH production. ACTH itself has wide-ranging effects on behavior. It influences the extinction of learned avoidance responces, strengthens passive avoidance responces, and can alter the rate of habituation of reflex responses.

The remaining article in this section presents overviews of drugs that have profound influences on behavior and experience. Frank Barron, Murray E. Jarvik, and Sterling Bunnell, Jr., focus on the hallucinogenic drugs, particularly mescaline, psylocybin, and LSD. At very low doses, these drugs alter consciousness and subjective sensations, which suggests that they have basic effects on synaptic transmission in the nervous system (see also the article in this section by Axelrod). For a time it was hoped that these hallucinogenic drugs would aid in the study of such severe mental illnesses as schizophrenia. Although this hope has not yet been realized, a clear understanding of the mechanisms by which hallucinogenic drugs act may someday yield fundamental insights into the basic brain mechanisms of awareness and conscious experience.

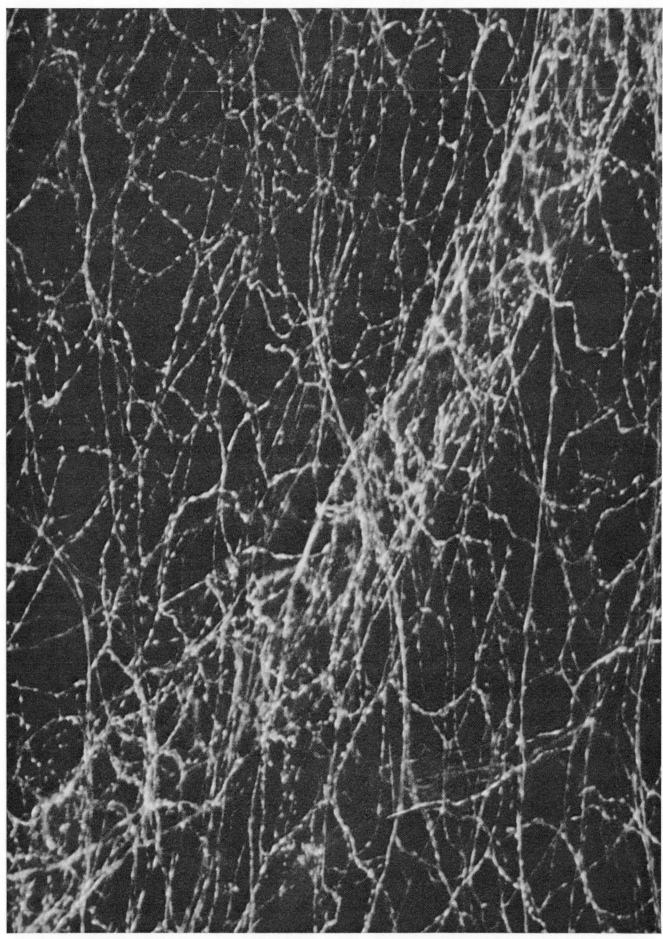

SYMPATHETIC-NERVE TERMINALS from the iris of a rat's eye emit a green glow after treatment with formaldehyde, showing that they contain noradrenaline, one of the neurotransmitters. The terminals, studded with varicosities where the noradrenaline is stored, are enlarged 2,400 diameters in this fluorescence micrograph made by David Jacobowitz of the National Institute of Mental Health.

Neurotransmitters

by Julius Axelrod
June 1974

*These chemicals released from nerve-fiber endings
are the messengers by means of which nerve cells
communicate. Neurotransmitters mediate functions
ranging from muscle contraction to the control
of behavior*

In 1901 the noted English physiologist J. N. Langley observed that the injection of an extract of the adrenal gland into an animal stimulated tissues innervated by the sympathetic nerves: the nerves of the autonomic nervous system that increase the heart rate, raise the blood pressure and cause smooth muscles to contract. Just three years before that John J. Abel of Johns Hopkins University had isolated the hormone adrenaline from the adrenal gland, and so Langley's observation prompted T. R. Elliott, his student at the University of Cambridge, to inject adrenaline into experimental animals. Elliott saw that the hormone, like the crude extract, produced a response in a number of organs that was similar to the response evoked by the electrical stimulation of sympathetic nerves. He thereupon made the brilliant and germinal suggestion that adrenaline might be released from sympathetic nerves and then cause a response in muscle cells with which the nerves form junctions. Elliott thus first enunciated the concept of neural communication by means of chemical transmitters. A neurotransmitter is a chemical that is discharged from a nerve-fiber ending. It reaches and is recognized by a receptor on the surface of a postsynaptic nerve cell or other excitable postjunctional cell and either stimulates or inhibits the second cell. Today it is clear that many different neurotransmitters influence a variety of tissues and physiological processes. Neurotransmitters make the heart beat faster or slower and make muscles contract or relax. They cause glands to synthesize hormone-producing enzymes or to secrete hormones. And they are the agents through which the brain regulates movement and changes mood and behavior.

Elliott's concept of chemical neurotransmission was accepted slowly. Langley, who disliked theories of any kind, discouraged further speculation by Elliott until more facts were available. That took time. The first definite evidence for neurochemical transmission was obtained in 1921 by Otto Loewi, who was then working at the University of Graz in Austria, through an elegant and crucial experiment. Loewi put the heart of a frog in a bath in which the heart could be kept beating. The fluid bathing the heart was allowed to perfuse a second heart. When Loewi stimulated the first heart's vagus nerve (a nerve of the parasympathetic system that reduces the heart rate), the beat of the second heart was slowed, showing that some substance was liberated from the stimulated vagus nerve, was transported by the fluid and influenced the perfused heart. The substance was later identified by Sir Henry Dale as acetylcholine, one of the first neurotransmitters to be recognized. In a similar experiment the stimulation of the accelerans nerve (the sympathetic nerve that increases the heart rate) of a frog heart speeded up the beat of an unstimulated perfused heart. In 1946 the Swedish physiologist Ulf von Euler isolated the neurotransmitter of the sympathetic system and identified it as noradrenaline.

The Transmitters

To be classed as a neurotransmitter a chemical should fulfill a certain set of criteria. Nerves should have the enzymes required to produce the chemical; when nerves are stimulated, they should liberate the chemical, which should then react with a specific receptor on the postjunctional cell and produce a biological response; mechanisms should be available to terminate the actions of the chemical rapidly. On the basis of these criteria two compounds are now established as neurotransmitters: acetylcholine and noradrenaline. Nerves that contain them are respectively called cholinergic and noradrenergic nerves. There are a number of other nerve chemicals that meet many of the listed criteria but have not yet been shown to meet them all. These "putative" transmitters are dopamine, adrenaline, serotonin, octopamine, histamine, gamma aminobutyric acid, glutamic acid, aspartic acid and glycine.

This article will deal mainly with one class of neurotransmitters, the catecholamines, since more is known about these compounds than about some other transmitters and since many of the principles governing their disposition appear to govern those of transmitters in general. The catecholamines include noradrenaline (also known as norepinephrine), dopamine and adrenaline (or epinephrine). They have in common a chemical structure that consists of a benzene ring on which there are two adjacent hydroxyl groups and an ethylamine side chain. Noradrenaline is present in peripheral nerves, the brain and the spinal cord and in the medulla, or inner core, of the adrenal gland. In peripheral tissues and in the brain noradrenaline acts as a neurotransmitter, that is, it exerts most of its effect locally on postjunctional cells. In the adrenal medulla it functions as a hormone, that is, it is released into the bloodstream and acts on distant target organs. Dopamine, once thought to be simply an intermediate in the synthesis of noradrenaline and adrenaline, is also a neurotransmitter in its own right in the brain, where it functions in nerves that influence movement and behavior. The third catecholamine, adrenaline, is largely concentrated in the adrenal medulla. It is discharged into the bloodstream in fear, anger or other stress and acts as a hormone on a number of organs, including the heart, the liver and the intestines. Just in the past year it has developed that adrenaline is probably also a neurotransmitter, since it is found in nerves in the brain.

Techniques developed a decade ago in Sweden made it possible to visualize catecholamines in neurons directly, by the fluorescent glow they emit after treatment with formaldehyde vapor. Fluorescence photomicrography, electron microscopy and radioautography have revealed the structure and functioning of the sympathetic nerve cell in great detail [see illustration below]. The neuron has a cell body and a long axon, or main fiber, that branches into a large number of terminals. Each nerve ending is studded with varicosities, or swellings, that look like beads on a string, so that a single sympathetic neuron can innervate thousands of other cells: "effector" cells.

In 1960 Georg Hertting, Gordon Whitby and I were able to show that radioactive noradrenaline (noradrenaline in which tritium, the radioactive isotope of hydrogen, has been substituted for some of the hydrogen atoms) is taken up selectively and retained in sympathetic nerves. In my laboratory at the National Institute of Mental Health we went on to find out where the neurotransmitter is stored within the nerve cell. Electron

micrographs of sympathetic-neuron varicosities reveal large numbers of vesicles with dark, granular cores. When photographic film was exposed to tissues from rats injected with labeled noradrenaline, the silver grains developed by the radiation from the radioactive hydrogen atoms were strikingly localized over the granulated vesicles [see illustrations on opposite page]. This indicated that it is in those vesicles that noradrenaline is stored within the nerve.

Synthesis and Release

The process leading to the synthesis of catecholamine transmitters begins in the cell body, which has the machinery for making the four enzymes needed for their formation: tyrosine hydroxylase, dopa decarboxylase, dopamine beta-hydroxylase (DBH) and phenylethanolamine N-methyltransferase (PNMT). The enzymes synthesized in the cell body are carried down the axon by a natural flowing process to the nerve endings, where the synthesis of the catecholamines is achieved.

The discharge of neurotransmitter from the nerve endings caps a complex series of events. When a nerve is stimulated, its membrane is depolarized, with sodium moving into the nerve as potassium comes out; the nerve signal propa-

gates as a wave of depolarization that moves along the nerve axon to the endings. As Bernhard Katz of University College London first showed for acetylcholine, the depolarization causes a quantum—a packet or spurt, as it were—of the transmitter to be discharged from the nerve ending into the synaptic cleft.

Biochemical evidence recently obtained in our laboratory and others shows that noradrenaline is released from nerves in much the same way. The vesicles in the endings contain not only noradrenaline but also the enzyme, DBH, that converts dopamine into noradrenaline. When the sympathetic nerve is stimulated electrically, noradrenaline and the enzyme are released in about the same proportions in which they are present in the vesicles. The only way that could happen would be through the fusion of the vesicle with the outer membrane of the nerve, followed by the formation of an opening large enough to allow molecules of noradrenaline to be extruded along with the much larger molecules of the enzyme. Such a release mechanism is called exocytosis. The detailed events whereby the vesicle fuses with the neural membrane and makes an opening to discharge its soluble contents are uncertain, as is the subsequent fate of the vesicle. We do know that certain conditions prevent the release of noradrenaline and DBH. One is the presence of vinblastin, a compound that breaks down the protein structures in nerve cells called neurotubules. Another is the presence of cytocholasin-beta, a substance that disrupts the function of the contractile filament system in cells. A third is the absence of calcium. These findings suggest that the long, tubelike protein structures may orient the vesicles to a site on the neuronal membrane from which the release occurs. It is well known that microfilaments in cells other than nerves, such as muscle cells, can be activated by calcium so that they contract. It is therefore possible that depolarization causes calcium to activate a contractile filament on the neural membrane, which thereupon contracts to make an opening large enough so that the soluble contents of the vesicle can be discharged.

The observation that DBH is released from nerves suggested to Richard Weinshilboum, a research associate in my laboratory, that the enzyme might find its way into the bloodstream. We devised a sensitive assay for the enzyme and found it is indeed present in the blood, and we and others went on to measure the amount of the enzyme (which is found specifically in sympathetic nerves) in a

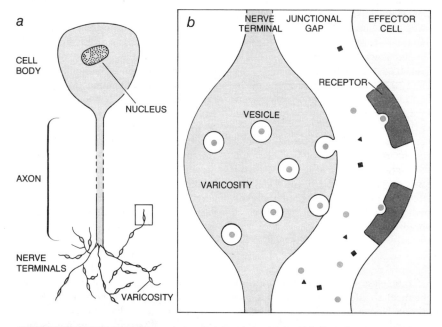

SYMPATHETIC NEURON, or nerve cell (a), consists of a cell body, a long axon and numerous nerve terminals studded with varicosities. Enzymes involved in the synthesis of the transmitters are made in the nucleus and transported down the axon to the varicosities, where the transmitters are manufactured and stored. A varicosity and its junction with another cell are enlarged (b). The transmitter (colored dots) is stored in vesicles. When the nerve is excited and depolarized, vesicles move to the cell membrane and fuse with it, releasing transmitter into the junctional gap. The transmitter reaches receptors on the effector cell that recognize only it, not any other chemicals (black shapes) that are present in the gap.

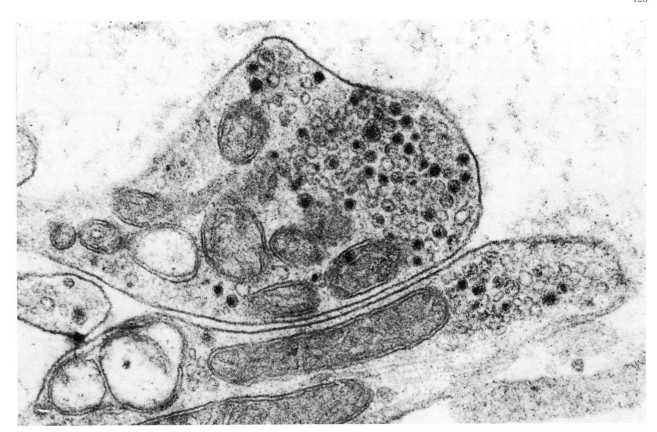

VARICOSITIES on noradrenaline-containing nerve endings from a rat pineal gland are enlarged 90,000 diameters in an electron micrograph made by Floyd Bloom of the National Institute of Mental Health. The varicosities contain vesicles, many with dense cores.

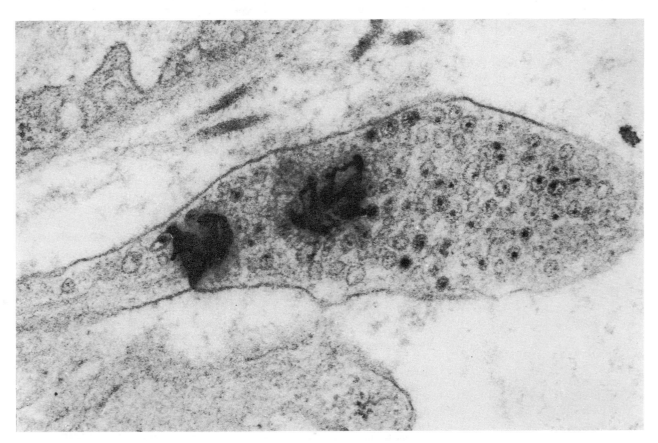

RADIOACTIVE NORADRENALINE is shown by radioautography to be localized in the vesicles. A pineal-tissue sample was taken from rats injected with labeled noradrenaline. The radioactivity developed silver grains (*black blots*) in a photographic film laid on the sample. The developed grains were strikingly localized over the vesicles, which were thus identified as sites of transmitter storage.

TYROSINE

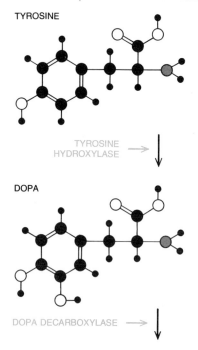

TYROSINE
HYDROXYLASE

DOPA

DOPA DECARBOXYLASE

DOPAMINE

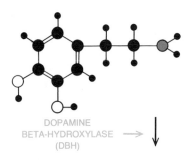

DOPAMINE
BETA-HYDROXYLASE
(DBH)

NORADRENALINE

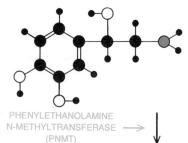

PHENYLETHANOLAMINE
N-METHYLTRANSFERASE
(PNMT)

ADRENALINE

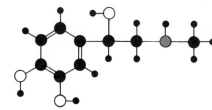

● HYDROGEN

○ OXYGEN

◉ NITROGEN

● CARBON

PRODUCTION of catecholamine transmitters is accomplished by four enzymes (color) in sympathetic-nerve terminals and in the adrenal gland. Tyrosine, an amino acid, is transformed into the intermediate dopa. Removal of a carboxyl (COOH) group forms dopamine, which is itself a transmitter and is also the precursor of the transmitter noradrenaline. In the adrenal gland the process continues with the addition of a methyl (CH₃) group to form adrenaline.

variety of disease states. It is low in the hereditary disorder of the autonomic system called familial dysautonomia and in Down's syndrome (mongolism), and it is high in torsion dystonia (a neurological disease involving muscle spasticity), in neuroblastoma (a cancer of nervous tissue) and in certain forms of hypertension. The findings suggest that in each of these diseases there are abnormalities in the functioning of the sympathetic nervous system.

Action and Inactivation

Once the neurortransmitter is liberated it diffuses across the cleft between the nerve terminal and adjacent cells. The capacity of a neighboring effector cell to respond to the transmitter then depends on the ability of a receptor on the postjunctional cell's surface to selectively recognize and combine with the neurotransmitter. When the receptor and transmitter interact, a series of events is triggered that causes the effector cell to carry out its special function. Some of these responses occur rapidly (in a fraction of a second), as in the propagation of nerve transmission across a synapse; others occur slowly, in minutes or sometimes hours, as in the synthesis of intracellular enzymes. There are two receptors that recognize noradrenaline, alpha and beta adrenergic receptors, and there is one for dopamine. These receptors can be distinguished from one another by the specific response each elicits and by the ability of specific drugs to block those responses.

The beta adrenergic receptors turn on an effector cell, and they do so by means of adenosine 3′5′ monophosphate, or cyclic AMP, the universal "second messenger" that mediates between hormones and many cellular activities elicited by those hormones [see "Cyclic AMP," by Ira Pastan; SCIENTIFIC AMERICAN Offprint 1256]. Investigators have traced several of the steps in the activation of the receptor by noradrenaline by studying the interaction of noradrenaline and fat cells or cells of the liver or of the

pineal gland. We have found the pineal, which makes a hormone called melatonin that inhibits the activity of sex glands, particularly suitable because it is heavily supplied with nerves containing noradrenaline [see "The Pineal Gland," by Richard J. Wurtman and Julius Axelrod; SCIENTIFIC AMERICAN Offprint 1015]. Melatonin is synthesized in a number of steps, one of which, the conversion of serotonin to N-acetylserotonin, is catalyzed by the enzyme serotonin N-acetyltransferase. It is that enzyme's synthesis that is controlled by the beta adrenergic receptor. When noradrenaline is released from a nerve innervating the pineal, it interacts with beta adrenergic receptors on the outside of the membrane of a pineal cell. Once a receptor is occupied by noradrenaline, the enzyme adenylate cyclase, on the inner surface of the cell membrane, is activated. The adenylate cyclase then converts the cellular energy carrier ATP to cyclic AMP, which in turn stimulates the synthesis of serotonin N-acetyltransferase [see illustration on opposite page]. This complex series of events can be turned off by propranolol, a drug that prevents the noradrenaline from combining with the beta adrenergic receptor.

The adenylate cyclase system is involved in scores of biological actions. The ability of the pineal cell to carry out its special function, the manufacture of melatonin, by utilizing the almost universal adenylate-cyclase system depends on the presence of receptors on the cell surface that can specifically recognize noradrenaline and of the enzyme hydroxyindole-O-methyltransferase, uniquely present in the pineal cell, that can convert N-acetylserotonin to melatonin.

Once the neurotransmitter has interacted with the postjunctional cell, its actions must be rapidly terminated; otherwise it would exert its effects for too long and precise control would be lost. In the cholinergic nervous system the acetylcholine is rapidly inactivated by the enzyme acetylcholinesterase, which metabolizes the transmitter. In the past 10 years it has become clear that the inactivation of neurotransmitters through enzymatic transformation is the exception rather than the rule. Catecholamine neurotransmitters are metabolized by two enzymes, catechol-O-methyltransferase (COMT) and monoamine oxidase (MAO); the latter is a particularly important enzyme that removes the amino (NH₂) group of a wide variety of compounds, including serotonin, noradrenaline, dopamine and adrenaline. There are enzyme-inhibiting chemicals that

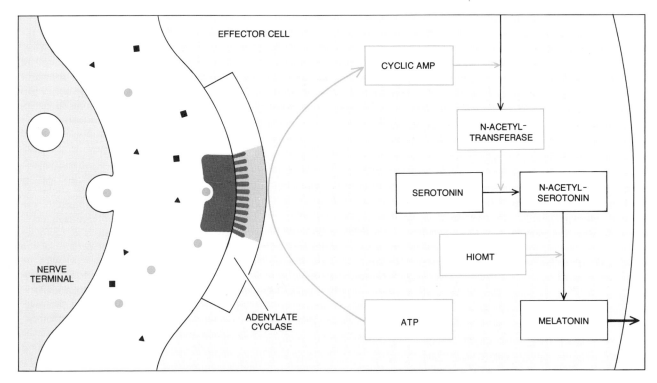

MODE OF ACTION of a transmitter is exemplified by the effect of noradrenaline on a pineal cell. Noradrenaline (*colored dots*) released from a nerve ending binds to a beta-adrenergic receptor on the pineal-cell surface. The receptor thereupon activates the enzyme adenylate cyclase on the inside of the pineal-cell membrane. The activated adenylate cyclase catalyzes the conversion of adeno-sine triphosphate (ATP) into cyclic adenosine monophosphate (AMP). The cyclic AMP stimulates synthesis of the enzyme N-acetyltransferase; the enzyme converts serotonin into N-acetyl-serotonin. This is transformed in turn by the pineal cell's specific enzyme, hydroxyindole-O-methyltransferase (HIOMT), to form melatonin, the pineal-gland hormone that acts on the sex glands.

can prevent COMT and MAO from carrying out their biochemical transformations; when such inhibitors were administered, the action of noradrenaline was found still to be rapidly terminated. There had to be a method of rapid inactivation other than enzymatic transformation.

In order to track down such a mechanism we injected a cat with radioactive noradrenaline. The labeled transmitter persisted in tissues that were rich in sympathetic nerves for many hours, long after its physiological actions were ended, indicating that radioactive noradrenaline was taken up in the sympathetic nerves and held there. My colleagues and I designed a simple experiment to prove this. Sympathetic nerves innervating the left salivary gland in rats were destroyed by removing the superior cervical ganglion on the left side of the neck; about seven days after this operation the noradrenaline nerves of the salivary gland on the right side were intact, whereas the nerves on the left side had completely disappeared. When radioactive noradrenaline was injected, the transmitter was found in the right salivary gland but not in the left one. We also found that in cats injected with radioactive noradrenaline the transmitter was re-leased when the sympathetic nerves were stimulated electrically. The experiments clearly demonstrated that noradrenaline is taken up into, as well as released from, sympathetic nerves. As a result of these experiments we postulated that noradrenaline is rapidly inactivated through its recapture by the sympathetic nerves; once it is back in the nerves, of course, the neurotransmitter cannot exert its effect on postjunctional cells. Leslie L. Iversen of the University of Cambridge has since shown that this neuronal recapture by sympathetic nerves is highly selective for noradrenaline or compounds resembling it in chemical structure. Recent work indicates that uptake by nerves may be the most general mechanism for the inactivation of neurotransmitters.

Regulation

Chemical transmitters in sympathetic nerves (and presumably in other nerves) are in a state of flux, continually being synthesized, released, metabolized and recaptured. The activity of nerves can also undergo marked fluctuation during periods of stress. In spite of all these dynamic changes the amount of cate-cholamines in tissues remains constant. This is owing to a variety of adaptive mechanisms that alter the formation, release and response of catecholamines. There are fast regulatory changes that require only fractions of a second and slower changes that take place after minutes or even hours.

When sympathetic nerves are stimulated, the conversion of tyrosine to noradrenaline in them is rapidly increased. The increased nervous activity specifically affects tyrosine hydroxylase, the enzyme that converts tyrosine to dopa, because its activity is inhibited by noradrenaline and dopamine. Any increase in nerve-firing brought on by stress, cold and certain drugs lowers the level of catecholamines in the nerve terminals. This reduces the negative-feedback effect of noradrenaline and dopamine on tyrosine hydroxylase, so that more tyrosine is converted to dopa, which in turn is converted to make more catecholamines. Conversely, when nerve activity is decreased, the catecholamine level rises, slowing down the conversion of tyrosine to dopa by once again inhibiting the tyrosine hydroxylase.

Another rapid regulation is accomplished at the nerve terminal itself, where the alpha adrenergic receptors are situated. When the alpha receptors are activated, they diminish the release of noradrenaline from nerve terminals into the synaptic cleft. When too much noradrenaline is released, it accumulates in the synaptic cleft; when the catecholamine level is high enough, it activates the alpha receptors on the presynaptic nerve terminals and shuts off further release of the neurotransmitter.

A slower regulatory process is brought on by prolonged firing of sympathetic nerves, which can step up the manufacture of the catecholamine-synthesizing enzymes tyrosine hydroxylase, DBH and (to a lesser extent) PNMT; the rise in the enzyme level enables the nerves to make more neurotransmitter. We discovered this phenomenon of increased enzyme synthesis when we gave animals reserpine, a versatile drug that lowers the blood pressure and incidentally increases sympathetic-nerve firing (which tends to raise the pressure) by a reflex action. The reserpine brought about a gradual increase in tyrosine hydroxylase and DBH in sympathetic nerves and the adrenal gland and of PNMT in the adrenal gland. Increases in these enzymes were also found in animals exposed to stress, cold, physical restraint, psychosocial stimulation or insulin injection. When the synthesis of proteins was prevented by drugs, on the other hand,

there was no elevation in enzyme activity after reserpine was given. This indicated that increased nerve activity stimulates the synthesis of new molecules of tyrosine hydroxylase, DBH and PNMT; with a greater need for neurotransmitters there is a compensatory increase in the synthesis of enzymes that catalyze the making of these transmitters.

In order to learn whether the command for increased synthesis of new tyrosine hydroxylase and DBH molecules can be transmitted from one nerve to another we cut the nerve innervating certain noradrenaline cell bodies—the superior cervical ganglia—on one side. When nerves were then stimulated reflexly by reserpine, there was an elevation of tyrosine hydroxylase and DBH levels in the innervated ganglia but not in the denervated ones. The experiment showed that one nerve can transmit information to another nerve (presumably by means of a chemical signal) that causes the postsynaptic nerve to make new enzyme molecules.

Sensitivity

In 1855 the German physiologist J. L. Budge observed that when the nerves leading to a rabbit's right eye were destroyed, the pupil of that eye became

more dilated than the left pupil. The phenomenon was later explained by the American physiologist Walter B. Cannon, who postulated that as a result of denervation the effector cells somehow become more responsive. He called this effect the "law of denervation supersensitivity." Subsequent work showed that denervation supersensitivity is caused by two separate mechanisms, one presynaptic and the other postsynaptic. When nerves are destroyed, presynaptic inactivation by recapture is abolished, thereby leaving the neurotransmitters to react with the postsynaptic site longer.

Denervation also causes a profound change in the degree of activity of the postjunctional cell. Recent work with the pineal gland in our laboratory has suggested a hypothesis for supersensitivity, and also for subsensitivity, in postjunctional cells. As we have seen, noradrenaline stimulates the synthesis of the enzyme serotonin N-acetyltransferase through a beta adrenergic receptor in the postjunctional pineal cell. When the nerves to pineal cells are destroyed (or depleted of noradrenaline by the administration of reserpine), the pineal cells become 10 times as responsive to noradrenaline; that is, when the postjunctional cell is deprived of its neurotransmitter for a period of time, it takes just

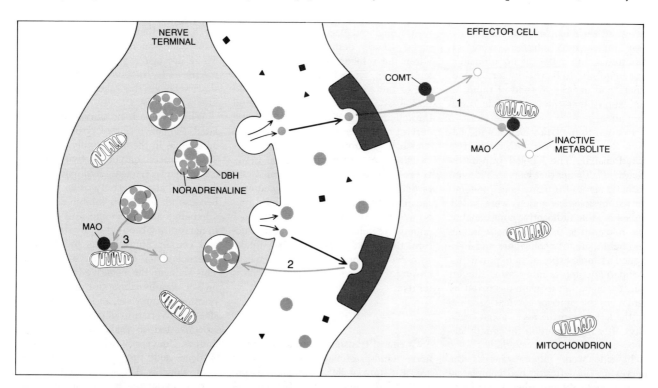

RELEASE AND INACTIVATION of the neurotransmitter noradrenaline is shown in more detail. The enzyme DBH is stored in the noradrenergic nerve terminals along with the transmitter and is released with it into the junctional gap. The noradrenaline binds to the receptors on the effector cell, eliciting that cell's response as shown in the illustration on the preceding page. Then the norad-

renaline's action is terminated either through metabolism (1) by the enzymes catechol-O-methyltransferase (COMT) and/or monoamine oxidase (MAO), or by recapture and storage (2) in the presynaptic sympathetic-nerve terminal; the latter is the more important process. MAO, stored in the membrane of mitochondria, also inactivates noradrenaline that leaks out of vesicles (3).

one packet of catecholamines to cause the same increase of N-acetyltransferase in the cell as 10 packets of transmitters would cause in a normally innervated cell. If, on the other hand, the pineal cell is exposed to an excessive amount of catecholamines for a period of time, it becomes less responsive: a larger amount of the transmitter is required to produce the same increase in N-acetyltransferase.

These experiments suggest that changes in the responsiveness of excitable cells are the result of an alteration in the "avidity" with which the receptor binds the neurotransmitters. If the receptor is exposed to small amounts of catecholamine for some time, it reacts with the neurotransmitter easily; if too many neurotransmitter molecules bombard the receptor, it becomes less responsive. Depending on the tissue, this change in sensitivity can come within hours or days, so that it is an effective adaptive mechanism for excitable cells. It is possible that the tolerance that is often developed to a drug taken in excess may reflect subsensitivity on the part of cells that respond to the drug.

Role in the Brain

The brain has billions of nerves that talk to one another by means of neurotransmitters. Neurobiologists are just beginning to unravel the complex biochemistry and physiology of chemical transmission in the brain. Many different neurotransmitters function in brain neurons, but because there are more precise methods of measuring catecholamines and drugs are available that perturb their formation, storage, release and metabolism, we know more about brain catecholamines than about the other neurotransmitters. Fluorescence photomicrography and drugs that selectively destroy catecholamine-containing nerves have made it possible to locate the noradrenaline, dopamine and serotonin cell bodies and trace the pathways of their axons and nerve endings [*see illustrations on page 131*]. The cell bodies of the dopamine-containing nerves are in the area of the brain stem called the substantia nigra, whence the dopaminergic axons course through the brain stem, many of them terminating in the caudate nucleus. The dopamine-containing tracts in the caudate nucleus play an important role in the integration of movement.

The elucidation of the biochemistry and pharmacology of dopamine in the brain has led to the development of a powerful treatment of a crippling disease, Parkinsonism. The Swedish pharmacologist Arvid Carlsson noted in 1959

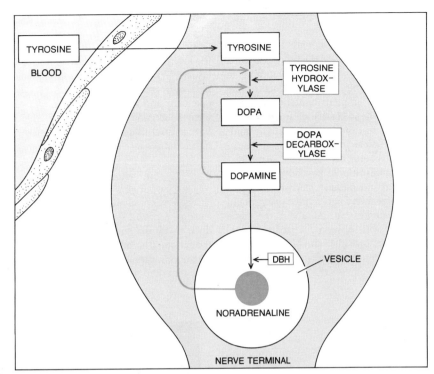

RAPID REGULATION of catecholamine synthesis is accomplished by a feedback mechanism: a buildup of dopamine and noradrenaline inhibits (*colored arrows*) the activity of tyrosine hydroxylase, which catalyzes the first step in the synthesis. An increase in nerve activity reduces the amount of dopamine and noradrenaline in the terminal, removing the inhibition; tyrosine hydroxylase activity increases and more transmitter is synthesized.

that when reserpine was given to rats, it sharply reduced the dopamine content of the caudate nucleus in the brain and also caused a Parkinson-like tremor. The administration of dopa, a dopamine precursor that can get from the blood into the brain more easily than dopamine, reversed the tremors. These findings prompted Oleh Hornykiewicz, who was then working at the University of Vienna, to measure the content of dopamine in the brain of patients who had died of Parkinson's disease. He found that there was virtually no dopamine in the caudate nucleus. The finding led directly to a major therapeutic advance by George C. Cotzias of the Brookhaven National Laboratory: when dopa, the dopamine precursor that can cross the blood-brain barrier, is administered, it makes up the dopamine deficiency and effectively relieves the symptoms of Parkinson's disease. This is a good example of how basic research can sometimes lead rapidly to a new treatment for a disease.

There are two main nerve tracts containing noradrenaline in the brain, the dorsal and ventral pathways. The cell bodies of the noradrenaline-containing tracts are found in the lower part of the brain in the area called the locus ceruleus, or "blue place." Noradrenaline-containing nerve tracts are highly branched

and reach many parts of the brain. Among the areas they innervate are the cerebellum and the cerebral cortex, which are concerned with the fine coordination of movement, alertness and emotion. Another part of the brain innervated by noradrenaline neurons is the hypothalamus, which controls many visceral functions of the body such as hunger, thirst, temperature regulation, blood pressure, reproduction and behavior. Manipulation of the noradrenaline levels in the brain can change many of the functions of the hypothalamus, particularly the "pleasure" centers. Noradrenaline tracts also appear to be involved in mood elevation and depression. Recently nerves containing adrenaline have also been observed in the brain stem. The next few years should show whether these adrenaline-containing tracts also control emotion, mood and behavior.

Drugs have been powerful tools for probing the action of neurotransmitters. As our knowledge concerning neurotransmitters has broadened, so has our understanding of the action of drugs on behavior and on the cardiovascular and motor systems; the two trends have interacted nicely. In the early 1950's pharmacologists recognized that the hallucinogenic agent lysergic acid diethylamine (LSD) not only resembles serotonin in chemical structure but also counteracts some of its pharmacologic actions (by occupying sites intended for serotonin). Several workers therefore proposed that serotonin must have something to do with insanity. Other hallucinogenic agents such as mescaline and amphetamine, on the other hand, are related in structure to noradrenaline. In the mid-1950's clinical investigators were learning that chemicals such as chlorpromazine could mitigate psychotic behavior, and that monoamine oxidase inhibitors and imipramine and related drugs could relieve depression. At about the same time it was observed that reserpine, which was proving valuable not only for hypertension but also for schizophrenia, markedly reduced the levels of noradrenaline and serotonin in the brain. The observations combined to suggest that these drugs exerted their actions on the brain by interfering with neurotransmitters. When my colleagues and I found that radioactive noradrenaline can be taken up and released from nerves, we were in a good position to investigate how a drug influences the disposition of injected radioactive transmitters.

Effect of Drugs

The first compound we examined was cocaine, a potent stimulant that can produce psychosis and that also intensifies the action of noradrenaline. When radioactive noradrenaline was injected into cats that had been given cocaine, the uptake of catecholamines by the sympathetic nerves was prevented, demonstrating that cocaine magnifies the effect of noradrenaline by preventing its capture and inactivation and leaving larger amounts of the catecholamine to react with the effector cell. Antidepressant drugs such as imipramine had the same effect: they blocked the uptake of noradrenaline into sympathetic nerves. By using radioactive noradrenaline we found that amphetamine, which is both a stimulant and a mind-altering drug, affects noradrenergic nerves in two ways: it blocks the uptake of noradrenaline and also promotes the release of the neurotransmitter from nerves.

Many drugs that are effective in the treatment of hypertension affect the

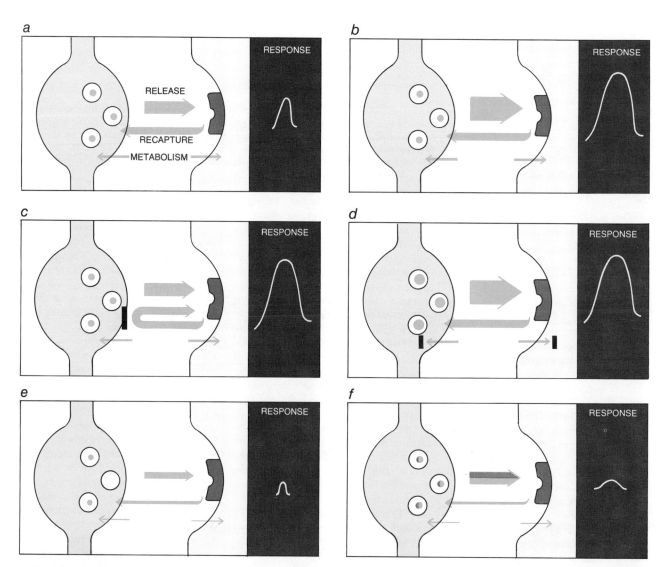

CERTAIN ADRENERGIC DRUGS increase or decrease the availability of noradrenaline at the adrenergic receptor. Normal release, recapture and metabolism (*colored arrows*) are illustrated, with a curve representing the normal response of a postjunctional cell (*a*). Antidepressant drugs enlarge that response in several ways, all of which increase the availability of noradrenaline at the synapse. Amphetamine does so by promoting the release of noradrenaline (*b*). Amphetamine and imipramine and related drugs block recapture (*c*); the monoamine-oxidase inhibitors interfere with inactivation through metabolism (*d*). Conversely, reserpine, which reduces blood pressure and may induce depression, reduces the response by depleting the noradrenaline in storage (*e*); alpha-methyldopa and other "false transmitters" are stored in the vesicles with noradrenaline and released with it, diluting its effect (*f*).

storage and release of noradrenergic transmitters. Reserpine and guanethidine reduce blood pressure by preventing the nerves that raise the pressure from storing noradrenaline. Antihypertensive drugs such as alpha methyl dopa, on the other hand, are transformed by enzymes in the nerve into substances that resemble the noradrenaline chemically. The "false transmitters" are stored and released along with natural neurotransmitters, diluting them and thus reducing their effect.

In the past 10 years many psychiatrists and pharmacologists have been struck by the fact that drugs that relieve mental depression also interfere with the uptake, storage, release or metabolism of noradrenaline. Whereas imipramine blocks the uptake of noradrenaline by nerves and amphetamine both releases noradrenaline and blocks its uptake, monoamine oxidase inhibitors, as their name implies, prevent the metabolism of the catecholamine. In other words, all these antidepressants produce similar results by different mechanisms: they increase the amount of catecholamine in the synaptic cleft, with the result that more transmitter is available to stimulate the receptor. Conversely, reserpine, a compound that decreases the amount of the chemical transmitters, sometimes produces depression. These considerations led to the proposal of a catecholamine hypothesis of depressive states, which holds that mental depression is associated with the decreased availability of brain catecholamine and is relieved by drugs that increase the amount of these transmitters at the adrenergic receptor. Although the hypothesis is not yet entirely substantiated, it has provided a valuable framework within which new approaches to understanding depression can be sought.

The introduction in the 1950's of antipsychotic drugs such as chlorpromazine and haloperidol revolutionized the treatment of schizophrenia, dramatically reducing the stay of schizophrenics in mental hospitals and saving many billions of dollars in hospital care. Research in the past decade has shown that antipsychotic drugs also exert their effect on the catecholamine neurotransmitters. Carlsson had observed that antischizophrenic drugs caused an increase in the formation of catecholamines in the rat brain, and he formed the hypothesis that this was owing to the drug's ability to block dopamine receptors. Work by other investigators has confirmed and extended this hypothesis. Antipsychotic drugs do block dopamine receptors in the brain, and there is a strong associa-

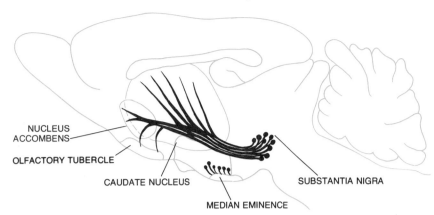

NUCLEUS ACCOMBENS

OLFACTORY TUBERCLE

CAUDATE NUCLEUS

MEDIAN EMINENCE

SUBSTANTIA NIGRA

DOPAMINE TRACTS, the main bundles of nerves containing dopamine, are shown (*black*) in a drawing of a longitudinal section along the midline of the rat brain. The cell bodies are concentrated in the substantia nigra, and the axons project primarily to the caudate nucleus. A dopamine deficiency in that region causes Parkinsonism, which can be treated with dopa.

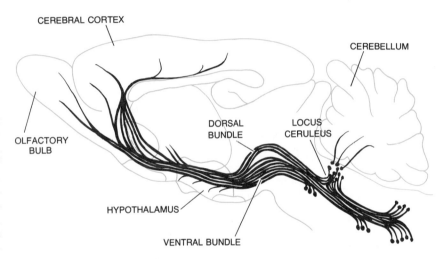

CEREBRAL CORTEX

CEREBELLUM

OLFACTORY BULB

DORSAL BUNDLE

LOCUS CERULEUS

HYPOTHALAMUS

VENTRAL BUNDLE

NORADRENALINE TRACTS arise primarily in the locus ceruleus and reach many brain centers, including the cerebellum, cerebral cortex and hypothalamus. Illustrations on this page are based on maps made by Urban Ungerstedt of Royal Caroline Institute in Sweden.

tion between the blocking ability of various drugs and their capacity to relieve schizophrenic symptoms. These findings point clearly to the involvement of the dopaminergic nerves in schizophrenia.

Amphetamine has also helped to clarify the nature of schizophrenia. Taken repeatedly in large amounts, amphetamine produces a psychosis manifested by repetitive and compulsive behavior and hallucinogenic delusions that are indistinguishable from the symptoms exhibited by paranoid schizophrenics. Amphetamine releases catecholamines from nerves in the brain to stimulate both noradrenergic and dopamine receptors. After doing experiments with two forms of amphetamine Solomon H. Snyder of the Johns Hopkins University Medical School hypothesized that the schizophrenia-like psychosis the drug induces is due to excessive release of dopamine.

The ability of antischizophrenia drugs, which block dopamine receptors, to relieve symptoms of amphetamine psychosis is consistent with this hypothesis.

Although there have been rapid advances in our knowledge of neurotransmitters in the past 20 years, much remains to be discovered about these compounds. Only a few of the chemical transmitters of the brain neurons have even been characterized. The role of neurotransmitters in behavior, mood, reproduction and learning and in diseases such as depression, schizophrenia, motor disorders and hypertension is beginning to evolve. If only the present trend toward reducing the funds committed to research support can be reversed, exciting new discoveries about neurotransmitters should soon be made, many of which will surely contribute directly toward the treatment or cure of some of man's most tragic afflictions.

13

The Hormones
of the Hypothalamus

by Roger Guillemin and Roger Burgus
November 1972

The anterior pituitary gland, which controls the peripheral endocrine glands, is itself regulated by "releasing factors" originating in the brain. Two of these hormones have now been isolated and synthesized

The pituitary gland is attached by a stalk to the region in the base of the brain known as the hypothalamus. Within the past year or so, after nearly 20 years of effort in many laboratories throughout the world, two substances have been isolated from animal brain tissue that represent the first of the long sought hypothalamic hormones. Because the molecular structure of the new hormones is fairly simple the substances can readily be synthesized in large quantities. Their availability and their high activity in humans has led physiologists and clinicians to consider that the hypothalamic hormones will open a new chapter in medicine.

It has long been known that the pituitary secretes several complex hormones that travel through the bloodstream to target organs, notably the thyroid gland, the gonads and the cortex of the adrenal glands. There the pituitary hormones stimulate the secretion into the bloodstream of the thyroid hormones, of the sex hormones by the gonads and of several steroid hormones such as hydrocortisone by the adrenal cortex. The secretion of the thyroid, sex and adrenocortical hormones thus has two stages beginning with the release of pituitary hormones. Studies going back some 50 years culminated in the demonstration that the process actually has three stages: the release of the pituitary hormones requires the prior release of another class of hormones manufactured in the hypothalamus. It is two of these hypothalamic hormones that have now been isolated, chemically identified and synthesized.

One of the hypothalamic hormones acts as the factor that triggers the release of the pituitary hormone thyrotropin, sometimes called the thyroid-stimulating hormone, or TSH. Thus the

hypothalamic hormone associated with TSH is called the TSH-releasing factor, or TRF. The other hormone is LRF. Here again "RF" stands for "releasing factor"; the "L" signifies that the substance releases the gonadotropic pituitary hormone LH, the luteinizing hormone. A third gonadotropic hormone, FSH (follicle-stimulating hormone), may have its own hypothalamic releasing factor, FRF, but that has not been demonstrated. It is known, however, that the hypothalamic hormone LRF stimulates the release of FSH as well as LH.

Studies are continuing aimed at characterizing several other hypothalamic hormones that are known to exist on the basis of physiological evidence but that have not yet been isolated. One of them regulates the secretion of adrenocorticotropin (ACTH), the pituitary hormone whose target is the adrenal cortex. Another hormone (possibly two hormones with opposing actions) regulates the release of prolactin, the pituitary hormone involved in pregnancy and lactation. Still another hormone (again possibly two hormones with opposing actions) regulates the release of the pituitary hormone involved in growth and structural development (growth hormone).

That the hypothalamus and the pituitary act in concert can be suspected not only from their physical proximity at the base of the brain but also from their development in the embryo. During the early embryological development of all mammals a small pouch forms in the upper part of the developing pharynx and migrates upward toward the developing brain. There it meets a similar formation, resembling the finger of a glove, that springs from the base of the primordial brain. Several months later the first pouch, now detached from

the upper oral cavity, has filled into a solid mass of cells differentiated into glandular types. At this point the second pouch, still connected to the base of the brain, is rich with hundreds of thousands of nerve fibers associated with a modified type of glial cell, not too unlike the glial cells found throughout the brain. The two organs are now enclosed in a single receptacle that has formed as an open spherical cavity within the sphenoid bone, on which the brain rests.

This double organ, now ensconced in the sphenoidal bone, is the pituitary gland, or hypophysis. The part that migrated from the brain is the posterior lobe, or neurohypophysis; the part that migrated from the pharynx is the anterior lobe, or adenohypophysis. Both parts of the gland remain connected to the brain by a common stalk that goes through the covering flap of the sphenoidal cavity. For many years after the double embryological origin of the pituitary gland was recognized the role of the gland was no more clearly understood than it had been in the old days. Indeed, the name "pituitary" had been given to it in the 16th century by Vesalius, who thought that the little organ had to do with secretion of *pituita:* the nasal fluid.

We know now that the anterior lobe of the pituitary gland controls the secretion and function of all the "periph-

HYPOTHALAMIC FRAGMENTS of sheep brains were the source from which the authors' laboratory extracted one milligram of TRF, the first hypothalamic hormone to be characterized and synthesized. The photograph is of about 30 frozen hypothalamic fragments; some five million such fragments, dissected from 500 tons of sheep brain tissue, were processed over a period of four years.

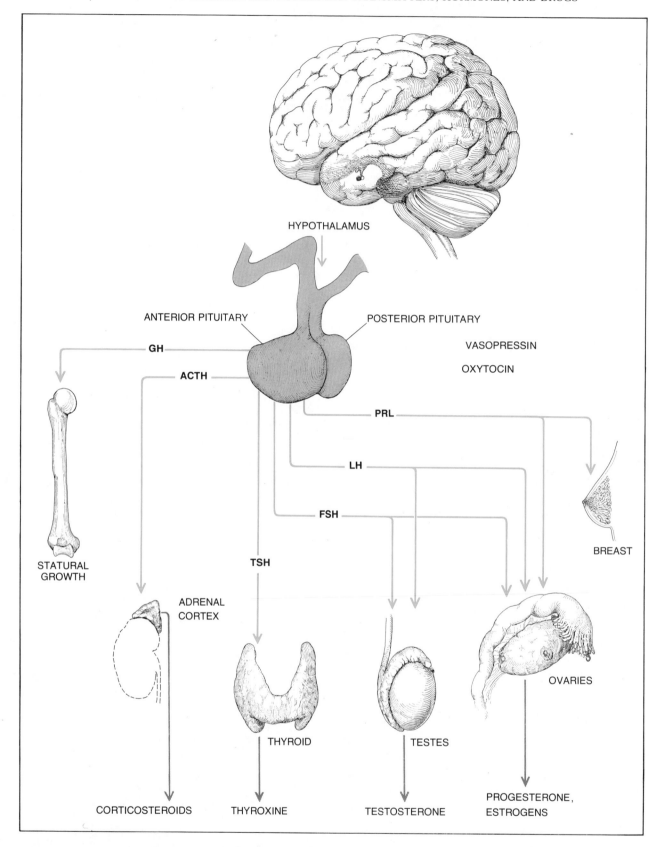

HYPOTHALAMUS

ANTERIOR PITUITARY

POSTERIOR PITUITARY

VASOPRESSIN

OXYTOCIN

GH

ACTH

PRL

LH

FSH

TSH

BREAST

STATURAL
GROWTH

ADRENAL
CORTEX

OVARIES

THYROID

TESTES

CORTICOSTEROIDS   THYROXINE   TESTOSTERONE   PROGESTERONE,
ESTROGENS

PITUITARY GLAND, connected to the hypothalamus at the base of the brain, has two lobes and two functions. The posterior lobe of the pituitary stores and passes on to the general circulation two hormones manufactured in the hypothalamus: vasopressin and oxytocin. The anterior lobe secretes a number of other hormones: growth hormone (GH), which promotes statural growth; adreno-corticotropic hormone (ACTH), which stimulates the cortex of the adrenal gland to secrete corticosteroids; thyroid-stimulating hormone (TSH), which stimulates secretions by the thyroid gland, and follicle-stimulating hormone (FSH), luteinizing hormone (LH) and prolactin (PRL), which in various combinations regulate lactation and the functioning of the gonads. Several of these anterior pituitary hormones are known to be controlled by releasing factors from the hypothalamus, two of which have now been synthesized.

eral" endocrine glands (the thyroid, the gonads and the adrenal cortex). It also controls the mammary glands and regulates the harmonious growth of the individual. It accomplishes all this by the secretion of a series of complex protein and glycoprotein hormones. All the pituitary hormones are manufactured and secreted by the anterior lobe. Why should this master endocrine gland have migrated so far in the course of evolution (a journey recapitulated in the embryo) to make contact with the brain? As we shall see, recent observations have answered the question.

The posterior lobe of the pituitary has been known for the past 50 years to secrete substances that affect the reabsorption of water from the kidney into the bloodstream. These secretions also stimulate the contraction of the uterus during childbirth and the release of milk during lactation. In the early 1950's Vincent Du Vigneaud and his co-workers at the Cornell University Medical College resolved a controversy of many years' standing by showing that the biological activities of the posterior lobe are attributable to two different molecules: vasopressin (or antidiuretic hormone) and oxytocin. The two molecules are octapeptides: structures made up of eight amino acids. Du Vigneaud's group showed that six of the eight amino acids in the two molecules are identical, which explains their closely related physicochemical properties and similar biological activity. Both hormones exhibit (in different ratios) all the major biological effects mentioned above: the reabsorption of water, the stimulation of uterine contractions and the release of milk.

As early as 1924 it was realized that the hormones secreted by the posterior lobe of the pituitary are also found in the hypothalamus: that part of the brain with which the lobe is connected by nerve fibers through the pituitary stalk. Later it was shown that the two hormones of the posterior pituitary are actually manufactured in some specialized nerve cells in the hypothalamus. They flow slowly down the pituitary stalk to the posterior pituitary through the axons, or long fibers, of the hypothalamic nerve cells [see top illustration on page 137]. They are stored in the posterior pituitary, which is now reduced to a storage organ rather than a manufacturing one. From it they are secreted into the bloodstream on the proper physiological stimulus.

These observations had led several

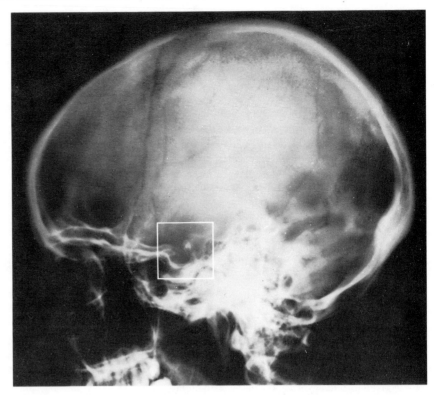

BONY RECEPTACLE in which the pituitary gland is enclosed is a cavity in the sphenoid bone, on which the base of the brain rests. White rectangle shows area diagrammed below.

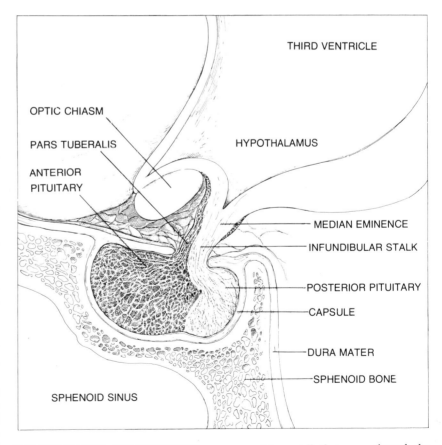

HYPOTHALAMUS AND PITUITARY are connected by a stalk that passes through the membranous lid of the receptacle in the sphenoid bone in which the pituitary rests. The double embryological origin of the two lobes of the pituitary is reflected in their differing tissues and functions and in the different ways that each is connected to the hypothalamus.

biologists, notably Ernst and Berta Scharrer, to the striking new concept of neurosecretion (the secretion of hormones by nerve cells). They suggested that specialized nerve cells might be able to manufacture and secrete true hormones, which would then be carried by the blood and would exert their effects in some target organ or tissue remote from their point of origin. The ability to manufacture hormones had traditionally been assigned to the endocrine glands: the thyroid, the gonads, the adrenals and so on. The suggestion that nerve cells could secrete hormones would endow them with a capacity far beyond their ability to liberate neurotransmitters such as epinephrine and acetylcholine at the submicroscopic regions (synapses) where they make contact with other nerve cells.

Even as these studies were in progress and these new concepts were being formulated other laboratories were reporting evidence that functions of the anterior lobe of the pituitary were somehow dependent on the structural integrity of the hypothalamic area and on a normal relation between the hypothalamus and the pituitary gland. For example, minute lesions of the hypothalamus, such as can be created by introducing

small electrodes into the base of the brain in an experimental animal and producing localized electrocoagulation, were found to abolish the secretion of anterior pituitary hormones. On the other hand, the electrical stimulation of nerve cells in the same regions dramatically increased the secretion of the hormones [see illustration below].

Thus the question was presented: Precisely how does the hypothalamus regulate the secretory activity of the anterior pituitary? The results produced by electrocoagulation and electrical stimulation of the hypothalamus suggested some kind of neural mechanism. One objection to this theory was rather hard to overcome. Careful anatomical studies over many years had clearly established that there were no nerve fibers extending from the hypothalamus to the anterior pituitary. The only nerve fibers found in the pituitary stalk were those that terminate in the posterior lobe.

A way out of the dilemma was provided by an entirely different working hypothesis, suggested by the discovery in 1936 of blood vessels of a peculiar type that were shown to extend from the floor of the hypothalamus through the pituitary stalk to the anterior pituitary [see bottom illustration on opposite

page]. If these tiny blood vessels were cut, the secretions of the anterior pituitary would instantly decrease. If the capillary vessels regenerated across the surgical cut, the secretions resumed.

Accordingly a new hypothesis was put forward about 1945 with which the name of the late G. W. Harris of the University of Oxford will remain associated. The hypothesis proposed that hypothalamic control of the secretory activity of the anterior pituitary could be neurochemical: some substance manufactured by nerve cells in the hypothalamus could be released into the capillary vessels that run from the hypothalamus to the anterior pituitary, where it could be delivered to the endocrine cells of the gland. On reaching these endocrine cells the substance of hypothalamic origin would somehow stimulate the secretion of the various anterior pituitary hormones.

The hypothesis that pituitary function is controlled by neurohormones originating in the hypothalamus was soon well established on the basis of intensive physiological studies in several laboratories. The next problem was therefore to isolate and characterize the postulated hypothalamic hormones. It was logical to guess that the hormones might be polypeptides of small molecular weight, since it had been well established that the two known neurosecretory products of hypothalamic origin, oxytocin and vasopressin, are each composed of eight amino acids. Indeed, in 1955 it was reported that crude aqueous hypothalamic extracts designed to contain polypeptides were able specifically to stimulate the secretion of ACTH, the pituitary hormone that controls the secretion of the steroid hormones of the adrenal cortex.

It was quickly demonstrated that none of the substances known to originate in the central nervous system (such as epinephrine, acetylcholine, vasopressin and oxytocin) could account for the ACTH-releasing activity observed in the extract of hypothalamic tissue. It therefore seemed reasonable to postulate the existence and involvement in this phenomenon of a new substance designated (adreno)corticotropin-releasing factor, or CRF. Several laboratories then undertook the apparently simple task of purifying CRF from hypothalamic extracts, with the final goal of isolating it and establishing its chemical structure. Seventeen years later the task still remains to be accomplished. Technical difficulties involving the methods

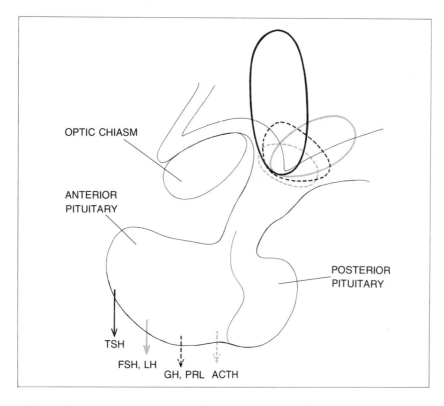

OPTIC CHIASM

ANTERIOR PITUITARY

POSTERIOR PITUITARY

TSH

FSH, LH

GH, PRL ACTH

RELATION between the hypothalamus and anterior pituitary was established experimentally. Lesions in specific regions of the hypothalamus interfere with secretion by the anterior lobe of specific hormones; electrical stimulation of those regions stimulates secretion of the hormones. The regions associated with each hormone are mapped schematically.

of assaying for CRF, together with certain peculiar characteristics of the molecule, have defied the enthusiasm, ingenuity and hard work of several groups of investigators.

More rewarding results were obtained in a closely related effort. About 1960 it was clearly established that the same crude extracts of hypothalamic tissue were able to stimulate the secretion of not only ACTH but also the three other pituitary hormones mentioned above: thyrotropin (TSH) and the two gonadotropins (LH and FSH). TSH is the pituitary hormone that controls the function of the thyroid gland, which in turn secretes the two hormones thyroxine and triiodothyronine. LH controls the secretion of the steroid hormones responsible for the male or female sexual characteristics; it also triggers ovulation. FSH controls the development and maturation of the germ cells: the spermatozoa and the ova. In reality the way in which LH and FSH work together is considerably more complicated than this somewhat simplistic description suggests.

Results obtained between 1960 and 1962 were best explained by proposing the existence of three separate hypothalamic releasing factors: TRF (the TSH-releasing factor), LRF (the LH-releasing factor) and FRF (the FSH-releasing factor). The effort began at once to isolate and characterize TRF, LRF and FRF. Whereas it was difficult to find a good assay for CRF, a simple and highly reliable biological assay was devised for TRF. At first, however, the assays for LRF and FRF still left much to be desired.

With a good method available for assaying TRF, progress was initially rapid. Within a few months after its discovery TRF had been prepared in a form many thousands of times purer. Preparations of TRF obtained from the brains of sheep showed biological activity in doses as small as one microgram. A great deal of physiological information was obtained with those early preparations. For example, the thyroid hormones somehow inhibit their own secretion when they reach a certain level in the blood. This fact had been known for 40 years and was the first evidence of a negative feedback in endocrine regulation. Studies with TRF showed that the feedback control takes place at the level of the pituitary gland as the result of some kind of competition between the number of available molecules of thyroid hormones and of TRF. Other significant observations were made on the gonadotropin-releasing factors when

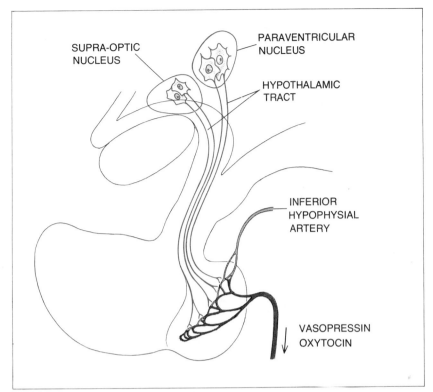

NEURAL CONNECTIONS could not explain the relation of the hypothalamus and the anterior lobe. The only significant nerve fibers connecting hypothalamus and pituitary run from two hypothalamic centers to the posterior lobe. They transmit oxytocin and vasopressin, two hormones manufactured in the hypothalamus and stored in the posterior lobe.

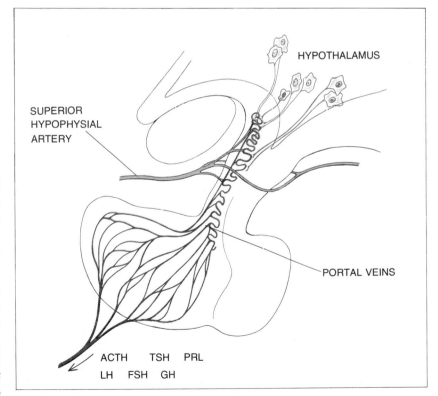

VASCULAR CONNECTIONS between hypothalamus and anterior lobe were eventually discovered: a network of capillaries reaching the base of the hypothalamus supplies portal veins that enter the anterior pituitary. Small hypothalamic nerve fibers apparently deliver to the capillaries releasing factors that stimulate secretion of the anterior-lobe hormones.

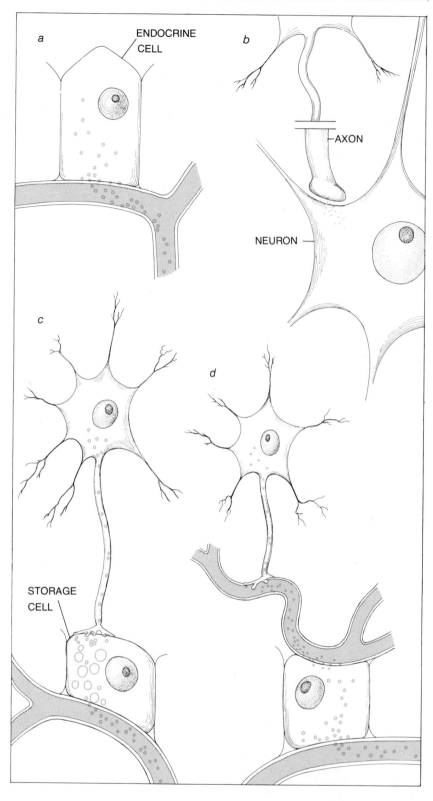

NEUROHUMORAL SECRETIONS involved in hypothalamic-pituitary interactions differ from classical hormone secretion and classical nerve-cell communication. A classical endocrine cell (such as those in the anterior pituitary or the adrenal cortex, for example) secretes its hormonal product directly into the bloodstream (*a*). At a classical synapse, the axon, or fiber, from one nerve cell releases locally a transmitter substance that activates the next cell (*b*). In neurosecretion of oxytocin or vasopressin the hormones are secreted by nerve cells and pass through their axons to storage cells in the posterior pituitary, eventually to be secreted into the bloodstream (*c*). Hypothalamic (releasing factor) hormones go from the neurons that secrete them into local capillaries, which carry them through portal veins to endocrine cells in the anterior lobe, whose secretions they in turn stimulate (*d*).

purified preparations, also active at microgram levels, were injected in experimental animals, for instance to produce ovulation.

It soon became apparent, however, that the isolation and chemical characterization of TRF, LRF and FRF would not be simple. The preparations active in microgram doses were chemically heterogeneous; they showed no clear-cut indication of a major component. It was also realized that each fragment of hypothalamus obtained from the brain of a sheep or another animal contained nearly infinitesimal quantities of the releasing factors. The isolation of enough of each factor to make its chemical characterization possible would therefore require the processing of an enormous number of hypothalamic fragments. Two groups of workers in the U.S. undertook this challenge: a group headed by A. V. Schally at the Tulane University School of Medicine and our own group, first at the Baylor University College of Medicine in Houston and then at the Salk Institute in La Jolla, Calif.

Over a period of four years the Tulane group worked with extracts from perhaps two million pig brains. Our laboratory collected, dissected and processed close to five million hypothalamic fragments from the brains of sheep. Since one sheep brain has a wet weight of about 100 grams, this meant handling 500 tons of brain tissue. From this amount we removed seven tons of hypothalamic tissue (about 1.5 grams per brain). Semi-industrial methods had to be developed in order to handle, extract and purify such large quantities of material. Finally in 1968 one milligram of a preparation of TRF was obtained that appeared to be homogeneous by all available criteria.

On careful measurement the entire milligram could be accounted for by the sole presence of three amino acids: histidine, glutamic acid and proline. Moreover, the three amino acids were present in equal amounts, which suggested that we were dealing with a relatively simple polypeptide perhaps as small as a tripeptide. In the determination of peptide sequences it is customary to subject the sample to attack by proteolytic enzymes, which cleave the peptide bonds holding the polypeptide chain together in well-established ways. Pure TRF, however, was shown to be resistant to all the proteolytic enzymes used. Since we could spare only a tiny amount of our precious one-milligram sample for studies of molecular weight, we could not obtain a

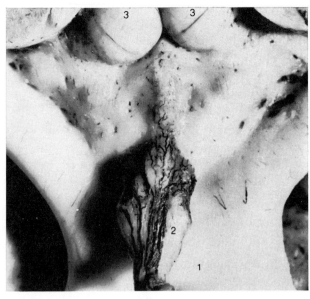

BLOOD VESSELS linking the hypothalamus and the anterior pituitary are seen in photographs made by Henri Duvernoy of the University of Besancon. The photomicrograph (*left*) shows some of the individual loops that characterize the capillary network at the base of the hypothalamus of a dog. The ascending branch of one loop is clearly seen (*1*); the loop comes close to the floor of the third ventricle (*2*) and then descends (*3*), carrying with it the releasing factors that are secreted by this region of the hypothalamus and entering the pars tuberalis of the anterior lobe (*4*). The photograph of the floor of the human hypothalamus (*right*) shows the optic chiasm (*1*), the posterior side of the pituitary stalk with its portal veins (*2*) and the mammillary bodies of the brain (*3*).

precise value for that important measurement. On the basis of inferential evidence, however, it seemed to be reasonable to assume that the molecular weight of TRF could not be more than 1,500.

With small molecules it is often possible to use methods based on the technique of mass spectrometry to obtain in a matter of hours the complete molecular structure of the compound under investigation. Because of the minute quantities of TRF available such efforts on our part were frustrated; the mass-spec-

trometric methods available to us in 1969 were not sensitive enough to indicate the structure of our unknown substance. Other approaches involve the use of infrared or nuclear magnetic-resonance spectrometry, which can provide direct insight into molecular structure. Here too the techniques then available were inadequate for providing clear-cut information about polypeptide samples that weighed only a few micrograms.

Confronted with nothing but dead ends, we decided on an entirely different

approach to finding the structure of TRF. That approach was first to synthesize each of six possible tripeptides composed of the three amino acids known to be present in TRF: histidine (abbreviated His), glutamic acid (Glu) and proline (Pro). The six tripeptides were then assayed for their biological activity. None showed any activity when they were injected at doses of up to a million times the level of the active natural TRF.

Was this another dead end? Not quite. Our synthetic polypeptides all had a

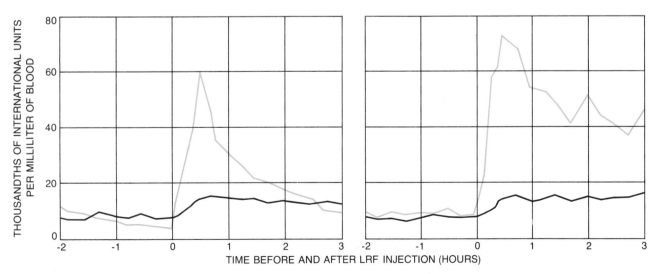

HYPOTHALAMIC HORMONES have clinical implications and applications. For example, women with no pituitary or ovarian defect respond to the administration of synthetic LRF by secreting normal amounts of the hormones LH and FSH. Curves show effect of LRF on secretion of LH (*color*) and FSH (*black*) in a normal woman on the third (*left*) and 11th (*right*) day of menstrual cycle.

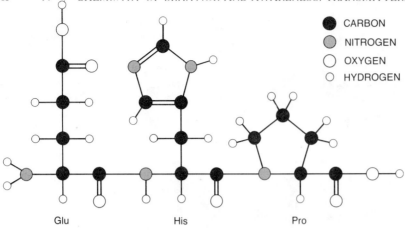

CARBON
NITROGEN
OXYGEN
HYDROGEN

Glu   His   Pro

AMINO ACID CONTENT of TRF, the releasing factor for thyroid-stimulating hormone (TSH), was established: glutamic acid, histidine and proline in equal proportions. Each of six possible tripeptides was synthesized; one is diagrammed. None was active biologically.

peptide at levels of only a few micrograms.

Meanwhile, armed with knowledge about the structure of other hormones, we modified the synthetic pGlu-His-Pro-OH to pGlu-His-Pro-NH$_2$ by replacing the hydroxyl group with an amino group (NH$_2$) to produce the primary amide [see top illustration on opposite page]. This substance proved to have the same biological activity as the natural TRF. At length the complete structure of the natural TRF was obtained by high-resolution mass spectrometry. It turned out to be the structure pGlu-His-Pro-NH$_2$. The time was late 1969. Thus TRF not only was the first of the hypothalamic hormones to be fully characterized but also was immediately available by synthesis in amounts many millions of times greater than the hormone present in one sheep hypothalamus. TRF from pig brains was subsequently shown to have the same molecular structure as TRF from sheep brains.

Characterization of the hypothalamic releasing factor LRF, which controls the secretion of the gonadotropin LH, followed rapidly. Isolated from the side fractions of the programs for the isolation of TRF, LRF was shown in 1971 to be a polypeptide composed of 10 amino acids. Six of the amino acids are not found in TRF: tryptophan (Trp), serine (Ser), tyrosine (Tyr), glycine (Gly), leucine (Leu) and arginine (Arg). The full sequence of LRF is pGlu-His-Trp-Ser-Tyr-Gly-Leu-Arg-Pro-Gly-NH$_2$ [see bottom illustration on these two pages]. Although this structure is more compli-

free amino group (NH$_2$) at the end of the molecule designated the N terminus. We knew that in several well-characterized hormones the N-terminus end was not free; it was blocked by a small substitute group of some kind. Indeed, we had evidence from the small quantity of natural TRF that its N terminus was also blocked. To block the N terminus of our six candidate polypeptides was not difficult: we heated them in the presence of acetic anhydride, which typically couples an acetyl group (CH$_3$CO) to the N terminus. When these "protected" tripeptides were tested, the results were unequivocal. The biological activity of the sequence Glu-His-Pro, and that sequence alone, was qualitatively indistinguishable from the activity of natural TRF. Quantitatively, how-

ever, there was still a considerable difference between the synthetic product and natural TRF. Next it was shown that the protective effect of heating Glu-His-Pro with the acetic anhydride had been to convert the glutamic acid at the N terminus into a ring-shaped form known as pyroglutamic acid (pGlu).

We now had available gram quantities of the synthetic tripeptide pGlu-His-Pro-OH. (The OH is a hydroxyl group at the end of the molecule opposite the N terminus.) Accordingly we could bring into play all the methods that had yielded no information with the microgram quantities of natural TRF. Several of the techniques were modified, particularly with the aim of obtaining mass spectra of the synthetic

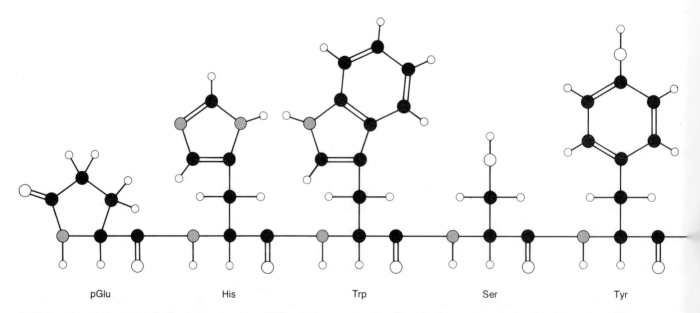

pGlu   His   Trp   Ser   Tyr

LRF, the releasing factor for the luteinizing hormone (LH), which affects the activity of the gonads, was characterized and synthesized

soon after. First the hormone was isolated and its amino acid content was determined. Then their intramolecular sequence was es-

cated than the structure of TRF, it begins with the same two amino acids (pGlu-His) and has the same group at the other terminus (NH_2).

It turns out that LRF also stimulates the secretion of the other gonadotropin, FSH, although not as powerfully as it stimulates the secretion of LH. It has been proposed that LRF may be the sole hypothalamic controller of the secretion of the two gonadotropins: LH and FSH.

There is good physiological evidence that the hypothalamus is also involved in the control of the secretion of the other two important pituitary hormones: prolactin and growth hormone. Curiously, prolactin is as plentiful in males as in females, but its role in male physiology is still a mystery. The hypothalamic mechanism involved in the control of the secretion of prolactin or growth hormone is not fully understood. It is quite possible that the secretion of these two pituitary hormones is controlled not by releasing factors alone but perhaps jointly by releasing factors and specific hypothalamic hormones that somehow act as inhibitors of the secretion of prolactin or growth hormone. If it should turn out that inhibitory hormones rather than stimulative ones are involved in the regulation of prolactin and growth hormone, one should not be too surprised. The brain provides many examples of inhibitory and stimulative systems working in parallel.

The hypothalamic hormones TRF and LRF are both now available by synthesis in unlimited quantities. Both are highly active in stimulating pituitary functions in humans. TRF is already a

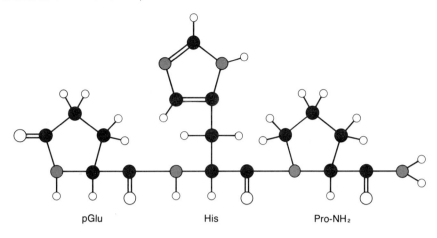

TRIPEPTIDES were modified in an effort to characterize the releasing factor. When the sequence glutamic acid–histidine-proline was modified by forming the glutamic acid into a ring and converting the proline end (*right*) to an amide, it was found to be TRF.

pGlu   His   Pro-NH₂

powerful tool for exploring pituitary functions in several diseases characterized by the abnormality of one or several of the pituitary secretions. There is increasing evidence that most patients with such abnormalities (primarily children) actually have normally functioning glands, since they respond promptly to the administration of synthetic hypothalamic hormones. Evidently their abnormalities are due to hypothalamic rather than pituitary deficiencies. These deficiencies can now be successfully treated by the administration of the hypothalamic polypeptide TRF.

Similarly, an increasing number of women who have no ovulatory menstrual cycle and who show no pituitary or ovarian defect begin to secrete normal amounts of the gonadotropins LH and FSH after the administration of LRF. The administration of synthetic LRF should therefore be the method of choice for the treatment of those cases of infertility where the functional defect resides in the hypothalamus-pituitary system. Indeed, ovulation can be induced in women by the administration of synthetic LRF. On the other hand, knowledge of the structure of the LRF molecule may open up an entirely novel approach to fertility control. Synthetic compounds closely related to LRF in structure may act as inhibitors of the native LRF. Two such analogues of LRF, made by modifying the histidine in the hormone, have been reported as antagonists of LRF. It is therefore possible that LRF antagonists will be used as contraceptives.

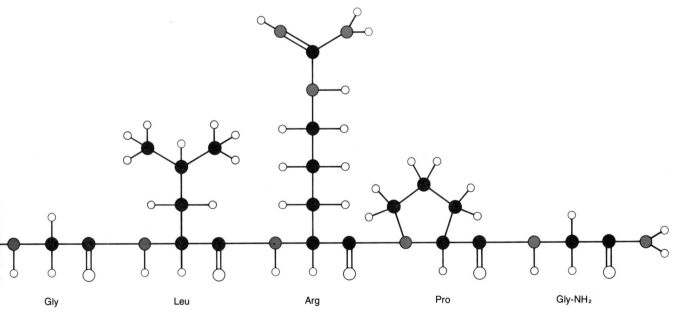

Gly   Leu   Arg   Pro   Gly-NH₂

tablished and reproduced by synthesis; the synthetic replicate shown here was found to have full biological activity. In addition to stimulating LH activity, LRF also stimulates the secretion of another gonadotropic hormone, FSH, although not so powerfully.

Stress and Behavior

by Seymour Levine
January 1971

*The chain of pituitary and adrenal hormones that
regulates responses to stress plays a major role in
learning and other behaviors. It may be that effective
behavior depends on some optimum level of stress*

Hans Selye's concept of the general "stress syndrome" has surely been one of the fruitful ideas of this era in biological and medical research. He showed that in response to stress the body of a mammal mobilizes a system of defensive reactions involving the pituitary and adrenal glands. The discovery illuminated the causes and symptoms of a number of diseases and disorders. More than that, it has opened a new outlook on the functions of the pituitary-adrenal system. One can readily understand how the hormones of this system may defend the body against physiological insult, for example by suppressing inflammation and thus preventing tissue damage. It is a striking fact, however, that the system's activity can be evoked by all kinds of stresses, not only by severe somatic stresses such as disease, burns, bone fractures, temperature extremes, surgery and drugs but also by a wide range of psychological conditions: fear, apprehension, anxiety, a loud noise, crowding, even mere exposure to a novel environment. Indeed, most of the situations that activate the pituitary-adrenal system do not involve tissue damage. It appears, therefore, that these hormones in animals, including man, may have many functions in addition to the defense of tissue integrity, and as a psychologist I have been investigating possible roles of the pituitary-adrenal system in the regulation of behavior.

The essentials of the system's operation in response to stress are as follows. Information concerning the stress (coming either from external sources through the sensory system or from internal sources such as a change in body temperature or in the blood's composition) is received and integrated by the central nervous system and is presumably delivered to the hypothalamus, the basal area of the brain. The hypothalamus secretes a substance called the corticotropin-releasing factor (CRF), which stimulates the pituitary to secrete the hormone ACTH. This in turn stimulates the cortex of the adrenal gland to step up its synthesis and secretion of hormones, particularly those known as glucocorticoids. In man the glucocorticoid is predominantly hydrocortisone; in many lower animals such as the rat it is corticosterone.

The entire mechanism is exquisitely controlled by a feedback system. When the glucocorticoid level in the circulating blood is elevated, the central nervous system, receiving the message, shuts off the process that leads to secretion of the stimulating hormone ACTH. Two experimental demonstrations have most clearly verified the existence of this feedback process. If the adrenal gland is removed from an animal, the pituitary puts out abnormal amounts of ACTH, presumably because the absence of the adrenal hormone frees it from restriction of this secretion. On the other hand, if crystals of glucocorticoid are implanted in the hypothalamus, the animal's secretion of ACTH stops almost completely, just as if the adrenal cortex were releasing large quantities of the glucocorticoid.

Now, it is well known that a high level of either of these hormones (ACTH or glucocorticoid) in the circulating blood can have dramatic effects on the brain. Patients who have received glucocorticoids for treatment of an illness have on occasion suffered severe mental changes, sometimes leading to psychosis. And patients with a diseased condition of the adrenal gland that caused it to secrete an abnormal amount of cortical hormone have also shown effects on the brain, including changes in the pattern of electrical activity and convulsions.

Two long-term studies of my own, previously reported in *Scientific American* [see "Stimulation in Infancy," Offprint 436, and "Sex Differences in the Brain," Offprint 498], strongly indicated that hormones play an important part in the development of behavior. One of these studies showed that rats subjected to shocks and other stresses in early life developed normally and were able to cope well with stresses later, whereas animals that received no stimulation in infancy grew up to be timid and deviant in behavior. At the adult stage the two groups differed sharply in the response of the pituitary-adrenal system to stress: the animals that had been stimulated in infancy showed a prompt and effective hormonal response; those that had not been stimulated responded slowly and ineffectively. The other study, based on the administration or deprivation of sex hormones at a critical early stage of development in male and female rats, indicated that these treatments markedly affected the animals' later behavior, nonsexual as well as sexual. It is noteworthy that the sex hormones are steroids rather similar to those produced by the adrenal cortex.

Direct evidence of the involvement of the pituitary-adrenal system in overt behavior was reported by two groups of experimenters some 15 years ago. Mortimer H. Appley, now at the University of Massachusetts, and his co-workers were investigating the learning of an avoidance response in rats. The animals were placed in a "shuttle box" divided into two compartments by a barrier. An electric shock was applied, and if the animals crossed the barrier, they could avoid or terminate the shock. The avoidance response consisted in making the move

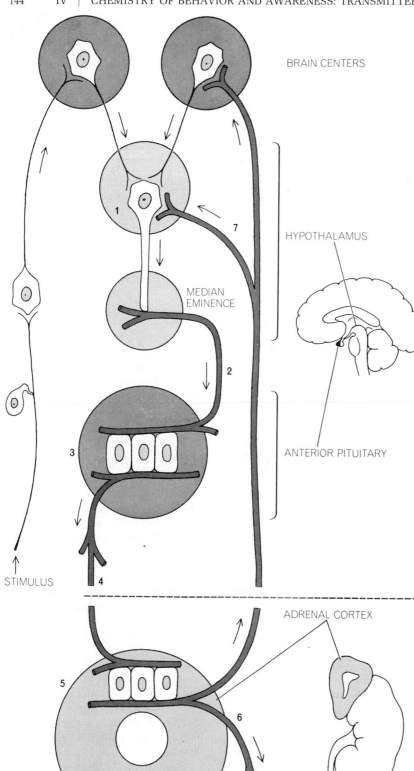

BRAIN CENTERS

HYPOTHALAMUS

MEDIAN EMINENCE

ANTERIOR PITUITARY

STIMULUS

ADRENAL CORTEX

PITUITARY-ADRENAL SYSTEM involves nerve cells and hormones in a feedback loop. A stress stimulus reaching neurosecretory cells of the hypothalamus in the base of the brain (*1*) stimulates them to release corticotropin-releasing factor (CRF), which moves through short blood vessels (*2*) to the anterior lobe of the pituitary gland (*3*). Pituitary cells thereupon release adrenocorticotrophic hormone (ACTH) into the circulation (*4*). The ACTH stimulates cells of the adrenal cortex (*5*) to secrete glucocorticoid hormones (primarily hydrocortisone in man) into the circulation (*6*). When glucocorticoids reach neurosecretory cells or other brain cells (it is not clear which), they modulate CRF production (*7*).

across the barrier when a conditioned stimulus, a buzzer signaling the onset of the shock, was sounded. Appley found that when the pituitary gland was removed surgically from rats, their learning of the avoidance response was severely retarded. It turned out that an injection of ACTH in pituitary-deprived rats could restore the learning ability to normal. At about the same time Robert E. Miller and Robert Murphy of the University of Pittsburgh reported experiments showing that ACTH could affect extinction of the avoidance response. Normally if the shocks are discontinued, so that the animal receives no shock when it fails to react to the conditioned stimulus (the buzzer in this case), the avoidance response to the buzzer is gradually extinguished. Miller and Murphy found that when they injected ACTH in animals during the learning period, the animals continued to make the avoidance response anyway, long after it was extinguished in animals that had not received the ACTH injection. In short, ACTH inhibited the extinction process.

These findings were not immediately followed up, perhaps mainly because little was known at the time about the details of the pituitary-adrenal system and only rudimentary techniques were available for studying it. Since then purified preparations of the hormones involved and new techniques for accurate measurement of these substances in the circulating blood have been developed, and the system is now under intensive study. Most of the experimental investigation is being conducted at three centers: in the Institute of Pharmacology at the University of Utrecht under David de Wied, in the Institute of Physiology at the University of Pecs in Hungary under Elemér Endroczi and in our own laboratories in the department of psychiatry at Stanford University.

The new explorations of the pituitary-adrenal system began where the ground had already been broken: in studies of the learning and extinction of the avoidance response, primarily by use of the shuttle box. De Wied verified the role of ACTH both in avoidance learning and in inhibiting extinction of the response. He did this in physiological terms by means of several experiments. He verified the fact that removal of the pituitary gland severely retards the learning of a conditioned avoidance response. He also removed the adrenal gland from rats and found that the response was then not extinguished, presumably because adrenal hormones were no longer present to restrict the pituitary's output of ACTH. When he excised the pituitary, thus eliminating the secretion of ACTH, the animals returned to near-normal behavior in the extinction of the avoidance response.

In further experiments De Wied injected glucocorticoids, including corticosterone, the principal steroid hormone of the rat's adrenal cortex, into animals that had had the adrenal gland, but not the pituitary, removed; as expected, this had the effect of speeding up the extinction of the avoidance response. Similarly, the administration to such animals of dexamethasone, a synthetic glucocorticoid that is known to be a potent inhibitor of ACTH, resulted in rapid extinction of the avoidance response; the larger the dose, the more rapid the extinction. Curiously, De Wied found that corticosterone and dexamethasone promoted extinction even in animals that lacked the pituitary gland, the source of ACTH. This indicated that the glucocorticoid can produce its effect not only through suppression of ACTH but also, in some way, by acting directly on the central nervous system. It has recently been found, on the other hand, that there may be secretions from the pituitary other than ACTH that can affect learning and

inhibit extinction of the avoidance response. The inhibition can be produced, for example, by a truncated portion of the ACTH molecule consisting of the first 10 amino acids in the sequence of 39 in the rat's ACTH—a molecular fragment that has no influence on the adrenal cortex. The same fragment, along with other smaller peptides recently isolated by De Wied, can also overcome the deficit in avoidance learning that is produced by ablation of the pituitary.

With an apparatus somewhat different from the shuttle box we obtained further light in our laboratory on ACTH's effects on behavior. We first train the animals to press a bar to obtain water. After this learning has been established the animal is given an electric shock on pressing the bar. This causes the animal to avoid approaching the bar (called "passive avoidance") for a time, but after several days the animal will usually return to it in the effort to get water and then will quickly lose its fear of the bar if it is not shocked. We found, however, that if the animal was given doses of ACTH after the shock, it generally failed to return to the bar at all, even though it was very thirsty. That is to say, ACTH suppressed the bar-pressing response, or, to put it another way, it strengthened the

passive-avoidance response. In animals with the pituitary gland removed, injections of ACTH suppressed a return to bar-pressing after a shock but injections of hydrocortisone did not have this effect.

The experiments I have described so far have involved behavior under the stress of fear and anxiety. Our investigations with the bar-pressing device go on to reveal that the pituitary-adrenal system also comes into play in the regulation of behavior based on "appetitive" responses (as opposed to avoidance responses). Suppose we eliminate the electric shock factor and simply arrange that after the animal has learned to press the bar for water it fails to obtain water on later trials. Normally the animal's bar-pressing behavior is then quickly extinguished. We found, however, that when we injected ACTH in the animals in these circumstances, the extinction of bar-pressing was delayed; the rats went on pressing the bar for some time although they received no water as reinforcement. Following up this finding, we measured the corticosterone levels in the blood of normal, untreated rats both when they were reinforced and when they were not reinforced on pressing the

WARNING
LIGHT

SPEAKER

SPEAKER

ELECTRIC GRID

PHOTOELECTRIC CELL

"SHUTTLE BOX" used for studying avoidance behavior is a two-compartment cage. The floor can be electrically charged. A shock is delivered on the side occupied by the rat (detected by the photocell). The rat can avoid the shock by learning to respond to the conditioned stimulus: a light and noise delivered briefly before the shock. The avoidance response, once learned, is slowly "extinguished" if the conditioned stimulus is no longer accompanied by a shock. Injections of ACTH inhibited the extinction process.

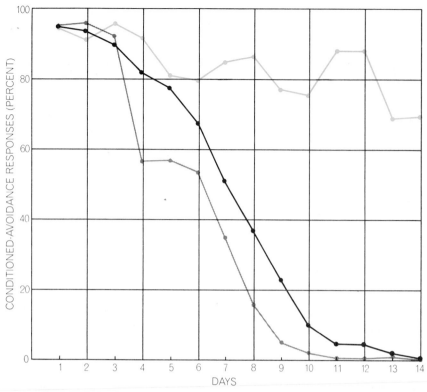

EXTINCTION of the avoidance response was studied by David de Wied of the University of Utrecht. Removal of the adrenal gland inhibited extinction (*color*); the rats responded to the conditioned stimulus in the absence of shock, presumably because adrenal hormones were not available to restrict ACTH output. When the pituitary was removed, the rate of extinction (*gray*) was about the same as in rats given only a sham operation (*black*).

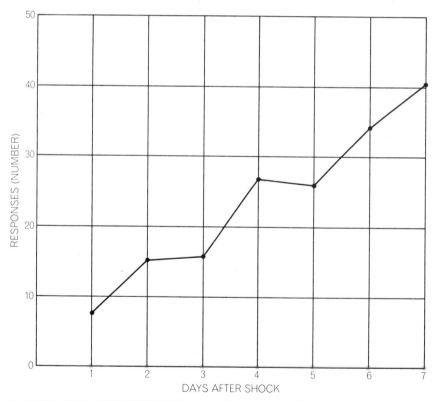

PASSIVE AVOIDANCE BEHAVIOR is studied by observing how rats, trained to press a bar for water, avoid the bar after they get a shock on pressing it. Before being shocked rats pressed the bar about 75 times a day. After the shock the control animals returned to the bar and, finding they were not shocked, gradually increased their responses (*black curve*). Rats injected with ACTH stayed away (*color*): ACTH strengthens the avoidance response.

bar. The animals that received no water reinforcement, with the result of rapid extinction of bar-pressing, showed a marked rise in activity of the pituitary-adrenal system during this period, whereas in animals that received water each time they pressed the bar there was no change in the hormonal output. In short, the extinction of appetitive behavior in this case clearly involved the pituitary-adrenal system.

Further investigations have now shown that the system affects a much wider range of behavior than learning and extinction. One of the areas that has been studied is habituation: the gradual subsidence of reactions that had appeared on first exposure to a novel stimulus when the stimulus is repeated. An organism presented with an unexpected stimulus usually exhibits what Ivan Pavlov called an orientation reflex, which includes increased electrical activity in the brain, a reduction of blood flow to the extremities, changes in the electrical resistance of the skin, a rise in the level of adrenal-steroid hormones in the blood and some overt motor activity of the body.

If the stimulus is repeated frequently, these reactions eventually disappear; the organism is then said to be habituated to the stimulus. Endroczi and his co-workers recently examined the influence of ACTH on habituation of one of the reactions in human subjects—the increase of electrical activity in the brain, as indicated by electroencephalography. The electrical activity evoked in the human brain by a novel sound or a flickering light generally subsides, after repetition of the stimulus, into a pattern known as electroencephalogram (EEG) synchronization, which is taken to be a sign of habituation. Endroczi's group found that treatment of their subjects with ACTH or the 10-amino-acid fragment of ACTH produced a marked delay in the appearance of the synchronization pattern, indicating that the hormone inhibits the process of habituation.

Experiments with animals in our laboratory support that finding. The stimulus we used was a sudden sound that produces a "startle" response in rats, which is evidenced by vigorous body movements. After a number of repetitions of the sound stimulus the startle response fades. It turned out that rats deprived of the adrenal gland (and consequently with a high level of ACTH in their circulation) took significantly longer than intact animals to habituate to the sound stimulus. An implant of the adrenal hormone hydrocortisone in the hy-

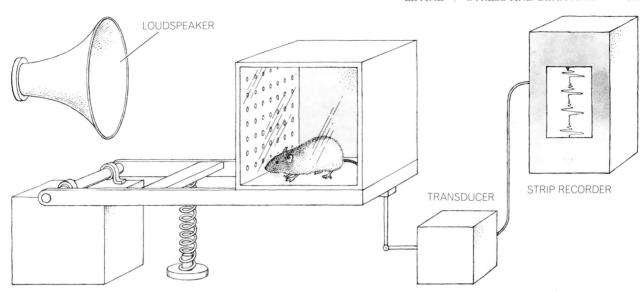

"STARTLE" RESPONSE is measured by placing a rat in a cage with a movable floor and exposing it to a sudden, loud noise. The rat tenses or jumps, and the resulting movement of the floor is transduced into movement of a pen on recording paper. After a number of repetitions of the noise the rat becomes habituated to it and the magnitude of the animal's startle response diminishes.

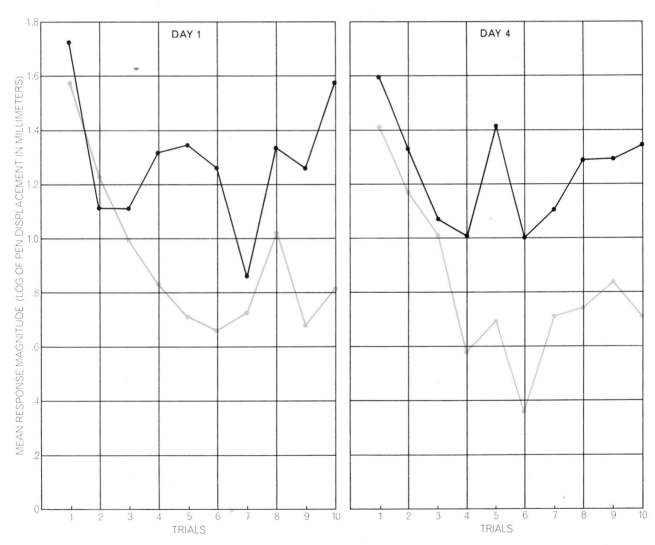

HABITUATION is affected by the pituitary-adrenal system. If a crystal of the adrenal hormone hydrocortisone is implanted in a rat's hypothalamus, preventing ACTH secretion, habituation is speeded up, as shown here. The mean startle response (shown as the logarithm of the recording pen's movement) falls away more rapidly in implanted rats (color) than in control animals (black).

pothalamus, on the other hand, speeded up habituation.

A series of studies by Robert I. Henkin of the National Heart Institute has demonstrated that hormones of the adrenal cortex play a crucial role in the sensory functions in man. Patients whose adrenal gland has been removed surgically or is functioning poorly show a marked increase in the ability to detect sensory signals, particularly in the senses of taste, smell, hearing and proprioception (sensing of internal signals). On the other hand, patients with Cushing's syndrome, marked by excessive secretion from the adrenal cortex, suffer a considerable dulling of the senses. Henkin showed that sensory detection and the integration of sensory signals are regulated by a complex feedback system involving interactions of the endocrine system and the nervous system. Although patients with a deficiency of adrenal cortex hormones are extraordinarily sensitive in the detection of sensory signals, they have difficulty integrating the signals, so that they cannot evaluate variations in properties such as loudness and tonal qualities and have some difficulty understanding speech. Proper treatment with steroid hormones of the adrenal gland can restore normal sensory detection and perception in such patients.

Henkin has been able to detect the effects of the adrenal corticosteroids on sensory perception even in normal subjects. There is a daily cycle of secretion of these steroid hormones by the adrenal cortex. Henkin finds that when adrenocortical secretion is at its highest level, taste detection and recognition is at its lowest, and vice versa.

In our laboratory we have found that the adrenal's steroid hormones can have a truly remarkable effect on the ability of animals to judge the passage of time. Some years ago Murray Sidman of the Harvard Medical School devised an experiment to test this capability. The animal is placed in an experimental chamber and every 20 seconds an electric shock is applied. By pressing a bar in the chamber the animal can prevent the shock from occurring, because the bar resets the triggering clock to postpone the shock for another 20 seconds. Thus the animal can avoid the shock altogether by appropriate timing of its presses on the bar. Adopting this device, we found that rats learned to press the bar at intervals averaging between 12 and 15 seconds. This prevented a majority of the shocks. We then gave the animals glucocorticoids and found that they became significantly more efficient!

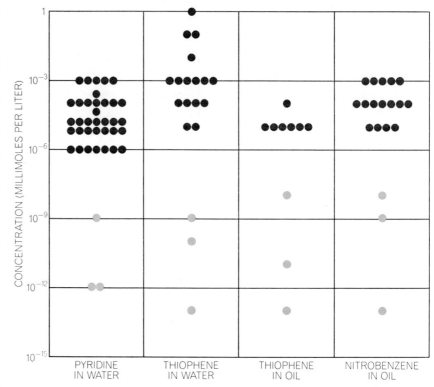

SENSORY FUNCTION is also affected by adrenocortical hormones. Robert I. Henkin of the National Heart Institute found that patients whose adrenal-hormone function is poor are much more sensitive to odor. Placing various chemicals in solution, he measured the detection threshold: the concentration at which an odor could be detected in the vapor. The threshold was much lower in the patients (*color*) than in normal volunteers (*black*).

They lengthened the interval between bar presses and took fewer shocks. Evidently under the influence of the hormones the rats were able to make finer discriminations concerning the passage of time. Monkeys also showed improvement in timing performance in response to treatment with ACTH.

The mechanism by which the pituitary-adrenal hormones act to regulate or influence behavior is still almost completely unknown. Obviously they must do so by acting on the brain. It is well known that hormones in general are targeted to specific sites and that the body tissues have a remarkable selectivity for them. The uterus, for instance, picks up and responds selectively to estrogen and progesterone among all the hormones circulating in the blood, and the seminal vesicles and prostate gland of the male select testosterone. There is now much evidence that organs of the brain may be similarly selective. Bruce Sherman McEwen of Rockefeller University has recently reported that the hippocampus, just below the cerebral cortex, appears to be a specific receptor site for hormones of the adrenal cortex, and other studies indicate that the lateral portion

of the hypothalamus may be a receptor site for gonadal hormones. We have the inviting prospect, therefore, that exploration of the brain to locate the receptor sites for the hormones of the pituitary-adrenal system, and studies of the hormones' action on the cells of these sites, may yield important information on how the system regulates behavior. Bela Bohun in Hungary has already demonstrated that implantation of small quantities of glucocorticoids in the reticular formation in the brain stem facilitates extinction of an avoidance response.

Since this system plays a key role in learning, habituation to novel stimuli, sensing and perception, it obviously has a high adaptive significance for mammals, including man. Its reactions to moderate stress may contribute greatly to the behavioral effectiveness and stability of the organism. Just as the studies of young animals showed, contrary to expectations, that some degree of stress in infancy is necessary for the development of normal, adaptive behavior, so the information we now have on the operations of the pituitary-adrenal system indicates that in many situations effective behavior in adult life may depend on exposure to some optimum level of stress.

The Hallucinogenic Drugs

by Frank Barron, Murray E. Jarvik and Sterling Bunnell, Jr.
April 1964

*These powerful alkaloids, tools for investigating
mental illness and perhaps for treating it, have become
the subject of a debate: Do their constructive
potentials outweigh their admitted hazards?*

Human beings have two powerful needs that are at odds with each other: to keep things the same, and to have something new happen. We like to feel secure, yet at times we like to be surprised. Too much predictability leads to monotony, but too little may lead to anxiety. To establish a balance between continuity and change is a task facing all organisms, individual and social, human and non-human.

Keeping things predictable is generally considered one of the functions of the ego. When a person perceives accurately, thinks clearly, plans wisely and acts appropriately—and represses maladaptive thoughts and emotions—we say that his ego is strong. But the strong ego is also inventive, open to many perceptions that at first may be disorganizing. Research on the personality traits of highly creative individuals has shown that they are particularly alert to the challenge of the contradictory and the unpredictable, and that they may even court the irrational in their own make-up as a source of new and unexpected insight. Indeed, through all recorded history and everywhere in the world men have gone to considerable lengths to seek unpredictability by disrupting the functioning of the ego. A change of scene, a change of heart, a change of mind: these are the popular prescriptions for getting out of a rut.

Among the common ways of changing "mind" must be reckoned the use of intoxicating substances. Alcohol has quite won the day for this purpose in the U.S. and much of the rest of the world. Consumed at a moderate rate and in sensible quantities, it can serve simultaneously as a euphoriant and tranquilizing agent before it finally dulls the faculties and puts one to sleep. In properly disposed individuals it may dissolve sexual inhibitions, relieve fear and anxiety, or stimulate meditation on the meaning of life. In spite of its costliness to individual and social health when it is used immoderately, alcohol retains its rank as first among the substances used by mankind to change mental experience. Its closest rivals in popularity are opium and its derivatives and various preparations of cannabis, such as hashish and marijuana.

This article deals with another group of such consciousness-altering substances: the "hallucinogens." The most important of these are mescaline, which comes from the peyote cactus *Lophophora williamsii;* psilocybin and psilocin, from such mushrooms as *Psilocybe mexicana* and *Stropharia cubensis;* and d-lysergic acid diethylamide (LSD), which is derived from ergot (*Claviceps purpurea*), a fungus that grows on rye and wheat. All are alkaloids more or less related to one another in chemical structure.

Various names have been applied to this class of substances. They produce distinctive changes in perception that are sometimes referred to as hallucinations, although usually the person under the influence of the drug can distinguish his visions from reality, and even when they seem quite compelling he is able to attribute them to the action of the drug. If, therefore, the term "hallucination" is reserved for perceptions that the perceiver himself firmly believes indicate the existence of a corresponding object or event, but for which other observers can find no objective basis, then the "hallucinogens" only rarely produce hallucinations. There are several other names for this class of drugs. They have been called "psychotomimetic" because in some cases the effects seem to mimic psychosis [see "Experimental Psychoses," by six staff members of the Boston Psychopathic Hospital; Scientific American, June, 1955]. Some observers prefer to use the term "psychedelic" to suggest that unsuspected capacities of the imagination are sometimes revealed in the perceptual changes.

The hallucinogens are currently a subject of intense debate and concern in medical and psychological circles. At issue is the degree of danger they present to the psychological health of the person who uses them. This has become an important question because of a rapidly increasing interest in the drugs among laymen. The recent controversy at Harvard University, stemming at first from methodological disagreements

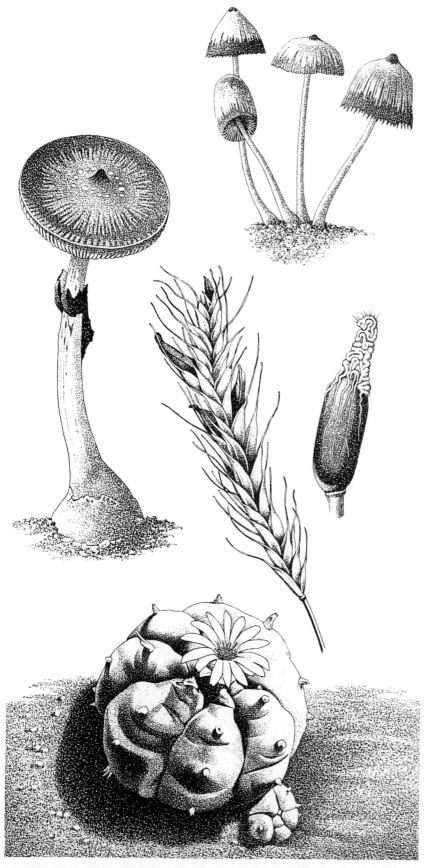

among investigators but subsequently involving the issue of protection of the mental health of the student body, indicated the scope of popular interest in taking the drugs and the consequent public concern over their possible misuse.

There are, on the other hand, constructive uses of the drugs. In spite of obvious differences between the "model psychoses" produced by these drugs and naturally occurring psychoses, there are enough similarities to warrant intensive investigation along these lines. The drugs also provide the only link, however tenuous, between human psychoses and aberrant behavior in animals, in which physiological mechanisms can be studied more readily than in man. Beyond this many therapists feel that there is a specialized role for the hallucinogens in the treatment of psychoneuroses. Other investigators are struck by the possibility of using the drugs to facilitate meditation and aesthetic discrimination and to stimulate the imagination. These possibilities, taken in conjunction with the known hazards, are the bases for the current professional concern and controversy.

In evaluating potential uses and misuses of the hallucinogens, one can draw on a considerable body of knowledge from such disciplines as anthropology, pharmacology, biochemistry, psychology and psychiatry.

In some primitive societies the plants from which the major hallucinogens are derived have been known for millenniums and have been utilized for divination, curing, communion with supernatural powers and meditation to improve self-understanding or social unity; they have also served such mundane purposes as allaying hunger and relieving discomfort or boredom. In the Western Hemisphere the ingestion of hallucinogenic plants in pre-Columbian times was limited to a zone extending from what is now the southwestern U.S. to the northwestern basin of the Amazon. Among the Aztecs there were professional diviners who achieved inspiration by eating either peyote, hallucinogenic mushrooms (which the Aztecs called *teo-nanacatyl,* or "god's flesh") or other hallucinogenic plants. *Teonanacatyl* was said to have been distributed at the coronation of Montezuma to make the ceremony seem more spectacular. In the years following the conquest of Mexico there were reports of communal mushroom rites among the Aztecs and other Indians of southern Mexico. The communal use has almost died out today, but in several

NATURAL SOURCES of the main hallucinogens are depicted. Psilocybin comes from the mushrooms *Stropharia cubensis* (*top left*) and *Psilocybe mexicana* (*top right*). LSD is synthesized from an alkaloid in ergot (*Claviceps purpurea*), a fungus that grows on cereal grains; an ergot-infested rye seed head is shown (*center*) together with a larger-scale drawing of the ergot fungus. Mescaline is from the peyote cactus *Lophophora williamsii* (*bottom*).

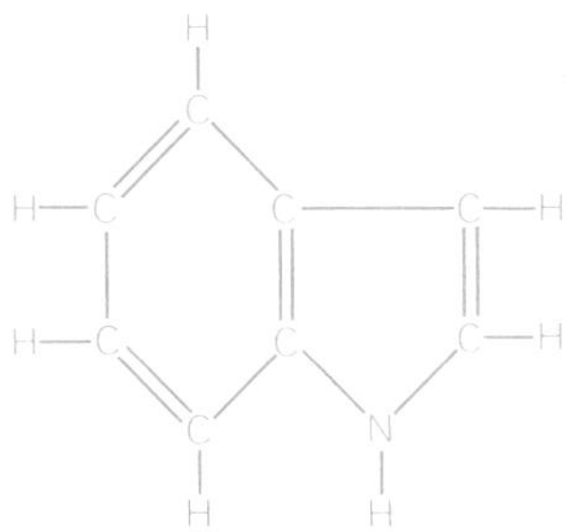

INDOLE RING

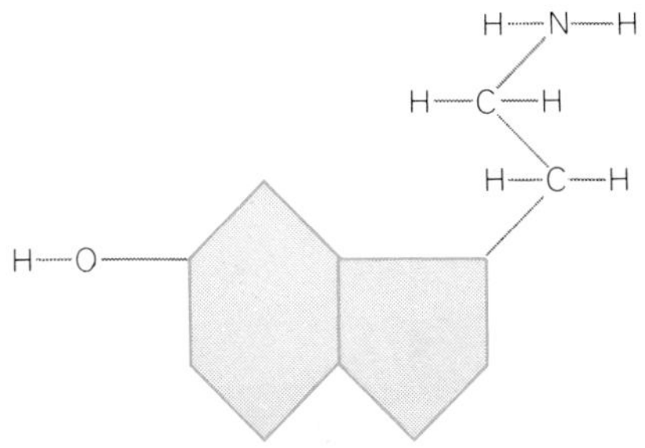

SEROTONIN

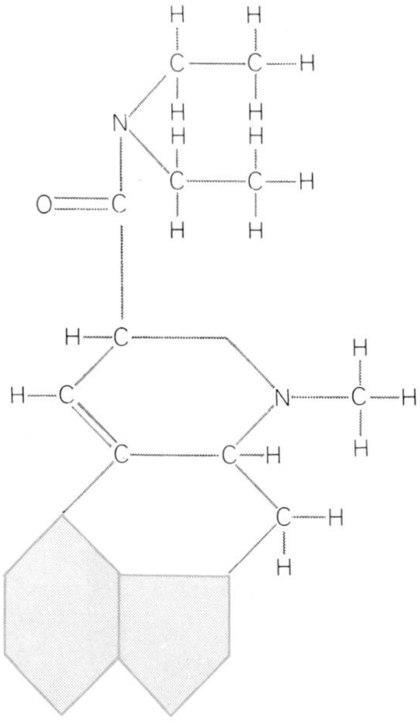

LSD

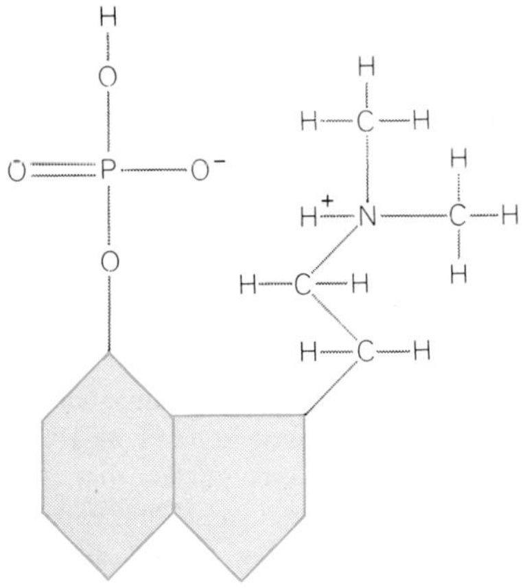

PSILOCYBIN

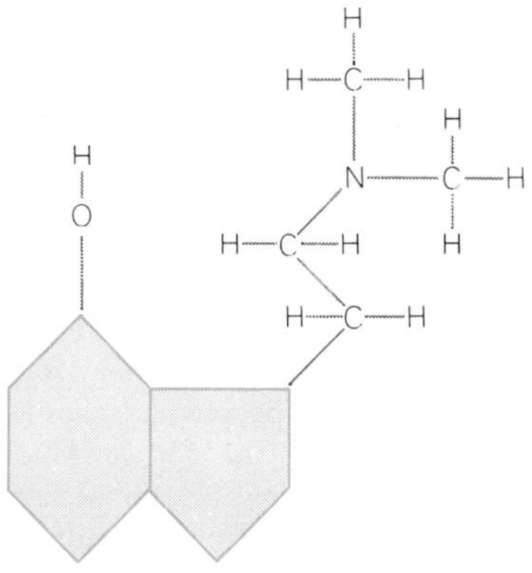

PSILOCIN

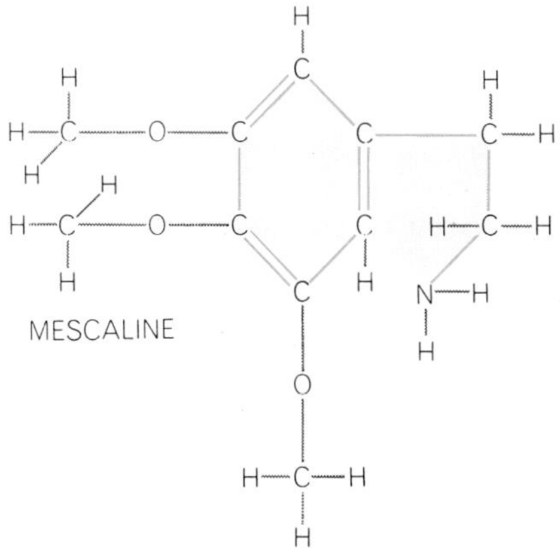

MESCALINE

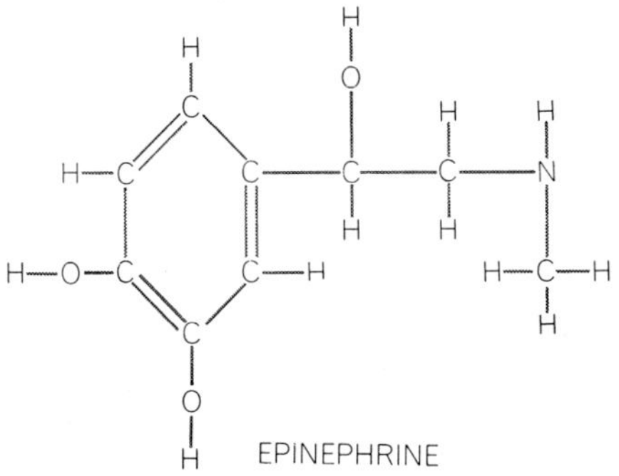

EPINEPHRINE

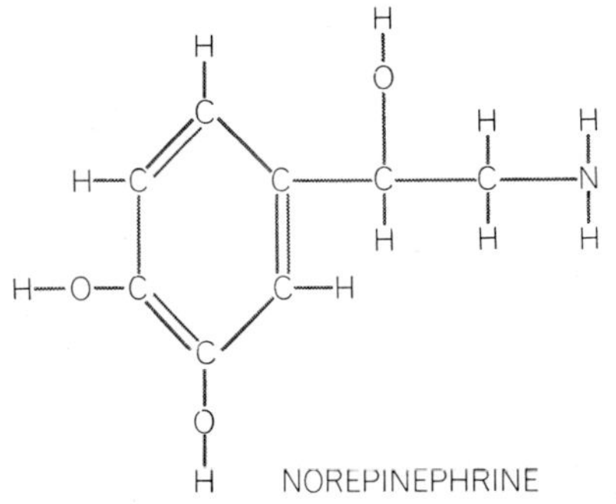

NOREPINEPHRINE

CHEMICAL RELATIONS among several of the hallucinogens and neurohumors are indicated by these structural diagrams. The indole ring (*in color at top*) is a basic structural unit; it appears, as indicated by the colored shapes, in serotonin, LSD, psilocybin and psilocin. Mescaline does not have an indole ring but, as shown by the light color, can be represented so as to suggest its relation to the ring. The close relation between mescaline and the two catechol amines epinephrine and norepinephrine is also apparent here.

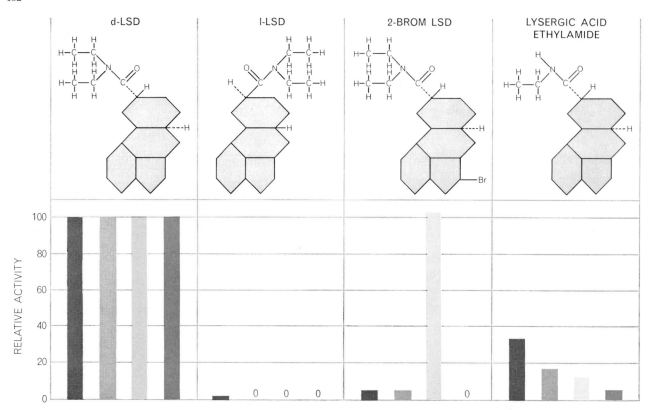

SLIGHT CHANGES in LSD molecule produce large changes in its properties. Here LSD (*left*) is used as a standard, with a "relative activity" of 100 in toxicity (*dark gray bar*), fever-producing effect (*light gray*), ability to antagonize serotonin (*light color*) and typical psychotomimetic effects (*dark color*). The stereoisomer of LSD (*second from left*) in which the positions of the side chains are reversed, shows almost no activity; the substitution of a bromine atom (*third from left*) reduces the psychotomimetic effect but not the serotonin antagonism; the removal of one of the two ethyl groups (*right*) sharply reduces activity in each of the areas.

tribes the medicine men or women (*curanderos*) still partake of *Psilocybe* and *Stropharia* in their rituals.

In the arid region between the Rio Grande and central Mexico, where the peyote cactus grows, the dried tops of the plants ("peyote buttons") were eaten by Indian shamans, or medicine men, and figured in tribal rituals. During the 19th century the Mescalero Apaches acquired the plant and developed a peyote rite. The peyotism of the Mescaleros (whence the name mescaline) spread to the Comanches and Kiowas, who transformed it into a religion with a doctrine and ethic as well as ritual. Peyotism, which spread rapidly through the Plains tribes, became fused with Christianity. Today its adherents worship God as the great spirit who controls the universe and put some of his power into peyote, and Jesus as the man who gave the plant to the Indians in a time of need. Saturday-night meetings, usually held in a traditional tepee, begin with the eating of the sacramental peyote; then the night is spent in prayer, ritual singing and introspective contemplation, and in the morning there is a communion breakfast of corn, game and fruit.

Recognizing the need for an effective organization to protect their form of worship, several peyote churches joined in 1918 to form the Native American Church, which now has about 225,000 members in tribes from Nevada to the East Coast and from the Mexican border to Saskatchewan. It preaches brotherly love, care of the family, self-reliance and abstinence from alcohol. The church has been able to defeat attempts, chiefly by the missionaries of other churches, to outlaw peyote by Federal legislation, and it has recently brought about the repeal of antipeyote legislation in several states.

The hallucinogens began to attract scholarly interest in the last decade of the 19th century, when the investigations and conceptions of such men as Francis Galton, J. M. Charcot, Sigmund Freud and William James, introduced a new spirit of serious inquiry into such subjects as hallucination, mystical experience and other "paranormal" psychic phenomena. Havelock Ellis and the psychiatrist Silas Weir Mitchell wrote accounts of the subjective effects of peyote, or Anhalonium, as it was then called. Such essays in turn stimulated

the interest of pharmacologists. The active principle of peyote, the alkaloid called mescaline, was isolated in 1896; in 1919 it was recognized that the molecular structure of mescaline was related to the structure of the adrenal hormone epinephrine.

This was an important turning point, because the interest in the hallucinogens as a possible key to naturally occurring psychoses is based on the chemical relations between the drugs and the neurohumors: substances that chemically transmit impulses across synapses between two neurons, or nerve cells, or between a neuron and an effector such as a muscle cell. Acetylcholine and the catechol amines epinephrine and norepinephrine have been shown to act in this manner in the peripheral nervous system of vertebrates; serotonin has the same effect in some invertebrates. It is frequently assumed that these substances also act as neurohumors in the central nervous system; at least they are present there, and injecting them into various parts of the brain seems to affect nervous activity.

The structural resemblance of mescaline and epinephrine suggested a possible link between the drug and mental illness: Might the early, excited stage of schizophrenia be produced or at least triggered by an error in metabolism that produced a mescaline-like substance? Techniques for gathering evidence on this question were not available, however, and the speculation on an "M-substance" did not lead to serious experimental work.

When LSD was discovered in 1943, its extraordinary potency again aroused interest in the possibility of finding a natural chemical activator of the schizophrenic process. The M-substance hypothesis was revived on the basis of reports that hallucinogenic effects were produced by adrenochrome and other breakdown products of epinephrine, and the hypothesis appeared to be strengthened by the isolation from human urine of some close analogues of hallucinogens. Adrenochrome has not, however, been detected in significant amounts in the human body, and it seems unlikely that the analogues could be produced in sufficient quantity to effect mental changes.

The relation between LSD and serotonin has given rise to the hypothesis that schizophrenia is caused by an imbalance in the metabolism of serotonin, with excitement and hallucinations resulting from an excess of serotonin in certain regions of the brain, and depressive and catatonic states resulting from a deficiency of serotonin. The idea arose in part from the observation that in some laboratory physiological preparations LSD acts rather like serotonin but in other preparations it is a powerful antagonist of serotonin; thus LSD might facilitate or block some neurohumoral action of serotonin in the brain.

The broad objection to the serotonin theory of schizophrenia is that it requires an oversimplified view of the disease's pattern of symptoms. Moreover, many congeners, or close analogues, of LSD, such as 2-brom lysergic acid, are equally effective or more effective antagonists of serotonin without being significantly active psychologically in man. This does not disprove the hypothesis, however. In man 2-brom LSD blocks the mental effects of a subsequent dose of LSD, and in the heart of a clam it blocks the action of both LSD and serotonin. Perhaps there are "keyholes" at the sites where neurohumors act; in the case of those for serotonin it may be that LSD fits the hole and opens the lock, whereas the psychologically inactive analogues merely occupy the keyhole, blocking the action of serotonin or LSD without mimicking their effects. Certainly the re-

semblance of most of the hallucinogens to serotonin is marked, and the correlations between chemical structure and pharmacological action deserve intensive investigation. The serotonin theory of schizophrenia is far from proved, but there is strong evidence for an organic factor of some kind in the disease; it may yet turn out to involve either a specific neurohumor or an imbalance among several neurohumors.

The ingestion of LSD, mescaline or psilocybin can produce a wide range of subjective and objective effects. The subjective effects apparently depend on at least three kinds of variable: the properties and potency of the drug itself; the basic personality traits and current mood of the person ingesting it, and the social and psychological context, including the meaning to the individual of his act in taking the drug and his interpretation of the motives of those who made it available. The discussion of subjective effects that follows is compiled from many different accounts of the drug experience; it should be considered an inventory of possible effects rather than a description of a typical episode.

One subjective experience that is frequently reported is a change in visual perception. When the eyes are open, the perception of light and space is affected: colors become more vivid and seem to glow; the space between objects becomes more apparent, as though space itself had become "real," and surface details appear to be more sharply defined. Many people feel a new awareness of the physical beauty of the world, particularly of visual harmonies, colors, the play of light and the exquisiteness of detail.

The visual effects are even more striking when the eyes are closed. A constantly changing display appears, its content ranging from abstract forms to dramatic scenes involving imagined people or animals, sometimes in exotic lands or ancient times. Different individuals have recalled seeing wavy lines, cobweb or chessboard designs, gratings, mosaics, carpets, floral designs, gems, windmills, mausoleums, landscapes, "arabesques spiraling into eternity," statuesque men of the past, chariots, sequences of dramatic action, the face of Buddha, the face of Christ, the Crucifixion, "the mythical dwelling places of the gods," the immensity and blackness of space. After taking peyote Silas Weir Mitchell wrote: "To give the faintest idea of the perfectly satisfying intensity and purity of these gorgeous color fruits

WATER COLORS were done, while under the influence of a relatively large dose of a hallucinogenic drug, by a person with no art training. Originals are bright yellow, purple, green and red as well as black.

154

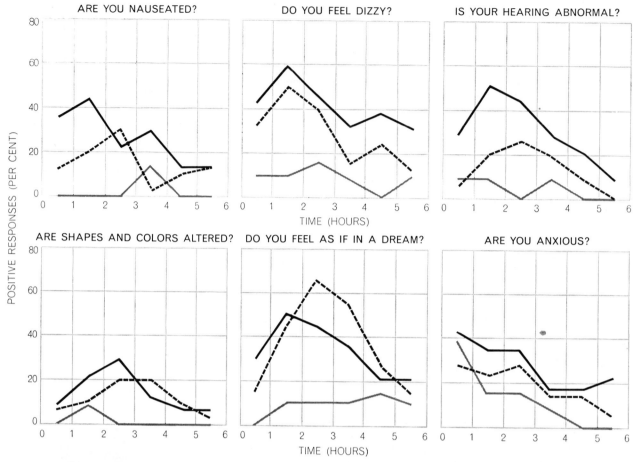

ARE YOU NAUSEATED? DO YOU FEEL DIZZY? IS YOUR HEARING ABNORMAL?

ARE SHAPES AND COLORS ALTERED? DO YOU FEEL AS IF IN A DREAM? ARE YOU ANXIOUS?

TIME (HOURS)

POSITIVE RESPONSES (PER CENT)

SUBJECTIVE REPORT on physiological and perceptual effects of LSD was obtained by means of a questionnaire containing 47 items, the results for six of which are presented. Volunteers were questioned at one-hour intervals beginning half an hour after they took the drug. The curves show the per cent of the group giving positive answers at each time. The gray curves are for those given an inactive substance, the broken black curves for between 25 and 75 micrograms and the solid black curves for between 100 and 225.

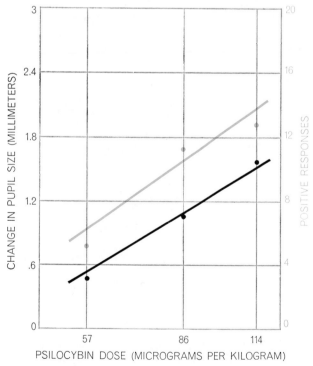

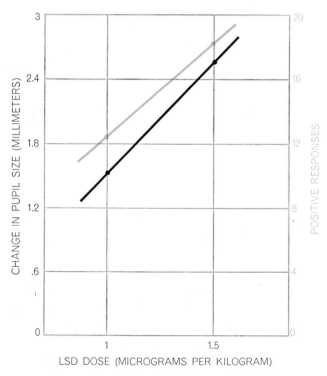

OBJECTIVE AND SUBJECTIVE effects vary with dosage as shown here. The data plotted in black are for the increase in size of pupil; the number of positive responses to questions like the ones at the top of the page are shown in color. The objective and subjective measures vary in a similar manner. The data are from an experiment done by Harris Isbell of the University of Kentucky.

is quite beyond my power." A painter described the waning hours of the effects of psilocybin as follows: "As the afternoon wore on I felt very content to simply sit and stare out of the window at the snow and the trees, and at that time I recall feeling that the snow, the fire in the fireplace, the darkened and book-lined room were so perfect as to seem almost unreal."

The changes in visual perception are not always pleasant. Aldous Huxley called one of his books about mescaline *Heaven and Hell* in recognition of the contradictory sensations induced by the drug. The "hellish" experiences include an impression of blackness accompanied by feelings of gloom and isolation, a garish modification of the glowing colors observed in the "heavenly" phase, a sense of sickly greens and ugly dark reds. The subject's perception of his own body may become unpleasant: his limbs may seem to be distorted or his flesh to be decaying; in a mirror his face may appear to be a mask, his smile a meaningless grimace. Sometimes all human movements appear to be mere puppetry, or everyone seems to be dead. These experiences can be so disturbing that a residue of fear and depression persists long after the effects of the drug have worn off.

Often there are complex auditory hallucinations as well as visual ones: lengthy conversations between imaginary people, perfectly orchestrated musical compositions the subject has never heard before, voices speaking foreign languages unknown to the subject. There have also been reports of hallucinatory odors and tastes and of visceral and other bodily sensations. Frequently patterns of association normally confined to a single sense will cross over to other senses: the sound of music evokes the visual impression of jets of colored light, a "cold" human voice makes the subject shiver, pricking the skin with a pin produces the visual impression of a circle, light glinting on a Christmas tree ornament seems to shatter and to evoke the sound of sleigh bells. The time sense is altered too. The passage of time may seem to be a slow and pleasant flow or to be intolerably tedious. A "sense of timelessness" is often reported; the subject feels outside of or beyond time, or time and space seem infinite.

In some individuals one of the most basic constancies in perception is affected: the distinction between subject and object. A firm sense of personal identity depends on knowing accurately the borders of the self and on being able to distinguish what is inside from what is outside. Paranoia is the most vivid pathological instance of the breakdown of this discrimination; the paranoiac attributes to personal and impersonal forces outside himself the impulses that actually are inside him. Mystical and transcendental experiences are marked by the loss of this same basic constancy. "All is one" is the prototype of a mystical utterance. In the mystical state the distinction between subject and object disappears; the subject is seen to be one with the object. The experience is usually one of rapture or ecstasy and in religious terms is described as "holy." When the subject thus achieves complete identification with the object, the experience seems beyond words.

Some people who have taken a large dose of a hallucinogenic drug report feelings of "emptiness" or "silence," pertaining either to the interior of the self or to an "interior" of the universe—or to both as one. Such individuals have a sense of being completely undifferentiated, as though it were their personal consciousness that had been "emptied," leaving none of the usual discriminations on which the functioning of the ego depends. One man who had this experience thought later that it had been an anticipation of death, and that the regaining of the basic discriminations was like a remembrance of the very first days of life after birth.

The effect of the hallucinogens on sexual experience is not well documented. One experiment that is often quoted seemed to provide evidence that mescaline is an anaphrodisiac, an inhibitor of sexual appetite; this conclusion seemed plausible because the drugs have so often been associated with rituals emphasizing asceticism and prayer. The fact is, however, that the drugs are probably neither anaphrodisiacs nor aphrodisiacs—if indeed any drug is. There is reason to believe that if the drug-taking situation is one in which sexual relations seem appropriate, the hallucinogens simply bring to the sexual experience the same kind of change in perception that occurs in other areas of experience.

The point is that in all the hallucinogen-produced experiences it is never the drug alone that is at work. As in the case of alcohol, the effects vary widely depending on when the drug is taken, where, in the presence of whom, in what dosage and—perhaps most important of all—by whom. What happens to the individual after he takes the drug, and his changing relations to the setting and the people in it during the episode, will further influence his experience.

Since the setting is so influential in these experiments, it sometimes happens that a person who is present when someone else is taking a hallucinogenic drug, but who does not take the drug himself, behaves as though he were under the influence of a hallucinogen. In view of this effect one might expect that a person given an inactive substance he thought was a drug would respond as though he had actually received the drug. Indeed, such responses have sometimes been noted. In controlled experiments, however, subjects given an inactive substance are readily distinguishable from those who take a drug; the difference is apparent in their appearance and behavior, their answers to questionnaires and their physiological responses. Such behavioral similarities as are observed can be explained largely by a certain apprehension felt by a person who receives an inactive substance he thinks is a drug, or by anticipation on the part of someone who has taken the drug before.

In addition to the various subjective effects of the hallucinogens there are a number of observable changes in physiological function and in performance that one can measure or at least describe objectively. The basic physiological effects are those typical of a mild excitement of the sympathetic nervous system. The hallucinogens usually dilate the pupils, constrict the peripheral arterioles and raise the systolic blood pressure; they may also increase the excitability of such spinal reflexes as the knee jerk. Electroencephalograms show that the effect on electrical brain waves is usually of a fairly nonspecific "arousal" nature: the pattern is similar to that of a normally alert, attentive and problem-oriented subject, and if rhythms characteristic of drowsiness or sleep have been present, they disappear when the drug is administered. (Insomnia is common the first night after one of the drugs has been taken.) Animal experiments suggest that LSD produces these effects by stimulating the reticular formation of the midbrain, not directly but by stepping up the sensory input.

Under the influence of one of the hallucinogens there is usually some reduction in performance on standard tests of reasoning, memory, arithmetic, spelling and drawing. These findings may not indicate an inability to perform well; after taking a drug many people simply refuse to co-operate with the tester. The very fact that someone should want to

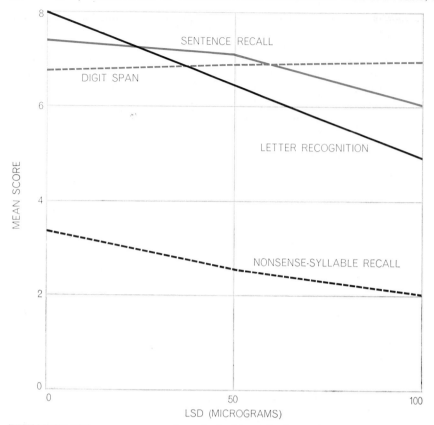

EFFECT OF LSD on memory was determined with standard tests. Curves show results of four tests for subjects given an inactive substance, 50 micrograms of the drug and 100 micrograms respectively. Effect of LSD was to decrease scores except in a test of digit-recall ability.

test them may seem absurd and may arouse either hostility or amusement. Studies by one of the authors in which tests of attention and concentration were administered to subjects who had been given different doses of LSD indicated that motivation was perhaps as important in determining scores as the subject's intellectual capacity.

The hallucinogenic drugs are not addictive—if one means by addiction that physiological dependence is established and the drug becomes necessary, usually in increasing amounts, for satisfactory physiological functioning. Some individuals become psychologically dependent on the drugs, however, and develop a "habit" in that sense; indeed, there is a tendency for those who ingest hallucinogens habitually to make the drug experience the center of all their activities. LSD, mescaline and psilocybin do produce physiological tolerance. If the same quantity of LSD is administered on three successive days, for example, it will not suffice by the third day to produce the same subjective or physiological effects; tolerance develops more slowly and less completely with mescaline and psilocybin. When an individual becomes tolerant to a given dos-

age of LSD, the ordinarily equivalent dose of psilocybin produces reduced effects. This phenomenon of cross-tolerance suggests that the two drugs have common pathways of action. Any tolerance established by daily administration of the drugs wears off rather rapidly, generally being dissipated within a few days if the drug is not taken.

The three major hallucinogens differ markedly in potency. The standard human doses—those that will cause the average adult male weighing about 150 pounds to show the full clinical effects—are 500 milligrams of mescaline, 20 milligrams of psilocybin and .1 milligram of LSD. It is assumed that in a large enough dose any of the hallucinogens would be lethal, but there are no documented cases of human deaths from the drugs alone. Death has been brought on in sensitive laboratory animals such as rabbits by LSD doses equivalent to 120 times the standard human dose. Some animals are much less susceptible; white rats have been given doses 1,000 times larger than the standard human dose without lasting harm. The maximum doses known by the authors to have been taken by human beings are 900 milligrams of mescaline, 70 milligrams

of psilocybin and two milligrams of LSD. No permanent effects were noted in these cases, but obviously no decisive studies of the upper limits of dosage have been undertaken.

There are also differences among the hallucinogens in the time of onset of effects and the duration of intoxication. When mescaline is given orally, the effects appear in two or three hours and last for 12 hours or more. LSD acts in less than an hour; some of its effects persist for eight or nine hours, and insomnia can last as long as 16 hours. Psilocybin usually acts within 20 or 30 minutes, and its full effect is felt for about five hours. All these estimates are for the standard dose administered orally; when any of the drugs is given intravenously, the first effects appear within minutes.

At the present time LSD and psilocybin are treated by the U.S. Food and Drug Administration like any other "experimental drug," which means that they can be legally distributed only to qualified investigators who will administer them in the course of an approved program of experimentation. In practice the drugs are legally available only to investigators working under a Government grant or for a state or Federal agency.

Nevertheless, there has probably been an increase during the past two or three years in the uncontrolled use of the drugs to satisfy personal curiosity or to experience novel sensations. This has led a number of responsible people in government, law, medicine and psychology to urge the imposition of stricter controls that would make the drugs more difficult to obtain even for basic research. These people emphasize the harmful possibilities of the drugs; citing the known cases of adverse reactions, they conclude that the prudent course is to curtail experimentation with hallucinogens.

Others—primarily those who have worked with the drugs—emphasize the constructive possibilities, insist that the hallucinogens have already opened up important leads in research and conclude that it would be shortsighted as well as contrary to the spirit of free scientific inquiry to restrict the activities of qualified investigators. Some go further, questioning whether citizens should be denied the opportunity of trying the drugs even without medical or psychological supervision and arguing that anyone who is mentally competent should have the right to explore the varieties of conscious experience if he can do so without harming himself or others.

The most systematic survey of the incidence of serious adverse reactions to hallucinogens covered nearly 5,000 cases, in which LSD was administered on more than 25,000 occasions. Psychotic reactions lasting more than 48 hours were observed in fewer than two-tenths of 1 per cent of the cases. The rate of attempted suicides was slightly over a tenth of 1 per cent, and these involved psychiatric patients with histories of instability. Among those who took the drug simply as subjects in experiments there were no attempted suicides and the psychotic reactions occurred in fewer than a tenth of 1 per cent of the cases.

Recent reports do indicate that the incidence of bad reactions has been increasing, perhaps because more individuals have been taking the hallucinogens in settings that emphasize sensation-seeking or even deliberate social delinquency. Since under such circumstances there is usually no one in attendance who knows how to avert dangerous developments, a person in this situation may find himself facing an extremely frightening hallucination with no one present who can help him to recognize where the hallucination ends and reality begins. Yet the question of what is a proper setting is not a simple one. One of the criticisms of the Harvard experiments was that some were conducted in private homes rather than in a laboratory or clinical setting. The experimenters defended this as an attempt to provide a feeling of naturalness and "psychological safety." Such a setting, they hypothesized, should reduce the likelihood of negative reactions such as fear and hostility and increase the positive experiences. Controlled studies of this hypothesis have not been carried out, however.

Many psychiatrists and psychologists who have administered hallucinogens in a therapeutic setting claim specific benefits in the treatment of psychoneuroses, alcoholism and social delinquency. The published studies are difficult to evaluate because almost none have employed control groups. One summary of the available statistics on the treatment of alcoholism does indicate that about 50 per cent of the patients treated with a combination of psychotherapy and LSD abstained from alcohol for at least a year, compared with 30 per cent of the patients treated by psychotherapy alone.

In another recent study the results of psychological testing before and after LSD therapy were comparable in most respects to the results obtained when conventional brief psychotherapy was employed. Single-treatment LSD therapy was significantly more effective, however, in relieving neurotic depression. If replicated, these results may provide an important basis for more directed study of the treatment of specific psychopathological conditions.

If the hallucinogens do have psychotherapeutic merit, it seems possible that they work by producing a shift in personal values. William James long ago noted that "the best cure for dipsomania is religiomania." There appear to be religious aspects of the drug experience that may bring about a change in behavior by causing a "change of heart." If this is so, one might be able to apply the hallucinogens in the service of moral regeneration while relying on more conventional techniques to give the patient insight into his habitual behavior patterns and motives.

In the light of the information now available about the uses and possible abuses of the hallucinogens, common sense surely decrees some form of social control. In considering such control it should always be emphasized that the reaction to these drugs depends not only on their chemical properties and biological activity but also on the context in which they are taken, the meaning of the act and the personality and mood of the individual who takes them. If taking the drug is defined by the group or individual, or by society, as immoral or criminal, one can expect guilt and aggression and further social delinquency to result; if the aim is to help or to be helped, the experience may be therapeutic and strengthening; if the subject fears psychosis, the drug could induce psychosis. The hallucinogens, like so many other discoveries of man, are analogous to fire, which can burn down the house or spread through the house life-sustaining warmth. Purpose, planning and constructive control make the difference. The immediate research challenge presented by the hallucinogens is a practical question: Can ways be found to minimize or eliminate the hazards, and to identify and develop further the constructive potentialities, of these powerful drugs?

NATIVE AMERICAN CHURCH members take part in a peyote ceremony in Saskatchewan, Canada. Under the influence of the drug, they gaze into the fire as they pray and meditate.

V

SENSORY PROCESSES

V   SENSORY PROCESSES

INTRODUCTION

Our sensory experience of the world around us—how it is that we come to see things as we do—is one of the fundamental problems in psychology and biology. Why do we identify and experience one stimulus complex as a Beethoven symphony and another as a chair or an interesting painting? To take a simple example, when you look at a chair, the chair obviously does not exist inside your head—it exists in the external world. However, there must be some kind of representational existence or image of the chair inside your head. In some manner, the pattern of light energy reflected from the chair activates a set of processes in your eyes, which in turn activates neurons to convey a pattern of nerve impulses into your brain. This pattern of impulses is transformed as it ascends to the visual areas of the cerebral cortex. Shortly thereafter, you have the experience of seeing the chair. Some of the more impressive recent advances in psychobiology have been in the analysis of sensory processes, particularly in terms of receptor processes and the coding that occurs in sensory nerve fibers and pathways of the brain. In this section we have limited our consideration to the visual system, largely because of the many exciting recent advances that have been made.

In the first article, "Three-pigment Color Vision," Edward F. MacNichol, Jr., reviews our current knowledge of the chemical receptor substances in the eye that are sensitive to different wavelengths of light energy. In essence there are three types of color receptor cells, or cones, in the retina of the eye. Each of these contains a different type of pigment substance. MacNichol describes the ingenious experiments used to identify the existence of these pigments in the human eye. Chemical analysis of comparable substances in the eyes of appropriate infrahuman animals by George Wald and associates at Harvard is in close agreement. These "three-pigment" data agree closely with the classical Young-Helmholtz theory and also fit well with electrophysiological data favoring an opponent-color system farther along the visual pathway, as in Hering's classical theory and its very important modern development by L. M. Hurvich and D. Jameson.

In the next article Floyd Ratliff discusses the fundamental problem of sensations of contour and contrast. We see contours when adjacent areas of the visual field appear to contrast. By the use of a simplified model system, the eye of the horseshoe crab (*Limulus*), Ratliff, H. K. Hartline, and their associates have been able to analyze some of the neuronal mechanisms that underlie the sensations of contour and contrast. His article is a clear survey of these fundamental mechanisms and how they can be applied to human sensation and perception.

In the next article, David H. Hubel discusses the visual cortex of the brain. In higher animals, as learned from studies on cats and humans, complex stimulus coding occurs not in the retina of the eye, but rather in the visual area of the cerebral cortex. Hubel and his colleague Torsten N. Wiesel first made the remarkable discovery that individual nerve cells in the visual region of the cerebral cortex respond as though they are encoding complex aspects of the visual world, ranging from edges and lines to right angles, tongues, and other dimensional stimuli. The manner in which these complex feature-detector neurons may be activated to yield such complex coding of visual sensation is described by Hubel.

The coding of complex stimuli by individual neurons in the brain is only a part of the story. Certain mammals, including man, have a three-dimensional visual world—they have depth perception. This requires binocular vision, with the visual fields of the two eyes overlapping and projecting to overlapping sets of neurons in the brain. In the last article of this section, John D. Pettigrew summarizes our current knowledge of the neurophysiology of binocular vision. By studying neurons in the visual cortex that respond to inputs from both eyes, it has been found that responses of the neurons are exceedingly sensitive to slight changes in the overlap of the stimulus fields of the two eyes. Such neuronal response to changes can aid in the coding of perception of depth.

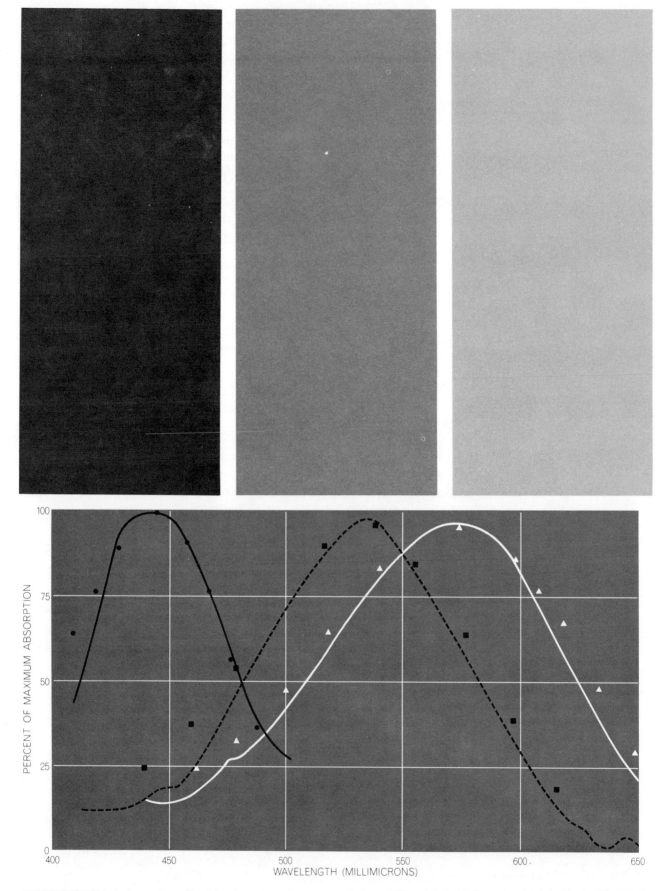

COLOR VISION in primates is mediated by three cone pigments responsible for sensing light in the blue, green and red portions of the spectrum. Their spectral-sensitivity curves are shown here; the color panels above correspond to the peak sensitivities: 447 millimicrons (blue-violet), 540 (green) and 577 (yellow). Although the "red" receptor peaks in the yellow, it extends far enough into the red to sense red well. Symbols accompanying curves trace shapes of hypothetical pigments with peaks at each wavelength (*see text*).

Three-Pigment Color Vision

16

by Edward F. MacNichol, Jr.
December 1964

*Direct measurements of the absorption of light
by individual cells show that color is discriminated
in vertebrate retinas by three pigments segregated
in three kinds of cone receptor*

Investigations completed during the past two years have established that color vision in vertebrates is mediated by three light-sensitive pigments segregated in three different kinds of receptor cell in the retina, and that one of these pigments is primarily responsible for sensing blue light, one for sensing green and one for red. These findings solve one of the central problems of color vision: the nature of the primary receptors that discriminate light of various wavelengths. Large questions remain to be answered: How is the information from the receptors coded in the retina? How is it transmitted to the brain? How is it decoded there?

In 1802 the English physicist Thomas Young suggested that the retina probably contains three different kinds of light-sensitive substances, each maximally sensitive in a different region of the spectrum, and that the information from the excitation of each substance is separately transmitted to the brain and there combined to reproduce the colors of the outside world. Over the years investigators accumulated a great deal of information on the mechanisms of vision without being able to prove or disprove Young's simple postulates. They learned that rod-shaped and cone-shaped receptor cells in the retina contain pigments that are bleached by light, that the rods are responsible for vision in faint light and that the cones distinguish colors. Psychophysical experiments, in which a human subject is presented with visual stimuli and asked to tell what he sees, established that any color could be matched by a combination of three colors in different parts of the spectrum. This supported Young's trichromatic theory, but other psychophysical studies seemed to support different theories. The fact is that psychophysical investigation tells only what the

visual system can do and not how it does it.

To learn what happens at various steps along the visual pathway one must measure directly the effect of light on the receptor cells and the generation of electrical impulses in the retinal nerve cells. Spectrophotometric measurements of individual cone cells in the retinas of the goldfish, the rhesus monkey and man, conducted in our laboratory at Johns Hopkins University and also at Harvard University and the University of Pennsylvania, have now confirmed Young's three-receptor hypothesis. Electrophysiological studies of nerve cells in the retina, on the other hand, suggest that Young was wrong about the transmission of color information to the brain along three discrete pathways.

A physiologist seeking to learn what message the eye sends the brain, and how, would like to start at the beginning—with the impact of light on a photoreceptor. Unfortunately the lack of suitable techniques ruled out this systematic approach: single-cell spectrophotometry has been possible only in very recent years. Electrophysiological methods, on the other hand, have been applicable since 1938, when H. K. Hartline, then at the University of Pennsylvania, isolated individual optic nerve fibers in the retina of the frog. Each such fiber originates in a single ganglion cell: a nerve cell that collects information from a large number of receptors. Hartline found that the ganglion cells responded to light by emitting showers of nerve impulses, and he classified the cells as "on," "off" or "on-off," depending on whether they responded to the onset or to the end of illumination or to both. In 1939 the Swedish physiologists Ragnar A. Granit and Gunnar Svaetichin and the Finnish physicist Alvar

Wilska developed microelectrodes that could record directly from a cell, and since then microelectrode techniques have been used to trace nerve messages through many parts of the visual pathway as well as in other parts of the nervous system.

The ganglion cells are "third order" nerve cells, two steps behind the receptor cells along the visual pathway (although in front of them anatomically; the receptor cells are at the back of the translucent retina). With the development of micropipette electrodes after World War II it became possible to probe more precisely into individual cells, and in the 1950's Svaetichin recorded, in the retinas of certain fishes, the most peripheral localized sign of electrical activity discovered up to that time: slow changes in potential in response to flashes of light. These S-potentials, as they came to be called, were of two types and were quite different from anything previously reported. One, which Svaetichin called the luminosity response, took the form of a sizable negative resting potential that increased in the presence of light; the wavelengths that are most effective in this regard are distributed in a broad peak across the center of the spectrum. The luminosity response has since been found in a large number of fishes and in the cat and the frog, and it probably occurs in all vertebrates. The other intraretinal response was similar in some respects: it was a steady negative resting potential that became more strongly negative when the stimulating light was at the short-wavelength, or blue, end of the spectrum. As progressively longer wavelengths were used for illumination, however, the responses diminished in amplitude until a neutral point was reached at which there was no sustained change in potential; any

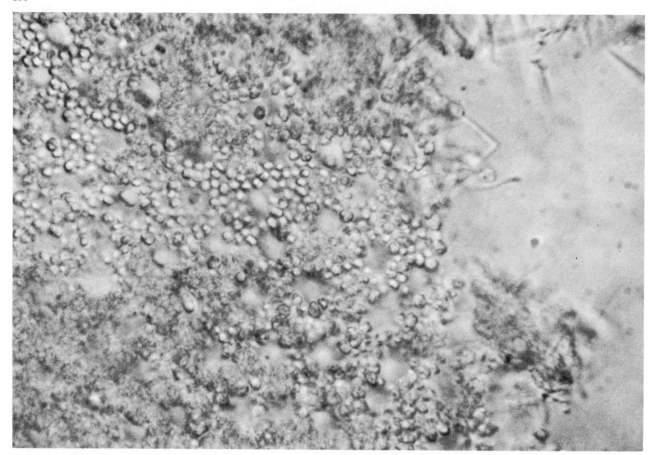

HUMAN RECEPTOR CELLS are seen end on in this photograph of a retinal specimen on the stage of the spectrophotometer that measures their light absorption. The well-defined small circles are the rod and cone outer segments, the parts of the receptors that contain the visual pigments. The rods are the more closely packed. The specimen is oriented so that the test beam of colored light comes through a cone outer segment (*green spot at middle left*) and the reference beam passes through an empty area (*right*).

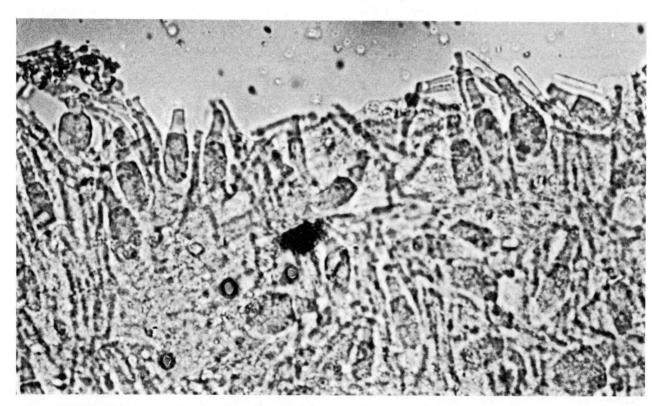

GOLDFISH RECEPTORS are seen from the side in a piece of retina squeezed between two cover slips and placed in the spectropho-tometer. The three-micron test and reference beams (*green spots*) pass through a cone outer segment (*upper left*) and a clear area.

increase in wavelength from that point on produced a positive potential! This unusual "chromatic" response suggested a possible mechanism of color vision. In 1957 I joined Svaetichin at the Venezuelan Institute for Scientific Research and we undertook a detailed study of both the nature and the exact source of the S-potentials.

We found the luminosity response in a number of different fishes but the chromatic response only in species that swim at levels to which a broad band of wavelengths, or colors, penetrates: no deeper than about 100 feet. The chromatic response of some fishes showed a negative peak in the green portion of the spectrum and a positive peak in the red; in other species the peaks were in the blue and yellow. Among the species we tested only the mullet (*Mugil*) had both the "green-red" and the "blue-yellow" response. Further analysis of these chromatic responses showed that each was made up of two opposed processes—negative in the blue or green and positive in the yellow or red—combined algebraically. The independence of the two processes was demonstrated by adaptation experiments. Illumination of a retina with a steady blue light, for example, diminished the chromatic response in the short-wavelength region and increased it in the yellow or red. Similar experiments did not change the shape of the luminosity response, only its amplitude. Clearly the chromatic response was made up of two distinct components, whereas the luminosity response was unitary.

To visualize the sites of origin we filled the micropipettes with dye that was forced out into the retinal tissue by electrophoresis after each recording. By sectioning and examining the specimens we could trace the luminosity response to the region just beyond the endings of the cone cells, where the fish retina has a layer of giant horizontal "glial" cells. The large size of the area in which the luminosity response arises, and the fact that it signals a change in brightness anywhere in an extensive area, seem to confirm its origin in these giant cells.

The chromatic response arises in the next layer of the retina. Genyo Mitarai of the University of Nagoya in Japan, working with Svaetichin, has secured evidence that they come from the so-called Müller fibers, which surround the "second order" nerve cells known as bipolar cells. The Müller fibers—like the giant horizontal cells—are glial elements: supporting or nutritive structures often seen in association with nerve cells.

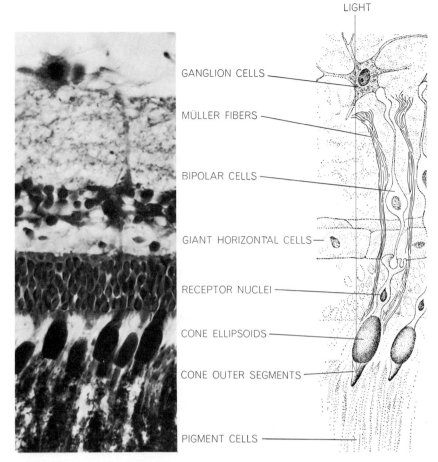

GOLDFISH RETINA, magnified about 1,000 diameters, is seen in section in the photomicrograph (*left*). The various elements of the retina are identified in the drawing (*right*). They have been rendered schematically in an effort to suggest the connections between them on the basis of the information available from recent electron microscope studies.

The S-potentials are quite different from the shower of short-lived "spike" impulses ordinarily emitted by nerve cells; Svaetichin has suggested that these slow changes in potential are signs of metabolic changes in the glial structures in which they originate, induced by the activity of adjacent nerve cells and able in turn to alter the nerve cells' activity. Glia have usually been assumed to play a passive role in the nervous system, but Holger Hydén of the University of Göteborg has shown that metabolic events in glial cells are correlated with certain forms of nervous activity and may even control them [see "Satellite Cells in the Nervous System," by Holger Hydén; SCIENTIFIC AMERICAN Offprint 134]. This is a challenging area for further experimentation.

Whatever their exact explanation, if these intraretinal S-potentials did have something to do with color vision, we thought they should be correlated with the discharge patterns of the ganglion cells, which appear to be the only source of messages from the retina to the brain. Russel L. DeValois of Indiana University had found that spontaneously active nerve cells in a visual center of the monkey brain increase their rate of discharge when the eye is stimulated by light at one end of the spectrum and decrease it when the eye is stimulated by light at the other end. No one, however, had obtained chromatic responses from the monkey retina for comparison. Together with M. L. Wolbarsht and H. G. Wagner of the Naval Medical Research Institute I studied the effects of wavelength on the responses of retinal ganglion cells in the goldfish (*Carassius auratus*), which had been shown to have a well-developed color sense.

First we established that the goldfish retina does produce both the luminosity and the chromatic S-potentials, both of them qualitatively the same as in the fishes we had studied previously. Then we went on to record with microelectrodes inserted into the ganglion cells. Most of these cells responded with a burst of impulses when a white light was turned on and an-

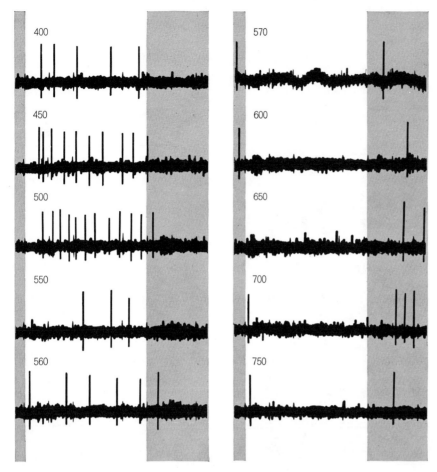

GANGLION-CELL RESPONSE varies with the wavelength of the stimulus, a half-second flash of light (*white area*). At short wavelengths (*left*) there is an "on" response, a burst of impulses during illumination. At long wavelengths (*right*) there is an "off" response instead. (Spikes at left side of some long-wavelength records are from preceding stimuli.)

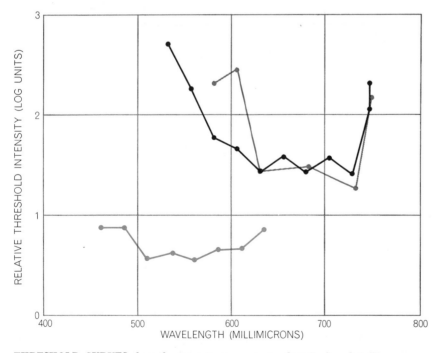

THRESHOLD CURVES show the intensity necessary to elicit "on" and "off" responses from a ganglion cell at different wavelengths. The "on" response (*color*) was obtained at short wavelengths, the "off" (*black*) at long wavelengths. In the overlap region the "off" response required a higher-intensity stimulus. Gray curve traces the inhibition threshold.

other burst when the light was turned off. Colored light brought a response that in the manner of the chromatic response was peculiarly dependent on wavelength. At short wavelengths, where the chromatic response was large and negative, a typical ganglion cell produced vigorous "on" discharges; at intermediate wavelengths, where the chromatic potential went to zero, there was a transition from "on" to "off"; at long wavelengths, where the chromatic response was large and positive, the "off" responses reached a maximum and there was a suppression of activity during illumination [*see top illustration at left*]. The short wavelengths caused excitation; the long wavelengths had an inhibitory effect during illumination that was followed by an "off" discharge that seemed to be a "postinhibitory rebound," a common phenomenon in nervous systems.

In addition to wavelength, the intensity of the stimulus also had an effect on the discharge. If we held the wavelength constant and increased the intensity of the illumination, the response pattern changed from excitation ("on") to both excitation and inhibition ("on-off") and eventually to inhibition alone ("off"). This held true only in a limited band of wavelengths.

The relation of these two factors—wavelength and intensity—became more evident when we ran a series of threshold experiments, adjusting the intensity of the stimulus to produce a constant response at various wavelengths; the intensity thus became a measure of the sensitivity of the process at a given wavelength. Measurements on a single ganglion cell usually defined two distinct luminosity functions of wavelength: the intensities for a constant "on" and for a constant "off" response. In one of our early experiments [*see bottom illustration at left*] the two curves overlapped from 530 to 610 millimicrons. It was in this region that a change in intensity was effective in converting "on" patterns to "off" patterns. The gray curve in the illustration traces the intensities that caused complete suppression of all activity during illumination; it is the "inhibition" curve. In the overlap region it illustrates the effect of increasing intensity mentioned above. Beyond that it coincides closely with the "off" response, again suggesting that the latter is a rebound phenomenon.

Experiments in which either the short-wavelength or the long-wavelength process was selectively light-adapted provided further evidence for the independence of the two processes and the idea that the "off" system is inhibitory in nature. Adaptation with red light, for example, depressed the "off" response and increased the sensitivity of the "on" process. The latter, moreover, could now be obtained throughout the spectrum: it had been released from inhibition.

The ganglion cells I have been discussing are "green-on, red-off" cells. We found others that gave an opposite response ("green-off, red-on"), but in both cases the "off" response was associated with the inhibition of nerve-impulse activity during illumination, whether it was spontaneous activity, the result of background illumination or a carry-over of the "on" burst elicited by a previous stimulus.

Our results made it clear that in the goldfish information with regard to wavelength is carried up the optic nerve in the form of discharges from ganglion cells that are acted on by groups of receptors having sensitivities in different parts of the spectrum. These groups of receptors, presumably acting through the second-order bipolar cells, exert either excitatory or inhibitory effects on the ganglion cells. A given ganglion cell may, for example, be excited primarily by a group of red-sensitive receptors and inhibited mainly by a number of green-sensitive receptors. Other cells would be conversely affected. Some ganglion cells show no wavelength dependence but have about equal "on" and "off" thresholds throughout the spectrum; one would expect that they receive equal numbers of excitatory and inhibitory connections from each type of receptor. A few cells maintain a discharge throughout illumination; these presumably have only excitatory connections. Others discharge in the dark and are inhibited throughout prolonged illumination; they may only have inhibitory connections. David Hubel and Torsten Wiesel at the Harvard Medical School have found similar color-coded "on" and "off" responses in the optic nerve fibers of monkeys. The kind of coding we discovered in the retinal ganglion cells of fishes presumably holds true in man as well.

At this point in our investigation we had identified, at the level of the *S*-potentials and again at the level of the ganglion-cell discharge, elements of an "opponent color" coding system. The 19th-century German physiologist Ewald Hering had developed a color-vision theory based on such a process, perhaps involving a yellow-blue, a red-green and a black-white receptor. Her-

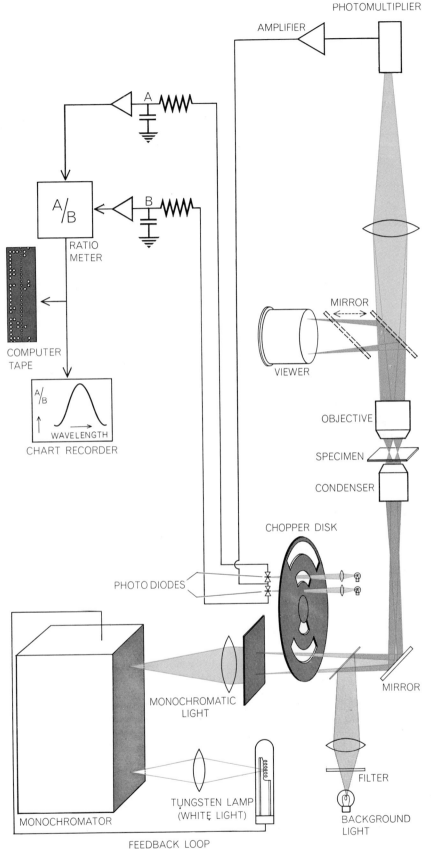

MICROSPECTROPHOTOMETER measures the absorption of light by a single cone. Monochromatic light, held to a constant flux by a feedback loop, is formed into two beams. A rotating chopper disk allows the "test" (*A*) and the "reference" (*B*) beams alternately to pass through the specimen to the photomultiplier tube. Depending on which beam is passing through, photodiodes switch the photomultiplier output into a test or a reference channel. The transmissivity of the specimen, *A* over *B*, is recorded and punched on tape.

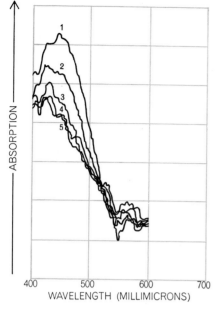

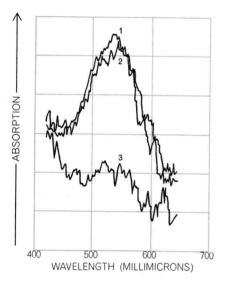

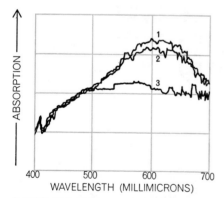

RAW DATA for blue (*top*), green (*middle*) and red (*bottom*) cones were recorded with varying gains and light intensities. The blue curves were done as described in the text and required correction for bleaching. Green and red curves *1* and *2*, recorded at low intensities, bleached very little; after deliberate flash bleaching, the final curves (*3*) were recorded. Subtracting the last from the first curves yields difference spectra.

ing's theory attempted to account for two-color phenomena—such as the fact that red and green (or blue and yellow) vary together in sensitivity and never appear subjectively mixed—that could not be easily explained by a trichromatic system of the sort suggested by Young and elaborated by Hering's contemporary Hermann von Helmholtz. There seemed to be no way to confirm or disprove either theory except by examining the sensitivity of the actual receptors at various wavelengths. This meant measuring the absorption characteristics of the pigments in the cones across the entire visible spectrum.

Cone pigments are difficult to extract and have yet to be separated from one another by standard biochemical methods. By analyzing a solution of chicken-retina pigments after partial bleaching, George Wald and his colleagues at Harvard University were able to distinguish a cone pigment, which they called iodopsin, from the known rod pigment rhodopsin, but this method has not been successful in mammals. The first successful method of distinguishing the various cone pigments *in situ* was devised by F. W. Campbell and W. A. H. Rushton at the University of Cambridge in 1955. They measured the intensity of light beamed into the human eye and reflected out again by the pigmented layer at the back of the retina. By selective bleaching and by comparing data from normal and color-blind people Rushton was able to identify two different pigments in the fovea, the central region of the retina where the cones are closely packed and there are no rods. One pigment, which he called chlorolabe, was most sensitive in the green part of the spectrum and another, erythrolabe, had its peak sensitivity in the yellow [see "Visual Pigments in Man," by W. A. H. Rushton; SCIENTIFIC AMERICAN Offprint 139]. At Harvard, Wald and Paul K. Brown were able to approach the problem even more directly, measuring with a spectrophotometer the absorption of light by dissected monkey and human foveas. They too were able to identify a green-sensitive and a red-sensitive pigment. Neither this method nor Rushton's, however, could specify whether the pigments were segregated in separate receptors or were mixed in a single receptor, nor could either method present clear evidence for any blue-sensitive pigment.

The best way to settle the question was somehow to measure with a spectrophotometer the absorption spectra of

the pigments in individual cone cells. This is simple conceptually but quite difficult in practice. The outer segment of a cone cell, which contains the pigment, has a diameter ranging from perhaps five microns to less than two microns in various species; the small amount of pigment present in each cone requires that the beam of light passed through it be of low intensity, and the quantized nature of light then makes for "photon noise" in the record. Nevertheless, two Japanese investigators, T. Hanaoka and K. Fujimoto, did manage in 1957 to examine single cones in the retina of the carp; they detected what appeared to be five or six different pigments, each in a different cone. For some reason they did not pursue this line of work. Brown at Harvard and Paul A. Liebman at the University of Pennsylvania made spectrophotometric measurements on the outer segment of frog rod cells, but their instruments were apparently not yet able to detect the pigments in the outer segment of cones, which are much smaller. William B. Marks and I set out to design an instrument sensitive enough to measure the absorption curves of goldfish cones.

Our microspectrophotometer directs two beams of colored light through a specimen of retinal tissue to a photomultiplier tube. The "test beam" passes through the outer segment of a cone; the "reference beam," through a clear area. The photomultiplier measures the amount of light transmitted by the cone pigment compared with the amount in the unobstructed reference beam [see illustration on preceding page]. Light generated in a monochromator passes through two small apertures in a piece of metal foil; the two resulting beams are focused on the specimen, a piece of goldfish retina squeezed flat between two glass cover slips. In order to keep the retina dark-adapted, or unbleached, we orient the specimen under infrared background illumination, viewing it with an infrared image converter.

A mechanical "chopper" alternately selects the test and reference beams for passage through the specimen to the photomultiplier; photodiodes on the chopper alternately switch the corresponding signal from the photomultiplier into a chart recorder that takes the ratio of the two signals. This ratio, a measure of the relative absorption of the cone pigment across the visible spectrum, is simultaneously digitized and punched on tape to be analyzed and corrected by computer.

The simple absorption spectrum of a

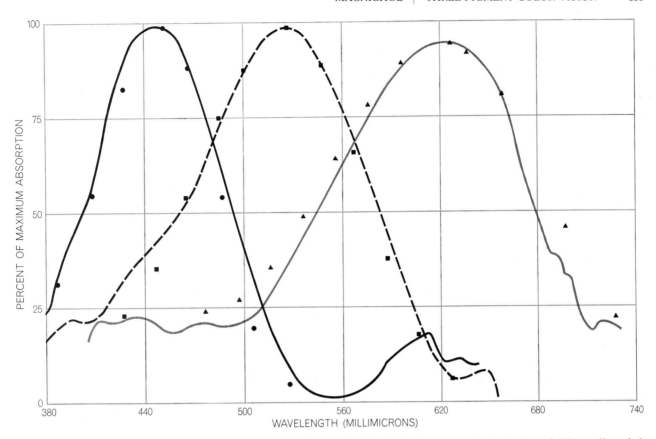

GOLDFISH CONE PIGMENT spectral sensitivities are shown by these curves, the averages of eight difference spectra peaking in the blue, 10 in the green and nine in the red. The small symbols outline the curves for hypothetical "Dartnall pigments" (*see text*).

visual pigment is distorted by the presence of extraneous nonbleaching pigments, by the wavelength-dependent scattering caused by particulate matter and by diffraction and chromatic aberration in the optical system. The usual way of minimizing such effects is to record an absorption spectrum, bleach the specimen with white light, record another absorption spectrum and subtract it from the first. If colored products are not created in the process (often they are and must be corrected for), the resulting "difference spectrum" should provide the true spectral absorption curve of the bleachable pigment. This method requires that the intensity of the test beam be low in order not to bleach the pigment during a scan. In the early stages of his investigation Marks found that he had to step up the intensity of the beam in order to overcome photon noise; therefore he allowed the test beam to bleach the pigment, making several scans [*see top record in illustration on opposite page*] and subtracting the last from the first to get a difference spectrum. The peak of such a spectrum was displaced from the correct wavelength because there was progressively less pigment available at successive points in the scan. Marks worked out a correction procedure: he

estimated the fraction of the original pigment remaining at each wavelength and divided the calculated difference at that point by the appropriate fraction. With W. E. Love, Marks wrote a computer program to perform the calculations, make the corrections and plot the corrected difference spectrum.

When a large number of difference spectra recorded in this way were printed together, it was evident that they fell into three groups with peaks in the blue, green and red. When he averaged the curves in each group, Marks came up with the three goldfish cone pigment spectra shown above, with peaks at wavelengths of about 455, 530 and 625 millimicrons. For evidence whether or not these curves represent the spectral sensitivities of three cone pigments, Marks compared them with the curves for three hypothetical visual pigments with peaks at these wavelengths. These curves are based on a translation of the curve of rhodopsin to the specified wavelengths according to a graph devised in 1953 by H. J. A. Dartnall of the Institute of Ophthalmology in London. Iodopsin and other visual pigments discovered since then have conformed to such curves. Our goldfish curves conform rather well, although not perfectly.

The primary conclusion we could draw from the goldfish investigation was that it unequivocally verified Young's three-receptor prediction, at least in one species known to be capable of color vision. Liebman has since performed similar experiments, employing light intensities that do not cause appreciable bleaching. He has provided independent confirmation of the work by developing curves that are in generally good agreement with Marks's results. Marks was also able to determine the density of the pigment in the cones: it is about a million molecules per cubic micron, or nearly the same as in the density of the rhodopsin in the rods. Since his measurements were made at right angles to the axis of the cones and could be repeated at several points in an outer segment with identical results, they showed further that the pigment is present throughout the outer segment (not concentrated in a minute granule, as Rushton had once suggested) and that such optical effects as filtering and focusing cannot play a significant role in color perception.

We were anxious to extend our investigation to individual human cone cells, not only because of the implicit interest of the human visual system but also because of the large amount of psychophysical data with which one can compare objective experimental results. William Dobelle, a graduate student, was able to obtain some human retinas through the cooperation of an eye bank, and along with them we used material from the rhesus monkeys *Macaca nemistrina* and *M. mulata*, obtained from the Naval Medical Research Institute. Monkey and human cones, like the cones of other primates, are much smaller than fish cones, measuring only about two microns in diameter at the base of the outer segment. If these cones were squeezed flat, as they were in the goldfish experiment, the light beam penetrated them from the side and not enough pigment molecules lay in its path to register a signal far enough above noise. Dobelle and Marks finally learned how to mount a piece of retina so that the cones are vertical and the beam of light traverses the main axis of the receptor, thus encountering more pigment molecules. They took specimens from the region of the retina just outside the fovea, where the cones are separated by closely packed rods, from which they can easily be discriminated, and proceeded to obtain difference spectra in the same way described earlier for goldfish cones.

When the computer printed out the corrected spectra for 10 primate cones, the curves fell once again into three clearly defined groups [*see illustration below*]. Marks has since made some corrections in these original results; the best averages to date for the three receptors are shown in the illustration on page 2, together with samples of the colors to which each receptor is most sensitive. The fact that in primates the "red" receptor's spectral curve peaks not in the red part of the spectrum but in the yellow seems remarkable but was not surprising. It had already been indicated by psychophysical results, notably those of W. S. Stiles of the National Physical Laboratory in England, who found a "red" maximum from 575 to 587 millimicrons. Although the curve peaks in the yellow, it extends far enough into the red to sense red light unambiguously. That is, these cones are at least substantially more sensitive to red than are the green receptors, and that is all that is necessary if red light is to stimulate the retina to send a message the brain can interpret as "red."

At about the same time as we were investigating primate cones, Brown and Wald at Harvard modified the instrument with which they had examined frog rods and primate foveas so that it could record from individual cones. Their measurements of four cones in a single human retina also revealed three distinct absorption curves, although the peaks of the curves were somewhat different from ours: 450, 525 and 555 millimicrons. This could have been because there are in fact substantial differences among individual cones of the same type or because the methods by which Brown and Wald produced and corrected their spectra were different from ours. Liebman has also obtained data from individual human cones, but we have not yet been able to analyze his results. Many more measurements will have to be made before the exact spectral sensitivities of primate color-vision pigments are determined.

Single-cell microspectrophotometry develops the curve of whatever pigment material is in an individual cone, and not necessarily the curve of an individual pigment. Recently Wald performed a series of psychophysical experiments to determine if the color sensitivity of the living human eye corresponds to the single-cone data. He measured threshold sensitivities after selective adaptation and derived three curves with peaks at 430, 540 and 575 millimicrons —in closer agreement with our spectrophotometric data than with his own. Since these pigment-specific curves obtained from the entire population of receptors agree so well with our cone-specific spectrophotometric data, it seems likely that there are indeed three types of cone, each of which contains principally one of three pigments.

Electrophysiological evidence of what goes on in the vertebrate receptor cell has been difficult to obtain, but last winter Tsuneo Tomita of Keio University in Japan recorded slow potential changes that he is fairly sure originated in receptors in the retina of the carp, which is closely related to the goldfish. These signals vary in response to illumination by light of different wavelengths. They seem to reach a maximum amplitude at three points in the spectrum. And the three peaks correspond rather well with those Marks derived for the pigments of the goldfish cones.

All the evidence for a three-color, three-receptor cone system comes up against the earlier electrophysiological evidence for an opponent-color system farther along the visual pathway. Color vision is apparently at least a two-stage process, consistent with the Young-Helmholz theory at the receptor level and with the Hering theory at the level of the optic nerve and beyond. Each receptor does not have its private route to the brain; three-color information is somehow processed in the retina and encoded into two-color on-off signals by each of the color-sensitive retinal ganglion cells for transmission to the higher visual centers.

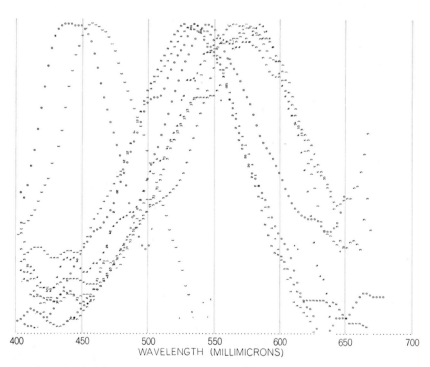

PRIMATE CONE difference spectra are shown as plotted from spectrophotometer tapes by a digital computer. One blue and one green human cone and eight rhesus monkey cones are represented. These curves, after correction, are the basis of the illustration on page 162.

17

Contour and Contrast

by Floyd Ratliff
June 1972

*We see contours when adjacent areas contrast
sharply. Surprisingly, certain contours, in turn, make
large areas appear lighter or darker than they really
are. What neural mechanisms underlie these effects?*

Contours are so dominant in our
visual perception that when we
draw an object, it is almost instinctive for us to begin by sketching its
outlines. The use of a line to depict a
contour may well have been one of the
earliest developments in art, as exemplified by the "line drawings" in the pic-
tographs and petroglyphs of prehistoric
artists. We see contours when there is a
contrast, or difference, in the brightness
or color between adjacent areas. How
contrast creates contours has been thoroughly studied by both scientists and
artists. How the contour itself can affect
the contrast of the areas it separates has
been known to artists for at least 1,000
years, but it is relatively new as a subject of scientific investigation. Although
the psychophysiological basis of how
contrast enables the visual system to distinguish contours has been studied for
the past century, it is only in the past
few years that psychologists and physiologists have started to examine systematically the influence of contour on
contrast.

You can readily observe how the visual system tends to abstract and accentuate contours in patterns of varying
contrast by paying close attention to the
edges of a shadow cast by an object in
strong sunlight. Stand with your back
to the sun and look closely at the shadow
of your head and shoulders on a side-
walk. You will see a narrow half-shadow
between the full shadow and the full
sunlight. Objectively the illumination in
the full shadow is uniformly low, in the
half-shadow it is more or less uniformly
graded and in the full sunlight it is uniformly high; within each area there are
no sharp maxima or minima. Yet you
will see a narrow dark band at the dark
edge of the half-shadow and a narrow
bright band at its bright edge. You can

enhance the effect by swaying from side
to side to produce a moving shadow.

These dark and bright strips, now
known as Mach bands, were first reported in the scientific literature some 100
years ago by the Austrian physicist,
philosopher and psychologist Ernst
Mach. They depend strictly on the distribution of the illumination. Mach formulated a simple principle for the effect:
"Whenever the light-intensity curve of
an illuminated surface (whose light intensity varies in only one direction) has
a concave or convex flection with respect to the abscissa, that place appears
brighter or darker, respectively, than its
surroundings" [*see bottom illustration
on page 173*].

The basic effect can be demonstrated
by holding an opaque card under an ordinary fluorescent desk lamp, preferably
in a dark room. If the shadow is cast on
a piece of paper, part of the paper is illuminated by light from the full length
of the lamp. Next to the illuminated area
is a half-shadow that gets progressively
darker until a full shadow is reached.
Ideally the distribution of light should
be uniformly high in the bright area,
uniformly low in the dark area and
smoothly graded between the bright and
the dark areas [*see top illustration on
page 173*]. If you now look closely at
the edges of the graded half-shadow,
you see a narrow bright band at the
bright edge and a narrow dark band at
the dark edge. These are the Mach
bands. Their appearance is so striking

that many people will not believe at first
that they are only a subjective phenomenon. Some will mistakenly try to explain
the appearance of the bands by saying
they are the result of multiple shadows
or diffraction.

Exact psychophysical measurements
of the subjective appearance of Mach
bands have been made by Adriana Fio-
rentini and her colleagues at the National Institute of Optics in Italy. Their technique consists in having an observer
adjust an independently variable spot of
light to match the brightness of areas in
and around the Mach bands. In general
they find that the bright band is distinctly narrower and more pronounced
than the dark band. The magnitude of
the effect, however, varies considerably
from person to person.

Since Mach bands delineate contours
we expect to see, only a careful observer, or someone who has reason to
objectively measure the light distribution at a shadow's edge, is likely to realize that the bands are a caricature of
the actual pattern of illumination. Artists
of the 19th-century Neo-Impressionist
school were unusually meticulous in
their observations, and this was reflected
in much of their work. A good example
is Paul Signac's "Le petit déjeuner." In
this painting there are numerous contrast effects in and around the shadows
and half-shadows. Particularly striking
is how some of the shadows are darkest
near their edges and quite light near

NEO-IMPRESSIONIST PAINTER Paul Signac was a meticulous observer of the contrast
effects in shadows and half-shadows. On the following page is a portion of his "Le petit
déjeuner" (1886–1887). Note how the shadow is darker near the unshaded tablecloth and
lighter next to the dark matchbox. Similar effects can be found in other shadows. The effects
change when the painting is viewed from various distances. The painting is in the Rijksmu-
seum Kröller-Müller at Otterlo in the Netherlands and is reproduced with its permission.

the object casting the shadow. Where Signac saw contrast he painted contrast, whether it was objectively present in the original scene or not. The effects we see in his painting depend of course partly on what Signac painted and partly on how our own eyes respond to contrast. When we view Signac's painting, our own eyes and brain further exaggerate the contrast he painted. As a result the painting appears to have even more contrast than the original scene could have had.

Without precise physical and psychophysical measurements it is difficult to tell how much of the contrast we perceive is objective and how much is subjective. Adding to the confusion is the fact that the subjective Mach bands can seemingly be photographed. All the photograph does, however, is to reproduce with considerable fidelity the original distribution of light in a scene, and it is this distribution of light and dark that gives rise to the subjective Mach bands. Moreover, the photographic process can itself introduce a spurious enhancement of contrast. Edge effects that closely resemble Mach bands can arise as the film is developed. Unlike Mach bands, they are an objective phenomenon consisting of actual variations in the density of the film, and the variations can be objectively measured.

On many occasions scientific investigators have mistaken Mach bands for objective phenomena. For example, shortly after W. K. Röntgen discovered X rays several workers attempted to measure the wavelength of the rays by passing them through ordinary diffraction slits and gratings and recording the resulting pattern on film. Several apparently succeeded in producing diffraction patterns of dark and light bands from which they could determine the wavelength of the X rays. All, however, was in error. As two Dutch physicists, H. Haga and C. H. Wind, showed later, the supposed diffraction patterns were subjective Mach bands.

As early as 1865 Mach proposed an explanation of the subjective band effect and other contrast phenomena in terms of opposed excitatory and inhibitory influences in neural networks in the retina and the brain. The means for direct investigation of such neural mechanisms did not become available, however, until the 1920's, when E. D. Adrian, Y. Zotterman and Detlev W. Bronk, working at the University of Cambridge, developed methods for recording the electrical activity of single nerve cells. The basic excitatory-inhibitory principle

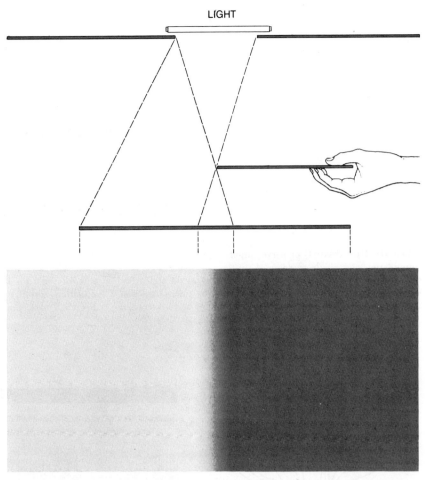

LIGHT

MACH BANDS can be produced with light from an ordinary fluorescent desk lamp (*upper illustration*). Place a sheet of white or gray paper on the desk and the light about a foot or so above it. Covering the ends of the lamp, which usually are not uniformly bright, may enhance the effect. Turn out the other lights in the room and hold an opaque card an inch or less above the paper. Various positions should be tried for optimum results. Note the narrow bright line and the broader dark line at the outer and inner edges of the half-shadow; these are the Mach bands. The lower illustration is a photograph of a half-shadow produced by the method described. The reproduction of the photograph does not retain all the characteristics of the original because of losses inherent in the reproduction process.

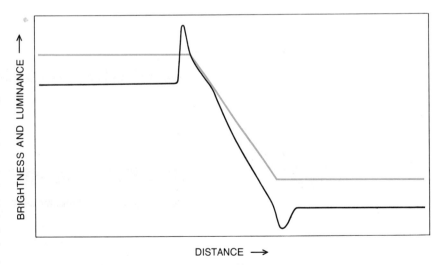

OBSERVED BRIGHTNESS CURVE obtained by psychophysical measurements (*black line*) has two sharp flections, one corresponding to the bright band and the other to the dark band. Measurement of actual luminance (*colored line*) across a half-shadow region reveals that the effect lies in the eye of the beholder and is not an objective phenomenon.

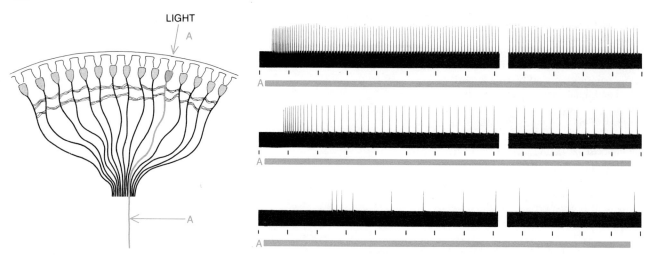

RATE OF DISCHARGE of nerve impulses produced by steady illumination of a single receptor, *A*, in the eye of the horseshoe crab *Limulus* is directly related to the intensity of the light. The nerve fibers from the receptor are separated by microdissection and connected to an electrode from an amplifier and a recorder.

The top record shows the response of *A* to steady, high-intensity light. The middle record shows the response to light of moderate intensity, and the lower record the response to low-intensity illumination. Duration of the light signal is indicated by the colored bar. Each mark above the colored bar indicates one-fifth of a second.

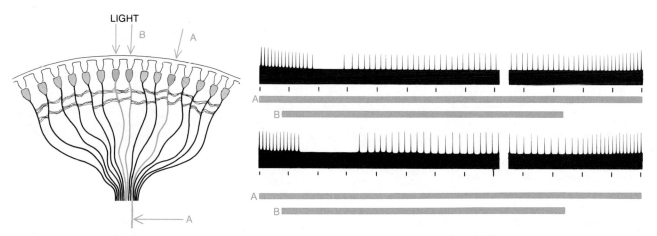

INHIBITION of receptor, *A*, steadily exposed to moderate illumination is produced when neighboring receptors, *B*, are also illuminated. The beginning and the end of the records show the initial and final rate of impulses by *A*. The colored bars indicate duration of light signals. The upper record shows the effects on *A* of moderate-intensity illumination of *B*. The lower record shows the effect on *A* of high-intensity illumination of *B*. The stronger the illumination on neighboring receptors, the stronger the inhibitory effect.

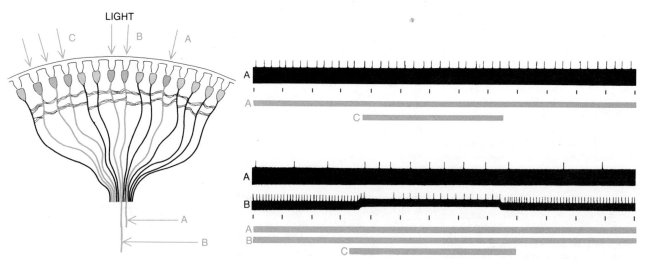

DISINHIBITION of receptor *A* occurs when the inhibition exerted on it by the *B* receptors is partially released by illuminating the large area *C*. The upper record shows that *A*'s activity is not affected when *C* also is illuminated because of the distance between them. The first part of the lower record shows the inhibitory effect of *B* on *A*, then the inhibition of *B* when *C* is illuminated and the concomitant disinhibition of *A*. When the illumination of *C* stops, *B* returns to a higher rate of activity and resumes its inhibition of *A*.

has been demonstrated to be essentially correct in experiments that H. K. Hartline and I, together with our colleagues, have carried out over the past 20 years.

We measured the responses of single neurons in the compound lateral eye of the horseshoe crab *Limulus*. (The animal also has two simple eyes in the front of its carapace near the midline.) The lateral eye of the horseshoe crab is comparatively large (about a centimeter in length) but otherwise it is much like the eye of a fly or a bee. It consists of about 1,000 ommatidia (literally "little eyes"), each of which appears to function as a single photoreceptor unit. Excitation does not spread from one receptor to another; it is confined to whatever receptor unit is illuminated. Nerve fibers arise from the receptors in small bundles that come together to form the optic nerve. Just behind the photoreceptors the small nerve bundles are interconnected by a network of nerve fibers. This network, or plexus, is a true retina even though its function is almost purely inhibitory.

Both the local excitatory and the extended inhibitory influences can be observed directly. A small bundle of fibers from a single receptor is separated by microdissection from the main trunk of the optic nerve and placed on an electrode. In this way the nerve impulses generated by light striking the receptor can be recorded. Weak stimulation produces a low rate of discharge; strong stimulation produces a high rate. These responses are typical of many simple sense organs.

In addition to the excitatory discharge there is a concomitant inhibitory effect. When a receptor unit fires, it inhibits its neighbors. This is a mutual effect: each unit inhibits others and in turn is inhibited by them. The strength of the inhibition depends on the level of activity of the interacting units and the distance between them. In general near neighbors affect one another more than distant neighbors, and the stronger the illumination, the stronger the inhibitory effect. We discovered that such an organization can produce a second-order effect that we call disinhibition. If two sets of receptors are close enough together to interact, they inhibit each other when both sets are illuminated. Now suppose a third set of receptors, far enough away so that it can interact with only one of the two sets of receptors, is illuminated. The activity of the third set will inhibit one set of the original pair, which in turn reduces the inhibition on

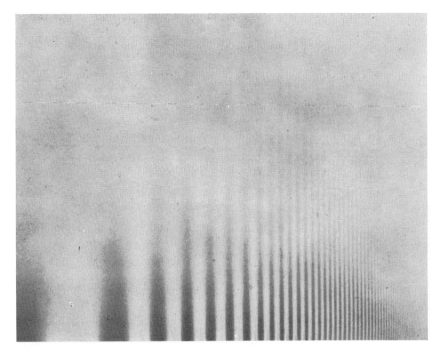

FILTER produced by lateral inhibition at low spatial frequencies and the lack of resolving power of the retina at high spatial frequencies causes intermediate spatial frequencies to be the most distinctly seen. The width of the vertical dark and light bands decreases in a logarithmic sinusoidal manner from the left to the right; the contrast varies logarithmically from less than 1 percent at the top to about 30 percent at the bottom. The objective contrast at any one height in the figure is the same for all spatial frequencies, yet the spatial frequencies in the middle appear more distinct than those at high or low frequencies; that is, the dark lines appear taller at the center of the figure. The effects of changes in viewing distance, luminance, adaptation and sharpness of eye focus can be demonstrated by the viewer.

MACH BAND PHENOMENON created with horizontal lines is shown here. In the illustration at left the black lines are a constant thickness from the left side to the midpoint and then thicken gradually. When the illustration is viewed from a distance, a vertical white "Mach band" appears down the middle. In the illustration at right the horizontal black lines are a constant thickness from the right side to the midpoint and then thin out. When viewed from a distance, the illustration appears to have a vertical black band down the middle.

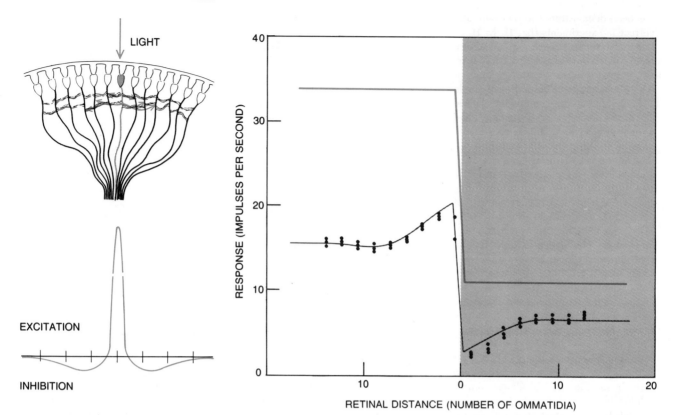

LIGHT

EXCITATION

INHIBITION

RESPONSE (IMPULSES PER SECOND)

RETINAL DISTANCE (NUMBER OF OMMATIDIA)

LATERAL INHIBITION in the eye of the horseshoe crab is strongest between receptors a short distance apart and grows weaker as the distance between receptors increases. Below the eye section is a graph of the type of excitatory and inhibitory fields that would be produced by the illumination of a single receptor. The colored line in the graph on the right shows what the retinal response would be to a sharp light-to-dark contour if lateral inhibition did not occur. The points on the graph show responses actually elicited by three scans of the pattern across the receptor in an experiment by Robert B. Barlow, Jr., of Syracuse University. The thin line shows the theoretical responses for lateral inhibition as computed by Donald A. Quarles, Jr., of the IBM Watson Research Center.

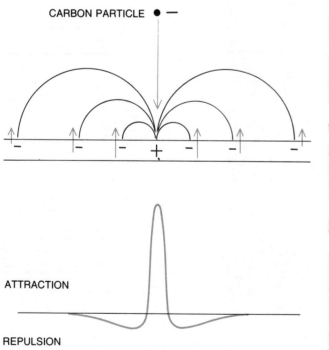

CARBON PARTICLE ● —

ATTRACTION

REPULSION

EDGE EFFECT in xerographic copying is the result of the shape of the electrostatic field (which is quite similar to that of the "neural" field in the top illustration) around a single charged point on the xerographic plate (*upper left*). The first panel on the right shows the original pattern. The middle panel shows a Xerox copy of the original. Note how contrast at the edges is greatly enhanced. The bottom panel shows a Xerox copy made with a halftone screen placed over the original so that the pattern is broken up into many dots.

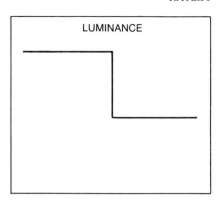

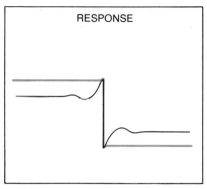

STEP PATTERN of illumination (*left*) also has a step-pattern luminance curve (as measured by a photometer) across the contour. A computer simulation of the response of the *Limulus* eye to the pattern (*black curve at right*) shows a maximum and a minimum that are the result of inhibitory interaction among the receptors. The colored curve at right shows how the pattern looks to a person; the small peak and dip in the curve indicate slight subjective contrast enhancement at the contour known as "border contrast."

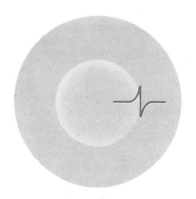

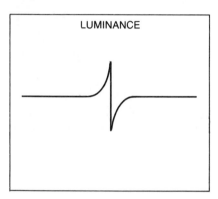

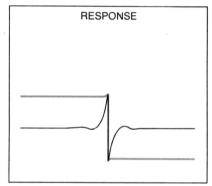

LUMINANCE on both sides of the Craik-O'Brien contour is the same but the inside (here simulated) is brighter. The human visual system may extrapolate (*colored curve*) from the maximum and minimum produced by inhibitory processes (*black curve at right*).

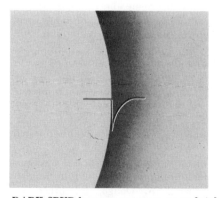

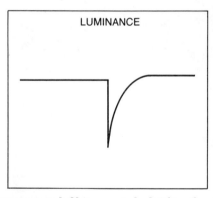

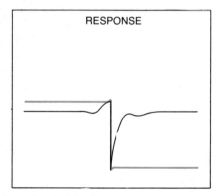

DARK SPUR between areas can create brightness reversal. Objectively the area at left of the contour is darker than the area at far right, but to an observer the left side (here simulated) will appear to be brighter than the right side. This brightness reversal agrees with the extrapolation (*colored curve*) from the maximum and minimum produced by inhibitory processes (*black curve at right*).

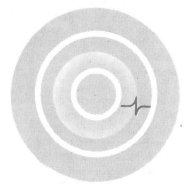

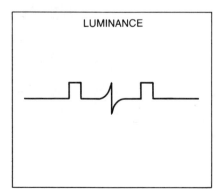

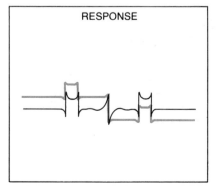

TWO BANDS OF LIGHT of equal intensity are superimposed on backgrounds of equal luminance separated by a Craik-O'Brien contour. The lights add their luminance to the apparent brightness (*colored curve*) and one band appears brighter than the other.

CRAIK-O'BRIEN EFFECT (this example is known as the Cornsweet illusion) is the result of a specific variation of luminance at the contour, which makes the outer zone appear slightly darker even though it has the same luminance as the inner zone. The effect here is less than in the original because of difficulty in reproducing the actual intensity relations.

RAPID ROTATION of this disk will create the Cornsweet illusion. The white spur creates a local variation near the contour between the two zones that causes the apparent brightness of the inner zone to increase. In the same way the dark spur creates a local variation that causes the outer zone to appear darker. Except in the spur region the objective luminance of the disk when it is rotating is the same in both the inner and the outer region.

the remaining set, thus increasing their rate of discharge [*see bottom illustration on page 174*]. Following the discovery of disinhibition in the eye of the horseshoe crab, Victor J. Wilson and Paul R. Burgess of Rockefeller University found that some increases in neural activity (called recurrent facilitation) that had been observed in spinal motoneurones in the cat were actually disinhibition. Subsequently M. Ito and his colleagues at the University of Tokyo observed a similar type of disinhibition in the action of the cerebellum on Deiter's nucleus in the cat.

The spatial distribution and relative magnitudes of the excitatory and inhibitory influences for any particular receptor unit in the eye of *Limulus* can be represented graphically as a narrow central field of excitatory influence surrounded by a more extensive but weaker field of inhibitory influence [*see top illustration on page 176*].

As Georg von Békésy has shown, the approximate response of an inhibitory network can be calculated graphically by superimposing the graphs for each of the interacting units, each graph scaled according to the intensity of the stimulus where it is centered. The summed effects of overlapping fields of excitation (positive values) and inhibition (negative values) at any particular point would determine the response at that point. In the limit of infinitesimally small separations of overlapping units, this would be mathematically equivalent to using the superposition theorem or the convolution integral to calculate the response. In fact, these inhibitory interactions may be expressed in a wide variety of essentially equivalent mathematical forms. The form Hartline and I used at first is a set of simultaneous equations—one equation for each of the interacting receptor units. Our colleagues Frederick A. Dodge, Jr., Bruce W. Knight, Jr., and Jun-ichi Toyoda have since that time expressed the properties of the inhibitory network in a less cumbersome and more general form: a transfer function relating the Fourier transform of the distribution of the intensity of the stimulus to the Fourier transform of the distribution of the magnitude of the response. This in effect treats the retinal network as a filter of the sinusoidal components in the stimulus, and can be applied equally well to both spatial and temporal variations. The overall filtering effect of the *Limulus* retina is to attenuate both the lowest and the highest spatial and temporal frequencies of the sinusoidal components.

It has long been known that spatial and temporal filtering effects of much the same kind occur in our own visual system. The main characteristics of the spatial "filter" can be seen by viewing the test pattern devised by Fergus W. Campbell and his colleagues at the University of Cambridge [*see top illustration on page 175*].

Even without considering the filter-like properties of neural networks it is possible to see how the subjective Mach bands can be produced by the interaction of narrow fields of excitation and broad fields of inhibition. Near the boundary between the light and dark fields some of the receptors will be inhibited not only by their dimly lit neighbors but also by some brightly lit receptors. The total inhibition of these boundary receptors will therefore be greater than the inhibition of dimly lit receptors farther from the boundary. Similarly, a brightly lit receptor near the boundary will be in the inhibitory field of some dimly lit receptors and as a result will have less inhibition acting on it than brightly lit receptors farther away from the boundary. Because of these differential effects near the boundary the response of the neural network in the *Limulus* retina will show a substantial maximum and minimum adjacent to the boundary even though the stimulus does not have such variations.

Opposed excitatory and inhibitory influences can mediate some highly specialized functions in higher animals. Depending on how these opposed influences are organized, they can detect motion, the orientation of a line or the difference between colors. No matter how complicated the visual system is, however, the basic contrast effects of the excitatory-inhibitory processes show up. For example, recent experiments by Russell L. De Valois and Paul L. Pease of the University of California at Berkeley show a contour enhancement similar to the bright Mach band in responses of monkey lateral geniculate cells. The simple lateral inhibition that produces contrast effects such as Mach bands may be a basic process in all the more highly evolved visual mechanisms.

Contrast phenomena are by no means found only in the nervous system. Indeed, contrast is found in any system of interacting components where opposed fields of positive (excitatory) and negative (inhibitory) influences exist. Whether the system is neural, electrical, chemical or an abstract mathematical model is irrelevant; all that is needed to produce a contrast effect is a certain distribution of the opposed influences. A familiar example is the contrast effect in xerography. The xerographic process does not reproduce solid black or gray areas very well. Only the edges of extended uniform areas are reproduced unless some special precautions are taken. This failing is inherent in the basic process itself. In the making of a xerographic copy a selenium plate is first electrostatically charged. Where light falls on the plate the electrostatic charge is lost; in dark areas the charge is retained. A black powder spread over the plate clings to the charged areas by electrostatic attraction and is eventually transferred and fused to paper to produce the final copy.

The electrostatic attraction of any point on the plate is determined not by the charge at that point alone but by the integrated effects of the electrostatic fields of all the charges in the neighborhood. Since the shapes of the positive and negative components of the individual fields happen to be very much like the shapes of the excitatory and inhibitory components of neural unit fields in the retina, the consequences are much the same too [*see bottom illustration on page 176*]. Contours are enhanced; uniform areas are lost. To obtain a xerographic copy of the uniform areas one merely has to put a halftone screen over the original. The screen breaks up the uniform areas into many small discontinuities, in effect many contours.

Similar contrast effects are seen in photography and in television. In photography a chemical by-product of the development process at one point can diffuse to neighboring points and inhibit further development there, causing spurious edge effects; in television the secondary emission of electrons from one point in the image on the signal plate in the camera can fall on neighboring points and "inhibit" them, creating negative "halos," or dark areas, around bright spots. The similarity of the contrast effects in such diverse systems is not a trivial coincidence. It is an indication of a universal principle: The enhancement of contours by contrast depends on particular relations among interacting elements in a system and not on the particular mechanisms that achieve those relations.

How a contour itself can affect the contrast of the areas it separates cannot be explained quite so easily. This effect of contour on contrast was first investigated by Kenneth Craik of the University of Cambridge and was described in

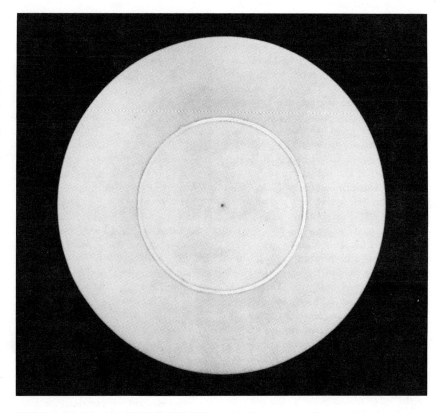

SOURCE OF CRAIK-O'BRIEN EFFECT can be demonstrated by covering the contour with a wire or string. When this is done, the inner and outer regions appear equally bright.

his doctoral dissertation of 1940. Craik's work was not published, however, and the same phenomenon (along with related ones) was rediscovered by Vivian O'Brien of Johns Hopkins University in 1958. The Craik-O'Brien effect, as I shall call it, has been of great interest to neurophysiologists and psychologists in recent years.

A particular example of this effect, sometimes called the Cornsweet illusion, is produced by separating two identical gray areas with a special contour that has a narrow bright spur and a narrow dark spur [see top illustration on page 178]. Although the two uniform areas away from the contour have the same objective luminance, the gray of the area adjacent to the light spur appears to be lighter than the gray of the area adjacent to the dark spur. When the contour is covered with a thick string, the grays of the two areas are seen to be the same. When the masking string is removed, the difference reappears but takes a few moments to develop. These effects can be very pronounced; not only can a contour cause contrast to appear when there actually is no difference in objective luminance but also a suitable contour can cause contrast to appear that is the reverse of the objective luminance.

With the choice of the proper contour a number of objectively different patterns can be made to appear similar in certain important respects [see illustrations on page 177]. It is reasonable to assume that in all these cases the dominant underlying neural events are also similar. With the mathematical equation for the response of a Limulus eye one can calculate the neural responses to be expected from each type of pattern when processed by a simple inhibitory network. When this is done, one finds that the calculated responses are all similar to one another. Each has a maximum on the left and a minimum on the right. Furthermore, there is a certain similarity between the calculated neural response and the subjective experience of a human observer viewing the patterns: where the computed response has a maximum, the pattern appears brighter on that side of the contour; where the computed response has a minimum, the pattern appears darker on that side of the contour. Indeed, merely by extending a line from the maximum out to the edge of that side of the pattern and a line from the minimum out to the edge of that side of the pattern one obtains a fair approximation to the apparent brightness. This correspon-

dence suggests that opposed excitatory and inhibitory influences in neural networks of our visual systems are again partly responsible for creating the effect. Even so, much would remain to be explained. Why should the influence of the contour be extended over the entire adjacent area rather than just locally? And why do three distinctly different stimuli, when used as contours, produce much the same subjective result?

The answer to both of these questions may be one and the same. Communication engineers have experimented with a number of sophisticated means of data compression to increase the efficiency of transmitting images containing large amounts of redundant information. For example, if a picture is being transmitted, only information about contours need be sent; the uniform areas between contours can be restored later by computer from information in the amplitudes of the maxima and minima at the contours. By the same token signals from the retina may be "compressed" and the redundant information extrapolated from the maximum and the minimum in the neural response. Such a process, which was postulated by Glenn A. Fry

KOREAN VASE from the 18th century provides an excellent example of the effect of a dark spur between areas. The moon appears to be brighter than the sky directly below it, but the actual luminance is just the reverse. If only a portion of the moon and an equal portion of the sky about one moon diameter below it are viewed through two identical small holes in a paper so that the dark contour is masked, the moon appears darker than the sky.

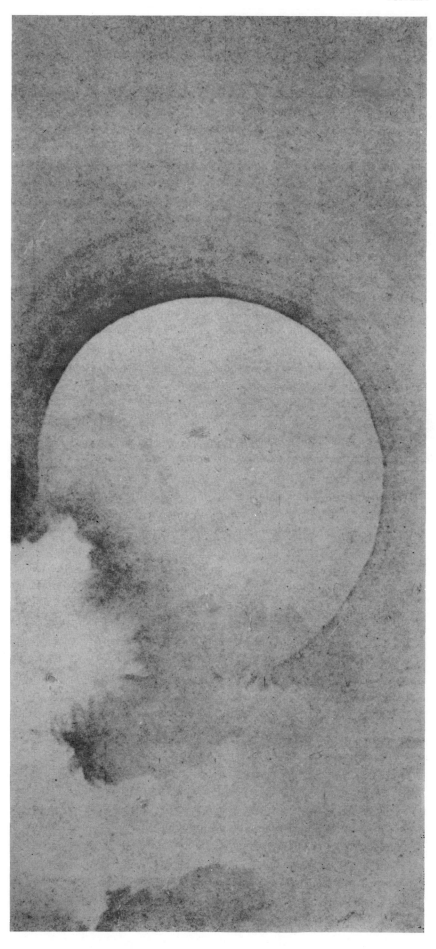

of Ohio State University many years ago, could explain the Craik-O'Brien effect.

What the actual mechanisms might be in our visual system that could "decode" the signals resulting from data compression by the retina and "restore" redundant information removed in the compression are empirical problems that have not yet been directly investigated by neurophysiologists. The problem as I have stated it may even be a will-o'-the-wisp; it is possible that there is no need to actually restore redundant information. The maximum and minimum in the retinal response may "set" brightness discriminators in the brain, and provided that there are no intervening maxima and minima (that is, visible contours) the apparent brightness of adjacent areas would not deviate from that set by the maximum or the minimum.

Some evidence that apparent brightness is actually set by the maximum and minimum at a contour or discontinuity and is then extrapolated to adjacent areas can be found in experiments conducted by L. E. Arend, J. N. Buehler and Gregory R. Lockhead at Duke University. They worked with patterns similar to those that create the Craik-O'Brien effect. On each side of the contour they produced an additional band of light. They found that the difference in apparent brightness between each band of light and its background depended only on the actual increment in luminance provided by the band, but that the apparent brightness of the two bands in relation to each other was determined by the apparent brightness of the background. For example, if two bands of equal luminance are superimposed on two backgrounds of equal luminance that are separated by a Craik-O'Brien contour, one of the bands of light will appear brighter than the other [*see bottom illustration on page 177*]. A number of related phenomena, in which contrast effects are propagated across several adjacent areas, are under investigation by Edwin H. Land and John H. McCann at the Polaroid Corporation. These experi-

JAPANESE INK PAINTING, "Autumn Moon" by Keinen, has a moon that objectively is only very slightly lighter than the sky. Much of the difference in apparent brightness is created by the moon's contour. The extent of the effect can be seen by covering the moon's edge with string. The painting, made about 1900, is in the collection of the late Akira Shimazu of Nara in Japan.

CHINESE TING YAO SAUCER is an example of the famous Ting white porcelain produced in the Sung dynasty of about A.D. 1000. Although the entire surface is covered with
only a single creamy white glaze, the incised lotus design appears brighter than the background because of the incisions, which have a sharp inner edge and a graded outer edge,
producing exactly the kind of contour that creates an apparent difference in brightness.

vase with a light meter under ordinary
room lights showed that the luminance
of the moon was 15 foot-lamberts and
the space one moon diameter below was
20 foot-lamberts. The contour effect is so
strong that the apparent brightness of
the two areas is just the reverse of the
objective luminance.

The contour-contrast effect can be
produced on a ceramic surface by still
another technique. This technique was
developed more than 1,000 years ago in
the Ting white porcelain of the Sung
dynasty and in the northern celadon cer-
amics of the same period. In the creation
of the effect a design was first incised in
the wet clay with a knife. The cut had a
sharp inner edge and a sloping outer
edge. The clay was then dried and covered with a white glaze. The slightly
creamy cast of the glaze inside the cuts
produces the necessary gradient to create the Craik-O'Brien effect. The result
is that the pattern appears slightly
brighter than the surround [see illustration at left]. Since the effect depends on
variations in the depth of the translucent
monochrome glaze, it is much more subtle than it is in the Japanese painting and
in the Korean vase. But then subtlety
and restraint were characteristic of the
Sung ceramists.

These examples of the effects of contrast and contour from the visual sciences and the visual arts illustrate the
need for a better understanding of how
elementary processes are organized into
complex systems. In recent years the
discipline of biology has become increasingly analytical. Much of the study
of life has become the study of the behavior of single cells and the molecular
events within them. Although the analytic approach has been remarkably pro-
ductive, it does not come to grips with
one of the fundamental problems facing
modern biological science: how unitary
structures and elementary processes are
organized into the complex functional
systems that make up living organs and
organisms. Fortunately, however, we are
not faced with an either-or choice. The
analytic and the organic approaches are
neither incompatible nor mutually exclusive; they are complementary, and advances in one frequently facilitate advances in the other. All that is required
to make biology truly a life science, no
matter what the level of analysis, is to
occasionally adopt a holistic or organic
approach. It is probably the elaborate
organization of unitary structures and
elementary processes that distinguishes
living beings from lifeless things.

ments lend further support to the general view outlined here.

Of course, the human visual system
is far too complex for the simple notion that apparent brightness is determined by difference at contours to be
the whole story. Nonetheless, the general idea contains at least the rudiments
of an explanation that is consistent with
known physiological mechanisms and
with the observed phenomena. Several
entirely different distributions of illumination may look much the same to the
human eye simply because the eye happens to abstract and send to the brain
only those features that the objectively
different patterns have in common. This
type of data compression may be a basic
principle common to many different
kinds of neural systems.

Even if the cause of the Craik-O'Brien
effect is in doubt, the effect itself is in-
controvertible. Although the effects of
contour on perceived contrast are relatively new to the scientific community,
the same effects have long been known
to artists and artisans. One can only

speculate on how the effects were discovered. Very likely they emerged in
some new artistic technique that was
developed for another purpose. Once
such a technique had been perfected, it
doubtless would have persisted and been
handed down from generation to generation. Furthermore, following the initial
discovery the technique would probably
have been applied in other media. In
any event such techniques date back as
far as the Sung dynasty of China (A.D.
960–1279), and they are still employed
in Oriental art. For example, in a Japanese ink painting made about 1900 a
single deft stroke of the brush greatly
increases the apparent brightness of the
moon [see illustration on preceding page].
If the contour is covered with a piece of
string, the apparent brightness of the
moon diminishes and that area is seen to
be very little brighter than its surround.

A similar effect is found in a scene on
an 18th-century Korean vase [see illustration on page 180]. Here the moon is
actually darker than the space below it.
Measurements of a photograph of the

The Visual Cortex of the Brain

18

November 1963

*A start toward understanding how it analyzes images
on the retina can be made through studies of the
responses that individual cells in the visual system
of the cat give to varying patterns of light*

An image of the outside world striking the retina of the eye activates a most intricate process that results in vision: the transformation of the retinal image into a perception. The transformation occurs partly in the retina but mostly in the brain, and it is, as one can recognize instantly by considering how modest in comparison is the achievement of a camera, a task of impressive magnitude.

The process begins with the responses of some 130 million light-sensitive receptor cells in each retina. From these cells messages are transmitted to other retinal cells and then sent on to the brain, where they must be analyzed and interpreted. To get an idea of the magnitude of the task, think what is involved in watching a moving animal, such as a horse. At a glance one takes in its size, form, color and rate of movement. From tiny differences in the two retinal images there results a three-dimensional picture. Somehow the brain manages to compare this picture with previous impressions; recognition occurs and then any appropriate action can be taken.

The organization of the visual system —a large, intricately connected population of nerve cells in the retina and brain —is still poorly understood. In recent years, however, various studies have begun to reveal something of the arrangement and function of these cells. A decade ago Stephen W. Kuffler, working with cats at the Johns Hopkins Hospital, discovered that some analysis of visual patterns takes place outside the brain, in the nerve cells of the retina. My colleague Torsten N. Wiesel and I at the Harvard Medical School, exploring the first stages of the processing that occurs in the brain of the cat, have mapped the visual pathway a little further: to what appears to be the sixth step from the retina to the cortex of the cerebrum. This kind of work falls far short of providing a full understanding of vision, but it does convey some idea of the mechanisms and circuitry of the visual system.

In broad outline the visual pathway is clearly defined [*see bottom illustration on opposite page*]. From the retina of each eye visual messages travel along the optic nerve, which consists of about a million nerve fibers. At the junction known as the chiasm about half of the nerves cross over into opposite hemispheres of the brain, the other nerves remaining on the same side. The optic nerve fibers lead to the first way stations in the brain: a pair of cell clusters called the lateral geniculate bodies. From here new fibers course back through the brain to the visual area of the cerebral cortex. It is convenient, although admittedly a gross oversimplification, to think of the pathway from retina to cortex as consisting of six types of nerve cells, of which three are in the retina, one is in the geniculate body and two are in the cortex.

Nerve cells, or neurons, transmit messages in the form of brief electrochemical impulses. These travel along the outer membrane of the cell, notably along the membrane of its long principal fiber, the axon. It is possible to obtain an electrical record of impulses of a single nerve cell by placing a fine electrode near the cell body or one of its fibers. Such measurements have shown that impulses travel along the nerves at velocities of between half a meter and 100 meters per second. The impulses in a given fiber all have about the same amplitude; the strength of the stimuli that give rise to them is reflected not in amplitude but in frequency.

At its terminus the fiber of a nerve cell makes contact with another nerve cell (or with a muscle cell or gland cell), forming the junction called the synapse. At most synapses an impulse on reaching the end of a fiber causes the release of a small amount of a specific substance, which diffuses outward to the membrane of the next cell. There the substance either excites the cell or inhibits it. In excitation the substance acts to bring the cell into a state in which it is more likely to "fire"; in inhibition the substance acts to prevent firing. For most synapses the substances that act as transmitters are unknown. Moreover, there is no sure way to determine from microscopic appearances alone whether a synapse is excitatory or inhibitory.

It is at the synapses that the modification and analysis of nerve messages take place. The kind of analysis depends partly on the nature of the synapse: on how many nerve fibers converge on a single cell and on how the excitatory and inhibitory endings distribute themselves. In most parts of the nervous system the anatomy is too intricate to reveal much about function. One way to circumvent this difficulty is to record impulses with microelectrodes in anesthetized animals, first from the fibers coming into a structure of neurons and then from the neurons themselves, or from the fibers they send onward. Comparison of the behavior of incoming and outgoing fibers provides a basis for learning what the structure does. Through such exploration of the different parts of the brain concerned with vision one can hope to build up some idea of how the entire visual system works.

That is what Wiesel and I have undertaken, mainly through studies of the visual system of the cat. In our experiments the anesthetized animal faces a wide screen 1.5 meters away, and we shine various patterns of white light on the screen with a projector. Simultane-

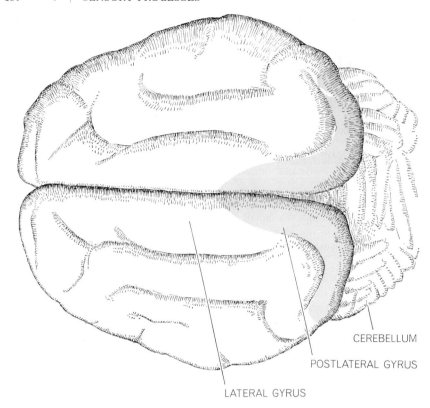

CEREBELLUM

POSTLATERAL GYRUS

LATERAL GYRUS

CORTEX OF CAT'S BRAIN is depicted as it would be seen from the top. The colored region indicates the cortical area that deals at least in a preliminary way with vision.

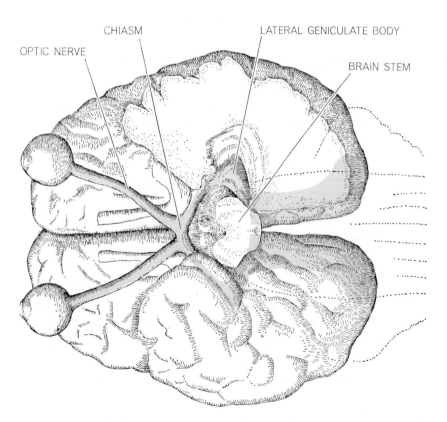

CHIASM   LATERAL GENICULATE BODY

OPTIC NERVE

BRAIN STEM

VISUAL SYSTEM appears in this representation of the human brain as viewed below. Visual pathway from retinas to cortex via the lateral geniculate body is shown in color.

ously we penetrate the visual portion of the cortex with microelectrodes. In that way we can record the responses of individual cells to the light patterns. Sometimes it takes many hours to find the region of the retina with which a particular visual cell is linked and to work out the optimum stimuli for that cell. The reader should bear in mind the relation between each visual cell—no matter how far along the visual pathway it may be—and the retina. It requires an image on the retina to evoke a meaningful response in any visual cell, however indirect and complex the linkage may be.

The retina is a complicated structure, in both its anatomy and its physiology, and the description I shall give is highly simplified. Light coming through the lens of the eye falls on the mosaic of receptor cells in the retina. The receptor cells do not send impulses directly through the optic nerve but instead connect with a set of retinal cells called bipolar cells. These in turn connect with retinal ganglion cells, and it is the latter set of cells, the third in the visual pathway, that sends its fibers—the optic nerve fibers—to the brain.

This series of cells and synapses is no simple bucket brigade for impulses: a receptor may send nerve endings to more than one bipolar cell, and several receptors may converge on one bipolar cell. The same holds for the synapses between the bipolar cells and the retinal ganglion cells. Stimulating a single receptor by light might therefore be expected to have an influence on many bipolar or ganglion cells; conversely, it should be possible to influence one bipolar or retinal ganglion cell from a number of receptors and hence from a substantial area of the retina.

The area of receptor mosaic in the retina feeding into a single visual cell is called the receptive field of the cell. This term is applied to any cell in the visual system to refer to the area of retina with which the cell is connected—the retinal area that on stimulation produces a response from the cell.

Any of the synapses with a particular cell may be excitatory or inhibitory, so that stimulation of a particular point on the retina may either increase or decrease the cell's firing rate. Moreover, a single cell may receive several excitatory and inhibitory impulses at once, with the result that it will respond according to the net effect of these inputs. In considering the behavior of a single cell an observer should remember that it is just one of a huge popu-

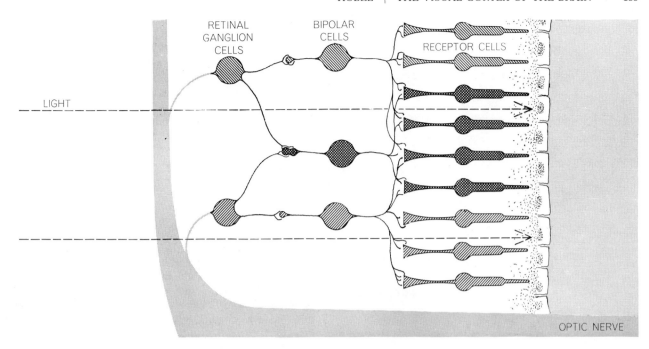

STRUCTURE OF RETINA is depicted schematically. Images fall on the receptor cells, of which there are about 130 million in each retina. Some analysis of an image occurs as the receptors transmit messages to the retinal ganglion cells via the bipolar cells. A group of receptors funnels into a particular ganglion cell, as indicated by the shading; that group forms the ganglion cell's receptive field. Inasmuch as the fields of several ganglion cells overlap, one receptor may send messages to several ganglion cells.

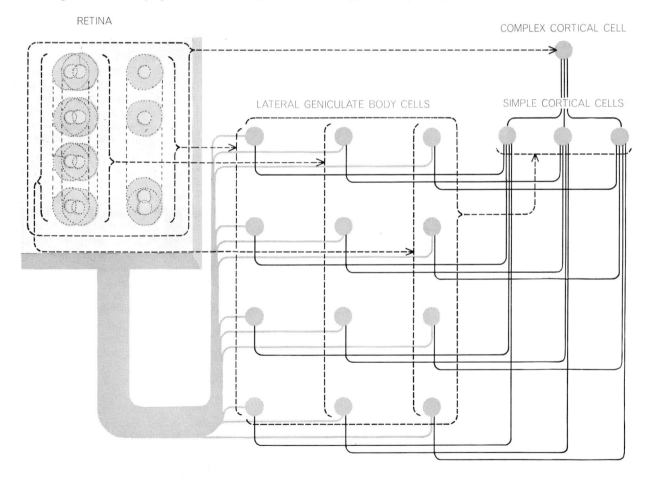

VISUAL PROCESSING BY BRAIN begins in the lateral geniculate body, which continues the analysis made by retinal cells. In the cortex "simple" cells respond strongly to line stimuli, provided that the position and orientation of the line are suitable for a particular cell. "Complex" cells respond well to line stimuli, but the position of the line is not critical and the cell continues to respond even if a properly oriented stimulus is moved, as long as it remains in the cell's receptive field. Broken lines indicate how receptive fields of all these cells overlap on the retina; solid lines, how several cells at one stage affect a single cell at the next stage.

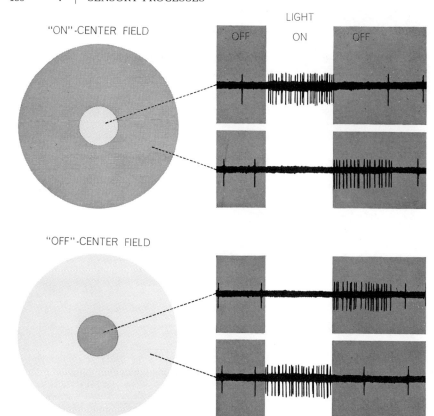

"ON"-CENTER FIELD

"OFF"-CENTER FIELD

LIGHT

OFF   ON   OFF

CONCENTRIC FIELDS are characteristic of retinal ganglion cells and of geniculate cells. At top an oscilloscope recording shows strong firing by an "on"-center type of cell when a spot of light strikes the field center; if the spot hits an "off" area, the firing is suppressed until the light goes off. At bottom are responses of another cell of the "off"-center type.

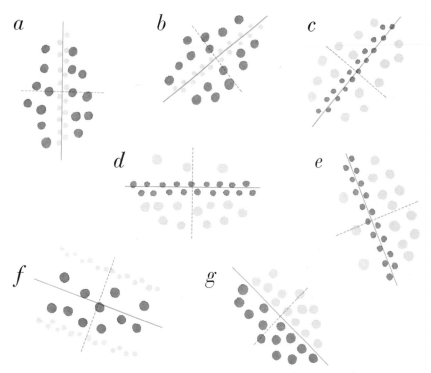

a   *b*   *c*

d   *e*

f   *g*

SIMPLE CORTICAL CELLS have receptive fields of various types. In all of them the "on" and "off" areas, represented by colored and gray dots respectively, are separated by straight boundaries. Orientations of fields vary, as indicated particularly at *a* and *b*. In the cat's visual system such fields are generally one millimeter or less in diameter.

lation of cells: a stimulus that excites one cell will undoubtedly excite many others, meanwhile inhibiting yet another array of cells and leaving others entirely unaffected.

For many years it has been known that retinal ganglion cells fire at a fairly steady rate even in the absence of any stimulation. Kuffler was the first to observe how the retinal ganglion cells of mammals are influenced by small spots of light. He found that the resting discharges of a cell were intensified or diminished by light in a small and more or less circular region of the retina. That region was of course the cell's receptive field. Depending on where in the field a spot of light fell, either of two responses could be produced. One was an "on" response, in which the cell's firing rate increased under the stimulus of light. The other was an "off" response, in which the stimulus of light decreased the cell's firing rate. Moreover, turning the light off usually evoked a burst of impulses from the cell. Kuffler called the retinal regions from which these responses could be evoked "on" regions and "off" regions.

On mapping the receptive fields of a large number of retinal ganglion cells into "on" and "off" regions, Kuffler discovered that there were two distinct cell types. In one the receptive field consisted of a small circular "on" area and a surrounding zone that gave "off" responses. Kuffler termed this an "on"-center cell. The second type, which he called "off"-center, had just the reverse form of field—an "off" center and an "on" periphery [*see top illustration on this page*]. For a given cell the effects of light varied markedly according to the place in which the light struck the receptive field. Two spots of light shone on separate parts of an "on" area produced a more vigorous "on" response than either spot alone, whereas if one spot was shone on an "on" area and the other on an "off" area, the two effects tended to neutralize each other, resulting in a very weak "on" or "off" response. In an "on"-center cell, illuminating the entire central "on" region evoked a maximum response; a smaller or larger spot of light was less effective.

Lighting up the whole retina diffusely, even though it may affect every receptor in the retina, does not affect a retinal ganglion cell nearly so strongly as a small circular spot of exactly the right size placed so as to cover precisely the receptive-field center. The main concern of these cells seems to be the contrast in illumination between one retinal region and surrounding regions.

Retinal ganglion cells differ greatly in the size of their receptive-field centers. Cells near the fovea (the part of the retina serving the center of gaze) are specialized for precise discrimination; in the monkey the field centers of these cells may be about the same size as a single cone—an area subtending a few minutes of arc at the cornea. On the other hand, some cells far out in the retinal periphery have field centers up to a millimeter or so in diameter. (In man one millimeter of retina corresponds to an arc of about three degrees in the 180-degree visual field.) Cells with such large receptive-field centers are probably specialized for work in very dim light, since they can sum up messages from a large number of receptors.

Given this knowledge of the kind of visual information brought to the brain by the optic nerve, our first problem was to learn how the messages were handled at the first central way station, the lateral geniculate body. Compared with the retina, the geniculate body is a relatively simple structure. In a sense there is only one synapse involved, since the incoming optic nerve fibers end in cells that send their fibers directly to the visual cortex. Yet in the cat many optic nerve fibers converge on each geniculate cell, and it is reasonable to expect some change in the visual messages from the optic nerve to the geniculate cells.

When we came to study the geniculate body, we found that the cells have many of the characteristics Kuffler described for retinal ganglion cells. Each geniculate cell is driven from a circumscribed retinal region (the receptive field) and has either an "on" center or an "off" center, with an opposing periphery. There are, however, differences between geniculate cells and retinal ganglion cells, the most important of which is the greatly enhanced capacity of the periphery of a geniculate cell's receptive field to cancel the effects of the center. This means that the lateral geniculate cells must be even more specialized than retinal ganglion cells in responding to spatial differences in retinal illumination rather than to the illumination itself. The lateral geniculate body, in short, has the function of increasing the disparity—already present in retinal ganglion cells—between responses to a small, centered spot and to diffuse light.

In contrast to the comparatively simple lateral geniculate body, the cerebral cortex is a structure of stupendous complexity. The cells of this great plate of

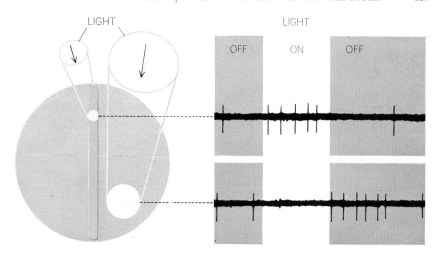

RESPONSE IS WEAK when a circular spot of light is shone on receptive field of a simple cortical cell. Such spots get a vigorous response from retinal and geniculate cells. This cell has a receptive field of type shown at *a* in bottom illustration on preceding page.

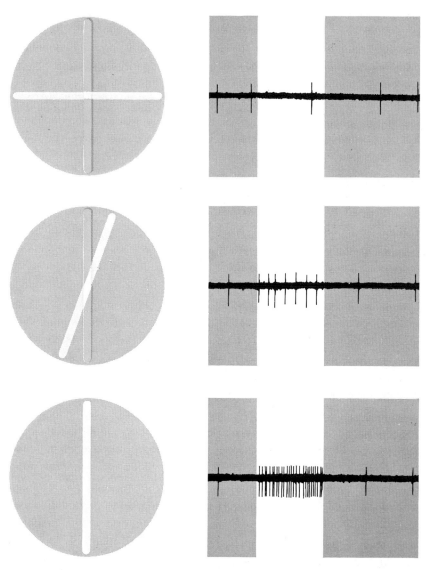

IMPORTANCE OF ORIENTATION to simple cortical cells is indicated by varying responses to a slit of light from a cell preferring a vertical orientation. Horizontal slit *(top)* produces no response, slight tilt a weak response, vertical slit a strong response.

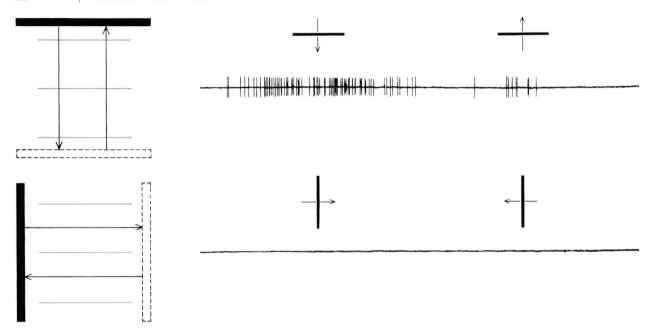

COMPLEX CORTICAL CELL responded vigorously to slow downward movement of a dark, horizontal bar. Upward movement of bar produced a weak response and horizontal movement of a vertical bar produced no response. For other shapes, orientations and movements there are other complex cells showing maximum response. Such cells may figure in perception of form and movement.

gray matter—a structure that would be about 20 square feet in area and a tenth of an inch thick if flattened out—are arranged in a number of more or less distinct layers. The millions of fibers that come in from the lateral geniculate body connect with cortical cells in the layer that is fourth from the top. From here the information is sooner or later disseminated to all layers of the cortex by rich interconnections between them. Many of the cells, particularly those of the third and fifth layers, send their fibers out of the cortex, projecting to centers deep in the brain or passing over to nearby cortical areas for further processing of the visual messages. Our problem was to learn how the information the visual cortex sends out differs from what it takes in.

Most connections between cortical cells are in a direction perpendicular to the surface; side-to-side connections are generally quite short. One might therefore predict that impulses arriving at a particular area of the cortex would exert their effects quite locally. Moreover, the retinas project to the visual cortex (via the lateral geniculate body) in a systematic topologic manner; that is, a given area of cortex gets its input ultimately from a circumscribed area of retina. These two observations suggest that a given cortical cell should have a small receptive field; it should be influenced from a circumscribed retinal region only, just as a geniculate or retinal ganglion cell is. Beyond this the anatomy provides no hint of what the cortex does

with the information it receives about an image on the retina.

In the face of the anatomical complexity of the cortex, it would have been surprising if the cells had proved to have the concentric receptive fields characteristic of cells in the retina and the lateral geniculate body. Indeed, in the cat we have observed no cortical cells with concentric receptive fields; instead there are many different cell types, with fields markedly different from anything seen in the retinal and geniculate cells.

The many varieties of cortical cells may, however, be classified by function into two large groups. One we have called "simple"; the function of these cells is to respond to line stimuli—such shapes as slits, which we define as light lines on a dark background; dark bars (dark lines on a light background), and edges (straight-line boundaries between light and dark regions). Whether or not a given cell responds depends on the orientation of the shape and its position on the cell's receptive field. A bar shone vertically on the screen may activate a given cell, whereas the same cell will fail to respond (but others will respond) if the bar is displaced to one side or moved appreciably out of the vertical. The second group of cortical cells we have called "complex"; they too respond best to bars, slits or edges, provided that, as with simple cells, the shape is suitably oriented for the particular cell under observation. Complex cells, how-

ever, are not so discriminating as to the exact position of the stimulus, provided that it is properly oriented. Moreover, unlike simple cells, they respond with sustained firing to moving lines.

From the preference of simple and complex cells for specific orientation of light stimuli, it follows that there must be a multiplicity of cell types to handle the great number of possible positions and orientations. Wiesel and I have found a large variety of cortical cell responses, even though the number of individual cells we have studied runs only into the hundreds compared with the millions that exist. Among simple cells, the retinal region over which a cell can be influenced—the receptive field—is, like the fields of retinal and geniculate cells, divided into "on" and "off" areas. In simple cells, however, these areas are far from being circularly symmetrical. In a typical example the receptive field consists of a very long and narrow "on" area, which is adjoined on each side by larger "off" regions. The magnitude of an "on" response depends, as with retinal and geniculate cells, on how much either type of region is covered by the stimulating light. A long, narrow slit that just fills the elongated "on" region produces a powerful "on" response. Stimulation with the slit in a different orientation produces a much weaker effect, because the slit is now no longer illuminating all the "on" region but instead includes some of the antagonistic "off" region. A slit at right angles to the optimum orientation for a cell of this type is usually completely ineffective.

In the simple cortical cells the process of pitting these two antagonistic parts of a receptive field against each other is carried still further than it is in the lateral geniculate body. As a rule a large spot of light—or what amounts to the same thing, diffuse light covering the whole retina—evokes no response at all in simple cortical cells. Here the "on" and "off" effects apparently balance out with great precision.

Some other common types of simple receptive fields include an "on" center with a large "off" area to one side and a small one to the other; an "on" and an "off" area side by side; a narrow "off" center with "on" sides; a wide "on" center with narrow "off" sides. All these fields have in common that the border or borders separating "on" and "off" regions are straight and parallel rather than circular [see bottom illustration on page 186]. The most efficient stimuli—slits, edges or dark bars—all involve straight lines. Each cell responds best to a particular orientation of line; other orientations produce less vigorous responses, and usually the orientation perpendicular to the optimum evokes no response at all. A particular cell's optimum, which we term the receptive-field orientation, is thus a property built into the cell by its connections. In general the receptive-field orientation differs from one cell to the next, and it may be vertical, horizontal or oblique. We have no evidence that any one orientation, such as vertical or horizontal, is more common than any other.

How can one explain this specificity of simple cortical cells? We are inclined to think they receive their input directly from the incoming lateral geniculate fibers. We suppose a typical simple cell has for its input a large number of lateral geniculate cells whose "on" centers are arranged along a straight line; a spot of light shone anywhere along that line will activate some of the geniculate cells and lead to activation of the cortical cell. A light shone over the entire area will activate all the geniculate cells and have a tremendous final impact on the cortical cell [see bottom illustration on page 185].

One can now begin to grasp the significance of the great number of cells in the visual cortex. Each cell seems to have its own specific duties; it takes care of one restricted part of the retina, responds best to one particular shape of stimulus and to one particular orientation. To look at the problem from the

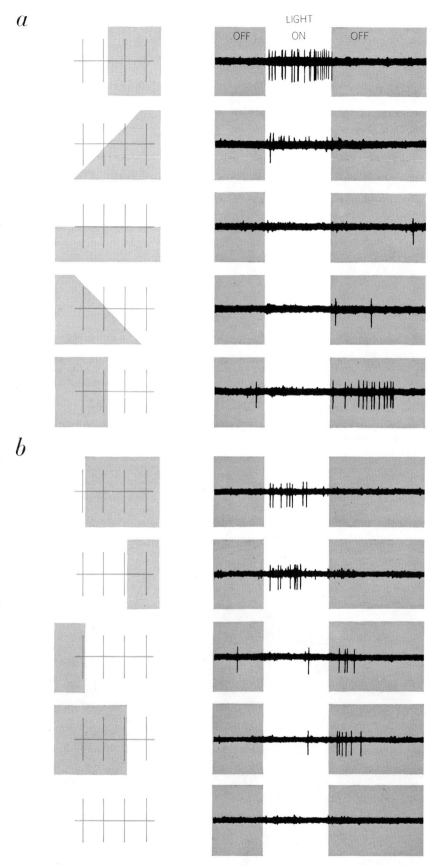

SINGLE COMPLEX CELL showed varying responses to an edge projected on the cell's receptive field in the retina. In group *a* the stimulus was presented in differing orientations. In group *b* all the edges were vertical and all but the last evoked responses regardless of where in the receptive field the light struck. When a large rectangle of light covered entire receptive field, however, as shown at bottom, cell failed to respond.

opposite direction, for each stimulus—each area of the retina stimulated, each type of line (edge, slit or bar) and each orientation of stimulus—there is a particular set of simple cortical cells that will respond; changing any of the stimulus arrangements will cause a whole new population of cells to respond. The number of populations responding successively as the eye watches a slowly rotating propeller is scarcely imaginable.

Such a profound rearrangement and analysis of the incoming messages might seem enough of a task for a single structure, but it turns out to be only part of what happens in the cortex. The next major transformation involves the cortical cells that occupy what is probably the sixth step in the visual pathway: the complex cells, which are also present in this cortical region and to some extent intermixed with the simple cells.

Complex cells are like simple ones in several ways. A cell responds to a stimulus only within a restricted region of retina: the receptive field. It responds best to the line stimuli (slits, edges or dark bars) and the stimulus must be oriented to suit the cell. But complex fields, unlike the simple ones, cannot be mapped into antagonistic "on" and "off" regions.

A typical complex cell we studied happened to fire to a vertical edge, and it gave "on" or "off" responses depending on whether light was to the left or to the right. Other orientations were almost completely without effect [see illustration on opposite page]. These re-

sponses are just what could be expected from a simple cell with a receptive field consisting of an excitatory area separated from an inhibitory one by a vertical boundary. In this case, however, the cell had an additional property that could not be explained by such an arrangement. A vertical edge evoked responses anywhere within the receptive field, "on" responses with light to the left, "off" responses with light to the right. Such behavior cannot be understood in terms of antagonistic "on" and "off" subdivisions of the receptive field, and when we explored the field with small spots we found no such regions. Instead the spot either produced responses at both "on" and "off" or evoked no responses at all.

Complex cells, then, respond like simple cells to one particular aspect of the stimulus, namely its orientation. But when the stimulus is moved, without changing the orientation, a complex cell differs from its simple counterpart chiefly in responding with sustained firing. The firing continues as the stimulus is moved over a substantial retinal area, usually the entire receptive field of the cell, whereas a simple cell will respond to movement only as the stimulus crosses a very narrow boundary separating "on" and "off" regions.

It is difficult to explain this behavior by any scheme in which geniculate cells project directly to complex cells. On the other hand, the findings can be explained fairly well by the supposition

that a complex cell receives its input from a large number of simple cells. This supposition requires only that the simple cells have the same field orientation and be all of the same general type. A complex cell responding to vertical edges, for example, would thus receive fibers from simple cells that have vertically oriented receptive fields. All such a scheme needs to have added is the requirement that the retinal positions of these simple fields be arranged throughout the area occupied by the complex field.

The main difficulty with such a scheme is that it presupposes an enormous degree of cortical organization. What a vast network of connections must be needed if a single complex cell is to receive fibers from just the right simple cells, all with the appropriate field arrangements, tilts and positions! Yet there is unexpected and compelling evidence that such a system of connections exists. It comes from a study of what can be called the functional architecture of the cortex. By penetrating with a microelectrode through the cortex in many directions, perhaps many times in a single tiny region of the brain, we learned that the cells are arranged not in a haphazard manner but with a high degree of order. The physiological results show that functionally the cortex is subdivided like a beehive into tiny columns, or segments [see illustration on next page], each of which extends from the surface to the white matter lower in the brain. A column is de-

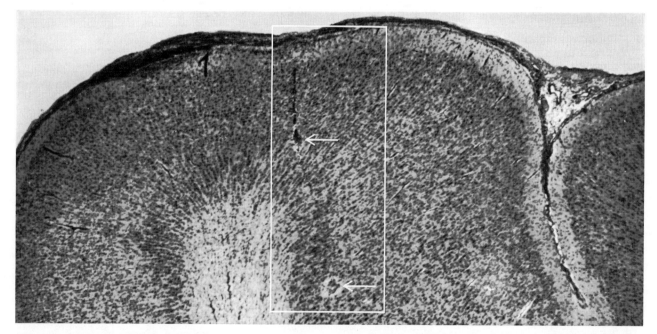

SECTION OF CAT'S VISUAL CORTEX shows track of micro-electrode penetration and, at arrows, two points along the track where lesions were made so that it would be possible to ascertain later where the tip of the electrode was at certain times. This section of cortex is from a single gyrus, or fold of the brain; it was six millimeters wide and is shown here enlarged 30 diameters.

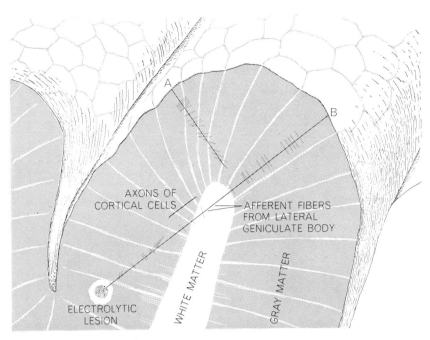

AXONS OF CORTICAL CELLS

AFFERENT FIBERS FROM LATERAL GENICULATE BODY

WHITE MATTER

GRAY MATTER

ELECTROLYTIC LESION

FUNCTIONAL ARRANGEMENT of cells in visual cortex resembled columns, although columnar structure is not apparent under a microscope. Lines *A* and *B* show paths of two microelectrode penetrations; colored lines show receptive-field orientations encountered. Cells in a single column had same orientation; change of orientation showed new column.

fined not by any anatomically obvious wall—no columns are visible under the microscope—but by the fact that the thousands of cells it contains all have the same receptive-field orientation. The evidence for this is that in a typical microelectrode penetration through the cortex the cells—recorded in sequence as the electrode is pushed ahead—all have the same field orientation, provided that the penetration is made in a direction perpendicular to the surface of the cortical segment. If the penetration is oblique, as we pass from column to column we record several cells with one field orientation, then a new sequence of cells with a new orientation, and then still another.

The columns are irregular in cross-sectional shape, and on the average they are about half a millimeter across. In respects other than receptive-field orientation the cells in a particular column tend to differ; some are simple, others complex; some respond to slits, others prefer dark bars or edges.

Returning to the proposed scheme for explaining the properties of complex cells, one sees that gathered together in a single column are the very cells one should expect to be interconnected: cells whose fields have the same orientation and the same general retinal position, although not the same position. Furthermore, it is known from

the anatomy that there are rich interconnections between neighboring cells, and the preponderance of these connections in a vertical direction fits well with the long, narrow, more or less cylindrical shape of the columns. This means that a column may be looked on as an independent functional unit of cortex, in which simple cells receive connections from lateral geniculate cells and send projections to complex cells.

It is possible to get an inkling of the part these different cell types play in vision by considering what must be happening in the brain when one looks at a form, such as, to take a relatively simple example, a black square on a white background. Suppose the eyes fix on some arbitrary point to the left of the square. On the reasonably safe assumption that the human visual cortex works something like the cat's and the monkey's, it can be predicted that the near edge of the square will activate a particular group of simple cells, namely cells that prefer edges with light to the left and dark to the right and whose fields are oriented vertically and are so placed on the retina that the boundary between "on" and "off" regions falls exactly along the image of the near edge of the square. Other populations of cells will obviously be called into action by the other three edges of the square. All the cell populations will change if the eye strays from the point fixed on, or if

the square is moved while the eye remains stationary, or if the square is rotated.

In the same way each edge will activate a population of complex cells, again cells that prefer edges in a specific orientation. But a given complex cell, unlike a simple cell, will continue to be activated when the eye moves or when the form moves, if the movement is not so large that the edge passes entirely outside the receptive field of the cell, and if there is no rotation. This means that the populations of complex cells affected by the whole square will be to some extent independent of the exact position of the image of the square on the retina.

Each of the cortical columns contains thousands of cells, some with simple fields and some with complex. Evidently the visual cortex analyzes an enormous amount of information, with each small region of visual field represented over and over again in column after column, first for one receptive-field orientation and then for another.

In sum, the visual cortex appears to have a rich assortment of functions. It rearranges the input from the lateral geniculate body in a way that makes lines and contours the most important stimuli. What appears to be a first step in perceptual generalization results from the response of cortical cells to the orientation of a stimulus, apart from its exact retinal position. Movement is also an important stimulus factor; its rate and direction must both be specified if a cell is to be effectively driven.

One cannot expect to "explain" vision, however, from a knowledge of the behavior of a single set of cells, geniculate or cortical, any more than one could understand a wood-pulp mill from an examination of the machine that cuts the logs into chips. We are now studying how still "higher" structures build on the information they receive from these cortical cells, rearranging it to produce an even greater complexity of response.

In all of this work we have been particularly encouraged to find that the areas we study can be understood in terms of comparatively simple concepts such as the nerve impulse, convergence of many nerves on a single cell, excitation and inhibition. Moreover, if the connections suggested by these studies are remotely close to reality, one can conclude that at least some parts of the brain can be followed relatively easily, without necessarily requiring higher mathematics, computers or a knowledge of network theories.

19

The Neurophysiology
of Binocular Vision

by John D. Pettigrew
August 1972

*The ability of certain mammals, including man, to
visually locate objects in the third dimension is traced
to the selective activity of single binocular nerve cells
in the visual cortex of the brain*

Man, along with cats, predatory birds and most other primates, is endowed with binocular vision. That is to say, both of his eyes look in the same direction and their visual fields (each about 170 degrees) overlap to a considerable extent. In contrast, many animals, such as rabbits, pigeons and chameleons, have their eyes placed so as to look in different directions, thereby providing a more panoramic field of view. Two questions come to mind: First, why do we have binocular vision instead of panoramic vision? Second, how is it that our single impression of the outside world results from the two different views we have of it by virtue of the separation of our eyes?

In answer to the first question, it is now known that binocular vision provides a powerful and accurate means of locating objects in space, a visual aptitude called stereopsis, or solid vision. Of course, it is possible to judge distance from the visual image of one eye by using indirect cues such as the angle subtended by an object of known size, the effort used in focusing the lens of the eye or the effect of motion parallax (in which the relative motions of near and far objects differ). These cues cannot be used in all situations, however, and they are not as accurate or as immediate as the powerful sensation of stereopsis, which is perhaps most familiar in the context of stereoscopic slide-viewers, three-dimensional motion pictures and so on. Some 2 percent of the population cannot enjoy stereopsis because of undefined anomalies of binocular vision. It is the aim of this article to give an account of recent work that shows how the brain achieves the very first stages of binocular depth discrimination.

Although it was not until the 19th century that the advantages of binoc-

ular vision were clearly demonstrated, man has pondered the arrangement of his eyes from earliest times. Of more concern to early investigators was not the first question, "Why binocular vision?" but rather "How does my single unified impression of the world result from the two views I have of it?" This second question is almost as difficult to answer today as it was when it was first asked by the ancient Greeks. The problem of "fusing" two slightly differing views of the world, however, is closely akin to the problem of using the slight differences between the views to achieve stereopsis. Thus a better understanding of the events in the nervous system underlying stereopsis should also throw some light on the problem of binocular fusion.

Galen taught in the second century that the fluid-filled ventricles of the brain were the seat of union, with a flow of visual spirit outward to both eyes. Galen's teachings were influential until the Renaissance, when scholars realized that the transfer of information is from the world to the eye, rather than in the reverse direction. René Descartes proposed in the 17th century that fibers from each eye might converge on the pineal gland for unification [*see illustration on page 195*]. His scheme, although incorrect, clearly indicates the now established principle that fibers from roughly corresponding regions of each eye converge on a single site in the brain. It was Isaac Newton who in 1704 first proposed that where the optic nerves cross in the optic chiasm there is an exchange of fibers. An early drawing of this concept, called partial decussation, shows how the fibers come together to carry information from corresponding parts of each eye [*see illustration on page 196*].

Newton's proposal, unlike that of Ga-

len or Descartes, has been extensively verified. The number of uncrossed fibers in the optic chiasm depends on the amount of overlap of the two visual fields, and this number tended to increase as animals evolved with eyes occupying a more frontal position [*see illustration on page 197*]. The rabbit, with only a tiny binocular portion in its visual field, has a very small number of ipsilateral, or uncrossed, fibers in the optic chiasm, whereas each of its cerebral hemispheres is heavily dominated by contralateral, or crossed, fibers from the opposite side. As the amount of binocular overlap increases from animal to animal, so does the number of ipsilateral fibers. In man there is almost complete overlap and 50 percent of the fibers of the optic nerve are uncrossed.

Although partial decussation provides the opportunity for the optic nerve fibers to come together in the brain, for a long time there was controversy over whether this coming together does in fact occur. For instance, at the first way station for the optic-nerve fibers in the brain, the lateral geniculate nucleus, the inputs from the two eyes are carefully segregated into layers. The more binocular overlap the animal has, the more obvious the layering is. The segregation is confirmed by physiological recordings that show that a neuron, or nerve cell, in a given layer can be excited by light stimuli falling on one eye only. The segregation is reinforced by inhibitory connections between corresponding neurons in adjacent layers.

At the level of the visual cortex of the brain, however, single neurons do receive excitatory inputs from both eyes. David H. Hubel and Torsten N. Wiesel of the Harvard Medical School demonstrated this effect for the first time in

194

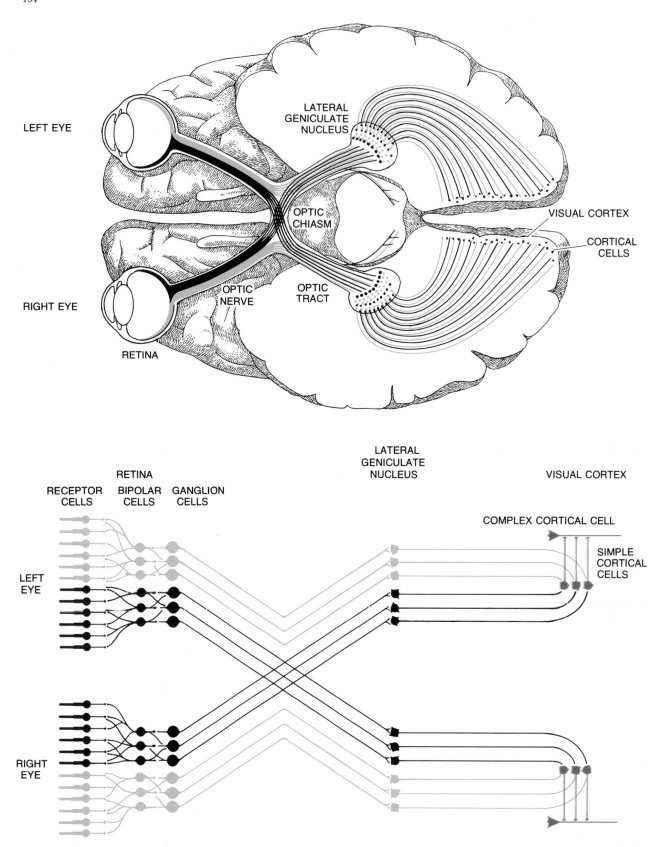

ANATOMY OF BINOCULAR VISION is represented in the drawing at top, which shows the human brain as viewed from below. The visual pathway from retina to cortex consists essentially of six types of neurons, or nerve cells, of which three are in the retina, one is in the lateral geniculate nucleus and two are in the cortex (*see schematic diagram at bottom*). Roughly half of the fibers of the optic nerve from each eye remain uncrossed at the optic chiasm.

These ipsilateral, or uncrossed, fibers (*color*) from the outer part of the retina of one eye join with the contralateral, or crossed, fibers (*black*) from the inner part of the retina of the other eye, and the two types of fiber travel together along the optic tract to the lateral geniculate nucleus, where fibers from each eye are segregated into layers. The fibers that emerge from this body carrying an input from both eyes converge on single neurons in the cortex.

1959 by recording from single neurons in the visual cortex of the cat [see the article "The Visual Cortex of the Brain," by David H. Hubel, beginning on page 183]. For almost every nerve cell studied two areas could be defined where light stimuli evoked a response, one associated with each eye. The proportion of binocularly activated neurons found has increased as the technique of presenting stimuli has become refined. Recent work by P. O. Bishop, Geoffrey H. Henry and John S. Coombs of the Australian National University shows that all the cells in the striate cortex of the cat receive an excitatory input from both eyes. Since each neuron in the striate cortex is simultaneously "looking" in two directions (one direction through each eye), the striate cortex can be regarded as the "cyclopean eye" of the binocular animal. The term cyclopean eye, derived from the mythological Cyclops, who had one eye in the center of his forehead, was first used by Ewald Hering and Hermann von Helmholtz in the 19th century to describe the way the visual cortex resolves the different directions of a given object as seen by each eye. Besides assessing visual direction, the cyclopean eye has an ability not possessed by either eye alone: it can use binocular parallax to ascertain the distance of an object.

Imagine looking down on an upturned bucket [see illustration on page 198]. If one directs each eye's fovea (the central high-resolution area of the retina) toward the cross at the center of the bucket, each eye will receive a slightly different view. The difference between the two views is called binocular parallax. Since each retinal image of the bottom of the bucket (small circles) is equidistant from the fovea, these two images must lie on exactly corresponding retinal points and are said to have zero disparity. Because of the horizontal separation between the eyes, the images of the rim of the bucket (large circles) are displaced horizontally with respect to the small circles and the foveas. These images lie on disparate retinal points. The retinal disparity between two such images is measured as an angle that corresponds to the difference between the angular separations of the two images from some known point such as the fovea (in the case of absolute disparity) or the smaller circle (in the case of relative disparity). If the disparity between the retinal images of the large circle is not too great, one sees not two large circles but a single large circle floating in depth behind the small one.

The basis of this powerful depth sensation of stereopsis was first demonstrated by Sir Charles Wheatstone (of

Wheatstone-bridge fame) in 1838. By providing very precise localization of objects in visual space, stereopsis can be regarded as the *raison d'être* of binocular vision. Whenever in evolution the need for the protection of panoramic vision was lessened (by the animal's taking to the trees as in the case of the primates, or by the animal's becoming predatory as in the case of the cats), then binocular vision developed to make it possible to use a depth cue more direct and accurate than the depth cues available to one eye alone. In addition, stereopsis enables a predator to penetrate the camouflage used by its prey, because monocular form perception is not a necessary prerequisite for stereoscopic vision. For example, an insect disguised as a leaf may be invisible monocularly but stand out in a different depth plane from real leaves when it is viewed stereoscopically. One can readily demonstrate this effect for oneself with the aid of random-dot stereograms devised by Bela Julesz of the Bell Telephone Laboratories [see "Texture and Visual Perception," by Bela Julesz; SCIENTIFIC AMERICAN Offprint 318]. Here a given pattern, such as a square, may be invisible to monocular inspection but stand out vividly when viewed stereoscopically.

The sole basis of stereopsis is the horizontal disparity between the two retinal

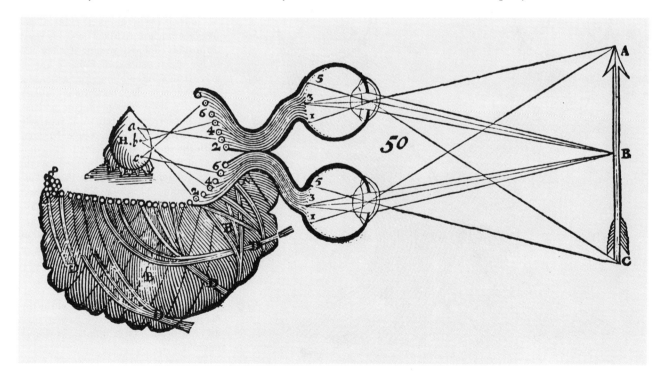

CONVERGENCE of nerve fibers from corresponding regions of each eye on a single site in the brain was proposed more than 300 years ago by René Descartes. In this early drawing of Descartes's scheme, reproduced from his study *Traite de l'Homme*, the optic nerve fibers from each eye are shown converging on the pineal gland (*H*), where they are rearranged, with those from corresponding retinal regions merging together. It is now known that fibers from both eyes do in fact converge, but not on the pineal.

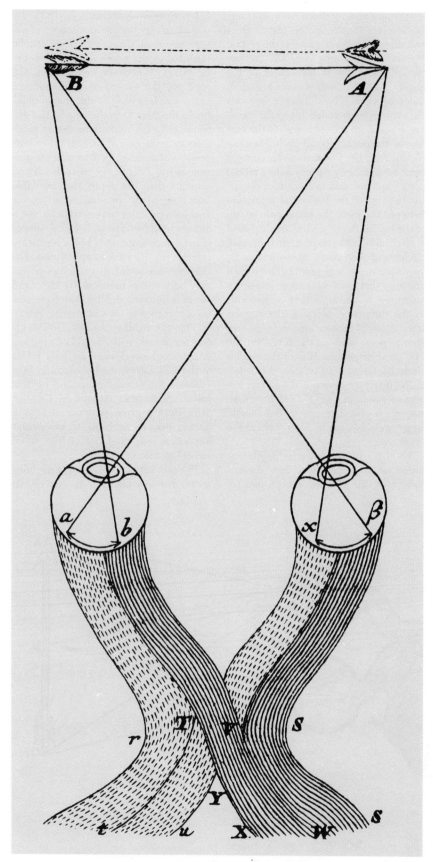

PARTIAL DECUSSATION, or crossover, of nerve fibers at the optic chiasm was first proposed by Isaac Newton in 1704. This drawing, made by a contemporary of Newton's, shows how fibers carrying information from corresponding parts of the eye come together on the same side of the brain in the interests of binocular vision. Newton's scheme was verified in the 19th century by the first ophthalmologists, Heinrich Müller and Bernhard von Gudden.

images. Of course, the brain must have a means by which it can first select those parts of the two images that belong to each other in the sense that they are images of the same feature in space. The horizontal disparities between the paired parts give the cue to depth. Julesz' experiments show that the binocular assessment of depth does not require the prior recognition of form, suggesting that the disparity information is processed by the brain fairly early in visual perception. Encouraged by this suggestion, neurophysiologists have examined the properties of binocularly activated neurons in the visual cortex, and over the past five years they have learned more about the neural mechanisms of binocular depth discrimination.

The experimental arrangement for studying binocularly activated neurons in the visual cortex is shown in the illustration on page 287. A cat that has been anesthetized and given a muscular paralyzing agent to prevent eye movements faces a screen onto which a variety of visual stimuli can be projected. A microelectrode inserted into the visual cortex samples activity from single nerve cells, and this activity is amplified so that it can be displayed on an oscilloscope, recorded and fed into a loudspeaker, in order that the experimenter can readily follow the response. Unlike neurons in the retina or the lateral geniculate nucleus, cortical neurons need exquisitely defined stimuli if they are to fire. Each cell requires that a line of a particular orientation (for instance a white slit on a dark background, a dark bar on a light background or a dark-light border) be placed on a narrowly defined region of each retina. Neurons with the same requirements for orientation of the stimulus are grouped together in columns that run from the surface of the brain to the brain's white matter. For some neurons within the column absolute position of the line is very important. Plotting with small spots of light suggests that such neurons receive a fairly direct input from the fibers coming into the cortex. These are "simple" neurons. Other neurons, called "complex," probably signal the output of the column; they behave as if they receive an input from a large number of simple neurons.

The speed and the direction of the moving stimulus are also important. Each of these stimulus requirements is more or less critical and each varies from neuron to neuron. As one slowly advances the electrode to pick up neurons, one must be continually moving a complicated pattern in front of the animal's eyes, in order to activate neurons that would otherwise be missed because of their lack of activity in the absence of the specific stimulus. (I sometimes wear a knitted sweater with a regular design as I move about in front of the cat.) Once one has found the specific stimulus for a given neuron, it is possible to define a region in the visual field of each eye where that stimulus will cause excitation of the cell. This region, called the response field, is plotted for each eye on a screen in front of the animal. The eye on the same side of the brain as the neuron in question is called ipsilateral; the eye on the opposite side is called contralateral. The study of a number of neurons in succession gives an array of ipsilateral and contralateral response fields [*see illustration on page 201*]. The arrays for each eye are separated on the screen because of the slightly divergent position the eyes assume in paralysis. Normally the eyes would be lined up so that the arrays could overlap and a single object might stimulate both response fields for a given neuron.

The highly specific stimulus requirements of cortical neurons could provide a means of identifying the parts of the two images corresponding to a single feature in object space. Because the number of identical features in a small part of the image in one eye is likely to be low, similar features lying in roughly corresponding regions in each eye can be assumed to belong to the same object. For example, a black line with a particular orientation and direction of movement in one image would be associated with a similar line at the most nearly corresponding position in the other image, because both are likely to be images of the same object. Since binocular cortical neurons have properties suited to the detection of the pair of retinal images produced by a given object, it was of great interest to see if they could also detect disparity between the pairs of images.

W hen one takes a close look at the position of each response field compared with the position of its partner in the opposite eye, it is immediately obvious that it is not possible to superimpose every response field on its partner simultaneously because of the greater scatter in the fields of the ipsilateral eye compared with those of the contralateral eye. The response fields therefore do not lie in corresponding regions of each retina and may be said to show disparity. I had

AMOUNT OF BINOCULAR OVERLAP of an animal's two visual fields is proportional to the percentage of uncrossed fibers in the optic chiasm. As animals evolved with eyes occupying a more frontal position this percentage tended to increase. The rabbit, for example, has only a tiny amount of binocular overlap and accordingly has a very small number of uncrossed fibers (*top*). The cat, in contrast, has a much larger binocular overlap and a correspondingly higher percentage of uncrossed fibers (*bottom*). In man there is almost complete binocular overlap and 50 percent of the fibers are uncrossed. The uncrossed nerve fibers carry information from the outer part of retina, the region responsible for binocular vision.

noticed this phenomenon in 1965 while working with Bishop at the University of Sydney and had considered the possibility that the variation in the position of one eye's response field with respect to the position of the corresponding response field of the opposite eye might play a role in the detection of retinal-image disparity and therefore in binocular depth discrimination. At that time, however, there were two major difficulties involved in the interpretation of the phenomenon.

The first difficulty was residual eye movement, which is present in small amounts even after the standard muscular paralyzing agents are applied. Since determination of the two response fields for one neuron can take hours (because one has to find the best stimulus orientation, speed of movement, exact position on the screen and so forth), one has to be sure that the eyes do not move in that time. Eye movement would produce spurious response-field disparities.

The second problem concerns the specificity of a neuron to binocular stimulation in the situation where a single stimulus is presented simultaneously to both eyes. It could be argued that the response-field disparities observed are not significant functionally since the neuron might tolerate large amounts of

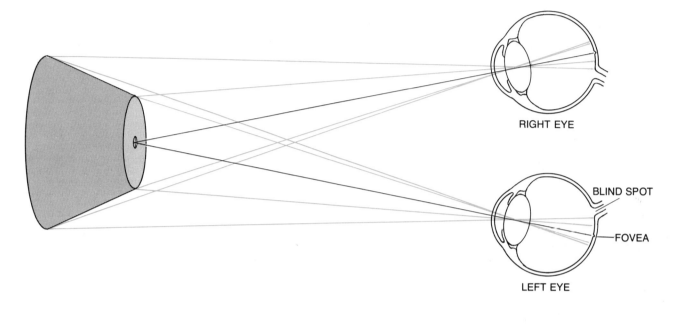

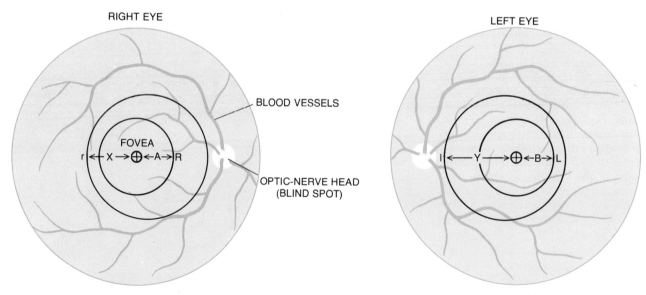

BINOCULAR PARALLAX is the term used to describe the disparity produced between two retinal images when one views a three-dimensional object. In this case a subject has been instructed to direct each eye toward the cross at the center of an upturned bucket (*top*). The drawings at bottom show how the fundus of each eye would look in an indirect ophthalmoscope. The fovea, the central high-resolution area of each retina, would appear as a shallow depression on which the cross would be imaged. The optic-nerve head, or blind spot, where the fibers of the optic nerve leave the retina and the blood vessels enter, would appear as a white disk. Since the small circles corresponding to the retinal images of the bottom of the bucket are each equidistant from the fovea (that is, distance A is equal to distance B), these two images must lie on exactly corresponding retinal points (R and L); these images are said to have zero disparity. The large circles corresponding to the images of the rim of the bucket, on the other hand, are displaced horizontally with respect to the small circles and the foveas (that is, distance X is not equal to distance Y); these images are said to lie on disparate retinal points (r and l). The amount of retinal disparity, usually expressed as an angle, is the difference between X and Y.

overlap of its receptive fields without changing its response. If the tolerated overlap were of the same order of magnitude as the variation in response-field disparity from neuron to neuron, then the latter variation would be of no use.

Both of these problems were worked out in the succeeding years by me in collaboration with Bishop and Tosaku Nikara at Sydney, and with Horace

B. Barlow and Colin Blakemore at the University of California at Berkeley. The problem of eye movement was solved by resorting to a number of measures simultaneously. A particularly potent mixture of neuromuscular blocking drugs was developed to reduce eye movement to a minimum without toxicity to the cat's heart and blood vessels. The sympathetic nerves to the orbit of the eye were cut to eliminate movements

due to the involuntary muscles near the eye. Any residual drift was carefully monitored by plotting the projection of some small blood vessel inside the eye onto a screen. Any tiny amount of movement between response-field plots could then be corrected. In the Berkeley experiments we carefully attached the margins of each eye to rigidly held rings, which kept the eyes fixed for the duration of the long measurements.

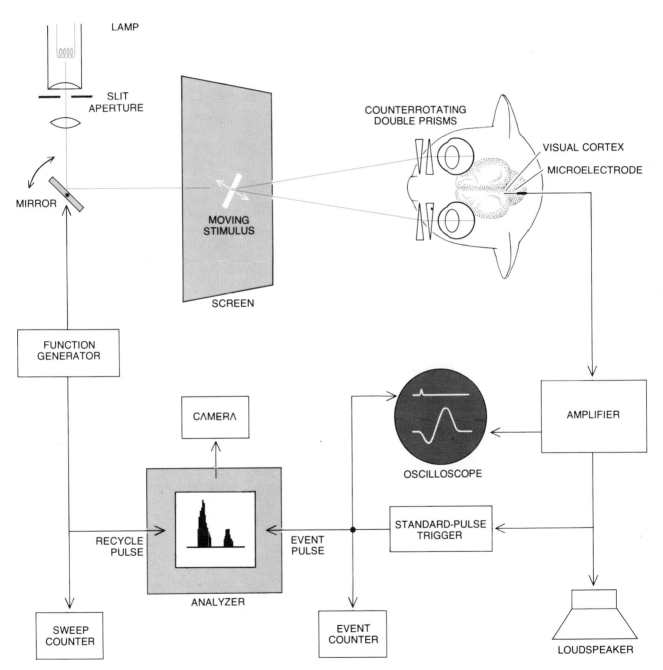

EXPERIMENTAL SETUP used by the author and his colleagues to study binocularly activated neurons in the visual cortex of the cat is depicted here. A cat that has been immobilized by a number of measures faces a screen onto which a moving line stimulus of any orientation, direction and speed can be projected from behind. A microelectrode inserted into the visual cortex samples activity from single neurons, and this activity is amplified so that it can be dis-

played on an oscilloscope, recorded and fed into a loudspeaker. Once a particular orientation and direction are discovered that will make the neuron fire, the stimulus is moved back and forth repeatedly while the neuron's response pattern is worked out. Counterrotating double prisms of variable power placed before the eyes enable the experimenter to determine the effect of changing retinal disparity as the stimulus moves in a fixed plane in front of the cat.

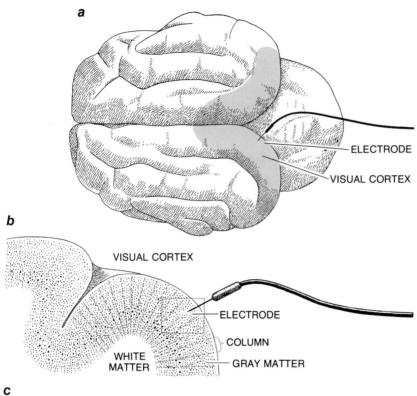

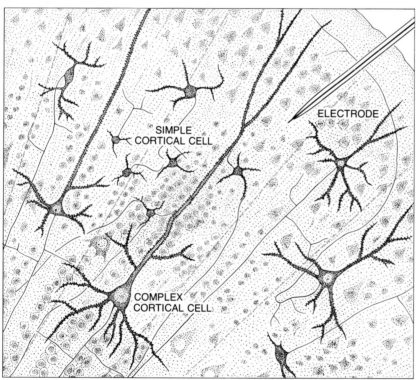

PENETRATION of the microelectrode through the cat's visual cortex is represented in this sequence of successively enlarged views. The top view of the entire brain (*a*) shows that the cortical region associated with vision (*color*) corresponds to a single gyrus, or fold, located toward the rear of each of the brain's two hemispheres. The cross section of this gyrus (*b*) reveals that the visual cortex is functionally divided into an array of tiny columns (*broken colored lines*) that run from the surface of the brain to the interior white matter. The magnified cross section (*c*) shows that each of these columns (which are not visible under the microscope) consists of a group of neurons with the same requirements for orientation of the stimulus. "Simple" neurons are those that appear to receive a fairly direct input from the fibers coming into the cortex. "Complex" neurons, which behave as if they receive an input from a large number of simple neurons, probably signal the output of the column.

The question "How specific is the response of a single neuron for the retinal disparity produced by a stimulus presented to both eyes?" was answered with the help of the following technique. The specific stimulus was swept forward and backward over both of the response fields of a cortical neuron when these had been lined up on the screen by the use of a double prism of variable power. The double prism was used to vary the visual direction of one eye (and therefore any response fields of that eye) in finely graded steps. Since the eyes are fixed, this maneuver changes the disparity between the retinal images of the moving stimulus, and if the change in prism power for one eye is in the horizontal plane, then the effect is identical with the one produced by a change in the distance of the stimulus along a line through the opposite eye and its response field.

We found that the binocular response of a particular cortical neuron in the left visual cortex to a moving slit of light varies considerably as the disparity is changed [*see illustration on page 203*] The responses were averaged for stimulation of each eye alone and for binocular stimulation when the two response fields have different amounts of overlap on the tangent screen where the light stimulus is moving forward and backward. The cortical neuron responded only to an oblique slit, and there was no response when the orientation was rotated more than 10 degrees in either direction. There was a response only as the slit moved across the screen from left to right and not in the reverse direction. Moreover, the response elicited from the left (ipsilateral) eye alone was weak.

The relative strength of the responses elicited from each eye varies from one neuron to another, and the particular neuron shown in the illustration is a case of extreme contralateral dominance. The inhibitory contribution from the ipsilateral eye is far from weak, however, as can be seen by the reduction of the binocular response when the response fields are stimulated in the "wrong" spatiotemporal relationship, as for example when the prism setting is such that the response fields are side by side instead of being superimposed.

Our findings demonstrated that the binocular response of the neuron is in fact very sensitive to slight changes in the overlap of its response fields in the plane of the stimulus. Since the response fields themselves are quite small (less than half a degree), this means a high

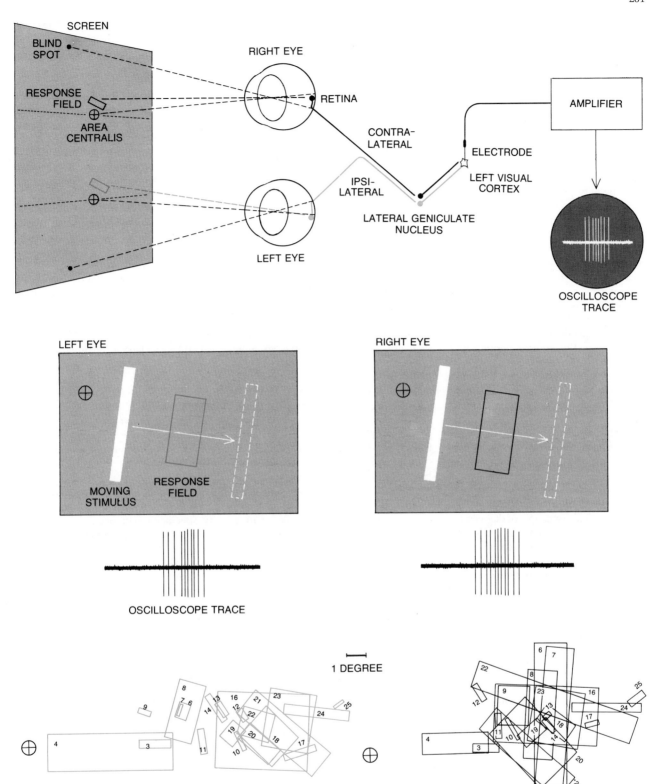

RESPONSE FIELDS FOR LEFT (IPSILATERAL) EYE

RESPONSE FIELDS FOR RIGHT (CONTRALATERAL) EYE

PAIRED RESPONSE FIELDS, one for each eye, can be plotted for a given neuron in the visual cortex of the cat (*top*). The response field of the neuron is defined as the region in the visual field of each eye where a specific stimulus will cause excitation of the cell (*middle*). In this illustration the response fields are separated on the screen because of the slightly divergent position the eyes assume in paralysis. Normally the fields would tend to overlap each other. By moving the microelectrode carefully through the cortex it is possible to record successively from a large number of different neurons; when the paired response fields of these neurons are plotted (*bottom*), those for the ipsilateral eye (the eye on the same side of the brain as the neuron in question) are more scattered than those for the contralateral eye (the eye on the opposite side). This means that it is not possible to superimpose all response fields on the same plane at the same time and that therefore different neurons would be optimally stimulated by objects in different planes.

level of disparity specificity. This particular neuron could indicate, by a marked decrease in firing rate, a disparity change as small as two minutes of arc, a feat approaching human performance. (The human threshold disparity is about 10 seconds of arc, or approximately 10 times better.)

It is perhaps not too surprising, in view of the very small size of the response fields, that the two retinal images of a binocularly presented stimulus must be very precisely located in order to produce a good response from the neuron. More surprising is the almost total suppression of the strong response from an appropriately located image in one eye if the image is inappropriately located in the other. This inhibition persists when the image is moved (for example by inserting the prism or by changing the distance of the stimulus) more than one degree of arc in either direction from the optimal position with respect to its correctly located partner in the other eye. In other words, binocular inhibition extends for more than one degree of retinal disparity on each side of the optimal disparity for a given neuron. The significance of this conclusion can be seen when one considers how nearby neurons behave with respect to one another in binocular vision; for those binocular neurons concerned with central vision the total range of optimal disparities is also a couple of degrees.

Let us now look at another disparity-specific binocular neuron recorded from the same column of tissue in the cortex as the one just described. Its stimulus requirements were quite similar (a slowly moving slit of light with the same orientation) except that the optimal disparity was 1.7 degrees more convergent because of the different position of its ipsilateral response field. Thus an oblique slit, in spite of the fact that it stimulates the contralateral response fields of both neurons, will under binocular viewing conditions excite one of them and inhibit the other, depending critically on its distance from the cat.

This binocular inhibition, operating over the same range as the range of disparity from one neuron to another, may be part of the explanation for the phenomenon of binocular fusion. A binocularly viewed target can be seen as being single in spite of the fact that it appears to lie in two different directions when the views from each eye alone are compared. In the upturned-bucket example, if the disparity between the retinal images of the larger circles is not too great, then one sees not two large circles but

a single (fused) large circle floating in depth. It is reasonable to suppose that the failure to see a second large circle is due to the binocular inhibition of those neurons that were activated monocularly by such a circle. The narrowing down of the amount of activity among different neurons narrows down in turn the number of stimulus possibilities from which the brain has to choose. In this case groups of binocular neurons associated with the same contour but with different retinal disparities are narrowed to one group and therefore a particular disparity.

Both of the neurons described above belong to Hubel and Wiesel's class of simple neurons, that is, neurons that respond only to stimuli on narrowly defined areas of the retina. It was particularly interesting to examine the binocular properties of complex neurons, since they are thought to receive an input from a number of simple neurons and therefore to respond over a wider area of retina. Would they also respond over a wider range of disparity?

Two types of disparity-specific complex neuron were found. In one group there was a high degree of specificity in spite of the large size of the response field. One binocular complex neuron had response fields six degrees across but could still detect changes of disparity as accurately as most simple neurons (which have fields less than one degree across). This astonishing precision means that the neuron would signal with a change in firing rate that a stimulus moving anywhere over a six-degree area had produced a change of just a few minutes of arc in retinal disparity. With the eyes in a constant position a disparity-specific complex neuron "looks" at a thin sheet suspended in space and fires if a stimulus with the correct orientation and speed of movement appears anywhere on the sheet (but not in front of or behind it).

Disparity-specific complex neurons behave as if they receive an input from a number of simple neurons with different absolute response-field positions in each eye but with the same relative position, so that they all have the same optimal disparity. In fact, we noticed groups of such neurons in the Berkeley experiments, and Hubel and Wiesel have recently shown that binocular neurons with the same disparity specificity in the monkey's cortex appear to be grouped in cortical columns similar to the columns for orientation specificity. We therefore have another example of the

cortical column as a system for extracting information about one specific type of stimulus while generalizing for others. A disparity-specific complex neuron can accordingly respond to a vertical edge moving over a wide region of the retina but over a very narrow depth in space. Directional specificity is lost but orientation and disparity information are retained.

There is some evidence for another type of binocular cortical column where all the neurons have response fields in the same position for the contralateral eye but have scattered fields for the ipsilateral eye. Blakemore calls these structures "constant direction" columns, because the neurons associated with them appear to respond at different disparities but to stimuli that are in the same direction from the contralateral eye. The output cell from such a column would presumably generalize for disparity but would be specific for the orientation and direction of the object.

Other complex binocular neurons responded over a wide range of disparity as well as of visual field. Since these neurons are active over the same range in which one observes binocular inhibition, they may be the source of the inhibition for simple neurons.

Once small residual eye movements had been accounted for and disparity specificity had been demonstrated, we were able to go ahead and compare the response-field pairs of a large number of different binocular neurons. In that way we could assess the total range of disparity variation. This was of particular interest because of a large body of observations obtained in psychophysical experiments on humans showing the range of disparity over which there is binocular fusion and the range of disparity over which stereopsis operates, both for central (foveal) vision and as one moves into the lower-resolution, peripheral visual field. The measurements were tedious because of the great length of time it takes to characterize a disparity-specific cortical neuron. In a typical experiment it took us three days to accumulate the 21 disparity-specific neurons whose response fields are shown in the illustration on the preceding page. All the neurons were recorded from the left striate cortex, and inspection of their response fields reveals a greater scatter in the fields of the left eye than in the fields of the right. This general observation that the ipsilateral receptive fields show more horizontal scatter is of interest in view of the fact that the ipsilateral

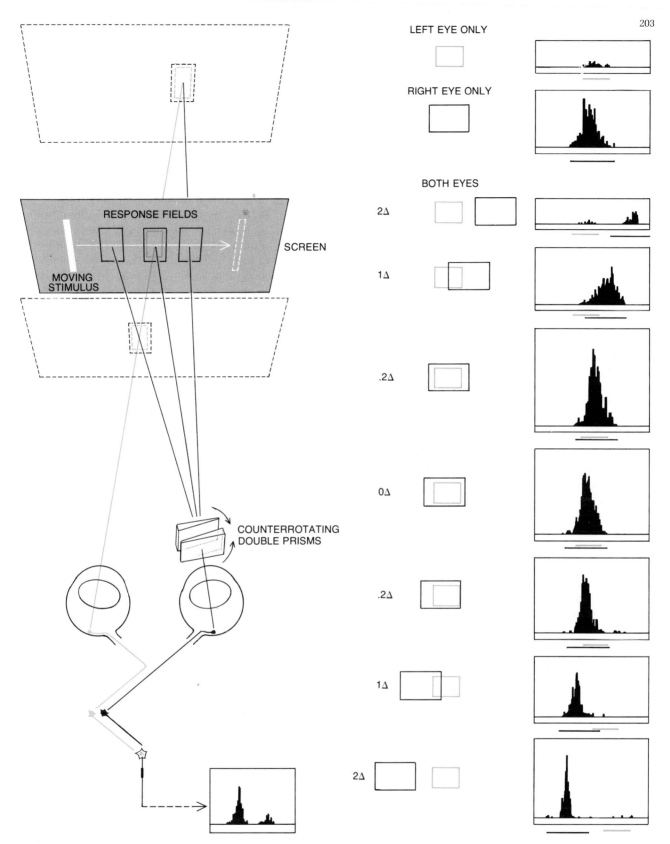

LEFT EYE ONLY

RIGHT EYE ONLY

BOTH EYES

2Δ

1Δ

.2Δ

0Δ

.2Δ

1Δ

2Δ

RESPONSE FIELDS

SCREEN

MOVING
STIMULUS

COUNTERROTATING
DOUBLE PRISMS

SPECIFICITY of a given binocular neuron for varying degrees of retinal disparity can be studied with the aid of counterrotating double prisms of variable power. The slight shifts of the two response fields with respect to each other in the plane of the moving stimulus are equivalent to setting that plane nearer to or farther from the animal (*left*). In this particular example, a case of extreme contralateral dominance, the response to a moving slit of light elicited from the left (ipsilateral) eye alone was weak; the inhibitory contribution from the ipsilateral eye is far from weak,

however, as can be seen from the reduction of the binocular response when the prism setting is such that the response fields are side by side instead of being superimposed (*right*). The response for this particular neuron falls off rapidly for disparities on the order of tenths of a degree; hence there would be good discrimination among neurons whose optimal disparities cover a range of several degrees. A prism setting of one diopter (Δ) is equal to a retinal disparity of one centimeter at a distance of one meter; expressed as an angle, a disparity of one Δ equals .57 degree.

fibers are the ones that have arisen most recently in the evolution of binocular vision.

One can get a measure of the range of disparity in the response fields by shifting each pair of fields horizontally so that all the left-eye fields are superimposed. It is clear that if there were no disparity between different pairs of response fields, then that would lead to superimposition of the right-eye fields also. The degree to which the fields do not superimpose can be measured, and in this case there was a range of six degrees of horizontal disparity and two degrees of vertical disparity. It is not immediately obvious why the neurons should cover a range of vertical disparity, since only the horizontal component can be used for stereopsis. The psychophysical studies show, however, that although the visual system cannot make use of vertical disparity, allowance must be made for such disparities so that the system can still operate when they are introduced. Vertical disparities arise at close viewing distances (where the image of a given object may be significantly larger on one retina) and also in the course of eye movements (where the two eyes may not remain perfectly aligned vertically).

The total range of disparity surveyed by a given cortical area varies according to retinal eccentricity. Binocular neurons concerned with the area centralis (the high-resolution part of the cat's retina that corresponds to the human fovea) cover a disparity range of two degrees compared with six degrees for those neurons dealing with the visual field about 10 degrees away from the midline. The small total range for the area centralis not only allows fine discrimination within that range but also requires fine control of eye movements so that the target being examined can be kept within the range. The range of disparities for central vision appears to be even narrower in humans and monkeys, where there is exquisite control of convergent and divergent eye movements so that the midpoint of the range can be varied. The fineness of the range is attested by the double vision that occurs if there is the slightest imbalance in the muscular system.

The preliminary results described here provide some insight into the initial operations performed by the visual cortex in extracting the information about disparity between small elements of the two retinal images. Much remains to be determined about how these first steps are utilized by the brain to yield our

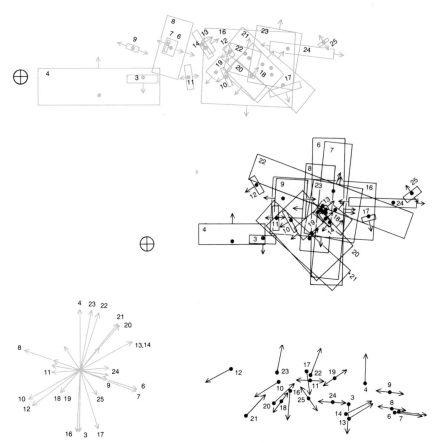

RANGE OF OPTIMAL RETINAL DISPARITIES for the 21 binocular neurons whose response field are plotted in the illustration on page 289 (and reproduced at the top of this illustration) can be calculated by shifting each pair of response fields horizontally so that the binocular centers (*black dots*) of all the left eye's field are superimposed (*bottom*). The scatter of the right eye's response fields then gives the range of disparities. For those fields located away from the central area there is a range of six degrees of horizontal disparity and two degrees of vertical disparity. For neurons with fields closer to the center of the retina the range is smaller and hence the neurons are capable of finer discrimination.

complete three-dimensional view of the world. Here are two examples of the kind of problem that remains to be solved: (1) Since convergent and divergent eye movements themselves produce changes in retinal disparity, how are these movements taken into account so that an absolute depth sense results that does not change with eye position? (2)

How is a synthesis achieved from the disparity information about the myriad contours of a visual scene? The answers to these and many more perplexing questions about the brain may be best answered by the combination of the approaches of psychophysics and neurophysiology that has proved fruitful thus far.

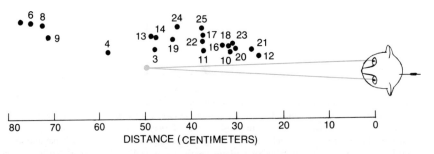

DISTANCE (CENTIMETERS)

DEPTH DISCRIMINATION attributable to binocular vision is represented by this plot of the points in space at which a correctly oriented contour would optimally stimulate the 21 binocular cortical neurons whose response fields are shown in the illustration at top of this page, provided that the cat's eyes are fixed on a point 50 centimeters in front (*colored dot*).

VI

MOTOR CONTROL SYSTEMS

VI MOTOR CONTROL SYSTEMS

INTRODUCTION

Essentially all behaviors that we can observe in other animals, including humans, are muscle movements—walking, running, ballet dancing, piano playing, and speaking—the list of movement is virtually endless. All of these are simply sequences of skeletal muscle contractions and relaxations. To the extent that psychobiology is the study of the physical basis of behavior, it is also the study of muscle movements. A number of brain structures can be described as having predominantly movement-control functions. Indeed, the English neurologist, Hughlings Jackson, asserted many years ago that the basic function of the nervous system is movement. In a very real sense all aspects of the nervous system are concerned with relating sensory input and ongoing activity of the brain to the movements that constitute behavior. The essential purpose of the brain is behavior. However, it is clear that some structures are much more important than others in the immediate control of movement.

In the first article in this section, entitled "How We Control the Contraction of Our Muscles," P. A. Merton presents a clear and up-to-date account of how voluntary muscular movements are regulated by feedback control systems. Consider a simple voluntary movement, such as picking up a pencil. Try to analyze your experiences as you do this. Initiation of the movement of your arm as you reach seems purely voluntary—you decide to reach and your arm reaches. We have no understanding at present of the mechanisms underlying this initiation of voluntary movement. However, once your arm movement begins, a number of feedback cues from receptors in joints and muscles, as well as visual information, guides the ongoing process of the movement. Merton focuses on these feedback systems in his article.

The next article, "Brain Mechanisms in Movement" by Edward V. Evarts, is concerned primarily with the region of the cerebral cortex most directly involved in the control of "voluntary" movement, the motor cortex and its major output system, the pyramidal tract. Evarts, using well-trained monkeys performing different kinds of movement tasks, has recorded the discharges of single nerve cells in the motor cortex that send their fibers down to the spinal cord to control muscle movements. He also discusses the interrelationships of two other major movement-control systems in the brain—the cerebellum and the basal ganglia—and provides examples of how these three control systems interact in the production of well-learned movements.

The final article in this section is "The Cortex of the Cerebellum" by Rodolfo R. Llinás. The cerebellum is one of the more intriguing structures in the brain. The basic interconnections in the cerebellum have remained relatively constant throughout the long course of evolution from reptiles to humans. The cerebellum seems to have a common function in these very diverse species. It is also one of the simpler structures of the brain in terms of its internal organization—the way in which the various neurons are hooked up together. In recent years we have achieved a rather good understanding of the way these neurons interact in the cerebellum and the kinds of functions the cerebellum performs in the regulation and control of "voluntary" movement. Llinás brings us up to date on our current understanding of how the cerebellum works as a movement-control system in the brain.

20

How We Control the Contraction of Our Muscles

by P. A. Merton
May 1972

Voluntary muscular movements are driven by a servomechanism similar in many respects to the automatic feedback system employed to control power-assisted steering in an automobile

Psychophysics is the branch of experimental science that deals with the relation between conscious mental events and physical events within and without the body. Most psychophysics is sensory psychophysics, which deals with the relation between a physical stimulus and the resulting sensation experienced by the subject. The object of sensory-psychophysical experiments is to gain understanding of the physiological mechanisms that lie between the stimulus and the sensation, and to be able to draw inferences about what goes on inside a sense organ, a nerve or the brain. Measurements of subjective sensory thresholds in any sensory mode (tactile, visual, auditory or whatever), perceptions of color matches and judgments of the pitch of a note or the direction of a sound are examples of sensory-psychophysical observations. Sensory psychophysics is an old and highly respectable subject. In the hands of such investigators as Thomas Young, Jan Purkinje, Hermann von Helmholtz, James Clerk Maxwell, Lord Rayleigh and their modern successors it has told us a great deal about vision, hearing and other senses. Young's celebrated three-color theory of color vision, published in 1802, was formulated entirely on psychophysical evidence and is the basis of modern color photography and color television.

The other branch of psychophysics, motor psychophysics, does not have these credentials. It deals with the reciprocal problem, the relation between a conscious effort of will and the resulting physical movement of the body. It is just as important to know how we move as how we feel, but on the motor side much less has been achieved, partly, I suspect, because physiologists for metaphysical reasons feel that conscious volition is a faintly disreputable thing for them to have dealings with.

In sensory psychophysics it is easy to find illustrative examples of sensory phenomena that have an analytical character, that is, examples that provide some insight into sensory mechanisms, but on the motor side it is not so easy. I can think of one striking instance. A motor psychophysical fact of immense everyday importance is the individuality of a person's signature. Whenever Mr. X makes the appropriate volitional effort and signs his name, it always comes out the same (or enough so to be recognizable) and different from what anyone can write if he tries to write the same name. This is not an analytical observation; it is just a mysterious physiological fact, which we take for granted because we are so familiar with it. What does tell us something, however, is the further observation that if Mr. X takes a piece of chalk and signs his name in large letters on a blackboard, it again comes out the same. The muscles used are different but the individuality remains. From this observation we learn something about the organization of the motor system.

In this article evidence from both branches of psychophysics is taken into account, but the main object is to redress the balance in favor of the motor side. In more concrete terms we ask: What has been learned by making observations on voluntary movements in man about the physiological mechanisms that make our muscles do what we expect of them? Not, of course, very much. The title of this article is somewhat pretentious, as titles will be. There are a few definite phenomena to describe. With them we reach a new point of view, from which I hope we can see a general line of advance. I shall stick to simple movements and not come close to explaining the individuality of handwriting. (That subject was introduced partly to advertise the fact that sensory physiologists do not have all the glamor problems.) It will be useful to start by drawing an analogy between the human body and an automobile.

In the old days the steering wheel of a motorcar was directly connected to the road wheels by a series of levers and linkages, and the brake pedal similarly applied pressure directly to the brake shoes. On coming to a hill a gearshift could be moved to engage a suitable pair of gears to climb the hill with.

Today, in order to enable the driver, no matter how frail, to control a massive vehicle with the flick of a wrist or ankle, sophisticated mechanisms have been developed to assist with steering, braking and gear-shifting. All these mechanisms have devices (sensors, we may call them) that measure some physical variable (for example brake pressure or engine revolutions) and use the "feedback" information from them to control the mechanism that assists the driver. Let us concentrate on the mechanism that assists with steering. In its essentials it works as follows. Each position of the steering wheel corresponds to a certain angle of the front road wheels that the driver would like them to assume with respect to the fore-and-aft axis of the chassis. A sensor at the bottom of the steering column detects the difference between this "demanded" position and the actual position of the road wheels. Signals from

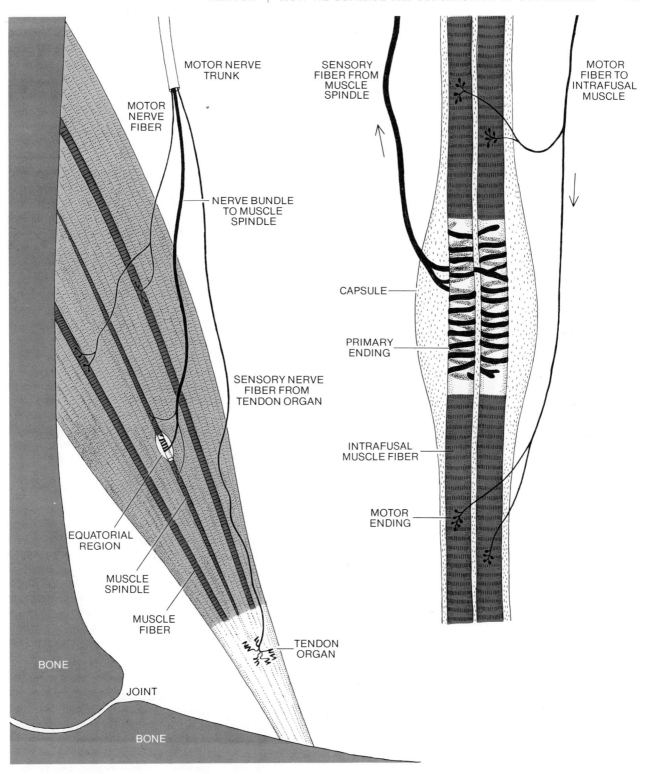

ARRANGEMENT OF SENSE ORGANS in a typical muscle is indicated in these simplified diagrams. The proportions in the diagram at left are highly distorted. A real muscle fiber is only about a tenth of a millimeter in diameter, but it is often several centimeters long. A muscle spindle is somewhat thinner; it consists of even finer specialized structures called intrafusal muscle fibers. Only two ordinary muscle fibers and one spindle are depicted in detail; a real muscle may contain tens of thousands of muscle fibers and hundreds of spindles. The diagram at right gives an enlarged view of the equatorial region of a muscle spindle. Wrapped around the intrafusal muscle fibers are the terminations of the sensory nerve fiber; the function of these sense endings is to respond to mechanical deformation by causing nerve impulses to be sent up the sensory nerve. In the equatorial region the cross striations, which are an indication of the presence of a contractile mechanism within the fiber, are absent. Hence when the intrafusal fibers contract, this region is extended and excites the sensory endings, just as if the region had been extended by stretching the entire muscle and the spindle within it. In this diagram only two intrafusal fibers are shown; a real spindle often has half a dozen or more. Moreover, intrafusal fibers come in two distinct varieties, only one of which is shown here. Another complication is the fact that there are three distinct kinds of motor nerve to the intrafusal fibers. In a real spindle the equatorial region is also much longer than depicted here. Photomicrographs showing the innervation of a tendon organ and the equatorial region of a muscle spindle appear on page 212.

the sensor, called the misalignment detector, are used to turn on a small servomotor (from the Latin *servus*, meaning slave), which turns the road wheels in such a direction as to cancel the misalignment. Thus the road wheels are made to point in the direction the driver wants, without his having to exert himself. As he turns the steering wheel the road wheels follow automatically.

Such is power-assisted steering. An engineer calls it a follow-up servomechanism. An important point to note is that, the function of the device being to help the driver automatically, he does not want to be bothered with the details of its operation; in particular he would only be distracted from his task of keeping his eyes on the road to see where to steer if signals from the sensor were relayed to him. They give information that is relevant only to the functioning of what ought to be a completely subservient mechanism, and they should remain private to that mechanism.

Power-assisted steering relieves the driver of physical effort only; other such devices relieve him of mental effort too. The automatic transmission, for example, does away with the need to decide when to change gear, as well as the need to perform the change. In an aircraft the automatic pilot does everything and leaves the human pilot completely free.

In the human body there are numerous automatic feedback mechanisms of this kind controlling physiological functions without any mental effort on our part. For instance, the blood pressure and the output of the heart are controlled so as to suit the current needs of the body; we are quite unaware of the functioning of these systems and of the signals from the pressure sensors in the walls of the arteries and elsewhere that are a part of them.

Such mechanisms are commonplace physiology; they are in the textbooks for medical students and nurses. When we come to muscle, however, the situation is different. To return to our analogy, in the case of the automobile we know what we want to control—direction, speed or retardation—and the problem is to design servomechanisms to help the driver, with appropriate sensors in each instance. The signals from the sensors are just part of the engineering technology, and so we do not display them on dials on the dashboard. They would only put the driver off. In the human machine we have muscles to control. How do we do it? Do the orders to contract go directly from the brain? Presumably not, since on examination it appears that muscles, like the automobile, are equipped with sensors of their own, of whose signals the owner of the muscles, like the owner of the automobile, remains unaware. Presumably, like the sensors in the automobile, they are taking part in automatic mechanisms that assist the subject in controlling his muscles. What are they helping to control? Muscle tension perhaps? It could be; some of them measure tension. Length? Others of them respond to changes in muscle length. A combination of tension and length? Sometimes tension and sometimes length? Now we see the nature of the problem. It is the inverse of the automobile designer's. We are presented with the sensors and we have to discover what the mechanism they are part of was designed to do. What precisely do we ask of our muscles that they need these confidential sensors to make them do it? It is by no means obvious.

Having thus briefly sketched the picture, let me now go into the physiology in more detail. It falls into two sections. The first presents the evidence that muscles incorporate sensory receptors of whose signals we are not consciously aware; the second discusses what is known of the mechanisms in which they take part.

In the 18th century the great Swiss physiologist Albrecht von Haller established for the first time that the internal organs of the body, such as the heart, the stomach and the brain, are in general insensitive to the kind of stimuli that are so readily felt by the skin: pricking, pinching, cutting, burning and so forth. It is this fact that enables surgeons to perform operations on, say, the brain substance with only local anesthesia around the incision. In his studies of muscle Haller found that stretching a muscle by pulling gently on the tendon exposed in a wound in a human subject did not cause sensations of either movement or tension. (Pulling hard, however, is painful.) Reflecting on Haller's observations, one can perceive that the viscera and the muscles are really in different categories. It is not at all surprising, when one comes to think of it, that the liver should be insensitive to cutting with a knife or burning with a cigarette; such stimuli would be so rare without the animal's getting an earlier and more effective warning from the abdominal skin that to develop a system to report them would give the animal a negligible evolutionary advantage, whereas sensitivity to mechanical contacts, which the skin preeminently possesses, would very likely be a positive disadvantage. Imagine what life would be like if throughout it one were as vividly aware of the beat of one's heart as the surgeon who puts a finger on it exposed during an operation! With muscle, however, it is quite otherwise. It might be useful for us to be conscious of how extended our muscles are at any moment, since that determines the position of our limbs, and also to know their rate of shortening or elongation and the tension in them. If we are to be-

STRIKING EXAMPLE of a simple experimental observation that provides some insight into the organization of the motor psychophysical system is represented by these two handwritten versions of a sentence taken from the text of this article. The sentence was written large on a wall with a felt-tipped pen (*top*) and small on a piece of paper with a fine mapping pen (*bottom*). The writing on the wall is about 10 times larger. The large writing was done by movements of the wrist, elbow and shoulder, whereas the small writing used muscles in the hand itself. Nevertheless, the character of the writing is the same in both cases.

lieve Haller, this is just what they do not tell us. For this and other reasons that will shortly emerge we find that, whereas the insentience of the viscera has long been received as physiological dogma with a status comparable to the circulation of the blood, the insentience of muscle has often been called in question and probably cannot be regarded as universally accepted even today.

For me the question was both raised and answered the day I read the arguments of Helmholtz, published in 1867 in his *Handbook of Physiological Optics.* Helmholtz reached the same conclusion as Haller by experiments with the eye, which have the merit that anyone can repeat them and convince himself of the facts. Helmholtz starts with the familiar observation that if one takes hold of the skin at the outer corner of the eyelids and jerks it sideways, the eye itself is moved and what one sees with that eye appears to jump about. On the other hand, we know that if one moves one's eyes voluntarily, the scene one is looking at does not appear to jump. Helmholtz argues as follows. In both cases the image of the external world moves over the retina as the eye moves. When one moves one's eyes actively, by voluntary effort, one allows for the eye movement and does not interpret the movement of the image on the retina as signifying a movement of the external world. When the eyes are moved passively by an external pull, however, one interprets what one sees as if the eye had remained still. The movement of the image on the retina is assumed to be due to a movement of the external world and not to a movement of the eye. Hence we only know in which direction our eyes are pointing when we move them voluntarily, and this must be because we make an unconscious estimate of the effort put into moving them. (We have a "sense of effort.") Sense organs in the eye muscles (or elsewhere around the eye, if there are any) do not tell us which way our eyes are pointing, because when the eyes are moved passively, we do not seem to know they have moved.

This argument, as it stands, is not conclusive, because when the eyelids are pulled, the sense organs in the eye muscles or elsewhere might not be excited in the same manner as when the eye is turned normally by the contraction of its muscles. The apparent movement of the external world during a passive movement of the eye might therefore be due to a misjudgment of the eye's direction rather than to a complete ignorance of its movement.

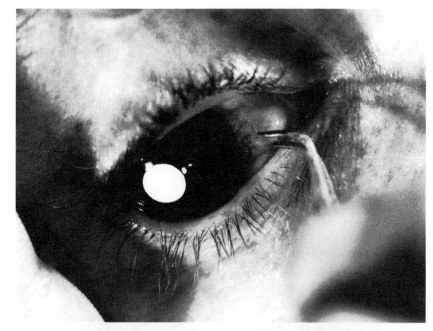

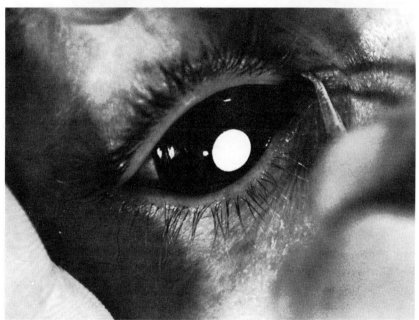

INSENTIENCE OF EYE MUSCLES was demonstrated a few years ago by means of an ingenious experiment devised by G. S. Brindley, now at the Maudsley Hospital in London. In these photographs, made in the course of the experiment, Brindley is manipulating the author's eye with forceps to test whether, after blinding it with a black cap, there was any awareness of passive movements. There was not. The white spot on the cap is to give an indication of eye position. The eye and the lids were treated with local anesthetic.

This objection, as Helmholtz argues, can be answered by considering afterimages. If one stares fixedly at a bright light for 15 to 30 seconds (please, not the sun!), then on looking elsewhere an afterimage of the bright light is perceived and persists for a minute or so. When an object is fixated steadily, the afterimage likewise stays still, but when the gaze is shifted, the afterimage also moves. This, of course, refers to active voluntary eye movements. In passive movements quite the opposite is found. No matter how hard one pulls on the eyelids the afterimage appears to remain completely stationary. In order to be certain of this phenomenon it is necessary to view the afterimage against a featureless background, such as a sheet of plain paper held close to the eye; otherwise the concomitant apparent jerking around of external objects may make the judgment difficult. Hence during passive movements we interpret what we see precisely as if the eye had not moved at all. It is not a matter of a quantitative misjudgment. The reader is encouraged to repeat for himself these crucial observations and reflect on the compelling conclusions Helmholtz drew from them.

A few years ago my friend G. S. Brindley (now at the Maudsley Hospital in London), who has a genius for settling or eliminating argument by incisive experiment, proposed that we confirm Helmholtz directly by blinding an eye with a black cap on the cornea (the eye's transparent front surface) and then moving the eye around with forceps to see if the subject could feel the movement. (Pain was prevented by instilling gener-

ous quantities of local-anesthetic eye drops.) The test proved that subjects are quite unaware of large passive rotations of the eye in its socket of 30 degrees or more; they do not know the eye is being manipulated at all unless the forceps happen to touch the eyelid. Another important point was that if the subject was invited to voluntarily move his eyeball while the forceps were gripping it, he was unable to tell whether the experimenter holding the forceps was allowing the movement to take place or was preventing the eye from moving.

The unequivocal conclusion of all these experiments is that we have no sense organs in the eye muscles or near them that tell us which way our eyes are pointing. We normally know which way

we are looking, but only because an internal "sense of effort" gives us an estimate of how much we have exerted our eye muscles. If voluntary movements are artificially impeded, or if passive movements are imposed, we absolutely do not know what is going on—unless we can see and reason back from the visual illusions we receive.

So much for the eyes. In the limbs the same facts are less easily demonstrated. To use Haller's method with patients whose tendons have been exposed under local anesthetic in the course of an orthopedic operation is one possibility, but it does not satisfy the powerful compulsion that all investigators in sensory physiology have to try it for themselves. A paper on visual illusions in which the author had not experienced the phenomena himself is almost unthinkable, and rightly so. What better way could he have of satisfying himself that they were correctly reported? Hence it is desirable to find a method for studying muscular sensibility in ordinary limb muscles of healthy subjects. The difficulty, of course, is to devise a way of stretching a muscle without the subject's knowing what is being done, since he can feel pressure on the skin or the movement of a joint. Local anesthesia of an extremity provides an answer. Investigators have variously injected local anesthetic around the joint at the base of the big toe or at the base of a finger, or have anesthetized the entire hand by cutting off the blood supply with a pneumatic tourniquet around the wrist for about 90 minutes. Movement of an anesthetized digit then stretches the muscles that move it, which lie above the anesthetized region. My collaborators and I use the top joint of the thumb, which has the advantage that only one muscle (lying well up in the forearm) flexes it, whereas the joints of the fingers are operated by more than one muscle, some in the hand and some in the forearm. Thus when the thumb is anesthetized by a tourniquet at the wrist, voluntary movements of the top joint are unimpaired in strength. We have also used injection of local anesthetic around the base of the thumb.

The uniform result of numerous experiments is that, with an adequate depth of anesthesia, the subject (whose eyes are shut) cannot tell in what position the experimenter is holding the top of his thumb, or whether he is bending it backward and forward. This is true only provided that the movement is not rapid and that the thumb is not forcibly extended or flexed at the limits of its range of movement. It is also the case

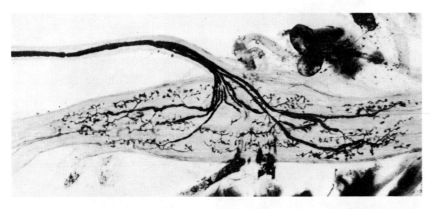

TENDON ORGAN contains sense endings that signal to the nervous system the tension in the part of the muscle in which they lie. A typical location of a tendon organ is shown in the diagram on page 299. The single sensory nerve fiber that services the tendon organ has been made to appear black in this photograph by means of a special silver stain. The nerve fiber divides many times, terminating in very fine branches with knobs at the ends. These structures, in some unknown way, sense the deformation produced by tension and cause nerve impulses to be sent up the sensory fiber at a rate that is determined by the tension. This tendon organ was dissected out of the leg muscle of a cat; it is about half a millimeter long. Surrounding one end are the remains of muscle fibers. Both photographs on this page were made by Colin Smith, Michael Stacey and David Barker of the University of Durham.

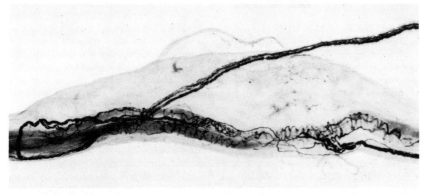

EQUATORIAL REGION of a muscle spindle dissected from the leg muscle of a rabbit appears in this photomicrograph; the part shown is about a millimeter long. Again the nerve fibers and nerve endings have been stained with a silver stain, making it possible to distinguish clearly the equatorial capsule, the intrafusal muscle fibers and the sensory endings wrapped around them. The nerve ending to the right is a primary ending; its sensory nerve fiber enters from lower right. The other ending is a secondary ending; its nerve fiber enters from upper right. The finer nerve fibers are part of the motor nervous system.

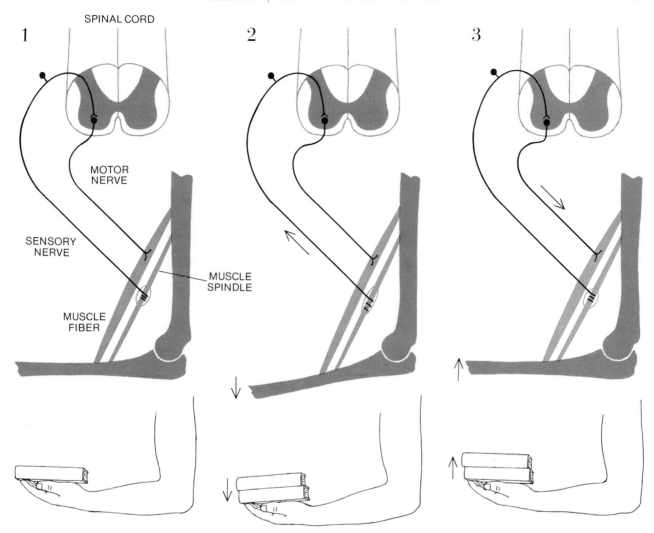

1

2

3

SPINAL CORD

MOTOR
NERVE

SENSORY
NERVE

MUSCLE
SPINDLE

MUSCLE
FIBER

STRETCH REFLEX is mediated by the nervous mechanism depicted in this highly schematic illustration. A muscle is under the influence of the stretch reflex when it is engaged in a steady contraction of a voluntary nature, as when a person's elbow is flexed steadily against a load (*1*). A sudden unexpected increase in the load (*2*) stretches the muscle, causing the sense ending on the muscle spindle to send nerve impulses to the spinal cord (*upward arrow*), where they impinge on a motor nerve cell at a synapse and excite it. As a result motor impulses are sent back down to the muscle (*downward arrow*), where they cause it to contract (*3*). More complicated nervous pathways than the one shown may also be involved in the stretch reflex. Any real muscle is, of course, supplied with many motor nerve fibers and spindles. In addition the synaptic connections to even a single motor nerve cell are multiple.

that if the subject attempts to flex his thumb, he cannot tell whether he has been successful, or whether the experimenter has prevented it from moving. Thus with skin and joint sensation eliminated the thumb behaves just like the eye. Muscle *is* insentient.

I have already argued that one would not on general grounds expect the liver, say, to have sensibility like the skin's. Indeed, if one looks at the liver through a microscope, it has none of the elaborate apparatus of sensibility seen in the skin—no network of branching nerve fibers ending in a variety of characteristic sensitive structures: the sense organs. The same goes for other viscera. Muscles are not so obliging. They are supposed to be insentient, but when we look inside them, they turn out to be full

of sense organs, and very fine sense organs at that. The principal kind, the muscle spindles, are the most elaborate sensory structures in the body outside of the eyes and ears. This deep paradox (for which the reader has already been prepared) is at the back of everything in this article. All the essential facts that create it have been known since 1894, when Sir Charles Sherrington proved conclusively that there were nerve fibers going to the muscle spindles that belonged to the body's system of sensory nerves, and hence established that the muscle spindles were sense organs. Unfortunately in those distant days Sherrington was insensitive to the class distinction between the information on the road sign that tells the driver to turn right and the information from the sensors in his power-assisted steering gear

that enables him to do so effortlessly (between, one might say, the different types of information required by the legislature and the executive). He allowed himself to be persuaded that Helmholtz had been wrong and that his own discovery showed that muscles were sentient after all.

Sherrington had thus taken the view that in effect there was no paradox, and his influence was so immense that it was 60 years before the true situation was at last clearly perceived. By this time the paradox had much less impact, since physiologists had discovered many of the facts about the muscle spindle needed for its resolution. Before going on to these facts I should finish the present story.

In the past few years the paradox has been given a further twist. Several groups of workers on both sides of the Atlantic, whose members are too numerous to name individually, have found that signals from muscle sense organs find their way to the cerebral cortex It seems that they get to the cortex but we remain unconscious of them. This is very surprising. No one imagines for a moment that we do not make use of all the information our eyes send to the cerebral cortex to build up the picture of the outside world we consciously perceive, and I am sure that a few years ago any ordinary physiologist would have been prepared to extend this point of view to sensory information of any kind that could be shown to get to the cortex.

The evidence for what I have just said is not complete. The animal most resembling man in which signals from muscle sense organs have been shown to reach the cortex is the baboon. It seems unlikely that they do not reach the cortex in man, and equally unlikely that a baboon should be conscious of the signals from its muscles when a man is not. A strong hint also comes from the cat. John F. Swett and C. M. Bourassa of the Upstate Medical Center of the State University of New York showed that muscle sense organs send signals to the cat's cerebral cortex, but unlike signals from the skin (or for that matter from the eyes or ears) they cannot be used to set up a conditioned reflex. Without explaining what is meant by this fact in detail one can say that it strongly suggests the cat is not conscious of the signals from its muscles.

The first part of this article was intended to introduce the reader to the idea that muscle organs function at a subconscious level in a purely subservient role. Like the perfect servant, they work so unobtrusively that we are unconscious of them, but the findings about cortical projection begin to strain the analogy. The eccentric 18th-century scientist Henry Cavendish reportedly dismissed any servant he caught sight of. He wrote down what food he wanted and it was put out for him. It would have been going too far to expect the butler to wait on him at table without betraying his presence, but that is what the muscle sense organs seem to manage to do!

Scarcely less remarkable than the mere existence of the muscle spindles is the fact that they (the most important of the two kinds of muscle sense organ) are themselves contractile. This is a unique property among sensory structures. That was perfectly clear to Sherrington in 1894, but it still remains one of the most challenging observations in the physiology of the motor system; even if the interpretations to be put forward later in this article are on the right lines, it is most improbable that they are more than one facet of the truth.

Muscle spindles (they are called spindles because they are long and thin and have pointed ends) consist of a bundle of modified muscle fibers, the intrafusal muscle fibers (from the Latin *fusus*, meaning spindle), with the sensory nerve fibers wrapped around a short specialized region somewhere near the middle of their length. The stimulus that excites a muscle spindle is the stretching of this specialized sensory region. Now, as I have said, the muscle spindles are contractile. They are not, however, equally contractile along their entire length; the contractile apparatus fades out in the sensory region, and the middle of the sensory region, where the sense endings connected to the largest nerve fibers lie, probably does not contract at all. When the spindle contracts, these sense endings (known as the primary endings) are stretched by the contraction of the remainder of the spindle and discharge nerve impulses.

The next point to observe is that the

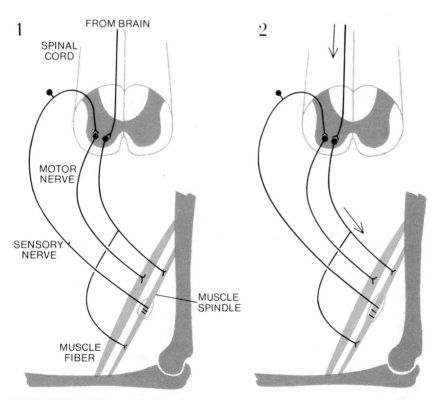
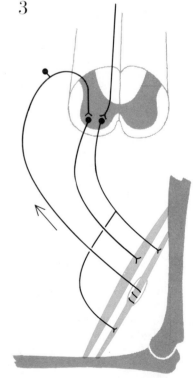

1   FROM BRAIN

SPINAL CORD

MOTOR NERVE

SENSORY NERVE

MUSCLE SPINDLE

MUSCLE FIBER

2

3

SERVOMECHANISM involved in the control of voluntary muscular contractions is shown here. The basic diagram (1) is the same as it is in the illustration of the stretch reflex, but with provision made for signals from the brain to cause the muscle spindle to contract by way of a special motor nerve fiber. When a signal is transmitted along this special fiber (2), the spindle contracts, exciting the spindle sensory ending, just as if the spindle had been stretched. Consequently a contraction of the main muscle is excited by way of the stretch-reflex pathway (3, 4). In a real muscle this picture is further complicated by the existence of a direct pathway

muscle spindles lie among the ordinary muscle fibers (the much larger red stringy structures, visible to the unaided eye, that actually do the work) and share their attachments to bone or tendon. Hence they change length as the main muscle fibers change length. If a contraction of a muscle spindle, which excites its primary ending, is succeeded by an equal contraction of the main muscle, the stretch will be taken off the sensory region and the ending will be silenced. The spindle primary, in fact, is sensitive to the difference in length between the spindle and the main muscle fibers; it is a misalignment detector. It discharges if contraction of the spindle is not matched by contraction of the main muscle, or, vice versa, if extension of the main muscle is not accompanied by relaxation of the spindle. There is no obligation for the muscle spindles and the main muscle to contract and relax together, because the motor nerve fibers that run to them and carry the nerve impulses from the central nervous system that cause them to contract are largely separate. The spindles could therefore be activated while the main muscle remained passive, and vice versa.

Having seen the circumstances under which nerve impulses are discharged by the spindle primary endings,

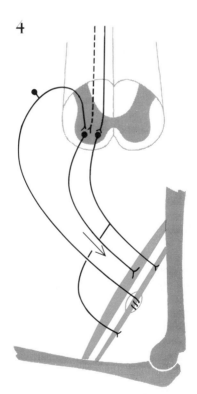

4

(broken line in diagram 4) from the brain to the main motor nerve cells. In the power-steering analogy this pathway corresponds to a direct connection between the steering wheel and the road wheels of an automobile.

the next question is: What do these impulses do when they reach the central nervous system? Their best-established function is to excite an automatic contraction—the stretch reflex—in the muscle from which they come. This they do, at least in part, by impinging directly on those nerve cells in the spinal cord that give rise to the motor nerve fibers to the muscle in question.

The most familiar manifestation of the stretch reflex is the knee jerk, widely used in medicine to test the state of the nervous pathways concerned. A physician strikes the tendon below the knee-cap with a rubber hammer, and in a healthy subject the muscles that straighten the knee briefly contract involuntarily. The effect of striking the tendon is slightly and suddenly to stretch these muscles, and so to excite their muscle spindles. The tendon itself has no part in the sensory mechanism. The tendon jerk is quite transient, but under suitable circumstances a slower, sustained extension of a muscle will result in a sustained reflex contraction. If the reaction in a patient who is otherwise relaxed is exaggerated, the limb is said to be "spastic," that is, affected by spasm.

Human muscles in general can be shown to be under the influence of the stretch reflex when they are engaged in steady contractions of a voluntary nature. The main evidence for this is that if a subject is invited, say, to flex his elbow steadily against a load, it is found that a sudden unexpected increase in the load, which causes his elbow to extend, calls up a larger contraction of his biceps muscle, and conversely a decrease in load causes a relaxation. Electrical recording methods reveal that these reactions begin so soon (within about a twentieth of a second) that they must be automatic, reflex responses.

It has been realized for half a century that the stretch reflex confers valuable self-regulating properties on a muscle, causing it automatically to adjust to changes in load, without any need for the orders that the brain sends down to be altered. Everyone believes the reason the horse does not sag at the knees when Douglas Fairbanks leaps from the castle parapet onto its back is that the horse's leg muscles immediately respond to the extra strain by way of their stretch reflexes. If this interpretation is correct, we have one answer to the question: What does the horse expect of its muscles? In this situation it expects them not only to exert enough force to support its body weight but also to adjust automatically to extra weight. Clearly what the horse really wants is for the

length of the muscles to be kept roughly constant so that posture is maintained. The stretch reflex can achieve this result for the horse because it is based on a sensor—the muscle spindle—that measures length, or, to be more exact, differences in length.

What happens when it is desired that the muscles should execute a movement, not merely maintain a stationary posture or some other steady contraction? The obvious trick is to cause the spindles to contract at the desired rate so that the sensory endings on the spindles will be excited if the main muscle does not itself keep up with the spindles, that is, does not contract at the desired rate. In this way the advantages of automatic compensation for changes of load by means of the stretch reflex could be retained during active shortening. Contraction of the spindles would in effect drive the main muscle by means of the stretch reflex, turning on more contraction if an unexpected obstruction were met with, or if the rate of shortening for any other reason fell behind, and, vice versa, damping down contraction automatically if the load unexpectedly diminished, or if for some other reason the movement undesirably accelerated. Within the past year C. D. Marsden, H. B. Morton and I have obtained direct evidence that this kind of rapid, reflex compensation does in fact occur during voluntary movements in man.

In this mode of operation the stretch reflex, as the reader will have perceived, functions as a follow-up servomechanism, closely analogous to power-assisted steering in an automobile. Contraction of the spindle corresponds to turning the steering wheel, shortening of the main muscle to turning of the road wheels, with the spindle sensory ending acting as the misalignment detector. The subject can demand of his muscles either a certain limb position or a certain rate of change of limb position, and within limits (limits not yet known in quantitative terms) his demands will be automatically met by his muscle servo.

That, in brief outline, is as far as we have gone in understanding how, when we make a voluntary effort, the muscle sense organs act at a subconscious level to ensure that our muscles do what we expect of them. Many facts have had to be left out and without doubt many more remain to be discovered. To attempt any account at this stage requires a certain presumption. I can only hope that when the whole truth emerges, it will prove to be an extension and not a contradiction of the story I have told here.

21

Brain Mechanisms in Movement

by Edward V. Evarts
July 1973

*The highest brain functions are generally thought to be
mediated in the cerebral cortex. In the control of the
muscles, however, the highest function may be served
by centers deeper in the brain*

The traditional view of the brain is that the highest level in its hierarchical organization is in the cortex, or outer part, of the cerebrum. It turns out that this is not true for the brain's motor functions: the control and integration of muscular movements. Brain research has gradually revealed that the motor area of the cerebral cortex is actually at a rather low level of the motor control system, not far removed from the muscular apparatus itself. Structures lying deep below the cortex are at a higher functional level of the system, as judged by their position in the neural chain of command that initiates and controls movement. The implication of these findings is that the primary function of the cerebral motor cortex may not be volition but rather the refined control of motor activity.

The current era of research on how the cerebral cortex controls movement began some 100 years ago with the studies of the British neurologist John Hughlings Jackson. Reasoning from the abnormal movements present in epilepsy and from the normal movements absent in apoplexy or stroke, he proposed that the brain was a sensory-motor machine divided into different centers for the coordination of sensation and movement. From the symptoms of stroke patients and the anatomical site of the blood clot or burst vessels that caused the symptoms he concluded that the part of the cerebral cortex most directly concerned with movement lay in the territory supplied by the middle cerebral artery. Experimental evidence for Jackson's theory was provided by Gustav Theodor Fritsch and Eduard Hitzig of Germany, who in 1870 reported that the electrical stimulation of a region in one cerebral hemisphere of a dog caused the contraction of muscles on the opposite side of the

dog's body. In 1874 Roberts Bartholow, an American physician, demonstrated that electrical stimulation of the cortical area proposed by Jackson as the site of motor control produced muscular contraction. That area is now called the motor cortex.

Jackson also devoted much study to focal epilepsy, a condition where convulsive movements are restricted to one part of the body, for example the thumb. He proposed that the localized movements result from excessive nerve discharges in localized areas of the cortex and that these discharges in turn give rise to localized muscular contractions without the volitional participation of the patient. Such localized epileptic attacks are now called Jacksonian epilepsy.

The discovery that muscular contraction could be produced by the electrical stimulation of a small region of the cerebral cortex came as a great surprise to the neurologists of that time. Before the work of Jackson, Fritsch and Hitzig it was generally believed that the highly convoluted cerebral cortex of man was involved in the generation of thoughts rather than of movements. The cerebral cortex was viewed as being man's highest organ of thought, and it was assumed that subcortical, or lower, centers were responsible for muscular contractions. Indeed, the intellectual climate of the day made it necessary for Fritsch and Hitzig to state that "contrary to the opinions of Flourens and most investigators who followed him, the soul in no case represents a sort of total function of the whole of the cerebrum, the expression of which might be destroyed by mechanical means *in toto*, but not in its individual parts. Individual psychological functions...depend for their entrance into matter, or for their formation from it,

upon circumscribed centers of the cerebral cortex."

Between 1900 and 1920 Charles S. Sherrington, the foremost neurophysiologist of the time, applied the technique of electrical stimulation to study how the cerebrum controlled movement. Although he made important discoveries with this procedure, he recognized its limitations: the movements produced by the electrical stimulation of the brain are nonvolitional, resembling the movements of epilepsy more than the movements of normal motor activity. Sherrington saw the need for new techniques, and he wrote that experiments leading to an understanding of the normal functioning of the cerebral motor centers would require "combining the methods of comparative psychology with the methods of experimental physiology...to furnish new data of importance toward the knowledge of movement as an outcome of the working of the brain."

The psychophysiological approach advocated by Sherrington was not feasible for nearly 50 years because of technical problems. As a result knowledge of the cerebral motor processes greatly lagged behind that of the cerebral sensory processes. One difficulty in studying volitional movement arose from the necessity of having the active participation of the experimental subject; that precluded the use of an anesthetized animal. Research on sensory processes moved ahead rapidly because sensory functions could be tested in such an animal. For example, the physiology of visual receptors could be studied in anesthetized animals but the physiology of eye movements could not, since such studies required animals capable of perception, attention and coordinated motor function.

Part of the problem was solved in the 1920's when physiological psychologists

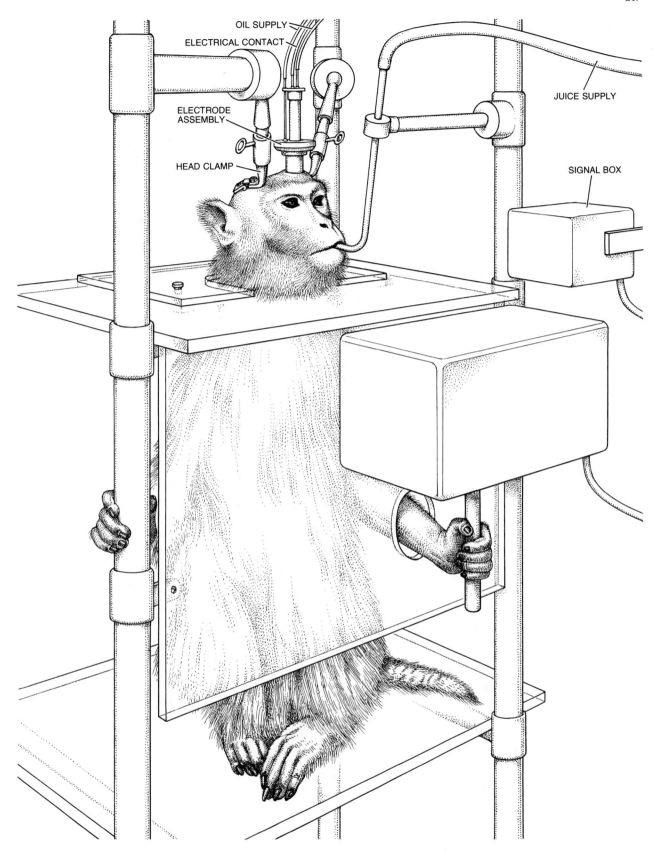

OIL SUPPLY
ELECTRICAL CONTACT
ELECTRODE ASSEMBLY
HEAD CLAMP
JUICE SUPPLY
SIGNAL BOX

RECORDINGS OF THE ACTIVITY of single nerve cells in the brain are obtained while a monkey performs a learned task in this specially designed "primate chair" in the author's laboratory at the National Institute of Mental Health. The monkey's head is painlessly immobilized so that the microelectrode in the brain does not change position during the experiment. The monkey has been trained to move the vertical rod by flexing its wrist when a light in the signal box comes on. If it makes the required movement within a specified time, it receives a reward of fruit juice through the tube in its mouth. Signals from the microelectrode implanted in the brain, along with data from the signal box and transducers connected to the vertical rod, are fed into a computer for analysis.

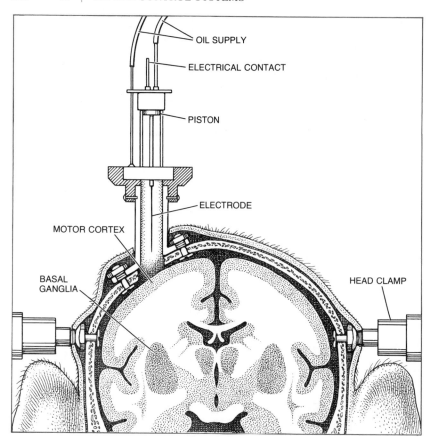

MICROELECTRODE ASSEMBLY consists of a fine platinum-iridium wire attached to a hydraulically actuated piston. A stainless-steel cylinder permanently attached to the monkey's skull provides access to the brain. The bolts on the sides of the skull are also permanently implanted. They are attached to clamps during the experiment to prevent head movement. After the electrode assembly is bolted to the cylinder the electrode is lowered by pumping oil into the inlet on the right and raised by pumping oil into the inlet on the left.

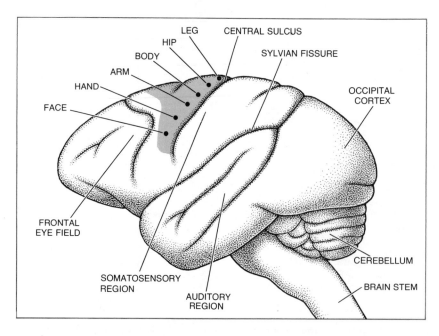

CEREBRAL CORTEX of a monkey's brain is depicted with the motor cortex, which controls muscular movement, in color. Electrical stimulation of the points indicated on the motor cortex causes involuntary contraction of the corresponding group of muscles on the opposite side of the body. Damage to an area of the motor cortex usually results in paralysis of the muscles controlled by that area. The frontal eye field is involved in eye movements.

developed techniques for conditioning animals to execute certain movements that could be systematically modified and that could be readily observed and recorded in the laboratory. The greatest stumbling block was finding a way to record the electrical activity of individual nerve cells in the brain of unanesthetized animals. Cerebral nerve cells are extremely small, and in order to record their electrical discharges a microelectrode must be placed within about 50 microns of the membrane of the nerve cell. In addition the microelectrode has to remain in position even when the animal moves. Some 15 years ago Herbert H. Jasper of the Montreal Neurological Institute worked out techniques for recording the activity of individual nerve cells in animals executing learned movements. His contribution consisted in miniaturizing the system for positioning the microelectrode in the brain. The entire apparatus he developed can be attached to the animal's skull, so that head movements do not displace the recording electrode [see top illustration at left].

The cerebral motor cortex was long the focal point for research on how the brain controls muscular movements, but today neurophysiological studies are concerned with the cerebellum and the basal ganglia as well [see illustrations on opposite page]. The objective of current research is to elucidate how these three interconnected parts of the brain—the motor cortex, the cerebellum and the basal ganglia—act together to control movement.

It is known that damage to the motor cortex causes paralysis but that damage to the basal ganglia or to the cerebellum produces abnormality rather than abolition of movement. For example, symptoms of Parkinson's disease, a neurological disorder resulting from damage to the basal ganglia, include active features such as tremor and muscular rigidity and negative features such as slowness in the initiation of movement and loss of the usual facial expression of emotions. The severity of the motor disorder depends not so much on what muscles are used as on how the muscles are used. A high-velocity movement can sometimes be carried out almost normally by a Parkinsonian patient who in the next moment may have great difficulty initiating a slow movement with the same muscles.

Damage to the cerebellum produces an abnormality of movement that is almost the opposite of the abnormality caused by damage to the basal ganglia. With a cerebellar disorder muscular tremor is most severe during voluntary movement and least marked when the muscles are at rest. It seems clear that the three motor control centers are functionally interdependent. But in what temporal order do they become active, and what aspect of movement does each control? These are questions that recordings of the activity of single nerve cells in the brain during the movement of specific muscles can help to answer.

One of the first microelectrode studies involved determining the time at which nerve cells in the motor cortex of monkeys discharged when the monkey executed a simple hand movement. The monkey was trained to depress a telegraph key and to watch for the appearance of a light, which came on at unpredictable times. If the monkey released the telegraph key within 350 milliseconds or less after the light came on, it was rewarded with a few drops of fruit juice. By simultaneously recording both the brain-cell discharges and the muscle discharges, it was found that cells in the motor cortex became active prior to muscular contraction. This, together with the known anatomical connections, indicates that cells in the motor cortex are components in the circuit that initiates the motor response.

Immediately adjacent to the motor cortex is the sensory cortex, which receives inputs from nerve endings in the skin and the joints. Recordings from nerve cells in the sensory receiving area showed activity after rather than before the initial muscular contraction, indicating that although these cells may play a part in guiding movement on the basis of feedback, they are not in the circuit that initiates the first muscular contraction. The sensory cortex is not the only region of the brain with strong inputs from peripheral receptors concerned with motor control. The cerebellum, for example, receives powerful inputs from the vestibular apparatus, which senses the equilibrium of the body, and from muscle receptors. It was commonly believed that the major role of the cerebellum was regulation of movement in response to feedback from the muscles after they had begun their contraction. It therefore came as a surprise when W. Thomas Thach, Jr., of the Yale University School of Medicine discovered that changes in cerebellar activity occurred prior to movement. Then Mahlon DeLong of the National Institute of Mental Health extended the studies to the basal ganglia and found that nerve cells in that region also become active in advance of muscular contraction.

The discovery that all three motor regions discharge prior to movement has

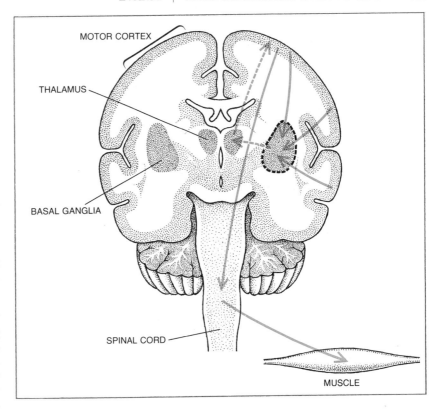

BASAL GANGLIA receive inputs from a wide area of the cerebral cortex and send signals to the motor cortex by way of the thalamus. When the functioning of the basal ganglia is impaired, faulty signals (*broken colored lines*) pass to the motor cortex and cause postural disturbances, muscular tremor at rest and difficulty in the initiation of movement.

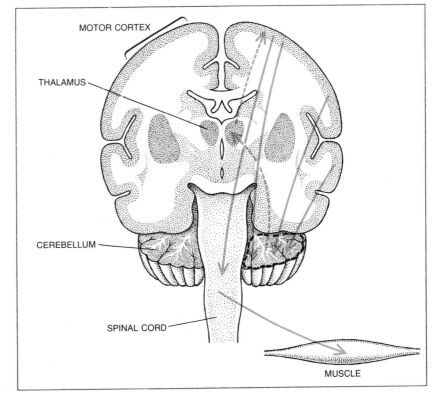

CEREBELLUM receives inputs from a wide area of the cerebral cortex. Damage to the cerebellum results in faulty signals to the motor cortex by way of the thalamus (*broken colored lines*). This causes muscular tremor that is most severe during voluntary movement.

led to a new notion of the functional relation of the three structures. The entire cerebral cortex sends fibers to both the basal ganglia and the cerebellum, and these two structures in turn send massive connections back to the motor cortex by way of the thalamus. Thus the basal ganglia and the cerebellum receive information from the somatosensory, visual and auditory regions of the cerebral cortex, transform this information and then send a new pattern of signals to the motor cortex. Whereas the traditional view held that the cerebral motor cortex was at the highest level of motor integration and that the subcortical structures were at a lower level, that is, closer to the muscle, it now appears that the situation is quite the reverse. The inputs going into the cerebellum and into the basal ganglia may be coded in a more abstract and complex manner than the inputs going into the motor cortex. In addition the motor cortex is more directly connected to spinal-cord motor neurons than either the cerebellum or the basal ganglia.

Although all three major motor regions of the brain become active prior to movement, each region is involved in quite different aspects of motor control. When studies were begun to determine the aspects of movement controlled by the motor cortex, there seemed to be two possible alternatives: control of muscle length or control of muscle tension. In other words, it was asked: Do impulses leaving the motor cortex specify the displacement to be produced or do they specify the force required to produce the displacement? Does the motor cortex control the direction and extent of the movement or does it control the direction and magnitude of the forces underlying the movement? A number of studies of motor performance in man have provided evidence for both possibilities. As one investigator, J. A. V. Bates of the National Hospital for Nervous Diseases in London, pointed out: "Force can be looked upon as the body's basic output quantity; velocity is thus the single integral of this, and displacement the double integral. To attempt a desired velocity and a desired displacement are thus in theory more complex operations than to attempt a desired force. But against this it might be emphasized that our everyday experience is a demand for accurate displacement outputs, i.e., practice in double integration."

In order to determine the primary output of the motor cortex my colleagues and I at the National Institute of Mental

Health devised an experiment that involved training a monkey to carry out a task in which the direction of force and the direction of displacement could be independently varied. A panel with a vertical rod that could be grasped with one hand was mounted on the monkey's cage. The monkey received a reward of fruit juice when the speed with which the handle was moved back and forth fell within certain time limits. The limits were narrowed as the monkey gained proficiency in carrying out the task. Ultimately the monkey was trained to displace the rod in more than 400 milliseconds but less than 700 milliseconds. Two successive displacements had to be made correctly before the monkey received a reward. The rod was displaced either by a bending of the wrist followed by a straightening of the wrist (flexion followed by extension) or vice versa.

The required cycle consisted of either flexion or extension displacement within the time limits followed by either extension or flexion, also within the time limits. A weight was attached to the rod with a string, and the string was passed over one of two pulleys. When it was passed over one pulley, the load opposed wrist flexion and tended to pull the wrist into an extended position. The monkey had to exert a force in the direction of flexion; even when the load was being lowered, the flexor muscles had to exert a force to prevent it from falling too rapidly. When the string was passed over the other pulley, the situation was reversed: the load now opposed the extensor muscles and as a result the monkey had to exert a net force in the direction of extension. During training both the size of the load and the direction in which it acted were varied so that the monkey learned to make movements of the required duration independently of these variables.

When the monkey was thoroughly trained in its home cage, it was then trained to carry out the same series of wrist movements in a special chair equipped with a recording apparatus. When the monkey's performance was satisfactory, a microelectrode was implanted in its brain. Recordings of a single nerve cell in the motor cortex were then made while the monkey performed the task. The results showed that the activity of nerve cells in the motor cortex was related to the amount and pattern of muscular contraction rather than to the displacement that the contraction produced [see bottom illustration at right].

The implication of this finding may be more readily grasped by imagining what

TEMPORAL RELATION between the discharge of a nerve cell in the motor cortex and a simple hand movement is shown at right. A monkey was trained to depress a

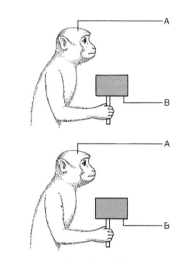

SELECTIVE ACTIVITY of a single nerve cell in the motor cortex during wrist displacement is shown at right. A monkey was trained to move a vertical rod between two stops within a certain time limit. When trace

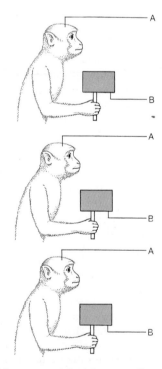

RELATION between activity of nerve cell in the motor cortex and the support of different weights by an arm is shown at right. A monkey was trained to hold a vertical handle between two stops. Weights were

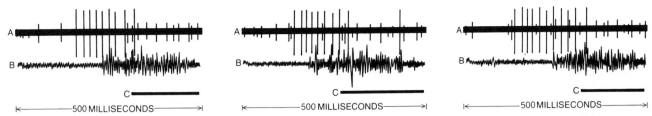

telegraph key and then to release it within 350 milliseconds after a light came on. The upper traces (*A*) show the activity of a single nerve cell in the arm region of the motor cortex, which was recorded by an implanted microelectrode. The traces start at the onset of the light signal. In a series of trials the nerve cell became active first, usually within 150 milliseconds of the signal. There followed a contraction of arm muscles (*B*), which was detected by an electromyograph. Trace (*C*) shows when the telegraph key opened.

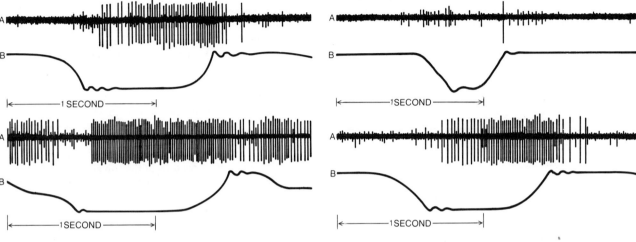

B is at its lowest, the wrist is extended. When the trace is at its highest, the wrist is flexed or bent forward. Recordings from a single nerve cell in the motor cortex (*A*) were made during the movements. When there was no weight opposing the movement (*top left*), the cell was active during flexion but not during extension. When a load of 400 grams opposing flexion was added (*bottom left*), the cell became much more active during both flexion and extension. When a 400-gram load opposed extension, however, the cell became almost totally "silent" (*top right*). With no opposing load the nerve cell again showed its initial pattern (*lower right*).

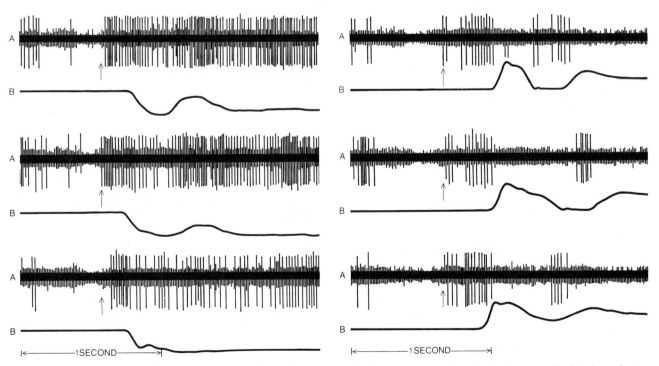

placed sometimes to oppose flexion of the wrist and sometimes to oppose extension. The magnitude of the load was also changed from time to time. Recordings from a single nerve cell in the motor cortex were made with a microelectrode (*A*). Displacement of the rod held is shown by the trace *B* and the arrow indicates when the monkey grasped the rod. The traces on the left from the top down show the activity of the nerve cell when the flexor muscles were respectively supporting weights of 400, 200 and 100 grams. The traces at right show the activity of the nerve cell when the extensor muscles supported the same sequence of weights.

happens when you lift different weights. Suppose in one case you hold a tennis ball and move your arm up and down over a fixed distance and at a fixed speed. Then you replace the tennis ball with a steel ball of the same size and repeat the arm motions exactly in the same manner. To an external observer there would be no difference between the arm movements with the two balls. Both movements would be over the same distance and at the same speed. The patterns of activity in your motor cortex would be quite different for the two movements, however, because the muscular contractions required to lift the heavy steel ball

are different from the contractions required to lift the light tennis ball.

Another question about how movements are controlled is whether the pattern of activity in a motor region is related only to the physical aspects of movement or whether there are different patterns of activity that are associated with the same physical movement. For example, when the muscular contractions are exactly the same, is the pattern of activity in the motor area the same for learned movements and for innate, reflex movements? When the cerebral motor cortex was thought to be the highest level of the motor control sys-

tem, it seemed logical to assume that its nerve cells would be more involved in learned movements than in reflexes. But when the activity of nerve cells in the motor cortex was recorded in association with natural movements such as scratching, eating and grooming, and also in association with highly learned movements such as reaction-time performance, it was found that the motor cortex participated in the control of movement regardless of whether the movement was innate or learned. In both types of movement the activity of the nerve cells in the motor cortex is related to what the muscles do rather than the circumstances in which they do it.

That does not mean that there is a one-to-one relation between the motor-cortex nerve cells and the spinal-cord motor nerve cells. On the contrary, there are a number of differences between the pattern of activity of nerve cells in the motor cortex and the activity of motor nerve cells in the spinal cord. It may be that the relation of the motor-cortex nerve cells to the spinal-cord motor nerve cells is similar to the relation between the cells in the lateral geniculate nucleus (a way station between the retina and the visual cortex) and the cells in the visual region of the cortex. Cells in both the lateral geniculate nucleus and the cortex respond to the location of the stimulus on the retina, but if there is a pattern in the stimulus, it will be processed by the visual cortex. In much the same way it appears that the activity of nerve cells in the motor cortex may be related to certain patterns of activity within a group of muscles, whereas the activity of a spinal-cord motor nerve cell is related only to a single set of fibers in one muscle.

In regions of the cerebral cortex outside the motor cortex, however, neural activity is sometimes more dependent on the context in which the movement occurs than on the muscular activity per se. By context is meant the mental circumstances or intentions associated with the movement of a set of muscles: whether the movement is voluntary or involuntary, learned or innate, fast or slow. For example, in the eye the same muscles serve for saccadic movements and for smooth pursuit movements. Saccadic eye movements are rapid jerks by which the gaze is shifted from one fixation point to another. Smooth pursuit movement is the tracking of a moving object so that the image remains stationary on the retina. Recordings made by Emilio Bizzi of the Massachusetts Institute of Technology from a frontal corti-

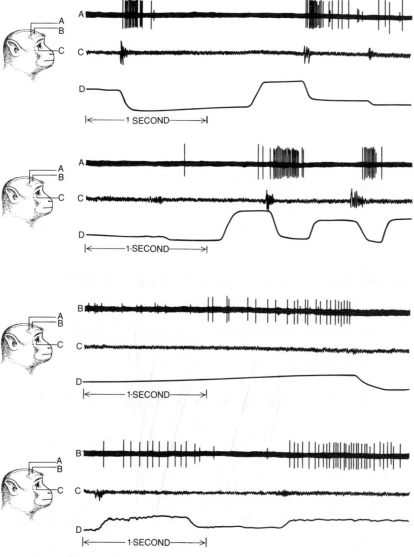

TWO TYPES OF NERVE CELL in the frontal eye field of the cerebral cortex exhibit different patterns of activity even though both are involved in controlling the same eye muscles. Recordings of the activity of single nerve cells in the frontal eye field by Emilio Bizzi of the Massachusetts Institute of Technology show that one type of cell (*A*) discharges during voluntary saccadic eye movement and a second type of cell (*B*) discharges during smooth pursuit eye movement and during maintained position. The electromyographic activity of an eye muscle (*C*) and eye movements (*D*) also were recorded. The top traces show a cell (*A*) discharging during saccadic movements. The bottom traces show the discharge of a different cell (*B*) during smooth pursuit (*upper B*) and maintained eye position (*lower B*).

cal region (outside the motor cortex) involved in controlling eye movements have revealed that one set of nerve cells participated in the saccadic movements and another set was involved in the pursuit movements even though the same muscles were serving both movements. Thus the activity of nerve cells in this frontal cortical region is not associated with the muscle activity, as it is in the motor cortex, but rather with the type of movement. In the motor cortex, on the other hand, the same set of nerve cells was found to control the contraction of arm muscles regardless of the circumstances or context of the movement.

Hans H. Kornhuber of the University of Ulm has proposed that cells in the cerebellum and in the basal ganglia are also differentially active depending on the type of movement rather than on the muscle activity. Drawing evidence both from patients with disorders of movement and from experimental studies in animals, Kornhuber in 1971 suggested that the major role of the cerebellum is to preprogram and initiate rapid saccadic or ballistic movements, whereas the major role of the basal ganglia is to generate slow movements. To test this hypothesis for the basal ganglia, DeLong carried out studies on the activity of individual cells in the basal ganglia of monkeys trained to make a quick limb movement in response to a red light and a slow, highly controlled movement in response to a green light. DeLong found that a high percentage of movement-related cells in a large portion of the basal ganglia discharged most strongly for the slow movement rather than for the fast one. Although the findings are consistent with Kornhuber's hypothesis, the exact role of these cells in the control of slow movements awaits further study. In any event it is clear that compared with the motor cortex, which is involved with both slow and fast movement, the basal ganglia are preferentially active in slow movements. The output of the basal ganglia, which presumably serves to modulate cortical output, goes to the motor cortex by way of the thalamus.

The cerebellum also projects fibers to the motor cortex by way of the thalamus, but we do not yet have direct experimental evidence on the special kinds of movement that the nerve cells of the cerebellum control. Clinical and anatomical data, however, suggest that the cerebellum may have a special role in quick, ballistic movements. Indeed, Kornhuber has proposed that the cerebellum and the basal ganglia are complementary structures, with the cerebellum control-

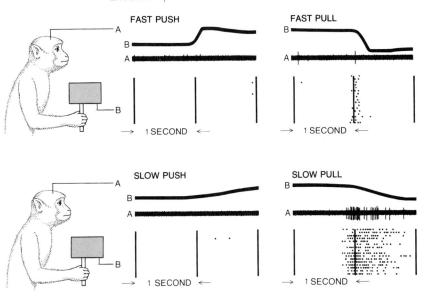

ACTIVITY OF A SINGLE NERVE CELL in the basal ganglia during pushing and pulling movements of the arm shown here was recorded by Mahlon DeLong of the National Institute of Mental Health. The traces labeled B show the position of the arm during the trials. The traces labeled A show the activity of the nerve cell in the basal ganglia during the same trial, and the lower portion shows the activity of the cell in raster form during a series of successive trials. The nerve cell discharged during the slow pulling movement but not during the slow pushing movement. During fast movements the cell discharged weakly.

ling quick movements and the basal ganglia controlling slow movements.

The results obtained so far from recording the activity of single nerve cells with microelectrodes and determining the relation between the recordings and the control of movement have been somewhat fragmentary. Their limitations serve to emphasize how much remains to be learned. A particularly promising area of investigation for the near future is the analysis of experimentally produced motor disturbances in monkeys, disturbances that are similar to the motor disturbances found in man, for example Parkinson's disease. Discovery of the neurophysiological errors in such experimental models of motor disturbances will be of value in developing and testing therapeutic drugs. Many patients with Parkinson's disease have shown a dramatic improvement after taking the drug L-dopa. With neurophysiological studies of Parkinsonism in monkeys it may be possible to determine exactly how L-dopa works. Analogous studies should be feasible for diseases involving the cerebellum.

People suffering from Parkinson's disease exhibit emotional as well as muscular disorders. Other basal-ganglia diseases, some of them genetically determined, are associated with psychological disorders. This indicates that the basal ganglia may be the region that provides the major associative link between the more specialized sensory division of the

nervous system and the motor division.

The implications of the studies I have described thus extend into the areas of psychology and psychiatry. Indeed, it seems possible that understanding of the human nervous system, even its most complex intellectual functions, may be enriched if the operation of the brain is analyzed in terms of its motor output rather than in terms of its sensory input. In the past most attempts to describe the higher functions of the brain have been made in terms of how sensory inputs are processed from the receptor on up to the higher cortical centers. A strong case for an alternative approach has been made by Roger W. Sperry of the California Institute of Technology. I shall end with his comment: "Instead of regarding motor activity as being subsidiary, that is, something to carry out, serve and satisfy the demands of the higher centers, we reverse this tendency and look upon the mental activity as only a means to an end, where the end is better regulation of overt response. Cerebration essentially serves to bring into motor behavior additional refinement, increased direction toward distant, future goals and greater overall adaptiveness and survival value. The evolutionary increase in man's capacity for perception, feeling, ideation, imagination and the like may be regarded not so much as an end in itself as something that has enabled us to behave, to act, more wisely and efficiently."

22

The Cortex
of the Cerebellum

by Rodolfo R. Llinás
January 1975

In this part of the brain the pattern of connections
between nerve cells has been determined in detail.
The pattern is now understood well enough to relate it
to the function of the neuronal networks

In the study of the brain a perennial goal is to infer function from structure, to relate the behavior of an animal to the form and organization of the cells in its central nervous system. At the highest level this task can be equated with the tantalizing problem of identifying the mind with the brain, a problem whose solution may well elude us for some time to come. On a more modest scale the operation of certain limited regions of the brain can already be interpreted in terms of cellular anatomy. For example, the sensory nerve circuits associated with the retina of the eye and the olfactory organs of the nasal cavity have been traced in detail, and our understanding of these circuits has helped to reveal how visual and olfactory information is processed.

The region of the brain where the correlation of anatomy with function has been determined with the greatest success is the cortex, or outer sheath, of the cerebellum. The cells of this structure have been classified according to their form and their position and orientation in the tissue. The properties of each kind of cell, and in particular their response to stimulation, have been investigated. Perhaps most important, a complete "wiring diagram" of the cerebellar nerve circuit has been drawn, showing how the several types of cells are interconnected. From this knowledge of the individual cell and of the pattern of connections between cells one can begin to predict the behavior of the system as a whole.

Of course, our knowledge of the cerebellum is far from complete. To begin with, a comprehensive explanation of the cerebellum would require an equally comprehensive understanding of other parts of the brain with which the cerebellum communicates; some of those

areas remain quite mysterious. Furthermore, our present model of the cerebellum is best suited to describing what happens when a single nerve impulse enters the cortex, and it must be somewhat vague in specifying the effect of a complex pattern of impulses. The model is valuable nevertheless; at the least it offers evidence that the functioning of the brain can be explained simply as the sum of the activities of its component cells, that in the final analysis all mental activity consists of known kinds of interactions between known kinds of nerve cells.

Anatomy of the Cerebellum

The cerebellum lies at the back of the skull behind the brain stem and under the great hemispheres of the cerebrum. Its name is a Latin diminutive of "cerebrum" and means simply "lesser brain." Superficially that is an adequate description of the cerebellum: it is much smaller than the cerebrum but shares certain morphological features with it. As in the cerebrum, the highest functions in the cerebellum are confined to the thin layer of gray matter that makes up the cortex and, as in the cerebrum, this layer is elaborately folded and wrinkled to increase its area. The folds are in fact much deeper and more closely spaced than those of the cerebral cortex. If the cerebellum is split down the middle, the folds form a pattern that resembles a tree, which medieval anatomists termed the *arbor vitae*, or tree of life [*see illustrations on page 227*].

Both the structure and the function of the cerebellum have been known, at least in terms of broad principles, since the end of the 19th century. The challenge to modern investigators has been in combining the two kinds of data and

discovering how a particular structure generates the observed behavior.

The fundamentals of cerebellar anatomy were established in 1888 by Santiago Ramón y Cajal of Spain. He employed a staining technique that had been developed in 1873 by Camillo Golgi of Italy, in which the tissue is impregnated with salts of silver, coloring some of the nerve cells deep brown or black. By studying many stained sections of tissue Ramón y Cajal identified the principal neurons, or nerve cells, of the cerebellar cortex and described their arrangement in space. The arrangement itself is remarkable: some elements of the system are arrayed at right angles to others with extraordinary precision and delicacy. Finally, Ramón y Cajal determined the nature of the connections between the neurons and recognized in them a stereotyped pattern, repeated throughout the cortex. The essential accuracy of his observations has been repeatedly confirmed, and the neuronal circuit he described has been found to be a universal feature of the cerebellum from the most primitive vertebrates to the most advanced.

The first reliable clue to the function of the cerebellum was provided by the Italian physiologist Luigi Luciani, who discovered that experimental animals deprived of a cerebellum suffer disturbances of coordination and equilibrium. Other investigators subsequently demonstrated that the cerebellum communicates with both the motor centers of the cerebrum and the proprioceptive organs of the body, the nerves that sense the relative position and tension of the muscles. By the end of the 19th century the English physiologist Charles Sherrington was able to conclude that the cerebellum coordinates the movements of the muscles but does not initiate them. Although

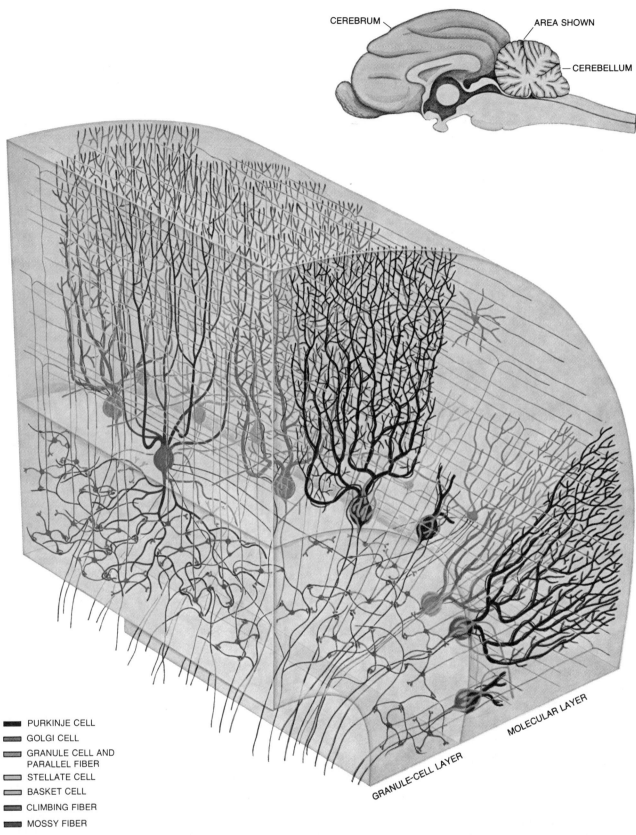

CEREBRUM

AREA SHOWN

CEREBELLUM

- ▬ PURKINJE CELL
- ▬ GOLGI CELL
- ▬ GRANULE CELL AND PARALLEL FIBER
- ▬ STELLATE CELL
- ▬ BASKET CELL
- ▬ CLIMBING FIBER
- ▬ MOSSY FIBER

MOLECULAR LAYER

GRANULE-CELL LAYER

ARCHITECTURE OF THE CORTEX of the cerebellum is diagrammed for a section of tissue from the brain of a cat. The location of the tissue section is indicated in the drawing at top right; the same array of cells is repeated throughout the cortex. Each cell type is identified by color in the key at bottom left. The cortex is organized around the Purkinje cells, whose somas, or cell bodies, define the border between the superficial molecular layer and the deeper granule-cell layer. In the molecular layer are the Purkinje-cell dendrites, which are arrayed in flattened networks like pressed leaves, and the parallel fibers, which pass through the dendrites perpendicularly. This layer also contains the stellate cells and the basket cells, which have similarly flattened arrays of dendrites. In the deeper layer are the granule cells, which give rise to the parallel fibers, and the Golgi cells, which are characterized by a cylindrical dendritic array. Input to the cortex is through the climbing fibers and mossy fibers; output is through the axons of Purkinje cells.

Sherrington's formulation can no longer be accepted entirely, it has been refined rather than refuted [see "The Cerebellum," by Ray S. Snider; SCIENTIFIC AMERICAN Offprint 38].

The Cerebellar Neurons

One reason the cerebellum is so well understood today is that its organization is much simpler than that of most other parts of the brain. The basic circuit of the cortex—with few modifications the circuit described by Ramón y Cajal—involves just seven nerve elements. Two of them conduct nerve impulses into the cortex; they are called the climbing fibers and the mossy fibers. Another

serves as the sole output of the system; it is the Purkinje-cell axon. The four remaining nerve elements are the granule cells, the Golgi cells, the basket cells and the stellate cells; they are entirely indigenous to the cerebellar cortex and run short distances between the other cells. The input terminals are often referred to as afferent fibers, the output cells as efferent neurons and the cells that serve as intermediaries as interneurons [see illustration below].

The discovery of a third afferent system, in addition to the climbing fibers and the mossy fibers, has recently been reported by F. E. Bloom and his colleagues at Saint Elizabeths Hospital in Washington. It consists of fibers arising

from a structure in the brain stem called the locus ceruleus. Because it is not yet clear how this system is related to the other functions of the cerebellum it will not be considered further here.

Neurons are diverse in form, but they all have certain structures in common. Each has a soma, or cell body, which contains the nucleus and usually a major portion of the cytoplasm as well. Extending from the soma are the dendrites (from the Greek for "tree"), which often branch repeatedly, and the axon, which can be quite long and may or may not branch. For the most part dendrites conduct nerve impulses toward the body of the cell and the axon conducts impulses away from it. The junction where the axon of one cell meets a dendrite of another is a synapse.

When a nerve impulse reaches the terminal point of the axon, it provokes the release of a transmitter substance, which passes across the synapse and alters the membrane of the dendrite of the next cell in the neural pathway, changing its permeability to certain ions. The resulting flow of ions across the membrane generates a small electric current, which propagates as a local electrical disturbance of the membrane down the dendrite to the soma. If the stimulating neuron is excitatory, and if the stimulation exceeds a threshold, the receiving cell will "fire" and the impulse will be conveyed through the axon to the next synapse. If the first cell is inhibitory, the probability that the receiving cell will fire is reduced.

The Purkinje cells were among the first neurons recognized in the nervous system; they are named for Johannes E. Purkinje, the Czech physiologist who described them in 1837. They are among the most complex of all neurons. Each has a large and extensive dendritic apparatus referring impulses to a bulblike soma, and a long, slender axon [see illustration on page 228]. The dendrites of a typical human Purkinje cell may form as many as 100,000 synapses with afferent fibers, more than those of any other cell in the central nervous system.

The Purkinje cells are the pivotal element in the neuronal network of the cerebellar cortex. They are found throughout the cortex, their cell bodies constituting a continuous sheath called the Purkinje-cell layer. The dendrites extend densely above the Purkinje-cell layer, toward the boundary of the cortex; this region is called the molecular layer. The axons extend in the opposite direction, into the deeper portion of the cortex called the granule-cell layer. The axons, in fact, penetrate far beyond this

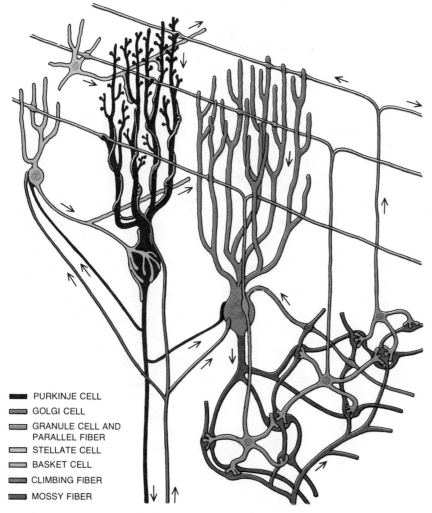

KEY:
- PURKINJE CELL
- GOLGI CELL
- GRANULE CELL AND PARALLEL FIBER
- STELLATE CELL
- BASKET CELL
- CLIMBING FIBER
- MOSSY FIBER

INTERCONNECTION OF NEURONS in the cortex follows an elaborate but stereotyped pattern. Each Purkinje cell is associated with a single climbing fiber and forms many synaptic junctions with it. The climbing fiber also branches to the basket cells and Golgi cells. Mossy fibers come in contact with the terminal "claws" of granule-cell dendrites in a structure called a cerebellar glomerulus. The axons of the granule cells ascend to the molecular layer, where they bifurcate to form parallel fibers. Each parallel fiber comes in contact with many Purkinje cells, but usually it forms only one synapse with each cell. The stellate cells connect the parallel fibers with the dendrites of the Purkinje cell, the basket cells mainly with the Purkinje-cell soma. Most Golgi-cell dendrites form junctions with the parallel fibers but some join the mossy fibers; Golgi-cell axons terminate at the cerebellar glomeruli. Cells are identified in the key at lower left; arrows indicate direction of nerve conduction.

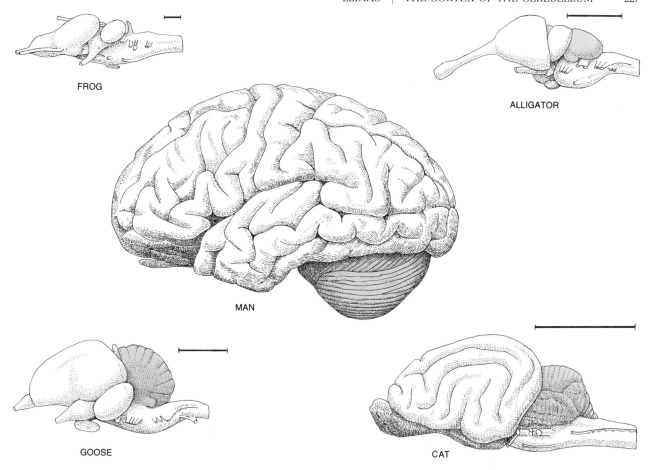

FROG

ALLIGATOR

MAN

GOOSE

CAT

EVOLUTION OF THE CEREBELLUM suggests that its function has become more important during the span of vertebrate history. From the amphibians through the reptiles and birds to the mammals it has become progressively larger, both in actual mass and in proportion to overall brain size. It has also become more convoluted, providing a greater area of cortex. In man it is a large and deeply fissured structure. The cerebellums are shown in color; the scale in relation to the human brain is indicated by horizontal bars.

region; they pass out of the cortex entirely, through the white matter in the core of the cerebellum, and eventually reach isolated lumps of gray matter called cerebellar nuclei. The nuclei are also supplied with side branches of the climbing-fiber and mossy-fiber input systems, so that they receive all the information going to the cortex. In the nuclei the incoming messages are blended with those returning from the cortex and are relayed to other parts of the brain and down the spinal cord to the rest of the body.

The dendrites of the Purkinje cells have an unusual arrangement that is at once the most conspicuous structural element in the cerebellar cortex and an important clue to its functioning. The entire mass of tangled, repeatedly bifurcating branches is confined to a single

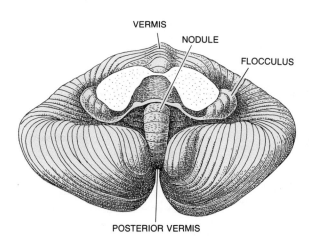

VERMIS

NODULE

FLOCCULUS

POSTERIOR VERMIS

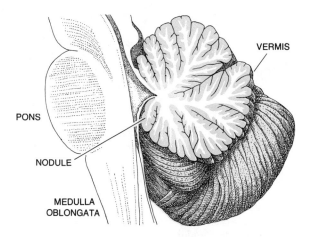

VERMIS

PONS

NODULE

MEDULLA
OBLONGATA

HUMAN CEREBELLUM consists of two hemispheres separated by a narrow girdle, the vermis. At left it is viewed from below; the brain stem has been removed to reveal the vermis, flocculus and nodule, which are involved in eye movement, among other functions. At right the cerebellum is sectioned through the vermis. The pattern of cortical folds is called the *arbor vitae* ("tree of life").

plane, as if it had been flattened like a pressed leaf. Moreover, the planes of all the dendrites in a given region are parallel, so that the dendritic arrays of the cells stack up in neat ranks; adjacent cells in a single plane form equally neat, but overlapping, files.

To a large extent this orderly array determines the nature and number of contacts made with other kinds of cells. As has been pointed out by Clement A. Fox of the Wayne State University School of Medicine, the dendrites are organized like a net to "catch" as many incoming signals as possible. Fibers running perpendicular to the plane of the dendrites will intersect a great many Purkinje cells, although they will touch each cell only once or at most a few times. Fibers oriented in this way do in fact constitute one of the afferent systems in the cortex. (Geometric arrays similar to the arrangement of the Purkinje-cell dendrites appear elsewhere in biology where a large surface area must be fitted into a small volume; an example is the antennae of moths.)

The Purkinje cell represents the output system of the cerebellar cortex, but it is not a mere transmitter or repeater of information originating elsewhere. It is part of an indivisible system of neurons whose activity is determined entirely by the way in which the other neurons are connected with the Purkinje cells and with one another.

The Climbing Fiber

The climbing fibers and the mossy fibers, the two afferent systems that ultimately direct impulses to the Purkinje cells, are distributed throughout the cerebellar cortex in a more or less orderly array. Their presence in all parts of the cortex was demonstrated by Jan Jansen and Alf Brodal and their colleagues at the Anatomical Institute at Oslo in Norway. These workers also showed that the two systems are apparently present in all members of the vertebrate subphylum. The systems are radically different; in some properties they represent opposite extremes among the neurons of the central nervous system.

The climbing fiber is virtually a private line to a given Purkinje cell. It begins outside the cerebellum in other regions of the brain such as the inferior olive, a compact collection of nerve cells alongside the medulla oblongata. The long, ramified axons of these cells extend into the cerebellar nuclei and cortex. In embryonic development the climbing fiber is the first afferent system to reach the Purkinje cell, and once it has "mated" with its particular cell it generally enforces monogamy. The union takes place early in the development of the cerebellum, and the formation of a junction with one climbing fiber apparently discourages others from attaching themselves to the same cell. As the Purkinje cell develops its net of dendrites the climbing fiber follows, matching the intricacy of the dendrites like a vine growing on the trunk and branches of a large tree. This behavior is the root of its name.

It was once believed the climbing fiber formed synapses with the smooth surface of the Purkinje-cell dendrites. It has now been demonstrated by Luis M. H. Larramendi and his colleagues at the University of Chicago, however, that the two cells are actually in contact only where small spines protrude in groups from the surface of the Purkinje-cell dendrite [see illustrations on opposite page]. There are many such spines on any one Purkinje cell. Dean E. Hillman of the University of Iowa has estimated that a Purkinje cell and its climbing fiber are probably in synaptic contact at about 300 points, which is a large number of junctions to be established between a cell and a single afferent fiber.

The action of the climbing fiber on the Purkinje cell was described in 1964 by John C. Eccles, K. Sasaki and me. Working at the Australian National University in Canberra, we found that stimulating a climbing fiber produced an exceedingly powerful excitation of the corresponding Purkinje cell. The Purkinje cell responded with a prolonged burst of high-frequency action potentials, the electrically recorded evidence that a nerve cell is discharging. The intensity of the response was not unexpected, considering the large number of synapses connecting the cells. The excitation was capable of overriding any ongoing activity in the Purkinje cell.

Recordings made with electrodes implanted in Purkinje cells showed that the action potential arises very quickly, then declines slowly and irregularly [see illustration on page 230]. The recorded pattern represents the firing of the cell body of the neuron and the generation of

PURKINJE CELLS sprout a dense network of overlapping dendrites, all confined to a single plane and extending above the cell bodies through the molecular layer to the surface of the cortex. In this section of tissue from the brain of a monkey the surface of the cortex is the bright diagonal strip; it is inside a fold and abuts another part of the cortex with its own Purkinje cells. The parallel fibers are not visible; they run perpendicular to the plane of the page. The Purkinje-cell axons are the small fibers extending from the cell bodies toward deeper strata. The tissue was prepared by staining it with silver salts; the photomicrograph was made by Clement A. Fox of the Wayne State University School of Medicine.

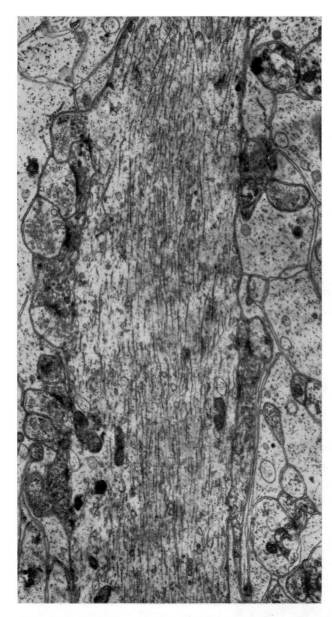

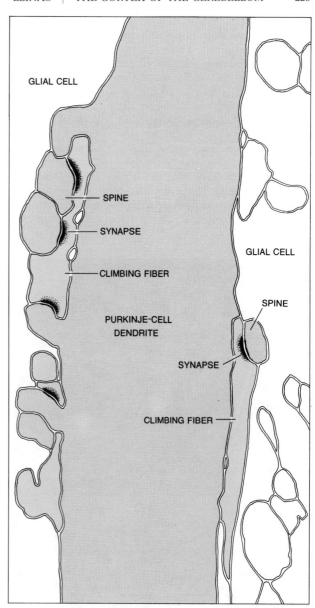

CLIMBING FIBER forms numerous synaptic junctions with a Purkinje-cell dendrite through spines that protrude in clusters from the surface of the dendrite. The structures visible in the electron micrograph at left are diagrammed and identified in the drawing at right. The several regions labeled "Climbing fiber" are segments of a single fiber that is wrapped around the dendrite. Nerve impulses are transmitted from the climbing fiber to the dendrite. Glial cells surrounding the synapse are not neurons but serve as a matrix in which the nerve cells are embedded. The photomicrograph was made by Dean E. Hillman of the University of Iowa.

many lesser action potentials in the dendrites as the cell is showered with synaptic transmitters released at many points by the climbing fiber. Because the response is provoked by a single impulse in a single afferent fiber, it is an all-or-nothing phenomenon, that is, it is present in full force or is absent altogether.

The Mossy Fiber

Whereas the climbing fiber generates many connections to a single Purkinje cell, the mossy fiber ultimately excites many Purkinje cells, but through only a few contacts with each of them. Among all the neurons of the central nervous system, the mossy fiber stimulates one of the largest numbers of cells to be activated by a single efferent fiber.

The mossy fibers do not terminate directly on Purkinje cells, as the climbing fibers do, but on small interneurons, the granule cells, which lie immediately under the Purkinje-cell layer. The granule cells serve as intermediaries, greatly increasing the number of Purkinje cells stimulated by a single afferent fiber.

One reason the granule cells can intersect so many Purkinje cells is that the granule cells are themselves exceedingly numerous. Valentino Braitenberg of the Max Planck Institute for Biological Cybernetics in Tübingen has calculated that the number of granule cells in the human cerebellar cortex may be 10 times greater than the number of cells previously believed to make up the entire brain. Sanford L. Palay of the Harvard Medical School has commented: "Of the 10^{10} cells in the brain, 10^{11} are in the granular layer of the cerebellar cortex!"

The axon of the granule cell projects upward, past the Purkinje-cell layer and into the molecular layer. There it splits, the two branches taking diametrically opposite directions, so that the axon assumes the form of a capital *T*. Fibers representing the horizontal portion of the *T* occupy all levels of the molecular layer. The orientation of these fibers is precisely determined: they are all parallel to one another (for that reason they are called parallel fibers), and they are perpendicular to the planes of the flattened Purkinje-cell dendrites [*see illustration on page 225*]. The arrangement of the cells is thus somewhat like an array of telephone poles (the Purkinje cells) strung with many telephone wires (the parallel fibers). The actual conformation is complicated by the curvature of the folds in the cortex.

The parallel fibers come in contact with the Purkinje cells through spines that emerge in enormous numbers from the terminal regions of the Purkinje-cell dendrites, regions called spiny branchlets [*see illustrations on opposite page*]. The junction is formed between the point of a spine and a globular expansion of the parallel fiber; the geometry of the synapse may resemble that of a ball joint, in which the spine penetrates the swollen part of the fiber.

Generally a parallel fiber comes in contact with a given Purkinje cell only once or (rarely) twice; nevertheless, most of the inputs to the Purkinje cells are through the parallel fibers. As I have noted, a single human Purkinje cell can receive as many as 100,000 parallel fibers (compared with a single climbing fiber).

Eccles, Sasaki and I have studied the effects of stimulating the mossy fibers. Like the climbing fiber, the mossy fiber is excitatory, and so is the granule cell it stimulates. Both afferent systems can therefore excite activity in the cerebellar cortex. The influence of the mossy fibers, however, is for obvious reasons diffuse and complex, in contrast to the sharply focused effect of the climbing fiber.

The Interneurons

Embedded in the matrix of the cerebellar circuitry are two sets of interneurons that, unlike the granule cells, have only short axons. One set is located in the molecular layer and consists of basket cells and stellate cells; the other is in the granule-cell layer and is represented by Golgi cells.

The basket and stellate cells are similar and can be considered members of a single class. Both receive impulses from the parallel fibers and act, through their axons, on Purkinje cells. The principal difference between the two types is that the basket cell establishes synaptic junctions with the Purkinje cell in the lower dendrites and on the soma, whereas the stellate cell is more or less confined to the dendrites. Perhaps the most significant anatomical observation on the basket and stellate cells pertains to the spatial distribution of their axons. They are perpendicular to the parallel fibers and are also perpendicular to the axis of the Purkinje cells. The network of cells in the molecular layer thus consists of three basic types of cell process all of which are mutually perpendicular.

In the granule-cell layer the remaining interneuron, the Golgi cell, also receives impulses from the parallel fibers, but its dendrites form synapses directly with the mossy fibers as well. The Golgi cells are components of a specialized synaptic linkage known as the cerebellar glomerulus, which is the basic functional unit of the granule-cell layer. It consists of a bulge or swelling in a mossy fiber, surrounded by the dendrites of granule cells, which in turn are surrounded by the axons of Golgi cells [*see illustrations on page 232*].

All three kinds of interneuron have been demonstrated to be inhibitory. The inhibitory effect of the basket cell on the soma of the Purkinje cell was initially shown by P. Andersen, Eccles and P. E.

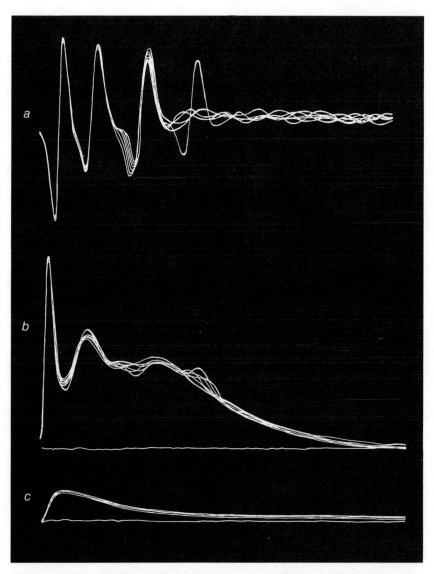

RESPONSE OF A PURKINJE CELL to stimulation by a climbing fiber is recorded electrically. Action potentials (voltages developed across the cell membrane) are measured from outside the cell (*a*) and from inside it (*b*). The response is strong and consistent; several repetitions are superposed here, revealing only small variations. It is an all-or-nothing response; if the climbing fiber fails to fire, only a straight line is recorded. Climbing-fiber stimulation provokes the firing of the Purkinje cell by depolarizing the cell membrane; the phenomenon can be recorded in isolation (*c*) in a damaged cell. The time span of the recordings is about 20 milliseconds. The voltages are not drawn to the same scale; those measured inside the cell (*b, c*) are actually many times larger than those measured outside (*a*).

Voorhoeve at the Australian National University in 1963; the inhibition of Purkinje-cell dendrites by stellate cells and the inhibition of granule cells by Golgi cells were demonstrated soon afterward by Eccles, Sasaki and me.

Organization of the Neurons

As we have seen, the activation of the cerebellar cortex through the climbing-fiber system is relatively straightforward: the stimulation of a single climbing fiber elicits a powerful response from a single Purkinje cell. The sequence of events that follows on the stimulation of a mossy fiber is not only more complicated but also inherently less predictable.

The initial sequence of events was first suggested by János Szentágothai of the Semmelweis University School of Medicine in Budapest: the stimulation of a small bunch of mossy fibers activates, through the granule cells and their parallel fibers, an extensive array of Purkinje cells and all three types of inhibitory interneuron. Subsequent interactions of the neurons tend to limit the extent and duration of the response. The activation of Purkinje cells through the parallel fibers is soon inhibited by the basket cells and the stellate cells, which are activated by the same parallel fibers. Because the axons of the basket and stellate cells run at right angles to the parallel fibers, the inhibition is not confined to the activated Purkinje cells; those on each side of the beam or column of stimulated Purkinje cells are also subject to strong inhibition. The effect of the inhibitory neurons is therefore to sharpen the boundary and increase the contrast between those cells that have been activated and those that have not.

At the same time the parallel fibers and the mossy fibers have activated the Golgi cells at the granule-cell level. The Golgi cells exert their inhibitory effect on the granule cells and thereby quench any further activity in the parallel fibers. This mechanism is one of negative feedback: through the Golgi cell the parallel fiber extinguishes its own stimulus. The net result of these interactions is the brief firing of a relatively large but sharply defined population of Purkinje cells.

At about the time the functional properties of these neuronal circuits were being elucidated an observation made by Masao Ito and his colleagues at the University of Tokyo changed our perspective on the behavior of the entire system. Ito and his co-workers discovered that the Purkinje cell is itself an inhibitory neuron. The entire output of the elabo-

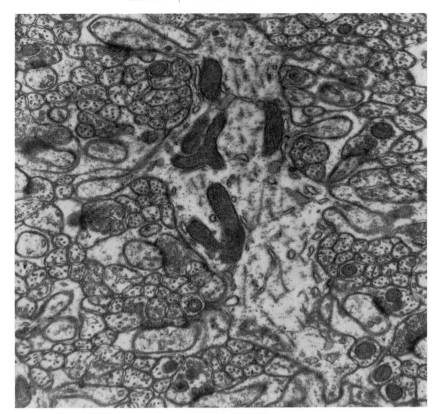

PARALLEL FIBERS attach to a Purkinje-cell dendrite in an electron micrograph made by Hillman. The dendrite is sectioned longitudinally; the parallel fibers are cut transversely.

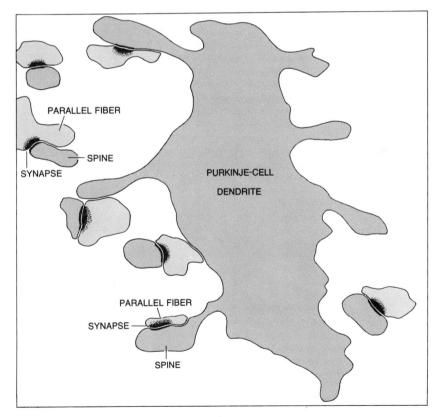

SYNAPSES between parallel fibers and the Purkinje-cell dendrite are indicated in a diagram identifying the elements of the electron micrograph at the top of the page. The region of the dendrite shown is called a spiny branchlet; the spines form junctions with the parallel fibers. Each parallel fiber ordinarily makes only one contact with a given Purkinje cell.

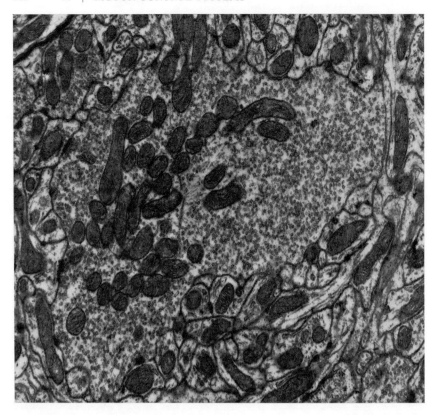

CEREBELLAR GLOMERULUS is seen in cross section in another electron micrograph made by Hillman. The cells of the mammalian tissue are identified in the diagram below.

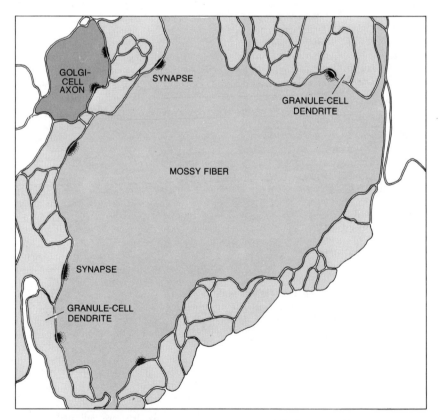

MOSSY FIBER forms synapses with the terminal dendrites of many granule cells in the cerebellar glomerulus. In addition the axons of Golgi cells make contact with the same granule-cell dendrites. The glomerulus forms on an enlarged segment of the mossy fiber.

rate neuronal network in the cerebellar cortex is therefore the organized, large-scale inhibition of other neurons in the cerebellar nuclei. Furthermore, it became evident that of the cells residing in the cortex only the granule cells are excitatory; all the rest are inhibitory. This work provided a fundamental insight into the functioning of the cortex. The firing of the nerve cells that give rise to the climbing fibers and the mossy fibers produces rapid activation of the cerebellar nuclei and through them of cerebral and spinal systems. This activity is abruptly terminated by the inhibitory signals from the cortex.

In several ways the model of the cerebellar cortex devised in these early studies was too simplistic. Although it described with some accuracy the neuronal response to an abrupt stimulus, such as an externally applied electrical potential, it was inadequate to describe the activity following the physiological stimuli constantly impinging on the cortex under ordinary circumstances. For example, the inhibitory interneurons of the molecular layer probably do not normally obliterate the activity of entire groups of Purkinje cells while allowing others to fire. It is more likely that they serve to set a threshold of excitability and thereby to regulate the dynamic range of activity in the cortex. The Golgi cell, on the other hand, is probably a central element in cerebellar organization. Through its direct contacts with the climbing fibers and the mossy fibers the Golgi cell probably "selects" what inputs reach the Purkinje-cell layer at a given time.

In spite of its limitations our study provided a foundation for constructing a theory of cerebellar function. The description of the interactions between the neuronal elements of the cortex was comprehensive and detailed, even if it was based on observations made under somewhat artificial circumstances. Furthermore, the study represented the first demonstration of a correlation between structure and function in a major lobe of the brain.

The Function of the Cerebellar Cortex

If we are finally to understand the significance of the neuronal circuits in the cerebellar cortex, we must analyze those circuits in terms of the kind of information they ordinarily receive. The techniques available for this task are necessarily less direct and less precise than dissection and staining or probing with an electrode, but they have nevertheless yielded important results. One of the most profitable techniques has been the mapping of projections onto the cerebellum. This consists in selecting a nerve fiber of known origin or destination outside the cerebellum and determining the point at which it impinges on the cerebellar cortex.

Each of the proprioceptive nerve endings in the skeletal muscles, for example, corresponds to a particular position on the surface of the cerebellum. When the sum of these positions is plotted, the result is a map such as the one that has been compiled over a period of many years by Olov Oscarsson of the University of Lund and by D. Armstrong and R. J. Harvey of the University of Bristol. By recording the projections of the climbing fibers they have discovered that these afferent cells are distributed with remarkable orderliness in the cerebellar cortex: they are organized in strips parallel to the median line and covering large areas distributed over many folds in the cortex [*see bottom illustration on next page*].

These maps confirm the earlier findings of Jan Voogd of the University of Leiden, who studied the effects of small lesions in the inferior olive, one of the principal sources of the climbing fibers. Nerve fibers radiating from a lesion usually degenerate, and Voogd found in this case that patterns of degenerating tissue on the cerebellar cortex assumed the form of long strips oriented from the front of the head to the back, that is, parallel to the median plane. His discovery suggests that the longitudinal strip is an important principle of organization in the projection of the climbing fibers onto the cerebellar cortex. The pattern has been detected in several vertebrate species.

A clue to the significance of this organizational pattern has recently been provided by pharmacological studies of the cortex. The experiments were performed by Y. Lamarre and C. de Montigny of the University of Montreal and by R. A. Volkind and me at the University of Iowa. They involved a drug called harmaline, derived from the herb harmal, which causes tremors; we have shown in the cat that the effects of the drug are traceable to the activation of the inferior olive. An immediate and obvious inference is that the inferior olive, with the fibers it projects to the cerebellar nuclei and the Purkinje cells, is part of a motor command system concerned with muscular movement. There is even a reasonable basis for speculation on what kind of movements are involved. When maps derived from the proprio-

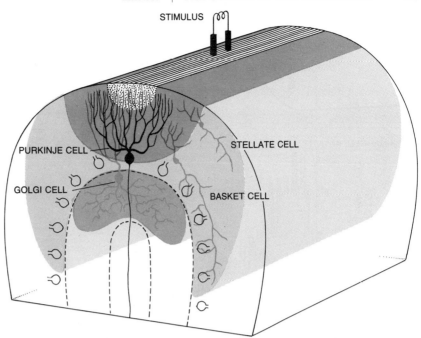

SPATIAL DISTRIBUTION of excitation in the cortex is determined largely by inhibitory neurons. When a brief electrical stimulus is applied to the surface of the cortex, a small bundle of parallel fibers (*stippled area*) is activated this bundle of fibers excites the dendrites of all the cells immediately under it (*gray*), that is, Purkinje cells, stellate cells, basket cells and Golgi cells. The firing of the Purkinje cells constitutes the sole output of the cortex; the other neurons serve to define which Purkinje cells can fire. Because the axons of basket cells and stellate cells extend at right angles to the parallel fibers in the molecular layer, they inhibit Purkinje cells in a wide area on both sides of the excited region (*light color*). The Golgi cells generate an area of inhibition in the granule cells directly under the activated array of parallel fibers (*dark color*). Because the parallel fibers are the axons of the granule cells, inhibition by Golgi cells tends to terminate the excitation.

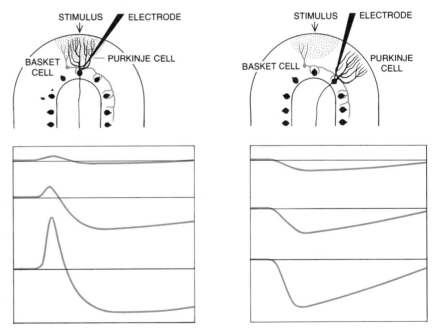

STIMULATION AND INHIBITION of Purkinje cells follow an established temporal sequence. When the response of a cell directly under the stimulated area is recorded (*left*), a brief period of activation is observed (*upward deflection*), followed by a longer period of inhibition (*downward deflection*). The activation results from the direct stimulation of the Purkinje cell by parallel fibers, the inhibition from the action of basket cells and stellate cells. The magnitude of the response varies with the intensity of the stimulation. When the response of a laterally located Purkinje cell is monitored (*right*), only the inhibition is observed, since only basket-cell axons, not stimulated parallel fibers, reach Purkinje cells.

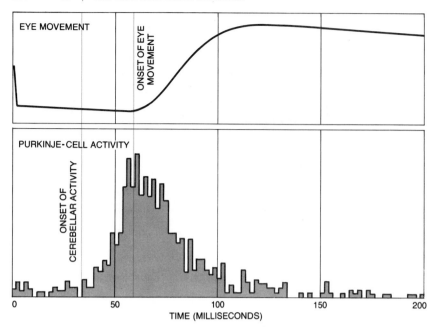

RAPID EYE MOVEMENTS called saccades are associated with activity in the cerebellar cortex. The top graph is an averaged record of 100 saccades; the bottom graph records the activity of a single Purkinje cell during the same 100 eye movements. Purkinje-cell activity begins to increase about 25 milliseconds before the movement is initiated, which suggests that the cerebellum can coordinate or correct such movements before they are generated.

ceptive sensors are superposed on the longitudinal strips that are associated with the climbing fibers, it is found that the climbing-fiber patterns overlap the projections of several areas of the body. It is the current hypothesis, therefore, that the climbing-fiber system is concerned with synchronous movements of groups of muscles, probably involving more than one limb. There is also reason to believe it mainly influences rapid movements. The inhibition of the cerebellar nuclei by the Purkinje cells should follow very soon after the activation of

the nuclei, generating a powerful but brief command signal.

A comprehensive analysis of the mossy-fiber system is more difficult to achieve. The effects of mossy-fiber stimulation are so different from those of the climbing fibers that it is possible the two systems are "time-sharing" the Purkinje cells, each employing them for quite different purposes. Not only do the mossy fibers activate large areas of the cortex instead of individual cells; they also enlist the aid of the inhibitory interneurons, which may modulate and detect patterns in incoming signals. The Golgi cells in particular may be involved in determining what kinds of information reach the cortex through the parallel fibers; moreover, in any time-sharing arrangement they could apportion the Purkinje cells between the two systems.

An example of a motor behavior that is linked with the mossy-fiber system has recently been encountered in studies of visual coordination. In organizing the delicate and precise movements of the eyes the cerebellum is evidently essential; cerebellar dysfunction often disrupts such movements. Two regions of the cerebellum are known to participate in these functions. One is the floccular-nodular area; it regulates the position of the eyes with respect to the orientation of the head and body, enabling one to stare at a fixed point while moving. The other is the cerebellar vermis, which is believed to control the rapid eye movements called saccades, which are important in visual tracking.

In a recent series of experiments at the Air Force School of Aerospace Medicine, James W. Wolfe and I showed that the activation of Purkinje cells by mossy fibers increases about 25 milliseconds before an eye movement begins [see top illustration at left]. The implication of this discovery is that cerebellar regulation of movement through the mossy-fiber system is capable of correcting mistakes before they have reached the muscles and have been expressed in actual movement. The cerebellum appears to correct these movements by acting as a brake.

Motor Coordination

There is no longer any doubt that the cerebellum is a central control point for the organization of movement. It does not initiate movement, and indeed movement can be generated in the absence of a cerebellum. It modulates or reorganizes motor commands, and by coordinating diverse signals it obtains the maximum efficiency from them. It is there-

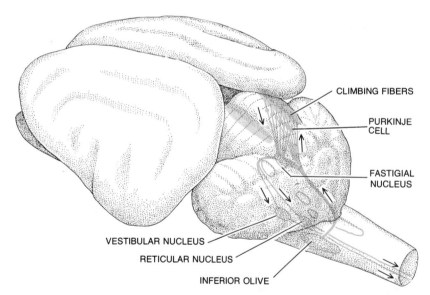

PROJECTION OF CLIMBING FIBERS onto the cerebellar cortex reveals an orderly distribution. The fibers originate in the two inferior olives of the brain stem. Fibers from each olive terminate in the opposite hemisphere of the cerebellum. There they are organized in longitudinal strips covering many cortical folds. The length and orientation of these strips suggest that the climbing-fiber system participates in the regulation of movements that involve several limbs, since each strip extends across areas known to be associated with several parts of the body. Branches of the climbing fibers also reach the cerebellar nuclei (the fastigial nucleus is shown here) and are joined there by the axons of Purkinje cells from the cortex. The output of the fastigial nucleus is applied to the vestibular and reticular nuclei.

fore an organ of regulation in the highest sense. It may in fact regulate more than motor performance. R. Nieuwenhuys and C. Nicholson of the Catholic University of Nijmegen have shown that in electric fish (family Mormyridae) employing an electric field as a sensory organ the cerebellum attains enormous size and fills most of the cranial cavity.

Without question the cerebellum is far more sophisticated than the simple control box, comparing muscle position with brain command, that Sherrington and his contemporaries supposed it to be. Israel Gelfand, M. L. Shik and their associates at the Institute of Information Transmission Systems in Moscow have shown that the cerebellum is capable of coordinating movement even in the absence of all information from the periphery of the body. They removed the forebrain and blocked proprioceptive sensation in experimental animals; as long as the cerebellum remained intact locomotion was possible, but it was disrupted when the cerebellum was removed. A series of experiments conducted by Anders Lundberg and his colleagues at the University of Göteborg provides a further indication that some cerebellar activity is concerned with the internal state of the central nervous system. They found that one of the main afferent tracts leading to the cerebellum, the ventral spinocerebellar tract, conveys information not about the state of the body or the external environment but about the activity of inhibitory interneurons in the spinal cord. Such an internal monitoring mechanism might be a necessity in a system intended to refine or revise motor commands before they reach the muscles, such as is observed in the cerebellar control of eye movement.

Excellence in motor coordination is obviously an adaptive advantage, and evidently it is enough of an advantage to sustain the development of a specialized brain center committed primarily to that purpose. The success of the motor coordination center is suggested by the calculations of Sherwood L. Washburn and R. S. Harding of the University of California at Berkeley. They report that the cerebellum has enlarged between threefold and fourfold in the past million years of human evolution.

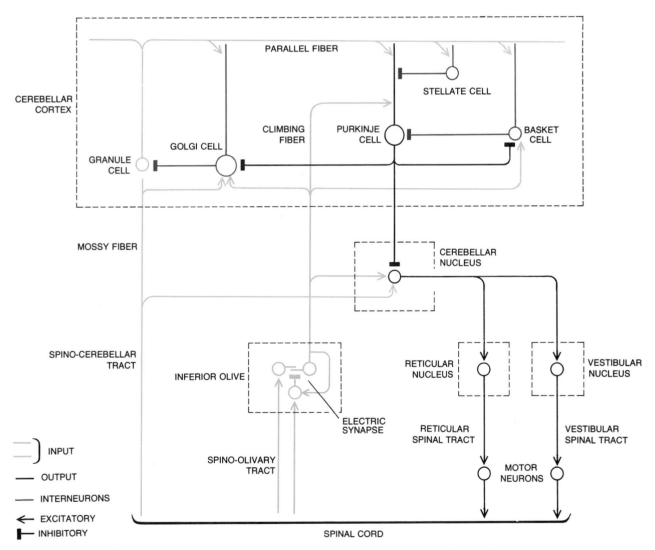

SCHEMATIC "WIRING DIAGRAM" of the cerebellar cortex and the brain centers with which it communicates relates the structure of the nerve-cell circuits to their function. The types of cells and synapses are identified in the key at lower left. Input to the cortex is through the climbing fibers and mossy fibers, both of which also send branches to the cerebellar nuclei. In the cortex both fibers ultimately act on the Purkinje cells; in addition the response of these cells is influenced by three kinds of interneurons, all of them inhibitory. Since the Purkinje cell is also inhibitory its effect on the cerebellar nuclei is to prevent the transmission of nerve impulses from the climbing fibers and mossy fibers that would otherwise reach the motor neurons and generate movement. Thus the cortex appears to be an organ of regulation, empowered to select certain motor commands for transmittal and to veto all others.

VII

PERCEPTION:
Sensory-Motor
Integration

VII PERCEPTION: Sensory-Motor Integration

INTRODUCTION

Some psychologists distinguish between *sensation* and *perception*—sensation refers to our immediate experience of the results of sensory processes, whereas perception is more complex, entailing the interpretation of sensations in the light of past experience. This distinction may be a little too simple. It is clear that perception involves not only sensory processes, but also behavioral responses. It involves a continuing set of transactions with the environment. Consequently, we have included articles on perception in the general category of sensory-motor integration. As we noted in Section V, a fundamental problem in psychology and biology has to do with our perception of the world. How is it that we see the world the way we do? It is clear that sensory processes play an important role in our perceptions. It is also clear that learning plays an important role. Furthermore, the actual responses we make seem to play a critical role in the determination of our perceptions of "reality."

It is often true that analysis of the neuronal substrates of behavior can be done more easily in simpler organisms. The interesting article by Jörg-Peter Ewert on the neural basis of visually guided behavior in the toad is a case in point. The toad has very little in the way of a visual cortex. Most visual processing appears to be done in the retina of the eye and in a lower brain region called the optic tectum. Ewert shows how the processing in the retina and the information transmitted up to the optic tectum guide the toad's movements in a very precise way. Indeed, it is clear from Ewert's article that the process whereby the toad sees, orients toward, strikes at, and catches a prey, is a continual set of transactions between the stimulus, the neuronal processing in the visual brain, and the resultant behavioral responses. Some psychologists may object to calling this behavior "perception of prey," but the toad behaves just as though he perceives the prey. As Ewert shows, the neuronal activity in the optic lobe is very tightly controlled, both by the sensory input and the motor movements the toad makes.

The importance of behavioral responding in perception in humans is emphasized in the article "Eye Movements and Visual Perception" by David Noton and Lawrence Stark. The article deals with the eye movements that occur when a person looks at a stationary picture. There are actually two sorts of eye movements: Very rapid but very small *nystagmic* movements that occur continuously and seem to be necessary for normal vision and *saccadic* movements that are rapid and extensive sweeps of the eyes as they shift from one fixation point to another within the picture. The authors describe these movements and develop a most interesting theory of visual memory in relation to the serial pattern of eye movements that a subject makes when looking at a picture.

A fundamental problem in the area of perception concerns the development of perception as an organism grows from birth to adulthood. To what extent does experience determine perception and to what extent is perception wired into the brain? As indicated in our discussion of visual coding in the introduction to Section V, some aspects of complex visual responses of neurons appear to be wired into the brain. In the next article in this section, "Plasticity in Sensory-motor Systems," Richard Held describes fascinating experiments that indicate that behavioral interaction with the environment may be necessary for the development of accurate responses to visual stimuli in humans. In short, experience plays an important role, but mere experience, *per se,* is not enough, one must engage in transactions with the environment.

Finally, we complete this section with the intriguing article by Fred Attneave entitled "Multistability in Perception." Some kinds of pictures and geometric forms, for example the Necker cube, spontaneously shift in their principal aspect when they are viewed. Attneave gives many examples of this phenomenon and discusses the perceptual principles and possible physical and neuronal mechanisms responsible for perceptual multistability. The examples given by Attneave provide interesting challenges for the psychobiologist. To what extent can we explain such complex perceptual phenomena on the basis of what we know about the neuronal functioning of the visual system?

23

The Neural Basis
of Visually Guided Behavior

by Jörg-Peter Ewert
March 1974

*Techniques from ethology and neurophysiology
are combined to show how an animal localizes
a visual object, discriminates its significance and then
makes the appropriate motor response*

Animals see things and then act on the basis of what they see. What chain of events connects some key stimulus with a specific fixed pattern of responses? In recent years workers in several laboratories have sought by many different means to analyze the nerve mechanisms by which animals interpret sensory signals and select the most appropriate response. The most effective way to understand the neural basis of behavior appears to be to apply a broad spectrum of experimental techniques: to combine ethological studies of an animal's behavior with experiments involving brain anatomy and brain-cell stimulation and the recording of individual nerve-cell activity.

For the past six years, in my laboratory first at the Technical University of Darmstadt and then at the University of Kassel, we have been taking this broad approach to learn about two kinds of visually controlled behavior in the toad: orienting (prey-catching) behavior and avoidance (escape) behavior. There are several good reasons for working with the toad. Amphibians are vertebrates, so that what we learn at their relatively low level of behavioral integration contributes to our understanding of more complex vertebrate functioning. Toads in particular have a limited and easily surveyed behavioral repertory. In response to specific stimuli one can repeatedly elicit predictable reactions, such as snapping at prey, fleeing from an enemy, clasping during courtship and making particular wiping motions after tactile stimulation. (The fickle European frog, in contrast, undergoes short-term changes in motivation and is not suitable for behavioral experiments.) Finally, the toad is not easily conditioned, so that its

innate behavioral functions can be measured in successive experiments for some time without being significantly affected by accumulated experience.

Toads respond to small objects, such as a piece of white cardboard moved over a black background, with a series of prey-catching reactions. First there is orientation toward the prey, then binocular fixation, then snapping, gulping and mouth-cleaning. Two basic processes are required to produce the overall orienting reaction: the identification of a stimulus and the location of it in space. The identification process determines the type of behavior. It is dependent on specific features of the stimulus such as its angular size, the orientation of the boundaries between light and dark, its angular velocity, its contrast with the background and so on. A detection process then localizes the stimulus and, together with the result of the identification process, determines the motor response, which can be either to turn toward the stimulus if it is identified as prey or to avoid it if it appears to be an enemy. In what follows I shall attempt to analyze the neurophysiological basis of signal identification, localization and the triggering of the associated instinctive actions.

To begin one must analyze quantitatively the key stimuli for orienting and avoidance behavior. This is done by changing various characteristics of a visual stimulus in an ordered way. The toad is placed in a cylindrical glass compartment where it observes a small square of black cardboard moving against a white background at a constant angular velocity, describing a circle around the animal at a distance of seven centimeters. The toad interprets such a stimulus as prey

and tries, through successive turning movements, to keep the object fixated in the center of its visual field. The degree of orienting activity is measured by counting the number of turning responses per minute.

The angular size of the stimulus—the angle it subtends—influences the orienting activity [*see illustration on page 242*]. Of a variety of square objects toads prefer those with an edge length of four to eight degrees. (The absolute size of such stimuli is five to 10 millimeters. Experiments where the distance between animal and stimulus is varied show that it is the absolute—not the angular—size that counts; in prey-catching behavior toads display "size constancy.") The toads turn away from objects larger than 30 degrees on a side, exhibiting the avoidance response. More particular information is obtained by substituting bars of various lengths for the square stimuli. As a two-by-two-degree stimulus is elongated along the horizontal axis the orienting activity increases until a saturation level is reached; wormlike objects turn out to be particularly attractive to toads. In contrast, the response decreases as a small stimulus is extended vertically, or perpendicularly to the direction of movement.

Other experiments indicate that toads discriminate prey from enemy objects through analysis of the visual stimulus in terms of point or edge configurations, also taking into consideration the direction of movement. A horizontal chain consisting of several two-by-two-degree units moving along the same path signifies prey. One such unit moving alone constitutes a prey stimulus just above the response threshold. When the horizontal chain is supplied with a separate vertical

BEHAVIORAL PATTERNS characteristic of the toad *Bufo bufo* are illustrated. The actions are commonly elicited in the animal by the sight of visual objects. These drawings, however, are based on photographs of toads whose brains were being stimulated electrically as part of the author's investigation of the neural bases of visually guided behavior. The electrode on the toad's head penetrates to the brain. An electric current applied to the optic tectum, a visual center in the brain, elicits a prey-catching sequence: orienting, or turning (*a*), snapping (*b*) and mouth-cleaning (*c*). Electrical stimulation, instead, of a site in the left or right thalamus brings a "planting-down" defensive posture (*d, e*) and stimulation of another part of the thalamus brings a crouching avoidance response (*f*).

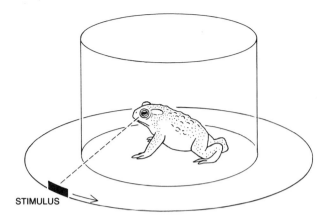

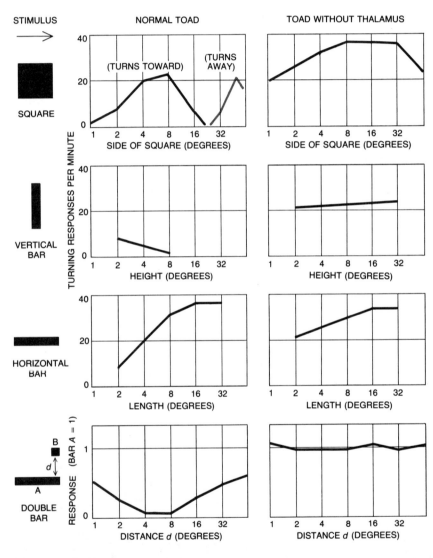

BEHAVIORAL RESPONSES of the toad to objects of various shapes and sizes were quantified. Small black objects were moved across the visual field at seven centimeters' distance and the orienting response was determined for normal toads (*left*) and those whose thalamus had been removed (*right*). Prey-catching responses (turning toward the object) were elicited most effectively in normal toads by squares with sides subtending four to eight degrees; the toads turned away from larger squares. Vertical bars were ineffective as prey objects—and increasingly ineffective with increasing height. Horizontal (wormlike) bars were increasingly effective as prey objects with increasing length, up to a limit. Double bars (a horizontal bar plus a vertical extension) were less attractive, the effect varying with distance between bars; the ratio of their effect to that of a single bar is shown (*bottom*). In toads lacking the thalamus the orienting response becomes "disinhibited." The animal tends to orient toward a target without discrimination, even if the target normally signals "danger."

extension (making it in effect an *L*-shaped structure moving on its long side), it loses efficiency as a prey-catching stimulus. The inhibitory effect of the vertical extension depends on its distance from the horizontal element. If a second vertical extension is introduced, in effect making the stimulus a shallow *U*-shaped structure, the total configuration signifies "enemy." The ethological interpretation is that it symbolizes a "swarm," and in the toad's brain inhibitory interactions first restrain prey-catching behavior and then induce escape behavior.

For constant form and angular velocity the behavioral activity generally increases as the amount of contrast between stimulus and background increases. White objects moving against a black background are normally more attractive as prey than black objects on white; the latter, on the other hand, are more effective in eliciting avoidance behavior. When the size and contrast are held constant, behavioral activity increases with increasing angular velocity, reaching a maximum at between 20 and 30 degrees per second. Stationary objects usually elicit no prey-catching or avoidance response. The common critical feature for key stimuli representing both prey and enemy is movement, and the two kinds of stimulus are differentiated primarily on the basis of their form: extension of the object in the horizontal direction of the movement generally means prey, whereas extension perpendicular to the direction of the movement signifies "not prey" or "enemy."

What does the toad's eye tell the toad's brain? This question was first formulated for the frog and dealt with in the fascinating research of Jerome Y. Lettvin and his colleagues at the Massachusetts Institute of Technology, and was later investigated quantitatively by O.-J. Grüsser and his co-workers at the Free University of Berlin. To ask the question is to open the "black box" of the toad's brain, or at least to examine the brain functions that participate in transforming input from visual stimuli into relevant behavioral patterns. At this point I shall describe neurophysiological findings concerning whether it is in the retina of the toad's eye that the key stimuli "prey" and "enemy" are encoded.

In the toad retina there are three types of ganglion cells that send their fibers by way of the optic nerve to the structure called the optic tectum in the midbrain. One can record the action potentials, or nerve signals, from the ends of these fibers by introducing a microelectrode into the tectum. John E. Dowling, then at

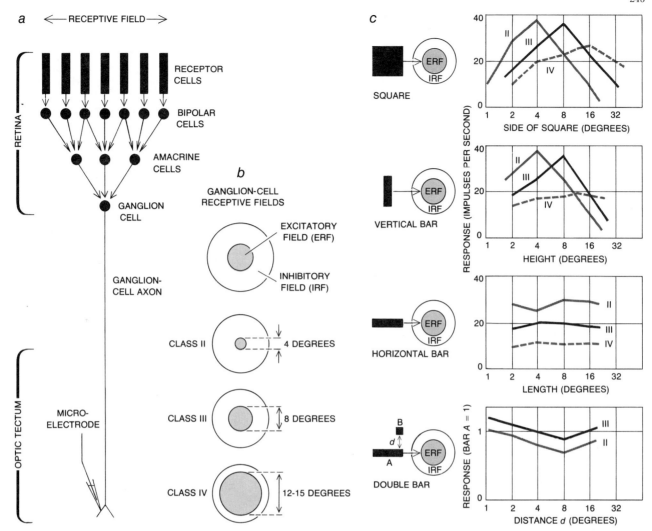

a ⟵ RECEPTIVE FIELD ⟶

RETINA

RECEPTOR CELLS

BIPOLAR CELLS

AMACRINE CELLS

GANGLION CELL

GANGLION-CELL AXON

OPTIC TECTUM

MICRO-ELECTRODE

b

GANGLION-CELL RECEPTIVE FIELDS

EXCITATORY FIELD (ERF)

INHIBITORY FIELD (IRF)

CLASS II — 4 DEGREES

CLASS III — 8 DEGREES

CLASS IV — 12-15 DEGREES

c

SQUARE — ERF / IRF

VERTICAL BAR — ERF / IRF

HORIZONTAL BAR — ERF / IRF

DOUBLE BAR — ERF / IRF

RESPONSE (IMPULSES PER SECOND)

SIDE OF SQUARE (DEGREES)

HEIGHT (DEGREES)

LENGTH (DEGREES)

RESPONSE (BAR A = 1)

DISTANCE *d* (DEGREES)

NEURAL RESPONSES of the toad to the same objects were measured with recording electrodes. The electrodes recorded impulses at the terminals in the optic tectum of fibers from individual ganglion cells, the cells in the retina of the eye on which signals from the receptor cells converge via intermediate cells (*a*). Each ganglion cell has an excitatory receptive field surrounded by an inhibitory receptive field. The diameter of the excitatory fields and the strength of the inhibitory surrounds are different for each of three classes of ganglion cells (*b*). For the square object and the vertical bar (which the ganglion cell "confuses"), maximum activity is elicited when the size of the object matches the excitatory-field size of each type of ganglion cell (*c*). Horizontal length does not much affect these cells' response. Vertical extension of a horizontal bar has less effect on these cells than on behavior (*opposite page*).

the Johns Hopkins University School of Medicine, showed through electron micrography that in the frog (or toad) retina each ganglion cell is connected to a number of receptor cells by bipolar and amacrine cells. Each ganglion cell is thus fed information from a particular part of the animal's visual field. Lateral connections established by horizontal and amacrine cells play a role in determining the properties of this receptive field. In toads as well as frogs the field consists of a central circular excitatory receptive field immediately surrounded by an inhibitory receptive field. The movement of an object through the excitatory field elicits a ganglion-cell discharge, which is inhibited if another object is simultaneously moving through the inhibitory field. The three ganglion-cell types in the toad (as in the frog) differ in several character-

istics, including in particular the diameter of their excitatory receptive fields: about four degrees for the so-called Class II ganglion cells, about eight degrees for Class III cells and from 12 to 15 degrees for Class IV cells. (Class I cells have been identified in frogs but not in toads.)

With microelectrodes we measure the rate of ganglion-cell discharge to see how it changes when objects (corresponding to those in the behavioral experiments described above) are moved through the receptive field of the cell. The impulse frequency increases with the length of the side of a square object until the length about equals the diameter of the excitatory field; then it decreases as the object becomes large enough to stimulate part of the surrounding inhibitory field. In accordance with the different sizes of the excitatory fields the maximum activa-

tion of each cell type is therefore elicited by objects of different sizes [*see illustration above*]. Extending a small square horizontally (making it a "worm") does not bring about any change in nerve-cell activation; this is in sharp contrast to the previously noted effect of extension on the behavioral response. The dependence of neuronal activation on the size of the stimulus is instead primarily a function of extension perpendicular to the direction of movement. Indeed, the discharge frequency is almost exactly the same in response to a narrow vertical bar as it is to a square with the same height as the bar. A retinal ganglion cell "confuses" the two stimuli—but the toad does not: the square excites behavioral activity and the bar inhibits it. When the object size is held constant, however, the dependence of the discharge rate on contrast between stimulus and background and on angular velocity is the same as it is in the behavioral experiments.

In summary, it is clear that the first important operations on the visual input from a prey stimulus or a threatening one are performed by the toad retina. For any particular prey or enemy stimulus the behavioral response to velocity and background contrast seems to depend on information processing in the retina. The size-dependent excitatory and inhibitory processes, however, which were noted in the behavioral experiments and which play an essential role in pattern discrimination, cannot be traced to the influence of the excitatory and inhibitory fields of retinal ganglion cells. There are no retinal "worm-detectors" as distinct from "enemy-detectors." The differential analysis, and thus the behaviorally relevant interpretation of the stimulus, must be achieved in nerve-cell populations beyond the retinal level.

Since different characteristics are coded by any one type of ganglion cell the question becomes: Where is that coding interpreted? What tells the central nervous system whether an increased rate of ganglion-cell firing stems, for example, from an increase in stimulus-

background contrast or from larger size? The differentiation can be made only if separate groups of cells receive different inputs from different optic-nerve fibers. In fact they do. The fibers of the optic nerve pass from each eye through the optic chiasm to the opposite side of the brain, ending in various parts of the forebrain and midbrain. Two of these destinations are of particular interest in our work. One, to which most optic-nerve fibers project, is in the surface layers of the optic tectum in the midbrain. The other is in the thalamus and the pretectal region of the diencephalon.

The optic tectum constitutes a localization system. In the tectum there is an exact topographical mapping of the retina and hence of the entire visual field. Movement of an object in a particular part of the visual field excites a corresponding region of the tectum, where the appropriate optic-nerve fibers terminate [see illustration on these two pages]. Recording from individual tectal neurons, or nerve cells, tells one how the individual retinal ganglion cells that excite them are reacting. In certain layers, for example, there are tectal neurons with excitatory receptive fields of about 10 to

27 degrees that are activated exclusively by moving objects. These neurons probably represent a localization system. This supposition is reinforced by experiments in which we stimulate the tectum of freely moving toads with trains of impulses delivered by means of an implanted electrode. Stimulation of a given region of the tectum always causes toads to turn toward a particular part of the visual field. Presumably the neurons we are thus activating have a direct connection with the animal's motor system, since (in contrast to the natural orienting movements made in response to a prey object) the electrically induced orienting is not disrupted by simultaneous presentation of a threatening object.

If the recording electrode is driven deeper into the tectum, it encounters neurons with larger receptive fields. Some of these cover the entire visual field on the opposite side, some the entire lower part of the field and some the entire field directly in front of the animal. Interestingly enough, all three types include the fixation point: the point of maximum visual acuity near the center of the visual field. The degree of activation of these three types of neurons could provide the toad with information about the

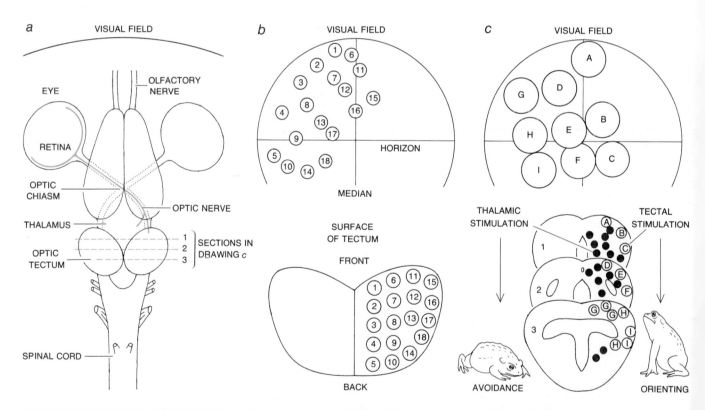

NEUROPHYSIOLOGICAL EXPERIMENTS yield data on the functions of different parts of the toad's visual system. Fibers of the retinal ganglion cells project primarily to the optic tectum and to the thalamus (a). The visual field of each eye is mapped (b), on a one-to-one basis (numbers), on the dorsal surface of the opposite side of the tectum. By the same token experimental electrical stim-

ulation (c) of various parts of the tectum (letters) causes the toad to turn to corresponding parts of the visual field. On the other hand stimulation (black disks) of the thalamus, which partially underlies the tectum, causes the opposite action: avoidance, or turning away. As a recording electrode penetrates below the surface of the tectum it encounters successive populations of cells with differ-

location of a large object, since whenever the three types are excited simultaneously the object must be at the fixation point.

In natural situations the behavior of toads can be influenced by sensory modalities other than vision. If, for example, a beetle crosses the field of vision, the toad's orienting reaction can be either accelerated or retarded by simultaneous vibratory and tactile stimuli. Such results can be obtained in experiments if prey models are presented together with acoustic or tactile stimuli. The area for producing such changes in behavioral activity seems to be in the subtectal region, where multisensory integration is achieved. In the area below the third ventricle of the midbrain there are large-field neurons with fields similar to those of the large-field tectal cells. These subtectal neurons receive additional inputs from neurons excited by tactile and vibratory stimuli. The "mechanoreceptive" field of one of these bimodal neurons is always localized on the same side as the visual receptive field. The additional inputs from nonvisual neurons could serve to lower the threshold of a part of the visual field in which a visual stimulus is anticipated and thus

in effect to raise the level of visual alertness.

The optic tectum also comprises a neuronal system that processes behaviorally relevant aspects of moving stimuli [see illustrations on next page]. The cells have excitatory receptive fields about 27 degrees in diameter. Those designated Type I tectal neurons are activated mainly if the stimulus surface of an object moved through the receptive field is extended in the direction of movement; extension perpendicular to direction of movement does not have the same effect. Other cells, the Type II tectal neurons, differ from Type I neurons in that their discharge rate actually diminishes with surface extension perpendicular to direction of movement. The response of these neurons constitutes the key stimulus "prey." That is, they can presumably be considered the trigger system for the prey-catching response.

The thalamic-pretectal region, the second major destination of fibers from the retina, apparently provides what can be called a "caution" system. I have recently identified four main types of visually sensitive neurons in the toad's thalamus by means of single-cell recordings.

They are activated respectively by four distinct stimulus situations: (1) movement of enemy objects extended perpendicularly to the direction of motion, excitatory receptive field of about 46 degrees; (2) movement of an object toward the toad, field about 90 degrees; (3) large stationary objects, field about 45 degrees; (4) stimulation of the balance sensors in the toad's ear by tilting. In general these thalamic neurons are activated principally in situations that tend to call for evasive movements—turning away from an enemy, sidestepping or compensating for tilting of the body. Brain-stimulation experiments support our feeling that the thalamic-pretectal region is one in which reactions can be assembled that lead to protective movements. Electrical stimulation of various sites in the region elicits the following reactions: closing of the eyelids, ducking, turning away, panicky springing away or tilting of the body.

We constructed a working hypothesis involving connections between the optic tectum and the thalamic-pretectal region: Electrical triggers in the tectum mainly elicit orienting, and triggers in the thalamic-pretectal region elicit avoidance. In a natural situation trigger impulses in particular layers of the tectum are evoked by small wormlike prey. Large objects extended perpendicularly to the direction of movement stimulate particular neurons in the thalamic-pretectal region, both directly through retinal inputs and indirectly by way of the optic tectum. These thalamic-pretectal neurons in turn inhibit the tectum and can also activate avoidance behavior [see illustration on page 247].

The existence of the postulated connections between the structures in the midbrain and the diencephalon has been demonstrated physiologically in two ways. One way is by direct electrical stimulation. Thalamic neurons that are sensitive to movement can also be activated by stimulation of points in the optic tectum. When the stimulating and recording electrodes are interchanged, the response of Type II neurons in the tectum to moving objects can be inhibited by the stimulation of cells in the thalamus. The other way is by surgical operation: if the optic tectum is removed, orienting movements are lost—and so are avoidance reactions, which is evidence for pathways from the tectum to the thalamus. If the thalamic-pretectal region is removed without damage to the tectum, then avoidance behavior is lost—and the orienting response is dramatically freed from inhibition even in the presence of enemy objects; this may be

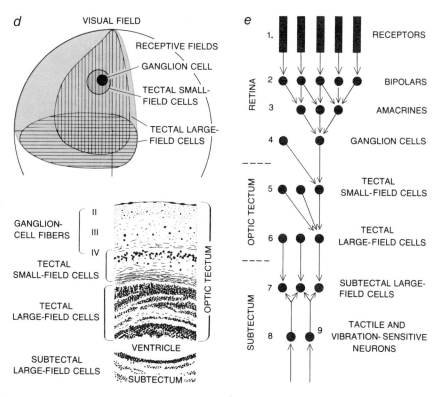

ent receptive fields (d). There are small-field cells with fields a little larger than those of ganglion cells and, lower down, three kinds of large-field cells, each with different coverage (color, horizontal hatching and vertical hatching). A drawing based on a stained brain section indicates the layers at which each of these is found. The final drawing (e) relates the various cell populations and shows another layer of large-field cells that receive inputs from visual cells above them and also from cells that respond to tactile or vibratory stimuli.

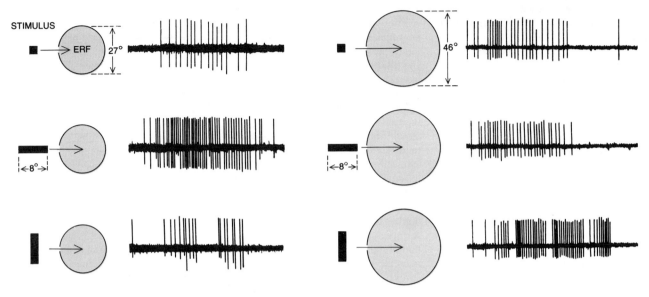

FEATURE DETECTION beyond the retinal level is accomplished by cells in the tectum and the thalamus. Recordings from individual cells indicate that tectal Type I neurons (*left*) are most activated if the object moving through the field is extended in the direction of movement. The cells in the thalamic area (*right*) respond most to an object extended perpendicularly to direction of movement.

evidence for the existence of inhibitory pathways from the thalamus to the optic tectum. In toads lacking the thalamic-pretectal region every moving stimulus elicits the orienting movements; the cautionary thalamic-pretectal system, which ordinarily allows orientation toward the stimulus only in behaviorally appropriate situations, is missing. If one lateral half of the thalamic-pretectal region is removed, the disinhibition extends to the entire visual field on the opposite side; small lesions in the thalamic-pretectal region affect only local small parts of the visual field. Quantitative experiments with toads lacking the thalamic-pretectal region make it clear that these animals cannot discriminate between stimuli that are behaviorally relevant and those that are irrelevant. The response of the Type II tectal cells to moving stimuli shows a similar "disinhibition" effect after thalamic-pretectal removal [*see illustrations on page 242 and below*].

The findings I have described so far suggest the following sequence of events: On the basis of retinal ganglion-cell input, the optic tectum tells the toad where in the visual field a stimulus is

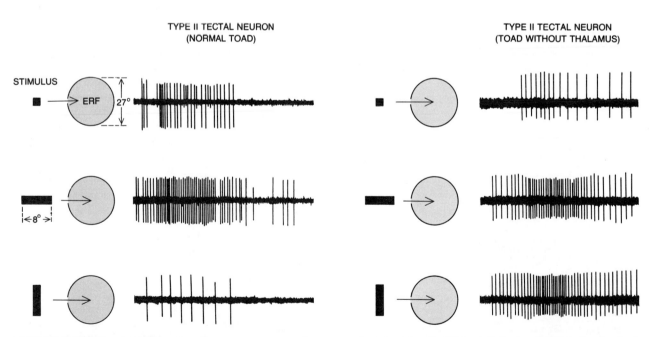

TRIGGER UNITS for the entire prey-catching response seem to be the Type II tectal neurons. In the normal toad (*left*) the cells are most activated by wormlike objects (*horizontal bar*). They are less activated (and the decrease is greater than in the case of Type I tectal neurons) by stimuli that in behavioral experiments are irrelevant for prey-catching (*vertical bar*). After removal of the thalamus, however (*right*), their response to those irrelevant stimuli is greatly increased, suggesting that the thalamic signal is inhibitory.

situated, how large it is, how strongly it contrasts with the background and how fast it is moving. The connections from the tectum to structures in the thalamic-pretectal region enable the toad to discern the significance to its behavior of the visual signals. The basic filtering process for the prey-enemy differentiation can be conceived of as passage through a series of "window discriminators" [*see illustration on next page*], each stage of which analyzes a particular aspect of the object in question. Each retinal ganglion cell acts as a vertical window that codes extension perpendicular to the direction of movement. The retinal analysis is repeated and amplified in the thalamic-pretectal region, where a neuron pool acts as another vertical window, this one with a certain minimum-response threshold. Extension in a horizontal direction is coded primarily by Type I tectal cells, which constitute a horizontal window. Type II tectal cells perform a summation, with signals arriving from the thalamic-pretectal region having an inhibitory effect and those from the Type I cells having an excitatory effect. The resultant signal acts as the trigger stimulus for the orienting movement. The triggering of avoidance behavior is probably achieved through the activation of still another pool of thalamic-pretectal neurons, the activation being proportional to an additive function of inputs from two of the window-discriminator pools.

One of the remarkable aspects of this system is a degree of plasticity, or changeability. During the summer months white prey objects moved against black backgrounds elicit orienting behavior much more effectively than do black objects against white. In fall and winter the situation is reversed, and at the same time the overall prey-catching activity of the toads decreases. Recently our recording electrodes revealed that the activation of single Class II ganglion cells in the retina exhibits this seasonal shift in white-black preference. In winter neurons with receptive fields in the lower part of the visual field are more strongly activated by black objects than by white ones; in the upper field the situation is reversed. In summer, however, the neurons whose receptive field is in the upper half of the visual field are activated primarily by black stimuli, whereas neurons receptive to the lower half of the visual field become more strongly activated by white stimuli and remain so until in the fall black stimuli again become dominant.

What is the biological significance of these observations? One can speculate that for toads, which are active at twilight, biologically important prey stimuli that appear in the lower half of the visual field are paler then their background; those in the upper part of the field, however, are for the most part relatively dark, or at least just as often dark as pale. Each of these contrast relations could be reflected in the sensitivity characteristics of the Class II retinal ganglion cells. With the approach of winter and the period of hibernation, toads stop catching prey. What makes them stop? One mechanism may be an inversion of ganglion-cell response characteristics, brought about by signals from the brain to the retina, such that the stimulus-background contrast relation is out of phase with the real world, making prey objects less visible. For the toad, in other words, identical objects appear to be dif-

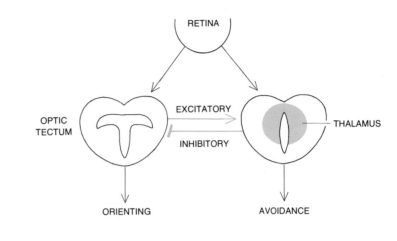

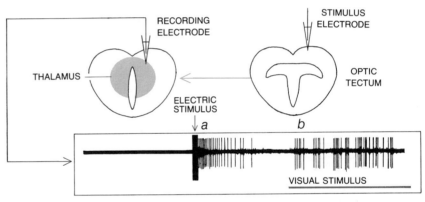

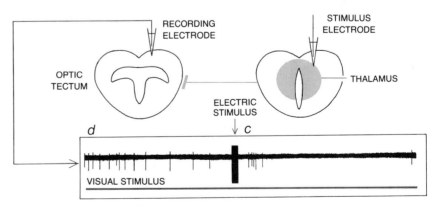

CONNECTIONS between the optic tectum and the thalamus were indicated by preceding experiments: signals from the retina excite both tectum and thalamus; subsequent impulses from Type I tectal neurons further excite cells in the thalamus, whereas signals from the thalamus inhibit activity in Type II tectal neurons. Two different kinds of motor activity are thereupon initiated by the two structures (*top*). Confirmatory evidence was obtained by electrical stimulation. Stimulation of the tectum (*middle*) elicits impulses (*a*) from cells in the thalamus that ordinarily respond to visual stimuli (*b*). Stimulation of the thalamus (*bottom*) inhibits (*c*) impulses normally elicited (*d*) in Type II neurons by moving objects.

ferent when they are seen in winter than when they are seen in summer, a reminder that an organism's picture of the environment is a product of its brain.

In contrast to the plasticity of the systems for the filtering and storage of information and for pattern recognition, brain mechanisms involved in instinctive actions are quite inflexible and do not adapt easily to changes in the stimulus situation. For each instinctive action in the behavioral repertory there is a pre-programmed "printed" neuronal circuit that coordinates the appropriate motor act—even if it becomes inappropriate! If such a circuit is triggered (either natural-ly or by electrode stimulation), the innate reaction proceeds automatically. Prey-catching behavior is a good example. On the basis of brain-stimulation experi-

ments we believe the sequence of events controlling a natural orientation response is about as follows: A pattern is formed by a natural stimulus on a portion of the retina that is outside the fixation region; the retinal locus has a corresponding projection locus in the optic tectum. If the filtering process described above has identified the object as prey, then the appropriate neuronal system is activated. A value corresponding to the distance between the prey's locus on the retina and the fixation point is transferred to the toad's motor system. The result is orientation: a turning movement such that the retinal representation of the prey is brought to the fixation point. That triggers a locus in the optic tectum that corresponds to the fixation point. As soon as this triggering reaches a threshold value

the rest of the prey-catching sequence is activated, quite independently of the result, or even of the short-term benefit to the animal, of such activation. For example, if an experimental prey object is removed at the instant when it is fixated by the toad, the entire normal prey-catching routine nevertheless proceeds. The toad snaps, gulps and wipes its mouth in spite of the "situational vacuum." The sequence is similar in its inevitability to what happens when the triggering region of the tectum is stimulated with an electrode.

As for avoidance behavior, the results of thalamic stimulation indicate that it is controlled by a single master program. The response consists in a firm planting of the extremities on one side of the toad's body and a gathering together of the limbs on the opposite side. With the toad in this stationary, poised position the additional behavior patterns for correcting tilting of the body or making the various evasive movements can be read-ily incorporated.

The evidence I have reviewed shows that in a lower vertebrate the neuro-nal processes for localization and iden-tification of a visual signal and for re-leasing the associated instinctive motor responses are separated topographically but are intimately connected with one another. In the course of evolution the centers for two of these processes, visual localization and instinctive action, have apparently remained in about their orig-inal positions. They occupy the same areas of the brain, the tectum and the thalamus, in monkeys and cats as they do in toads. The organization of these parts of the brain, to which both neurophysi-ological and ethological methods have provided investigative access, shows re-markable constancy in all classes of ver-tebrates. That is not the case, however, for stimulus identification. In toads this process takes place primarily in the tha-lamic-pretectal region and also in the retina and the tectum. Mammals, how-ever, underwent further evolution, cor-responding to the importance of pattern recognition in the evolution of their be-havior. A new substrate developed for two associated but highly specialized processes, filtering and storage of infor-mation: the visual cortex. From the in-vestigations of Gerald E. Schneider at M.I.T. we learn that in this case ontog-eny reflects phylogeny. In newborn ham-sters subcortical pathways between the tectum and the thalamus are implicated in pattern discrimination. In adult ani-mals, on the other hand, pattern discrim-ination takes place in the cortex.

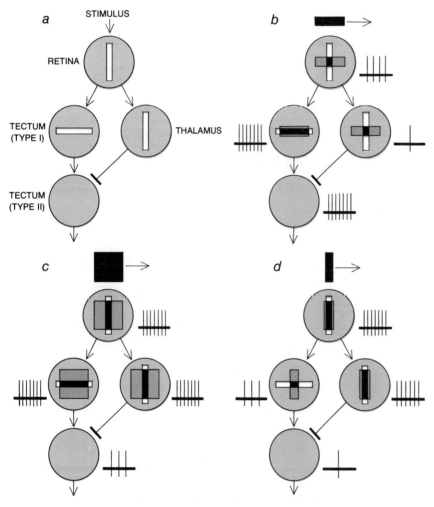

IDENTIFICATION OF AN OBJECT AS PREY OR ENEMY is symbolized as a series of operations by "window discriminators" (*a*). A ganglion cell in the retina codes vertical ex-tension (perpendicular to direction of movement), in effect responding to as much of a vi-sual object as appears in a vertical window; extension beyond the window has an inhibitory effect. Cells in the thalamus do the same thing. In the tectum Type I cells code horizontal extension (in the direction of movement). Type II tectal cells sum the excitatory signal from Type I cells and the inhibitory signal from the thalamus, and the resultant signal trig-gers an orienting movement. At each stage the cell discharge depends on the relation be-tween the object and the window that senses its extension either in or perpendicular to the direction of movement (*b, c, d*). (The cell-discharge patterns shown here are schematic.)

24

Eye Movements
and Visual Perception

by David Noton and Lawrence Stark
June 1971

Recordings of the points inspected in the scanning of a picture and of the path the eyes follow in the inspection provide clues to the process whereby the brain perceives and recognizes objects

The eyes are the most active of all human sense organs. Other sensory receptors, such as the ears, accept rather passively whatever signals come their way, but the eyes are continually moving as they scan and inspect the details of the visual world. The movements of the eyes play an important role in visual perception, and analyzing them can reveal a great deal about the process of perception.

We have recently been recording the eye movements of human subjects as they first inspected unfamiliar objects and then later recognized them. In essence we found that every person has a characteristic way of looking at an object that is familiar to him. For each object he has a preferred path that his eyes tend to follow when he inspects or recognizes the object. Our results suggest a new hypothesis about visual learning and recognition. Before describing and explaining our experiments more fully we shall set the stage by outlining some earlier experiments that have aided the interpretation of our results.

Eye movements are necessary for a physiological reason: detailed visual information can be obtained only through the fovea, the small central area of the retina that has the highest concentration of photoreceptors. Therefore the eyes must move in order to provide information about objects that are to be inspected in any detail (except when the object is quite small in terms of the angle it subtends in the visual field). The eye-movement muscles, under the control of the brain, aim the eyes at points of interest [see "Control Mechanisms of the Eye," by Derek H. Fender, SCIENTIFIC AMERICAN, July 1964, and "Movements of the Eye," by E. Llewellyn Thomas, SCIENTIFIC AMERICAN Offprint 516].

During normal viewing of stationary objects the eyes alternate between fixa-tions, when they are aimed at a fixed point in the visual field, and rapid movements called saccades. Each saccade leads to a new fixation on a different point in the visual field. Typically there are two or three saccades per second. The movements are so fast that they occupy only about 10 percent of the viewing time.

Visual learning and recognition involve storing and retrieving memories. By way of the lens, the retina and the optic nerve, nerve cells in the visual cortex of the brain are activated and an image of the object being viewed is formed there. (The image is of course in the form of neural activity and is quite unlike the retinal image of the object.) The memory system of the brain must contain an internal representation of every object that is to be recognized. Learning or becoming familiar with an object is the process of constructing this representation. Recognition of an object when it is encountered again is the process of matching it with its internal representation in the memory system.

A certain amount of controversy surrounds the question of whether visual recognition is a parallel, one-step process or a serial, step-by-step one. Psychologists of the Gestalt school have maintained that objects are recognized as wholes, without any need for analysis into component parts. This argument implies that the internal representation of each object is a unitary whole that is matched with the object in a single operation. More recently other psychologists have proposed that the internal representation is a piecemeal affair—an assemblage of parts or features. During recognition the features are matched serially with the features of the object step by step. Successful matching of all the features completes recognition.

The serial-recognition hypothesis is supported mainly by the results of experiments that measure the time taken by a subject to recognize different objects. Typically the subject scans an array of objects (usually abstract figures) looking for a previously memorized "target" object. The time he spends considering each object (either recognizing it as a target object or rejecting it as being different) is measured. That time is normally quite short, but it can be measured in various ways with adequate accuracy. Each object is small enough to be recognized with a single fixation, so that eye movements do not contribute to the time spent on recognition.

Experiments of this kind yield two general results. First, it is found that on the average the subject takes longer to recognize a target object than he does to reject a nontarget object. That is the result to be expected if objects are recognized serially, feature by feature. When an object is compared mentally with the internal representation of the target object, a nontarget object will fail to match some feature of the internal representation and will be rejected without further checking of features, whereas target objects will be checked on all features. The result seems inconsistent with the Gestalt hypothesis of a holistic internal representation matched with the object in a single operation. Presumably in such an operation the subject would take no longer to recognize an object than he would to reject it.

A second result is obtained by varying the complexity of the memorized target object. It is found that the subject takes longer to recognize complex target objects than to recognize simple ones. This result too is consistent with the serial-recognition hypothesis, since more features must be checked in the more complex object. By the same token the result also appears to be inconsistent with the Gestalt hypothesis.

It would be incorrect to give the impression that the serial nature of object recognition is firmly established to the exclusion of the unitary concept advanced by Gestalt psychologists. They have shown convincingly that there is indeed some "primitive unity" to an object, so that the object can often be singled out as a separate entity even before true recognition begins. Moreover, some of the recognition-time experiments described above provide evidence, at least with very simple objects, that as an object becomes well known its internal representation becomes more holistic and the recognition process correspondingly becomes more parallel. Nonetheless, the weight of evidence seems to support the serial hypothesis, at least for objects that are not notably simple and familiar.

If the internal representation of an object in memory is an assemblage of features, two questions naturally suggest themselves. First, what are these features, that is, what components of an object does the brain select as the key items for identifying the object? Second, how are such features integrated and related to one another to form the complete internal representation of the object? The study of eye movements during visual perception yields considerable evidence on these two points.

In experiments relating to the first question the general approach is to present to a subject a picture or another object that is sufficiently large and close to the eyes so that it cannot all be registered on the foveas in one fixation. For example, a picture 35 centimeters wide and 100 centimeters from the eyes subtends a horizontal angle of 20 degrees at each eye—roughly the angle subtended by a page of this magazine held at arm's length. This is far wider than the one to two degrees of visual field that are brought to focus on the fovea.

Under these conditions the subject must move his eyes and look around the picture, fixating each part he wants to see clearly. The assumption is that he looks mainly at the parts of the picture he regards as being its features; they are the parts that hold for him the most information about the picture. Features are tentatively located by peripheral vision and then fixated directly for detailed inspection. (It is important to note that in these experiments and in the others we shall describe the subject is given only general instructions, such as "Just look at the pictures," or even no instructions at all. More specific instructions, requiring him to inspect and describe some specific aspect of the picture, usually result in appropriately directed fixations, as might be expected.)

When subjects freely view simple pictures, such as line drawings, under these conditions, it is found that their fixations tend to cluster around the angles of the picture. For example, Leonard Zusne and Kenneth M. Michels performed an experiment of this type at Purdue University, using as pictures line drawings of simple polygons [see illustration on

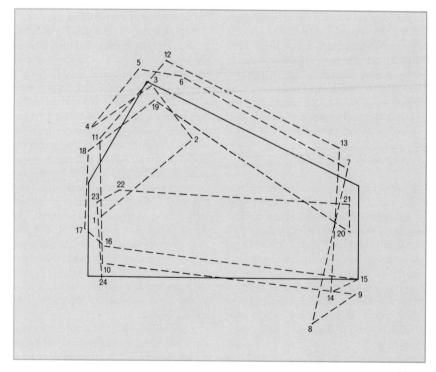

IMPORTANCE OF ANGLES as features that the brain employs in memorizing and recognizing an object was apparent in experiments by Leonard Zusne and Kenneth M. Michels at Purdue University. They recorded fixations while subjects looked at drawings of polygons for eight seconds. At top is one of the polygons; the dots indicate the fixations of seven subjects. Sequence of fixations by one subject in an eight-second viewing appears at bottom.

opposite page]. From the fixations made by their subjects in viewing such figures it is clear that the angles of the drawings attracted the eyes most strongly.

Our tentative conclusion is that, at least with such line drawings, the angles are the principal features the brain employs to store and recognize the drawing. Certainly angles would be an efficient choice for features. In 1954 Fred Attneave III of the University of Oregon pointed out that the most informative parts of a line drawing are the angles and sharp curves. To illustrate his argument he presented a picture that was obtained by selecting the 38 points of greatest curvature in a picture of a sleeping cat and joining the points with straight lines [*see illustration at right*]. The result is clearly recognizable.

Additional evidence that angles and sharp curves are features has come from electrophysiologists who have investigated the activity of individual brain cells. For example, in the late 1950's Jerome Y. Lettvin, H. R. Maturana, W. S. McCulloch and W. H. Pitts of the Massachusetts Institute of Technology found angle-detecting neurons in the frog's retina. More recently David H. Hubel and Torsten N. Wiesel of the Harvard Medical School have extended this result to cats and monkeys (whose angle-detecting cells are in the visual cortex rather than the retina). And recordings obtained from the human visual cortex by Elwin Marg of the University of California at Berkeley give preliminary indications that these results can be extended to man.

Somewhat analogous results have been obtained with pictures more complex than simple line drawings. It is not surprising that in such cases the features are also more complex. As a result no formal description of them has been achieved. Again, however, high information content seems to be the criterion. Norman H. Mackworth and A. J. Morandi made a series of recordings at Harvard University of fixations by subjects viewing two complex photographs. They concluded that the fixations were concentrated on unpredictable or unusual details, in particular on unpredictable contours. An unpredictable contour is one that changes direction rapidly and irregularly and therefore has a high information content.

We conclude, then, that angles and other informative details are the features selected by the brain for remembering and recognizing an object. The next question concerns how these

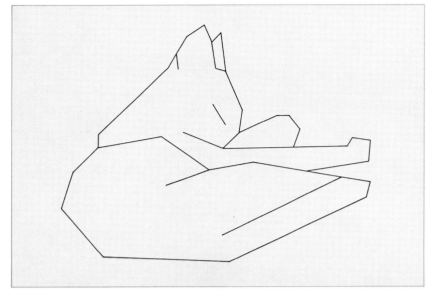

SHARP CURVES are also important as features for visual identification, as shown by Fred Attneave III of the University of Oregon in a picture made by selecting the 38 points of greatest curvature in a picture of a sleeping cat and joining them with straight lines, thus eliminating all other curves. The result is still easily recognizable, suggesting that points of sharp curvature provide highly useful information to the brain in visual perception.

features are integrated by the brain into a whole—the internal representation—so that one sees the object as a whole, as an object rather than an unconnected sequence of features. Once again useful evidence comes from recordings of eye movements. Just as study of the locations of fixations indicated the probable nature of the features, so analysis of the order of fixations suggests a format for the interconnection of features into the overall internal representation.

The illustration at left shows the fixations made by a subject while viewing a photograph of a bust of the Egyptian queen Nefertiti. It is one of a series of recordings made by Alfred L. Yarbus of the Institute for Problems of Information Transmission of the Academy of Sciences of the U.S.S.R. The illustration

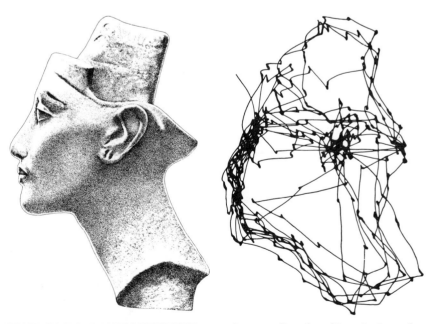

REGULARITIES OF EYE MOVEMENT appear in a recording of a subject viewing a photograph of a bust of Queen Nefertiti. At left is a drawing of what the subject saw; at right are his eye movements as recorded by Alfred L. Yarbus of the Institute for Problems of Information Transmission in Moscow. The eyes seem to visit the features of the head cyclically, following fairly regular pathways, rather than crisscrossing the picture at random.

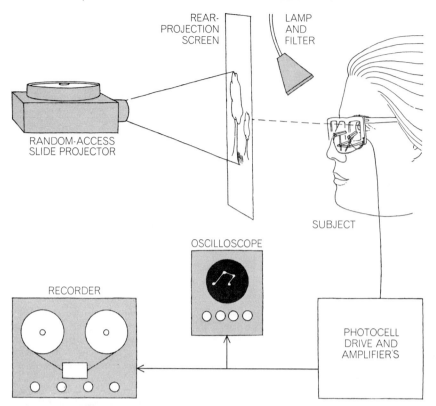

EXPERIMENTAL PROCEDURE employed by the authors is depicted schematically. The subject viewed pictures displayed on a rear-projection screen by a random-access slide projector. Diffuse infrared light was shined on his eyes; his eye movements were recorded by photocells, mounted on a spectacle frame, that detected reflections of the infrared light from one eyeball. Eye movements were displayed on oscilloscope and also recorded on tape.

image on a screen that was fully exposed to the ordinary light in the laboratory. In this way we produced an image of low visibility and could be sure that the subject would have to look directly (foveally) at each feature that interested him, thus revealing to our recording equipment the locus of his attention.

Our initial results amply confirmed the previous impression of cycles of eye movements. We found that when a subject viewed a picture under these conditions, his eyes usually scanned it following—intermittently but repeatedly —a fixed path, which we have termed his "scan path" for that picture [see illustration on page 254]. The occurrences of the scan path were separated by periods in which the fixations were ordered in a less regular manner.

Each scan path was characteristic of a given subject viewing a given picture. A subject had a different scan path for every picture he viewed, and for a given picture each subject had a different scan path. A typical scan path for our pictures consisted of about 10 fixations and lasted for from three to five seconds. Scan paths usually occupied from 25 to 35 percent of the subject's viewing time, the rest being devoted to less regular eye movements.

It must be added that scan paths were not always observed. Certain pictures (one of a telephone, for example) seemed often not to provoke a repetitive response, although no definite common characteristic could be discerned in such pictures. The commonest reaction, however, was to exhibit a scan path. It was interesting now for us to refer back to the earlier recordings by Zusne and Michels, where we observed scan paths that had previously passed unnoticed. For instance, in the illustration on page 250 fixations No. 4 through No. 11 and No. 11 through No. 18 appear to be two occurrences of a scan path. They are identical, even to the inclusion of the small reverse movement in the lower right-hand corner of the figure.

This demonstration of the existence of scan paths strengthened and clarified our ideas about visual perception. In accordance with the serial hypothesis, we assume that the internal representation of an object in the memory system is an assemblage of features. To this we add a crucial hypothesis: that the features are assembled in a format we have termed a "feature ring" [see illustration on page 255]. The ring is a sequence of sensory and motor memory traces, alternately recording a feature of

shows clearly an important aspect of eye movement during visual perception, namely that the order of the fixations is by no means random. The lines representing the saccades form broad bands from point to point and do not crisscross the picture at random as would be expected if the eyes visited the different features repetitively in a random order. It appears that fixation on any one feature, such as Nefertiti's eye, is usually followed by fixation on the same next feature, such as her mouth. The overall record seems to indicate a series of cycles; in each cycle the eyes visit the main features of the picture, following rather regular pathways from feature to feature.

Recently at the University of California at Berkeley we have developed a hypothesis about visual perception that predicts and explains this apparent regularity of eye movement. Essentially we propose that in the internal representation or memory of the picture the features are linked together in sequence by the memory of the eye movement required to look from one feature to the next. Thus the eyes would tend to move from feature to feature in a fixed order, scanning the picture.

Most of Yarbus' recordings are summaries of many fixations and do not contain complete information on the ordering of the fixations. Thus the regularities of eye movements predicted by our hypothesis could not be definitely confirmed from his data. To eliminate this constraint and to subject our hypothesis to a more specific test we recently made a new series of recordings of eye movements during visual perception.

Our subjects viewed line drawings of simple objects and abstract symbols as we measured their eye movements (using photocells to determine the movements of the "white" of the eye) and recorded them on magnetic tape [see illustration above]. We thereby obtained a permanent record of the order of fixations made by the subjects and could play it back later at a lower speed, analyzing it at length for cycles and other regularities of movement. As in the earlier experiments, the drawings were fairly large and close to the subject's eyes, a typical drawing subtending about 20 degrees at the eye. In addition we drew the pictures with quite thin lines and displayed them with an underpowered slide projector, throwing a dim

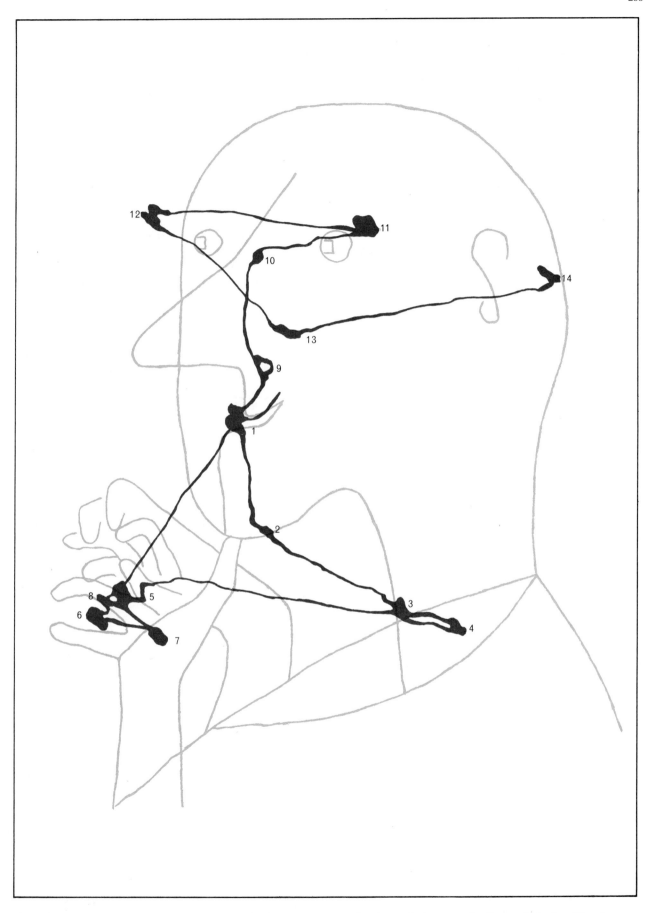

EYE MOVEMENTS made by a subject viewing for the first time a drawing adapted from Paul Klee's "Old Man Figuring" appear in black. Numbers show the order of the subject's visual fixations on the picture during part of a 20-second viewing. Lines between them represent saccades, or rapid movements of eyes from one fixation to the next. Saccades occupy about 10 percent of viewing time.

the object and the eye movement required to reach the next feature. The feature ring establishes a fixed ordering of features and eye movements, corresponding to a scan path on the object.

Our hypothesis states that as a subject views an object for the first time and becomes familiar with it he scans it with his eyes and develops a scan path for it. During this time he lays down the memory traces of the feature ring, which records both the sensory activity and the motor activity. When he subsequently encounters the same object again, he recognizes it by matching it with the feature ring, which is its internal representation in his memory. Matching consists in verifying the successive features and carrying out the intervening eye

movements, as directed by the feature ring.

This hypothesis not only offers a plausible format for the internal representation of objects—a format consistent with the existence of scan paths—but also has certain other attractive features. For example, it enables us to draw an interesting analogy between perception and behavior, in which both are seen to involve the alternation of sensory and motor activity. In the case of behavior, such as the performance of a learned sequence of activities, the sensing of a situation alternates with motor activity designed to bring about an expected new situation. In the case of perception (or, more specifically, recognition) of an object the verification of features alternates with

movement of the eyes to the expected new feature.

The feature-ring hypothesis also makes a verifiable prediction concerning eye movements during recognition: The successive eye movements and feature verifications, being directed by the feature ring, should trace out the same scan path that was established for the object during the initial viewing. Confirmation of the prediction would further strengthen the case for the hypothesis. Since the prediction is subject to experimental confirmation we designed an experiment to test it.

The experiment had two phases, which we called the learning phase and the recognition phase. (We did not, of course, use any such suggestive terms

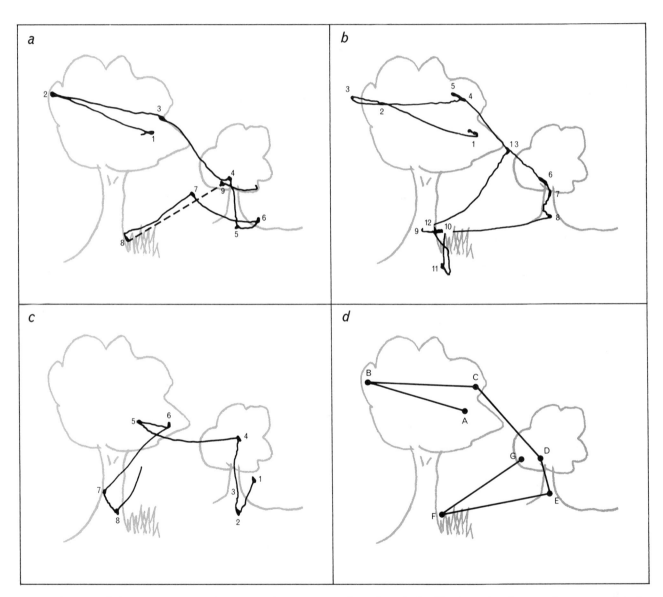

REGULAR PATTERN of eye movement by a given subject viewing a given picture was termed the subject's "scan path" for that picture. Two of five observed occurrences of one subject's scan path as he looked at a simple drawing of trees for 75 seconds are shown here (a, b). The dotted line between fixations 8 and 9 of a indicates that the recording of this saccade was interrupted by a blink. Less regular eye movements made between these appearances of the scan path are at c. Subject's scan path is idealized at d.

in briefing the subjects; as before, they were simply told to look at the pictures.) In the learning phase the subject viewed five pictures he had not seen before, each for 20 seconds. The pictures and viewing conditions were similar to those of the first experiment. For the recognition phase, which followed immediately, the five pictures were mixed with five others the subject had not seen. This was to make the recognition task less easy. The set of 10 pictures was then presented to the subject three times in random order; he had five seconds to look at each picture. Eye movements were recorded during both the learning phase and the recognition phase.

When we analyzed the recordings, we were pleased to find that to a large extent our predictions were confirmed. Scan paths appeared in the subject's eye movements during the learning phase, and during the recognition phase his first few eye movements on viewing a picture (presumably during the time he was recognizing it) usually followed the same scan path he had established for that picture during the learning phase [see illustration on following page]. In terms of our hypothesis the subject was forming a feature ring during the learning-phase occurrences of the scan path; in the recognition phase he was matching the feature ring with the picture, following the scan path dictated by the feature ring.

An additional result of this experiment was to demonstrate that different subjects have different scan paths for a given picture and, conversely, that a given subject has different scan paths for different pictures [see illustration on page 257]. These findings help to discount certain alternative explanations that might be advanced to account for the occurrence of scan paths. The fact that a subject has quite different scan paths for different pictures suggests that the scan paths are not the result of some fixed habit of eye movement, such as reading Chinese vertically, brought to each picture but rather that they come from a more specific source, such as learned feature rings. Similarly, the differences among subjects in scan paths used for a given picture suggest that the scan paths do not result from peripheral feature detectors that control eye movements independent of the recognition process, since these detectors might be expected to operate in much the same way in all subjects.

Although the results of the second experiment provided considerable support for our ideas on visual percep-

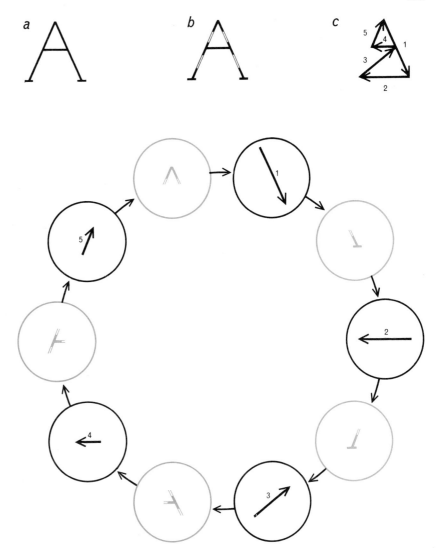

FEATURE RING is proposed by the authors as a format for the internal representation of an object. The object (a) is identified by its principal features (b) and is represented in the memory by them and by the recollection of the scan path (c) whereby they were viewed. The feature ring therefore consists of sensory memory traces (color) recording the features and motor memory traces (black) of the eye movements from one feature to the next.

tion, certain things remain unexplained. For example, sometimes no scan path was observed during the learning phase. Even when we did find a scan path, it did not always reappear in the recognition phase. On the average the appropriate scan path appeared in about 65 percent of the recognition-phase viewings. This is a rather strong result in view of the many possible paths around each picture, but it leaves 35 percent of

the viewings, when no scan path appeared, in need of explanation.

Probably the basic idea of the feature ring needs elaboration. If provision were made for memory traces recording other eye movements between features not adjacent in the ring, and if the original ring represented the preferred and habitual order of processing rather than the inevitable order, the occasional substitution of an abnormal order for the

RECURRENCE OF SCAN PATH during recognition of an object is predicted by the feature-ring hypothesis (see illustration on next page). A subject viewed the adaptation of Klee's drawing (a). A scan path appeared while he was familiarizing himself with the picture (b, c). It also appeared (d, e) during the recognition phase each time he identified the picture as he viewed a sequence of familiar and unfamiliar scenes depicted in similar drawings. This particular experimental subject's scan path for this particular picture is presented in idealized form at f.

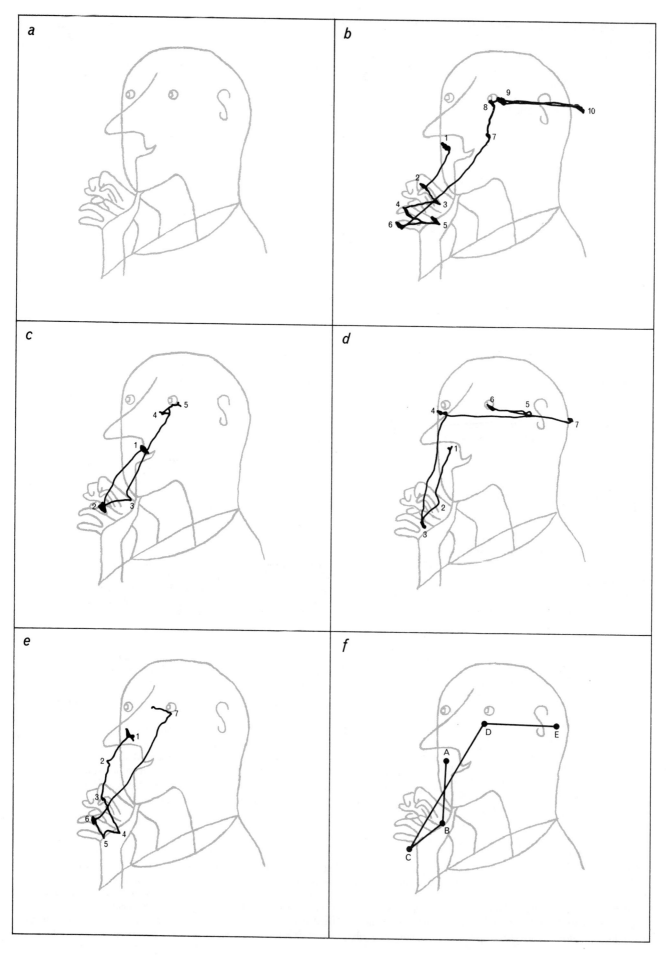

scan path would be explained [*see top illustration on following page*].

It must also be remembered that the eye-movement recordings in our experiments were made while the subjects viewed pictures that were rather large and close to their eyes, forcing them to look around in the picture to see its features clearly. In the more normal viewing situation, with a picture or an object small enough to be wholly visible with a single fixation, no eye movements are necessary for recognition. We assume

that in such a case the steps in perception are parallel up to the point where an image of the object is formed in the visual cortex and that thereafter (as would seem evident from the experiments on recognition time) the matching of the image and the internal representation is carried out serially, feature by feature. Now, however, we must postulate instead of eye movements from feature to feature a sequence of internal shifts of attention, processing the features serially and following the scan

path dictated by the feature ring. Thus each motor memory trace in the feature ring records a shift of attention that can be executed either externally, as an eye movement, or internally, depending on the extent of the shift required.

In this connection several recordings made by Lloyd Kaufman and Whitman Richards at M.I.T. are of interest. Their subjects viewed simple figures, such as a drawing of a cube, that could be taken in with a single fixation. At 10 randomly chosen moments the subject was asked

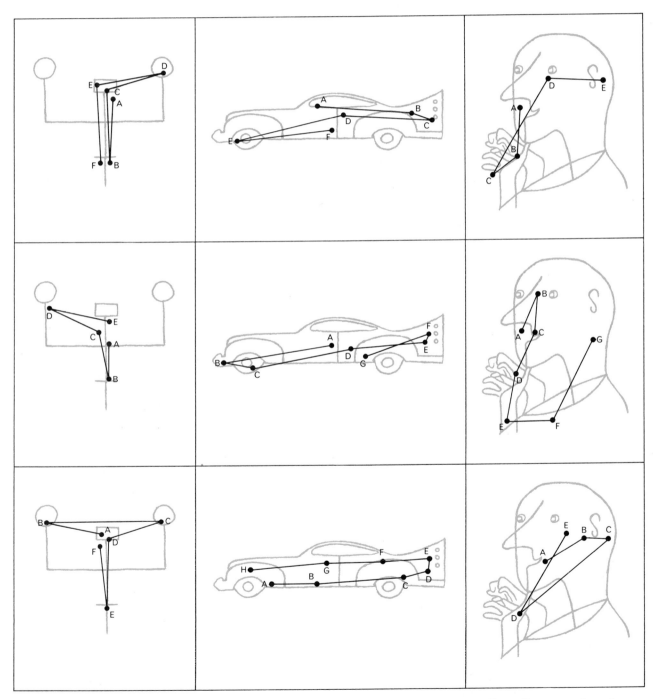

VARIETY IN SCAN PATHS is shown for three subjects and three pictures. Each horizontal row depicts the scan paths used by one subject for the three pictures. Vertically one sees how the scan paths of the three subjects for any one picture also varied widely.

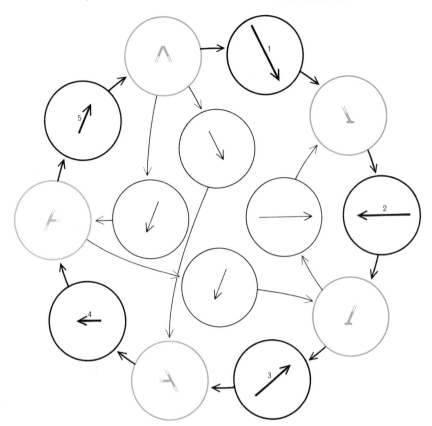

MODIFIED FEATURE RING takes into account less regular eye movements that do not conform to scan path. Several movements, which appeared in 35 percent of recognition viewings, are in center of this ring. Outside ring, consisting of sensory (*color*) and motor memory traces (*black*), represents scan path and remains preferred order of processing.

to indicate where he thought he was looking. His answer presumably showed what part of the picture he was attending to visually. His actual fixation point was then recorded at another 10 randomly selected moments [*see the illustration below*]. The results suggest that the subject's attention moved around the picture but his fixation remained fairly steady near the center of the picture. This finding is consistent with the view that smaller objects too

are processed serially, by internal shifts of attention, even though little or no eye movement is involved.

It is important to note, however, that neither these results nor ours prove that recognition of objects and pictures is necessarily a serial process under normal conditions, when the object is not so large and close as to force serial processing by eye movements. The experiments on recognition time support the serial hypothesis, but it cannot yet be regard-

ed as being conclusively established. In our experiments we provided a situation that forced the subject to view and recognize pictures serially with eye movements, thus revealing the order of feature processing, and we assumed that the results would be relevant to recognition under more normal conditions. Our results suggest a more detailed explanation of serial processing—the feature ring producing the scan path—but this explanation remains conditional on the serial hypothesis.

In sum, we believe the experimental results so far obtained support three main conclusions concerning the visual recognition of objects and pictures. First, the internal representation or memory of an object is a piecemeal affair: an assemblage of features or, more strictly, of memory traces of features; during recognition the internal representation is matched serially with the object, feature by feature. Second, the features of an object are the parts of it (such as the angles and curves of line drawings) that yield the most information. Third, the memory traces recording the features are assembled into the complete internal representation by being connected by other memory traces that record the shifts of attention required to pass from feature to feature, either with eye movements or with internal shifts of attention; the attention shifts connect the features in a preferred order, forming a feature ring and resulting in a scan path, which is usually followed when verifying the features during recognition.

Clearly these conclusions indicate a distinctly serial conception of visual learning and recognition. In the trend to look toward serial concepts to advance the understanding of visual perception one can note the influence of current work in computerized pattern recognition, where the serial approach has long been favored. Indeed, computer and information-processing concepts, usually serial in nature, are having an increasing influence on brain research in general.

Our own thoughts on visual recognition offer a case in point. We have developed them simultaneously with an analogous system for computerized pattern recognition. Although the system has not been implemented in working form, a somewhat similar scheme is being used in the visual-recognition system of a robot being developed by a group at the Stanford Research Institute. We believe this fruitful interaction between biology and engineering can be expected to continue, to the enrichment of both.

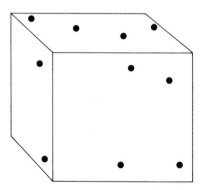 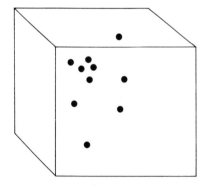

INTERNAL SHIFTS OF ATTENTION apparently replace eye movements in processing of objects small enough to be viewed with single fixation. A subject's attention, represented by statements of where he thought he was looking, moved around picture (*left*), whereas measured fixation point (*right*) remained relatively stationary. Illustration is based on work by Lloyd Kaufman and Whitman Richards at the Massachusetts Institute of Technology.

25

Plasticity in Sensory-Motor Systems

by Richard Held
November 1965

*An animal's own movements change what it sees
and hears. Laboratory experiments that tamper
with this feedback loop show that it is a key
to developing and maintaining spatial orientation
in advanced mammals*

Anyone who has worn eyeglasses is likely to have experienced distorted vision the first time he put them on. The distortion may have been severe enough to cause him trouble in motor coordination, as in reaching out to touch something or in being sure of where he stepped. Such a person will also recall, however, that in a day or two the distortion disappeared. Evidently his central nervous system had made some adjustment so that the things he saw through the glasses looked normal again and he could have renewed confidence in his touch and step.

This process of adjustment, particularly as it operates in recovery from radical transformations of vision (as when the world is made to appear upside down or greatly shifted to one side by special goggles), has attracted the attention of scientists at least since the time of the great 19th-century investigator Hermann von Helmholtz. What has intrigued us all is the finding that correct perception of space and accurate visually guided action in space are in the long run not dependent on unique and permanently fixed optical properties of the paths taken by light rays traveling from object to eye. This finding, however, must be squared with the normally high order of precision in spatial vision and its stability over a period of time. How can the visual control of spatially coordinated action be stable under normal circumstances and yet sufficiently modifiable to allow recovery from transformation? Recovery takes time and renewed contact with the environment. Adaptation must result from information drawn from this contact with the environment. If the end product of adaptation is recovery of the former stability of perception, then the information on which that recovery is

based must be as reliable and unvarying as its end product. The investigations my colleagues and I have undertaken (first at Brandeis University and more recently at the Massachusetts Institute of Technology) have been directed toward discovering this source of information and elucidating the mechanism of its use by the perceiving organism. A useful tool in our work has been deliberate distortion of visual and auditory signals, a technique we call rearrangement.

Visual rearrangement can be produced experimentally with prisms [see "Experiments with Goggles," by Ivo Kohler; SCIENTIFIC AMERICAN Offprint 465]. Similarly, the apparent direction of sounds can be distorted in the laboratory by suitable apparatus. We have used such devices to show that in many cases the viewer or the listener subjected to these distortions soon adapts to them, provided that during the experiment he has been allowed to make voluntary use of his muscles in a more or less normal way.

The proviso suggests that there is more to the mechanism of perceptual adaptation than a change in the way the sensory parts of the central nervous system process data from the eyes and ears. The muscles and motor parts of the nervous system are evidently involved in the adaptation too—a revelation that has been very important in our efforts to discover the responsible source of information. The concept of a relation between sensory and motor activities in the adaptive process is reinforced by what happens when humans and certain other mammals undergo sensory deprivation through prolonged isolation in monotonous environments, or motor deprivation through prolonged immobilization. Their performance on perceptual

and motor tasks declines. By the same token, the young of higher mammals fail to develop normal behavior if they undergo sensory or motor deprivation.

Taken together, these findings by various experimenters suggested to us that a single mechanism is involved in three processes: (1) the development of normal sensory-motor control in the young, (2) the maintenance of that control once it has developed and (3) the adaptation to changes or apparent changes in the data reported by the senses of sight and hearing. A demonstration that such a mechanism exists would be of value in understanding these processes. Moreover, it would help to explain a phenomenon that otherwise could be accounted for only by the existence of enormous amounts of genetically coded information. That phenomenon is the adjustment of the central nervous system to the growth of the body—on the sensory side to the fact that the afferent, or input, signals must change with the increasing separation between the eyes and between the ears, and on the motor side to the fact that the growth of bone and muscle must call for a gradual modification of the efferent, or output, signals required to accomplish a particular movement. This problem is especially critical for animals that grow slowly and have many jointed bones. The possibility that the need for genetically coded information has been reduced by some such mechanism is of course contingent on the assumption that the animal's environment is fairly stable. For these reasons it is not surprising that clear evidence for adaptation to rearrangement and for dependence of the young on environmental contact in developing coordination has been found only in primates and in cats.

Such, in brief, is the background of

our effort to discover the operating conditions of the suspected mechanism. Our conclusion has been that a key to its operation is the availability of "reafference." This word was coined by the German physiologists Erich von Holst and Horst Mittelstädt to describe neural excitation following sensory stimulation that is systematically dependent on movements initiated by the sensing animal; von Holst and Mittelstädt also used the word "exafference" to describe the result of stimulation that is inde-pendent of self-produced movement. "Afference" alone refers to any excitation of afferent nerves. These concepts should become clearer to the reader from the remainder of this article.

Among the contributions von Helmholtz made to science were many that were later incorporated into psychology. His experiments included work on the displacement of visual images by prisms. He was the first to report that the misreaching caused by such a dis-placement is progressively reduced during repeated efforts and that on removal of the prism the subject who has succeeded in adapting to this displacement will at first misreach in the opposite direction.

Helmholtz' findings and those of similar experiments by many other workers have often been interpreted as resulting from recognition of error and consequent correction. We doubted this interpretation because of our conviction that a single mechanism underlies both

ACTIVE AND PASSIVE MOVEMENTS of kittens were compared in this apparatus. The active kitten walked about more or less freely; its gross movements were transmitted to the passive kitten by the chain and bar. The passive kitten, carried in a gondola, received essentially the same visual stimulation as the active kitten because of the unvarying pattern on the wall and on the center post. Active kittens developed normal sensory-motor coordination; passive kittens failed to do so until after being freed for several days.

adaptation to rearrangement in the adult and the development of the young. An error-correcting process could hardly explain the original acquisition of coordination. If an infant initially has no sense of the spatial relation between his efforts to move his hand and their visual consequences, he cannot recognize a visible error in reaching. Yet infants do acquire eye-hand coordination in their earliest months. Hence we suspected that error recognition was no more necessary for adaptation in the adult than it was in the development of the infant's coordination. To test this assumption we designed an experiment that prevented the subject from recognizing his error. If he still managed to correct his reach to allow for a displaced image, it would be evident that there was more to the matter of adaptation than the simple fact that the subject could see his error directly.

With this objective in mind we designed the apparatus shown in the top illustration at the left. In this apparatus the subject saw the image of a square target reflected by a mirror and was asked to mark on a piece of paper under the mirror the apparent position of the corners of the square. Because of the mirror, he could see neither the marks nor his hand. After he had marked each point 10 times, withdrawing his hand between markings so that he would have to position it anew each time, the mirror and marking sheet were removed and a prism was substituted. Looking through the prism, the subject then spent several minutes moving his hand in various ways, none of which involved deliberate reaching for a target. Thereafter the original situation was restored and the subject made more marks under the mirror. These marks revealed that each of the subjects was making some correction for the displacement of image that had been caused by the prism.

Having thus established that at least partial adaptation can occur in the absence of direct recognition of error, we used the apparatus to test the role of motor-sensory feedback in adaptation. Our main purpose was to see what degree of adaptation would occur under the respective conditions of active and passive movement—in other words, under conditions of reafference and exafference in which the afference was equivalent. In these experiments the subject's writing arm was strapped to a board pivoted at his elbow to allow left and right movement. He then looked at his hand through a prism under three

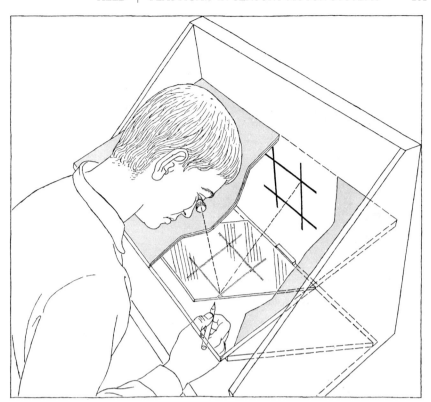

MIRROR APPARATUS tests subject's ability to guide his unseen hand to a visible target. Subject first marks under the mirror the apparent location of the corners of the square as he sees them in the mirror. He then looks through a prism, as depicted in the illustration below, after which he makes more marks. They show his adaptation to the prism effect.

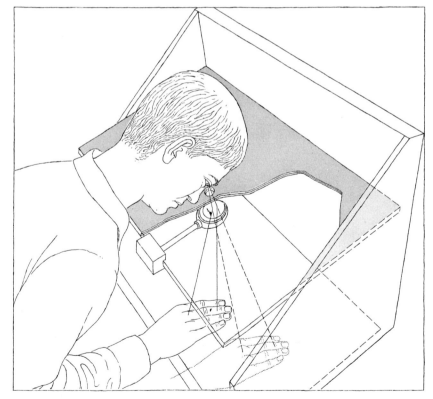

VIEW THROUGH PRISM displaces a visual image. Some subjects looked at their motionless hand, some moved the arm back and forth in a left-right arc, and some had the arm moved passively in a similar arc. They then made marks under the mirror as shown in the illustration at the top of the page. Typical results appear in illustrations on following page.

BEFORE   AFTER

NO MOTION

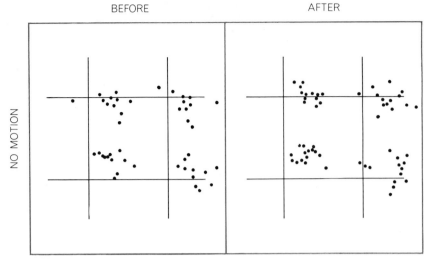

MARKINGS made by a subject before and after looking through a prism as described in illustrations on opposite page are shown. He kept hand still while viewing it through prism.

BEFORE   AFTER

PASSIVE MOTION

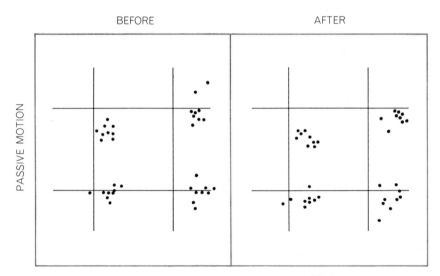

PASSIVE MOVEMENT of subject's hand as he viewed it through prism produced these marks. They show no adaptation to horizontal displacement of images caused by the prism.

BEFORE   AFTER

ACTIVE MOTION

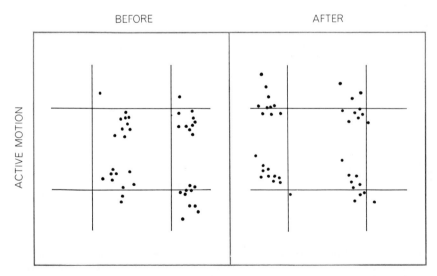

ACTIVE MOVEMENT of subject's hand produced a clear adaptation to displacement of images by prism. Tests showed importance of such movement in sensorimotor coordination.

conditions: (1) no movement, (2) active movement, in which he moved the arm back and forth himself, and (3) passive movement, in which he kept his arm limp and it was moved back and forth by the experimenter. In each case he marked the apparent location of points under the mirror before and after looking through the prism.

Comparison of these marks showed that a few minutes of active movement produced substantial compensatory shifts [*see illustrations at left*]. Indeed, many of the subjects showed full adaptation, meaning exact compensation for the displacement caused by the prism, within half an hour. In contrast, the subjects in the condition of passive movement showed no adaptation. Even though the eye received the same information from both active and passive conditions, the evidently crucial connection between motor output and sensory input was lacking in the passive condition. These experiments showed that movement alone, in the absence of the opportunity for recognition of error, does not suffice to produce adaptation; it must be self-produced movement. From the point of view of our approach this kind of movement, with its contingent reafferent stimulation, is the critical factor in compensating for displaced visual images.

What about an adaptive situation involving movements of the entire body rather than just the arm and hand? We explored this situation in two ways, using an apparatus in which the subject judged the direction of a target only in reference to himself and not to other visible objects [*see top illustration on next page*]. This kind of direction-finding is sometimes called egocentric localization.

The apparatus consisted initially of a drum that could be rotated by the experimenter, after which the subject, sitting in a chair that he could rotate, was asked to position himself so that a target appeared directly in front of him. Later we dispensed with the drum and merely put the subject in a rotatable chair in a small room. After the experimenter had randomly positioned the target, which was a dimly illuminated slit, the subject rotated himself to find the target.

The first of the two ways in which we tested the role of reafferent stimulation involving movement of the whole body was an experiment in adaptation to short-term exposure to prisms. After several trials at locating the target, the subject put on prism goggles. He then walked for an hour along an outdoor path or sat in a wheelchair that was pushed along the same path for the same length of time. Thereupon he removed the goggles and went back to the target-finding apparatus for more tests. Any error in target-finding after wearing the prism goggles would be a measure of the adaptation the subject had made to the visual displacements produced by the prisms.

Again the degree of adaptation achieved by the subjects who had been involved in active movement was far greater than that of the subjects who had been carried in the wheelchair. This was true both when one subject had been exposed to the active condition and another to the passive and when a single subject had been exposed successively to each condition. Even more striking contrasts appeared in our second test, which involved wearing prisms for several hours at a time under conditions of active and passive movement. In these circumstances several of the subjects who were able to move voluntarily achieved full adaptation, whereas subjects whose movements were passive achieved virtually no adaptation.

In this connection it will be useful to mention an experiment we conducted on directional hearing. The sound emanating from a localized source reaches the listener's nearer ear a fraction of a second sooner than it reaches his farther ear. This small difference in the time of arrival of the sound at the two ears is the first stage in ascertaining the direction from which the sound comes. If, then, a subject's ears could be in effect displaced around the vertical axis of his head by a small angle, he would err by an equivalent angle in his location of the sound. This effect can be produced artificially by a device called the pseudophone, in which microphones substitute for the external ears. Subjects who have worn a pseudophone for several hours in a normally noisy environment show compensatory shifts in locating sounds, provided that they have been able to move voluntarily. In addition they occasionally report that they hear two sources of sound when only one is present. When measurements are made of the two apparent directions of the source, they differ by approximately the angle at which the ears were displaced around the center of the head during the exposure period. I have called the effect diplophonia.

The reports of doubled localization

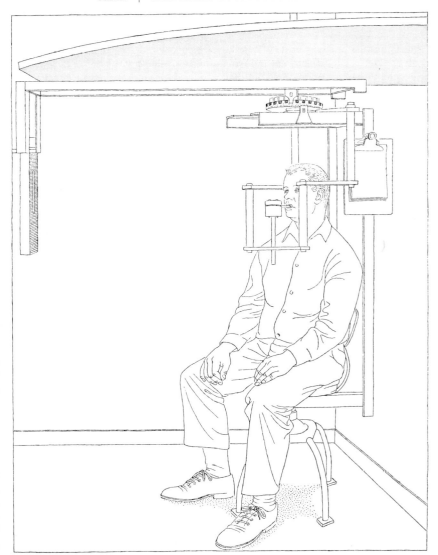

DIRECTION-FINDING by egocentric localization, in which a subject judges the direction of a target only in relation to himself and not to other visual cues, uses this apparatus. Target is randomly positioned at subject's eye level; he then rotates himself so that the target is directly in front of him. He does this before and after wearing prism goggles with which he either walks on an outdoor path or is pushed along the same path in a wheelchair. Change in direction-finding after wearing prisms measures adaptation to the prisms.

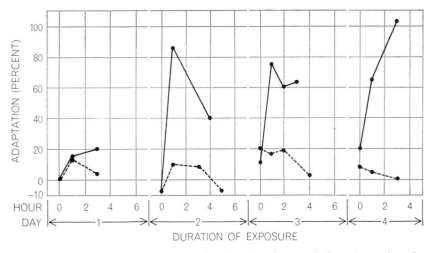

PROLONGED EXPOSURE to prisms produced varying degrees of adaptation to them depending on whether a subject's movement was active (solid lines) or passive (broken lines).

following adaptation suggest that compensation for rearrangement consists in the acquisition of a new mode of coordination that is objectively accurate for the condition of rearrangement but that coexists along with the older and more habitual mode. If this is true, the

gradual and progressive course of adaptation usually found in experiments must be considered the result of a slow shift by the subject from the older direction of localization to the newer direction.

All these experiments strongly suggested the role in adaptation of the

close correlation between signals from the motor nervous system, producing active physical movement, and the consequent sensory feedback. This correlation results from the fact that the feedback signals are causally related to movement and that in a stable environ-

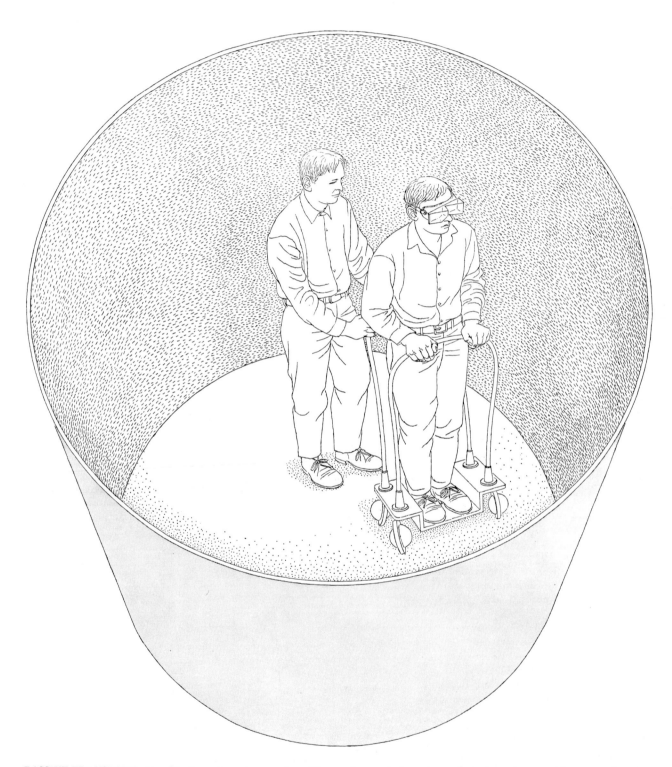

PASSIVE TRANSPORT of a subject wearing prism goggles while viewing a random scene is depicted. Purpose of the apparatus was to test the hypothesis that subjects moving actively through such a scene, which looks the same with or without prisms, would show a

degree of adaptation to the prisms whereas subjects moved passively would not. That is what happened. Tests showed a link between visual and motor processes in the central nervous system by altering the correlation between motor outflow and visual feedback.

ment there is a unique feedback signal for any particular movement. The correlation is reduced by environmental instability: the presence either of objects that themselves move or of passive movements of the body that are produced by external forces. Under these conditions more than one feedback signal may accompany any particular movement.

From a theoretical point of view the importance of body movement and particularly of self-produced movement derives from the fact that only an organism that can take account of the output signals to its own musculature is in a position to detect and factor out the decorrelating effects of both moving objects and externally imposed body movement. One way to verify the importance of the correlation would be to set up an experimental situation in which the correlation was impaired or deliberately decorrelated. If the consequence was a loss of coordination, evidence for the role of normally correlated reafference in maintaining normal coordination would be strengthened.

We conducted such an experiment in visual perception by means of an apparatus that provided a prism effect of continually varying power [*see top illustration at right*]. In such an apparatus an object such as the hand seems to move constantly, and the movement perceived is wholly independent of whatever actual motion may be taking place. The same arm movement made at different times will produce different retinal feedbacks. Since the subject does not control the continual changes in his visual input that are produced by the prism, his nervous system has no means of distinguishing these changes in the input from those that are self-initiated.

With this apparatus we conducted various experiments, again including active and passive arm movements of the type described previously. We found that the coordination between eye and hand was significantly degraded under conditions of active movement but not under conditions of passive movement. Similar results appeared in tests made by Sanford Freedman of Tufts University of the effect of decorrelation on hearing. Again the performance of subjects who were allowed to move actively during decorrelation deteriorated badly, whereas the performance of subjects whose bodily movements were restricted did not deteriorate. Both the visual and the auditory experiments confirmed the importance of the correlation between

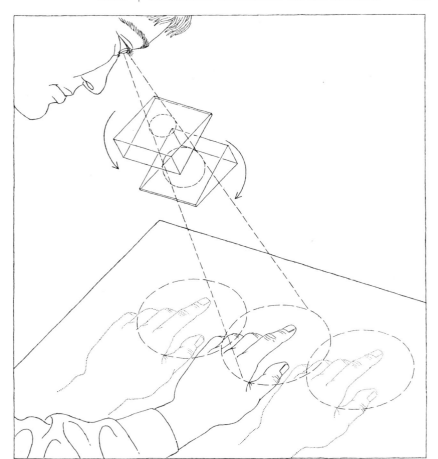

VERIFICATION EXPERIMENT sought to show role of correlation of sensory feedback and active physical movement by impairing it. Means of decorrelation was the rotating-prism apparatus shown here. It produces apparently continuous movement of subject's hand in one dimension, thus breaking the link between actual movement and visual feedback.

	VERTICAL DISPLACEMENT		HORIZONTAL DISPLACEMENT	
BEFORE EXPOSURE				
AFTER EXPOSURE				

RESULTS OF DECORRELATION are shown in markings made by a subject before and after looking through rotating prism. In one condition (*left*) prisms displaced images vertically; in another (*right*), horizontally. Markings after long exposure are spread out in the direction of displacement, showing a loss of precision in visual-motor coordination.

movement and sensory feedback in maintaining accurate coordination.

In another test of our hypothesis about reafference we undertook to see what would happen when subjects looked through prisms at a random scene, lacking in the lines and curves that provide normal visual cues. The straight lines characteristic of normal scenes look curved when viewed through a prism. When the prism is removed, such lines seem to curve in the opposite direction. What if straight lines looked curved after a subject had removed prism goggles through which he had viewed a random scene?

Our hypothesis was that such an effect would be produced in subjects who moved actively while viewing the random field but not in those whose movements were passive. If such a result occurred, we would have shown that the subjective geometry of the visual field can be altered by reafference. This finding would have the surprising implication that a motor factor is involved in a process traditionally regarded as purely visual. We would have demonstrated in another way the close, one-to-one correlation between movement and visual feedback and would have further evidence of a link between motor and visual mechanisms in the central nervous system.

Our apparatus for testing this hypothesis consisted of a large drum that had on its inside surface an irregular array of small spots [see illustration on page 264]. These spots looked the same whether viewed with a prism or not. Each subject, before putting on prism goggles and entering the drum, was tested for his perception of a vertical line; we did this by having him indicate when a grating of bars given varying curvatures by prisms appeared straight. Thereafter, entering the drum with the goggles on, the subject either walked around in the drum or was transported on a cart. He stayed in the drum for half an hour and then, after removing the goggles, again took the test with the grating of bars. Without exception the active subjects perceived curvature when looking at lines that were actually straight, whereas the passive subjects perceived little or none.

Having established by these various means the role of reafference in adaptation to changed sensory inputs, we decided to examine its role in the development of visually controlled coordination in the newborn. The contribution of experience to the development of perceived space and of spatially oriented behavior has been debated for some centuries. During the past few decades a number of experimental approaches to the issue have been made. The technique most often used involves depriving very young animals of sensory contact with the environment. It has been hoped that the procedure would decide whether or not sensory experience, as opposed to maturation alone in the absence of such experience, is required for the development of spatial discrimination.

In certain species of higher mammals, including man, various forms of visual deprivation ranging from total absence of light to mere absence of gross movement in a normally illuminated environment have all resulted in deficiencies in visually guided behavior. Unfortunately these deficiencies are not easily interpreted. They can be attributed, at least in part, to several alternative causes, including pathological changes in the anatomy of the retina and its projections to the brain. Since our findings implicated movement-produced stimulation, they enabled us to test this factor without depriving animals of normal visual stimulation.

The experiments my colleague Alan Hein and I have performed to study the earliest development of vision originated from observations made by Austin H. Riesen of the University of California at Riverside and his collaborators. Riesen's research demonstrated that kittens restrained from walking from the time of their earliest exposure to light develop marked deficiencies in the visual control of behavior compared with unrestrained animals reared normally. The deficiencies of Riesen's animals may have resulted either from the lack of variation in visual stimulation, which was the explanation he preferred, or from the lack of visual stimulation correlated with movement, which was our own hypothesis.

To decide between these alternatives we devised an apparatus in which the gross movements of a kitten moving more or less normally were transmitted to a second kitten that was carried in a gondola [see illustration on page 260]. These gross movements included turns to left and right, circular progress around the center post of the apparatus and any up-and-down motions made by the first kitten. The second kitten was allowed to move its head, since prior experimenters had reported that head movement alone was not sufficient to produce normal behavior in kittens, and it could also move its legs inside the gondola. Both kittens received essentially the same visual stimulation because the pattern on the walls and the center post of the apparatus was unvarying.

Eight pairs of kittens were reared in darkness until the active member of each pair had enough strength and coordination to move the other kitten in the apparatus; the ages at which that state was attained ranged from eight to 12 weeks. Two other pairs were exposed to patterned light for three hours a day between the ages of two and 10 weeks; during exposure they were in a holder that prevented locomotion. Thereafter all 10 pairs spent three hours a day in the apparatus under the experimental condition; when they were not in the apparatus, they were kept with their mothers and littermates in unlighted cages.

After an average of about 30 hours in the apparatus the active member of each pair showed normal behavior in several visually guided tasks. It blinked at an approaching object; it put out its forepaws as if to ward off collision when gently carried downward toward a surface, and it avoided the deep side of a visual cliff—an apparatus in which two depths, one shallow and the other a sharp drop, appear beneath a sheet of glass [see "The 'Visual Cliff,'" by Eleanor J. Gibson and Richard D. Walk; SCIENTIFIC AMERICAN Offprint 402]. After the same period of exposure each of the passive kittens failed to show these types of behavior. The passive kittens did, however, develop such types of behavior within days after they were allowed to run about in a normal environment.

In sum, the experiments I have described have led us to conclude that the correlation entailed in the sensory feedback accompanying movement—reafference—plays a vital role in perceptual adaptation. It helps the newborn to develop motor coordination; it figures in the adjustment to the changed relation between afferent and efferent signals resulting from growth; it operates in the maintenance of normal coordination, and it is of major importance in coping with altered visual and auditory inputs. The importance of the correlation in all these functions has been revealed by experiments that tamper with its normal operation. In the process these experiments have uncovered a fundamental role of the motor-sensory feedback loop.

26

Multistability in Perception

by Fred Attneave
December 1971

*Some kinds of pictures and geometric forms
spontaneously shift in their principal aspect
when they are looked at steadily. The reason
probably lies in the physical organization
of the perceptual system*

Pictures and geometric figures that spontaneously change in appearance have a peculiar fascination. A classic example is the line drawing of a transparent cube on this page. When you first look at the cube, one of its faces seems to be at the front and the other at the back. Then if you look steadily at the drawing for a while, it will suddenly reverse in depth and what was the back face now is the front one. The two orientations will alternate spontaneously; sometimes one is seen, sometimes the other, but never both at once.

When we look steadily at a picture or a geometric figure, the information received by the retina of the eye is relatively constant and what the brain perceives usually does not change. If the figure we are viewing happens to be an ambiguous figure, what the brain perceives may change swiftly without any change in the message it is receiving from the eye. The psychologist is interested in these perceptual alternations not as a curiosity but for what they can tell us about the nature of the perceptual system.

It is the business of the brain to represent the outside world. Perceiving is not just sensing but rather an effect of sensory input on the representational system. An ambiguous figure provides the viewer with an input for which there are two or more possible representations that are quite different and about equally good, by whatever criteria the perceptual system employs. When alternative representations or descriptions of the input are equally good, the perceptual system will sometimes adopt one and sometimes another. In other words, the perception is multistable. There are a number of physical systems that have the same kind of multistable characteristics, and a comparison of multistability in physical and perceptual situations

may yield some significant clues to the basic processes of perception. First, however, let us consider several kinds of situations that produce perceptual multistability.

Figure-ground reversal has long been used in puzzle pictures. It is often illustrated by a drawing that can be seen as either a goblet or a pair of faces [*see top illustration on page 269*]. This figure was introduced by the Danish psychologist Edgar Rubin. Many of the drawings and etchings of the Dutch artist Maurits C. Escher are particularly elegant examples of figure-ground reversal [*see bottom illustration on page 269*]. These examples are somewhat misleading because they suggest that the components of a figure-ground reversal must be familiar objects. Actually you can make a perfectly good reversing figure by scribbling a meaningless line down the middle of a circle. The line will be seen as a contour or a boundary, and its appearance is quite different depending on which side of the contour is seen as the inside and which as the outside [*see top illustration on page 271*]. The difference is so fundamental that if a person first sees one side of the contour as the object or figure, the probability of his recognizing the same contour when it is shown as part of the other half of the field is little better than if he had never seen it at all; this was demonstrated by Rubin in a classic study of the figure-ground dichotomy.

Note that it is quite impossible to see both sides of the contour as figures at the same time. Trying to think of the halves as two pieces of a jigsaw puzzle that fit together does not help; the pieces are still seen alternately and not simultaneously. What seems to be involved here is an attribution of surface properties to some parts of a field but not to others. This kind of distinction is of cen-

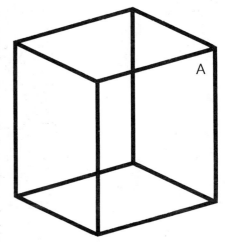

NECKER CUBE, a classic example of perspective reversal, is named after Louis Albert Necker, who in 1832 reported that line drawings of crystals appeared to reverse in depth spontaneously. Corner *A* alternates from front to back when gazed at steadily.

tral importance in the problem of scene analysis that Marvin Lee Minsky of the Massachusetts Institute of Technology and other investigators of computer simulation have been grappling with lately. The figure made by drawing a line through a circle is actually tristable rather than bistable; the third possibility is being able to see the line as a thing in itself, as a twisted wire rather than the boundary of a figure.

PAINTING BY SALVADOR DALI on the following page is an example of the use of ambiguous figures by a serious artist. The illustration is a portion of "Slave Market with Apparition of the Invisible Bust of Voltaire." It is reproduced with the permission of the Dali Museum in Cleveland. When viewed at close range, the figures of people predominate; when viewed at a distance, bust of Voltaire becomes apparent.

The point of basic interest in figure-ground reversal is that one line can have two shapes. Since an artist's line drawing is readily identifiable with the object it is supposed to portray, and since a shape has much the same appearance whether it is white on black, black on white or otherwise colored, many workers have suggested that the visual system represents or encodes objects primarily in terms of their contours. As we have seen, however, a contour can be part of two shapes. The perceptual representation of a contour is specific to which side is regarded as the figure and which as the ground. Shape may be invariant over a black-white reversal, but it is not invariant over an inside-outside reversal.

Under natural conditions many factors cooperate to determine the figure-ground relationship, and ambiguity is rare. For example, if one area encloses another, the enclosed area is likely to be seen as the figure. If a figure is divided into two areas, the smaller of the areas

The visual field usually consists of many objects that overlap and occlude one another. The perceptual system has an impressive ability to segregate and sort such objects from one another. Along with distinguishing figure from ground, the system must group the fragments of visual information it receives into separate sets that correspond to real objects. Elements that are close to one another or alike or homogeneous in certain respects tend to be grouped together. When alternative groupings are about equally good, ambiguity results.

For example, if a set of dots are aligned, the perceptual system tends to group them on the basis of this regularity. When the dots are in regular rows and columns, they will be seen as rows if the vertical distance between the dots is greater than the horizontal distance, and they will seem to be in columns if the horizontal distance is greater than the vertical distance. When the spacing both ways is the same, the two groupings—rows and columns—tend to alternate. What is interesting and rather puzzling about the situation is that vertical and horizontal groupings are competitive at all. Geometrically the dots form both rows and columns; why, then, does seeing them in rows preclude seeing them in columns at the same moment? Whatever the reason is in terms of perceptual mechanisms, the principle involved appears to be a general one: When elements are grouped percep-

REVERSIBLE GOBLET was introduced by Edgar Rubin in 1915 and is still a favorite demonstration of figure-ground reversal. Either a goblet or a pair of silhouetted faces is seen.

WOODCUT by Maurits C. Escher titled "Circle Limit IV (Heaven and Hell)" is a striking example of both figure-ground reversal and competition between rival-object schemata. Devils and angels alternate repeatedly but neither seems to be able to overpower the other.

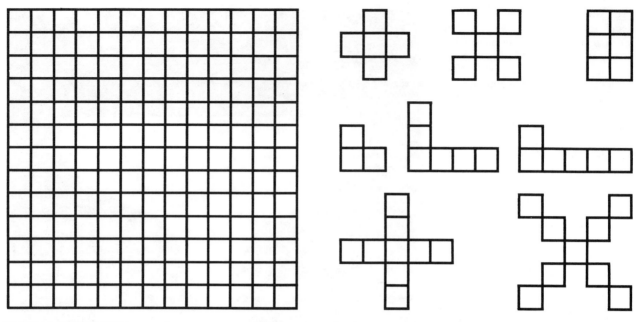

FIGURAL GROUPINGS occur when one stares at a matrix of squares. The simple figures organize themselves spontaneously and with effort more complex figures can be perceived. Some figures, however, are so complex that they are difficult to maintain.

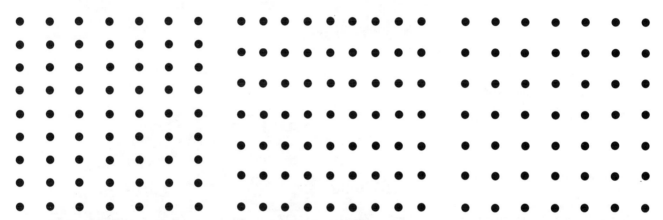

ALIGNED DOTS fall into a regular pattern when viewed. Depending on the spacing, dots can be seen as columns (*left*) or as rows (*middle*). When vertical and horizontal spacing are equal, dots can be seen as rows or columns but not as both at the same time.

EQUILATERAL TRIANGLES appear in one of three orientations depending on the dominant axis of symmetry (*left*). Usually all point in the same direction at one time, although the direction can change spontaneously. The scalene triangles (*middle*) fluctuate in orientation even though they are asymmetrical because they can also appear as isosceles or right triangles that point down or up. The same shape can be seen as either diamonds or tilted squares (*right*) depending on the orientation of the local reference system.

tually, they are partitioned; they are not simultaneously cross-classified.

A related case of multistability involves apparent movement. Four lights are arranged in a square so that the diagonally opposite pairs of lights flash simultaneously. If the two diagonal pairs of lights are flashed alternately, it will appear to an observer as if the lights are moving. The apparent motion can take either of two forms: the observer will see motion along the vertical sides of the square, with two pairs of lights, one on the left and the other on the right, moving in opposite directions up and down, or he will see two sets of lights moving back and forth horizontally in opposite directions. If he continues to watch for a while, the motion will switch from vertical to horizontal and vice versa. When one apparent motion gives way to the other, the two perceptions are subjectively so different that the unsuspecting observer is likely to believe there has been some physical change. Apparent movement involves the grouping of events that are separated in both space and time, but the events so grouped are represented as having a common identity; specifically it appears that the same light has moved to a new place. The rivalry between the horizontal and the vertical movement is thus easier to comprehend than the rivalry between rows and columns of dots: if the representational system reflects the laws of the world it represents, the same object cannot traverse two different paths simultaneously or occupy two different places at once.

Ambiguities of grouping are also evident in fields of repetitive elements such as a floor with hexagonal tiles or even a matrix of squares drawn on paper [*see top illustration on opposite page*]. If one stares at the matrix for a while, certain subsets of the squares will spontaneously organize themselves into simple figures. With voluntary effort one can attain fairly stable perceptions of rather complex figures. The most readily seen figures, however, tend to be simple, compact and symmetrical.

Some of the most striking and amusing ambiguous figures are pictures (which may or may not involve figure-ground reversal) that can be seen as either of two familiar objects, for example a duck or a rabbit, a young girl or an old woman, and a man or a girl [*see illustrations on next two pages*]. What is meant by "familiar" in this context is that the visual inputs can be matched to some acquired or learned schemata of classes of objects. Just what such class

REVERSING FIGURE can be made by scribbling a line through a circle. The shape of the contour formed depends on which side of the line is regarded as part of the figure.

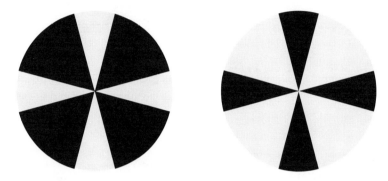

LARGER AREA of a figure is more likely to be seen as the background. Either the large crosses or the small ones may be seen as the figure, but the small crosses have the advantage.

REVERSAL AND ROTATION occur simultaneously in this ingenious design. When the stylized maple-leaf pattern alternates between black and white, it also rotates 90 degrees.

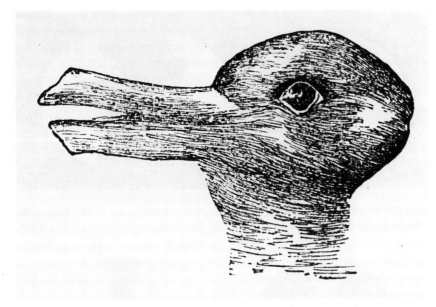

RABBIT-DUCK FIGURE was used in 1900 by psychologist Joseph Jastrow as an example of rival-schemata ambiguity. When it is a rabbit, the face looks to the right; when it is a duck, the face looks to the left. It is difficult to see both duck and rabbit at the same time.

YOUNG GIRL–OLD WOMAN was brought to the attention of psychologists by Edwin G. Boring in 1930. Created by cartoonist W. E. Hill, it was originally published in *Puck* in 1915 as "My Wife and My Mother-in-law." The young woman's chin is the old woman's nose.

schemata consist of—whether they are like composite photographs or like lists of properties—remains a matter of controversy. In any case the process of identification must involve some kind of matching between the visual input and a stored schema. If two schemata match the visual input about equally well, they compete for its perceptual interpretation; sometimes one of the objects is seen and sometimes the other. Therefore one reason ambiguity exists is that a single input can be matched to different schemata.

In certain ambiguous figures we can clearly see the nature of the positive feedback loop that accounts for the "locking in," or stabilization, of one or another aspect of the figure at any given time. For example, if in the young girl–old woman figure a certain line is tentatively identified as a nose, then a line below it must be the mouth and the shapes above must be the eyes. These partial identifications mutually support one another to form a stable perception of an old woman. If, however, the line we started with is seen as a chin instead of as a nose, then the perception formed is that of a young woman. The identification of wholes and of parts will likewise be reciprocally supportive, contributing further to the locking-in process.

Why one aspect of an ambiguous figure, once it is locked in, should ever give way to the other is a fundamental question. Indeed, a person can look for quite a long time at an ambiguous figure and see only one aspect of it. Robert Leeper of the University of Oregon showed that if a subject was first exposed to a version of the figure that was biased in favor of one of the interpretations, he would almost always see only that aspect in the ambiguous version. Not until the other aspect was pointed out would the figure spontaneously alternate. It is only after the input has made contact with both schemata that they become competitive. Making the initial contact and the associated organization must entail a type of learning.

Ambiguities of depth characterize a large class of multistable figures, of which the cube on page 99 is the most familiar. In 1832 a Swiss geologist, Louis Albert Necker, pointed out that a drawing of a transparent rhomboid crystal could be seen in either of two different ways, that the viewer often experiences "a sudden and involuntary change in the apparent position of a crystal or solid represented by an engraved figure." Necker concluded that the aspect seen depends entirely on the point of

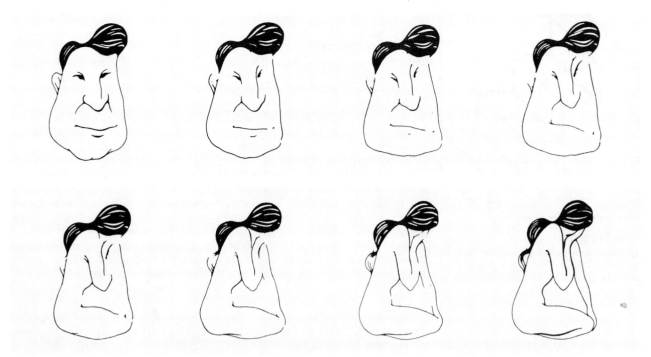

MAN-GIRL FIGURES are part of a series of progressively modified drawings devised by Gerald Fisher in 1967. He found that the last drawing in the top row has equal probability of being seen as a man or as a girl. Perception of middle pictures can be biased toward the man by viewing series in sequence beginning from top left and can be biased toward the girl by starting from bottom right.

fixation, "the point of distinct vision" being perceived as the closer. Although the fixation point is indeed important, it has been shown that depth reversal will readily occur without eye movement.

If we want to understand how depth relationships can be multistable, we must first consider the more general question of how the perceptual system can derive a three-dimensional representation from a two-dimensional drawing. A straight line in the outside world casts a straight line on the retina. A given straight line on the retina, however, could be the image of any one of an infinite number of external lines, and not necessarily straight lines, that lie in a common plane with one another and the eye. The image on a single retina is always two-dimensional, exactly as a photograph is. We should not be surprised, therefore, that depth is sometimes ambiguous; it is far more remarkable that the perceptual system is able to select a particular orientation for a line segment (or at worst to vacillate between two or three orientations) out of the infinite number of legitimate possibilities that exist.

On what basis does the system perform this feat? According to the Gestalt psychologists the answer is to be found in a principle of *Prägnanz:* one perceives the "best" figure that is consistent with a given image. For most practical purposes "best" may be taken to mean "simplest." The advantage of this interpretation is that it is easier to find objective standards for complexity than for such qualities as being "best." One observes a particular configuration of lines on paper, such as the Necker cube, and assigns a three-dimensional orientation to the lines such that the whole becomes a cube (although an infinite number of noncubical forms could project the same form) because a cube is the simplest of the possibilities. In a cube the lines (edges) are all the same length; they take only three directions, and the angles they form are all equal and right

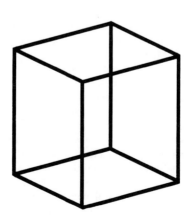
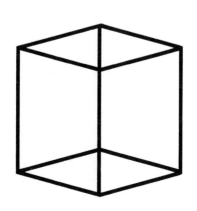
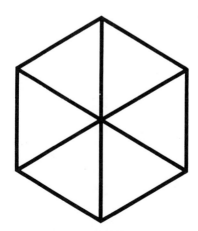

PROJECTIONS OF A CUBE onto a two-dimensional surface are nearly always seen in depth when they resemble the Necker cube *(left)*. As the projection becomes simpler and more regular it is more likely to be seen as a flat figure, such as a hexagon *(right)*.

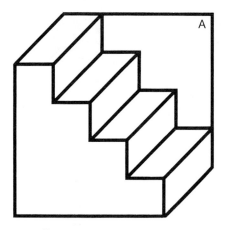

SCHRÖDER STAIRS line drawing is another classic example of perspective reversal. Corner *A* is part of the rear wall when the staircase goes up to the left; when reversal occurs, corner *A* becomes part of the front wall and the bottom of the stairway is seen.

angles. No other interpretation of the figure, including the two-dimensional aspect itself, is as simple and regular. In cases of reversible perspective two maximally simple tridimensional constructions are permissible, each being symmetrical with the other in depth.

If this reasoning is correct, simple projections of a given solid should be perceived as being flat more often than complex projections of the same solid. Julian Hochberg and his colleagues at Cornell University studied various two-dimensional projections of a cube and other regular solids [*see bottom illustra-*

tion on preceding page]. Relatively complex projections are nearly always perceived in depth. A figure such as a regular hexagon divided into equilateral triangles, which is simple and regular in two dimensions, stays two-dimensional because seeing it as a cube does not make it any simpler. Intermediate figures become tristable; they are sometimes seen as being flat and sometimes as being one or another aspect of a cube. The measure of complexity devised by Hochberg and Virginia Brooks involved the number of continuous lines in the figure, the number of interior angles and the number of different angles. This measure predicted with considerable accuracy the proportion of the time that a figure was seen in depth rather than as being flat.

I have been emphasizing the importance of simplicity, but it is obvious that familiarity also plays an important role in instances of ambiguous depth. The two factors are hard to disentangle. Simple structures are experienced with great frequency, particularly in man-made environments. As Alvin G. Goldstein of the University of Missouri has shown by experiment, within limits a nonsense shape is judged to be simpler the more often it is experienced. In my view familiarity and simplicity become functionally equivalent in the perceptual system when a given input corresponds closely to a schema that is already well established by experience and can therefore be encoded or described (in the lan-

guage of the nervous system) most simply in terms of that schema.

Depth reversal does not occur only with two-dimensional pictures. As the Austrian physicist and philosopher Ernst Mach pointed out, the perspective of many real objects will reverse when the object is viewed steadily with one eye. A transparent glass half-filled with water is a particularly dramatic example, but it requires considerable effort to achieve the reversal and the stability of the reversal is precarious. Mach discovered an easier reversal that is actually more instructive. Take a white card or a small piece of stiff paper and fold it once along its longitudinal axis [*see bottom illustration on this page*]. Place the folded card or paper in front of you on a table so that it makes a rooflike structure. Close one eye and view the card steadily for a while from directly above. It will reverse (or you can make it reverse) so that it appears as if the fold is at the bottom instead of the top. Now view the card with one eye from above at about a 45-degree angle so that the front of the folded card can be seen. After a few seconds the card will reverse and stand up on end like an open book with the inside toward you. If the card is asymmetrically illuminated and is seen in correct perspective, it will appear to be more or less white all over, as it is in reality, in spite of the fact that the illuminated plane reflects more light than the shadowed one. When the reversal occurs, the shadowed plane looks gray instead of white and the illuminated plane may appear luminous. In the perspective reversal the perceptual mechanism that preserves the constancy of reflectance is fooled; in order to maintain the relation between light source and the surfaces the perceptual system makes corrections that are erroneous because they are based on incorrect information.

Another remarkable phenomenon involving the folded card seems to have escaped Mach's notice. Recently Murray Eden of the Massachusetts Institute of Technology found that if after you make the folded card reverse you move your head slowly from side to side, the card will appear to rock back and forth quite as convincingly as if it were physically in motion. The explanation, very roughly, is that the mechanism that makes allowance for head movements, so that still objects appear still even though the head moves, is operating properly but on erroneous premises when the perspective is reversed. The perceived rocking of the card is exactly what would

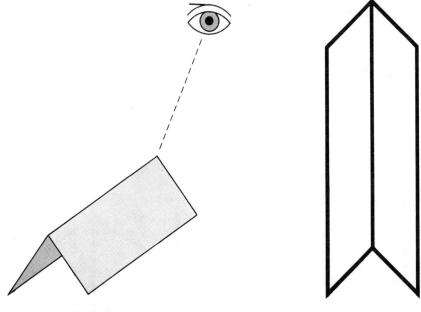

DEPTH REVERSAL OF A REAL OBJECT can occur when it is viewed from above with one eye, an effect discovered by Ernst Mach. When a folded card is viewed from above and the front, it will appear to stand on end like an open book when it reverses. The same kind of depth reversal occurs with a simple line drawing of a folded card (*above right*).

have to happen objectively if the card were really reversed to account for the sequence of retinal images accompanying head movement. What is remarkable about this is not that the mechanism can be wrong but rather that it can function so efficiently as a "lightning calculator" of complex problems in projective geometry and compensate so completely to maintain the perceived orientation. It seems to me that this capacity is a good argument for the existence of some kind of working model of three-dimensional space within the nervous system that solves problems of this type by analogue operations. Indeed, the basic concept of *Prägnanz*, of a system that finds its way to stable states that are simple by tridimensional criteria, is difficult to explain without also postulating a neural analogue model of three-dimensional space. We have no good theory at present of the nature of the neural organization that might subserve such a model.

A few years ago I stumbled on a principle of ambiguity that is different from any we have been considering. While planning an experiment on perceptual grouping I drew a number of equilateral triangles. After looking at them for a time I noticed that they kept changing in their orientation, sometimes pointing one way, sometimes another and sometimes a third way [*see bottom illustration on page 270*]. The basis for this tristable ambiguity seems to be that the perceptual system can represent symmetry about only one axis at a time, even though an equilateral triangle is objectively symmetrical about three axes. In other words, an equilateral triangle is always perceived as being merely an isosceles triangle in some particular orientation. Compare any two sides or any two angles of an equilateral triangle and you will find that the triangle immediately points in the direction around which the sides and angles are symmetrical. When a group of equilateral triangles points upward, the triangles cease to fluctuate; the perceptual system strongly prefers the vertical axis of symmetry. Indeed, any perceived axis of symmetry seems to have the character of a locally rotated vertical.

When scalene triangles (triangles with three unequal sides) are grouped together with their corresponding sides parallel, they also appear to fluctuate in orientation after a brief inspection [*see bottom illustration on page 207*]. This is at first puzzling since they have no axes of symmetry at all. The answer to the puzzle involves the third dimension: When the triangles are seen to

point in a given direction, they simultaneously go into depth in such a way that they look like isosceles triangles seen at an angle. Perspective reversal doubles the possibilities, so that there are six ways the scalene triangles can be seen as isosceles. The same triangles may also be seen as right triangles in depth, with the obtuse angles most easily becoming the right angles.

These observations begin to make sense if we suppose the perceptual system employs something quite like a Cartesian coordinate system to locate and describe things in space. (To call the system Cartesian is really putting the issue backward, since Descartes clearly took the primary perceptual directions of up-down, left-right and front-back as his reference axes.) The multistable states of triangles thus appear to involve simple relations between the figure and the reference system. The reference system may be tilted or rotated locally by the perceptual system and produce the apparent depth or orientation of the triangles.

In the same way we can explain how the same shape can appear to be so different when it is seen as a square or as a diamond. The square is perceived as having horizontal and vertical axes along its sides; the diamond is perceived as being symmetrical about a vertical axis running through opposite corners. Yet in certain kinds of grouping the perceptual axes can be locally rotated and the diamond can look like a tilted square [*see bottom illustration on page 270*].

It should be evident by now that some principle of *Prägnanz*, or minimum complexity, runs as a common thread through most of the cases. It seems likely that the perceptual machinery is a teleological system that is "motivated" to represent the outside world as economically as possible, within the constraints of the input received and the limitations of its encoding capabilities.

A good reason for invoking the concept of multistability to characterize figural ambiguity is that we know a great deal about multistable physical and electronic systems and may hope to apply some of this knowledge to the perceptual processes. The multistable behavior of the perceptual system displays two notable characteristics. The first is that at any one moment only one aspect of the ambiguous figure can be seen; mixtures or intermediate states occur fleetingly if at all. The second is that the different percepts alternate periodically. What accounts for this spontaneous alternation? Once the percep-

tual system locks into one aspect of the figure, why does it not remain in that state? An analogous physical system is a trapdoor that is stable only when it is either open or closed.

As Necker pointed out, changing the point of visual fixation may cause perspective to reverse. In the instances where the input is being matched against more than one schema visual fixation on a feature that is more critical to one representation than the other may lock perception into only one aspect of the ambiguous figure. Since the percepts can alternate without a change in the point of fixation, however, some additional explanation is needed. The most likely is that the alternative aspects of the figure are represented by activity in different neural structures, and that when one such structure becomes "fatigued," or satiated or adapted, it gives way to another that is fresher and more excitable. Several investigators have noted that a reversing figure alternates more rapidly the longer it is looked at, presumably because both alternative neural structures build up some kind of fatigue. In some respects the neural structures behave like a multistable electronic circuit. A common example of multistability in electronic circuitry is the multivibrator flip-flop circuit, which can incorporate either vacuum tubes or transistors. In the vacuum tube version [*see illustration on following page*] when one tube is conducting a current, the other tube is prevented from conducting by the low voltage on its grid. The plates and the grids of the two tubes are cross-coupled through capacitors, and one tube continues to conduct until the charge leaks from the coupling capacitor sufficiently for the other tube to start conducting. Once this tube begins to conduct, the positive feedback loop quickly makes it fully conducting and the other tube is cut off and becomes

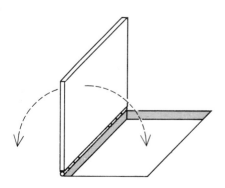

PHYSICAL SYSTEM that exhibits a simple form of multistability is a trapdoor that is stable only when it is either open or shut.

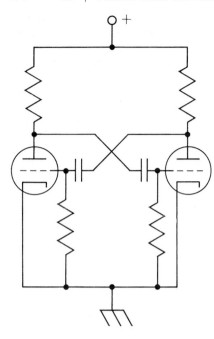

nonconducting. The process reverses and the system flip-flops between one state and the other.

What is "fatigued" in the multivibrator is the suppressive linkage. In other words, the inhibition of the nonconducting tube slowly weakens until it is no longer strong enough to prevent conduction. The possibility of an analogous neural process, in which the inhibition

MULTIVIBRATOR CIRCUIT spontaneously alternates between two states. When one vacuum tube is conducting, the other is inhibited. A charge leaking from the coupling capacitor eventually starts the inhibited tube conducting. The positive feedback loop quickly makes it fully conducting and cuts off conduction in the first tube. The entire process is repeated in reverse, and the circuit flops from one state to the other.

of the alternative neural structure progressively weakens, is worth considering.

Brain lesions may affect the perception of ambiguous figures. The finding most generally reported is that in people who have suffered brain damage the rate of alternation is lower, more or less independently of the locus of the lesion. On the other hand, a study of a group of brain-damaged war veterans conducted by Leonard Cohen at New York University indicated that damage to both frontal lobes increases the rate of alternation of a reversible figure, whereas damage to only one frontal lobe decreases the rate. The theoretical implications of these neurological findings are quite obscure and will doubtless remain so until we have some fundamental picture of the way the nervous system represents form and space.

VIII

LEARNING
AND MEMORY

VIII LEARNING AND MEMORY

INTRODUCTION

Learning is the most important thing that people do. Language, society, and culture are all learned, and their continued existence depends on the learning of each new individual. As the articles in the earlier sections indicate, we have a good beginning for understanding the basic processes of communication among neurons and the neuronal mechanisms that may underlie sensation, the control of movement, and the more complex aspects of sensory-motor integration that we have labeled perception. Unfortunately we do not yet have a very good understanding of the neural mechanisms that underlie learning.

Human beings are qualitatively different from all other animals because of what they can learn. We learn much more than apes. Apes, in turn, learn much more than rats, who learn a great deal more than flies. It is largely for this reason that psychology has emphasized the study of learning. A classic question in physiological psychology concerns the engram—the physical changes in the brain that accompany learning. Learning is broadly conceived as changes in behavior resulting from experience. It is convenient to distinguish between learning and memory: Learning refers to the acquisition or development of new responses and memory refers to the retention or recall of the learned responses. The articles in this section represent four major approaches to the fundamental problem of understanding the neural basis of learning and memory: The use of simplified model neuronal systems, the use of structural and anatomical measures, the use of chemical measures, and finally the measurement of electrical activity in nervous systems.

In the first article of this section, "Nerve Cells and Behavior," by Eric R. Kandel, the model-system approach to the problem of simple changes in behavior is illustrated. He uses portions of the nervous system of a very primitive invertebrate, the seahare, or *Aplysia*, which has relatively few giant neurons that can be studied and identified individually. He shows how some of the pathways can be traced out and the particular neurons identified. He selects a system that shows the properties of behavioral habituation—a simple form of learning—and analyzes the possible neuronal mechanisms that may underlie habituation in this very simple beast.

In the next article, by Mark R. Rosenzweig, Edward L. Bennett, and Marion Cleeves Diamond, entitled "Brain Changes in Response to Experience," structural and chemical changes that develop in the brain as a result of experience are studied. Rosenzweig and his associates developed the now famous "rich rat" and "poor rat" environments. Rich rat environments are group living cages with toys and interesting stimulus objects and plenty of space to explore. Poor rat environments are bare laboratory cages, such as house most rats in laboratories. When investigators compare rats that have been living in the two environments, they find very substantial and important differences in a number of brain measurements—such things as brain weight, chemical contents, the number of glial cells, and other properties of the brain. The rich environment seems to favor increased development of the brain. These studies have profound implications for human development. It is clear that experience is critically important in brain development in the individual as he grows from birth.

In the next article, Bernard W. Agranoff considers the chemical mechanisms that may underlie long-term memory in his article, "Memory and Protein Synthesis." Goldfish were trained to cross a barrier in order to avoid electric shock and were then given brain injections of substances that interfere with the manufacture of protein in the brain. Under certain conditions this treatment appears to abolish the learned response. Agranoff concludes that protein synthesis is a necessary substrate for the establishment of long-term memory.

Karl H. Pribram, the eminent neuropsychologist, is the author of the last article in this section, "The Neurophysiology of Remembering." Pribram addresses the basic issue first raised in 1929 by Lashley in the search for the engram. Lashley's work indicated that although the engram very clearly developed in the cerebral cortex, learning could not be localized to specific local circuits. Thus, visual memory is retained as long as some small piece of visual cortex remains intact, regardless of the location of that piece. Pribram and his associates have studied the changes in electrophysiological activity of the visual cortex and other regions of the brain of the monkey as it learns visual discrimination. Their results lead them to suggest that holography may provide the missing clue. Pribram summarizes a number of studies from his laboratory that bear on this critical issue of how the brain stores memory.

Nerve Cells and Behavior

by Eric R. Kandel
July 1970

*Can memory and learning be studied at the level
of nerve cells and their interconnections? A beginning
is made by relating changes in the activity
of nerve cells to the modification of simple behaviors*

The application of biological techniques to behavior has its roots in the writings of Charles Darwin, who argued that since man had evolved from lower animals, human behaviors must have parallels in the behaviors of lower forms. Darwin's radical insights stimulated studies of animal behavior, opening the way to experimentation that was not feasible in man. The studies dealt both with the comparative aspects of behavior in different species and with the analysis of brain mechanisms, two lines of investigation that for a while developed independently.

The comparative studies of behavior proved almost immediately rewarding. It soon became evident that in spite of great variations in the behavioral capabilities of different animals, certain basic response patterns essential for survival—such as feeding, escape and sexual behaviors—were almost universal. Surprising parallels in the details of these behaviors were found in higher and lower animals. Even simple forms of learning seemed to be governed by principles applicable to widely different species.

The analysis of brain mechanisms progressed more slowly at first, but after World War II the development of techniques for studying individual nerve cells revolutionized the neural sciences and made it possible to analyze progressively more complex neuronal processes. As a result a very good understanding has been achieved of the biophysical functioning of the nerve cell and of synaptic transmission, the mechanism whereby one nerve cell communicates with another [see the article "The Synapse," by Sir John Eccles, beginning on page 89]. In addition insights have been gained into the organization of interconnected groups of neurons from cellular studies of sensory and motor systems [see the article "The Visual Cortex of the Brain," by David H. Hubel, beginning on page 183].

In recent years the investigative tradition of comparative behavior and the tradition of brain mechanisms have begun to converge. Advances in the concepts and techniques for studying individual nerve cells and interconnected groups of cells have encouraged neural scientists to apply these methods to studying complete behavioral acts and modifications of behaviors produced by learning. Guided by the lessons of the comparative behaviorists, investigators have sought to study very general behaviors, characteristic of those found in most animals, in species whose nervous systems are amenable to detailed cellular analyses. This led to an interest in certain invertebrates, such as crayfish, leeches, various insects and snails, that have the great advantage that their nervous system is made up of relatively few nerve cells (perhaps 10,000 or 100,000 compared with the trillion or so in higher animals). In these animals one can begin to trace, at the level of individual cells, not only the sensory information coming into the nervous system and the motor actions coming out of it but also the total sequence of events that underlies a behavioral response. By combining psychological techniques for demonstrating the behavioral capabilities of simple animals with cellular techniques for analyzing neural mechanisms, it is now becoming possible to clarify some relations between neural mechanisms and learning. Although cellular concepts and techniques are still far from explaining behavior and learning in higher animals, they are beginning to be useful in understanding elementary forms of behavioral modification in simple animals.

In this article I shall first outline some of the theoretical issues that have influenced modern studies of the mechanism of learning and describe how cellular neurophysiological techniques helped to clarify these issues by revealing that the synapses of nerve cells are functionally modifiable. I shall then try to illustrate how the combined use of cellular and behavioral techniques makes it possible to relate synaptic modifications in certain nerve cells to short-term modification of behavior in an invertebrate.

Cellular-Connection Approach

When investigators first began applying biological techniques to the study of the neural mechanisms of learning, several quite different strategies evolved, but only one of them—the cellular-connection approach—has proved consistently useful. The cellular-connection approach assumes that both the transformation of neural information and its storage as memory involve only nerve cells and their interconnections. This approach derives from morphological studies of the nervous system by the Spanish anatomist Santiago Ramón y Cajal, who held that the nervous system was constructed from discrete cellular units, the neurons, and that the way to understand the brain was to analyze its functional architecture—its wiring diagram. Proponents of this view have therefore focused on the properties of individual neurons, paying particular attention to the synapse, the connection between the nerve cells.

The importance of specific neuronal interconnections in behavior was first demonstrated impressively by R. W. Sperry at the University of Chicago in the 1940's. In a series of studies on the regeneration of neural connections in lower vertebrates, Sperry showed that visual perception and motor coordination could best be explained in terms of highly specific cellular interconnections.

Moreover, these connections seemed invariant and appeared not to be affected by experience [see "The Growth of Nerve Circuits," by R. W. Sperry; SCIENTIFIC AMERICAN Offprint 72].

These studies presented an interesting paradox. If the development of connections between most neurons in the nervous system is rigidly determined, how then is behavior modified? How does one reconcile the known malleability of behavior with a preprogrammed and rigidly "wired" nervous system? One of the characteristic features of learning and other behavioral modifications is their long time course; even a simple behavioral modification lasts for several minutes and certain types of learning may endure for many years. How is the modified neural activity sustained in a set of prewired connections? Do memory and learning require some further additions to the wiring diagram?

Plastic and Dynamic Change

A number of solutions for this dilemma have been proposed. The two that have proved most interesting experimentally are based on notions of the plastic and the dynamic capabilities of neurons. The plasticity hypothesis was first put forward by Cajal and several other neuroanatomists and then in more modern form by two psychologists, Jerzy Kornorski in Poland and Donald O. Hebb in Canada. A current version of

this hypothesis states that even though the anatomical connections between neurons may develop according to a rigid plan, the strength or effectiveness of the connections is not entirely predetermined and the effectiveness of synapses and other properties of neurons can be altered by experience. This hypothesis predicted that neurons, and in particular their synapses, should be able to change their functional properties as a result of altered activity.

The dynamic hypothesis derived from the anatomical studies of Rafael Lorente de Nó of Rockefeller University, who showed that neurons are often interconnected in the form of closed chains. Neural activity could therefore be sustained by the circulation or reverberation of impulses within a closed chain of interconnected, self-reexciting neurons. This again would not require anatomical change; in fact, the hypothesis does not even require a functional change in the properties of neurons.

The possibility that dynamic changes could account for persistent neural activity was initially very attractive to neurophysiologists because there were many examples in the nervous system of neurons connected to one another in circular paths. As studies of the physiological functions of neural networks advanced, however, it became clear that neurons can mediate inhibition as well as excitation—can tend to quench as well as to fire a nerve impulse. What appeared ana-

tomically to be a self-reexciting loop might therefore contain one or more inhibitory connections that could prevent reexcitation. In addition, memory was shown to survive a number of drastic experimental manipulations, such as cooling of the brain and epileptic convulsions, that would be likely to interrupt the circulation of impulses in closed chains of neurons. As a result of these findings the possibility that dynamic activity provides the neural basis of even short-term memory now seems less likely, although it has not been excluded. Studies of the plastic capabilities of neurons, on the other hand, have turned out to be surprisingly rewarding, since experiments have shown that a remarkable capacity for short-term functional modifications is built into the structure of many synapses.

The first demonstration of the plastic capability of a synapse was provided in 1947 by Martin G. Larrabee and Detlev W. Bronk, then at Johns Hopkins University. They studied a simple "monosynaptic" pathway, that is, one consisting of a single class of neurons directly connected to another class of neurons through a single set of synapses. They tetanized (repetitively stimulated at a high frequency) certain fibers leading to the stellate ganglion in the autonomic nervous system of the cat and found that the responsiveness of the stimulated monosynaptic pathway was greatly facilitated, or enhanced, for a few minutes whereas neighboring, unstimulated pathways were unaffected [see illustration on this page]. They called this phenomenon posttetanic potentiation.

A few minutes is clearly not very long compared with the duration of most learning processes, but it is long compared with the millisecond events that had characterized nerve actions known up to that time. Some behavioral modifications are indeed relatively short-lived, and a plastic mechanism such as posttetanic potentiation might underlie them. Moreover, Larrabee and Bronk showed that the duration of posttetanic potentiation could be extended by longer periods of stimulation. Recently W. Alden Spencer and Reuben Wigdor of the New York University School of Medicine and F. B. Beswick and R. T. W. L. Conroy in Britain have found that posttetanic potentiation can last for as long as two hours after a period of tetanization lasting for from 15 to 30 minutes.

After the discovery of posttetanic potentiation, a number of investigators examined other monosynaptic pathways and encountered an opposite phenomenon, a posttetanic depression, whereby

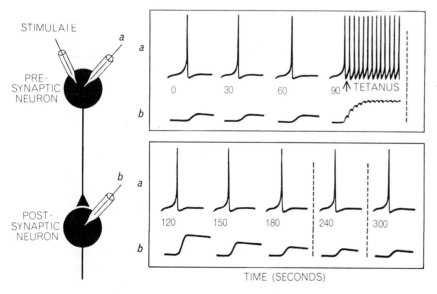

POSTTETANIC POTENTIATION is a form of plastic change in neural activity. It can be studied in some monosynaptic pathways in which both presynaptic and postsynaptic cells can be impaled with microelectrodes. Stimulation of a presynaptic neuron produces an action potential in it (*a*) that propagates to the nerve terminal and leads to generation of a synaptic potential in the postsynaptic cell (*b*). Repetitive high-frequency stimulation greatly increases the effectiveness of the stimulated pathway, as indicated by the increase in the amplitude of the postsynaptic potential. The increase persists several minutes after tetanus.

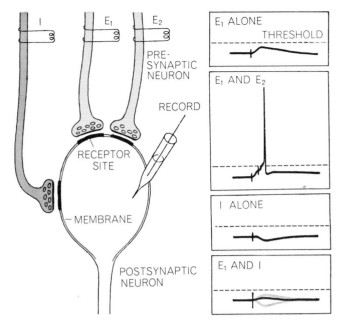

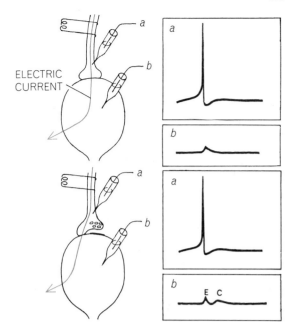

SYNAPSE is the junction between two nerve cells. Most synapses are chemical (*left*), but some are electrical (*top right*) or conjoint (*lower right*). A chemical synapse may be excitatory (*light color*) or inhibitory (*gray*). After a characteristic delay an arriving nerve impulse releases transmitter molecules, thought to be stored in vesicles in the synaptic knob of the presynaptic fiber, that diffuse across the synaptic gap to receptor sites on the postsynaptic cell membrane, increasing its permeability to certain ions and thus changing the electrical potentials of the postsynaptic cell. An impulse in one excitatory fiber (E_1) may produce only a small excitatory postsynaptic potential (EPSP) in the postsynaptic cell. Sequential impulses from two excitatory endings (E_1 and E_2) may combine to depolarize the membrane enough to reach threshold, firing the cell. An inhibitory fiber (I) changes the membrane potential in the opposite direction, counteracting any excitatory action arriving at the same time (E_1 and I). At an electrical synapse the gap between the presynaptic and postsynaptic neuron is reduced and the current produced by the action potential in the presynaptic neuron flows directly into the postsynaptic cell and out across its membrane, depolarizing it. A presynaptic impulse (a) can therefore produce an immediate electrical postsynaptic potential (b). In a conjoint synapse, both chemical and electrical, the presynaptic impulse (a) produces (b) first an electrical synaptic potential (E) and then, after a delay, a chemical synaptic potential (C).

repetitive stimulation leads to a decrease in synaptic effectiveness that sometimes lasts for an hour or more. Other synaptic pathways were found that do not require high-frequency stimulation to undergo plastic changes; they undergo a low-frequency depression when they are stimulated at low rates. For example, Jan Bruner and Ladislav Tauc, at the Marey Institute in Paris, recently described a profound low-frequency depression in a monosynaptic system in the marine invertebrate *Aplysia*. In some synapses one stimulus frequency produces depression and another frequency leads to facilitation. Moreover, plastic changes are not limited to excitatory synapses; they can also occur at inhibitory synapses.

The Synapse

The great advantage of monosynaptic systems is that their anatomical simplicity allows them to be examined directly. It was in monosynaptic systems that Sir Bernhard Katz and his colleagues at University College London and Sir John Eccles and his collaborators at the Australian National University first worked out the general principles that underlie chemical synaptic transmission. They showed that at the synapse the action potential, or nerve impulse, in the termi-

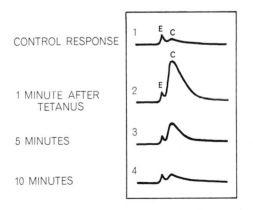

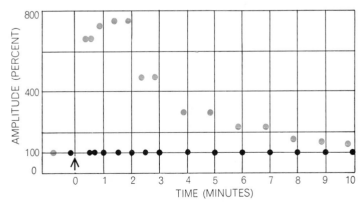

CONJOINT SYNAPSE experiment by Robert Martin and Guillermo R. J. Pilar demonstrated that the chemical synapse is subject to posttetanic potentiation but the electrical synapse is not. The electrical and chemical potential are shown in their usual relation (*1 at left*). After a brief tetanus the chemical synaptic potential is increased but not the electrical (*2*); the chemical synaptic potential remains elevated for more than 10 minutes (*3 and 4*). The chart (*right*) shows the quantitative results of the complete experiment. The arrow indicates the tetanus. The electrical EPSP (*black*) is unaffected; the chemical EPSP (*color*) rises and declines.

nal part of the neuron leading to the synapse (the presynaptic neuron) triggers the release of a "chemical messenger," or transmitter substance, such as acetylcholine [*see top illustration on preceding page*]. The chemical transmitter diffuses across the gap separating the two neurons at the synapse and interacts with a receptor site on the outer surface of the membrane of the postsynaptic cell. This interaction leads to a change in the permeability of the membrane to certain ions.

At an excitatory synapse the transmitter-receptor interaction produces an increase in the permeability of the membrane to sodium and potassium ions, resulting in a depolarizing potential change: the excitatory postsynaptic potential (EPSP). This makes the membrane potential less negative, moving it toward the threshold at which a new ac-

tion potential will be discharged in the postsynaptic cell. If the EPSP is large enough, the threshold is exceeded and an all-or-none action potential is triggered. At an inhibitory synapse the transmitter-receptor interaction increases the permeability to potassium or chloride ions, resulting in a hyperpolarizing potential change: the inhibitory postsynaptic potential (IPSP). This moves the membrane potential away from the critical threshold potential, thereby decreasing the possibility of the postsynaptic cell's discharging an action potential.

Studies of monosynaptic systems provided a basis for analyzing the cellular mechanisms of plastic change. In all instances examined plasticity of synaptic pathways has been shown to involve a change in the amplitude of the postsynaptic potential. Detailed study of mechanisms has been possible in the

case of posttetanic potentiation. O. F. Hutter of University College London found that the characteristic increase in the EPSP results from an increased amount of transmitter substance released by the presynaptic terminals with each impulse; the sensitivity of the receptor to the transmitter was unaltered. Similarly, posttetanic depression and low-frequency depression seem to be due to a decrease in the amount of transmitter released and not to a change in receptor sensitivity, but the evidence here is less complete.

In 1957 Edwin J. Furshpan and David D. Potter, then at University College London, found that the central nervous system contained not only chemical but also electrical synapses. The two classes of synapses have a number of properties in common, but the electrical synapses (which are less numerous) do not utilize a chemical transmitter; there is a direct flow of current from the presynaptic to the postsynaptic cell [*see top illustration on preceding page*]. The finding of a second class of synapses made possible further exploration of the mechanisms of plastic change. If synaptic plasticity resulted from changes in the action of transmitter substances, then electrical synapses, lacking these transmitters, should have restricted capabilities for plastic change. This hypothesis was soon tested by Robert Martin and Guillermo R. J. Pilar of the University of Utah, who compared electrical and chemical transmission in a "conjoint" synapse of the ciliary ganglion of the chick, where electrical and chemical transmission occur together. Martin and Pilar found that following repetitive stimulation only the chemically mediated EPSP changed; the electrically mediated synaptic potential was not affected. Michael V. L. Bennett of the Albert Einstein College of Medicine reached the same conclusion independently after detailed studies of more than a dozen electrical synapses.

These and other experiments suggest that the predominance of chemical over electrical transmission in the central nervous system may in part be related to the ability of many (perhaps all) chemical synapses to undergo prolonged alterations in efficacy as a result of earlier activity, and thereby to serve as elementary sites for information storage. The striking distinction between the plastic capabilities of electrical and of chemical synapses also strengthens the impression, which emerges from studies of different chemical synapses, that different synaptic pathways can vary greatly in the type and amount of the plastic change they are capable of.

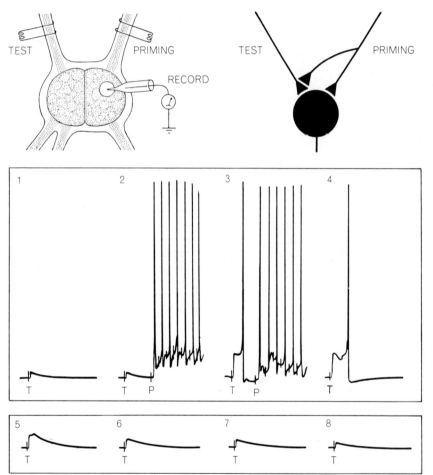

PROLONGED HETEROSYNAPTIC facilitation is studied in the abdominal ganglion of the snail *Aplysia* (*top left*). A test pathway is weakly stimulated and produces a small EPSP (*1*). When a different, "priming" pathway is strongly and repetitively stimulated, it produces a larger synaptic potential, firing the cell (*2*). Priming facilitates the test pathway; it too produces a large EPSP that fires the cell (*3*). Ten seconds after priming, the test pathway alone fires the cell (*4*). It continues to produce a larger potential than control after 3.5, 10 and 20 minutes (*5, 6, 7*), reverting to control size after 30 minutes (*8*). A model postulated for this facilitation has a terminal of the priming pathway ending on the presynaptic terminal of the test pathway, controlling its transmitter release (*top right*).

The finding that the pattern of activity along a given pathway can lead to changes in synaptic efficacy at chemical synapses in that pathway was an important step toward understanding how behavior might be modified. With post-tetanic potentiation or low-frequency depression, however, the changes in effectiveness are restricted to the repetitively stimulated synaptic pathway. Even simple behavioral modifications characteristically involve activity in two different pathways. Might activity in one pathway produce plastic changes in the synaptic activity of another pathway?

Heterosynaptic Facilitation

To examine this question, Tauc and I, working at the Marey Institute, investigated the effects of a more complex stimulus sequence on a number of different cells in the abdominal ganglion of *Aplysia*. In a particular cell we found that an EPSP produced by stimulation of one pathway could be greatly facilitated by activity in another pathway. We called this process heterosynaptic facilitation. Although not specific to or dependent on a precise pairing of the stimuli, the stimulus sequence used in these experiments begins to resemble the sequences used in learning experiments. The results provide a neural analogue of quasi-conditioning, or sensitization, the process whereby a strong stimulus enhances other responses.

As was the case for posttetanic potentiation, heterosynaptic facilitation did not result from a change in the threshold or in the biophysical characteristics of the postsynaptic cell membrane during facilitation. The facilitation could be produced in a pathway consisting of only a single fiber (as shown by the fact that it produced an elementary, or unitary, EPSP in the postsynaptic cell), indicating that the synaptic efficacy of the pathway was being directly controlled by the activity of another pathway. Tauc and I therefore proposed that fibers of the facilitating pathway synapse on the presynaptic terminals of the facilitated pathway, and that this presynaptic synapse acts as a governor regulating the long-term release of the chemical transmitter substance in the facilitated pathway [*see illustration on opposite page*].

The idea that activity in one pathway could control activity in another one was not new. A few years earlier Joseph Dudel and Stephen W. Kuffler of the Harvard Medical School and others had reported that some synapses undergo presynaptic inhibition, a mechanism whereby activity in one pathway de-

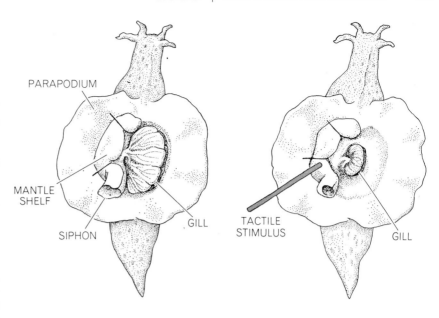

APLYSIA, a marine snail, has a vestigial shell in the mantle shelf. At rest, the gill is partially covered by the mantle shelf (*left*). When the siphon or shelf is touched, the siphon contracts and the gill retracts underneath the shelf in a typical defensive reflex (*right*).

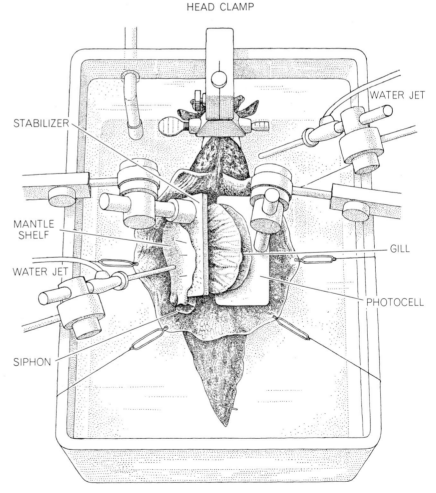

GILL-WITHDRAWAL REFLEX was studied by clamping the animal in a small aquarium and recording the extent of gill contraction with a photocell. When the siphon or shelf was stimulated by a jet of water, the gill contracted, exposing the photocell to light from above.

presses synaptic transmission in another [see "Inhibition in the Central Nervous System," by Victor J. Wilson; SCIENTIFIC AMERICAN, May, 1966]. That process generally lasts for only a few hundred milliseconds. The studies of *Aplysia* showed that certain pathways could exert a prolonged influence on the activity of others, and that this influence could be facilitatory as well as inhibitory.

To summarize, different types of plastic change lasting for many minutes and even hours occur at chemical synapses, and there is some evidence that the changes involve two types of regulatory mechanism within the presynaptic terminals that control transmitter release. One class of regulatory mechanisms underlies low-frequency depression, posttetanic depression and posttetanic facilitation and is responsive to activity limited to the stimulated (homosynaptic) pathway. The second class underlies heterosynaptic facilitation and heterosynaptic depression, and involves alterations in one synaptic pathway following activity in an adjacent pathway. The evidence for presynaptic mechanisms is incomplete, however; in several instances there remains an alternate possibility that the change in synaptic effectiveness may be due to a change in the receptor-site sensitivity of the postsynaptic cell.

The detailed study of the plastic capabilities of neurons is only beginning. It is likely that other aspects of neuronal function—such as a cell's threshold or spontaneous firing pattern—may also prove capable of plastic change. It is clear, however, that an important prediction of the cellular-connection hypothesis has been supported: neurons and their synapses have at least some capabilities for plastic change.

Plasticity and Behavior

Given that some synapses can show plastic capabilities, how do these changes in a single nerve cell relate to behavior and its modification? In order to bridge the gap between cellular plasticity and behavior, a detailed knowledge of the anatomy and physiology of the specific neural circuit that mediates the behavior is required. This requirement is very difficult to meet in the intact brain of higher animals because these brains contain an enormous number of cells and an even larger number of interconnections. Moreover, the vertebrate brain mediates highly complex behaviors. One way around these problems is to study simple behaviors under the control of numerically reduced neural populations—either isolated portions of the vertebrate nervous system or simple invertebrate ganglia (discrete collections of cells). The most consistent progress has come from studies of habituation and dishabituation in the spinal cord of the cat and the abdominal ganglion of *Aplysia*.

Habituation, sometimes considered the most elementary form of learning, is a decrease in a behavioral response that occurs when an initially novel stimulus is presented repeatedly. A common example is the habituation of an "orienting response" to a new stimulus. When a stimulus such as a sudden noise is presented for the first time, one's attention is immediately drawn to it, and one's heart rate and respiratory rate increase. As the same noise is repeated, one's attention and bodily responses gradually diminish (which is why one can become accustomed to working in a noisy office). In this sense habituation is learning to accommodate to stimuli that have lost novelty or meaning. Besides being important in its own right, habituation is frequently involved in more complex learning, which consists not only in acquiring new responses but also in eliminating incorrect responses. Once a response is habituated two processes can lead to its restoration. One is spontaneous recovery, which occurs as a result of withholding the stimulus to which the animal has habituated. The other is dishabituation, which occurs as a result of changing the stimulus pattern, for example by presenting a stronger stimulus to another pathway. Similar types of response decrement and restoration, last-

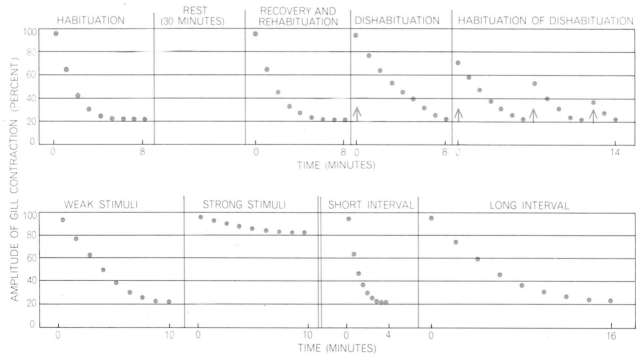

HABITUATION AND DISHABITUATION in the gill-withdrawal reflex have properties characteristic of these behavioral modifications in higher animals. The response decreased (habituation) with successive stimulations, recovered slowly after a rest period and then rehabituated when repeated stimuli were reintroduced. It could also be restored rapidly to control value (dishabituation) by the presentation of a strong new stimulus (*arrow*). The dishabituatory stimulus habituated in turn after repetition. The reflex also habituated more rapidly with weak rather than strong stimuli and with short rather than long intervals between stimuli.

ing for from several minutes to several hours, have been demonstrated for a wide variety of behaviors in all animals that have been examined, including man. The existence of such general ways of modifying behavior suggests that their neuronal mechanisms may also prove to be quite general.

The first neural analysis of habituation was undertaken in the spinal cord of the cat. The spinal cord mediates the reflex responses underlying posture and locomotion in vertebrates. In the course of analyzing the neural mechanism of spinal reflexes, Sir Charles Sherrington, the great British physiologist, found that certain reflex responses, such as the flexion withdrawal of a limb in response to stimulation of the skin, decreased with repeated stimulation and recovered only after many seconds of rest. Sherrington was greatly influenced by Cajal's work, and he tried to develop his notions of reflex action in relation to the anatomical diagrams Cajal had worked out. (In fact, it was Sherrington who coined the term "synapse" for the zone of apposition between two neurons, which Cajal had described.) Sherrington had the great insight to appreciate that neural reactions within the spinal cord differed from those in the peripheral nerves because of the numerous synaptic connections within the cord. It was therefore perhaps only natural for him to attribute the decrease in the responsiveness of the withdrawal reflex to a decrease in function at the synapses through which the motor neuron responsible for flexion was repeatedly activated. In other words, as early as 1908 Sherrington had suggested that a plastic change at central synapses could underlie response decrement. He was able to show that the decrement was not due to fatigue of either the muscles or the sensory receptors but, with the neurophysiological techniques then available, he could not fully test his intriguing synaptic hypothesis.

The problem was reinvestigated by C. Ladd Prosser and Walter Hunter of Brown University, who found that the habituated flexion withdrawal can be restored to full size (dishabituated) by the application of a strong new stimulus to another part of the skin. More recently Alden Spencer, Richard F. Thompson and Duncan R. Neilson, Jr., then at the University of Oregon, found that dishabituation is not simply a transient wiping out of habituation but an independent facilitatory process superimposed on habituation, and they established that spinal-reflex habituation resembled the habituation of more complex behavioral responses. Spencer and his colleagues

also began the cellular analysis of habituation. By recording intracellularly from a motor neuron they showed that response decrement involved a change not in the properties of the motor neurons but in the synaptic impingement on them. They could not localize the critical

changes precisely, however, because the central synaptic pathways of the flexion withdrawal reflex in the cat are complex, involving many connections between sensory and motor cells through interneurons that have not yet been worked out. Barbara Wikelgren of the Massa-

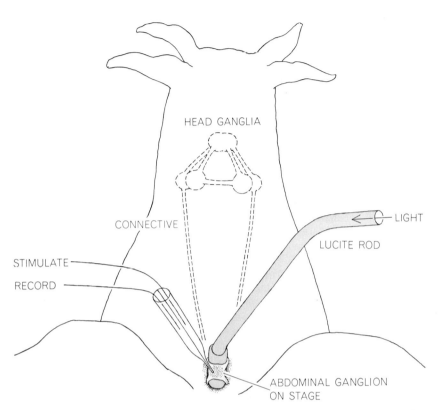

ABDOMINAL GANGLION of *Aplysia* is a group of some 1,800 cells at the forward end of the animal's abdomen, near the head. It is connected to the head ganglia by connective nerves. To study the individual cells of the abdominal ganglion, the author and his colleagues cut a slit in the skin and lift ganglion out on a stage lighted by a curved Lucite rod.

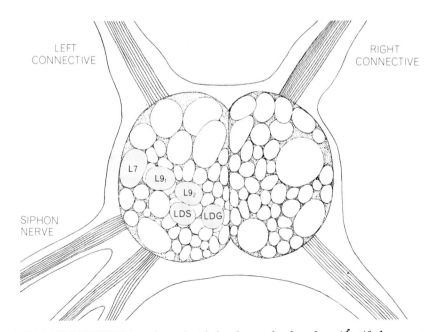

CELLS OF GANGLION have been classified and a number have been identified as recognizable individuals. By firing cells one at a time with a microelectrode, five cells (*color*) in one part of the ganglion were identified that produced movements of the withdrawal reflex.

chusetts Institute of Technology has gone on to examine several populations of interneurons and has shown that decremental changes occur only in certain classes of them, but the complexity of the pathways has still prevented her from distinguishing between plastic and dynamic changes in neuronal activity or specifying whether inhibitory or excitatory synaptic transmission is altered.

Gill Withdrawal in *Aplysia*

The further analysis of habituation required a still simpler system, one where the components of the behavioral response could be reduced to one or more monosynaptic systems. In search of such systems, a number of researchers have been attracted to the invertebrate nervous system because these systems contain relatively few cells, thus reducing the task of a behavioral analysis [see "Small Systems of Nerve Cells," by Donald Kennedy; SCIENTIFIC AMERICAN Offprint 1073]. The nervous system of marine gastropod mollusks is particularly advantageous because it contains cells that are unusually large (some reach almost one millimeter in diameter) and therefore are suitable for study with intracellular microelectrodes. For this reason my colleagues and I at the New York University School of Medicine have worked on the abdominal ganglion of *Aplysia*, a giant marine snail that grows to about a foot in size. An opisthobranch, *Aplysia* differs from the better-known pulmonate snails in having only a very small residual shell. Like some other marine mollusks, such as the octopus and the squid, *Aplysia* gives off a brilliant

purple ink when it is overly perturbed.

The abdominal ganglion of *Aplysia* has only about 1,800 cells and yet is capable of generating a number of interesting behaviors. Wesley T. Frazier, Irving Kupfermann, Rafiq Waziri and I collaborated with Richard E. Coggeshall, an anatomist at the Harvard Medical School, to classify the cells in this ganglion into different functional clusters. We also identified 30 cells as unique individuals and mapped a number of their central connections. This provided a good starting point for an attempt to examine the cellular changes in habituation and dishabituation. Our plan was to delineate a behavior that is controlled by cells in the abdominal ganglion and that undergoes habituation, to analyze the neural circuit of this behavior and then to try to specify the locus and the nature of the functional change in the neural circuit that underlies the modification of behavior. Kupfermann and I initiated this work and we were soon joined by Harold Pinsker and Vincent Castellucci.

An *Aplysia* shows a defensive withdrawal response that is in some ways analogous to the flexion withdrawal response in the cat. The snail's gill, an external respiratory organ, is partially covered by the mantle shelf, which contains the thin residual shell. When either the mantle shelf or the anal siphon, a fleshy continuation of the mantle shelf, is gently touched, the siphon contracts and the gill withdraws into the cavity underneath the mantle shelf. If the stimulus is very strong, it brings in other behavioral components, such as ink production. The defensive purpose of this reflex is clear: it protects the gill, a vital and delicate

organ, from possible damage. Gill withdrawal is therefore analogous to the withdrawal of a man's hand from a potentially damaging stimulus. As in the case of these other defensive responses, the gill-withdrawal reflex habituates when it is repeatedly elicited by a weak or harmless stimulus.

When Thompson and Spencer reviewed the literature on habituation in vertebrates, they described nine features that characterize this simple behavioral modification. We found six of these characteristic features in the gill-withdrawal reflex in *Aplysia*: (1) response decrement, typically a negative exponential function of the number of stimulus presentations; (2) recovery with rest; (3) dishabituation; (4) habituation of the dishabituatory stimulus as it is repeated; (5) greater habituation with weak rather than strong stimuli, and (6) greater habituation with short rather than long stimulus intervals.

The fit between short-term habituation in *Aplysia* and in mammals was encouraging, and we went on to analyze the neural circuit of this behavior. To this end Kupfermann and I made a small slit just forward of the snail's mantle region through which the abdominal ganglion, with its connectives and peripheral nerves attached, was lifted out on an illuminated stage [*see top illustration on preceding page*] so that various neurons could be impaled with double-barreled microelectrodes for recording and direct stimulation.

First we searched for the motor neurons of the reflex—the component leading outward from the central nervous system. We did this by firing different cells one at a time with the microelectrode and observing whether or not they produced movements of the external organs of the mantle cavity. By this means we identified five motor cells, clustered together in one part of the ganglion, that produced contractions of the gill, the siphon or the mantle shelf. Three of the five cells produced movements limited to the gill, one cell produced movement of the siphon only and one cell produced movement of the gill, the siphon and the mantle shelf [*see illustration at left*]. The motor component of this reflex, then, consists of individual elements with both restricted and overlapping distributions; it is redundant, as are other motor systems that have been described in invertebrates. Turning to the afferent component of the reflex, which leads toward the central nervous system, we next mapped the sensory receptive field of the motor cells by stimulating the surface of the animal's body with light brush-

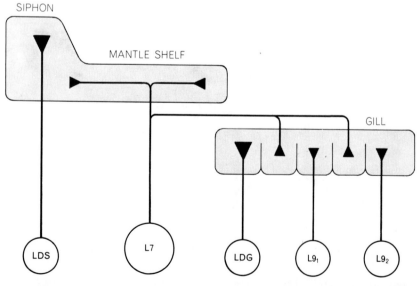

INDIVIDUAL ACTIONS of the five cells are shown. Three produce movement of the gill alone; one, movement of the siphon alone, and one, movement of gill, siphon and shelf.

strokes. We found that all five motor cells received large EPSP's, producing a brisk repetitive spike discharge, when the siphon or the mantle shelf was stimulated. The tactile receptive field of these five motor cells was identical with that of the defensive withdrawal reflex. Our analysis suggested a simple pathway for the excitatory input, in part monosynaptic and in part mediated by interneurons [*see top illustration on this page*]. At this early stage we could not exclude the possibility of an underlying inhibitory component.

The Nature of the Changes

Having analyzed at least part of the wiring diagram of the total withdrawal reflex, we next examined the changes that accompany habituation and dishabituation of the gill component of the total reflex. These changes could occur at a number of points in the circuit. The first possibility, that habituation was due to changes outside the central nervous system either in the muscle or in the sensory receptors in the skin, was quite readily excluded. Stimulation of the individual motor neurons or of the peripheral nerves innervating the gill at rates that are effective in producing habituation did not give rise to a significant decrease in gill contraction. Moreover, the size of this directly evoked gill response was the same before, during and after habituation or dishabituation of the reflex response. Finally, single sensory axons recorded in the peripheral nerves did not change their rate of firing when the sensory stimulus was repeated at rates that produced reflex habituation.

Since neither muscle fatigue nor sensory accommodation could account for the habituation of the gill reflex, habituation must result from some functional change within the central nervous system. We therefore examined the EPSP produced in the major motor neurons of the gill by tactile stimulation of the siphon or mantle shelf and found that it underwent characteristic changes that were causally related to habituation, to recovery and to dishabituation. When a tactile stimulus was repeated to produce habituation at the behavioral level, the resulting EPSP in the gill motor neuron gradually decreased in size, and the amount and frequency of the spike activity it evoked decreased correspondingly. Recovery of reflex responsiveness, produced either by rest or by a dishabituatory stimulus, was associated with an increase of the EPSP and a corresponding increase in spike activity.

We next began a more detailed ex-

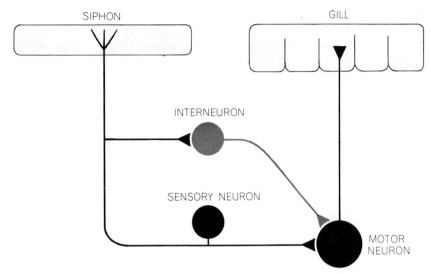

SIMPLE WIRING DIAGRAM for the gill component of the withdrawal reflex shows how the excitatory input from the sensory cells could fire the motor cells both directly and via intervening excitatory interneurons. (In *Aplysia* and other invertebrates the presynaptic neuron normally ends on the beginning of the fiber of the postsynaptic cell, as in the upper illustration on the next page. Here the synapse is indicated schematically, on the cell body.)

amination of the mechanism underlying these changes in the synaptic potential. First we examined whether the synaptic changes resulted from alteration of the synaptic impingement on the motor neuron or from a change in the biophysical properties of the motor neuron itself. The amplitude of any synaptic potential is determined by the amount of synaptic current that flows across the resistance provided by the cell membrane outside the synaptic area [*see top illustration on page 283*]. A synaptic potential can therefore be altered in two ways: (1) by a direct change in synaptic current, produced either by a change in the amount of transmitter released by presynaptic neurons or by a change in the sensitivity

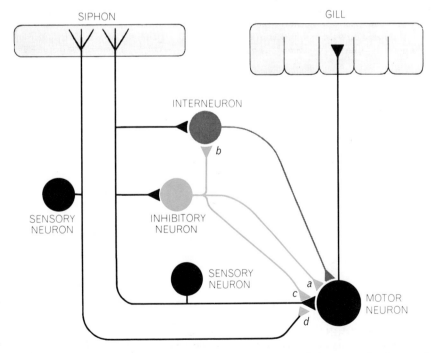

INHIBITION might reduce the excitation of motor neurons and thus cause the decreased responses of habituation. If an inhibitory interneuron were involved in the pathway, it might operate on the motor neuron itself (*a*), on an excitatory interneuron (*b*) or on the terminals of the afferent sensory fiber (*c*). Alternatively, parallel sensory fibers in a different pathway, activated by the same stimulus, might effect presynaptic inhibition (*d*).

of the postsynaptic neuron's receptor sites; (2) by a change in the resistance of the membrane of the postsynaptic cell. To distinguish between these two possibilities we measured the resistance of the postsynaptic cell and found that it was unaltered during habituation and dishabituation. The changes in the synaptic potential during habituation and dishabituation must therefore reflect changes in the synaptic current. This could have been caused by a change in receptor sensitivity or, what is more likely, by a change in the amount of transmitter that is released by the total synaptic impingement on the motor neuron.

Many elements impinge on a motor neuron and a change in synaptic impingement could therefore be caused by one of a number of factors. If for the moment we consider only habituation, then the decrease in the amplitude of the EPSP might be due to a decrease, caused by inhibition, in the number of active excitatory elements impinging on the motor neuron and thus contributing to the total synaptic potential. If the afferent fibers that excite the motor neuron also activated a side chain consisting of one or more inhibitory neurons, an inhibitory neuron could reduce the excitatory activity by acting on the motor neuron directly, on an excitatory interneuron or on the excitatory terminals of the sensory fiber [see bottom illustration on preceding page]. If repeated stimulation then produced a sustained increase in inhibitory action (by either dynamic or plastic means), it would result in progressive suppression of either the motor neuron or the excitatory interneuron that helps to discharge the motor neuron. Alternatively, habituation could occur without any increase of active inhibition; there might simply be a progressive decrease in the effectiveness of the individual excitatory synaptic actions.

Eliminating Inhibition

In order to distinguish between these two possibilities it was necessary to examine an individual excitatory element in isolation to see whether, in the complete absence of inhibition, the EPSP it produced would show the characteristic decrement, paralleling behavioral habituation, in the course of repeated stimulation. To this end we radically simplified the afferent component of the reflex pathway by separating a small piece of siphon skin that is part of the receptive field of the reflex together with its afferent nerve to the ganglion, and isolating the ganglion from the rest of the nervous system by removing it from the animal to an experimental chamber [see upper illustration at left]. In this simplified preparation we searched the skin until we found a responsive region that when stimulated produced an "elementary" EPSP in the motor neuron, that is, a unitary signal reflecting the synaptic response produced by a single sensory fiber. When this elementary EPSP was repeatedly evoked, it paralleled the gill response, decreased with repeated stimulation and recovered following rest.

This established that the change in potential was not the result of inhibition in the direct pathway from sensory to motor nerve. Inhibition was not yet ruled out, however. Since the stimulus that produced the elementary EPSP might also be activating other sensory fibers, the decrement in the synaptic potential might be due to presynaptic inhibition from parallel afferent fibers [see bottom illustration on preceding page]. To eliminate this last possibility we had to stimulate a single sensory neuron in isolation, thereby ensuring that it was acting alone.

This appeared at first to be a difficult experimental objective. It could best be

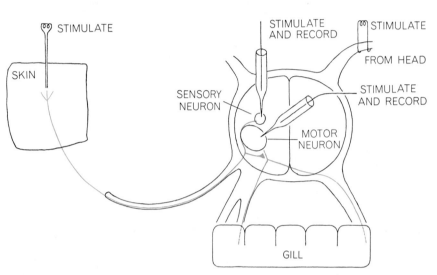

INDIVIDUAL EXCITATORY ELEMENT was isolated to eliminate inhibitory neurons in the pathway as sources of habituation. A piece of skin was probed to produce in the motor neuron an "elementary" EPSP, one clearly evoked by a single cell. This EPSP showed decrement. In another experiment the cell body of an individual sensory neuron was identified and stimulated directly, and its decrement was observed. Dishabituation was also studied in this pathway, with electrical stimulation to the connective as the dishabituatory stimulus.

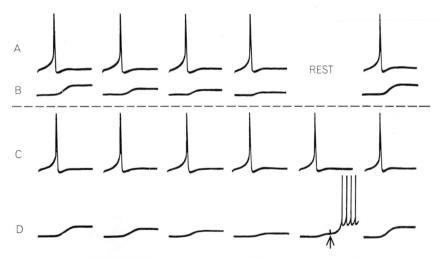

NEURAL DETERMINANTS of habituation and dishabituation are seen in these traces from an individual sensory neuron and motor neuron. Stimulation produces an action potential in the sensory neuron (A) that induces an elementary EPSP in the motor neuron (B); repeated stimulation produces a decrement of the EPSP; rest brings about recovery. Dishabituation was demonstrated by firing the sensory nerve (C) to produce habituation (D), then delivering a stronger stimulus (arrow) to a head connective, increasing the EPSP.

achieved by stimulating the cell body of a sensory neuron with an intracellular electrode, and the cell bodies of mechanoreceptor neurons were believed to be located in the skin, where they are difficult to isolate for recording and stimulation. Soon after we started work on this problem, however, John G. Nicholls and Denis A. Baylor of the Yale University School of Medicine reported that the cell bodies of mechanoreceptor neurons in the leech were located not in the skin but in the central ganglia; fortunately we found a similar situation in the abdominal ganglion of *Aplysia*. We identified a group of sensory cells that were excited by mechanical stimulation of small regions of the skin of the siphon and that had properties consistent with their being primary sensory neurons of the gill-withdrawal reflex. By stimulating and recording from one of these mechanosensory neurons and simultaneously recording from a gill motor neuron, we finally were able to reduce the gill reflex to its most elementary monosynaptic components and to examine the two cells in turn as well as their interaction [*see upper illustration on opposite page*].

Stimulation of one of the mechanoreceptor neurons produced a fairly large elementary EPSP in the motor neuron. Repeated stimulation produced a dramatic decrease in the amplitude of the potential; as in the case of stimulation of the skin, the potential produced by direct stimulation of the sensory neuron sometimes diminished so markedly that after a few stimuli it was barely visible. Rest led to recovery [*see lower illustration on opposite page*]. These data make it very unlikely that inhibition is involved and suggest that decrement of the EPSP is due to a plastic change in excitatory synaptic efficacy. This could result from either a decrease in the amount of transmitter released with each impulse or a decrease in the sensitivity of the postsynaptic receptor sites.

Dishabituation, the facilitation of a decreased response that occurs when a strong new stimulus is applied to another part of the receptive field, has also been studied in the isolated ganglion. We found that an EPSP that had decreased through habituation could be restored by a strong stimulus to the right or left connective nerve, which carry fibers from the head ganglia; at times the facilitated synaptic potential was even larger than it had been before habituation. In studies of the individual mechanoreceptor neurons we found that the dishabituation took place without a change in the fre-

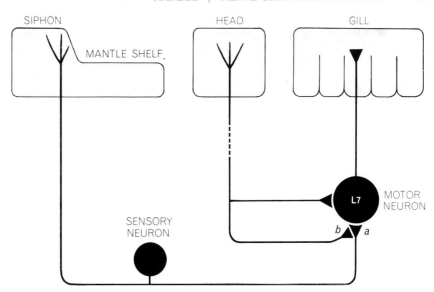

PROPOSED WIRING DIAGRAM for the elementary withdrawal reflex does not involve inhibition. The plastic change of habituation occurs at the excitatory synapse between sensory and motor neuron (*a*). Stimulation of head causes dishabituation, apparently by acting presynaptically at the synapse (*b*), increasing transmitter release from sensory terminals.

quency of firing of the sensory neuron [*see lower illustration on opposite page*]. This excludes posttetanic potentiation as a mechanism for the facilitation and suggests that dishabituation involves a heterosynaptic (presynaptic) facilitation.

As in the case of the gill-withdrawal reflex in the intact animal, the elementary monosynaptic EPSP's produced by individual sensory neurons had many of the accepted characteristics of habituation and dishabituation: (1) decrement with repeated stimulation; (2) recovery with rest; (3) facilitation following a strong stimulus to another pathway; (4) decrement of the facilitatory effect with repetition; (5) greater decrement with short rather than with long interstimulus intervals. (We have not examined the effects of the sixth variable, stimulus intensity, on the elementary EPSP.)

The Wiring Diagram

We can now propose a simplified circuit diagram to illustrate the locus and mechanism of the various plastic changes that accompany habituation and dishabituation of the gill-withdrawal reflex [*see illustration above*]. The motor neuron is *L7*, on which the work with the elementary EPSP was done. Repetitive stimulation of sensory receptors leads to habituation by producing a plastic change at the synapse between the sensory neuron and the motor neuron. The exact mechanism of the synaptic change is uncertain. We still cannot exclude a change in receptor sensitivity

but, by analogy with the brief low-frequency synaptic depression analyzed in detail in vertebrate and crayfish neuromuscular junctions, we tend to think the decrement of the elementary EPSP represents a decrease in the release of excitatory transmitter from the presynaptic terminal. Unlike the brief low-frequency depression, however, the decrement in the habituation pathway is remarkably large and prolonged. These features suggest that perhaps additional elements operate in synapses of the habituatory pathway. Stimulation of the head leads to dishabituation by producing heterosynaptic facilitation at the same synapse. This facilitation appears to operate presynaptically, perhaps by enhancing the release of transmitter substance.

We have used the monosynaptic pathway between the mechanoreceptor neurons and one of the motor neurons (*L7*) as a model for studying the total reflex. Comparable experiments with monosynaptic inputs still need to be done on other gill motor neurons and on the polysynaptic pathway in order to account quantitatively for the complete behavioral modifications. It is clear already that the unhabituated elementary EPSP's produced by a single spike in individual sensory neurons are relatively large and often trigger an action potential in the motor neuron. In addition there are at least 10 such sensory neurons that synapse on the motor neuron. It therefore seems likely that a substantial portion of the total EPSP in the gill motor neuron *L7* is due to the monosynaptic EPSP's from mechanoreceptor neurons. Furthermore, the spike activity of $L7$ contributes a substantial part of the total gill contraction. Since changes in the spike activity of the motor neuron $L7$ are directly produced by changes in EPSP amplitude, a substantial part of the habituation and dishabituation of the early component of the withdrawal reflex can be explained by alterations in the efficacy of excitatory synapses between the sensory and the motor neurons. Indeed, if similar processes occur on the other motor neurons and on the interneurons, these mechanisms could explain all the habituation and dishabituation.

Our data lead to some more general conclusions. First, habituation and dishabituation appear to involve a change in the functional effectiveness of previously existing excitatory connections. In these simple cases, at least, it therefore seems unnecessary to explain the behavioral modifications by invoking the growth of new connections or dynamic activity in a group of cells. The capability for behavioral modification seems to be built directly into the neural architecture of the behavioral reflex. Since the architecture is redundant and distributed, the capability for modification is redundant and distributed too.

Second, although a number of investigators have postulated on the basis of indirect evidence that habituation involves active inhibition, in *Aplysia*, where a major component of the synaptic mechanism of habituation can be studied directly, neither presynaptic nor postsynaptic inhibition appears to be critically involved.

Third, these experiments indicate that habituation and dishabituation are separate processes and that dishabituation is not merely an interruption of the decrease associated with habituation but an independent facilitatory process superimposed on the habituation. (Seen in this perspective, dishabituation is essentially a special case of quasi-conditioning.) Although habituation and dishabituation are independent, they do not involve different neurons with overlapping fields of action. Rather, the two processes appear to represent two independent regulatory mechanisms acting at the same synapse.

Finally, these studies strengthen the assumption that a prerequisite for studying behavioral modification is understanding the neural circuit underlying the behavior. Once the wiring diagram of the behavior is known, analysis of its modifications is simplified. The same strategy may be applicable to biochemical studies of learning that will eventually describe its mechanisms at a molecular level.

More Complex Behaviors

Studies of habituation of defensive reflexes in the cat and in *Aplysia* span six decades of research, but they represent only a small beginning; we are still far from understanding the neuronal mechanism of long-term memory and of higher learning. It would seem nevertheless that cellular approaches directed toward working out the wiring diagram of behavioral responses can now be applied to more complex learning processes. I have here considered only reflexive behaviors. Animals also display a wide variety of instinctive behaviors, or "fixed-action patterns," that are sometimes triggered by sensory stimuli but that do not require sensory information for the patterning of their behavioral sequence.

For example, in addition to its role in reflex withdrawal, the gill of *Aplysia* participates in a spontaneous withdrawal sequence that has the properties of a fixed-action pattern: it is centrally generated and highly stereotyped, and it occurs in almost identical form in the absence of sensory input in the completely isolated ganglion. Kupfermann, Waziri and I (and more recently Bertram Peretz at the University of Kentucky Medical School) have specified parts of the wiring diagram of this behavior, and it is already apparent that it is different from the reflex withdrawal and considerably more complex; it involves one or more as yet unidentified pattern-generating neurons. An even more complex fixed-action pattern, an escape response consisting of several sequential stereotypically patterned movements, occurs in *Tritonia*, a mollusk closely related to *Aplysia*. A. O. D. Willows of the University of Washington is well on the way toward providing a wiring diagram of even this higher order of instinctive behavior. It may therefore soon be possible to contrast the neural organization of several reflexive and instinctive behaviors in closely related mollusks. If the instinctive behaviors prove to be modifiable, it may then be possible to compare the mechanisms involved in the modification of reflexive and instinctive behaviors.

It would be unrealistic to expect soon a complete set of solutions to as varied and deep a set of problems as learning presents. The pace has quickened, however, and neurobiology may soon provide increasingly complete analyses of progressively more complex instances of learning.

28

Brain Changes in Response to Experience

by Mark R. Rosenzweig, Edward L. Bennett
and Marian Cleeves Diamond
February 1972

*Rats kept in a lively environment for 30 days show
distinct changes in brain anatomy and chemistry
compared with animals kept in a dull environment.
The implications of these effects for man are assessed*

Does experience produce any observable change in the brain? The hypothesis that changes occur in brain anatomy as a result of experience is an old one, but convincing evidence of such changes has been found only in the past decade. It has now been shown that placing an experimental animal in enriched or impoverished environments causes measurable changes in brain anatomy and chemistry. How these changes are related to learning and memory mechanisms is currently being studied by an interdisciplinary approach that involves neurochemical, neuroanatomical and behavioral techniques.

The earliest scientific account of brain changes as a result of experience that we have been able to find was written in the 1780's by an Italian anatomist, Michele Gaetano Malacarne. His experimental design is worth describing briefly, since it resembles the one we are using in our laboratory at the University of California at Berkeley. He worked with two dogs from the same litter and with two parrots, two goldfinches and two blackbirds, each pair of birds from the same clutch of eggs. He trained one member of each pair for a long period; the other member of the pair was left untrained. He then killed the animals and examined their brains. He reported that there were more folds in the cerebellum of the trained animals than in that of the untrained ones. Although his study was noted by some of his contemporaries, we have not found any evidence that others attempted to carry out similar experiments. Knowledge of Malacarne's experiment quickly faded away.

During the 19th century there was considerable interest in the relation between the size of the human head and intellectual ability and training. In the 1870's Paul Broca, a famous French physician and anthropologist, compared the head circumference of medical students and male nurses and found that the students had larger heads. Since he believed the two sets of young men were equal in ability, he concluded that the differences in head size must have been due to the differences in training. Clearly Broca's logic was not impeccable, and there are other possible explanations for the differences he found. His critics pointed to the lack of correspondence between skull size and brain volume, the important roles of age and body size in determining brain size and the relative stability of the size of the brain in comparison with the size of most other organs. By the beginning of the 20th century not only had experimenters failed to prove that training resulted in changes in the gross anatomy of the brain but also a consensus had developed that such changes could not be detected, and so the search was generally abandoned.

With the development of new biochemical tools and techniques in the 1950's, some investigators began to ask if chemical changes in the brain following training could be detected. They looked for changes at the synapses that transmit impulses from one nerve cell to another or for changes in the nucleic acids (RNA and DNA) of nerve cells. The techniques used to find chemical or anatomical changes in the brain following experience are not difficult in principle but they must be carried out with precision because many of the changes that occur are not large. Here is how a basic experiment is conducted with laboratory rats of a given strain. (In our experiments we have worked with several strains of rats and with laboratory mice and gerbils; we have observed similar effects in all these animals.) At a given age, often at weaning, sets of three males are taken from each litter. Usually

a dozen sets of three males are used in an experiment. This yields stabler and more reliable results than working with a single set, as Malacarne did.

The use of rodents for these studies is convenient for several reasons. Brain dissection is simpler in rodents than it is in carnivores or primates because the cerebral cortex of rodents is smooth and not convoluted like the cortex of higher mammals. The gray cortex can be stripped away from the underlying white matter more readily in rodents than it can in higher mammals. Rodents are small, inexpensive and bear large litters, so that littermates with the same genetic background can be assigned to different conditions. In addition, geneticists have developed inbred lines of rats and mice, and working with these inbred lines gives us further control over the genetic background.

The three male rats from each litter are assigned at random so that one rat remains in the standard laboratory colony cage, one rat is placed in an enriched environment and the third is put in an impoverished environment. It should be noted that "enriched" and "impoverished" are not used in an absolute sense but only in relation to the standard laboratory colony environment that is the usual baseline for studies in anatomy, biochemistry, physiology, nutrition and behavior.

In the standard laboratory conditions a few rats live in a cage of adequate size with food and water always present [see *illustration on following page*]. In the enriched environment several rats live in a large cage furnished with a variety of objects they can play with. A new set of playthings, drawn out of a pool of 25 objects, is placed in the cage every day. In the impoverished environment each rat lives alone in a cage. Originally the isolated rats were kept in a separate quiet room, but this turned out to be unnecessary.

At the end of a predetermined experimental period, which can be from a few days to several months, the rats are sacrificed and their brains are removed. The brain dissection and analysis of each set of three littermates are done in immediate succession but in a random order and identified only by code number so that the person doing the dissection does not know which cage the rat comes from. With practice a skillful worker can do dissections with considerable precision and reliability. To delineate the various cortical regions a small plastic calibrated T square is used [*see illustration on page 296*]. Samples removed from a cortical region are weighed to the nearest tenth of a milligram and then placed on dry ice. The samples are kept frozen until chemical analysis is performed to determine the activity of the neurotransmitter enzymes in them.

If the rat brains are to be used for anatomical studies, the animal is anesthetized and perfused with a fixative solution. Later sections of the brain are prepared for microscopy.

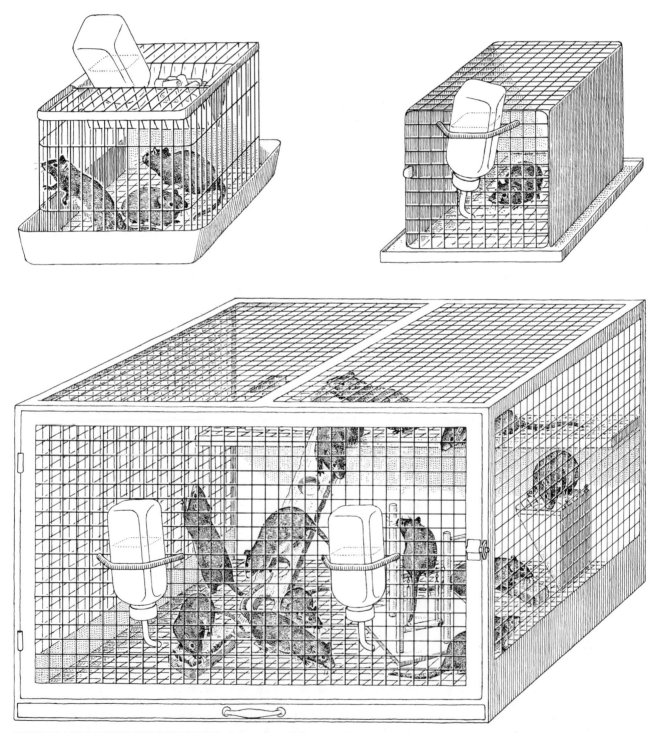

THREE LABORATORY ENVIRONMENTS that produce differences in brain anatomy of littermate rats are depicted. In the standard laboratory colony there are usually three rats in a cage (*upper left*). In the impoverished environment (*upper right*) a rat is kept alone in a cage. In the enriched environment 12 rats live together in a large cage furnished with playthings that are changed daily. Food and water are freely available in all three environments. The rats typically remain in the same environment for 30 days or more.

In the 1950's we had been attempting to relate individual differences in the problem-solving behavior of rats to individual differences in the amount of the enzyme acetylcholinesterase in the brain. (At the time and until 1966 the psychologist David Krech was a member of the research group.) The enzyme rapidly breaks down acetylcholine, a substance that acts as a transmitter between nerve cells. The excess transmitter must be neutralized quickly because nerve impulses can follow each other at a rate of hundreds per second. This enzymatic activity is often measured in terms of tissue weight, and so in our early experiments we recorded the weight of each sample of brain tissue we took for chemical analysis. We found indications that the level of brain acetylcholinesterase was altered by problem-solving tests, and this led us to look for effects of more extensive experience. To our surprise we found that different experiences not only affected the enzymatic activity but also altered the weight of the brain samples.

By 1964 we had found that rats that had spent from four to 10 weeks in the enriched or the impoverished environments differed in the following ways: rats with enriched experience had a greater weight of cerebral cortex, a greater thickness of cortex and a greater total activity of acetylcholinesterase but less activity of the enzyme per unit of tissue weight. Moreover, rats with enriched experience had considerably greater activity of another enzyme: cholinesterase, which is found in the glial cells and blood capillaries that surround the nerve cells. Glial cells (named from the Greek word for "glue") perform a variety of functions, including transportation of materials between capillaries and nerve cells, formation of the fatty insulating sheath around the neural axons and removal of dead neural tissue.

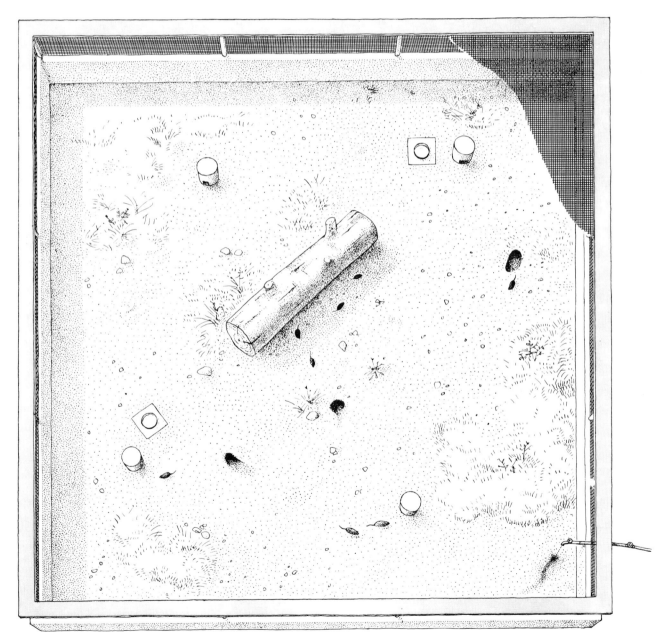

SEMINATURAL ENVIRONMENT for studying the effects of experience on the brain is provided by outdoor enclosures at the Field Station for Research in Animal Behavior at the University of California at Berkeley. The enclosures have a concrete base 30 feet by 30 feet with a screen over the top. Inbred laboratory rats thrive in the outdoor setting when food and water are provided. The rats revert to burrowing, something that their ancestors, which had lived in laboratory cages, had not done for more than 100 generations.

We later found that there were more glial cells in rats from the enriched environment than there were in rats from the impoverished one, and this may account for the increased activity of cholinesterase. Although differences in experience did not change the number of nerve cells per unit of tissue, the enriched environment produced larger cell bodies and nuclei. These larger cell bodies indicate higher metabolic activity. Further chemical measures involving RNA and DNA pointed in the same direction. The amount of DNA per milligram of tissue decreased, presumably because the bulk of the cortex increased as the number of neurons, whose nuclei contain a fixed amount of DNA, remained relatively constant. The amount of RNA per milligram remained virtually unchanged, yielding a significant increase in the ratio of RNA to DNA, and this suggests a higher metabolic activity. In most of the experiments the greatest differences between enriched and impoverished experience were found in the occipital cortex, which is roughly the rear third of the cortical surface.

We do not know why the occipital region of the cortex is affected by enriched experience more than other regions. At first we thought that differences in visual stimulation might be responsible, but when we used blinded rats, the occipital cortex still showed significant differences between littermates from the enriched and the impoverished environments. We found the same effects when normal rats were placed in the different environments and kept in darkness for the entire period. This is not to say that deprivation of vision did not have an effect on the anatomy and chemistry of the brain. The occipital cortex of rats that were blinded or kept totally in the dark gained less weight than the occipital cortex of littermates that were raised in standard colony conditions with a normal light-dark cycle, but this did not prevent the occurrence of the enrichment-impoverishment effect.

Although the brain differences induced by environment are not large, we are confident that they are genuine. When the experiments are replicated, the same pattern of differences is found repeatedly. For example, in 16 replications between 1960 and 1969 of the basic enriched-environment-v.-impoverished-environment experiment, using the same strain of rat exposed to the experimental conditions from the age of 25 to 105 days, each experiment resulted in a greater occipital-cortex weight for the rats in the enriched environment. Twelve

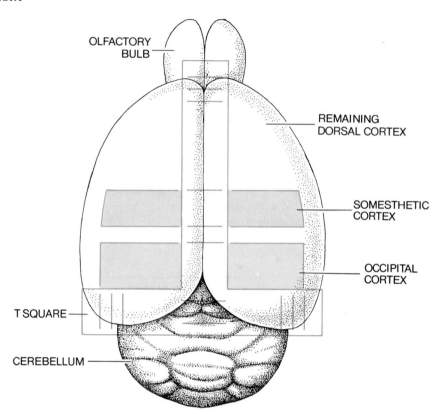

CORTICAL AREAS of a rat brain are located for dissection with the aid of a calibrated plastic T square to ensure uniform samples. The desired sections are removed, weighed and stored on dry ice. The remaining cortex and the subcortex also are weighed and frozen.

of the 16 replications were significantly at better than the .05 level, that is, for each of the 12 experiments there was less than one chance in 20 that the difference was due simply to chance or biological variability. For weight of the total cortex, 13 of the 16 experiments showed significant differences [see top illustration on opposite page].

The most consistent effect of experience on the brain that we found was the ratio of the weight of the cortex to the weight of the rest of the brain: the subcortex. It appears that the cortex increases in weight quite readily in response to an enriched environment, whereas the weight of the rest of the brain changes little. Moreover, since rats with larger bodies tend to have both a heavier cortex and a heavier subcortex than smaller rats, the ratio of the cortex to the rest of the brain tends to cancel the influence of body weight. For animals of a given strain, sex, age and environment the cortex/subcortex ratio tends to be the same even if the animals differ in body weight. When the environment is such that the cortex grows, the cortex/subcortex ratio shows the change very clearly and reliably. On this measure 14 of the 16 experiments were significant at the .01 level.

One of the major problems for mea-

suring the effects of experience on the brain is finding an appropriate baseline. Initially we took the standard laboratory colony condition as the baseline, as most other investigators have. The cortex/subcortex-weight ratio in rats from the enriched environment is greater than the ratio in rats from the standard colony environment, and this ratio in turn is greater than the ratio in rats from the impoverished environment. Where thickness of cortex is concerned, both environmental enrichment and impoverishment are effective but on different regions of the cortex.

Suppose that the natural environment in which the animals evolved were taken as the baseline. Compared with the laboratory environments, even the enriched one, a natural environment may be much richer in learning experiences. For inbred laboratory animals, however, it is no longer clear what the natural environment is. Laboratory rats and mice have been kept for more than 100 generations in protected environments, and inbreeding has made their gene pool different from the natural one. For this reason we have begun to study wild deer mice (*Peromyscus*). The mice are trapped in the San Francisco area and brought to our laboratory; some are kept in almost

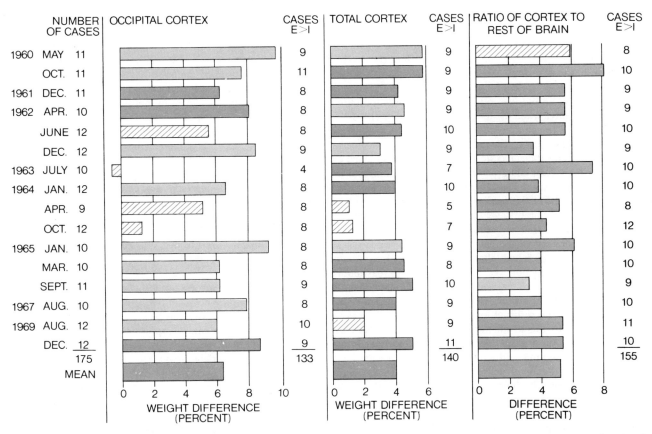

BRAIN-WEIGHT DIFFERENCES between rats from enriched environments and their littermates from impoverished environments were replicated in 16 successive experiments between 1960 and 1969 involving an 80-day period and the same strain of rat. For the occipital cortex, weight differences in three of the replications were significant at the probability level of .01 or better (*dark colored bars*), nine were significant at the .05 level (*light colored bars*) and four were not significant (*hatched bars*). The ratio of the weight of the cortex to the rest of the brain proved to be the most reliable measure, with 14 of the 16 replications significant at the .01 level.

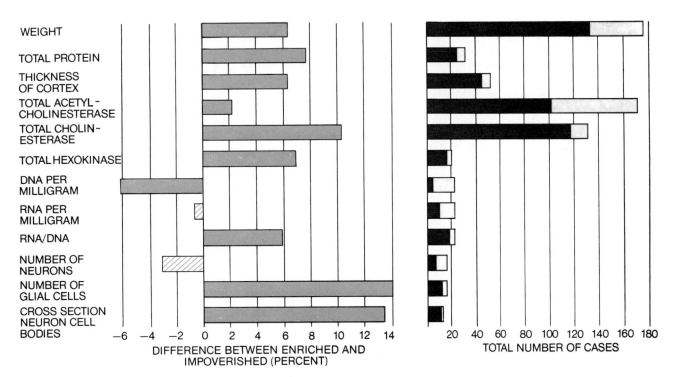

OCCIPITAL CORTEX of rats kept in enriched or impoverished environments from 25 to 105 days showed the effects of the different experiences. The occipital cortex of rats from the enriched environment, compared with that of rats from the impoverished one, was 6.4 percent heavier. This was significant at the .01 level or better, as were most other measures (*dark colored bars*). Only two measures were not significant (*hatched bars*). The dark gray bars on the right show the number of cases in which the rat from the enriched environment exceeded its littermate from the impoverished environment in each of the measures that are listed.

natural conditions at an outdoor station and others are put into laboratory cages. The work with deer mice is still in progress, but we have also placed laboratory rats in the outdoor setting. We found that when food is provided, laboratory rats can thrive in an outdoor enclosure even in a wet winter when the temperature drops to the freezing point. When the ground was not too wet, the rats dug burrows, something their ancestors had not done for more than 100 generations. In each of eight experiments the rats kept for one month in the outdoor setting showed a greater brain development than their littermates that had been kept in enriched laboratory cages. This indicates that even the enriched laboratory environment is indeed impoverished in comparison with a natural environment.

It is possible that the brain changes we found are not the result of learning and memory but are due to other aspects of the experimental situation, such as the amount of handling and stress, or perhaps an altered rate of maturation. For example, simply handling rats, particularly young ones, is known to increase the weight of their adrenal glands. Rats in the enriched environment are handled each day when they are removed from their cage while their playthings are being changed, whereas rats in the impoverished environment are handled only once a week for weighing. We tested the effects of handling on brain changes some years ago. Some rats were handled for several minutes a day for either 30 or 60 days; their littermates were never handled. There were no differences between the handled rats and the nonhandled ones in brain weight or brain-enzyme activity. More recently rats from both the enriched and the impoverished environments were handled once a day and the usual brain differences developed.

Stress was another possible cause of the cerebral effects. Rats from the impoverished environment might have suffered from "isolation stress" and rats from the enriched environment may have been stressed by "information overload." To test this notion Walter H. Riege subjected rats to a daily routine of stress. The rats were briefly tumbled in a revolving drum or given a mild electric shock. The stress produced a significant increase in the weight of the adrenal glands but did not give rise to changes in the brain measures that we use. It seems clear that stress is not responsible for the cerebral changes we have found.

It was also possible, since some of the brain changes we have found go in the same direction as changes that occur in normal maturation, that enriched experience simply accelerates maturation or that isolation retards it. Changes in the depth of the cerebral cortex and certain other changes resulting from an enriched environment go in the opposite direction to what is found in normal growth. The cortical thickness of standard colony rats reaches a maximum at 25 days after birth and then decreases slightly with age, whereas enriched experience causes cortical thickness to increase even in year-old rats. In fact, Riege has found that an enriched environment will produce as great an increase in brain weight in fully mature rats as it does in young rats, although the adult rats require a longer period of environmental stimulation to show the maximum effect.

The effect of enriched environment on very young rats has been tested by Dennis Malkasian. He puts sets of three litters of six-day-old rat pups and their mother either into an unfurnished cage or into a cage containing play objects. Brains were taken for anatomical analysis at 14, 19 and 28 days of age. At each age pups from the enriched environment showed a greater thickness of cerebral cortex, and in some parts of the cortex the differences were larger than those found in experiments with rats examined after weaning.

When we first reported our results other investigators were understandably skeptical, since the effect of experience on the brain had not been previously demonstrated. After our findings had been replicated, some investigators began to think that the brain may be so plastic that almost any treatment can modify it, for example merely placing a rat for 15 minutes a day in any apparatus other than its home cage. This does not happen; although cerebral changes are easier to induce than we had supposed at first, a moderate amount of experience is still necessary. We recently demonstrated that two hours of daily enriched experience over a 30-day period is sufficient to produce the typical changes in brain weight. On the other hand, placing a group of 12 rats in a large unfurnished cage for two hours a day for 30 days did not bring about significant changes in our usual brain measures. Moreover, putting rats alone in large cages with play objects for two hours a day is not very effective, probably because a single rat does not play with the objects much and tends to rest or to groom itself. The enriched environment will produce cerebral changes in a single rat if the rat is stimulated to interact with the objects. This can be done by giving the rat a moderate dose of an excitant drug or by putting it into the enriched environment during the dark part of its daily cycle (rats are nocturnal animals). A recent experiment indicates that cerebral changes can also be achieved by putting the rat into the enriched environment after several hours of food deprivation and placing tiny pellets of food on and in the play objects.

There can now be no doubt that many aspects of brain anatomy and brain chemistry are changed by experience. Some of our most recent efforts have been directed toward determining the changes that occur at the synaptic level in the occipital cortex, a region of the brain that shows relatively large changes with experience in enriched environments. Over the past few years Albert Globus of the University of California at Irvine has been counting the number of dendritic spines in brain sections from rats that have been exposed to an enriched environment or an impoverished one in our laboratory. Most of the synaptic contacts between nerve cells in the cortex are made on the branchlike dendrites of the receiving cell or on the dendritic spines, which are small projections from the dendrites. Globus made his counts on the cortical neuron called a pyramidal cell [see top illustration on opposite page]. He found more spines, particularly on the basal dendrites, in rats exposed to an enriched environment than in littermates from the impoverished environment.

An even more detailed view of changes in the synaptic junctions has come out of a study we have done in collaboration with Kjeld Møllgaard of the University of Copenhagen, who spent a year in our laboratory. He prepared electron micrographs of brain sections from the third layer of the occipital cortex of rats. Measurement of the synaptic junctions revealed that rats from enriched environments had junctions that averaged approximately 50 percent larger in cross section than similar junctions in littermates from impoverished environments. The latter, however, had more synapses per unit area [see illustration on page 300].

William T. Greenough, Roger West and T. Blaise Fleischmann of the University of Illinois have also found that there is increased synaptic contact in enriched-experience rats. Some other workers have reported that increased size of synapse is associated with a decreased number of synapses, whereas decreased size of synapse is associated with an increased number. It seems that memory or learning may be encoded in the brain either by the selective addition of contacts between nerve cells or by the selective removal of contacts, and that both processes may go on at the same time.

Does an enriched environment or an impoverished environment alter learning ability? Although some studies suggest that experience in an enriched environment usually improves subsequent learning, the effects are often short-lived. The result depends on many factors, for example the measure of learning that is used, the age at which the enriched experience is provided and the type of task that is learned. Early enrichment may improve subsequent learning of one task, have no effect on another task and actually impair learning in a third. Perhaps we should not expect much transfer of capacity among entirely different kinds of behavior. Nor should we expect experience in an enriched environment to lead to an increase in "general ability"; every environment is specific and so are abilities. Harry F. Harlow of the University of Wisconsin has shown that early problem-solving in monkeys may have the deleterious effect of fixating infantile behavior patterns; such monkeys may never reach the efficient adult performance that they would have attained without the early training. Again, this result is specific and should be generalized only with caution.

Formal training of rats, such as teaching them to press a lever in response to a signal or to run a maze, produces changes in brain anatomy and chemistry, but the type of training seems to determine the kind of changes. Victor Fedorov and his associates at the Pavlov Institute of Physiology near Leningrad found changes in brain weight and in the activity of acetylcholinesterase and cholinesterase after prolonged training of rats, but the pattern of changes is different from what we found with enriched and impoverished environments. In our laboratory we have given rats daily formal training in either operant-conditioning devices or in a series of mazes for a month or more and have found changes in brain weight and brain enzymes. These changes, however, were rather small and also had a pattern different from the changes induced by environmental experience. This is clearly a problem that requires more research.

The effect of experimental environments on the brains of animals has sometimes been cited as bearing on problems of human education. We should like to sound a cautionary note in this regard. It is difficult to extrapolate from an

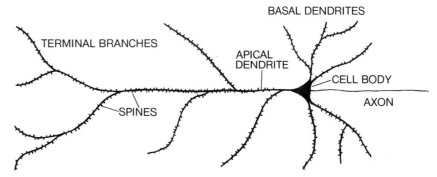

DENDRITIC SPINES, tiny "thorns," or projections, from the dendrites of a nerve cell, serve as receivers in many of the synaptic contacts between neurons. The drawing is of a type of cortical neuron known as the pyramidal cell. Rats from an enriched environment have more spines on these cells than their littermates from an impoverished environment.

experiment with rats under one set of conditions to the behavior of rats under another set of conditions, and it is much riskier to extrapolate from a rat to a mouse to a monkey to a human. We have found generally similar brain changes as a result of experience in several species of rodents, and this appears to have fostered the assumption that similar results may be found with carnivores and with primates, including man. Only further research will show whether or not this is so. Animal research raises questions and allows us to test concepts and techniques, some of which may later prove useful in research with human subjects.

If this research leads to knowledge of how memories are stored in the brain, it will have obvious implications for the study of conditions that favor learning

and memory and also of conditions that impair learning and the laying down of memories. Among the unfavorable conditions that are of great social concern are mental retardation and senile decline in ability to form new memories. Clues to the prevention or amelioration of these conditions could be of great social value. Let us also consider two other areas into which such research on brain plasticity may extend.

One of these areas concerns the effects of malnutrition on the development of the brain and of intelligence. Some investigators, such as R. H. Barnes and David A. Levitsky of the Cornell University Graduate School of Nutrition, have proposed that certain effects of malnutrition may actually be secondary effects of environmental impoverishment. That is,

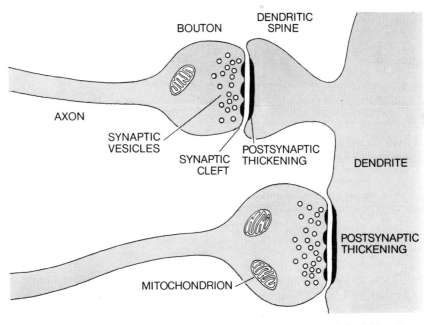

SYNAPTIC JUNCTIONS between nerve cells can be between axon and dendritic spine or between axon and the dendrite itself. The vesicles contain a chemical transmitter that is released when an electrical signal from the axon reaches the end bouton. The transmitter moves across the synaptic cleft and stimulates the postsynaptic receptor sites in the dendrite. The size of the postsynaptic membrane is thought to be an indicator of synaptic activity.

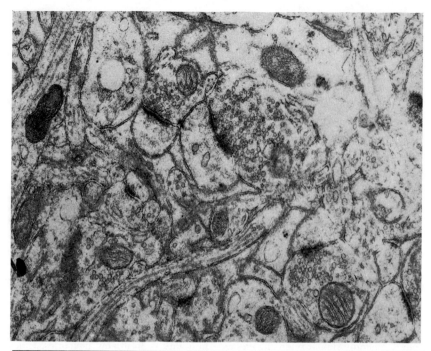

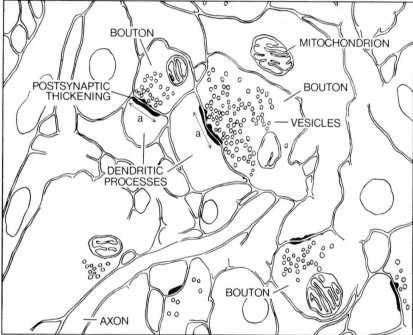

BRAIN SECTION from the occipital cortex of a rat is enlarged 37,000 times in this electron micrograph by Kjeld Møllgaard. The map identifies some of the components. Measurement of the postsynaptic thickening is shown in the map of the section by the arrow (*a*). The number of synaptic junctions was also counted. It was found that rats reared in an enriched environment had junctions approximately 50 percent larger than littermates from an impoverished environment, and the latter had more junctions, although smaller ones, per unit area.

cation on the postmortem examination of the brain of a blind deaf-mute, Laura Bridgman. It was found that the parts of her cortex that were involved in vision and hearing were thin and lacked the pattern of folding found in the normal human brain. In contrast, the region of her cortex devoted to touch had a normal appearance. It would be of interest to see if such results could be generalized by a large-scale modern postmortem study of brains of people who had been deprived of one or more senses. It would be even more interesting to find out if heightened employment of a sense leads to supranormal development of the associated brain region. Would musicians as a group, for example, show an enhanced development of the auditory cortex?

The human brain, because of the specialization of the two cerebral hemispheres, is more likely to provide answers to such questions than animal brains. Spoken words are analyzed in the auditory region of the left cerebral hemisphere, whereas music is analyzed in the auditory region of the right hemisphere. (These hemispheric functions are reversed in a few people.) The relative development of different regions in the same brain could be measured, so that the subjects would be their own control. In recent investigations Norman Geschwind and Walter Levitsky of the Harvard Medical School have found that 65 percent of the human brains they examined showed a greater anatomical development of the auditory area in the left hemisphere, 11 percent showed a greater auditory development in the right hemisphere and 24 percent showed equal development on the two sides. On the other hand, behavioral and physiological tests indicate that 96 percent of the people tested have left-hemisphere speech dominance and presumably have a greater development of the auditory area on that side. Is it possible that people with musical training account for most of the cases in which size of the right auditory area equals or exceeds the size of the left? In order to find out investigators will have to measure sufficient numbers of brains of individuals whose major abilities and disabilities are known. In fact, such a program was proposed 100 years ago by Broca, but the techniques available then were not adequate to carrying out the project. Today the results of our animal studies can serve as a guide, and investigators can look more penetratingly for the anatomical and chemical changes in the human brain that are correlated with experience and learning.

since a prominent effect of malnutrition is to make the person or animal apathetic and unresponsive to the environment, the individual then suffers from lack of stimulation, and this may be the direct cause of some of the symptoms usually associated with malnutrition. Current research suggests that some of the effects of malnutrition may be offset by programs of environmental stimula-

tion or increased by environmental impoverishment.

Another possibly beneficial result of our research findings would be to stimulate a resurgence of attempts to determine relations between experience and brain anatomy in man. This was a topic of some interest late in the 19th century, and a number of reports were published. For example, in 1892 there was a publi-

29

Memory and Protein Synthesis

by Bernard W. Agranoff
June 1967

*If a goldfish is trained to perform a simple task
and shortly thereafter a substance that blocks the
manufacture of protein is injected into its skull,
it forgets what it has been taught*

What is the mechanism of memory? The question has not yet been answered, but the kind of evidence needed to answer it has slowly been accumulating. One important fact that has emerged is that there are two types of memory: short-term and long-term. To put it another way, the process of learning is different from the process of memory-storage; what is learned must somehow be fixed or consolidated before it can be remembered. For example, people who have received shock treatment in the course of psychiatric care report that they cannot remember experiences they had immediately before the treatment. It is as though the shock treatment had disrupted the process of

consolidating their memory of the experiences.

In our laboratory at the University of Michigan we have demonstrated that there is a connection between the consolidation of memory and the manufacture of protein in the brain. Our experimental animal is the common goldfish (*Carassius auratus*). Basically what we do is train a large number of goldfish to perform a simple task and at various times before, during and after the training inject into their skulls a substance that interferes with the synthesis of protein. Then we observe the effect of the injections on the goldfish's performance.

Why seek a connection between memory and protein synthesis? For one thing,

enzymes are proteins, and enzymes catalyze all the chemical reactions of life. It would seem reasonable to expect that memory, like all other life processes, is dependent on enzyme-catalyzed reactions. What is perhaps more to the point, the manufacture of new enzymes is characteristic of long-term changes in living organisms, such as growth and the differentiation of cells in the embryo. And long-term memory is by definition a long-term change.

The investigation of a connection between memory and protein synthesis is made possible by the profound advances in knowledge of protein synthesis that have come in the past 10 years. A molecule of protein is made from 20 differ-

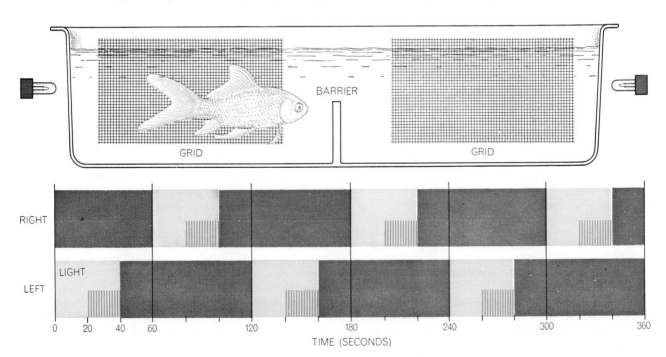

TRAINING TANK the author used was designed so that goldfish learned to swim from the light end to the dark end. A learning trial began with the illumination of the left end of the tank (*chart at bottom*), followed after a pause by mild electric shocks (*colored vertical lines*) from grids at that end. At first a fish would swim over the central barrier in response to shock; then increasingly the fish came to respond to light cue alone as sequence of light, shock and darkness was alternately repeated at each end of the tank.

1   2   3

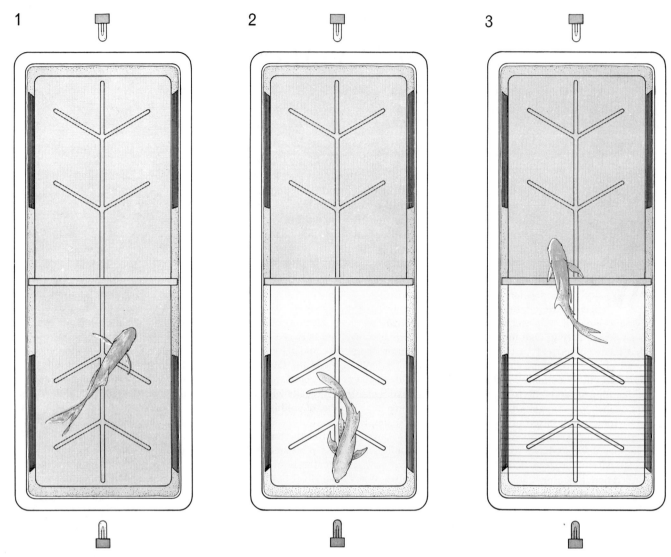

GOLDFISH LEARN in successive trials to solve the problem the shuttle box presents. Following 20 seconds of darkness (1) the end of the box where the fish is swimming is lighted for an equal period of time (2). The fish fails to respond, swimming over the barrier

ent kinds of amino acid molecule, strung together in a polypeptide chain. The stringing is done in the small bodies in the living cell called ribosomes. Each amino acid molecule is brought to the ribosome by a molecule of transfer RNA, a form of ribonucleic acid. The instructions according to which the amino acids are linked in a specific sequence are brought to the ribosome by another form of ribonucleic acid: messenger RNA. These instructions have been transcribed by the messenger RNA from deoxyribonucleic acid (DNA), the cell's central library of information.

With this much knowledge of protein synthesis one can begin to think of examining the process by interfering with it in selective ways. Such interference can be accomplished with antibiotics. Whereas some substances that interfere with the machinery of the cell, such as cyanide, are quite general in their ef-

fects, antibiotics can be highly selective. Indeed, some of them block only one step in cellular metabolism. As an example, the antibiotic puromycin simply stops the growth of the polypeptide chain in the ribosome. This it does by virtue of the fact that its molecule resembles one end of the transfer RNA molecule with an amino acid attached to it. Accordingly the puromycin molecule is joined to the growing end of the polypeptide chain and blocks its further growth. The truncated chain is released attached to the puromycin molecule.

Numerous workers have had the idea of using agents such as puromycin to block protein synthesis in animals and then observing the effects on the animals' behavior. Among them have been C. Wesley Dingman II and M. B. Sporn of the National Institutes of Health, who injected 8-azaguanine into rats; T. J. Chamberlain, G. H. Rothschild and

Ralph W. Gerard of the University of Michigan, who administered the same substance to rats, and Josefa B. Flexner, Louis B. Flexner and Eliot Stellar of the University of Pennsylvania, who injected puromycin into mice. Such experiments encouraged us to try our hand with the goldfish.

We chose the goldfish for our experiments because it is readily available and can be accommodated in the laboratory in large numbers. Moreover, a simple and automatically controlled training task for goldfish had already been developed by M. E. Bitterman of Bryn Mawr College. One might wonder if a fish has such a thing as long-term memory; in the opinion of numerous psychologists and anglers there can be no doubt of it.

Our training apparatus is called a shuttle box. It is an oblong plastic tank

4   **5**   **6**

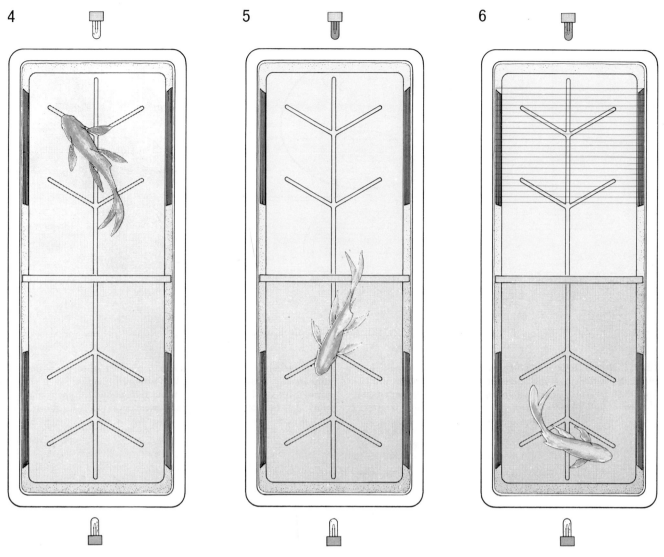

only after the shock period heralded by light has begun (*3*). When the same events are repeated at the other end of the box (*4, 5 and 6*), the fish shown here succeeds in crossing the barrier during the 20 seconds of light that precede the period of intermittent shock.

divided into two compartments by a barrier that comes to within an inch of the water surface [*see illustration on page 301*]. At each end of the box is a light that can be turned on and off. On opposite sides of each compartment are grids by means of which the fish can be given a mild electric shock through the water.

The task to be learned by the fish is that when it is in one compartment and the light goes on at that end of the box, it should swim over the barrier into the other compartment. In our initial experiments we left the fish in the dark for five minutes and then gave it five one-minute trials. Each trial consisted in (1) turning on the light at the fish's end of the box, (2) 20 seconds later intermittently turning on the shocking grids and (3) 20 seconds after that turning off both the shocking grids and the light. If the fish crossed the barrier into the other

compartment during the first 20 seconds, it *avoided* the shock; if it crossed the barrier during the second 20 seconds, it *escaped* the shock.

An untrained goldfish almost always escaped the shock, that is, it swam across the barrier only when the shock began. Whether the fish escaped the shock or avoided it, it crossed the barrier into the other compartment. Then, after 20 seconds of darkness, the light at that end was turned on to start the second trial. Thus the fish shuttled back and forth with each trial. If a fish failed to either avoid or escape, it missed the next trial. Such missed trials were rare and generally came only at the beginning of training.

In these experiments the goldfish went through five consecutive cycles of five minutes of darkness followed by five training trials; accordingly they received a total of 20 trials in 40 minutes. They

were then placed in individual "home" tanks—plastic tanks that are slightly smaller than the shuttle boxes—and kept there for three days. On the third day they were returned to the shuttle box, where they were given 10 more trials in 20 minutes.

The fish readily learned to move from one compartment to the other when the light went on, thereby avoiding the shock. Untrained fish avoided the shock in about 20 percent of the first 10 trials and continued to improve with further trials. If they were allowed to perform the task day after day, the curve of learning flattened out at about 80 percent correct responses.

What was even more significant for our experiments was what happened when we changed the interval between the first cycle of trials and the second, that is, between the 20th and the 21st of the 30 trials. If the second cycle was

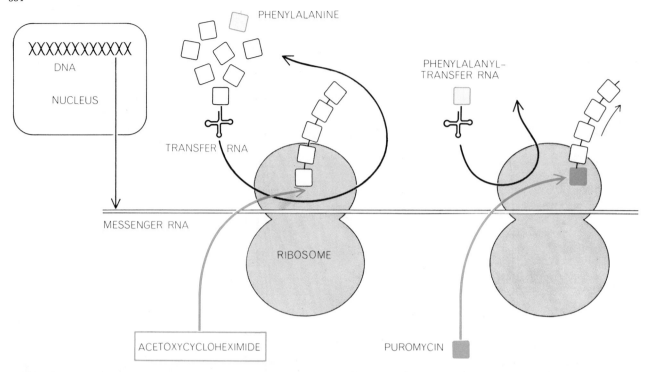

PHENYLALANINE

PHENYLALANYL-
TRANSFER RNA

DNA

NUCLEUS

TRANSFER RNA

MESSENGER RNA

RIBOSOME

ACETOXYCYCLOHEXIMIDE

PUROMYCIN

PROTEIN-BLOCKING AGENTS can interrupt the formation of molecules at the ribosome, where the amino acid units of protein are linked according to instructions embodied in messenger ribonucleic acid (mRNA). One agent, acetoxycycloheximide, interferes with the bonding mechanism that links amino acids brought to the ribosome by transfer RNA (tRNA). Puromycin, another agent, resembles the combination of tRNA and the amino acid phenylalanine. Thus it is taken into chain and prematurely halts its growth.

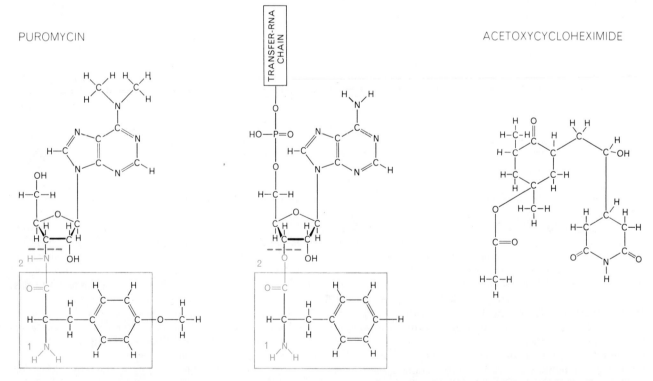

PHENYLALANYL-
TRANSFER RNA

PUROMYCIN

TRANSFER-RNA CHAIN

ACETOXYCYCLOHEXIMIDE

MOLECULAR DIAGRAMS show the resemblance between puromycin and the combination phenylalanyl-tRNA. In both cases the portion of the molecule below the broken line is incorporated into a growing protein molecule, joining at the free amino group (1). But in puromycin the CONH group (2), unlike the corresponding group (COO) of phenylalanyl, will not accept another amino acid and the chain is broken. Acetoxycycloheximide does not resemble amino acid but slows rate at which the chain forms.

begun a full month after the first, the fish performed as well as they did on the third day. If the second cycle was begun on the day after the first, the fish performed equally well, as one would expect. In short, the fish had perfect memory of their training.

We found that we could predict the training scores of groups of fish on the third day on the basis of their scores on the first day. This made it easier for us to determine the effect of antibiotics on the fish's memory: we could compare the training scores of fish receiving antibiotics with the predicted scores. Since we conducted these initial experiments we have made several improvements in our procedure. We now record the escapes and avoidances automatically with photodetectors, and we have arranged matters so that a fish does not miss a trial if it fails to escape. We have altered the trial sequence and the time interval between the turning on of the light and the turning on of the shocking grid. The results obtained with these improved procedures are essentially the same as our earlier ones.

The principal antibiotic we use in our experiments is puromycin, whose effect on protein synthesis was described earlier. We inject the drug directly into the skull of the goldfish with a hypodermic syringe. A thin needle easily penetrates the skull; 10 microliters of solution is then injected over the fish's brain (not into it). In an early series of experiments we injected 170 micrograms of puromycin in that amount of solution at various stages in our training procedures.

We found that if the puromycin was injected immediately after training, memory of the training was obliterated. If the same amount of the drug was injected an hour after training, on the other hand, memory was unaffected. Injection 30 minutes after training produced an intermediate effect. Reducing the amount of puromycin caused a smaller loss of memory.

After the injection the fish seemed to swim normally. We were therefore encouraged to test whether or not puromycin interferes with the changes that occur in the brain as the fish is being trained. This we did by injecting the fish before their initial training. We found that they learned the task at a normal rate, that is, their improvement during the first 20 trials was normal. Fish tested three days later, however, showed a profound loss of memory. This indicated to us that puromycin did not block the short-term memory demonstrated during

TRACE FROM RECORDER shows the performances of 10 goldfish in 30 trials. Each horizontal row represents a trial, beginning at the bottom with trial 1. A blip (*left side*) indicates that a fish either escaped or avoided the shock; a dash in the same row (*right*) signifies an avoidance, that is, a correct response for the trial. These fish learned at the normal rate.

learning but did interfere with the consolidation of long-term memory. And since an injection an hour after training has no effect on long-term memory, whereas an injection immediately after training obliterates it, it appears that consolidation can take place within an hour.

One observation puzzled us. The animals had received their initial training during a 40-minute period, 20 minutes of which was spent in the dark. Puromycin could erase all memory of this training; none of the memory was consolidated. Yet the experiment in which we injected puromycin 30 minutes after training had shown that more than half of the memory was consolidated during that period. How was it that no memory at all was consolidated at least toward the end of the 40-minute training period? To be sure, the fish that had been injected 30 minutes after the training period had been removed from the shuttle boxes and placed in their home tanks. But what was different about the time spent in the shuttle box and the time spent in the home tank that memory could be consolidated in the home tank

but could not be in the shuttle box?

Roger E. Davis of our laboratory undertook further experiments to clarify the phenomenon. He found that fish that were allowed to remain in the shuttle box for several hours after training and were then returned to their home tank showed no loss of memory when they were tested four days later. On the other hand, fish that were allowed to remain in the shuttle box for the same length of time and were then injected with puromycin and returned to their home tank had a marked memory loss! In other words, the fish in the first group did not consolidate memory of their training until after they had been placed in their home tank. It appears that simply being in the shuttle box prevents the fixation of memory. Subsequent studies have led us to the idea that memory fixation is blocked when the organism is in an environment associated with a high level of stimulation. This effect indicates that the formation of memory is environment-dependent, just as the consolidation of memory is time-dependent.

We conclude from all these experiments that long-term memory of training in the goldfish is formed by a puromycin-sensitive step that begins after training and requires that the animal be removed from the training environment. The initial acquisition of information by the fish is puromycin-insensitive and is a qualitatively different process. But what does the action of puromycin on memory formation have to do with its known biochemical effect: the inhibition of protein synthesis?

We undertook to establish that puromycin blocks protein synthesis in the goldfish brain under the conditions of our experiments. This we did in the following manner. First we injected puromycin into the skull of the fish. Next we injected into the abdominal cavity of the fish leucine that had been labeled with tritium, or radioactive hydrogen. Now, leucine is an amino acid, and if labeled leucine is injected into a goldfish's abdominal cavity, it will be incorporated into whatever protein is being synthesized throughout the goldfish's body. By measuring the amount of labeled leucine incorporated into protein after, say, 30 minutes, one can determine the rate of protein synthesis during that time.

We compared the amount of labeled leucine incorporated into protein in goldfish that had received an injection of puromycin with the amount incorporated in fish that had received either no injection or an injection of inactive salt solution. We found that protein synthesis in the brain of fish that had been injected with puromycin was deeply inhibited. The effects of different doses of puromycin and the length of time it took the drug to act did not, however, closely correspond to what we had observed in our experiments involving the behavioral performance of the goldfish. In retrospect this result is not surprising. Various experiments, including our own, had shown that the rate of memory consolidation can be altered by changes in the conditions of training. Moreover, the rate of leucine incorporation can be affected by complex physiological factors.

Another way to check whether or not puromycin exerts its effects on memory by inhibiting protein synthesis would be to perform the memory experiments with a second drug known to inhibit such synthesis. Then if puromycin blocks long-term memory by some other mechanism, the second drug would have no effect on memory. It would be even better if the second drug did not resemble puromycin in molecular structure, so that its effect on protein synthesis would not be the same as puromycin's. Such a drug exists in acetoxycycloheximide. Where puromycin blocks the growth of the polypeptide chain by taking the place of an amino acid, acetoxycycloheximide simply slows down the rate at which the amino acids are linked together. We found that a small amount of this drug (.1 microgram, or one 1,700th the weight of the amount of puromycin we had been using) produced a measurable memory deficit in goldfish. Moreover, it commensurately inhibited the synthesis of protein in the goldfish brain.

These experiments suggest that protein synthesis is required for the consolidation of memory, but they are not conclusive. Louis Flexner and his colleagues have found that puromycin can interfere with memory in mice. On the other hand, they find that acetoxycycloheximide has no such effect. They conclude that protein is required for the expression of memory but that experience acts not on protein synthesis directly but on messenger RNA. The conditions of their experiments and the fact that they are working with a different animal do not allow any ready comparison with our experiments.

Our studies of the goldfish have led us to view learning and memory as a form of biological development. One may think of the brain of an animal as being completely "wired" by heredity; all possible pathways are present, but not all are "soldered." It may be that in short-term memory, pathways are selected rapidly but impermanently. In that case protein synthesis would not be required, which may explain why puromycin has no effect on short-term memory. If the consolidation of memory calls for more permanent connections among pathways, it seems reasonable that protein synthesis would be involved. The formation of such connections, of course, would be blocked by puromycin and acetoxycycloheximide.

Another possibility is that the drugs block not the formation of permanent pathways but the transmission of a signal to fix what has just been learned. There is some evidence for this notion in what happens to people who suffer damage to certain parts of the brain (the mammillary bodies and the hippocampus). They retain older memories and are capable of new learning, but they cannot form new long-term memories. Experiments with animals also provide some evidence for a "fix" signal. We are currently doing experiments in the hope of determining which of these hypotheses best fits the effects of puromycin and acetoxycycloheximide on memory in the goldfish.

Quite apart from our own work, it has been suggested by others that it is possible to transfer patterns of behavior

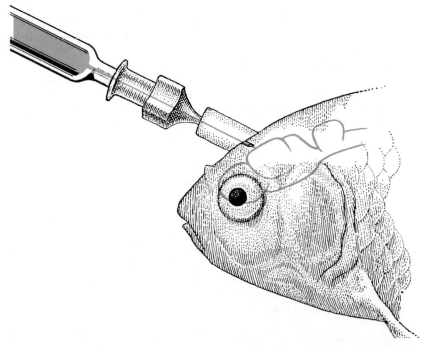

ANTIBIOTIC WAS INJECTED through the thin skull of a goldfish and over rather than into the brain. The antibiotic was puromycin, which inhibits protein synthesis. Following its injection the fish were able to swim normally. They could then be tested for memory loss.

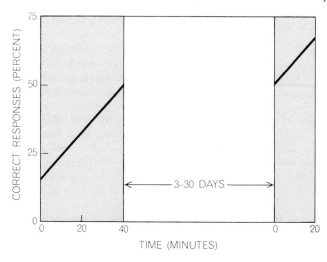

NORMAL LEARNING RATE of goldfish in 30 shuttle-box trials is shown by the black curve. Whether the last 10 trials were given three days after the first 20 (the regular procedure) or as much as a month later, fish demonstrated the same rate of improvement.

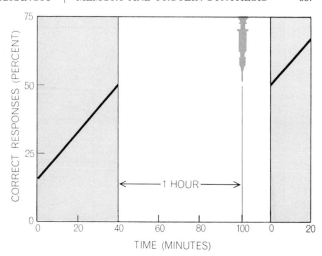

INJECTION WITH PUROMYCIN one hour after completion of 20 learning trials did not disrupt memory. Goldfish given the antibiotic at this point scored as well as those in the control group in the sequence of 10 trials that followed three days afterward.

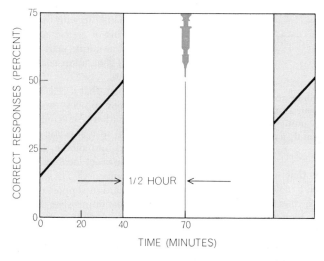

INJECTION HALF AN HOUR AFTER the first 20 trials cut the level of correct responses to half the level without such injection.

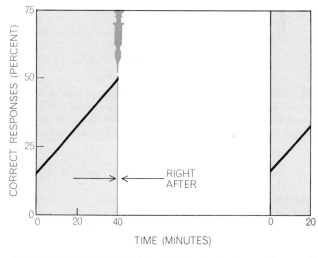

INJECTION IMMEDIATELY AFTER the first 20 trials erased all memory of training. The fish scored at the untrained level.

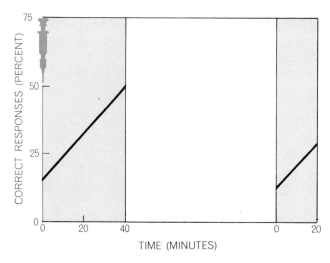

INJECTION PRIOR TO TRAINING did not affect the rate at which goldfish learned to solve the shuttle-box problem. But puromycin given at this point did suppress the formation of long-term memory, as shown by the drop in the scores three days afterward.

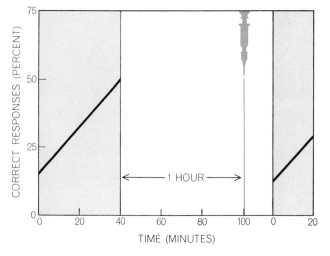

ENVIRONMENTAL FACTOR in the formation of lasting memory was seen when fish remained in training (instead of "home") tanks during the fixation period. Under these conditions fixation did not occur. Puromycin given at end of period still erased memory.

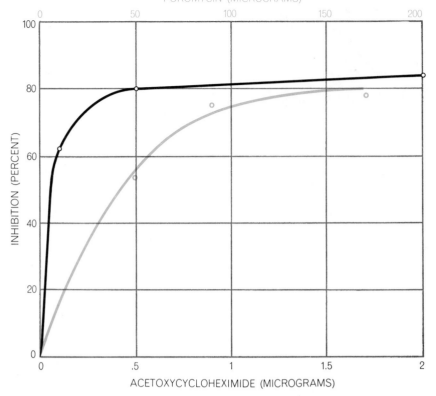

PUROMYCIN (MICROGRAMS)

ACETOXYCYCLOHEXIMIDE (MICROGRAMS)

SLOWED PROTEIN SYNTHESIS in the brain of goldfish is induced both by acetoxycyclo-heximide (*black line*) and the antibiotic puromycin (*colored line*), agents that block the fixation of memory. The author tested the effect on goldfish of various quantities of the two drugs; acetoxycycloheximide was found several hundred times more potent than puromycin.

from one animal to another (even to an animal of a different species) by inject-ing RNA or protein from the brain of a trained animal into the brain (or even the abdominal cavity) of an untrained one. If such transfers of behavior pat-terns can actually be accomplished, they imply that memory resides in molecules of RNA or protein. Nothing we have learned with the goldfish argues for or against the possibility that a behavior pattern is stored in such a molecule.

It can be observed, however, that there is no precedent in biology for such storage. What could be required would be a kind of somatic mutation: a change in the cell's store of information that would give rise to a protein with a new sequence of amino acids. It seems un-likely that such a process could operate at the speed required for learning.

It might also be that learning and memory involve the formation of short segments of RNA or protein that some-how label an individual brain cell. Rich-ard Santen of our laboratory has calcu-lated (on the basis of DNA content) the number of cells in the brain of a rat: it comes to 500 million. With this figure one can calculate further that a poly-peptide chain of seven amino acids, ar-ranged in every possible sequence, could provide each cell in the rat's brain with two unique markers.

The concept that each nerve cell has its own chemical marker is supported by experiments on the regeneration of the optic nerve performed by Roger W. Sperry of the California Institute of Technology. If the optic nerve of a frog is cut and the two ends of the nerve are put back together rotated 180 degrees with respect to each other, the severed fibers of the nerve link up with the same fiber as before. This of course suggests that each fiber has a unique marker that in the course of regeneration enables it to recognize its mate.

Is it possible, then, that a cell "turned on" by the learning process manufac-tures a chemical marker? And could such a process give rise to a substance that, when it is injected into another animal, finds its way to the exact location where it can effectuate memory? Thus far the evidence put forward in support of such ideas has not been impressive. In this exciting period of discovery in brain re-search clear-cut experiments are more important than theories. Certain long-term memories held by investigators in this area may be more of a hindrance than a help in exploring all its possibili-ties.

30

The Neurophysiology of Remembering

by Karl H. Pribram
January 1969

Experiments with monkeys have identified the brain areas involved in the recall of various learned tasks. Memory may take the form of interference patterns that resemble laser-produced holograms

In 1950, toward the end of a busy life devoted to investigating the neurophysiology of memory, Karl S. Lashley wrote: "I sometimes feel, in reviewing the evidence on the localization of the memory trace, that the necessary conclusion is that learning just is not possible at all. Nevertheless, in spite of such evidence against it, learning does sometimes occur." That same year Edwin G. Boring, a leading psychologist of Lashley's generation, pointed out the deep impact that this failure to find physiological evidence for the memory trace had had on psychology. "Where or how," he asked, "does the brain store its memories? That is the great mystery. How can learning persist unreproduced, being affected by other learning while it waits? On the proper occasion what was learned reappears somewhat modified. Where was it in the meantime?... The physiology of memory has been so baffling a problem that most psychologists in facing it have gone positivistic, being content with hypothesized intervening variables or with empty correlations."

Hardly were these bleak observations in print before new research tools became available and were promptly applied in experiments on the neurophysiology of memory. As in all research that produces results important to workers in more than one discipline, however, dissemination across traditional boundaries is slowed by differences in vocabulary, in research technique and in the way a problem is subtly influenced by the subjects and materials employed by workers in different disciplines. As a result one finds even today that many psychologists (even those kindly disposed toward physiology) have the impression that little or no progress has been made in the effort to establish the neurophysiological basis of memory. This stems from the fact that psychologists have addressed themselves primarily to questions about *process*, whereas neurophysiologists and neurochemists have addressed themselves primarily to the question of how the brain achieves short-term and long-term *storage*.

My own research has sought to answer more directly the questions posed by psychologists: What kinds of memory process must exist in the brain to allow remembering to take place? The results of this research have cast doubt on at least some of the assumptions about brain mechanisms (explicit and implicit) that are held by both psychologists and physiologists and that in my view have impeded any coming to grips with the problem of process.

Neurophysiologists had over several decades extensively mapped the brain with electrical recording devices and with weak electric currents to trace nerve pathways. As a result of such experiments on cats, monkeys and even men (performed during neurosurgery) physiologists could speak with some confidence of visual, auditory and somesthetic and motor areas in the cerebral cortex. Although they remained baffled by the "memory trace," they still felt they could describe the nerve pathways from a stimulus input (say the flash of a light) to a muscular response. The success of these studies often blinded the investigators to the fact that many of these presumed pathways could hardly be reconciled with Lashley's experiments dating back to the 1920's, which showed that rats could remember and could perform complex activities even after major nerve pathways in the brain had been cut and after as much as 90 percent of the primary visual cortex had been surgically removed.

As a neurosurgeon I had no reason to challenge the prevailing views of physiologists until I met Lashley and was convinced that we knew less than we thought. I soon resolved to continue his general line of investigation, working with monkeys rather than with rats, and in addition to make an effort to follow recordable changes of the electrical activity of the brain as the animals were trained to perform various tasks. Although this work has gone slowly at times (one experiment I shall describe took seven years), my co-workers and I have now gathered neurophysiological data from more than 950 monkeys. The results of these experiments are forcing many revisions in traditional concepts of how the brain works when tasks are learned and later remembered.

Beyond this I believe there is now available a hypothesis about the nature of the memory trace that satisfies the known physiological requirements and that can be tested by experiment. It is perhaps not surprising that the brain may exploit, among other things, the most sophisticated principle of information storage yet known: the principle of the hologram. In a hologram the information in a scene is recorded on a photographic plate in the form of a complex interference, or diffraction, pattern that appears meaningless. When the pattern is illuminated by coherent light, however, the original image is reconstructed. What makes the hologram unique as a storage device is that every element in the original image is distributed over the entire photographic plate. The hypothesis is attractive because remembering or recollecting literally implies a reconstructive process—the assembly of dismembered mnemic events. In what follows, therefore, I shall give first the evidence for believing that

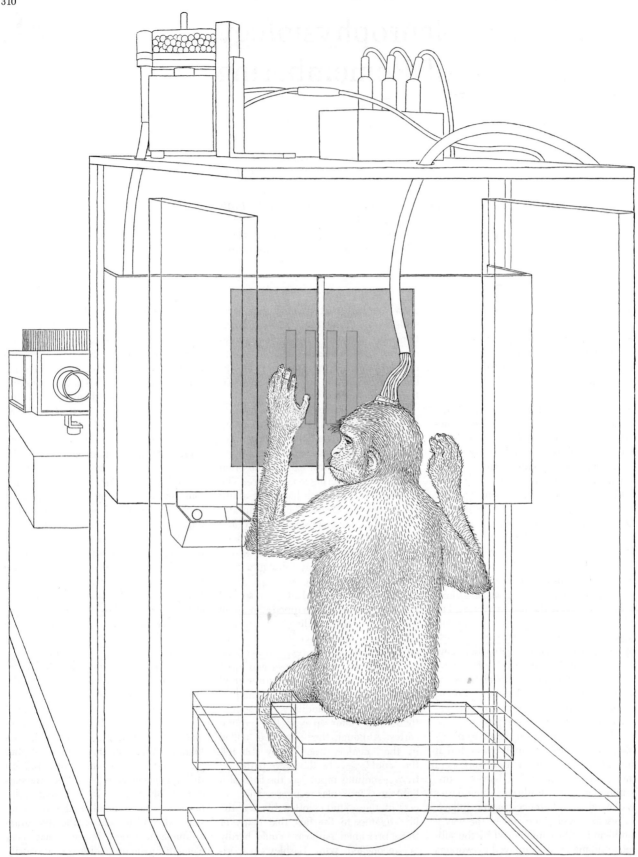

VISUAL-DISCRIMINATION TASK developed in the author's laboratory at Stanford University School of Medicine is depicted in this illustration. On the translucent panel in front of him the monkey sees either a circle or a series of vertical stripes, which have been projected from the rear. He is rewarded with a peanut, which drops into the receptacle at his left elbow, if he presses the right half of the panel when he sees the circle or the left half when he sees the stripes. Electrodes record the wave forms that appear in the monkey's visual cortex as he develops skill at this task. Early in the experiments the wave forms show whether the monkey sees the circle or stripes. Eventually they reveal in advance which half of the panel the monkey will press (*see illustration on page 312*).

mnemic events are distributed in the brain and then describe experiments that tell us something about the way these mnemic events become re-collected into useful memory processes.

The abuses that the brain can survive and still function successfully have been documented many times since Lashley's pioneering experiments. Human testimony is provided daily in the neurological clinic of every large hospital when diseased or damaged brain tissue has to be removed. In the laboratory the brain seems to mock the ingenuity of the experimenter. Robert Galambos of the University of California at San Diego has severed up to 98 percent of the optic tract of cats without seriously impairing the cats' ability to perform skillfully on tests requiring them to differentiate between highly similar figures. Roger W. Sperry of the California Institute of Technology has surgically crosshatched sensory receiving areas in the cortex of monkeys without disturbing the presumed organization of the input system. In other experiments the system continued to function even when Sperry inserted strips of mica in the crosshatched troughs in an effort to electrically insulate small squares of tissue from one another. Conversely, Lashley, Kao Liang Chow and Josephine Semmes tried, without success, to short-circuit the electrical activity of the brain by placing strips of gold foil over the receiving areas. To accomplish a similar end I injected a minute amount of aluminum hydroxide cream at a number of points within a receiving area of an animal's cerebral cortex to produce electrical discharges resembling those seen in electroencephalograms during an epileptic seizure. Although these multiple discharging foci sharply retarded the animal's ability to learn a task of pattern discrimination, they did not interfere with recognition of these patterns when the multiple lesions were produced after learning.

Such experiments have been interpreted as showing that each sensory system has considerable reserve capacity. Since it seems to make little difference in terms of performance which parts of the system are destroyed, it has been suggested that this reserve is distributed throughout the system, that the information needed to discriminate patterns is duplicated in many locations. According to this hypothesis, the discharging foci produced by injections of aluminum hydroxide cream interfere in some way with the reduplication that normally

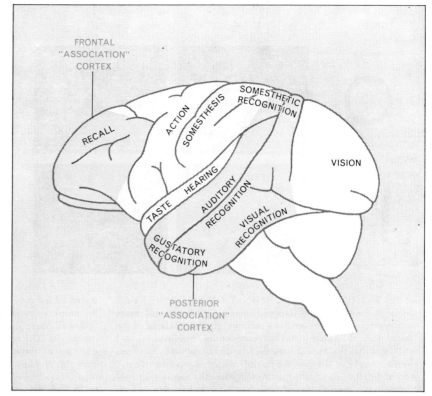

LOCALIZATIONS OF FUNCTION in the cerebral cortex of monkeys have been known in general for many years. The evidence has been supplied in part by anatomical tracing of nerve pathways and more recently by electrical recording of wave forms, both through the intact skull and by use of implanted electrodes. Somesthesis refers to the sense of touch.

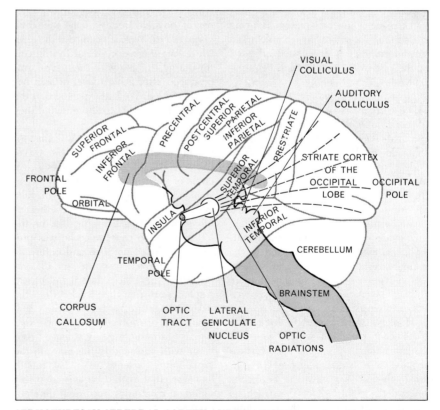

STRUCTURES IN CEREBRAL CORTEX AND BRAINSTEM mentioned in the text can be identified with the help of this illustration. Most of the cortical areas are labeled in adjectival form, the word "cortex" being omitted. The brainstem and its structures are shown in color. The corpus callosum is a bundle of nerve fibers that connects the two hemispheres of the brain. The lateral geniculate nucleus is the major relay station in the visual input system.

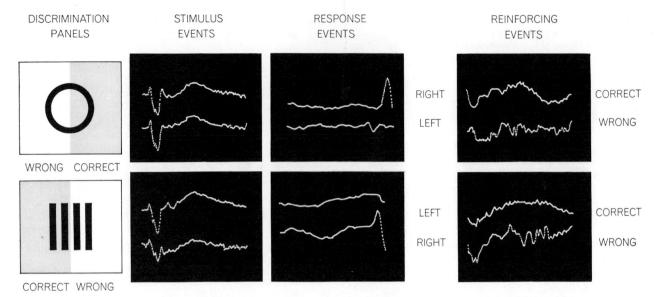

| DISCRIMINATION PANELS | STIMULUS EVENTS | RESPONSE EVENTS | | REINFORCING EVENTS | |

RESULTS OF VISUAL-DISCRIMINATION EXPERIMENT are shown in the wave forms recorded from the striate (visual) cortex of a monkey. The waves are those recorded after he has learned the task illustrated on page 388. The records under "Stimulus events" are wave forms that appear immediately after the monkey has been shown a circle or stripes. The records under "Response events" were generated just prior to the moment when the monkey actually responded by pressing either the left or the right half of the panel. The records under "Reinforcing events" were produced when the monkey was rewarded with a peanut if he was correct or not rewarded if he was wrong. The correct response was to press the right half of the panel on seeing a circle, the left half on seeing stripes.

A slight difference in the "stimulus" wave forms indicates whether the monkey has seen stripes or a circle. After he has learned his task well sharp differences appear in the response and reinforcing panels. The response wave forms, which are actually "intention" waves, show one pattern (the one with the sharp peak) whenever the monkey is about to press the right half of the panel, regardless of whether he has seen a circle or stripes. If he has actually seen stripes, of course, pressing the right half of the panel is the wrong response. Thus the wave forms reflect his intention to press a particular half of the panel. They could hardly reveal whether his response is going to be right or wrong because at this point he still "thinks" he is about to make the correct response.

takes place when information is being stored, but once storage is complete and the information is distributed all parts of the system are more or less "equipotent."

The correctness of this view has now been put to direct test. Over the past few years Nico Spinelli and I have shown that electrical activity recorded from widely distributed points in the striate, or visual, cortex of monkeys shows distinctive responses to different stimuli. Moreover, other widely distributed points within the cortex and brainstem give evidence that they have participated in storing information linked to the animal's response to particular stimuli. Let me describe the experiment more fully. (This is the one that took seven years to complete.)

Monkeys were placed in front of a translucent panel on which we could project either a circle or four vertical stripes [see illustration on page 310]. If, when the monkey saw the circle, he pressed the right half of the panel, he would be rewarded with a peanut. He would be similarly rewarded if he pressed the left side of the panel when the stripes appeared. Before the training begins we painlessly implant a number of tiny electrodes in the monkey's visual cortex. We then compare the electrical wave forms produced by the cortex during training with the wave forms produced after a high level of skill has been attained. We had expected that the wave forms would be different, and they were.

What we did not expect was that we would be able to tell from the waveform records whether the monkey saw a circle or vertical stripes, whether he responded correctly or made a mistake and, most surprising of all, whether he *intended* to press the right half or the left half of the panel once he was presented with the problem and *before* he initiated an overt response [see illustration above]. All these differing electrical responses arose in the visual cortex—the part of the brain that receives the visual input. We are forced to conclude that signals representing experience converge with and modify the input to the visual-input systems. We also found, however, that within the visual cortex different electrodes recorded different events.

Thus we now have direct evidence that signals become distributed within the input system. What we see (or at least what the monkey sees) is not a pure and simple coding of the light patterns that are focused on the retina. Somewhere between the retina and the visual cortex the inflowing signals are modified to provide information that is already linked to a learned response, for example the monkey's intention to press one panel or another. Evidently what reaches the visual cortex is evoked by the external world but is hardly a direct or simple replica of it. Further, the information inherent in the input becomes distributed over wide regions of the visual cortex.

How might such a distribution of information occur? A possible clue to the puzzle came from an optical artifact, the hologram, which was then being made for the first time with the help of coherent laser light [see "Photography by Laser," by Emmett N. Leith and Juris Upatnieks; SCIENTIFIC AMERICAN Offprint 300]. The interference pattern of the hologram is created when a beam of coherent light is split so that a "reference" portion of the beam can interact with a portion reflected from a scene or an object. I reasoned (much as Lashley had) that neuronal events might interact in some way to produce complex patterns within the brain; the hologram now provided an explicit model.

Evidence for some such patterning of neuronal events, at least in the visual channels, has been provided by the work of R. W. Rodieck of the University of Sydney. He has shown that the initiating events in the visual channel that express the relations between the excitation of one receptor in the retina and the activity of neighboring points can be described mathematically through the use of "convolutional integrals," expressions somewhat similar to the familiar Fourier transformations. For example, the shape of the visual receptive field of a single retinal ganglion cell represents the convolution of a derivative of the shape of the retinal image produced at that point [*see illustration on this page*]. Convolutional integrals and Fourier transformations provide the mathematical basis on which holography was founded. Thus at least a first step has been taken to show that interference effects may operate in the central nervous system.

The question remains: How can interference effects be produced in the brain? One can imagine that when nerve impulses arrive at synapses (the junction between two nerve cells), they produce electrical events on the other side of the synapse that take the form of momentary standing wave fronts. Typically the junctions made by a nerve fiber number in the dozens, if not hundreds. The patterns set up by arriving nerve impulses presumably form a microstructure of wave forms that can interact with similar microstructures arising in overlapping junctional contacts. These other microstructures are derived from the spontaneous changes in electrical potential that ceaselessly occur in nerve tissue, and from other sources within the brain. Immediate cross-correlations result, and these can add in turn to produce new patterns of nerve impulses.

The hypothesis presented here is that the totality of this process has a more or less lasting effect on protein molecules and perhaps other macromolecules at the synaptic junctions and can serve as a neural hologram from which, given the appropriate input, an image can be reconstructed. The attractive feature of the hypothesis is that the information is distributed throughout the stored hologram and is thus resistant to insult. If even a small corner of a hologram is illuminated by the appropriate input, the entire original scene reappears. Moreover, holograms can be layered one on top of the other and yet be separately reconstructed.

The holographic hypothesis imme-

diately raises many questions. Do the mathematical expressions that interpret the shape of visual receptive fields at the ganglion-cell layer of the retina yield equally useful interpretations at more central stations in the visual system? What kind of neural reference mechanism plays the role of the coherent light source needed to make and display holograms? Perhaps a kind of coherence results from the anatomical fact that the retina and the visual cortex are linked by many thousands of fibers arranged in parallel pathways. Or it could be that the nerve cells in the visual channel achieve coherence by rhythmic firing. Still another possibility is that coherence results from the operation of the variety of detectors that respond to such simple aspects of stimuli as the tilt of a line and movement that have recently received so much attention [see the article "The Visual Cortex of the Brain," by David H. Hubel, beginning on page 183].

Other questions that flow from the holographic hypothesis are concerned with the storage of the memory trace. Two alternatives come to mind. The first involves a "tuning" of cell assemblies by changing synaptic characteristics so that a particular circuit will somehow resonate when it receives a familiar "note"; the second is some form of molecular storage, perhaps involving a change in structure at the synapses. Of course circuit-tuning may be secondary to just such structural changes, or the job may be done by a mechanism as yet unimagined. Such questions can be and are being investigated in the laboratory with techniques available today.

There is another line of investigation demonstrating that representations of

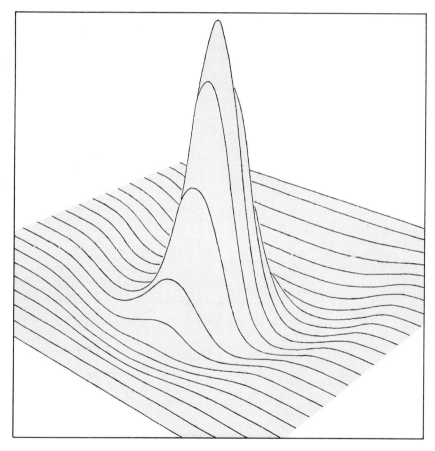

IDEALIZED MAP OF VISUAL RECEPTIVE FIELD represents recordings made from a single ganglion cell in the retina of the eye when a point source of light is presented in various parts of the visual field. The map contains smooth contour lines because the ganglion cell integrates the response of its neighbors, with which it is interconnected. The height of the contour at any point represents the number of times the individual nerve cell fires when the location of the point light source corresponds to that position on the map. Maximum firing occurs when the position of the light corresponds to that of the central peak. In mathematical terms, each contour line represents the "convolutional integral" of the first derivative of the shape of the stimulus figure. The interaction of many such convolutional integrals may produce hologram-like interference patterns within the visual system and elsewhere in the brain. Storage of such patterns could provide the basis of memory.

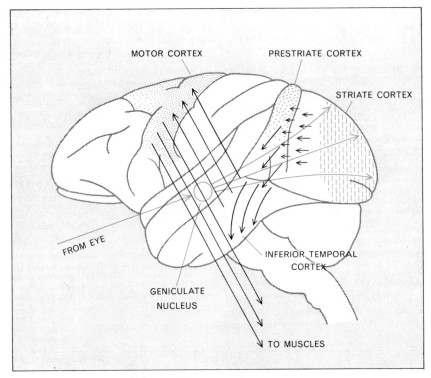

OLD VIEW OF VISUAL-RECOGNITION MECHANISM assumed that after visual information reached the striate cortex it was transferred to the prestriate cortex in two steps and from there to the inferior temporal cortex. Muscular response, according to the old view, then required that a message travel from the inferior temporal cortex to the precentral cortex (the motor cortex), which responded by sending signals down the brainstem to the muscles.

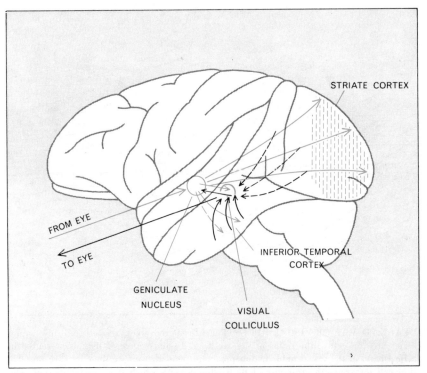

NEW VIEW OF VISUAL-RECOGNITION MECHANISM emphasizes the recent evidence that impulses from the inferior temporal cortex directly modify the visual input *before* it reaches the striate cortex (*see illustration on page 316*). This modification takes place subcortically through tracts leading to the visual colliculus and through interactions between that part of the brainstem and the lateral geniculate nucleus. There is also some evidence for an indirect pathway from the retina to the inferior temporal cortex. Visual information also seems to flow from the visual cortex to the visual colliculus. In the new view the body's muscle responses are relatively independent of the visual-recognition mechanism.

experience are distributed after entering the brain. The experiments I have described thus far demonstrated a distribution in space. There is also distribution in time; there are mechanisms in the brain for temporally distributing, or holding, events long enough so that they can be firmly registered. The evidence comes from an important group of experiments showing how animals (including man) gradually become habituated to a novel stimulus. Until recently habituation was thought to be due to a fatiguing of the nervous system. Eugene Sokolov of the University of Moscow showed, however, that when one is habituated, one can be dishabituated, that is, "oriented" anew, by a lowering in the intensity of the stimulus or even by complete silence when stimuli are expected. I like to call it the "Bowery-el phenomenon." For many years there was an elevated railway line (the "el") on Third Avenue in New York that made a fearful racket; when it was torn down, people who had been living in apartments along the line awakened periodically out of a sound sleep to call the police about some strange occurrence they could not properly define. Many such calls came at the times the trains had formerly rumbled past. The strange occurrences were of course the deafening silence that had replaced the expected noise.

In laboratory studies of this phenomenon the physiological concomitants of the orienting reaction are recorded and their reduction allows habituation to be investigated. The orienting reaction includes, among other things, changes in the conductivity of the skin (the galvanic skin response), changes in heart rate and respiratory rate, and changes in the electroencephalogram. Muriel H. Bagshaw and I found that we had to separate these physiological indicators of the orienting reaction into two classes. This was necessary because after we had surgically removed the frontal lobes of a monkey's brain, or the brainstem region known as the amygdala, the orienting stimulus no longer evoked the galvanic skin response or changes in heart rate and respiratory rate. (The responses themselves were not destroyed, because they could be evoked under other conditions.) On the other hand, surgery did not eliminate certain changes in the electroencephalogram and certain behavioral changes that also occur as a part of the orienting reaction. Surgery also interfered with habituation: a monkey lacking his frontal lobes or his amygdala continued much longer to show the behavioral and electroencephalographic orienting reactions. These results suggested that the loss of

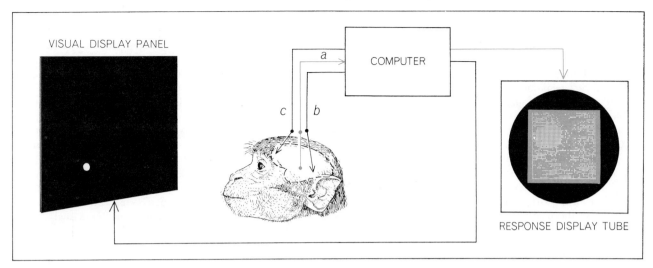

INVESTIGATION OF VISUAL RECEPTIVE FIELDS is carried out by presenting a monkey with a small source of light that is systematically moved from point to point in a raster-like pattern. At each point the response of a single cell in the lateral geniculate nucleus is recorded by a microelectrode (*a*). During this mapping a weak electrical stimulus can be delivered to other parts of the brain, such as the inferior temporal cortex (*b*) or the frontal cortex (*c*), to see if there is any effect. Some typical results are illustrated on the next page. The technique, which relies heavily on the computer, was developed by the author's colleague Nico Spinelli.

galvanic skin responses and heart and respiratory changes precluded habituation; when these indicators of orienting were not present, the stimulus, although perceived, failed to be registered in memory.

We have all had the experience of being preoccupied while a friend is recounting his experiences to us. Finally in exasperation he may say, "You aren't listening." Caught unaware, you may still be able quickly to repeat your friend's last sentence and from this even reconstruct what the "conversation" was about. If, however, your reverie is allowed to continue, much of what reached your ears will have been irretrievably lost; things just did not register. Thus there are two classes of indicators of orienting: the one concerned with just "sampling" the input, the other with its "registration," or storage.

E. D. Homskaya in the laboratory of A. R. Luria in Moscow and Mrs. Bagshaw in our laboratory at the Stanford University School of Medicine have also demonstrated that removal of the frontal lobes or the amygdala interferes with the indicators of registration when they appear in classical conditioning experiments. In normal animals the conditioning cue (such as a bell or a light) evokes changes in the galvanic skin response, in heart rate and in respiratory rate, as well as in the electroencephalogram. As the conditioning trials continue, these changes take place earlier and earlier until they actually precede the conditioning cue. It is as if the subject of the experiment were rehearsing the situation, anticipating what is coming next. After removal of the frontal lobes or the amyg-

dala, however, this rehearsal apparently ceases. Thus one can demonstrate that both anticipation and registration—a temporal distribution of mnemic events—take place in a normal subject, and that these processes are impaired by surgery in certain parts of the brain. There is as yet little evidence to indicate how these parts of the brain bring about this temporal distribution of mnemic events.

Given the fact that mnemic events become distributed in the brain, what happens during remembering? Some kind of organizing process is clearly required. Experimental data make it likely that this process involves the "association cortex" of primates such as monkeys and man [*see top illustration on page 311*]. These regions are not to be confused with the "polysensory association cortex" that immediately surrounds the sensory projection areas and that has been studied so intensively in cats. The primate association areas consist of two general classes: the frontal and the posterior. The posterior association areas are located among the various primary sensory areas and consist of subareas that are specific for each of the senses.

In operations on several hundred monkeys my colleagues and I have made many kinds of lesion in this posterior system; the type, the size and the location of the lesions were based on a variety of anatomical and physiological criteria. These monkeys have been tested for their ability to learn and to retain discrimination tasks involving four senses. Vision is studied with a variety of patterns, colors and brightnesses; touch, with unseen objects of different shapes

and textures; taste, with samples differing in bitterness or sweetness; hearing, with different sound patterns. From the results of such experiments we are able to subdivide the posterior association cortex into areas, each serving a particular sense. These investigations show that the parieto-occipital area is concerned with touch, the anterior temporal cortex with taste, the middle temporal region with hearing. The inferior temporal cortex is important to visual discrimination [*see illustrations on page 311*].

These results present a number of questions. Why, following the removal of the inferior temporal cortex, do monkeys fail completely to accomplish visual discriminations while being perfectly able to accomplish discriminations in other senses and to perform more complex tasks, such as tasks involving delayed reactions and alternation of response? The problem is complicated by the following facts. Visual information passes from the retina to a relay point called the lateral geniculate nucleus and thence to the occipital (or striate) cortex. It had long been taught that the occipital cortex then sends information out to the surrounding areas, and that the information finally reaches the inferior temporal cortex. Since our monkeys fail in visual discrimination tasks after the removal of the inferior temporal cortex, the classical teaching would seem to be supported. Other considerations nonetheless argue that the classical view must be wrong.

First of all, the anatomical evidence shows that nerve impulses would have to be relayed by three synapses in traveling from the occipital cortex to the inferior temporal region. Three synapses, however, can get a signal from anywhere to almost anywhere else in the brain, so that this is hardly sufficient evidence for a mechanism that demands strict sensory specificity. Second, Chow, in a series of experiments confirmed by my own, removed all the tissue surrounding the occipital cortex in monkeys, so that the primary visual receiving area is totally isolated from the inferior temporal cortex. Such animals show no loss of visual performance in spite of the fact that a lesion in the inferior temporal cortex only a third or a quarter the size of the one made in the disconnection experiment will cause serious impairment on the same tasks. This makes it most unlikely that impulses reaching the inferior temporal cortex from the upper regions of the visual system account for the importance of this cortex in vision.

What, then, is the mechanism that enables the inferior temporal cortex to play such a key role in the performance of visual tasks? Where does it get its information and where does it send it? The available evidence (much of which I have had to omit in this brief account) has led me to propose that the inferior temporal cortex exerts its control by organizing the traffic in the primary visual system. Recently the pathways from the inferior temporal cortex to the visual system have been traced. Applying the methods of electrophysiology, Spinelli and I have found, for example, that we can change the size and shape of visual receptive fields by stimulating the inferior temporal cortex [*see illustration below*]. These and other experiments demonstrate beyond doubt that the inferior temporal cortex is not the passive recipient of data relayed from the primary visual cortex, as was long believed, but actively influences what enters the visual cortex. Similar results have been obtained in the auditory system by James H. Dewson in my laboratory.

An experiment that tells us a little about the meaning of this control over input is currently being completed by my associate Lauren Gerbrandt. A monkey sits in a chair inside a box that can be opened, so that he can see out, or closed. He can be stimulated through an electrode placed in the lateral geniculate nucleus (the relay station in the visual input system) while we record the level of activity in the visual cortex. When the box is closed, geniculate stimulation evokes only a small response in the cortex. When the box is open, the response is large. Gerbrandt found, however, that he could augment the strength of the cortical response when the box is closed (and only then) by stimulation of

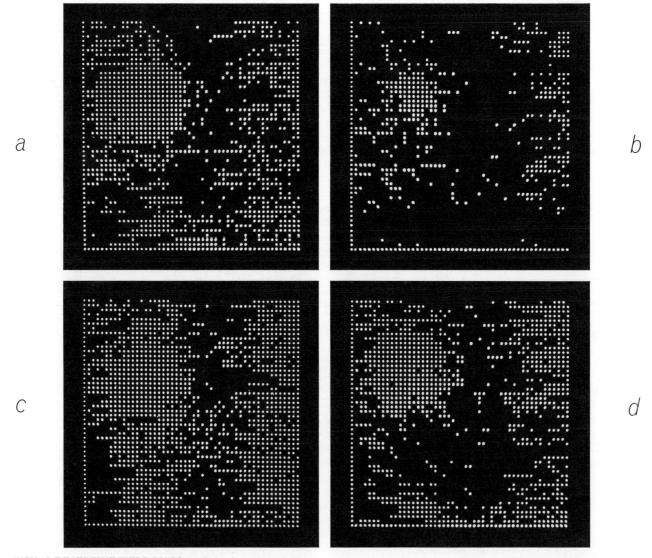

VISUAL-RECEPTIVE-FIELD MAPS, made by the technique illustrated on the preceding page, show how information flowing through the primary visual pathway is altered by stimulation elsewhere in the brain. Map *a* is the normal response of a cell in the geniculate nucleus when a light source is moved through a rasterlike pattern. Map *b* shows how the field is contracted by stimulation of the inferior temporal cortex. Map *c* shows the expansion produced by stimulation of the frontal cortex. Map *d* is a final control.

the inferior temporal cortex. The response is then as strong as when the monkey is alertly looking about, examining the world around him. This suggests to us that electrical stimulation of the association cortex crudely reproduces the neural activity that goes on naturally when the animal is actively engaged in sampling and attending his visual environment.

A detailed and satisfactory mechanism for explaining these results remains to be worked out. A tentative hypothesis supported by considerable anatomical evidence, and very recently by limited electrophysiological evidence, might go something like this. There is evidently an input from the visual pathway, rather separate from the primary visual pathway, that leads to the inferior temporal cortex. This visual input to the inferior temporal cortex triggers a process that feeds back into the primary visual system and there exercises a control over the flow of visual impulses to the visual cortex [*see bottom illustration on page 314*]. This view is based on such evidence as our ability to change the size and shape of the visual fields in the optic nerve and lateral geniculate nucleus by stimulation of the inferior temporal cortex.

This, however, can be only a part of the story. A satisfactory hypothesis also has to explain the first experiment I described, in which recordings from the visual cortex foreshadowed the monkey's intention to press either the right or the left panel when he was presented with a circle or vertical stripes. Here we have evidence that the frontal cortex and the amygdala, which are involved in registration, also affect the visual mechanism, often in a direction just opposite to what is produced by stimulation of the inferior temporal cortex.

Pathways from the visual cortex to the superior colliculus of the brainstem are well known. Recently we have traced similar pathways from the inferior temporal cortex to this same superior colliculus, which is an important structure in the visual system. (In birds the collicular region plays a role comparable to the role of the cerebral cortex in primates.) One can now begin to see how surgically isolating the visual cortex from the inferior temporal cortex does not destroy an animal's capacity to perform visual tasks. Evidently the communication link between the visual cortex and the inferior temporal cortex (which is essential to the retention of visual discriminations) is buried deep within the brainstem. Just as the brainstem serves

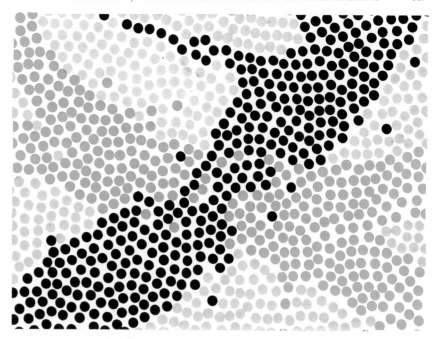

INTERSECTION OF NERVE PATHWAYS in the visual-input channel can be depicted schematically in two dimensions by an array of dots, each representing a single nerve cell. The response of each cell in turn can be visualized as corresponding to the patterns shown in the visual-receptive-field maps presented on page 316. At a given instant a stimulus arising in a particular part of the visual field will cause a certain group of cells (*color*) to respond. Simultaneously a stimulus in another part of the field will excite a different group (*black*). Gray cells are inactive at this instant. As long as the scene in the visual field remains constant, these same groups of cells will "flash" off and on many times a second. The interference patterns resulting from the interacting fields of the flashing cells may provide the opportunity for the formation of holographic patterns. This diagram first appeared in "The Physiology of Imagination," by John C. Eccles; SCIENTIFIC AMERICAN Offprint 65.

as a convergence station for the visual system, it serves (on the basis of Dewson's evidence) a similar function in hearing. The importance of such subcortical convergences, which in turn alter the input to the cortex, has been highlighted by these experiments.

Further evidence for this cortico-subcortical mode of operation of the brain (as opposed to a transcortical mode) comes from the same group of experiments in which our animals learned to distinguish between circles and stripes while a record of their brain waves was being made. The reason for doing these experiments in the first place was that I wanted to see how the wave forms recorded from various parts of the brain would be altered by making lesions in the inferior temporal cortex after the monkeys had learned their task. I fully expected that a lesion would selectively affect one of the wave forms and would leave others unchanged. Thus (I hoped) we would be able to identify the mechanism that accounted for the monkey's failure to perform satisfactorily after the lesion. We might conclude, for example, that the lesion had interfered with the monkey's capacity to differentiate between circles and stripes or that it had

interfered with some process linked to reinforcement or response. This is not what happened.

Instead of finding a selective change in one or another of these electrical waves, we found that the electrodes that provided the best differential recordings in advance of surgery subsequently showed no such differences; other electrodes whose wave forms had been undifferentiated now showed persistent and reliable differences. These differences turned out to be associated, for the most part, with responses, but in very peculiar ways that we have not as yet been able to decipher clearly.

It seems as if the frame of reference within which the brain activity had been working before the lesions were made was now shifted, and in fact was shifting from time to time. Judging by their behavior, the monkeys were as surprised by the effects of the surgery as we were. They approached their task confident of their ability to solve the problems, only to find they made errors (and hence received no peanut). This resulted in spurts, hesitations and variability in performance. It seemed as if they were completely baffled, not realizing, of course, that it was the inside of their

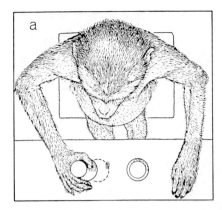 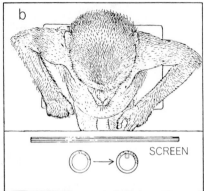 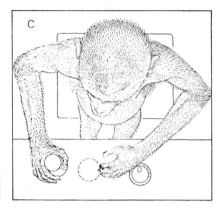

ALTERNATION TASK requires that a monkey remember which cup he lifted last in order to lift the correct one on his next trial and be rewarded with a peanut. Normally he is rewarded if he remembers to lift the cups in a simple alternating sequence: left, right, left and so on. After each trial a screen comes between him and the cups and remains there for periods that can be varied from seconds to many minutes. In part *c* of this sequence the monkey has forgotten to alternate his response. Experiments demonstrate that certain brain lesions interfere with a monkey's ability to remember what he did even a few seconds earlier. By changing the task only slightly, however, the author found that brain-damaged monkeys were no longer perplexed (*see illustration on facing page*).

heads and not the situation that we had changed. What is the explanation?

Whatever the transformations of input (holographic or otherwise) that occur in the nervous system, such transformations are in effect coding operations. In order for a code to work, that is, to be decipherable, it must be framed within a context. This context must remain stable or the information conveyed by the code will be destroyed by successive transformations. Our reading of the recordings of the electrical brain activity of the monkeys who had their inferior temporal cortex removed is that the framework within which their discriminations had been made before surgery was now disrupted and shifting. The events observed by these monkeys no longer conveyed information because their brains had in a sense become unstable.

As a hypothesis this can be tested. We are about to investigate means of providing externally the stability that the brains of the brain-damaged monkeys evidently lack. Sandra Reitz, a student in my laboratory, recently suggested that this could be done simply by increasing the spatial redundancy of the visual cues (that is, the number of identical displays) that we present to our monkeys on a discrimination task. The expectation is, if our view is correct, that this change in the task will overcome the difficulty in discrimination experienced by the monkeys with lesions of the inferior temporal cortex.

Therefore a beginning has been made in specifying the structures that participate in the organization of memory inside the brain. The next task is to discover *how* these structures accomplish the physiological processes we call remembering, whether by holographic

representations or by some process even more subtle. In our concern with the storage mechanism, however, we should never overlook that aspect of memory which is of overriding importance to the process of effective remembering: the method of organizing or coding what is to be remembered.

In everyday life there are many homely examples to show that a given message is easier to remember in one form than in another. For example, rhymes are often employed in aphorisms ("A stitch in time saves nine"); many people cannot remember the number of days in the month without first recalling the jingle of their childhood. A more important example of the value of efficient coding is found in the 0–9 method of writing down numbers compared with the clumsy system of the Romans. By employing the concept of zero to indicate multiples of 10 our mathematical tasks are vastly simplified.

A coding mechanism need not necessarily be very complicated. Take, for example, the following "poem," which the neurophysiologist Warren McCulloch likes to intone with bishop-like solemnity: INMUDEELSARE/INCLAYNONEARE/INPINETARIS/INOAKNONEIS. When spaces are inserted where they belong, the message instantly becomes clear: IN MUD EELS ARE/IN CLAY NONE ARE/IN PINE TAR IS/IN OAK NONE IS. The passage has been decoded by the simple procedure of parsing, or what the psychologist George A. Miller, my sometime collaborator who is now at Rockefeller University, calls "chunking" [see "Information and Memory," by George A. Miller; SCIENTIFIC AMERICAN Offprint 419].

Many experiments with monkeys demonstrate that the frontal cortex—long regarded as the site of the "highest

mental faculties" in man and primates—plays an important role in short-term memory, whatever else it may be doing. When sufficiently complex tests, comparable to those used with monkeys, are given to lobotomized patients, they too show this memory disturbance. My experiments provide strong evidence that the primate frontal cortex performs its role by means of a coding operation that seems to resemble parsing, or chunking. When the frontal cortex of a monkey is damaged, the animal has difficulty performing tasks in which he has to remember what happened just a few seconds earlier.

Typical of such tasks is one in which the monkey faces two identical cups with lids that he must raise in a particular sequence to obtain a peanut [*see illustration above*]. In the simplest case he is rewarded with a peanut at each trial if he simply remembers to lift the lids alternately: left, right, left and so on. Then he must wait a specified interval, which can be varied from a few seconds to hours, between each trial, and while he is waiting an opaque screen is interposed between him and the cups. His task, then, is to remember which lid he lifted last so that he can lift the other one on the next trial. A monkey whose frontal cortex has been resected will fail at this simple task even when the interval between trials is reduced to three seconds.

It occurred to me that perhaps the task appears to these monkeys much as an unparsed passage does to us. I therefore changed the task so that the rewarded sequence became left-right (long interval), left-right (long interval) and so on. There was still a mandatory pause with the screen interposed of five seconds between each left-right trial, but now a longer interval of 15 seconds was inserted between *pairs* of trials. Immediately the monkeys with frontal cortex damage performed as successfully as the control animals whose brains were intact [*see illustration below*]. That time-parsing was the key to the success of the brain-damaged monkeys was shown by other experiments in which the interval between trials was held constant but some other clue, such as a red light or a buzzer, was presented at every other trial. The clues were ignored; the monkeys with frontal lobe resections still failed at the task.

The experiment is important in several respects. First, it demonstrates at least one function of the frontal lobes, a function that may be basic to other functions. Second, it suggests that the difficulty the brain-damaged monkey has in recalling what he did last is not due simply to a premature fading of the memory trace; after all, he improved quickly when a longer interval was interposed, provided that the task was adequately structured. Third, this structuring, organizing or coding is in fact crucial to the process of recall.

Other studies show that the frontal cortex, like the posterior association cortex, exercises control over sensory information flowing into the cortical receiving areas. In many instances, as I have noted, electrical stimulation of the frontal cortex produces effects that are opposite to those produced by posterior stimulation. Our studies are not advanced enough as yet to specify which pathways from the frontal lobes may be involved. Recent work done by Donald B. Lindsley and Carmine D. Clemente at the Brain Research Institute of the University of California at Los Angeles indicates that the pathway involved may be a large tract of fibers (running in the medial forebrain bundle) that carries inhibitory impulses to the reticular formation of the brainstem. I have on occasion attempted to spell out some possible relations between neural inhibitory processes and short-term memory but such efforts are at best tentative.

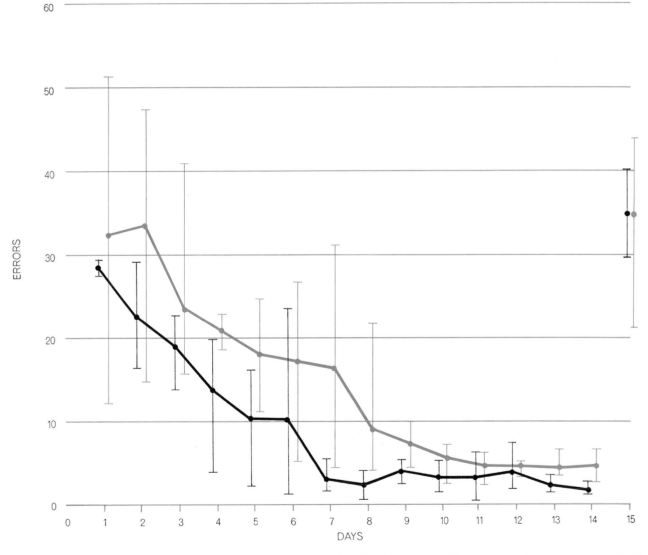

MODIFIED ALTERNATION TASK could be mastered as readily by monkeys with part of their frontal cortex removed (*colored curve*) as by normal monkeys (*black curve*). The brain-damaged monkeys had been unable to solve the standard left-right alternation task (*described in the illustration on page 318*) even when the interval between trials was only a few seconds. The task was then modified so that the interval between each left-and-right trial was kept brief (*five seconds*) but a 15-second pause was inserted after every right-hand trial. When this change was made, brain-damaged monkeys performed about as well as normal monkeys, as shown here. Errors are the number made each day before a monkey achieved 40 successful trials. Bars indicate the range of errors made by different monkeys. Data for the 15th day show the result when all the trials were again separated by equal intervals of five seconds.

Coding and recoding are thus found to be essential operations in both memory storage and remembering. I have described evidence showing clearly that storage is distributed throughout a sensory system. I have also mentioned some evidence suggesting that the transformations (coding operations) that are performed within the input channels can be described in terms of convolutional integrals. The basic premise involved is that neighboring neural elements do not work independently of one another. By virtue of lateral interactions, neural elements spatially superpose the excitatory and inhibitory electrical potentials that arise among neighboring nerve cells. These transformations generate a microstructure of postsynaptic events, which can be regarded as wave fronts that set up interference patterns with other (preexisting or internally generated) wave fronts, producing in their totality something resembling a hologram. Given a mechanism capable of storing this hologram, an image could be evoked at some later time by the appropriate input. In order to be effective as codes, transformations must take place within some stable framework. To an extent this framework can be provided by the stored microstructure itself, by the parallel pathways of the input system, by the specific detector sensitivities of units in the system and by the very redundancy of the external environment. (We have no trouble recognizing automobiles because there are so many of them and they are so much alike.)

For complex and novel events, however, a more powerful organizer must come into action. Experiments conducted in my laboratory and elsewhere suggest that this organizing mechanism critically involves the association areas of the cerebral cortex. The mechanism does not, however, seem to reside within these areas. Rather, the association areas exercise control on the input system by way of deeper structures in the brainstem. In short, the function of the association areas of the cortex turns out to be that of providing a major part of the organizing process necessary to remembering: the reconstruction of an image from distributed mnemic events.

IX

COMMUNICATION
AND LANGUAGE

IX COMMUNICATION AND LANGUAGE

INTRODUCTION

Language is the supreme and unique accomplishment of the species *Homo sapiens*. Although many animals communicate, their communication does not approach human language. Language is much more than merely communication from one organism to another—it possesses structural as well as functional properties. It has a grammatical structure, *syntax*. Some linguists today feel that this may be universal for *Homo sapiens*—that all languages may have similar fundamental structural properties. Linguistic studies of the development of language in the individual suggest that, for normal persons living in the company of others, language is an inevitable consequence of possessing a human brain. Because we use language with such great ease and because of its complexity, we tend to forget that it, like our other behaviors, is a biological phenomenon; in particular, it is an expression of the complexity of the organization and functions of the brain.

In the first article, Edward O. Wilson sets the stage with a broad-ranging and fascinating discussion of animal communication. Animals ranging from insects to man communicate by means of chemicals, movements, and sounds. There are many species-specific kinds of communications, limited to one particular species. Others may be broader. For example, the handwave greeting seems to be common to all higher primates and not limited simply to man. However, as Wilson emphasizes at the end of his article, human language is qualitatively different from forms of communication in any other species.

Can an ape learn language? The next article, written by Ann and David Premack, "Teaching Language to an Ape," explores this fascinating question. There have actually been several different approaches to teaching language to chimpanzees. In earlier studies much effort was devoted to raising chimps with human families from infancy and attempting to teach them to speak verbally. Chimpanzees develop motor skills more rapidly than human babies do, but none have learned to use more than two or three words. They learned a great deal about appropriate behavior in the family and about the meanings of words and gestures, but they could not learn to *speak* language. In recent years, two quite novel approaches have indicated that it is possible to teach chimpanzees very complex languagelike communication. Allen and Beatrice Gardner have taught American Sign Language to chimpanzees. Chimps are much better at using their hands than at generating verbal sounds. The Gardner's best chimp, Washoe, has learned more than 150 words in American Sign Language and does communicate very effectively. The Premacks adopted a different approach and trained their chimpanzee, Sarah, to learn geometric forms as symbols for words. Sarah now has a reading and writing vocabulary of about 130 words and seems to have quite good understanding of the use of these words in communication with the experimenters. Whether these fascinating attempts at language training in chimps have succeeded in training the animals to use *language* or merely to use a method of communication that is an elaboration of conditioned responses *à la* Pavlov, is not yet clear, but the experiments are fascinating.

In the last article in this section Norman Geschwind considers the relation between language and the brain. Most of our information about the brain substrates of language in humans has come from studies of unfortunate persons who have received brain damage of one kind or another and who exhibit deficits in speech and language. It is of very considerable interest to note that the two fundamental aspects of language, namely the structure, or *syntax* (grammar), and the meaning, or *semantics,* seem to have different localized brain substrates. In particular, the syntactic aspect of language seems to depend upon an anterior speech area called Broca's area and the semantic aspect seems to depend on a posterior brain area called Wernicke's area. Both of these areas are in the cerebral cortex. Geschwind reviews the current status of our knowledge of the brain substrates of language in humans.

Animal Communication

by Edward O. Wilson

*Animals ranging from insects to mammals
communicate by means of chemicals, movements, and
sounds. Man also uses these modes of communication,
but he adds his own unique kind of language.*

The most instructive way to view the communication systems of animals is to compare these systems first with human language. With our own unique verbal system as a standard of reference we can define the limits of animal communication in terms of the properties it rarely—or never—displays. Consider the way I address you now. Each word I use has been assigned a specific meaning by a particular culture and transmitted to us down through generations by learning. What is truly unique is the very large number of such words and the potential for creating new ones to denote any number of additional objects and concepts. This potential is quite literally infinite. To take an example from mathematics, we can coin a nonsense word for any number we choose (as in the case of the googol, which designates a 1 followed by 100 zeros). Human beings utter their words sequentially in phrases and sentences that generate, according to complex rules also determined at least partly by the culture, a vastly larger array of messages than is provided by the mere summed meanings of the words themselves. With these messages it is possible to talk about the language itself, an achievement we are utilizing here. It is also possible to project an endless number of unreal images: fiction or lies, speculation or fraud, idealism or demagogy, the definition depending on whether or not the communicator informs the listener of his intention to speak falsely.

Now contrast this with one of the most sophisticated of all animal communication systems, the celebrated waggle dance of the honeybee (*Apis mellifera*), first decoded in 1945 by the German biologist Karl von Frisch. When a foraging worker bee returns from the field after discovering a food source (or, in the course of swarming, a desirable new nest site) at some distance from the hive, she indicates the location of this target to her fellow workers by performing the waggle dance. The pattern of her movement is a figure eight repeated over and over again in the midst of crowds of sister workers. The most distinctive and informative element of the dance is the straight run (the middle of the figure eight), which is given a particular emphasis by a rapid lateral vibration of the body (the waggle) that is greatest at the tip of the abdomen and least marked at the head.

The complete back-and-forth shake of the body is performed 13 to 15 times per second. At the same time the bee emits an audible buzzing sound by vibrating its wings. The straight run represents, quite simply, a miniaturized version of the flight from the hive to the target. It points directly at the target if the bee is dancing outside the hive on a horizontal surface. (The position of the sun with respect to the straight run provides the required orientation.) If the bee is on a vertical surface inside the darkened hive, the straight run points at the appropriate angle away from the vertical,

so that gravity temporarily replaces the sun as the orientation cue.

The straight run also provides information on the distance of the target from the hive, by means of the following additional parameter: the farther away the goal lies, the longer the straight run lasts. In the Carniolan race of the honeybee a straight run lasting a second indicates a target about 500 meters away, and a run lasting two seconds indicates a target two kilometers away. During the dance the follower bees extend their antennae and touch the dancer repeatedly. Within minutes some begin to leave the nest and fly to the target. Their searching is respectably accurate: the great majority come down to search close to the ground within 20 percent of the correct distance.

Superficially the waggle dance of the honeybee may seem to possess some of the more advanced properties of human language. Symbolism occurs in the form of the ritualized straight run, and the communicator can generate new messages at will by means of the symbolism. Furthermore, the target is "spoken of" abstractly: it is an object removed in time and space. Nevertheless, the waggle dance, like all other forms of nonhuman communication studied so far, is severely limited in comparison with the verbal language of human beings. The straight run is after all just a reenactment of the flight the bees will take, complete with wing-buzzing to represent the actual motor activity required. The separate messages are not devised arbitrarily. The rules they follow are genetically fixed and always designate, with a one-to-one correspondence, a certain direction and distance. .

In other words, the messages cannot be manipulated to provide new classes of information. Moreover, within this

COURTSHIP RITUAL of grebes is climaxed by the "penguin dance" shown on the opposite page. In this ritual the male and the female present each other with a beakful of the waterweed that is used as a nest-building material. A pair-bonding display, the dance may have originated as "displacement" behavior, in this instance a pantomime of nest-building triggered by the conflict within each partner between hostility and sexual attraction. The penguin dance was first analyzed in 1914 by Julian Huxley, who observed the ritual among great crested grebes in Europe. Shown here are western grebes in southern Saskatchewan.

rigid context the messages are far from being infinitely divisible. Because of errors both in the dance and in the subsequent searches by the followers, only about three bits of information are transmitted with respect to distance and four bits with respect to direction. This is the equivalent of a human communication system in which distance would be gauged on a scale with eight divisions and direction would be defined in terms of a compass with 16 points. Northeast could be distinguished from north by northeast, or west from west by southwest, but no more refined indication of direction would be possible.

The waggle dance, in particular the duration of the straight run denoting distance, illustrates a simple principle that operates through much of animal communication: the greater the magnitude to be communicated, the more intense and prolonged the signal given. This graduated (or analogue) form of communication is perhaps most strikingly developed in aggressive displays among animals. In the rhesus monkey, for example, a low-intensity aggressive display is a simple stare. The hard look a human receives when he approaches a caged rhesus is not so much a sign of curiosity as it is a cautious display of hostility.

Rhesus monkeys in the wild frequently threaten one another not only with stares but also with additional displays on an ascending scale of intensity. To the human observer these displays are increasingly obvious in their meaning. The new components are added one by one or in combination: the mouth opens, the head bobs up and down, characteristic sounds are uttered and the hands slap the ground. By the time the monkey combines all these components, and perhaps begins to make little forward lunges as well, it is likely to carry through with an actual attack. Its opponent responds either by retreating or by escalating its own displays. These hostile exchanges play a key role in maintaining dominance relationships in the rhesus society.

Birds often indicate hostility by ruffling their feathers or spreading their wings, which creates the temporary illusion that they are larger than they really are. Many fishes achieve the same deception by spreading their fins or extending their gill covers. Lizards raise their crest, lower their dewlaps or flatten the sides of their body to give an impression of greater depth. In short, the more hostile the animal, the more likely it is to attack and the bigger it seems to become. Such exhibitions are often accompanied by graded changes both in color and in vocalization, and even by the release of characteristic odors.

The communication systems of insects, of other invertebrates and of the lower vertebrates (such as fishes and amphibians) are characteristically stereotyped. This means that for each signal there is only one response or very few responses, that each response can be evoked by only a very limited number of signals and that the signaling behavior and the responses are nearly constant throughout entire populations of the same species. An extreme example of this rule is seen in the phenomenon of chemical sex attraction in moths. The female silkworm moth draws males to her by emitting minute quantities of a complex alcohol from glands at the tip of her abdomen. The secretion is called bombykol (from the name of the moth, *Bombyx mori*), and its chemical structure is *trans*-10-*cis*-12-hexadecadienol.

Bombykol is a remarkably powerful biological agent. According to estimates made by Dietrich Schneider and his co-workers at the Max Planck Institute for Comparative Physiology at Seewiesen in Germany, the male silkworm moths start searching for the females when they are immersed in as few as 14,000 molecules of bombykol per cubic centimeter of air. The male catches the molecules on some 10,000 distinctive sensory hairs on each of its two feathery antennae. Each hair is innervated by one or two receptor cells that lead inward to the main antennal nerve and ultimately through connecting nerve cells to centers in the brain. The extraordinary fact that emerged from the study by the Seewiesen group is that only a single molecule of bombykol is required to activate a receptor cell. Furthermore, the cell will respond to virtually no stimulus other than molecules of bombykol. When about 200 cells in each antenna are activated, the male moth starts its motor response. Tightly bound by this extreme signal specificity, the male performs as little more than a sexual guided missile, programmed to home on an increasing gradient of bombykol centered on the tip of the female's abdomen—the principal goal of the male's adult life.

Such highly stereotyped communication systems are particularly important in evolutionary theory because of the possible role the systems play in the origin of new species. Conceivably one small change in the sex-attractant molecule induced by a genetic mutation, together with a corresponding change in the antennal receptor cell, could result in the creation of a population of individuals that would be reproductively isolated from the parental stock. Persuasive

WAGGLE DANCE of the honeybee, first decoded by Karl von Frisch in 1945, is performed by a foraging worker bee on its return to the hive after the discovery of a food source. The pattern of the dance is a repeated figure eight. During the straight run in the middle of the figure the forager waggles its abdomen rapidly and vibrates its wings. As is shown in the illustrations on the opposite page, the direction of the straight run indicates the line of flight to the food source. The duration of the straight run shows workers how far to fly.

evidence for the feasibility of such a mutational change has recently been adduced by Wendell L. Roelofs and Andre Comeau of Cornell University. They found two closely related species of moths (members of the genus *Bryotopha* in the family Gelechiidae) whose females' sex attractants differ only by the configuration of a single carbon atom adjacent to a double bond. In other words, the attractants are simply different geometric isomers. Field tests showed not only that a *Bryotopha* male responds solely to the isomer of its own species but also that its response is inhibited if some of the other species' isomer is also present.

A qualitatively different kind of specificity is encountered among birds and mammals. Unlike the insects, many of these higher vertebrates are able to distinguish one another as individuals on the basis of idiosyncrasies in the way they deliver signals. Indigo buntings and certain other songbirds learn to discriminate the territorial calls of their neighbors from those of strangers that occupy territories farther away. When a recording of the song of a neighbor is played near them, they show no unusual reactions, but a recording of a stranger's song elicits an agitated aggressive response.

Families of seabirds depend on a similar capacity for recognition to keep together as a unit in the large, clamorous colonies where they nest. Beat Tschanz of the University of Bern has demonstrated that the young of the common murre (*Uria aalge*), a large auk, learn to react selectively to the call of their parents in the first few days of their life and that the parents also quickly learn to distinguish their own young. There is some evidence that the young murres can even learn certain aspects of the adult calls while they are still in the egg. An equally striking phenomenon is the intercommunication between African shrikes (of the genus *Laniarius*) recently analyzed by W. H. Thorpe of the University of Cambridge. Mated pairs of these birds keep in contact by calling antiphonally back and forth, the first bird vocalizing one or more notes and its mate instantly responding with a variation of the first call. So fast is the exchange, sometimes taking no more than a fraction of a second, that unless an observer stands between the two birds he does not realize that more than one bird is singing. In at least one of the species, the boubou shrike (*Laniarius aethiopicus*), the members of the pair learn to sing duets with each other. They work out combinations of phrases that are sufficiently individual

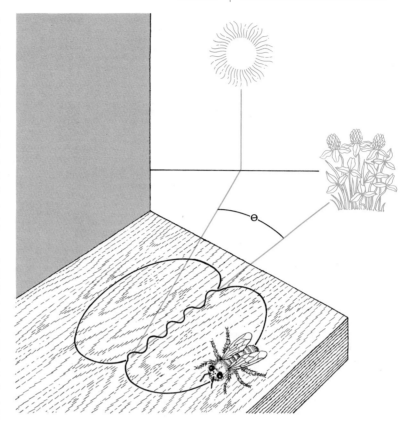

DANCING OUTSIDE THE HIVE on a horizontal surface, the forager makes the straight run of its waggle dance point directly at the source of food. In this illustration the food is located some 20 degrees to the right of the sun. The forager's fellow workers maintain the same orientation with respect to the sun as they leave for the reported source of food.

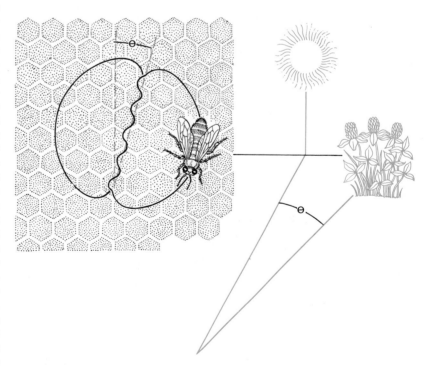

DANCING INSIDE THE HIVE on the vertical face of the honeycomb, the forager uses gravity for orientation. The straight line of the waggle dance that shows the line of flight to the source of food is oriented some 20 degrees away from the vertical. On leaving the hive, the bee's fellow workers relate the indicated orientation angle to the position of the sun.

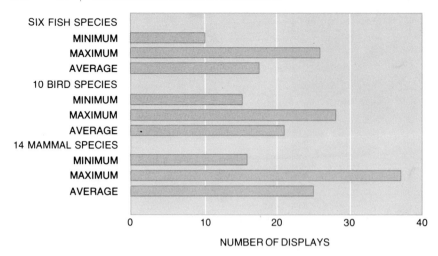

COMMUNICATIVE DISPLAYS used by 30 species of vertebrate animals whose "languages" have been studied vary widely within each of the classes of animals represented: fishes, birds and mammals. The average differences between the classes, however, are comparatively small. The largest and smallest number of displays within each class and the average for each class are shown in this graph. Six of the fish species that have been studied use an average of some 17 displays, compared with an average of 21 displays used by 10 species of birds and an average of 25 displays among 14 species of mammals. Martin H. Moynihan of the Smithsonian Institution compiled the display data. The 30 vertebrates and the number of displays that each uses are illustrated on the opposite page and on page 270.

to enable them to recognize each other even though both are invisible in the dense vegetation the species normally inhabits.

Mammals are at least equally adept at discriminating among individuals of their own kind. A wide range of cues are employed by different species to distinguish mates, offspring and in the case of social mammals the subordinate or dominant rank of the peers ranged around them. In some species special secretions are employed to impart a personal odor signature to part of the environment or to other members in the social group. As all dog owners know, their pet urinates at regular locations within its territory at a rate that seems to exceed physiological needs. What is less well appreciated is the communicative function this compulsive behavior serves: a scent included in the urine identifies the animal and announces its presence to potential intruders of the same species.

Males of the sugar glider (Petaurus breviceps), a New Guinea marsupial with a striking but superficial resemblance to the flying squirrel, go even further. They mark their mate with a secretion from a gland on the front of their head. Other secretions originating in glands on the male's feet, on its chest and near its arms, together with its saliva, are used to mark its territory. In both instances the odors are distinctive enough for the male to distinguish them from those of other sugar gliders.

As a rule we find that the more highly social the mammal is, the more complex the communication codes are and the more the codes are utilized in establishing and maintaining individual relationships. It is no doubt significant that one of the rare examples of persistent individual recognition among the lower animals is the colony odor of the social insects: ants and termites and certain social bees and wasps. Even here, however, it is the colony as a whole that is recognized. The separate members of the colony respond automatically to certain caste distinctions, but they do not ordinarily learn to discriminate among their nestmates as individuals.

By human standards the number of signals employed by each species of animal is severely limited. One of the most curious facts revealed by recent field studies is that even the most highly social vertebrates rarely have more than 30 or 35 separate displays in their entire repertory. Data compiled by Martin H. Moynihan of the Smithsonian Institution indicate that among most vertebrates the number of displays varies by a factor of only three or four from species to species. The number ranges from a minimum of 10 in certain fishes to a maximum of 37 in the rhesus monkey, one of the primates closest to man in the complexity of their social organization. The full significance of this rule of relative inflexibility is not yet clear. It may be that the maximum number of messages any animal needs in order to be fully adaptive in any ordinary environment, even a social one, is no more than

30 or 40. Or it may be, as Moynihan has suggested, that each number represents the largest amount of signal diversity the particular animal's brain can handle efficiently in quickly changing social interactions.

In the extent of their signal diversity the vertebrates are closely approached by social insects, particularly honeybees and ants. Analyses by Charles G. Butler at the Rothamsted Experimental Station in England, by me at Harvard University and by others have brought the number of individual known signal categories within single species of these insects to between 10 and 20. The honeybee has been the most thoroughly studied of all the social insects. Apart from the waggle dance its known communicative acts are mediated primarily by pheromones: chemical compounds transmitted to other members of the same species as signals. The glandular sources of these and other socially important substances are now largely established. Other honeybee signals include the distinctive colony odor mentioned above, tactile cues involved in food exchange and several dances that are different in form and function from the waggle dance.

Of the known honeybee pheromones the "queen substances" are outstanding in the complexity and pervasiveness of their role in social organization. They include trans-9-keto-2-decenoic acid, which is released from the queen's mandibular glands and evokes at least three separate effects according to the context of its presentation. The pheromone is spread through the colony when workers lick the queen's body and regurgitate the material back and forth to one another. For the substance to be effective in the colony as a whole the queen must dispense enough for each worker bee to receive approximately a tenth of a microgram per day.

The first effect of the ketodecenoic acid is to keep workers from rearing larvae in a way that would result in their becoming new queens, thus preventing the creation of potential rivals to the mother queen. The second effect is that when the worker bees eat the substance, their own ovaries fail to develop; they cannot lay eggs and as a result they too are eliminated as potential rivals. Indirect evidence indicates that ingestion of the substance affects the corpora allata, the endocrine glands that partly control the development of the ovaries, but the exact chain of events remains to be worked out. The third effect of the pheromone is that it acts as a sex attractant. When a virgin queen flies from

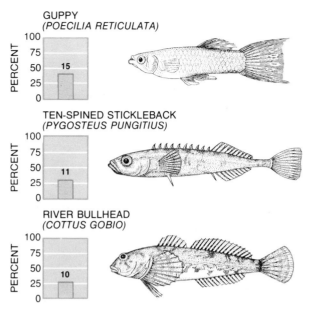
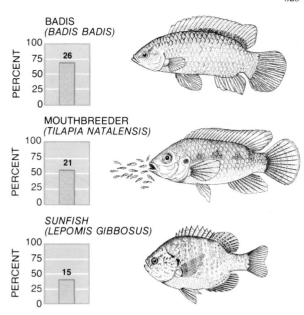

GUPPY
(POECILIA RETICULATA)

TEN-SPINED STICKLEBACK
(PYGOSTEUS PUNGITIUS)

RIVER BULLHEAD
(COTTUS GOBIO)

BADIS
(BADIS BADIS)

MOUTHBREEDER
(TILAPIA NATALENSIS)

SUNFISH
(LEPOMIS GIBBOSUS)

DISPLAYS BY FISHES range from a minimum of 10, used by the river bullhead (*bottom left*), to a maximum of 26, used by the badis (*top right*). The badis repertory is thus more extensive than those of eight of the 10 birds and nine of the 14 mammals studied. The bar beside each fish expressed the number of its displays in percent; 37 displays, the maximum in the study, equal 100 percent.

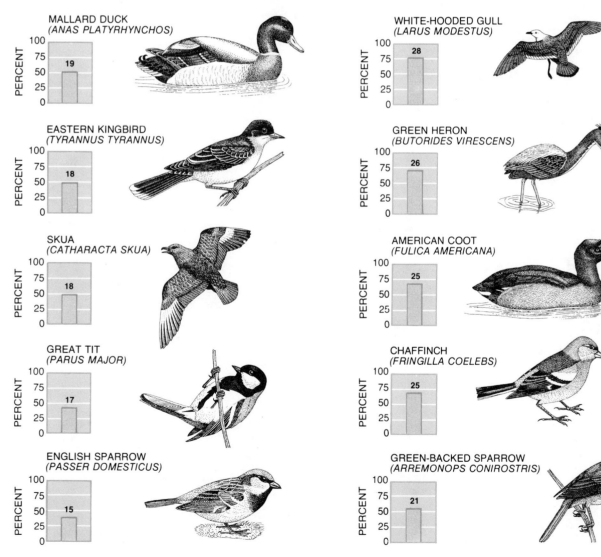

MALLARD DUCK
(ANAS PLATYRHYNCHOS)

EASTERN KINGBIRD
(TYRANNUS TYRANNUS)

SKUA
(CATHARACTA SKUA)

GREAT TIT
(PARUS MAJOR)

ENGLISH SPARROW
(PASSER DOMESTICUS)

WHITE-HOODED GULL
(LARUS MODESTUS)

GREEN HERON
(BUTORIDES VIRESCENS)

AMERICAN COOT
(FULICA AMERICANA)

CHAFFINCH
(FRINGILLA COELEBS)

GREEN-BACKED SPARROW
(ARREMONOPS CONIROSTRIS)

DISPLAYS BY BIRDS range from a minimum of 15, used by the English sparrow (*bottom left*), to a maximum of 28, used by the white-headed gull (*top right*). The maximum repertory among birds thus proves to be little greater than the fishes' maximum.

330

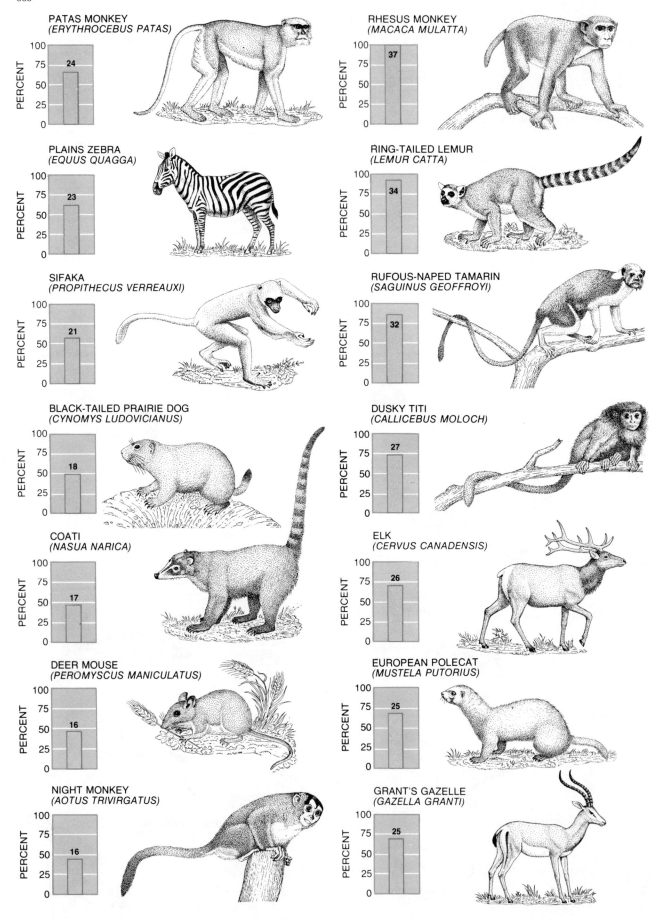

PATAS MONKEY
(ERYTHROCEBUS PATAS)

PERCENT — 24

PLAINS ZEBRA
(EQUUS QUAGGA)

PERCENT — 23

SIFAKA
(PROPITHECUS VERREAUXI)

PERCENT — 21

BLACK-TAILED PRAIRIE DOG
(CYNOMYS LUDOVICIANUS)

PERCENT — 18

COATI
(NASUA NARICA)

PERCENT — 17

DEER MOUSE
(PEROMYSCUS MANICULATUS)

PERCENT — 16

NIGHT MONKEY
(AOTUS TRIVIRGATUS)

PERCENT — 16

RHESUS MONKEY
(MACACA MULATTA)

PERCENT — 37

RING-TAILED LEMUR
(LEMUR CATTA)

PERCENT — 34

RUFOUS-NAPED TAMARIN
(SAGUINUS GEOFFROYI)

PERCENT — 32

DUSKY TITI
(CALLICEBUS MOLOCH)

PERCENT — 27

ELK
(CERVUS CANADENSIS)

PERCENT — 26

EUROPEAN POLECAT
(MUSTELA PUTORIUS)

PERCENT — 25

GRANT'S GAZELLE
(GAZELLA GRANTI)

PERCENT — 25

DISPLAYS BY MAMMALS range from a minimum of 16, used both by the deer mouse and by the night monkey (*left, bottom and next to bottom*), to a maximum of 37, used by the rhesus monkey (*top right*). Two other primates rank next in number of displays.

the hive on her nuptial flight, she releases a vapor trail of the ketodecenoic acid in the air. The smell of the substance not only attracts drones to the queen but also induces them to copulate with her.

W here do such communication codes come from in the first place? By comparing the signaling behavior of closely related species zoologists are often able to piece together the sequence of evolutionary steps that leads to even the most bizarre communication systems. The evolutionary process by which a behavior pattern becomes increasingly effective as a signal is called "ritualization." Commonly, and perhaps invariably, the process begins when some movement, some anatomical feature or some physiological trait that is functional in quite another context acquires a secondary value as a signal. For example, one can begin by recognizing an open mouth as a threat or by interpreting the turning away of the body in the midst of conflict as an intention to flee. During ritualization such movements are altered in some way that makes their communicative function still more effective. In extreme cases the new behavior pattern may be so modified from its ancestral state that its evolutionary history is all but impossible to imagine. Like the epaulets, shako plumes and piping that garnish military dress uniforms, the practical functions that originally existed have long since been obliterated in order to maximize efficiency in display.

The ritualization of vertebrate behavior commonly begins in circumstances of conflict, particularly when an animal is undecided whether or not to complete an act. Hesitation in behavior communicates the animal's state of mind—or, to be more precise, its probable future course of action—to onlooking members of the same species. The advertisement may begin its evolution as a simple intention movement. Birds intending to fly, for example, typically crouch, raise their tail and spread their wings slightly just before taking off. Many species have ritualized these movements into effective signals. In some species white rump feathers produce a conspicuous flash when the tail is raised. In other species the wing tips are flicked repeatedly downward, uncovering conspicuous areas on the primary feathers of the wings. The signals serve to coordinate the movement of flock members, and also may warn of approaching predators.

Signals also evolve from the ambivalence created by the conflict between two or more behavioral tendencies.

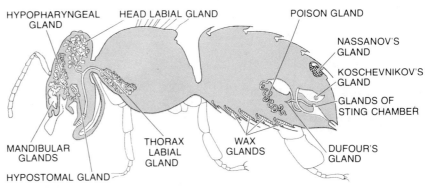

PHEROMONES OF THE HONEYBEE are produced by the glands shown in this cutaway figure of a worker. The glands perform different functions in different castes. In workers, for example, the secretion of the mandibular glands serves as an alarm signal. In a queen, however, the mandibular secretion that is spread through the colony as a result of grooming inhibits workers from raising new queens and also prevents workers from becoming egg-layers. It is also released as a vaporous sex attractant when the new queen leaves the hive on her nuptial flight. The "royal jelly" secreted by the hypopharyngeal gland serves as a food and also acts as a caste determinant. The labial glands of head and thorax secrete a substance utilized for grooming, cleaning and dissolving. Action of the hypostomal-gland secretion is unknown, as is the action of Dufour's gland. The wax glands yield nest-building material, the poison gland is for defense and the sting-chamber glands provide an alarm signal. The secretion of Nassanov's gland assists in assembling workers in conjunction with the waggle dance; that of Koschevnikov's gland renders queens attractive to workers.

When a male faces an opponent, unable to decide whether to attack or to flee, or approaches a potential mate with strong tendencies both to threaten and to court, he may at first make neither choice. Instead he performs a third, seemingly irrelevant act. The aggression is redirected at a meaningless object nearby, such as a pebble, a blade of grass or a bystander that serves as a scapegoat. Or the animal may abruptly commence a "displacement" activity: a behavior pattern with no relevance whatever to the circumstance in which the animal finds itself. The animal may preen, start ineffectual nest-building movements or pantomime feeding or drinking.

Such redirected and displacement activities have often been ritualized into strikingly clear signals. Two classic examples involve the formation of a pair bond between courting grebes. They were among the first such signals to be recognized; Julian Huxley, the originator of the concept of ritualization, analyzed the behavior among European great crested grebes in 1914. The first ritual is "mutual headshaking." It is apparently derived from more elementary movements, aimed at reducing hostility, wherein each bird simply directs its bill away from its partner. The second ritual, called by Huxley the "penguin dance," includes headshaking, diving and the mutual presentation by each partner to its mate of the waterweeds that serve as nesting material. The collection and presentation of the waterweeds may have evolved from displacement nesting behavior initially produced by the conflict between hostility and sexuality.

A perhaps even more instructive example of how ritualization proceeds is provided by the courtship behavior of the "dance flies." These insects include a large number of carnivorous species of dipterans that entomologists classify together as the family Empididae. Many of the species engage in a kind of courtship that consists in a simple approach by the male; this approach is followed by copulation. Among other species the male first captures an insect of the kind that normally falls prey to empids and presents it to the female before copulation. This act appears to reduce the chances of the male himself becoming a victim of the predatory impulses of the female. In other species the male fastens threads or globules of silk to the freshly captured offering, rendering it more distinctive in appearance, a clear step in the direction of ritualization.

Increasing degrees of ritualization can be observed among still other species of dance flies. In one of these species the male totally encloses the dead prey in a sheet of silk. In another the size of the offered prey is smaller but its silken covering remains as large as before: it is now a partly empty "balloon." The male of another species does not bother to capture any prey object but simply offers the female an empty balloon. The last display is so far removed from the original behavior pattern that its evolutionary origin in this empid species might have remained a permanent mystery if biolo-

AGGRESSIVE DISPLAYS by a rhesus monkey (*top*) and a green heron (*bottom*) illustrate a major principle of animal communication: the greater the magnitude to be communicated, the more prolonged and intense the signal is. In the rhesus what begins as a display of low intensity, a hard stare (*left*), is gradually escalated as the monkey rises to a standing position (*middle*) and then, with an open mouth, bobs its head up and down (*right*) and slaps the ground with its hands. If the opponent has not retreated by now, the monkey may actually attack. A similarly graduated aggressive display is characteristic of the green heron. At first (*middle*) the heron raises the feathers that form its crest and twitches the feathers of its tail. If the opponent does not retreat, the heron opens its beak, erects its crest fully, ruffles all its plumage to give the illusion of increased size and violently twitches its tail (*right*). Thus in both animals the likelier the attack, the more intense the aggressive display. Andrew J. Meyerriecks of the University of South Florida conducted the study of heron display and Stuart A. Altmann of the University of Chicago conducted the rhesus display study.

gists had not discovered what appears to be the full story of its development preserved step by step in the behavior of related species.

One of the most important and most difficult questions raised by behavioral biology can be phrased in the evolutionary terms just introduced as follows: Can we hope to trace the origin of human language back through intermediate steps in our fellow higher primates—our closest living relatives, the apes and monkeys—in the same way that entomologists have deduced the origin of the empty-balloon display among the dance flies? The answer would seem to be a very limited and qualified yes. The most probable links to investigate exist within human paralinguistics: the extensive array of facial expressions, body postures, hand signals and vocal tones and emphases that we use to supplement verbal speech. It might be possible to match some of these auxiliary signals with the more basic displays in apes and monkeys. J. A. R. A. M. van Hooff of the State University of Utrecht, for example,

has argued persuasively that laughter originated from the primitive "relaxed open-mouth display" used by the higher primates to indicate their intention to participate in mock aggression or play (as distinct from the hostile open-mouth posture described earlier as a low-intensity threat display in the rhesus monkey). Smiling, on the other hand, van Hooff derives from the primitive "silent bared-teeth display," which denotes submission or at least nonhostility.

What about verbal speech? Chimpanzees taught from infancy by human trainers are reported to be able to master the use of human words. The words are represented in some instances by sign language and in others by metal-backed plastic symbols that are pushed about on a magnetized board. The chimpanzees are also capable of learning rudimentary rules of syntax and even of inventing short questions and statements of their own. Sarah, a chimpanzee trained with plastic symbols by David Premack at the University of California at Santa Barbara, acquired a vocabulary of 128 "words," including a different "name"

for each of eight individuals, both human and chimpanzee, and other signs representative of 12 verbs, six colors, 21 foods and a rich variety of miscellaneous objects, concepts, adjectives and adverbs. Although Sarah's achievement is truly remarkable, an enormous gulf still separates this most intelligent of the anthropoid apes from man. Sarah's words are given to her, and she must use them in a rigid and artificial context. No chimpanzee has demonstrated anything close to the capacity and drive to experiment with language that is possessed by a normal human child.

The difference may be quantitative rather than qualitative, but at the very least our own species must still be ranked as unique in its capacity to concatenate a large vocabulary into sentences that touch on virtually every experience and thought. Future studies of animal communication should continue to prove useful in helping us to understand the steps that led man across such a vast linguistic chasm in what was surely the central event in the evolution of the human mind.

32

Teaching Language to an Ape

by Ann James Premack and David Premack

October 1972

Sarah, a young chimpanzee, has a reading and writing vocabulary of about 130 "words." Her understanding goes beyond the meaning of words and includes the concepts of class and sentence structure

O ver the past 40 years several efforts have been made to teach a chimpanzee human language. In the early 1930's Winthrop and Luella Kellogg raised a female chimpanzee named Gua along with their infant son; at the age of 16 months Gua could understand about 100 words, but she never did try to speak them. In the 1940's Keith and Cathy Hayes raised a chimpanzee named Vicki in their home; she learned a large number of words and with some difficulty could mouth the words "mama," "papa" and "cup." More recently Allen and Beatrice Gardner have taught their chimpanzee Washoe to communicate in the American Sign Language with her fingers and hands. Since 1966 in our laboratory at the University of California at Santa Barbara we have been teaching Sarah to read and write with variously shaped and colored pieces of plastic, each representing a word; Sarah has a vocabulary of about 130 terms that she uses with a reliability of between 75 and 80 percent.

Why try to teach human language to an ape? In our own case the motive was to better define the fundamental nature of language. It is often said that language is unique to the human species. Yet it is now well known that many other animals have elaborate communication systems of their own. It seems clear that language is a general system of which human language is a particular, albeit remarkably refined, form. Indeed, it is possible that certain features of human language that are considered to be uniquely human belong to the more general system, and that these features can be distinguished from those that are unique to the human information-processing regime. If, for example, an ape can be taught the rudiments of human language, it should clarify the dividing line between the general system and the human one.

There was much evidence that the chimpanzee was a good candidate for the acquisition of language before we began our project. In their natural environment chimpanzees have an extensive vocal "call system." In captivity the chimpanzee has been taught to sort pictures into classes: animate and inanimate, old and young, male and female. Moreover, the animal can classify the same item in different ways depending

SARAH, after reading the message "Sarah insert apple pail banana dish" on the magnetic board, performed the appropriate actions. To be able to make the correct interpretation that she should put the apple in the pail and the banana in the dish (not the apple, pail and banana in the dish) the chimpanzee had to understand sentence structure rather than just word order. In actual tests most symbols were colored (*see illustration on following page*).

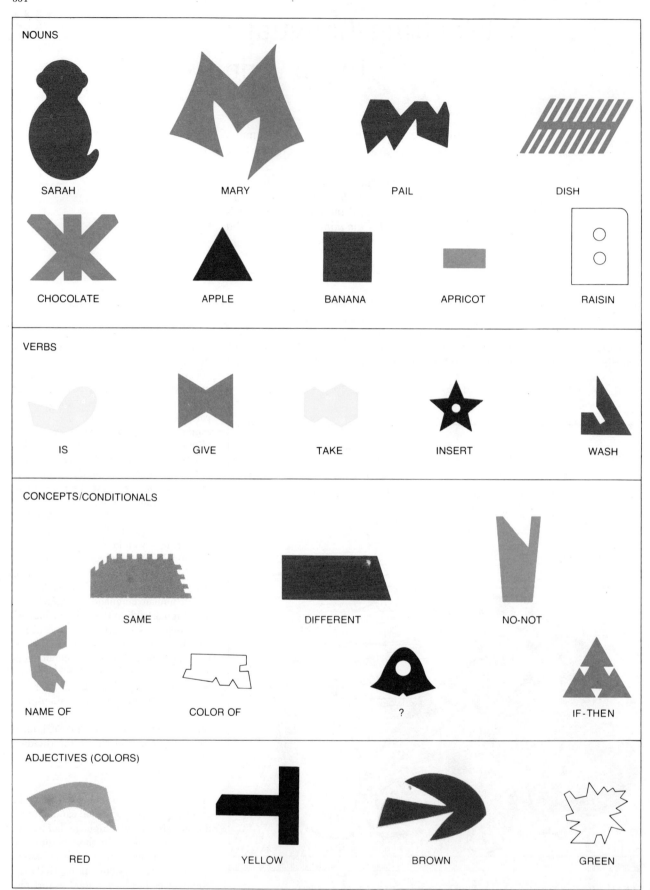

NOUNS

SARAH MARY PAIL DISH

CHOCOLATE APPLE BANANA APRICOT RAISIN

VERBS

IS GIVE TAKE INSERT WASH

CONCEPTS/CONDITIONALS

SAME DIFFERENT NO-NOT

NAME OF COLOR OF ? IF-THEN

ADJECTIVES (COLORS)

RED YELLOW BROWN GREEN

PLASTIC SYMBOLS that varied in color, shape and size were chosen as the language units to be taught to Sarah. The plastic pieces were backed with metal so that they would adhere to a magnetic board. Each plastic symbol stood for a specific word or concept. A "Chinese" convention of writing sentences vertically from top to bottom was adopted because at the beginning of her training Sarah seemed to prefer it. Sarah had to put the words in proper sequence but the orientation of the word symbols was not important.

on the alternatives offered. Watermelon is classified as fruit in one set of alternatives, as food in another set and as big in a third set. On the basis of these demonstrated conceptual abilities we made the assumption that the chimpanzee could be taught not only the names of specific members of a class but also the names for the classes themselves.

It is not necessary for the names to be vocal. They can just as well be based on gestures, written letters or colored stones. The important thing is to shape the language to fit the information-processing capacities of the chimpanzee. To a large extent teaching language to an animal is simply mapping out the conceptual structures the animal already possesses. By using a system of naming that suits the chimpanzee we hope to find out more about its conceptual world. Ultimately the benefit of language experiments with animals will be realized in an understanding of intelligence in terms not of scores on tests but of the underlying brain mechanisms. Only then can cognitive mechanisms for classifying stimuli, for storing and retrieving information and for problem-solving be studied in a comparative way.

The first step in teaching language is to exploit knowledge that is already present. In teaching Sarah we first mapped the simple social transaction of giving, which is something the chimpanzee does both in nature and in the laboratory. Considered in terms of cognitive and perceptual elements, the verb "give" involves a relation between two individuals and one object, that is, between the donor, the recipient and the object being transferred. In order to carry out the act of giving an animal must recognize the difference between individuals (between "Mary" and "Randy") and must perceive the difference between donors and recipients (between "Mary gives Randy" and "Randy gives Mary"). In order to be able to map out the entire transaction of giving the animal has to distinguish agents from objects, agents from one another, objects from one another and itself from others.

The trainer began the process of mapping the social transaction by placing a slice of banana between himself and Sarah. The chimpanzee, which was then about five years old, was allowed to eat the tasty morsel while the trainer looked on affectionately. After the transaction had become routine, a language element consisting of a pink plastic square was placed close to Sarah while the slice of banana was moved beyond her reach. To obtain the fruit Sarah now had to put the plastic piece on a "language board" on the side of her cage. (The board was magnetic and the plastic square was backed with a thin piece of steel so that it would stick.) After Sarah had learned this routine the fruit was changed to an apple and she had to place a blue plastic word for apple on the board. Later several other fruits, the verb "give" and the plastic words that named each of them were introduced.

To be certain that Sarah knew the meaning of "give" it was necessary to contrast "give" with other verbs, such as "wash," "cut" and "insert." When Sarah indicated "Give apple," she was given a piece of apple. When she put "Wash apple" on the board, the apple was placed in a bowl of water and washed. In that way Sarah learned what action went with what verb.

In the first stage Sarah was required to put only one word on the board; the name of the fruit was a sufficient indicator of the social transaction. When names for different actions—verbs—were introduced, Sarah had to place two words on the board in vertical sequence. In order to be given an apple she had to write "Give apple." When recipients were named, two-word sentences were not accepted by the trainer; Sarah had to use three words. There were several trainers, and Sarah had to learn the name of each one. To facilitate the teaching of personal names, both the chimpanzees and the trainers wore their plastic-word names on a string necklace. Sarah learned the names of some of the recipients the hard way. Once she wrote "Give apple Gussie," and the trainer promptly gave the apple to another chimpanzee named Gussie. Sarah never repeated the sentence. At every stage she was required to observe the proper word sequence. "Give apple" was accepted but "Apple give" was not. When donors were to be named, Sarah had to identify all the members of the social transaction: "Mary give apple Sarah."

The interrogative was introduced with the help of the concepts "same" and "different." Sarah was given a cup and a spoon. When another cup was added, she was taught to put the two cups together. Other sets of three objects were given to her, and she had to pair the two objects that were alike. Then she was taught to place the plastic word for "same" between any two similar objects and the plastic word for "different" between unlike objects. Next what amounted to a question mark was placed between pairs of objects. This plastic shape (which bore no resemblance to the usual kind of question mark) made the question explicit rather than implicit, as it had been in the simple matching tests. When the interrogative element was placed between a pair of cups, it meant: "What is the relation between cup A and cup B?" The choices provided Sarah were the plastic words "same" and "different." She learned to remove the interrogative particle and substitute the correct word [see top illustration on page 339]. Sarah was able to transfer what she had learned and apply the word "same" or "different" to numerous pairs of objects that had not been used in her training.

Any construction is potentially a question. From the viewpoint of structural linguistics any construction where one or more elements are deleted becomes a question. The constructions we used with Sarah were "A same A" and "A different B." Elements in these constructions were removed and the deletion was marked with the interrogative symbol; Sarah was then supplied with a choice of missing elements with which she could restore the construction to its familiar form. In principle interrogation can be taught either by removing an element from a familiar situation in the animal's world or by removing the element from a language that maps the animal's world. It is probable that one can induce questions by purposively removing key elements from a familiar situation. Suppose a chimpanzee received its daily ration of food at a specific time and place, and then one day the food was not there. A chimpanzee trained in the interrogative might inquire "Where is my food?" or, in Sarah's case, "My food is?" Sarah was never put in a situation that might induce such interrogation because for our purposes it was easier to teach Sarah to answer questions.

At first Sarah learned all her words in the context of social exchange. Later, when she had learned the concepts "name of" and "not name of," it was possible to introduce new words in a more direct way. To teach her that objects had names, the plastic word for "apple" and a real apple were placed on the table and Sarah was required to put the plastic word for "name of" between them. The same procedure was repeated for banana. After she had responded correctly several times, the symbol for "apple" and a real banana were placed on the table and Sarah had to put "not

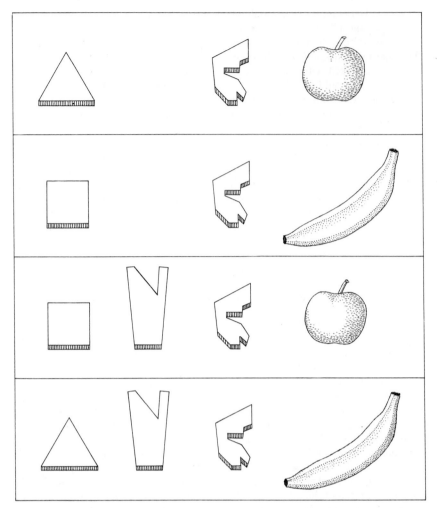

TEACHING LANGUAGE WITH LANGUAGE was the next step. Sarah was taught to put the symbol for "name of" between the word for "apple" and an apple and also between the word for "banana" and a banana. She learned the concept "not name of" in the same way. Thereafter Sarah could be taught new nouns by introducing them with "name of."

name of" between them. After she was able to perform both operations correctly new nouns could be taught quickly and explicitly. The plastic words for "raisin" and "name of" could be placed next to a real raisin and Sarah would learn the noun. Evidence of such learning came when Sarah subsequently requested "Mary give raisin Sarah" or set down "Raisin different apple."

An equally interesting linguistic leap occurred when Sarah learned the predicate adjective and could write such sentences as "Red color of apple," "Round shape of apple" and "Large size of apple." When asked for the relation between "Apple is red ? Red color of apple" and given "same" and "different" as choices, she judged the sentences to be the same. When given "Apple is red ? Apple is round," she judged the sentences to be different. The distinctions between similar and different, first learned with actual objects, was later

applied by Sarah in linguistic constructions.

In English the conditional consists of the discontinuous elements "if-then," which are inconvenient and conceptually unnecessary. In symbolic logic the conditional consists of the single sign ⊃, and we taught Sarah the conditional relation with the use of a single plastic word. Before being given language training in the conditional, she was given contingency training in which she was rewarded for doing one thing but not another. For example, she was given a choice between an apple and a banana, and only when she chose the apple was she given chocolate (which she dearly loved). "If apple, then chocolate, if banana, then no chocolate" were the relations she learned; the same relations were subsequently used in sentences to teach her the name for the conditional relation.

The subject was introduced with the

written construction: "Sarah take apple ? Mary give chocolate Sarah." Sarah was provided with only one plastic word: the conditional particle. She had to remove the question mark and substitute the conditional in its place to earn the apple and the chocolate. Now she was presented with: "Sarah take banana ? Mary no give chocolate Sarah." Again only the conditional symbol was provided. When Sarah replaced the question mark with the conditional symbol, she received a banana but no chocolate. After several such tests she was given a series of trials on each of the following pairs of sentences: "Sarah take apple if-then Mary give chocolate Sarah" coupled with "Sarah take banana if-then Mary no give chocolate Sarah," or "Sarah take apple if-then Mary no give chocolate Sarah" coupled with "Sarah take banana if-then Mary give chocolate Sarah."

At first Sarah made many errors, taking the wrong fruit and failing to get her beloved chocolate. After several of her strategies had failed she paid closer attention to the sentences and began choosing the fruit that gave her the chocolate. Once the conditional relation had been learned she was able to apply it to other types of sentence, for example "Mary take red if-then Sarah take apple" and "Mary take green if-then Sarah take banana." Here Sarah had to watch Mary's choice closely in order to take the correct action. With the paired sentences "Red is on green if-then Sarah take apple" and "Green is on red if-then Sarah take banana," which involved a change in the position of two colored cards, Sarah was not confused and performed well.

As a preliminary to learning the class concepts of color, shape and size Sarah was taught to identify members of the classes red and yellow, round and square and large and small. Objects that varied in most dimensions but had a particular property in common were used. Thus for teaching the word "red" a set of dissimilar, unnamed objects (a ball, a toy car, a Life Saver and so on) that had no property in common except redness were put before the chimpanzee. The only plastic word available to her was "red." After several trials on identifying red with a set of red objects and yellow with a set of yellow objects, Sarah was shifted to trials where she had to choose between "red" and "yellow" when she was shown a colored object. Finally completely new red and yellow objects were presented to her, including small cards that were identical except for their color.

Again she performed at her usual level of accuracy.

Sarah was subsequently taught the names of shapes, "round" and "square," as well as the size names "large" and "small." These words formed the basis for teaching her the names of the class concepts "color of," "shape of" and "size of." Given the interrogative "Red ? apple" or "Yellow ? banana," Sarah was required to substitute the plastic word for "color of" for the question mark. In teaching class names a good many sentences were not written on the board but were presented as hybrids. The hybrid sentences consisted of a combination of plastic words and real objects arranged in the proper sentence sequence on Sarah's worktable. Typical sentences were "Yellow ?" beside a real yellow balloon or "Red ?" beside a red wood block.

The hybrid sentences did not deter Sarah in the least. Her good performance showed that she was able to move with facility from symbols for objects to actual objects. Her behavior with hybrid constructions recalls the activity of young children, who sometimes combine spoken words with real objects they are unable to name by pointing at the objects.

Was Sarah able to think in the plastic-word language? Could she store information using the plastic words or use them to solve certain kinds of problem that she could not solve otherwise? Additional research is needed before we shall have definitive answers, but Sarah's performance suggests that the answers to both questions may be a qualified yes. To think with language requires being able to generate the meaning of words in the absence of their external representation. For Sarah to be able to match "apple" to an actual apple or "Mary" to a picture of Mary indicates that she knows the meaning of these words. It does not prove, however, that when she is given the word "apple" and no apple is present, she can think "apple," that is, mentally represent the meaning of the word to herself. The ability to achieve such mental representation is of major importance because it frees language from simple dependence on the outside world. It involves displacement: the ability to talk about things that are not actually there. That is a critical feature of language.

The hint that Sarah was able to understand words in the absence of their external referents came early in her language training. When she was given a piece of fruit and two plastic words, she was required to put the correct word for the fruit on the board before she was allowed to eat it. Surprisingly often, however, she chose the wrong word. It then dawned on us that her poor performance might be due not to errors but to her trying to express her preferences in fruit. We conducted a series of tests to determine her fruit preferences, using actual fruits in one test and only fruit names in the other. Sarah's choices between the words were much the same as her choices between the actual fruits. This result strongly suggests that she could generate the meaning of the fruit names from the plastic symbols alone.

We obtained clearer evidence at a later stage of Sarah's language training. In the same way that she could use

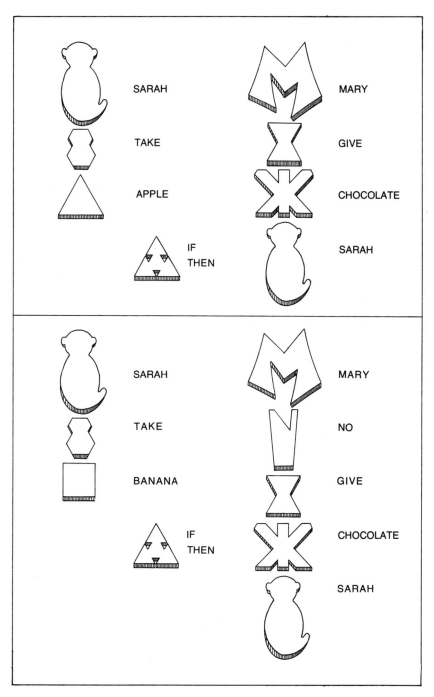

CONDITIONAL RELATION, which in English is expressed "if...then," was taught to Sarah as a single word. The plastic symbol for the conditional relation was placed between two sentences. Sarah had to pay attention to the meaning of both sentences very closely in order to make the choice that would give her a reward. Once the conditional relation was learned by means of this procedure, the chimpanzee was able to apply it to other situations.

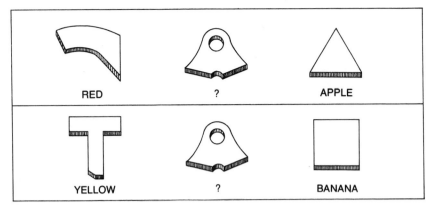

CLASS CONCEPT OF COLOR was taught with the aid of sentences such as "Red ? apple" and "Yellow ? banana." Sarah had to replace the interrogative symbol with "color of."

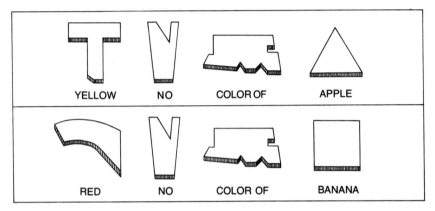

NEGATIVE CONCEPT was introduced with "no-not." When asked "Yellow ? apple" or "Red ? banana," Sarah had to replace interrogative symbol with "color of" or "not color of."

ALTERNATIVE FEATURES			
RED	GREEN	RED	RED
○	□	○	○

FEATURE ANALYSIS of an actual apple and the plastic word for "apple" was conducted. Sarah was shown an apple or the word and made to choose from alternative features: red or green, round or square, square with stem or plain square and square with stem or round. Sarah gave plastic word for "apple" same attributes she had earlier assigned to apple.

"name of" to learn new nouns, she was able to use "color of" to learn the names of new colors. For instance, the names "brown" and "green" were introduced in the sentences "Brown color of chocolate" and "Green color of grape." The only new words at this point were "brown" and "green." Later Sarah was confronted with four disks, only one of which was brown, and when she was instructed with the plastic symbols "Take brown," she took the brown disk. Since chocolate was not present at any time during the introduction of the color name "brown," the word "chocolate" in the definition must have been sufficient to have Sarah generate or picture the property brown.

What form does Sarah's supposed internal representation take? Some indication is provided by the results of a test of ability to analyze the features of an object. First Sarah was shown an actual apple and was given a series of paired comparisons that described the features of the apple, such as red v. green, round v. square and so on. She had to pick the descriptive feature that belonged to the apple. Her feature analysis of a real apple agreed nicely with our own, which is evidence of the interesting fact that a chimpanzee is capable of decomposing a complex object into features. Next the apple was removed and the blue plastic triangle that was the word for "apple" was placed before her and again she was given a paired-comparison test. She assigned the same features to the word that she had earlier assigned to the object. Her feature analysis revealed that it was not the physical properties of the word (blue and triangle) that she was describing but rather the object that was represented by the word [see bottom illustration at left].

To test Sarah's sentence comprehension she was taught to correctly follow these written instructions: "Sarah insert apple pail," "Sarah insert banana pail," "Sarah insert apple dish" and "Sarah insert banana dish." Next instructions were combined in a one-line vertical sequence ("Sarah insert apple pail Sarah insert banana dish"). The chimpanzee responded appropriately. Then the second "Sarah" and the second verb "insert" were deleted to yield the compound sentence: "Sarah insert apple pail banana dish." Sarah followed the complicated instructions at her usual level of accuracy.

The test with the compound sentence is of considerable importance, because it provides the answer to whether or not

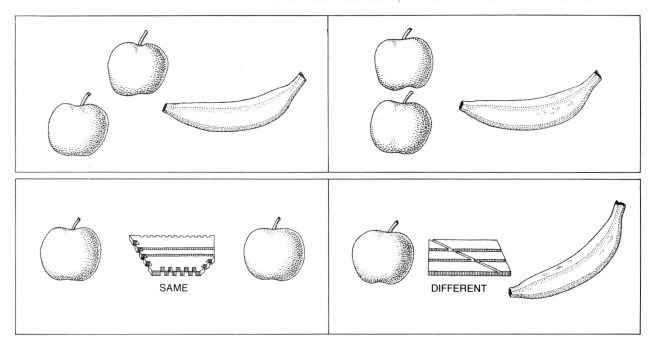

CONCEPTS "SAME" AND "DIFFERENT" were introduced into Sarah's vocabulary by teaching her to pair objects that were alike (*top illustration*). Then two identical objects, for example apples, were placed before her and she was given plastic word for "same" and induced to place word between the two objects. She was also taught to place the word for "different" between unlike objects.

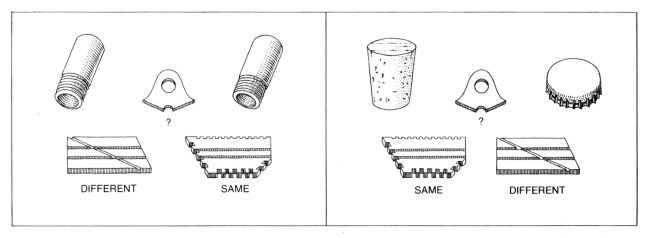

THE INTERROGATIVE was introduced with the help of the concepts "same" and "different." A plastic piece that meant "question mark" was placed between two objects and Sarah had to replace it with either the word for "same" or the word for "different."

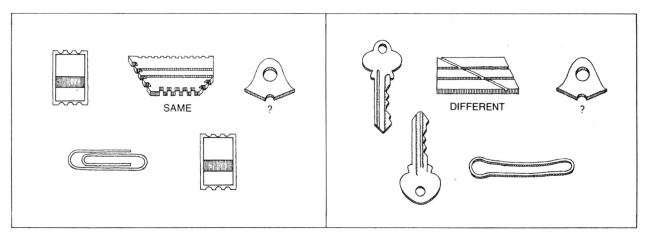

NEW VERSION OF THE INTERROGATIVE was taught by arranging an object and plastic symbols to form questions: "What is [Object A] the same as?" or "What is [Object A] different from?" Sarah had to replace question marker with the appropriate object.

Sarah could understand the notion of constituent structure: the hierarchical organization of a sentence. The correct interpretation of the compound sentence was "Sarah put the apple in the pail and the banana in the dish." To take the correct actions Sarah must understand that "apple" and "pail" go together but not "pail" and "banana," even though the terms appear side by side. Moreover, she must understand that the verb "insert" is at a higher level of organization and refers to both "apple" and "banana." Finally, Sarah must understand that she, as the head noun, must carry out all the actions. If Sarah were capable only of linking words in a simple chain, she would never be able to interpret the compound sentence with its deletions. The fact is that she interprets them correctly. If a child were to carry out the instructions in the same way, we would not hesitate to say that he recognizes the various levels of sentence organization: that the subject dominates the predicate and the verb in the predicate dominates the objects.

Sarah had managed to learn a code, a simple language that nevertheless included some of the characteristic features of natural language. Each step of the training program was made as simple as possible. The objective was to reduce complex notions to a series of simple and highly learnable steps. The same program that was used to teach Sarah to communicate has been successfully applied with people who have language difficulties caused by brain damage. It may also be of benefit to the autistic child

In assessing the results of the experiment with Sarah one must be careful not to require of Sarah what one would require of a human adult. Compared with a two-year-old child, however, Sarah holds her own in language ability. In fact, language demands were made of Sarah that would never be made of a child. Man is understandably prejudiced in favor of his own species, and members of other species must perform Herculean feats before they are recognized as having similar abilities, particularly language abilities. Linguists and others who study the development of language tend to exaggerate the child's understanding of language and to be extremely skeptical of the experimentally demonstrated language abilities of the chimpanzee. It is our hope that our findings will dispel such prejudices and lead to new attempts to teach suitable languages to animals other than man.

Language and the Brain

by Norman Geschwind
April 1972

*Aphasias are speech disorders caused by brain
damage. The relations between these disorders and
specific kinds of brain damage suggest a model of how
the language areas of the human brain are organized*

Virtually everything we know of how the functions of language are organized in the human brain has been learned from abnormal conditions or under abnormal circumstances: brain damage, brain surgery, electrical stimulation of brains exposed during surgery and the effects of drugs on the brain. Of these the most fruitful has been the study of language disorders, followed by postmortem analysis of the brain, in patients who have suffered brain damage. From these studies has emerged a model of how the language areas of the brain are interconnected and what each area does.

A disturbance of language resulting from damage to the brain is called aphasia. Such disorders are not rare. Aphasia is a common aftereffect of the obstruction or rupture of blood vessels in the brain, which is the third leading cause of death in the U.S. Although loss of speech from damage to the brain had been described occasionally before the 19th century, the medical study of such cases was begun by a remarkable Frenchman, Paul Broca, who in 1861 published the first of a series of papers on language and the brain. Broca was the first to point out that damage to a specific portion of the brain results in disturbance of language output. The portion he identified, lying in the third frontal gyrus of the cerebral cortex, is now called Broca's area [*see illustration on page 343*].

Broca's area lies immediately in front of the portion of the motor cortex that controls the muscles of the face, the jaw, the tongue, the palate and the larynx, in other words, the muscles involved in speech production. The region is often called the "motor face area." It might therefore seem that loss of speech from damage to Broca's area is the result of paralysis of these muscles. This explana-

tion, however, is not the correct one. Direct damage to the area that controls these muscles often produces only mild weakness of the lower facial muscles on the side opposite the damage and no permanent weakness of the jaw, the tongue, the palate or the vocal cords. The reason is that most of these muscles can be controlled by either side of the brain. Damage to the motor face area on one side of the brain can be compensated by the control center on the opposite side. Broca named the lesion-produced language disorder "aphemia," but this term was soon replaced by "aphasia," which was suggested by Armand Trousseau.

In 1865 Broca made a second major contribution to the study of language and the brain. He reported that damage to specific areas of the left half of the brain led to disorder of spoken language but that destruction of corresponding areas in the right side of the brain left language abilities intact. Broca based his conclusion on eight consecutive cases of aphasia, and in the century since his report his observation has been amply confirmed. Only rarely does damage to the right hemisphere of the brain lead to language disorder; out of 100 people with permanent language disorder caused by brain lesions approximately 97 will have damage on the left side. This unilateral control of certain functions is called cerebral dominance. As far as we know man is the only mammal in

which learned behavior is controlled by one half of the brain. Fernando Nottebohm of Rockefeller University has found unilateral neural control of birdsong. It is an interesting fact that a person with aphasia of the Broca type who can utter at most only one or two slurred words may be able to sing a melody rapidly, correctly and even with elegance. This is another proof that aphasia is not the result of muscle paralysis.

In the decade following Broca's first report on brain lesions and language there was a profusion of papers on aphasias of the Broca type. In fact, there was a tendency to believe all aphasias were the result of damage to Broca's area. At this point another great pioneer of the brain appeared on the scene. Unlike Broca, who already had a reputation at the time of his first paper on aphasia, Carl Wernicke was an unknown with no previous publications; he was only 26 years old and a junior assistant in the neurological service in Breslau. In spite of his youth and obscurity his paper on aphasia, published in 1874, gained immediate attention. Wernicke described damage at a site in the left hemisphere outside Broca's area that results in a language disorder differing from Broca's aphasia.

In Broca's aphasia speech is slow and labored. Articulation is crude. Characteristically, small grammatical words and the endings of nouns and verbs are

LOCATION OF SOME LESIONS in the brain can be determined by injecting into the bloodstream a radioactive isotope of mercury, which is taken up by damaged brain tissue. The damaged region is identified by scanning the head for areas of high radioactivity. The top scan on the following page was made from the back of the head; the white area on the left shows that the damage is in the left hemisphere. The bottom scan is of the left side of the head and shows that the uptake of mercury was predominantly in the first temporal gyrus, indicating damage to Wernicke's speech area by occlusion of blood vessels. David Patten and Martin Albert of the Boston Veterans Administration Hospital supplied the scans.

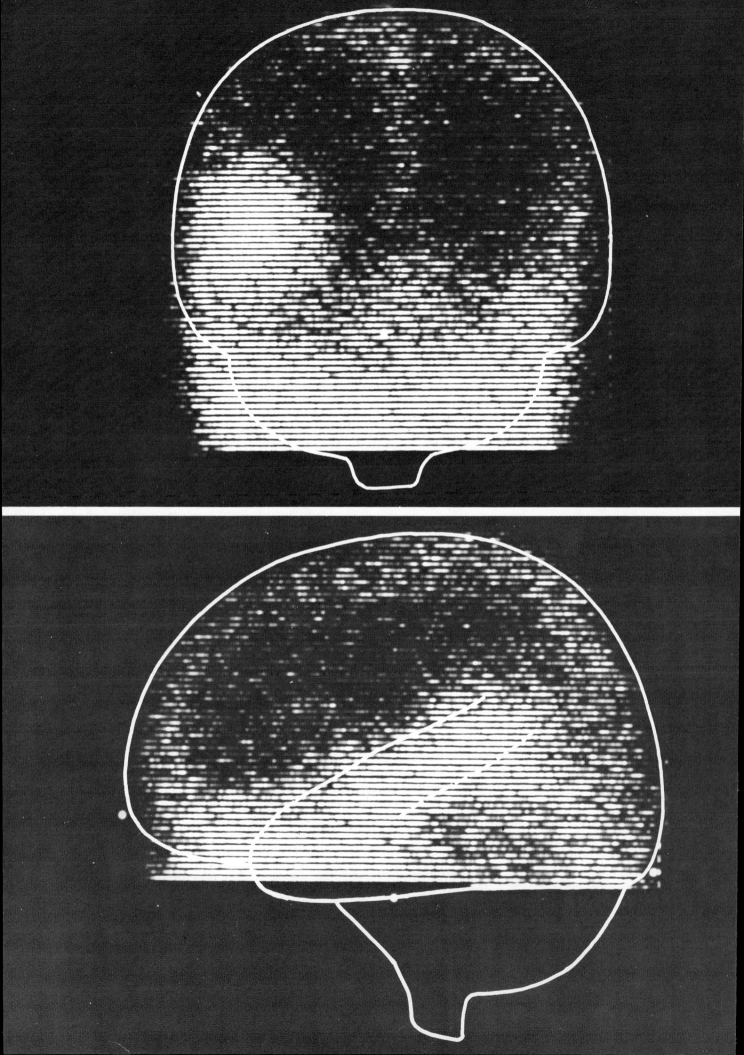

omitted, so that the speech has a telegraphic style. Asked to describe a trip he has taken, the patient may say "New York." When urged to produce a sentence, he may do no better than "Go... New York." This difficulty is not simply a desire to economize effort, as some have suggested. Even when the patient does his best to cooperate in repeating words, he has difficulty with certain grammatical words and phrases. "If he were here, I would go" is more difficult than "The general commands the army." The hardest phrase for such patients to repeat is "No ifs, ands or buts."

The aphasia described by Wernicke is quite different. The patient may speak very rapidly, preserving rhythm, grammar and articulation. The speech, if not listened to closely, may almost sound normal. For example, the patient may say: "Before I was in the one here, I was over in the other one. My sister had the department in the other one." It is abnormal in that it is remarkably devoid of content. The patient fails to use the correct word and substitutes for it by

circumlocutory phrases ("what you use to cut with" for "knife") and empty words ("thing"). He also suffers from paraphasia, which is of two kinds. Verbal paraphasia is the substitution of one word or phrase for another, sometimes related in meaning ("knife" for "fork") and sometimes unrelated ("hammer" for "paper"). Literal or phonemic paraphasia is the substitution of incorrect sounds in otherwise correct words ("kench" for "wrench"). If there are several incorrect sounds in a word, it becomes a neologism, for example "pluver" or "flieber."

Wernicke also noted another difference between these aphasic patients and those with Broca's aphasia. A person with Broca's aphasia may have an essentially normal comprehension of language. Indeed, Broca had argued that no single lesion in the brain could cause a loss of comprehension. He was wrong. A lesion in Wernicke's area can produce a severe loss of understanding, even though hearing of nonverbal sounds and music may be fully normal.

Perhaps the most important contribu-

tion made by Wernicke was his model of how the language areas in the brain are connected. Wernicke modestly stated that his ideas were based on the teachings of Theodor Meynert, a Viennese neuroanatomist who had attempted to correlate the nervous system's structure with its function. Since Broca's area was adjacent to the cortical region of the brain that controlled the muscles of speech, it was reasonable to assume, Wernicke argued, that Broca's area incorporated the programs for complex coordination of these muscles. In addition Wernicke's area lay adjacent to the cortical region that received auditory stimuli [see illustration below]. Wernicke made the natural assumption that Broca's area and Wernicke's area must be connected. We now know that the two areas are indeed connected, by a bundle of nerve fibers known as the arcuate fasciculus. One can hypothesize that in the repetition of a heard word the auditory patterns are relayed from Wernicke's area to Broca's area.

Comprehension of written language

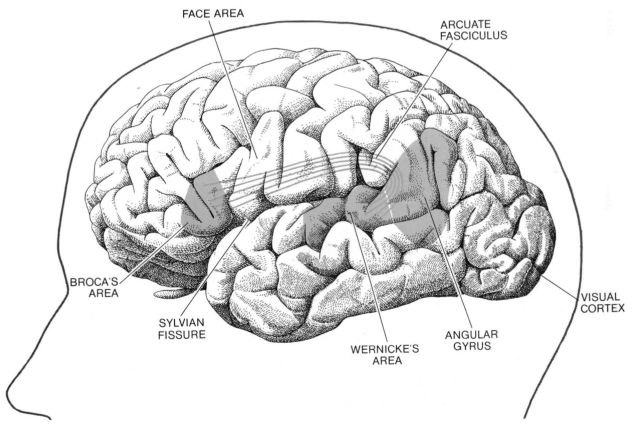

FACE AREA

ARCUATE FASCICULUS

BROCA'S AREA

SYLVIAN FISSURE

WERNICKE'S AREA

ANGULAR GYRUS

VISUAL CORTEX

PRIMARY LANGUAGE AREAS of the human brain are thought to be located in the left hemisphere, because only rarely does damage to the right hemisphere cause language disorders. Broca's area, which is adjacent to the region of the motor cortex that controls the movement of the muscles of the lips, the jaw, the tongue, the soft palate and the vocal cords, apparently incorporates programs for the coordination of these muscles in speech. Damage to Broca's area results in slow and labored speech, but comprehension of

language remains intact. Wernicke's area lies between Heschl's gyrus, which is the primary receiver of auditory stimuli, and the angular gyrus, which acts as a way station between the auditory and the visual regions. When Wernicke's area is damaged, speech is fluent but has little content and comprehension is usually lost. Wernicke and Broca areas are joined by a nerve bundle called the arcuate fasciculus. When it is damaged, speech is fluent but abnormal, and patient can comprehend words but cannot repeat them.

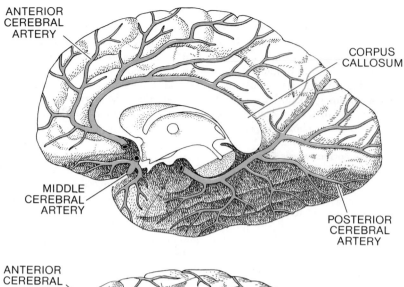

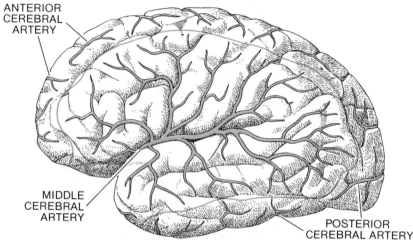

CEREBRAL AREAS are nourished by several arteries, each supplying blood to a specific region. The speech and auditory region is nourished by the middle cerebral artery. The visual areas at the rear are supplied by the posterior cerebral artery. In patients who suffer from inadequate oxygen supply to the brain the damage is often not within the area of a single blood vessel but rather in the "border zones" (*colored lines*). These are the regions between the areas served by the major arteries where the blood supply is marginal.

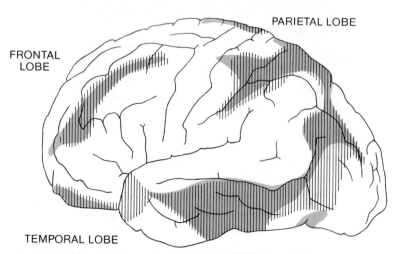

ISOLATION OF SPEECH AREA by a large *C*-shaped lesion produced a remarkable syndrome in a woman who suffered from severe carbon monoxide poisoning. She could repeat words and learn new songs but could not comprehend the meaning of words. Postmortem examination of her brain revealed that in the regions surrounding the speech areas of the left hemisphere, either the cortex (*colored areas*) or the underlying white matter (*hatched areas*) was destroyed but that the cortical structures related to the production of language (Broca's area and Wernicke's area) and the connections between them were left intact.

would require connections from the visual regions to the speech regions. This function is served by the angular gyrus, a cortical region just behind Wernicke's area. It acts in some way to convert a visual stimulus into the appropriate auditory form.

We can now deduce from the model what happens in the brain during the production of language. When a word is heard, the output from the primary auditory area of the cortex is received by Wernicke's area. If the word is to be spoken, the pattern is transmitted from Wernicke's area to Broca's area, where the articulatory form is aroused and passed on to the motor area that controls the movement of the muscles of speech. If the spoken word is to be spelled, the auditory pattern is passed to the angular gyrus, where it elicits the visual pattern. When a word is read, the output from the primary visual areas passes to the angular gyrus, which in turn arouses the corresponding auditory form of the word in Wernicke's area. It should be noted that in most people comprehension of a written word involves arousal of the auditory form in Wernicke's area. Wernicke argued that this was the result of the way most people learn written language. He thought, however, that in people who were born deaf, but had learned to read, Wernicke's area would not be in the circuit.

According to this model, if Wernicke's area is damaged, the person would have difficulty comprehending both spoken and written language. He should be unable to speak, repeat and write correctly. The fact that in such cases speech is fluent and well articulated suggests that Broca's area is intact but receiving inadequate information. If the damage were in Broca's area, the effect of the lesion would be to disrupt articulation. Speech would be slow and labored but comprehension should remain intact.

This model may appear to be rather simple, but it has shown itself to be remarkably fruitful. It is possible to use it to predict the sites of brain lesions on the basis of the type of language disorder. Moreover, it gave rise to some definite predictions that lesions in certain sites should produce types of aphasia not previously described. For example, if a lesion disconnected Wernicke's area from Broca's area while leaving the two areas intact, a special type of aphasia should be the result. Since Broca's area is preserved, speech should be fluent but abnormal. On the other hand, comprehension should be intact because Wernicke's area is still functioning. Repetition of spoken language, however, should be grossly impaired. This syndrome has in fact been found. It is termed conduction aphasia.

The basic pattern of speech localization in the brain has been supported by the work of many investigators. A. R. Luria of the U.S.S.R. studied a large number of patients who suffered brain wounds during World War II [see the article "The Functional Organization of the Brain," by A. R. Luria, beginning on page 375]. When the wound site lay over Wernicke's or Broca's area, Luria found that the result was almost always severe and permanent aphasia. When the wounds were in other areas, aphasia was less frequent and less severe.

A remarkable case of aphasia has provided striking confirmation of Wernicke's model. The case, described by Fred Quadfasel, Jose Segarra and myself, involved a woman who had suffered from accidental carbon monoxide poisoning. During the nine years we studied her she was totally helpless and required complete nursing care. She never uttered speech spontaneously and showed no evidence of comprehending words. She could, however, repeat perfectly sentences that had just been said to her. In addition she would complete certain phrases. For example, if she heard "Roses are red," she would say "Roses are red, violets are blue, sugar is sweet and so are you." Even more surprising was her ability to learn songs. A song that had been written after her illness would be played to her and after a few repetitions she would begin to sing along with it. Eventually she would begin to sing as soon as the song started. If the song was stopped after a few bars, she would continue singing the song through to the end, making no errors in either words or melody.

On the basis of Wernicke's model we predicted that the lesions caused by the carbon monoxide poisoning lay outside the speech and auditory regions, and that both Broca's area and Wernicke's area were intact. Postmortem examination revealed a remarkable lesion that isolated the speech area from the rest of the cortex. The lesion fitted the prediction. Broca's area, Wernicke's area and the connection between them were intact. Also intact were the auditory pathways and the motor pathways to the speech organs. Around the speech area, however, either the cortex or the underlying white matter was destroyed [see bottom illustration on facing page]. The woman could not comprehend speech because the words did not arouse

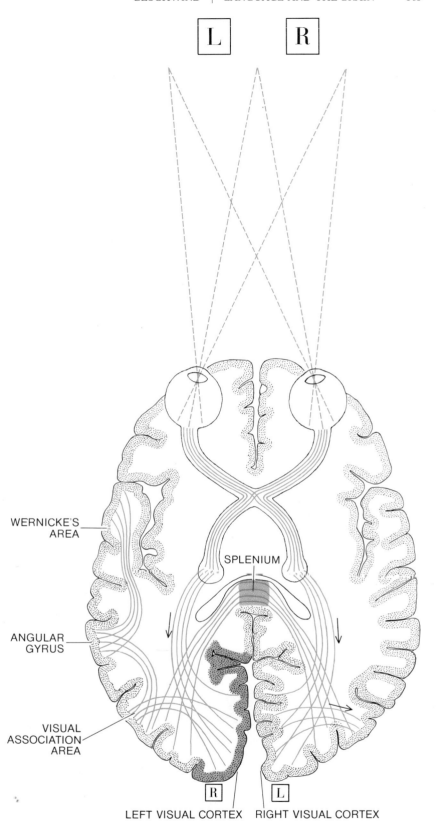

CLASSIC CASE of a man who lost the ability to read even though he had normal visual acuity and could copy written words was described in 1892 by Joseph Jules Dejerine. Postmortem analysis of the man's brain showed that the left visual cortex and the splenium (*dark colored areas*) were destroyed as a result of an occlusion of the left posterior cerebral artery. The splenium is the section of the corpus callosum that transfers visual information between the two hemispheres. The man's left visual cortex was inoperative, making him blind in his right visual field. Words in his left visual field were properly received by the right visual cortex, but could not cross over to the language areas in the left hemisphere because of the damaged splenium. Thus words seen by the man remained as meaningless patterns.

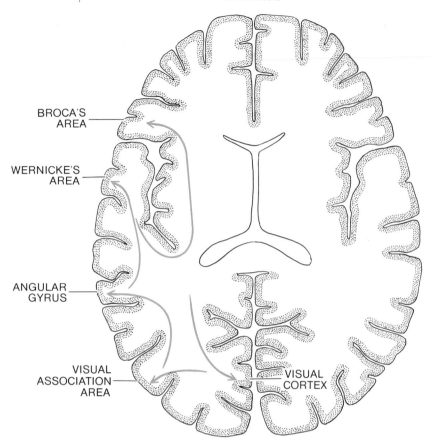

SAYING THE NAME of a seen object, according to Wernicke's model, involves the transfer of the visual pattern to the angular gyrus, which contains the "rules" for arousing the auditory form of the pattern in Wernicke's area. From here the auditory form is transmitted by way of the arcuate fasciculus to Broca's area. There the articulatory form is aroused, is passed on to the face area of the motor cortex and the word then is spoken.

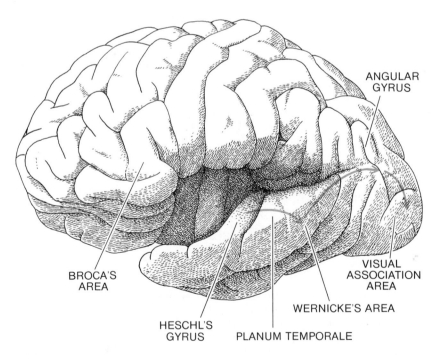

UNDERSTANDING the spoken name of an object involves the transfer of the auditory stimuli from Heschl's gyrus (the primary auditory cortex) to Wernicke's area and then to the angular gyrus, which arouses the comparable visual pattern in the visual association cortex. Here the Sylvian fissure has been spread apart to show the pathway more clearly.

associations in other portions of the cortex. She could repeat speech correctly because the internal connections of the speech region were intact. Presumably well-learned word sequences stored in Broca's area could be triggered by the beginning phrases. This syndrome is called isolation of the speech area.

Two important extensions of the Wernicke model were advanced by a French neurologist, Joseph Jules Dejerine. In 1891 he described a disorder called alexia with agraphia: the loss of the ability to read and write. The patient could, however, speak and understand spoken language. Postmortem examination showed that there was a lesion in the angular gyrus of the left hemisphere, the area of the brain that acts as a way station between the visual and the auditory region. A lesion here would separate the visual and auditory language areas. Although words and letters would be seen correctly, they would be meaningless visual patterns, since the visual pattern must first be converted to the auditory form before the word can be comprehended. Conversely, the auditory pattern for a word must be transformed into the visual pattern before the word can be spelled. Patients suffering from alexia with agraphia cannot recognize words spelled aloud to them nor can they themselves spell aloud a spoken word.

Dejerine's second contribution was showing the importance of information transfer between the hemispheres. His patient was an intelligent businessman who had awakened one morning to discover that he could no longer read. It was found that the man was blind in the right half of the visual field. Since the right half of the field is projected to the left cerebral hemisphere, it was obvious that the man suffered damage to the visual pathways on the left side of the brain [see illustration on preceding page]. He could speak and comprehend spoken language and could write, but he could not read even though he had normal visual acuity. In fact, although he could not comprehend written words, he could copy them correctly. Postmortem examination of the man's brain by Dejerine revealed two lesions that were the result of the occlusion of the left posterior cerebral artery. The visual cortex of the left hemisphere was totally destroyed. Also destroyed was a portion of the corpus callosum: the mass of nerve fibers that interconnect the two cerebral hemispheres. That portion was the splenium, which carries the visual information between the hemispheres. The destruction of the splenium prevented stimuli from the visual cortex of the right hemisphere from reaching the angular gyrus of the left hemisphere. According to Wernicke's model, it is the left angular gyrus that converts the visual pattern of a word into the auditory pattern; without such conversion a seen word cannot be comprehended. Other workers have since shown that when a person is blind in the right half of the visual field but is still capable of reading, the portion of the corpus callosum that transfers visual information between the hemispheres is not damaged.

In 1937 the first case in which surgical section of the corpus callosum stopped the transfer of information between the hemispheres was reported by John Trescher and Frank Ford. The patient had the rear portion of his corpus callosum severed during an operation to remove a brain tumor. According to Wernicke's model, this should have resulted in the loss of reading ability in the left half of the visual field. Trescher and Ford found that the patient could read normally when words appeared in his right visual field but could not read at all in his left visual field.

Hugo Liepmann, who was one of Wernicke's assistants in Breslau, made an extensive study of syndromes of the corpus callosum, and descriptions of these disorders were a standard part of German neurology before World War I. Much of this work was neglected, and only recently has its full importance been appreciated. Liepmann's analysis of corpus callosum syndromes was based on Wernicke's model. In cases such as those described by Liepmann the front four-fifths of the corpus callosum is destroyed by occlusion of the cerebral artery that nourishes it. Since the splenium is preserved the patient can read in either visual field. Such a lesion, however, gives rise to three characteristic disorders. The patient writes correctly with his right hand but incorrectly with the left. He carries out commands with his right arm but not with the left; although the left hemisphere can understand the command, it cannot transmit the message to the right hemisphere. Finally, the patient cannot name objects held in his left hand because the somesthetic sensations cannot reach the verbal centers in the left hemisphere.

The problem of cerebral dominance in humans has intrigued investigators since Broca first discovered it. Many early neurologists claimed that there were anatomical differences between the hemispheres, but in the past few decades there has been a tendency to assume that the left and right hemispheres are

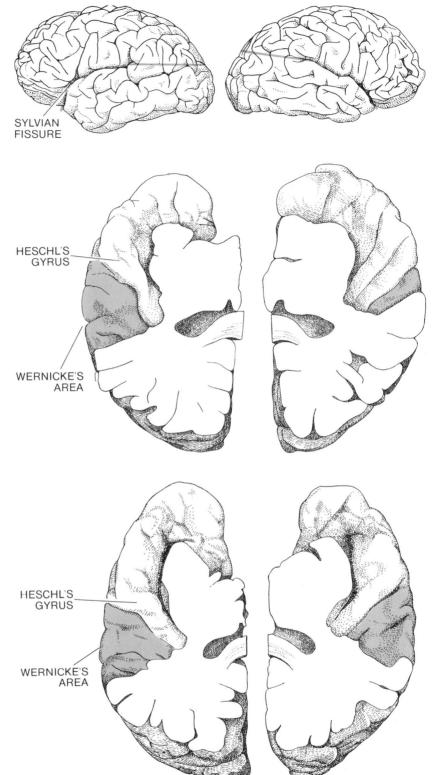

ANATOMICAL DIFFERENCES between the two hemispheres of the human brain are found on the upper surface of the temporal lobe, which cannot be seen in an intact brain because it lies within the Sylvian fissure. Typically the Sylvian fissure in the left hemisphere appears to be pushed down compared with the Sylvian fissure on the right side (top illustration). In order to expose the surface of the temporal lobe a knife is moved along the fissure (broken line) and then through the brain, cutting away the top portion (solid line). The region studied was the planum temporale (colored areas), an extension of Wernicke's area. The middle illustration shows a brain with a larger left planum; the bottom illustration shows left and right planums of about the same size. In a study of 100 normal human brains planum temporale was larger on the left side in 65 percent of the cases, equal on both sides in 24 percent of the cases and larger on the right side in 11 percent.

MEANING	BROCA'S APHASIA				WERNICKE'S APHASIA
	KANA		KANJI		
	PATIENT'S	CORRECT	PATIENT'S	CORRECT	
INK	キンス (KINSU)	インキ (INKI)	墨 (SUMI)	墨	参 答 微 乂土 久 (LONG TIME)
UNIVERSITY	タイ (TAI)	ダイガク (DAIGAKU)	大學	大学 (GREAT LEARNING)	兵 (SOLDIER) 美
TOKYO	トウ (TOU)	トウキヨウ (TOKYO)	東京	東京 (EAST CAPITAL)	

JAPANESE APHASICS display some characteristics rarely found in Western patients because of the unique writing system used in Japan. There are two separate forms of such writing. One is Kana, which is syllabic. The other is Kanji, which is ideographic. Kana words are articulated syllable by syllable and are not easily identified at a glance, whereas each Kanji character simultaneously represents both a sound and a meaning. A patient with Broca's aphasia, studied by Tsuneo Imura and his colleagues at the Nihon University College of Medicine, was able to write a dictated word correctly in Kanji but not in Kana (*top left*). When the patient was asked to write the word "ink," even though there is no Kanji character for the word, his first effort was the Kanji character "sumi," which means india ink. When required to write in Kana, the symbols he produced were correct but the word was wrong. Another patient who had Wernicke's aphasia wrote Kanji quickly and without hesitation. He was completely unaware that he was producing meaningless ideograms, as are patients who exhibit paraphasias in speech. Only two of characters had meaning (*top right*).

symmetrical. It has been thought that cerebral dominance is based on undetected subtle physiological differences not reflected in gross structure. Walter Levitsky and I decided to look again into the possibility that the human brain is anatomically asymmetrical. We studied 100 normal human brains, and we were surprised to find that striking asymmetries were readily visible. The area we studied was the upper surface of the temporal lobe, which is not seen in the intact brain because it lies within the depths of the Sylvian fissure. The asymmetrical area we found and measured was the planum temporale, an extension of Wernicke's area [see illustration on preceding page]. This region was larger on the left side of the brain in 65 percent of the cases, equal in 24 percent and larger on the right side in 11 percent. In absolute terms the left planum was nine millimeters longer on the average than the right planum. In relative terms the left planum was one-third longer than the right. Statistically all the differences were highly significant. Juhn A. Wada of the University of British Columbia subsequently reported a study that confirmed our results. In addition Wada studied a series of brains from infants who had died soon after birth and found that the planum asymmetry was present. It seems likely that the asymmetries of the brain are genetically determined.

It is sometimes asserted that the anatomical approach neglects the plasticity of the nervous system and makes the likelihood of therapy for language disorders rather hopeless. This is not the case. Even the earliest investigators of aphasia were aware that some patients developed symptoms that were much milder than expected. Other patients recovered completely from a lesion that normally would have produced permanent aphasia. There is recovery or partial recovery of language functions in some cases, as Luria's large-scale study of the war wounded has shown. Of all the patients with wounds in the primary speech area of the left hemisphere, 97.2 percent were aphasic when Luria first examined them. A follow-up examination found that 93.3 percent were still aphasic, although in most cases they were aphasic to a lesser degree.

How does one account for the apparent recovery of language function in some cases? Some partial answers are available. Children have been known to make a much better recovery than adults with the same type of lesion. This suggests that at least in childhood the right hemisphere has some capacity to take over speech functions. Some cases of adult recovery are patients who had suffered brain damage in childhood. A number of patients who have undergone surgical removal of portions of the speech area for the control of epileptic seizures often show milder language disorders than had been expected. This probably is owing to the fact that the patients had suffered from left temporal epilepsy involving the left side of the brain from childhood and had been using the right hemisphere for language functions to a considerable degree.

Left-handed people also show on the average milder disorders than expected when the speech regions are damaged, even though for most left-handers the left hemisphere is dominant for speech just as it is for right-handers. It is an interesting fact that right-handers with a strong family history of left-handedness show better speech recovery than people without left-handed inheritance.

Effective and safe methods for studying cerebral dominance and localization of language function in the intact, normal human brain have begun to appear. Doreen Kimura of the University of Western Ontario has adapted the technique of dichotic listening to investigate the auditory asymmetries of the brain. More recently several investigators have found increased electrical activity over the speech areas of the left hemisphere during the production or perception of speech. Refinement of these techniques could lead to a better understanding of how the normal human brain is organized for language. A deeper understanding of the neural mechanisms of speech should lead in turn to more precise methods of dealing with disorders of man's most characteristic attribute, language.

X

ATTENTION, AWARENESS, AND THOUGHT

X ATTENTION, AWARENESS, AND THOUGHT

INTRODUCTION

We have just begun in recent years to gain some understanding of possible brain mechanisms that may underlie the most complex processes in human behavior and experience, such phenomena as attention, awareness or consciousness, and the processes of thought. Some of these areas have been particularly difficult to analyze because it is hard to find adequate animal models. Like language, thought processes in humans are in many ways qualitatively different from those in lower animals. This is not to say that animals do not think. Indeed, chimpanzees appear to think very well under certain conditions. However, human thought is extricably bound up with language. Awareness or consciousness is the toughest issue of all to deal with. We must rely on verbal reports from human subjects. There seems to be no other satisfactory way of measuring consciousness. Attention is a process that is easy to study in humans—it is easy to find out whether a person is attending or not by simply asking him—but extraordinarily difficult to study in animals. Analysis of brain mechanisms of these complex processes has only begun.

In the first article, Donald E. Broadbent considers attention and the perception of speech. We have made most progress in recent years in the area of attention in studies on selective listening in humans. This approach was really begun by Broadbent. The normal child learns language entirely through hearing it spoken. Reading, writing, and other elaborations of speech are secondary. Consequently, to understand language we must also understand the biological mechanisms that underlie the perception of speech. Broadbent surveys the auditory system in terms of how it responds to speech sounds and develops an analysis of how we perceive speech. A basic fact about speech is that we can really only attend to one voice message at a time. Our listening is selective. Broadbent analyzes the processes of selective listening in experiments on comprehension of two different voice messages presented simultaneously to the two ears. His work provides a solid empirical base of information about attention in humans.

In the next article Doreen Kimura considers the implications of the asymmetry of the human brain. One of the most remarkable things about the human brain and the brains of all other higher animals is that there are in fact two brains in each head. The two hemispheres, the two sides of the brain, are virtually mirror images of each other—most structures are present on both sides—and are interconnected by massive bands of fiber systems. It has become increasingly clear in recent years that one hemisphere tends to dominate the other in many aspects of behavior and experience. We learned in the last section that language is localized in the left hemisphere in most humans. The left hemisphere is also dominant in the control of many other behaviors. Most people are right-handed; since the control pathway crosses from one side of the body to the other side of the brain, the left motor cortex controls the right hand. However, the right hemisphere also has its areas of specialization. It seems clear that the right hemisphere is superior to the left in terms of analyzing information about where objects are located in space. Interestingly, the right hemisphere seems to be dominant for appreciation of music as well. Melodies are processed more in the right hemisphere than in the left. Although information from each ear gets to both hemispheres, the information that has crossed is more effective. Consequently, after performing a "dichotic" listening task—for example, listening to two different melodies in the two different ears—most subjects are later able to recognize the melody presented to the left ear better than the one presented to the right ear. Kimura reviews these various aspects of cerebral dominance in her article.

Perhaps the most striking and important studies of recent years on human consciousness are those by R. W. Sperry, Michael S. Gazzaniga, and their associates at the California Institute of Technology. These studies are described by Gazzaniga in his article, "The Split Brain in Man." They studied patients in which the interconnecting fibers between the two hemispheres were surgically severed to prevent the spread of epileptic seizures from one hemisphere to the other. The treatment was successful in preventing epilepsy for several patients. Of greater importance in this context, the split-brain patients behaved as though the two hemispheres were in fact responsible for two separate awarenesses or consciousnesses. The left hemisphere is highly verbal, rational, and normally dominant, and the right hemisphere is visual-spatial, impulsive, and occasionally struggled for control. Normally, the interconnecting fibers permit the two hemispheres to function smoothly together. Gazzaniga's article is a fascinating account of these experiments.

In the final article, A. R. Luria, a leading Soviet brain scientist, discusses the functional organization of the brain. Luria focuses on the functions of the most complex regions of the cerebral cortex, the association areas. These are the areas of the brain that have developed most in primate evolution. The great expansion of these areas in man is the primary neurological feature that distinguishes man from apes. Luria is concerned with all aspects of the functioning of the association cortex—its role in thought, language, and behavior. His article provides an excellent summary of our current understanding of the complex functions of association areas of the brain.

34

Attention and the Perception of Speech

by Donald E. Broadbent
April 1962

*If an individual listens to two voice messages
at one time, he usually understands only one.
This indicates that the brain has an "attention
mechanism" for selecting the desired information*

Paying attention—and not paying attention—are surely two of the most important abilities of human beings. Yet in spite of their crucial role in learning, and in a host of other intelligent activities, psychologists for many years did not consider them proper topics of study. Attention seemed a subjective quality, associated historically with the introspective method of investigation. That method tends to give inconsistent results and so fell into disrepute among experimental psychologists. Correspondingly, most respectable theorists failed to make use of any concept resembling attention; and, since research in psychology tends to be dominated by theory, there was little experimentation along lines that might have revived the idea.

In the past 10 years, however, the concept of attention has begun to force itself on the attention of psychologists in various ways. One is through studies of the efficiency of control systems such as those concerned with the regulation of air traffic at airports. A major cause of failure in these systems is that the human operator has too much information to handle simultaneously, or that he reacts to an unimportant signal when he should be dealing with an important one. These problems require some understanding of phenomena that would commonly be described under the heading of "attention." There is now accumulating a wide variety of experimental results that clarify these phenomena, although the larger part of the work remains to be done. In this article I shall describe some of the research on attention to spoken messages.

One of the earliest findings, and one that agrees with everyday experience, is that it is harder to understand two messages arriving simultaneously than two messages arriving one after the other.

One might be tempted to explain this as a purely physical interference between the two stimuli; for example, the louder passages of one message might drown out the softer passages of the other and vice versa, rendering them both unintelligible. Actually the matter is not so simple. By recording the messages on tape and playing them for different subjects instructed to respond in different ways, the intelligibility is shown to depend on psychological factors. Specifically, either message becomes understandable if the listener is instructed to ignore the other. But the two messages together cannot both be understood, even though the necessary information is available to the ear. Another way of making the same point is to insert the words of one message into spaces between the words from the other: "Oh God say save can our you gracious see Queen." Each message is hard to understand, but each word is spoken separately and is fully audible. The difficulty evidently lies inside the nervous system, which somehow prevents an adequate response to signals that are "heard" satisfactorily.

Further experiments demonstrate that comprehension improves if the two messages differ in certain physical characteristics. For instance, it is better if a man speaks one message and a woman speaks the other; or if the loudspeaker removes the lower tones from one voice but not the other. Spatial separation of the two voices gives the best result of all. The different messages should not come through the same loudspeaker or even from separate speakers mounted one above the other; the two speakers should be separated as far as possible from each other in the horizontal plane. Interestingly enough, a listener also comprehends simultaneous spoken messages

better when they come from a stereophonic system than when they are played over a single loudspeaker. (This effect, rather than the doubtful gain in realism, is for many people the main advantage of stereophonic high-fidelity systems: the listener can pay attention to different musical instruments played at the same time.)

Physical distinctions are most helpful in promoting understanding when one message has no importance for the listener and does not have to be answered. It would seem that the differences allow the brain to filter the incoming sounds and select some for response while ignoring others.

The need to throw away part of the available information can perhaps be understood by comparing the brain with man-made communication systems. Engineers nowadays talk of capacity for transmitting information, by which they mean the number of equally probable messages of which one can be sent in a specified time. Suppose, for example, that two complicated military plans have been prepared and an order is to be sent to carry out one of them. A simple communication system consisting of a red and a green lamp can transmit the message with maximum efficiency by the lighting of a single lamp. If there were four plans instead of two, however, it would be impossible to give the order by lighting one of the two lamps no matter how simple each plan might be. Either there must be more lamps or more time is needed for sending the order. In the most efficient code for two lamps, two successive flashes of the red lamp would mean one plan, a red flash followed by a green flash would mean another, and so on. One of four possible messages can be transmitted with two lamps, but only by taking two units of time. With eight pos-

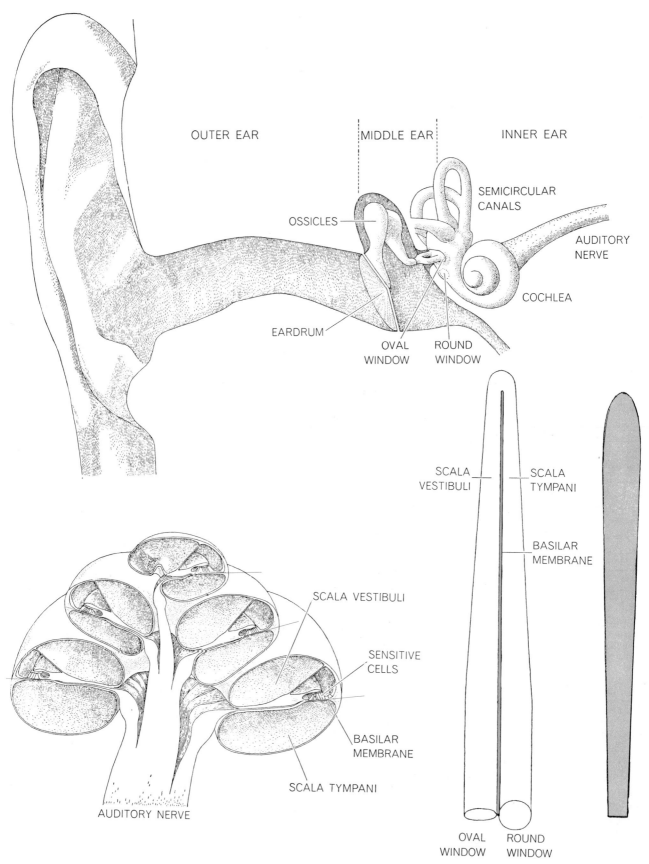

OUTER EAR
MIDDLE EAR
INNER EAR

SEMICIRCULAR
CANALS

OSSICLES

AUDITORY
NERVE

COCHLEA

EARDRUM

OVAL
WINDOW

ROUND
WINDOW

SCALA
VESTIBULI

SCALA
TYMPANI

BASILAR
MEMBRANE

SCALA VESTIBULI

SENSITIVE
CELLS

BASILAR
MEMBRANE

SCALA TYMPANI

AUDITORY NERVE

OVAL
WINDOW

ROUND
WINDOW

PERCEPTION OF SPEECH begins in the ear, shown at top in simplified cross section. The eardrum transmits sound vibrations to the three small bones called ossicles, which cause waves in fluid in the cochlea. The cochlea, seen in cross section at bottom left, contains the basilar membrane (*color*), on which rest the sensitive cells that excite auditory-nerve fibers. At bottom center cochlea is rolled out, with basilar membrane in side view. Front view of the basilar membrane (*bottom right*) shows that it is wider at one end than the other. The wide region vibrates in response to low frequencies, whereas the narrow region responds to high frequencies.

sible messages the code would call for three flashes of the two lamps, taking three units of time; 16 possible messages would require four flashes, and so forth.

Although the human brain has far more than the two states represented by the red and the green lamp, the number of its possible states is presumably limited. One would expect, then, that there is a limit to the number of different possibilities among which it can distinguish in a given time. Indeed, a number of experiments suggest a close parallel with the two-lamp system: in many cases a man's reaction time in responding to one of several possible signals increases by an equal amount every time the number of possible signals is doubled. Since there is a maximum speed at which one signal can be distinguished from others, the brain limits the number of possibilities being considered at any one time by selecting only part of the information reaching the ears. Therefore the degree of difficulty in dealing with two simultaneous spoken messages depends on the number of other messages that might have arrived instead of the two that did arrive. If only a few other messages are possible, the two messages together may not exceed the capacity of the brain and the listener may understand both. On the other hand, if each message is drawn from a very large range of possibilities, it may be all the listener can do to respond appropriately to one of them.

Several studies support these conclusions. John C. Webster and his associates at the U.S. Navy Electronics Laboratory in San Diego, Calif., observed that control-tower operators in San Diego could sometimes identify two aircraft call signs arriving at the same time but could understand only one of the two messages that followed. The call signs penetrated because the operators knew pretty well which aircraft might call. They did not know what the pilots would say.

An experiment at the Applied Psychology Research Unit in Cambridge, England, required a listener to answer a rapid series of questions while pressing a key in response to an intermittent buzzer. The interference produced by the buzzer in the ability to answer questions increased after the subject had been told that he would also have to respond to a bell. Even when the bell did not ring, the subject found the questions harder to answer than when he was expecting only the buzzer.

These results help to explain why a person can sometimes listen to two things at once and sometimes cannot pay atten-

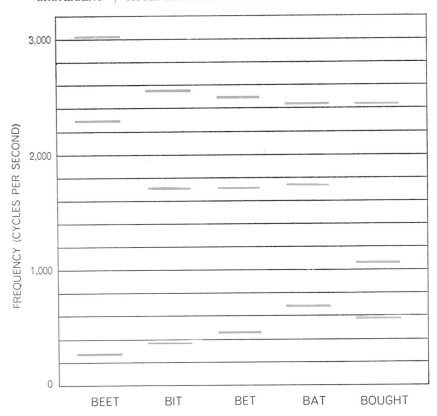

VOWEL FORMANTS, or frequencies that make up each vowel sound, are shown here for five different vowels. The values given are averages for male voices. Actually they differ from person to person. Although three formants are shown here for each sound, quite recognizable vowels can be produced by mechanisms using two filters to make two formants.

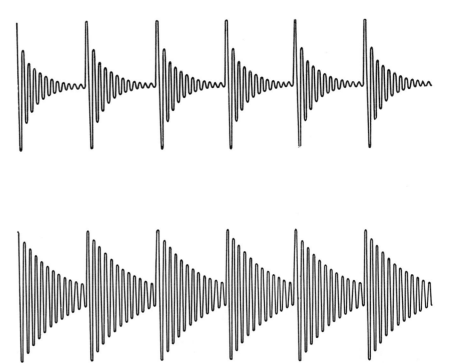

DECAY RATE of pulses from vocal cords affects quality of speech. Waves of highest amplitude mark beginning of each pulse. At top, pulses decay rapidly, helping to give the voice a crisp or sharp sound. At bottom, the decay is much slower, giving the voice a mellow quality. In both cases the frequencies of the pulses and the vibrations are exactly the same.

tion to more than one. When the listener is thoroughly familiar with a situation, so that he knows to within a small number of alternatives what each message will be, he can comprehend two simultaneous messages. But when one or both messages are drawn from a large number of possibilities, the filter in the brain lets only one message come through.

How does the filter work? As yet the answer is not known. Enough is known, however, about the physical characteristics of speech and the physiology of hearing to make possible some reasonable speculation. Human speech is produced by the combined action of the vocal cords and the vocal tract, which consists of the cavities of the throat, mouth and nose. Taut vocal cords produce a buzz when air is forced through them. The buzz consists of brief pulses, or puffs of air, at the rate of 100 or more per second, each pulse containing energy at many frequencies. These pulses excite into vibration the air in the cavities of the throat, nose and mouth. The cavities can be tuned to different frequencies by changing the position of the tongue, cheeks, jaw and lips. What emerges is a train of waves that contains a particular group of frequencies and is pulsed about 100 times per second. Each pulse starts out at full strength and decays rapidly until the sound energy is renewed by the next one [see bottom illustration on preceding page].

Many vowel sounds contain waves at two or more widely separated frequencies. For example, when the greatest energy is at 375 and 1,700 cycles per second, the vowel sound in the word "bit" is produced; frequencies of 450

and 1,700 cycles per second give the vowel in "bet." (These figures apply to a typical male voice. In the voices of women and children the whole range of frequencies may be higher but the listener takes this into account.) On reaching the ear, the sounds stimulate sense organs arranged along the basilar membrane in the cochlea [see illustration on page 354]. Low frequencies stimulate organs at one end of the membrane; high frequencies affect those at the other end. A complex sound made up of several frequencies energizes several different regions of the basilar membrane. Each sense organ on the membrane connects with particular nerve fibers going to the brain; thus the word "bit" stimulates one combination of fibers and the word "bet" another combination.

If both words reach the ear simultaneously, both combinations of fibers would come into play and the brain would have the problem of deciding which belong together. It might seem then that two or more voices would produce so much confusion in the ear that the brain could not select one voice for special attention. Of course, certain obvious features help distinguish one speaker from another: accent, rate of speaking, loudness or softness. But one cannot make use of these features until one knows which frequencies belong to which voice. Thus the problem remains: How does the brain manage to focus attention on one voice? Studies of the artificial generation of speech sounds have begun to throw some light on this problem.

Peter Ladefoged of the University of Edinburgh and I have been experimenting with a device that was developed by Walter Lawrence of the Signals Re-

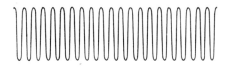

LOW FILTER FREQUENCY

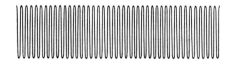

HIGH FILTER FREQUENCY

SPEECH SOUNDS consist of pulses of energy from the voice, shown here as high and

search Development Establishment in England. Our version of the apparatus sends a series of electrical pulses (analogous to pulses from the vocal cords) through two filter circuits, each of which passes primarily one frequency. The waves from one filter circuit, which are like those from the largest human speech cavity, are mixed with waves from the other, which imitate the frequencies produced by the second largest cavity. To-

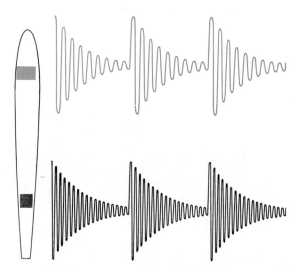

DIFFERENT FILTER FREQUENCIES but same rate of pulsation or modulation from voice excites two different regions of a basilar membrane (left). Listener reports he hears one vowel sound.

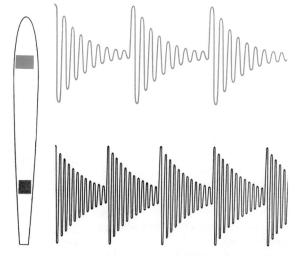

DIFFERENT PULSATION RATES and different filter frequencies make the listener hear two different sounds, even though only one ear or basilar membrane is actually being used for hearing.

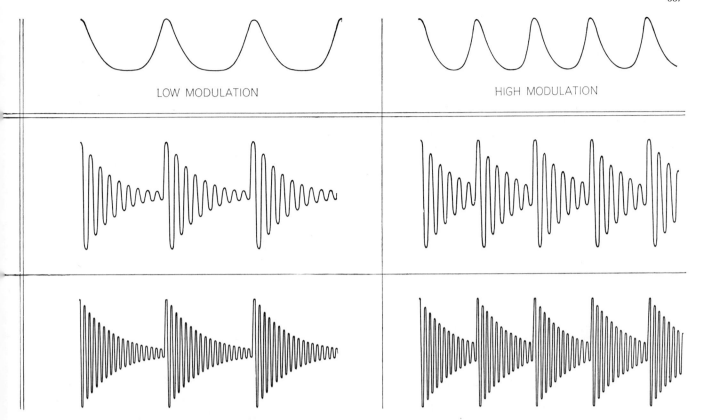

LOW MODULATION

HIGH MODULATION

low modulations (*across top*), and of specific frequencies emitted by the mouth and throat "filters," or cavities (*far left*). These two

types of wave combine in patterns like those in this diagram. Effects of such waves are shown across bottom of these two pages.

gether the two wave trains are heard as quite acceptable vowel sounds that can be changed by tuning the filters to different frequencies. Varying the pulse rate used to excite the filters alters the apparent pitch or intonation of the "speech": it rises with faster pulse rates and falls with slower ones.

When the same pulses excite both filters, a listener hears the output as readily identifiable vowel sounds. This is true

even when the low frequency is fed into one ear and the high frequency into the other. But if the two filters are pulsed at slightly different rates, the "speech" becomes unacceptable and listeners say that they are hearing two sounds coming from two sources rather than a single vowel sound.

Other experiments on the fusion of

sounds at the two ears, conducted by Colin A. Cherry and his colleagues at the Imperial College of Science and Technology in London, also support the idea that when the rate of pulsing, or modulation, is the same for two sounds, the hearer perceives them as one sound. It seems reasonable to suppose, therefore, that a man can listen to one person

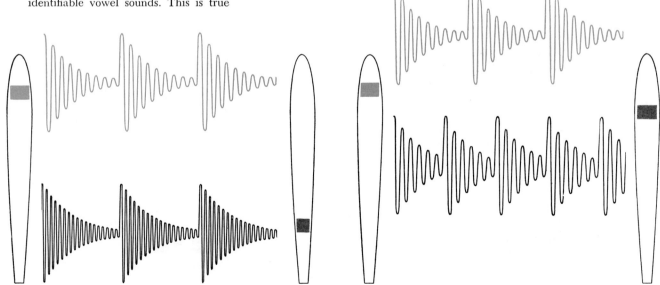

USING BOTH EARS, listener will hear one vowel sound, although right ear hears one filter frequency and left ear hears another. The pulsation or modulation rate has to be the same.

TWO PULSATION RATES, combined with same filter frequency and fed into each ear separately, produce two distinct sounds. The brain evidently focuses its attention on the rate of pulsation.

and ignore another primarily by selecting from the mass of sounds entering his ears all those frequencies that are being modulated at the same rate. Since it is most unlikely that the vocal cords of two speakers would vibrate at exactly the same rate at any moment, modulation would almost always provide an important (if not the sole) means of separating a pair of voices.

It is now a generally accepted principle of neurophysiology that messages traveling along a particular nerve can differ either by involving different nerve fibers or by producing a different number of impulses per second in the fibers. High-frequency and low-frequency sounds stimulate different fibers. It may be that the rate at which the sounds are pulsed controls the rate of firing of the fibers. If so, the brain could pick out one voice from others by focusing its attention on all auditory nerve fibers that are firing at the same rate.

A further indication of the importance of modulation is that it, rather than the frequency of the waves being modulated, seems under certain conditions to determine the pitch of a voice. This can be demonstrated with the artificial speech generator. A filter tuned to, say, 3,000 cycles per second is pulsed at the rate of 100 cycles per second. A listener is asked to match the pitch of the sound with either of two simple sound waves, one at 100 cycles per second and the oth-

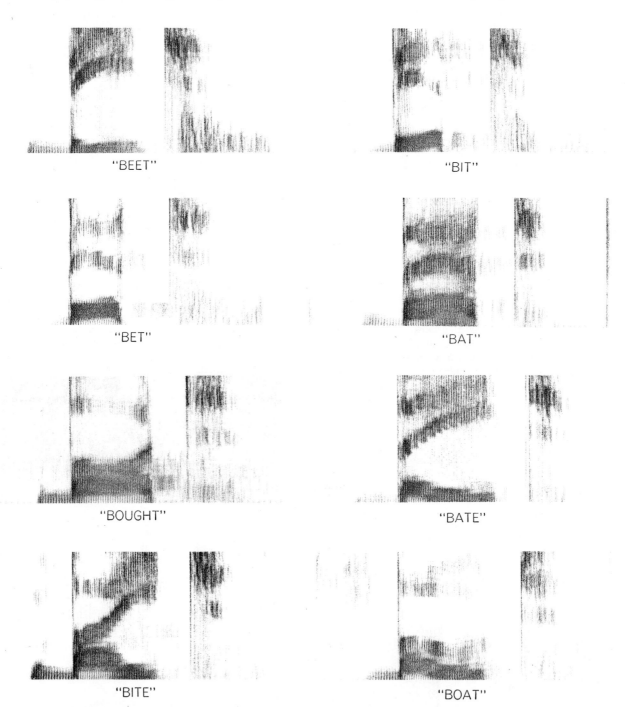

"BEET"

"BIT"

"BET"

"BAT"

"BOUGHT"

"BATE"

"BITE"

"BOAT"

SOUND SPECTROGRAMS show that various vowel sounds are made of several different frequencies. Time is shown horizontally, frequencies vertically and intensity of sound by relative darkness. The "b" of each word appears at lowest frequency. Vowel begins suddenly as lips open. After vowel there is a quiet period followed by a burst of noise primarily at high frequency as the "t" explodes. Frequency shifts in "bate" and "bite" are diphthongs. Spectrograms were made by H. K. Dunn of Bell Telephone Laboratories.

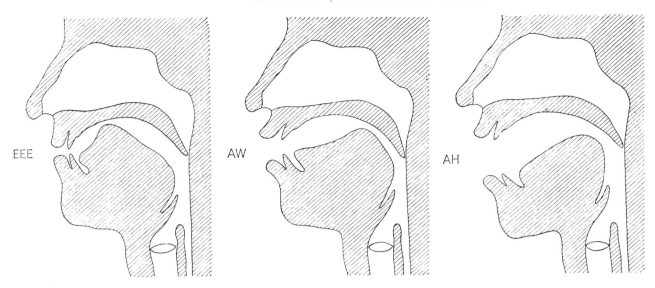

SHAPE OF CAVITIES in the mouth is primarily responsible for the production of different vowel sounds. Three other factors that play a key role in this process are the configuration of the tongue, the size of the opening of the mouth and the position of the lips.

er at 3,000. Usually he selects the 100-cycle sound.

The selection mechanism that has been described is still hypothetical, but I believe that something much like it must exist. There can be no doubt, however, that it is not the only basis for auditory attention. Several experiments have served to make this clear. In one, a listener is equipped with earphones that feed one voice into the right ear and another voice into the left. Normally the subject has no difficulty in understanding the message entering one ear and ignoring the other. But under certain conditions sound from the ear being ignored can break into consciousness. For example, Neville Moray of the University of Oxford has demonstrated that a man fully occupied in listening to speech entering one ear will hear his own name in the other ear even though

he remains quite unresponsive to any other word in that ear. Under similar circumstances Anne M. Treisman of the University of Oxford has found that speech entering the rejected ear can break through to the subject's attention if it consists of words that would probably follow the words that have just been heard by the ear that is receiving attention. In these cases the content of the speech has taken precedence over its physical characteristics.

How the brain focuses attention on meaning or content is as yet an almost complete mystery. One thing is clear. If the method proposed for choosing between voices is correct, there must be two attention mechanisms. Selection on the basis of content involves examining a stimulus for its possible appropriateness to a particular set of responses

rather than for the presence or absence of a physical marker. At one moment, for example, a person might be ready to write down any of the digits one through nine and highly unready to write anything else, or indeed to respond in any other way. If he hears a sound from any direction or in any voice that can be interpreted as the name of one of the digits, he will respond by writing it down; only if the sound cannot be so interpreted will he not respond. At another time he might be ready to write down letters of the alphabet but not numbers, and so on.

Both types of attention are now the subject of intensive research. The next few years should yield more definite clues to the nature of each and at least a tentative answer to the question of whether or not they depend on different mechanisms.

35

The Asymmetry of the Human Brain

by Doreen Kimura
March 1973

The cerebral hemispheres, though physically alike, have different functions: the right is specialized for analyzing information about the environment and the left for skilled motor acts, including speech

In most animals the structure of the nervous system is essentially symmetrical. In mammals the symmetry is made more striking by the prominence of the uppermost part of the brain: the cerebral hemispheres. In man, however, the two cerebral hemispheres differ greatly in their functions. It is well known that the left hemisphere plays a dominant role in speech [see the article "Language and the Brain," by Norman Geschwind, beginning on page 341]. The right hemisphere also has specialized functions, but until recently we have had less information about them because of the emphasis on studying language disorders. It turns out that the right hemisphere plays a dominant role in man's perception of his environment.

For more than a century the principal source of knowledge about the division of labor between the two cerebral hemispheres of man has been malfunctions of the brain caused by accident, surgery or disease. Although studies of intellectual impairments in patients with various kinds of brain lesion have provided much valuable information, such studies have the disadvantage that the damage may have affected not only the specific functional systems but also their interaction. In the past few years I have been involved in developing methods for studying the asymmetry of hemispheric functions in normal people.

I first became aware of the possibility that some aspects of brain function could be readily studied in normal people while I was doing research with patients at the Montreal Neurological Institute. One of the tests administered to the patients was a modification of a dichotic listening technique devised by Donald E. Broadbent of the British Medical Research Council's Applied Psychology Research Unit. His technique involves simultaneously presenting a spoken digit to one ear and a different spoken digit to the other ear. Three such pairs are usually delivered in sequence during one trial, and the subject is asked to report all the numbers he has heard. Patients with damage to the left temporal region of the brain reported fewer digits correctly than patients with damage to the right temporal region. A quite unexpected and intriguing finding was that most patients, no matter what part of the brain had been damaged, reported the words they had heard with their right ear more accurately than those they had heard with their left. The same turned out to be true for a group of normal people. There is evidence from numerous studies of pure-tone thresholds that the left and right ears do not differ in their basic capacity for detecting sounds, and so we concluded that the perceptual superiority of the right ear for words was somehow related to that ear's connections with the brain.

A peculiarity of the human nervous system is that each cerebral hemisphere receives information primarily from the opposite half of the body. Man's visual system is so arranged that vision to the right of a fixation point is mediated by the left half of the brain and vice versa. The auditory system is somewhat less crossed in that each half of the brain receives input from both ears, but the crossed connections are nevertheless stronger than the uncrossed ones. The tactual and motor systems of the brain are almost completely crossed: sensations from the left half of the body and movement of the left half of the body are served primarily by the right cerebral hemisphere and vice versa. The two hemispheres are themselves interconnected by nerve pathways. These pathways, the largest of which is the corpus callosum, play an important role in coordinating the activities of the hemispheres.

Since the auditory system is a predominantly crossed system, the neural input from the right ear to the left cerebral hemisphere should be stronger than that from the right ear to the right hemisphere. And since the left hemisphere usually contains the neural system for perception of speech, it is reasonable to suppose speech sounds presented to the right ear would have readier access to the speech-perception system. This supposition can be directly tested by observing people whose speech functions are not in the left hemisphere but in the right. Which side serves speech can be determined by the sodium amytal test, devised by Juhn A. Wada. The test involves injecting sodium amytal (a sedative) into the carotid artery of one side of the neck or the other. The drug disturbs the functioning of the cerebral hemisphere on that side for a few minutes, and if the subject's speech is disturbed as well one infers that speech is represented in that hemisphere.

Thirteen patients whom I tested at the Montreal Neurological Institute were found to have speech represented in the right hemisphere rather than in the left. The scores of these patients on the dichotic listening task were higher for the left ear. The results supported the hypothesis that the superiority of the right ear in normal subjects is due to better connections between that ear and the left (speech) hemisphere than between that ear and the right hemisphere.

We found further evidence that the superior performance of one ear on dichotic listening tasks did in fact reflect a hemispheric specialization of function. Brenda Milner of the Montreal Neurological Institute found that whereas damage to the left temporal lobe of the brain impaired comprehension of spoken material, damage to the right temporal lobe impaired the perception of certain other kinds of auditory material, particularly the discrimination of tonal quality and tonal pattern. I developed a dichotic listening task in which a headset was used to simultaneously play one melodic pattern to one ear and a different melodic pattern to the other ear. The subject was then asked to pick out the two melodies he (or she) had just heard from four melodies, each of which was played one at a time to both ears. Since melodies are processed predominantly by the right temporal lobe, normal subjects were able to pick out the melody presented to the left ear better than the one presented to the right ear.

The results were particularly exciting because they opened the way for exploration of the characteristics of verbal and nonverbal processes in the brain with relatively simple techniques. Although it has been known for more than a century that the left hemisphere is involved in speech functions, we still do not have a very clear idea of what the characteristics of those functions are. The traditional way of distinguishing them is to use a term such as "symbolic," which implies that the defining characteristics have to do with the capacity to let an event stand for something else. When we applied the dichotic listening technique, we got a rather different answer. The right ear was found to be superior for nonsense syllables and nonsensical sounds (such as recorded speech played backward or a foreign language unknown to the subject). Donald Shankweiler and Michael Studdert-Kennedy of the Haskins Laboratories in New Haven, Conn., have also applied the dichotic method to the problems of defining the characteristics of speech. They found that there was no right-ear superiority for the perception of isolated vowels but that there was such an effect for consonant-vowel syllables. It is difficult to reconcile all these findings with the notion that the left-hemisphere speech system primarily processes symbolic material. Why should vowels, which can have symbolic value, be processed equally well by both hemispheres whereas nonsense sounds such as speech played backward, which do not have a symbolic value, are apparently processed primarily by the left hemisphere?

One is forced to conclude that in auditory perception the left hemisphere is specialized for the perception of certain kinds of sound generated by the human vocal cords and vocal tract. By cutting a tape recording of natural speech into small segments Laurain King and I found that the briefest duration that yielded a right-ear superiority was about 200 milliseconds, or about the duration of an average spoken syllable: a consonant and a vowel. That size of unit seems to be necessary, although not always sufficient, for asymmetrical processing, and it supports the notion that the syllable is a basic unit in speech.

We further studied the dichotic perception of different vocal nonspeech sounds, such as coughing, laughing and crying. Instead of finding a right-ear superiority with these sounds, we ob-

DICHOTIC LISTENING TASK consists in simultaneously playing one melody to one ear and a different melody to the other ear. The subject is then asked to select these melodies from a series of four melodies that are played subsequently one at a time to both ears. The melodies are played through earphones connected to a dual-channel tape recorder. Other dichotic listening tasks involved listening to pairs of digits, words, nonsense syllables, vowels, backward speech and vocal sounds such as laughing and crying.

tained a left-ear superiority. This result suggests that these sounds are processed primarily by the right hemisphere, just as melodic patterns are. Melodies hummed by another person were also identified better when heard by the left ear. Therefore if the left hemisphere distinguishes sounds by their articulatory features, these features must be rather specific.

With some justification speech is generally regarded as being primarily an auditory-vocal system. Insofar as comprehension of a written word is a consequence of prior experience with the spoken equivalent, one might expect the speech system to take part in the processing of printed and written material. In actuality when reading abilities are thoroughly tested, disturbances of speech are nearly always accompanied by at least a mild disorder in reading. We set out to find whether or not there were visual perceptual asymmetries analogous to the right- and left-ear effects we had found in the auditory modality. Some earlier studies had in fact shown that words and letters are more accurately reported from the right half of the field of vision than from the

left half, but the effects were explained as being caused by reading habits. In order to relate such effects specifically to the asymmetry of cerebral function, we needed to find tasks that tapped right-hemisphere visual functions as well.

Although the visual system is crossed, its connections are different from those of the auditory system. The connections are not from each eye to the opposite half of the brain but from each half of the visual field to the visual cortex on the opposite side [see illustration on opposite page]. Vision to the left of the point of fixation is received by the right half of each retina and the neural pathways from the right side of both retinas go to the visual cortex of the right hemisphere. Obviously the fibers from the right half of the retina of the left eye must cross the midline of the brain to get to the right hemisphere but the fibers from the right half of the retina of the right eye do not cross.

An important difference between vision and audition is that when the head is motionless, the ears are stationary but the eyes are not. Since the eyes are con-

stantly moving, under normal viewing conditions one cannot present an image in only one visual field. In order to overcome this difficulty stimuli must be presented very rapidly during some period when the point of fixation is known. This can be done with the instrument known as the tachistoscope [see illustration on page 364]. The subject looks into the instrument and is asked to fixate on a designated point. While he is fixating, a visual stimulus is presented very rapidly either to the left of the point or to the right. Before the subject can make a new fixation to look at the stimulus, the stimulus has disappeared. As a result only one side of each of the retinas and only one cerebral hemisphere are directly stimulated.

In most of our tachistoscope experiments we did not use competition between two stimuli, as we had in the dichotic listening tests. In fact, our findings have been less ambiguous when only one visual field is stimulated. In normal people, then, words and letters are reported more accurately from the right visual field than from the left, a finding compatible with the right-ear superiority for the recognition of spoken sounds. That is, the recognition of visual verbal material is also more accurate when such material initially stimulates the left hemisphere.

Much of our work with visual perception has dealt with uncovering some of the specialized functions of the right hemisphere. It has been known for some time that injury to the right posterior part of the brain (the parieto-occipital region) results in the impairment of complex abilities such as drawing, finding one's way from place to place and building models from a plan or picture. In our studies with normal subjects we found evidence that the right hemisphere is also primary for some very fundamental visual processes. We find, for example, that in the simplest kind of spatial task—the location of a single point in a two-dimensional area—the right hemisphere is dominant. We tested for this ability by presenting dots one at a time either in the left visual field or in the right for a hundredth of a second. The dot was presented at various locations within a circle drawn on a plain white card. The subject then identified the location of the dot on a similar card outside the tachistoscope. The scores for correctly locating dots were higher for dots presented in the left field than for dots presented in the right field. Moreover, ascertaining the number of dots and of geometric forms was more accurate for the left field.

AUDITORY PATHWAYS from the ears to the cerebral auditory receiving areas in the right and left hemispheres are partially crossed. Although each hemisphere can receive input from both ears, the neural connections from one ear to the hemisphere on the opposite side are stronger than the connections to the hemisphere on the same side. When ipsilateral (same side) and contralateral (opposite side) inputs compete in the auditory neural system, it is thought that the stronger contralateral input inhibits or occludes the ipsilateral signals.

This ability is not due merely to some kind of heightened attention to stimuli on the left, since the simple detection of dots is no more accurate in one field than in the other. Detection was tested either by having the subject report whether or not a dot was present on any one trial with a fixed exposure time, or by determining the exposure time required for detection of a dot. In neither case is there a difference between the detection accuracy of the left field and of the right. It appears instead that the right hemisphere incorporates important components of a system of spatial coordinates that facilitates the location of a point in space. Of course, stimuli arriving at both visual cortexes must ordinarily have access to this system, but when input is deliberately limited to one visual field, it is possible to determine if one hemisphere has a functional advantage.

We then asked if the right hemisphere might also be important for depth perception. Locating objects in three dimensions can be mediated by one or more of several cues. Most of these cues are monocular, that is, they can be distinguished by one eye. The cues include the relative sizes of retinal images, the obscuring of one object by another or the relative speed with which two objects move across the field of vision. Another important cue to depth, binocular disparity, requires both eyes. Binocular disparity refers to the fact that because the two eyes are separated each eye receives a slightly different retinal image. The disparity between the two images can provide information about the depth of an object because nearer objects have a larger binocular disparity than farther ones.

Margaret Durnford and I initiated some studies in depth perception by attaching a classical depth-perception box to the back of the tachistoscope. The box contains a fixed vertical central rod in line with the fixation point. On each side of the central rod is a track on which another vertical rod can be moved. The movable rod is seen with both eyes for only a fraction of a second, and the subject was asked whether it was nearer than the central rod or farther. When the variable rod was in the left visual field, that is, when the information went to the right hemisphere, the reports were more accurate. Thus spatial information in the third dimension also is processed more accurately by the right hemisphere than by the left.

When the movable rod was viewed with only one eye, there was no difference in accuracy between the left field

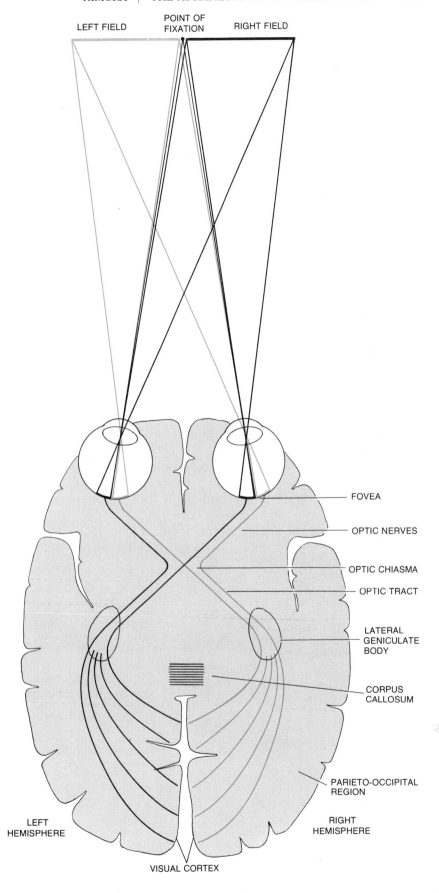

VISUAL PATHWAYS are completely crossed, so that when the eyes are fixated on a point, all of the field to the left of the fixation point excites the visual cortex in the right hemisphere and stimuli from the right visual field excite the left visual cortex. The visual cortexes can communicate via the corpus callosum, which connects the two hemispheres.

and the right. This result suggested that binocular information was processed primarily by the right hemisphere and that monocular information was processed by each hemisphere. As a further test of the specificity of hemispheric asymmetry we presented visual stimuli in which the only cue to depth was binocular disparity. When two slightly different views of a two-dimensional picture are seen separately by the two eyes by means of a stereoscope, the natural binocular disparity can be simulated. The subject reports seeing the two as being fused and as possessing the characteristics of depth that neither image alone yields.

Random-dot stereograms developed by Bela Julesz of the Bell Telephone Laboratories are ideal for this purpose, since each monocular image appears as a random array of dots. When the two images are viewed stereoscopically, a form such as a square or a triangle appears either in front of the rest of the array or behind it. A series of such stereograms with different forms was tachistoscopically presented to either the left or the right visual field, and the subject was asked to identify the form that stood out. For example, on a left-field trial one random-dot image would be presented to the left field of the left eye and its stereogram partner to the left field of the right eye. The two patterns thus presented are initially processed in the right cerebral hemisphere. A presentation to the right field, on the other hand, leads to stereoscopic processing in the left hemisphere.

We had anticipated some difficulty in getting binocular fusion because of the brief exposure (100 milliseconds) we had to use, but somewhat to our surprise most people we tested could do the task. The identification of stereoscopic stimuli was clearly better when stimuli were presented to the left visual field, that is, when the disparate images went to the right hemisphere. It may be, then, that the right-hemisphere processing of depth information is rather specifically connected to the utilization of such binocular cues.

Clearly the right hemisphere works better than the left hemisphere in analyzing information about where objects are located in space. The probability that we were tapping functions fundamental to orientation in space encouraged us to study hemispheric specialization for still another basic visual process: the perception of the slant of a line. Very short lines were presented one at a time in either the left visual field or the right. The lines varied in slope from 15 degrees to 165 degrees in 15-degree steps. After the subject had seen the line he was asked to pick it out of a multiple-choice array of slanted lines on a sheet of paper. There was a small but consistent superiority for slope identification in the left visual field, again suggesting that this information is asymmetrically processed in the brain. David H. Hubel and Torsten N. Wiesel of the Harvard Medical School have suggested that the initial processing of the orientation of a line is done in the visual cortex. The fact that we found a hemispheric asymmetry for such perceptual tasks opens the possibility that there may be some functional asymmetry between the hemispheres in primary processes as well as in the more complex associative processes.

We do not know precisely what neural systems in the brain we are sampling with our perceptual techniques. The evidence we have suggests that with the

EXPOSURE FIELD

LEFT FIELD   RIGHT FIELD

LIGHTS

PARTIALLY
SILVERED
MIRROR

FIXATION
POINT

RIGHT
VISUAL CORTEX

TWO-FIELD TACHISTOSCOPE is used for study of visual perception. When the fixation field is lighted, an observer sees a reflection of the field in the partially silvered mirror. He is asked to fixate on a point in the center of the field. Then the fixation-field light is turned off and the exposure-field light is simultaneously turned on for a few milliseconds. The image on the exposure field passes through the partially silvered mirror and is briefly seen by the observer. At the end of the exposure the fixation-field light comes on and the exposure-field light goes off. By placing the exposure image in the left or right visual field as desired the experimenter can selectively stimulate either the right or the left visual cortex.

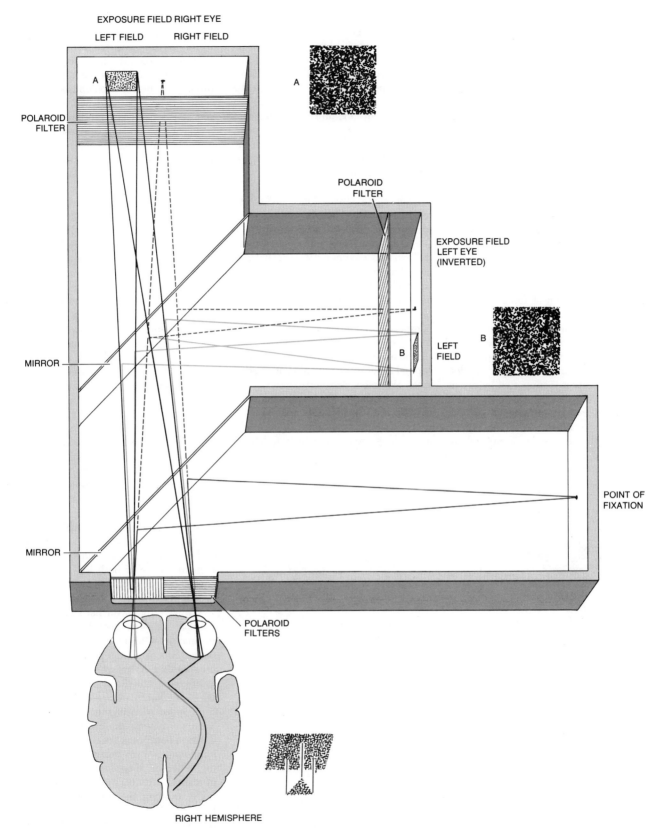

EXPOSURE FIELD RIGHT EYE

LEFT FIELD   RIGHT FIELD

A

POLAROID
FILTER

POLAROID
FILTER

EXPOSURE FIELD
LEFT EYE
(INVERTED)

A

MIRROR

LEFT
FIELD

B

B

MIRROR

POINT OF
FIXATION

POLAROID
FILTERS

RIGHT HEMISPHERE

THREE-FIELD TACHISTOSCOPE is used in studies of depth perception. The subject initially fixates on a point, which he sees as a reflection from a partially silvered mirror. The two exposure fields become visible when the light on the fixation field is turned off and the lights near the exposure fields are flashed on. The Polaroid filters are arranged so that each eye receives a different image. Using a technique developed by Bela Julesz of the Bell Telephone Laboratories, the author presented one random-dot pattern to the right hemiretina of the right eye and a slightly different random-dot pattern to the right hemiretina of the left eye. In other trials the pattern was presented to the left hemiretinas. When each pattern is viewed alone, no shapes or depth can be seen, but when the two patterns are fused somewhere in the visual system, the subject in this case sees a triangle floating in front of the background dot pattern. Most people are better at identifying the stereoscopic figure when the images are flashed onto the left visual field than when they are flashed onto the right visual field, indicating that the right hemisphere may be better at processing depth information.

tachistoscopic tests we are tapping the function of regions near the striate cortex, the major visual pathway to the hemispheres, rather than more remote regions such as the temporal lobes, which also have visual functions. With the auditory dichotic tests, on the other hand, we are probably tapping the functions of the temporal lobe area.

A related point of interest is that we have not found any left-visual-field superiority for the perception of form, although we have tried in several tests. We know that damage to the right temporal lobe impairs the perception of nonsense designs, suggesting that some portions of the right hemisphere may indeed be critical for form perception. The tachistoscopic methods we used, however, do not sample the function of the systems for perception of form. Apparently the neural systems involved in spatial processing are relatively independent of those involved in form perception, a suggestion that was made many years ago by the British neurologist Gordon Holmes and that is supported by recent studies of visual perception in hamsters conducted by Gerald Schneider of the Massachusetts Institute of Technology.

Although we have concentrated on visual and auditory perception, it appears that there is an analogous asymmetry in tactual perception. Beata Hermelin and Neil O'Connor of the Medical Research Council's Developmental Psychology Unit have reported that the tactual perception of Braille dot patterns by blind people is more rapid with the left hand than with the right. Diana Ingram in our laboratory has found that when one arm is used to locate a point out of sight under a table on which the location of the point is indicated, the left arm performs more accurately than the right.

From these observations and others one can conclude that the posterior part of the right hemisphere is involved in the direct analysis of information about the external environment. The parietooccipital area is particularly critical for the kinds of behavior that are dependent on spatial relations, whereas the temporal region takes part in processing nonspatial stimuli such as melodic patterns and nonsense designs. An important secondary process in the analysis of perceptual input is the attaching of a verbal label. We know that verbal transformation of information involves the left hemisphere, but we still have much to learn about the transfer from right-to-left-hemisphere processing and from left-to-right-hemisphere processing. For example, we can demonstrate left-visual-

field superiority in spatial perception in spite of the fact that the subject ultimately gives us a verbal response that is controlled from his left hemisphere. We explain this result by saying that the primary analysis is accomplished by the right hemisphere, and the verbal response is secondary. In other situations, however, the mode of response (manual or vocal) can influence which field dominates. Hence we do not yet have a completely satisfactory explanation.

We have seen that the left hemisphere is critical for the production and perception of certain sounds made by the human speech system. Recently my colleagues and I have obtained evidence from patients with cerebral strokes that the left hemisphere may also be essential for some types of movements of the hand. We found that patients with left-sided cerebral damage have difficulty copying a series of hand movements, whether the movements are meaningful or not. Moreover, there are reports in the clinical literature of deaf mutes who used hand movements as a means of communication and who, after suffering damage to the left hemisphere, displayed disturbances of these movements that were analogous to disturbances of speech. That the left hemisphere has a special control over some aspects of manual behavior is further suggested by the fact that most people use their right hand for many skilled acts. Although the relation between speech lateralization and hand preference is not perfect, the high incidence of both left-hemisphere control of speech and right-hand preference is probably not coincidental.

We have found further support for a relation between speech and certain manual activities by observing the hand movements of normal people while they are speaking. As everyone knows, speech is often accompanied by gestures, in which the hands are moved around freely in space without touching anything. Such movements are hardly ever seen during a nonspeech vocal activity such as humming. In both humming and speaking, however, there may be other kinds of manual activity, such as touching the body, rubbing the nose or scratching. Equally interesting is the fact that the free movements during speech are made primarily by the hand opposite the hemisphere that controls speech (as determined by means of the dichotic verbal method). If speech is controlled by the left hemisphere, as it is in most people, the right hand makes more of the free movements, whereas if speech is controlled by the right hemisphere, the left

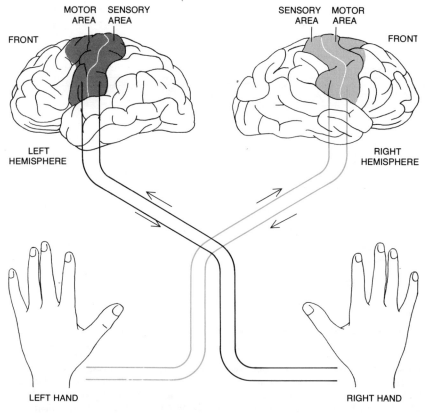

MOTOR AND SENSORY PATHWAYS from the hands are almost completely crossed, so that each hand is served primarily by the cerebral hemisphere on the opposite side.

GESTURES DURING SPEECH are made primarily by the hand that is opposite the cerebral hemisphere controlling speech. In most people speech is controlled by the left hemisphere, and the right hand of such people makes more free movements than the left hand during speech, as is shown in these pictures from a video tape recording made by the author during an experiment. The asymmetrical use of the hands during speech has been found only when the hands move freely in space without touching the body.

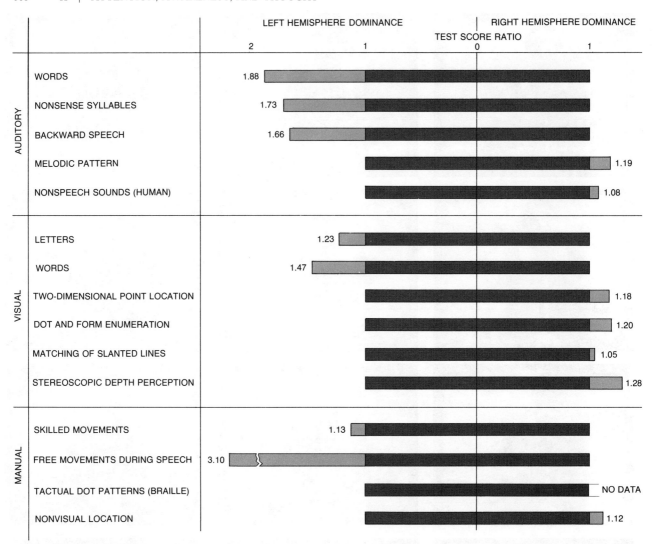

FUNCTIONAL ASYMMETRIES of the cerebral hemispheres in normal, right-handed people are found in the auditory, visual and manual modalities. Test scores for the left and right sides were converted to ratios for comparison. The ratio for left-hemisphere dominance for perception of spoken words is 1.88 : 1, whereas the ratio for right-hemisphere dominance for melodies is 1.19 : 1. These ratios are not fixed values since they vary with the type of stimulus, the kind of response required and the difficulty of the task.

hand makes more of the free movements. Curiously, this asymmetry is restricted to free movements; it does not appear in self-touching movements. These findings and the clinical findings I have mentioned suggest that there is indeed some overlap between the speaking system in a hemisphere and the system controlling certain kinds of manual activity. It may be that the left hemisphere is particularly well adapted not for the symbolic function in itself but for the execution of some categories of motor activity that happen to lend themselves readily to communication.

In our work on cerebral asymmetry in normal people we have occasionally encountered sex differences. In right-hemisphere tasks males tend to have a greater left-visual-field superiority for dot location and dot enumeration than females. We also know that males are

superior to females in certain visual-spatial tasks. It may be that right-hemisphere specialization is more pronounced in males than in females, and that such specialization may sometimes be advantageous. Recently Jeannette McGlone and Wilda Davidson in my laboratory at the University of Western Ontario found some evidence in favor of this idea. They administered a standard test of spatial perception in which the subject must identify a design after it has been rotated. They found, as is usual in this task, that males usually performed better than females. The females who did particularly poorly on the test were those who showed some left-hemispheric specialization for spatial functions (as inferred from the tachistoscopic dot-enumeration test). Usually such functions are controlled by the right hemisphere.

In contrast, females tend to have greater verbal fluency than males. There

is no evidence, however, that adult females are more asymmetrical in speech lateralization than males. Dichotic studies nonetheless suggest that speech lateralization may develop earlier in girls than in boys. It appears that for some intellectual functions the brains of males and females may be differently organized. Most of human evolution must have taken place under conditions where for the male hunting members of society accurate information about both the immediate and the distant environment was of paramount importance. For the females, who presumably stayed closer to home with other nonhunting members of the group, similar selection processes may not have operated. It will be interesting to discover whether or not the sex differences in verbal and nonverbal asymmetries we have uncovered with our relatively simple techniques hold true for other cultures.

The Split Brain in Man

by Michael S. Gazzaniga
August 1967

*The human brain is actually two brains, each capable
of advanced mental functions. When the cerebrum
is divided surgically, it is as if the cranium contained
two separate spheres of consciousness*

The brain of the higher animals, including man, is a double organ, consisting of right and left hemispheres connected by an isthmus of nerve tissue called the corpus callosum. Some 15 years ago Ronald E. Myers and R. W. Sperry, then at the University of Chicago, made a surprising discovery: When this connection between the two halves of the cerebrum was cut, each hemisphere functioned independently as if it were a complete brain. The phenomenon was first investigated in a cat in which not only the brain but also the optic chiasm, the crossover of the optic nerves, was divided, so that visual information from the left eye was dispatched only to the left brain and information from the right eye only to the right brain. Working on a problem with one eye, the animal could respond normally and learn to perform a task; when that eye was covered and the same problem was presented to the other eye, the animal evinced no recognition of the problem and had to learn it again from the beginning with the other half of the brain.

The finding introduced entirely new questions in the study of brain mechanisms. Was the corpus callosum responsible for integration of the operations of the two cerebral hemispheres in the intact brain? Did it serve to keep each hemisphere informed about what was going on in the other? To put the question another way, would cutting the corpus callosum literally result in the right hand not knowing what the left was doing? To what extent were the two half-brains actually independent when they were separated? Could they have separate thoughts, even separate emotions?

Such questions have been pursued by Sperry and his co-workers in a wide-ranging series of animal studies at the California Institute of Technology over

the past decade [see "The Great Cerebral Commissure," by R. W. Sperry; SCIENTIFIC AMERICAN Offprint 174]. Recently these questions have been investigated in human patients who underwent the brain-splitting operation for medical reasons. The demonstration in experimental animals that sectioning of the corpus callosum did not seriously impair mental faculties had encouraged surgeons to resort to this operation for people afflicted with uncontrollable epilepsy. The hope was to confine a seizure to one hemisphere. The operation proved to be remarkably successful; curiously there is an almost total elimination of all attacks, including unilateral ones. It is as if the intact callosum had served in these patients to facilitate seizure activity.

This article is a brief survey of investigations Sperry and I have carried out at Cal Tech over the past five years with some of these patients. The operations were performed by P. J. Vogel and J. E. Bogen of the California College of Medicine. Our studies date back to 1961, when the first patient, a 48-year-old war veteran, underwent the operation: cutting of the corpus callosum and other commissure structures connecting the two halves of the cerebral cortex [*see illustration on page 371*]. As of today 10 patients have had the operation, and we have examined four thoroughly over a long period with many tests.

From the beginning one of the most striking observations was that the operation produced no noticeable change in the patients' temperament, personality or general intelligence. In the first case the patient could not speak for 30 days after the operation, but he then recovered his speech. More typical was the third case: on awaking from the surgery the patient quipped that he had a "splitting headache," and in his still drowsy

state he was able to repeat the tongue twister "Peter Piper picked a peck of pickled peppers."

Close observation, however, soon revealed some changes in the patients' everyday behavior. For example, it could be seen that in moving about and responding to sensory stimuli the patients favored the right side of the body, which is controlled by the dominant left half of the brain. For a considerable period after the operation the left side of the body rarely showed spontaneous activity, and the patient generally did not respond to stimulation of that side: when he brushed against something with his left side he did not notice that he had done so, and when an object was placed in his left hand he generally denied its presence.

More specific tests identified the main features of the bisected-brain syndrome. One of these tests examined responses to visual stimulation. While the patient fixed his gaze on a central point on a board, spots of light were flashed (for a tenth of a second) in a row across the board that spanned both the left and the right half of his visual field. The patient was asked to tell what he had seen. Each patient reported that lights had been flashed in the right half of the visual field. When lights were flashed only in the left half of the field, however, the patients generally denied having seen any lights. Since the right side of the visual field is normally projected to the left hemisphere of the brain and the left field to the right hemisphere, one might have concluded that in these patients with divided brains the right hemisphere was in effect blind. We found, however, that this was not the case when the patients were directed to point to the lights that had flashed instead of giving a verbal report. With this manual response they were able to indicate when lights had

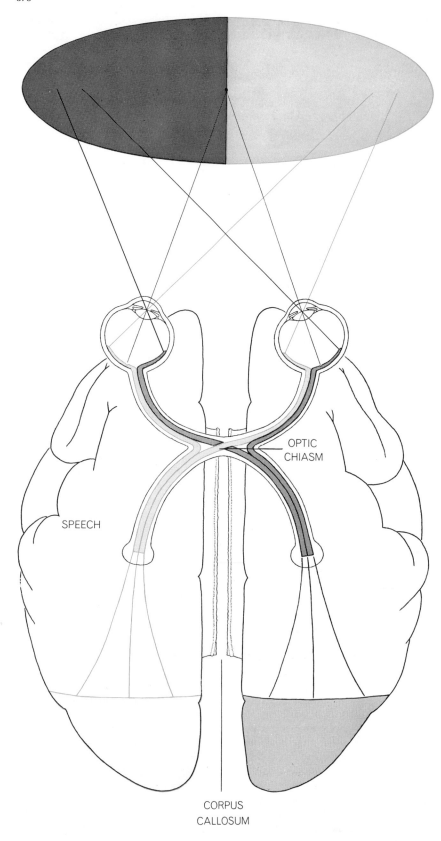

SPEECH

OPTIC CHIASM

CORPUS CALLOSUM

VISUAL INPUT to bisected brain was limited to one hemisphere by presenting information only in one visual field. The right and left fields of view are projected, via the optic chiasm, to the left and right hemispheres of the brain respectively. If a person fixes his gaze on a point, therefore, information to the left of the point goes only to the right hemisphere and information to the right of the point goes to the left hemisphere. Stimuli in the left visual field cannot be described by a split-brain patient because of the disconnection between the right hemisphere and the speech center, which is in the left hemisphere.

been flashed in the left visual field, and perception with the brain's right hemisphere proved to be almost equal to perception with the left. Clearly, then, the patients' failure to report the right hemisphere's perception verbally was due to the fact that the speech centers of the brain are located in the left hemisphere.

Our tests of the patients' ability to recognize objects by touch at first resulted in the same general finding. When the object was held in the right hand, from which sensory information is sent to the left hemisphere, the patient was able to name and describe the object. When it was held in the left hand (from which information goes primarily to the right hemisphere), the patient could not describe the object verbally but was able to identify it in a nonverbal test—matching it, for example, to the same object in a varied collection of things. We soon realized, however, that each hemisphere receives, in addition to the main input from the opposite side of the body, some input from the same side. This "ipsilateral" input is crude; it is apparently good mainly for "cuing in" the hemisphere as to the presence or absence of stimulation and relaying fairly gross information about the location of a stimulus on the surface of the body. It is unable, as a rule, to relay information concerning the qualitative nature of an object.

Tests of motor control in these split-brain patients revealed that the left hemisphere of the brain exercised normal control over the right hand but had less than full control of the left hand (for instance, it was poor at directing individual movements of the fingers). Similarly, the right hemisphere had full control of the left hand but not of the right hand. When the two hemispheres were in conflict, dictating different movements for the same hand, the hemisphere on the side opposite the hand generally took charge and overruled the orders of the side of the brain with the weaker control. In general the motor findings in the human patients were much the same as those in split-brain monkeys.

We come now to the main question on which we centered our studies, namely how the separation of the hemispheres affects the mental capacities of the human brain. For these psychological tests we used two different devices. One was visual: a picture or written information was flashed (for a tenth of a second) in either the right or the left visual field, so that the information was transmitted only to the left or to the right brain hemisphere [see illustration on page 372]. The other type of test was

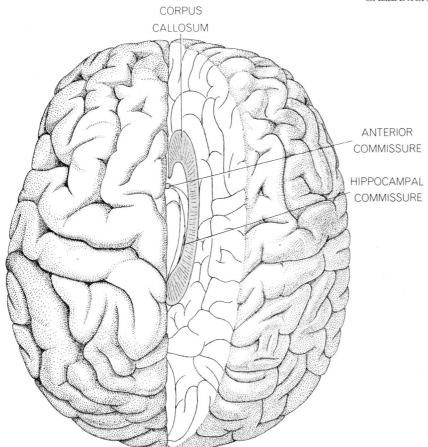

CORPUS
CALLOSUM

ANTERIOR
COMMISSURE

HIPPOCAMPAL
COMMISSURE

TWO HEMISPHERES of the human brain are divided by neurosurgeons to control epileptic seizures. In this top view of the brain the right hemisphere is retracted and the corpus callosum and other commissures, or connectors, that are generally cut are shown in color.

tactile: an object was placed out of view in the patient's right or left hand, again for the purpose of conveying the information to just one hemisphere—the hemisphere on the side opposite the hand.

When the information (visual or tactile) was presented to the dominant left hemisphere, the patients were able to deal with and describe it quite normally, both orally and in writing. For example, when a picture of a spoon was shown in the right visual field or a spoon was placed in the right hand, all the patients readily identified and described it. They were able to read out written messages and to perform problems in calculation that were presented to the left hemisphere.

In contrast, when the same information was presented to the right hemisphere, it failed to elicit such spoken or written responses. A picture transmitted to the right hemisphere evoked either a haphazard guess or no verbal response at all. Similarly, a pencil placed in the left hand (behind a screen that cut off vision) might be called a can opener or a cigarette lighter, or the patient might not

even attempt to describe it. The verbal guesses presumably came not from the right hemisphere but from the left, which had no perception of the object but might attempt to identify it from indirect clues.

Did this impotence of the right hemisphere mean that its surgical separation from the left had reduced its mental powers to an imbecilic level? The earlier tests of its nonverbal capacities suggested that this was almost certainly not so. Indeed, when we switched to asking for nonverbal answers to the visual and tactile information presented in our new psychological tests, the right hemisphere in several patients showed considerable capacity for accurate performance. For example, when a picture of a spoon was presented to the right hemisphere, the patients were able to feel around with the left hand among a varied group of objects (screened from sight) and select a spoon as a match for the picture. Furthermore, when they were shown a picture of a cigarette they succeeded in selecting an ashtray, from

a group of 10 objects that did not include a cigarette, as the article most closely related to the picture. Oddly enough, however, even after their correct response, and while they were holding the spoon or the ashtray in their left hand, they were unable to name or describe the object or the picture. Evidently the left hemisphere was completely divorced, in perception and knowledge, from the right.

Other tests showed that the right hemisphere did possess a certain amount of language comprehension. For example, when the word "pencil" was flashed to the right hemisphere, the patients were able to pick out a pencil from a group of unseen objects with the left hand. And when a patient held an object in the left hand (out of view), although he could not say its name or describe it, he was later able to point to a card on which the name of the object was written.

In one particularly interesting test the word "heart" was flashed across the center of the visual field, with the "he" portion to the left of the center and "art" to the right. Asked to tell what the word was, the patients would say they had seen "art"—the portion projected to the left brain hemisphere (which is responsible for speech). Curiously when, after "heart" had been flashed in the same way, the patients were asked to point with the left hand to one of two cards—"art" or "he"—to identify the word they had seen, they invariably pointed to "he." The experiment showed clearly that both hemispheres had simultaneously observed the portions of the word available to them and that in this particular case the right hemisphere, when it had had the opportunity to express itself, had prevailed over the left.

Because an auditory input to one ear goes to both sides of the brain, we conducted tests for the comprehension of words presented audibly to the right hemisphere not by trying to limit the original input but by limiting the ability to answer to the right hemisphere. This was done most easily by having a patient use his left hand to retrieve, from a grab bag held out of view, an object named by the examiner. We found that the patients could easily retrieve such objects as a watch, comb, marble or coin. The object to be retrieved did not even have to be named; it might simply be described or alluded to. For example, the command "Retrieve the fruit monkeys like best" results in the patients' pulling out a banana from a grab bag full of plastic fruit; at the command "Sunkist sells a lot of them" the patients retrieve an orange. We knew that touch information from the left hand was going exclusively to the right hemisphere because moments later, when the patients were asked to name various pieces of fruit placed in the left hand, they were unable to score above a chance level.

The upper limit of linguistic abilities in each hemisphere varies from subject to subject. In one case there was little or no evidence for language abilities in the right hemisphere, whereas in the other three the amount and extent of the capacities varied. The most adept patient showed some evidence of even being able to spell simple words by placing plastic letters on a table with his left hand. The subject was told to spell a word such as "pie," and the examiner then placed the three appropriate letters, one at a time in a random order, in his left hand to be arranged on the table. The patient was able to spell even more abstract words such as "how," "what" and "the." In another test three or four letters were placed in a pile, again out of view, to be felt with the left hand. The letters available in each trial would spell only one word, and the instructions to the subject were "Spell a word." The patient was able to spell such words as "cup" and "love." Yet after he had completed this task, the patient was unable to name the word he had just spelled!

The possibility that the right hemisphere has not only some language but even some speech capabilities cannot be ruled out, although at present there is no firm evidence for this. It would not be surprising to discover that the patients are capable of a few simple exclamatory remarks, particularly when under emotional stress. The possibility also remains, of course, that speech of some type could be trained into the right hemisphere. Tests aimed at this question, however, would have to be closely scrutinized and controlled.

The reason is that here, as in many of the tests, "cross-cuing" from one hemisphere to the other could be held responsible for any positive findings. We had a case of such cross-cuing during a series of tests of whether the right hemisphere could respond verbally to simple red or green stimuli. At first, after either a red or a green light was flashed to the right hemisphere, the patient would guess the color at a chance level, as might be expected if the speech mechanism is solely represented in the left hemisphere. After a few trials, however, the score improved whenever the examiner allowed a second guess.

We soon caught on to the strategy the patient used. If a red light was flashed and the patient by chance guessed red, he would stick with that answer. If the flashed light was red and the patient by chance guessed green, he would frown,

shake his head and then say, "Oh no, I meant red." What was happening was that the right hemisphere saw the red light and heard the left hemisphere make the guess "green." Knowing that the answer was wrong, the right hemisphere precipitated a frown and a shake of the head, which in turn cued in the left hemisphere to the fact that the answer was wrong and that it had better correct itself! We have learned that this cross-cuing mechanism can become extremely refined. The realization that the neurological patient has various strategies at his command emphasizes how difficult it is to obtain a clear neurological description of a human being with brain damage.

Is the language comprehension by the right hemisphere that the patients exhibited in these tests a normal capability of that hemisphere or was it acquired by learning after their operation, perhaps during the course of the experiments themselves? The issue is difficult to decide. We must remember that we are examining a half of the human brain, a system easily capable of learning from a single trial in a test. We do know that the right hemisphere is decidedly inferior to the left in its overall command of language. We have established, for instance, that although the right hemisphere can respond to a concrete noun such as "pencil," it cannot do as well with verbs; patients are unable to re-

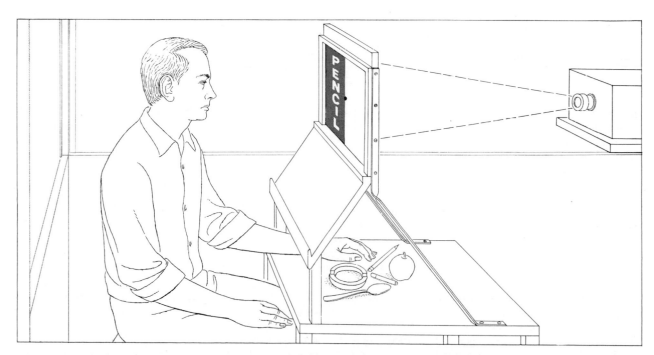

RESPONSE TO VISUAL STIMULUS is tested by flashing a word or a picture of an object on a translucent screen. The examiner first checks the subject's gaze to be sure it is fixed on a dot that marks the center of the visual field. The examiner may call for a verbal response—reading the flashed word, for example—or for a nonverbal one, such as picking up the object that is named from among a number of things spread on the table. The objects are hidden from the subject's view so that they can be identified only by touch.

spond appropriately to simple printed instructions, such as "smile" or "frown," when these words are flashed to the right hemisphere, nor can they point to a picture that corresponds to a flashed verb. Some of our recent studies at the University of California at Santa Barbara also indicate that the right hemisphere has a very poorly developed grammar; it seems to be incapable of forming the plural of a given word, for example.

In general, then, the extent of language present in the adult right hemisphere in no way compares with that present in the left hemisphere or, for that matter, with the extent of language present in the child's right hemisphere. Up to the age of four or so, it would appear from a variety of neurological observations, the right hemisphere is about as proficient in handling language as the left. Moreover, studies of the child's development of language, particularly with respect to grammar, strongly suggest that the foundations of grammar—a ground plan for language, so to speak—are somehow inherent in the human organism and are fully realized between the ages of two and three. In other words, in the young child each hemisphere is about equally developed with respect to language and speech function. We are thus faced with the interesting question of why the right hemisphere at an early age and stage of development possesses substantial language capacity whereas at a more adult stage it possesses a rather poor capacity. It is difficult indeed to conceive of the underlying neurological mechanism that would allow for the establishment of a capacity of a high order in a particular hemisphere on a temporary basis. The implication is that during maturation the processes and systems active in making this capacity manifest are somehow inhibited and dismantled in the right hemisphere and allowed to reside only in the dominant left hemisphere.

Yet the right hemisphere is not in all respects inferior or subordinate to the left. Tests have demonstrated that it excels the left in some specialized functions. As an example, tests by us and by Bogen have shown that in these patients the left hand is capable of arranging blocks to match a pictured design and of drawing a cube in three dimensions, whereas the right hand, deprived of instructions from the right hemisphere, could not perform either of these tasks.

It is of interest to note, however, that although the patients (our first subject in particular) could not execute such tasks

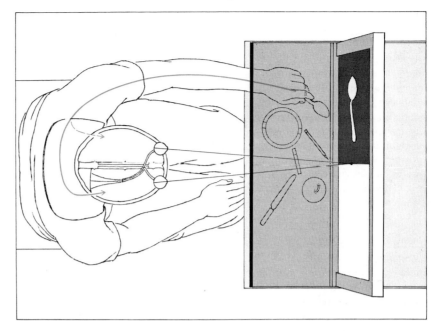

VISUAL-TACTILE ASSOCIATION is performed by a split-brain patient. A picture of a spoon is flashed to the right hemisphere; with the left hand he retrieves a spoon from behind the screen. The touch information from the left hand projects (*color*) mainly to the right hemisphere, but a weak "ipsilateral" component goes to the left hemisphere. This is usually not enough to enable him to say (using the left hemisphere) what he has picked up.

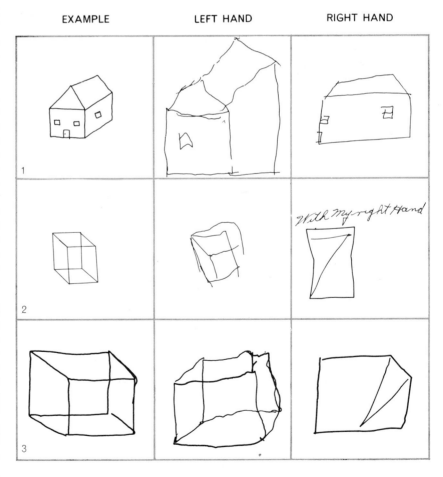

EXAMPLE   LEFT HAND   RIGHT HAND

"VISUAL-CONSTRUCTIONAL" tasks are handled better by the right hemisphere. This was seen most clearly in the first patient, who had poor ipsilateral control of his right hand. Although right-handed, he could copy the examples only with his left hand.

with the right hand, they were capable of matching a test stimulus to the correct design when it appeared among five related patterns presented in their right visual field. This showed that the dominant left hemisphere is capable of discriminating between correct and incorrect stimuli. Since it is also true that the patients have no motor problems with their right hand, the patients' inability to perform these tasks must reflect a breakdown of an integrative process somewhere between the sensory system and the motor system.

We found that in certain other mental processes the right hemisphere is on a par with the left. In particular, it can independently generate an emotional reaction. In one of our experiments exploring the matter we would present a series of ordinary objects and then suddenly flash a picture of a nude woman. This evoked an amused reaction regardless of whether the picture was presented to the left hemisphere or to the right. When the picture was flashed to the left hemisphere of a female patient, she laughed and verbally identified the picture as a nude. When it was later presented to the right hemisphere, she said in reply to a question that she saw nothing, but almost immediately a sly smile spread over her face and she began to chuckle. Asked what she was laughing at, she said: "I don't know...nothing...oh—that funny machine." Although the right hemisphere could not describe what it had seen, the sight nevertheless elicited an emotional response like the one evoked from the left hemisphere.

Taken together, our studies seem to demonstrate conclusively that in a split-brain situation we are really dealing with two brains, each separately capable of mental functions of a high order. This implies that the two brains should have twice as large a span of attention—that is, should be able to handle twice as much information—as a normal whole brain. We have not yet tested this precisely in human patients, but E. D. Young and I have found that a split-brain monkey can indeed deal with nearly twice as much information as a normal animal [see illustration below]. We have so far determined also that brain-bisected patients can carry out two tasks as fast as a normal person can do one.

Just how does the corpus callosum of the intact brain combine and integrate the perceptions and knowledge of the two cerebral hemispheres? This has been investigated recently by Giovanni Berlucchi, Giacomo Rizzolati and me at the Istituto di Fisiologia Umana in Pisa. We made recordings of neural activity in the posterior part of the callosum of the cat with the hope of relating the responses of that structure to stimulation of the animal's visual fields. The kinds of responses recorded turned out to be similar to those observed in the visual cortex of the cat. In other words, the results suggest that visual pattern information can be transmitted through the callosum. This finding militates against the notion that learning and memory are transferred across the callosum, as has usually been suggested. Instead, it looks as though in animals with an intact callosum a copy of the visual world as seen in one hemisphere is sent over to the other, with the result that both hemispheres can learn together a discrimination presented to just one hemisphere. In the split-brain animal this extension of the visual pathway is cut off; this would explain rather simply why no learning proceeds in the visually isolated hemisphere and why it has to learn the discrimination from scratch.

Curiously, however, the neural activity in the callosum came only in response to stimuli at the midline of the visual field. This finding raises difficult questions. How can it be reconciled with the well-established observation that the left hemisphere of a normal person can give a running description of all the visual information presented throughout the entire half-field projected to the right hemisphere? For this reason alone one is wearily driven back to the conclusion that somewhere and somehow all or part of the callosum transmits not only a visual scene but also a complicated neural code of a higher order.

All the evidence indicates that separation of the hemispheres creates two independent spheres of consciousness within a single cranium, that is to say, within a single organism. This conclusion is disturbing to some people who view consciousness as an indivisible property of the human brain. It seems premature to others, who insist that the capacities revealed thus far for the right hemisphere are at the level of an automaton. There is, to be sure, hemispheric inequality in the present cases, but it may well be a characteristic of the individuals we have studied. It is entirely possible that if a human brain were divided in a very young person, both hemispheres could as a result separately and independently develop mental functions of a high order at the level attained only in the left hemisphere of normal individuals.

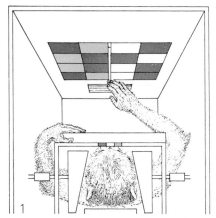 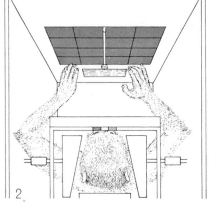 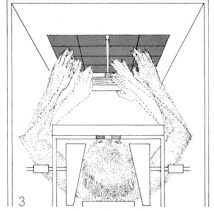

SPLIT-BRAIN MONKEYS can handle more visual information than normal animals. When the monkey pulls a knob (1), eight of the 16 panels light momentarily. The monkey must then start at the bottom and punch the lights that were lit and no others (2). With the panels lit for 600 milliseconds normal monkeys get up to the third row from the bottom before forgetting which panels were lit (3). Split-brain monkeys complete the entire task with the panels lit only 200 milliseconds. The monkeys look at the panels through filters; since the optic chiasm is cut in these animals, the filters allow each hemisphere to see the colored panels on one side only.

The Functional Organization of the Brain

by A. R. Luria
March 1970

The sensory and motor functions of the human brain are well localized, but more complex functions such as speech and writing remain obscure. Injuries to the brain provide clues to how such systems are organized

The functional organization of the human brain is a problem that is far from solved. I shall describe in this article some recent advances in the mapping of the brain. They open up a new field of exploration having to do with the structures of the brain involved in complex forms of behavior.

So far as sensory and motor functions are concerned, the brain, as is well known, has been mapped in precise detail. Studies by neurologists and psychologists over the past century have defined the centers that are responsible for some elementary functions such as seeing, hearing, other sensory functions and the control of the various muscular systems of the body. From outward symptoms or simple tests disclosing a disturbance of one of these functions it is possible to deduce the location of the lesion (a tumor or a hemorrhage, for example) causing the disturbance. Such a finding is of major importance in neurology and neurosurgery. The sensory and motor centers, however, account for only a small part of the area of the cerebral cortex. At least three-quarters of the cortex has nothing to do with sensory functions or muscle actions. In order to proceed further with the mapping of the brain's functions we must look into the systems responsible for the higher, more complex behavioral processes.

It is obvious that these processes, being social in origin and highly complex in structure and involving the elaboration and storage of information and the programming and control of actions, are not localized in particular centers of the brain. Plainly they must be managed by an elaborate apparatus consisting of various brain structures. Modern psychological investigations have made it clear that each behavioral process is a complex functional system based on a plan or program of operations that leads to a definite goal. The system is self-regulating: the brain judges the result of every action in relation to the basic plan and calls an end to the activity when it arrives at a successful completion of the program. This mechanism is equally applicable to elementary, involuntary forms of behavior such as breathing and walking and to complicated, voluntary ones such as reading, writing, decision-making and problem-solving.

What is the organizational form of this system in the brain? Our present knowledge of neurology indicates that the apparatus directing a complex behavioral process comprises a number of brain structures, each playing a highly specific role and all under coordinated control. One should therefore expect that lesions of the structures involved might result in changes in the behavior, and that the nature of the change would vary according to the particular structure that is damaged.

A New Approach

This concept forms the basis of our new approach to exploration of the functional organization of the brain—a study we call neuropsychology. The study has two objectives. First, by pinpointing the brain lesions responsible for specific behavioral disorders we hope to develop a means of early diagnosis and precise location of brain injuries (including those from tumors or from hemorrhage) so that they can be treated by surgery as soon as possible. Second, neuropsychological investigation should provide us with a factor analysis that will lead to better understanding of the components of complex psychological functions for which the operations of the different parts of the brain are responsible.

The human brain can be considered to be made up of three main blocks incorporating basic functions. Let us examine the responsibilities of each block in turn.

The first block regulates the energy level and tone of the cortex, providing it with a stable basis for the organization of its various processes. The brilliant researches of Horace W. Magoun, Giuseppe Moruzzi, Herbert H. Jasper and Donald B. Lindsley located the components of the first block in the upper and lower parts of the brain stem and particularly in the reticular formation, which controls wakefulness. If an injury occurs in some part of the first block, the cortex goes into a pathological state: the stability of its dynamic processes breaks down, there is a marked deterioration of wakefulness and memory traces become disorganized.

I. P. Pavlov observed that when the normal tone of the cortex is lowered, the "law of force" is lost and much of the brain's ability to discriminate among stimuli suffers. Normally the cortex reacts powerfully to strong or significant stimuli and responds hardly at all to feeble or insignificant stimuli, which are easily suppressed. A weakened cortex, on the other hand, has about the same response to insignificant stimuli as to significant ones, and in an extremely weakened state it may react even more strongly to weak stimuli than to strong ones. We all know about this loss of the brain's selectivity from common experience. Recall how diffuse and disorganized our thoughts become when we are drowsy, and what bizarre associations the mind may form in a state of fatigue or in dreams.

Obviously the results of injury to the first block in the brain, namely the loss of the selectivity of cortical actions and of normal discrimination of stimuli, will bring about marked changes in behavior. The control of behavior becomes deranged. In our common work with Macdonald Critchley of England such disturbances have been observed in patients who had tumors of the middle parts of the frontal lobes, and other investigators in our laboratory in Moscow have since reported similar effects from lesions in deep parts of the brain.

The Second Block

The second block of the brain has received much more study, and its role in the organization of behavior is better known. Located in the rear parts of the cortex, it plays a decisive role in the analysis, coding and storage of information. In contrast to the functions of the first block, which are mainly of a general nature (for example controlling wakefulness), the systems of the second block have highly specific assignments.

We can easily identify areas in the second block that are respectively responsible for the analysis of optic, acoustic, cutaneous and kinesthetic stimuli. Each of these cortical areas has a hierarchical organization: a primary zone that sorts and records the sensory information, a secondary zone that organizes the information further and codes it and a tertiary zone where the data from different sources overlap and are combined to lay the groundwork for the organization of behavior.

Injuries to the parts of the second block produce much more specific effects than lesions in the first block do. An injury in a primary zone of the second block results in a sensory defect (in seeing or hearing, for example); it does not, however, bring about a marked change in complex forms of behavior. A lesion

in a secondary zone produces more complicated disturbances. It interferes with analysis of the sensory stimuli the zone receives and, because the coding function is impaired, the lesion leads to disorganization of all the behavioral processes that would normally respond to these particular stimuli. It does not disturb any other behavioral processes, however, which is an important aid for locating the lesion.

Of the various lesions in the second block of the brain those in the tertiary zones are particularly interesting to us as neuropsychologists. Since these zones are responsible for the synthesis of a collection of information inputs from different sources into a coherent whole, a lesion of a tertiary zone can cause such complex disturbances as visual disorientation in space. The lesion seriously im-

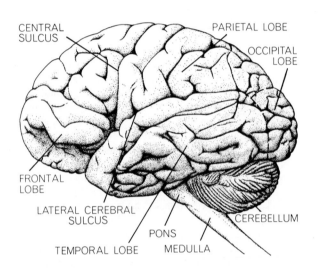

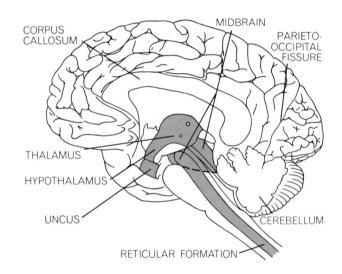

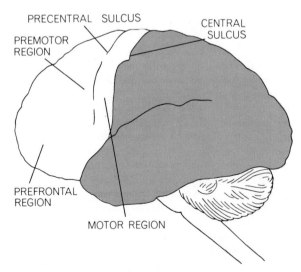

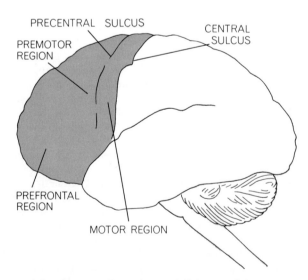

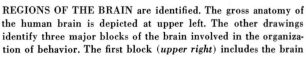

REGIONS OF THE BRAIN are identified. The gross anatomy of the human brain is depicted at upper left. The other drawings identify three major blocks of the brain involved in the organization of behavior. The first block (*upper right*) includes the brain stem and the old cortex. It regulates wakefulness and the response to stimuli. The second block (*lower left*) plays a key role in the analysis, coding and storage of information. The third block (*lower right*) is involved in the formation of intentions and programs.

pairs the ability to handle complex problems that entail an organization of input in simultaneous matrixes. That is why these lesions may render a person incapable of performing complex operations with numbers or of coping with a complexity in grammar logic or language structure.

The Third Block

The third block of the brain, comprising the frontal lobes, is involved in the formation of intentions and programs for behavior. Important contributions to elucidation of the functions of the frontal lobes have been made by S. I. Franz, L. Bianchi, Karl H. Pribram and Jerzy Konorski through studies of animals and by V. M. Bekhterev, C. Kleist and Derek E. Denny-Brown through clinical observations. We have devoted much study to the roles of the third block in our laboratory.

The frontal lobes perform no sensory or motor functions; sensation, movement, perception, speech and similar processes remain entirely unimpaired even after severe injury to these lobes. Nevertheless, the frontal lobes of the human brain are by no means silent. Our findings make it clear that they participate to a highly important degree in every complex behavioral process.

Intimately connected with the brain stem, including its reticular formation, the frontal lobes serve primarily to activate the brain. They regulate attention and concentration. W. Grey Walter showed a number of years ago that the activity of the brain could be measured by the appearance of certain slow brain waves in an electroencephalogram; these waves are evoked when a subject is stimulated to active expectancy and disappear when the subject's attention is exhausted [see "The Electrical Activity of the Brain," by W. Grey Walter; SCIENTIFIC AMERICAN Offprint 73]. At about the same time M. N. Livanov, a Russian investigator, found that mental activity is signaled by a complex of electrical excitations in the frontal cortex and that these excitations disappear when the subject subsides to a passive state or is lulled with tranquilizers.

Functional Systems

Now that we have reviewed the functions of the brain's basic blocks, let us see what we can learn about the location of specific parts of the various functional systems. It is clear that every complex form of behavior depends on the joint operation of several faculties located in different zones of the brain. A disturbance of any one faculty will affect the behavior, but each failure of a specific factor presumably will change the behavior in a different way. We have explored these effects in detail with a number of psychological experiments.

To illustrate our findings I shall discuss the results of a neuropsychological analysis of two processes. One is voluntary movement; the other is speech and in particular one of its forms, namely writing.

It was long supposed that voluntary movements are a function of the motor cortex, that is, the large pyramidal cells of the cortex of the anterior convolution of the brain. These cells, discovered by the Russian anatomist V. A. Betz more than 100 years ago, have exceptionally long axons that conduct the excitation toward the roots of the spinal cord. Impulses from these cells result in the constriction of muscles and are supposed to be the neurophysiological basis of voluntary movement.

Up to a certain point this is true, but the mechanism of the formation of a voluntary movement is much more complicated. To think that a voluntary action is formed in the narrow field of the motor cortex would be a mistake similar to an assumption that all the goods exported through a terminal are produced in the terminal. The system of cortical zones participating in the creation of a voluntary movement includes a complex of subcortical and cortical zones, each playing a highly specific role in the whole functional system. That is why lesions of different parts of the brain can result in the disturbance of different voluntary movements.

Let us examine the components of voluntary movement and see how it is affected differently by lesions in different parts of the brain. The first component is a precisely organized system of afferent (sensory) signals. The Russian physiologist N. A. Bernstein has shown in a series of studies that it is impossible to regulate a voluntary movement only by way of efferent impulses from the brain to the muscles. At every moment of the movement the position of the limb is different, and so is the density of the muscles. The brain has to receive feedback from the muscles and joints to correct the program of impulses directed to the motor apparatus. One can recognize the nature of the problem by recalling how difficult it is to start a leg movement if

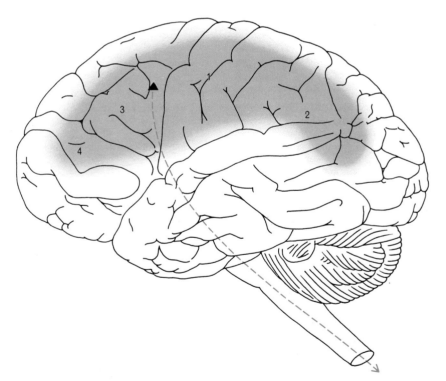

VOLUNTARY MOVEMENT is controlled by a complex of cortical and subcortical zones. The classical theory was that voluntary movement originated with the large pyramidal cells (*arrowhead*) of the cortex; they have long axons that conduct impulses to the spinal cord. It is now known that other zones participating in voluntary movement are the postcentral zone (*1*), which deals with sensory feedback from the muscles; the parieto-occipital zone (*2*), which is involved in the spatial orientation of movement; the premotor zone (*3*), which deals with the separate links of motor behavior, and the frontal zone (*4*), which programs movements. Lesions in different zones give rise to different behavioral aberrations.

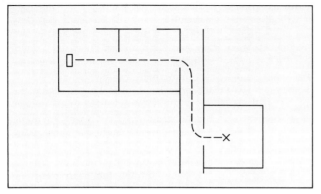

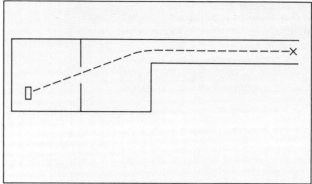

SPATIAL DISORGANIZATION is evident in a patient who had a gunshot wound of the right parieto-occipital part of the brain. The patient was asked to depict the layout of his hospital ward. His visualization is at right and the actual layout of the ward is at left.

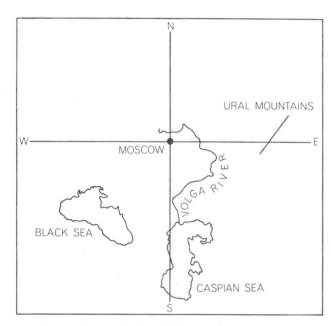

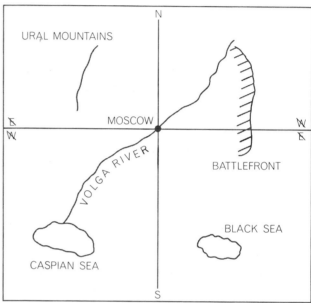

CONFUSION OVER DIRECTIONS was manifested by another patient with a gunshot wound of the right parieto-occipital zone. He was asked to draw a map of the region of the U.S.S.R. where he had been involved in fighting during World War II. The actual geographical relations are shown at left; the patient's view is at right. The line of battle represented on his map was in fact west of Moscow. In addition to reversing most of the locations, the patient could not make up his mind on the labeling of east and west.

the leg has become numb. This sensory or proprioceptive base is provided by a special part of the brain: the postcentral sensory cortex. If this part of the cortex is destroyed by a wound or other injury, the patient not only loses sensation in the limb but also is unable to fulfill a well-organized voluntary movement.

One of our co-workers has studied the physiological mechanism of such a disturbance and has shown that in lesions of the sensory part of the cortex every voluntary impulse loses its specific "address" and arrives equally at all muscles, both flexors and extensors. No organized movement can be elicited in such conditions. That is why neurologists have called this kind of motor disturbance afferent paresis.

A second component of voluntary movement is the spatial field. The movement has to be precisely oriented toward a certain point in space. Spatial analysis is done in another zone of the cortex: the tertiary parts of the parieto-occipital areas. Lesions of these highly complicated parts of the cortex result in a different kind of disturbance of voluntary movement. The sensory base of the movement remains intact, but the patient fails in a precise spatial organization of the movement. He loses the ability to evaluate spatial relations and confuses left and right. Such a patient may be unable to find his way in a familiar place or may be confused in such matters as evaluating the position of the hands of a watch or in distinguishing east and west on a map.

The sensory and spatial factors in the organization of a movement are basic but still insufficient to allow the completion of the movement. A voluntary movement is the result of a sequence of events. A skilled movement is really a kinetic melody of such interchangeable links. Only if one already fulfilled part of the movement is blocked and the impulse is shifted to another link can an organized skilled movement be made.

An important finding, first described by Karl S. Lashley and John F. Fulton and carefully studied in our laboratory for many years, is that a totally different part of the brain—the premotor cortex—is responsible for sequential interchanges of separate links of motor behavior. A skilled movement disintegrates when this part of the brain is injured. Such a patient still has sensory feedback and spatial orientation, but he loses the ability to arrest one of the steps of the movement and to make a transition from one step to the next.

Even now I have not fully described the brain's organization of a voluntary movement. Every movement has to be subordinated to a stable program or a stable intention. They are provided in the prefrontal lobes of the brain (included in the third block). If the frontal lobes are injured, the sensory base, spatial organization and plasticity of the movement remain but goal-linked actions are replaced by meaningless repetitions of already fulfilled movements or impulsive answers to outside stimuli. The whole purposive conduct of the patient is disturbed.

Speech and Writing

Let us now analyze a more complex psychological process: the ability to speak, and particularly the ability to write. It used to be thought that the operation of writing is controlled by a certain area (called Exher's center) in the middle of the premotor zone of the brain's left hemisphere (for a right-handed writer). It has since been learned, however, that this is not the case, and that a broad area of the left hemisphere is involved. We must therefore consider the effects of lesions in all parts of this region on writing.

Let us start by a psychological analysis of the processes involved in writing something in response to an instruction. Suppose one is asked to write a given word. The interpretation of the oral request turns out to be in itself a complex process. A word is composed of individual sounds, or phonemes, each coded by a letter or combination of letters. The recognition of a word may depend on the perception of very slight differences between phonemes, or acoustic cues. Consider, for example, "vine" and "wine," "special" and "spatial," "bull" and "pull," "bark" and "park." The practiced brain readily distinguishes between similar sounds, and to a person brought up in the English language the two words in these pairs sound quite different from each other. Obviously the brain must perform a sharp analysis of phonemes on the basis of learning. We become impressed with this fact when we see how difficult it is to sense distinctions in listening to a foreign language. To an English-speaking or French-speaking person, for example, three words in the Russian language—*pyl*, meaning "ardor," *pyl'* (with the *l* palatalized), meaning "dust," and *pil* (with a hard *l*), meaning "he drank"—sound almost exactly the same, yet a Russian has no difficulty distinguishing these words. Much more remarkable instances of subtle distinctions the mind is called on to make can be

cited in other languages. In Chinese *ma* and *ma* have the opposite meaning ("to buy" and "to sell"), although the only difference is in the tone of the vowel. In the Vietnamese language the phoneme *tü* has at least six different meanings, depending on the pitch of the voice!

What part of the brain is responsible for recognizing phonemes? Our observations on many hundreds of patients with local brain wounds or tumors who underwent word-writing tests established clearly that the critical region lies in the secondary zones of the left temporal lobe, which are intimately connected with other parts of the brain's speech area. People with lesions in this region cannot distinguish *b* from *p* or *t* from *d*, and they may write "pull" instead of "bull" or "tome" instead of "dome." Moreover, they may make unsuccessful attempts to find the contents of the sounds of words they try to write. Interestingly enough, Chinese patients with severe injury of the acoustic region have no such difficulty, because their writing is based on ideographs instead of on words that call for the coding of phonemes.

Continuing our dissection of the process of word recognition, we must note that people commonly pronounce an unfamiliar word before writing it, and in the case of an unfamiliar name they are likely to ask the person to spell it. Articulation of the sounds helps to clarify the word's acoustic structure. A class of Russian elementary schoolchildren during a lesson in the early stages of learning to write is generally abuzz with their mouthing of the words. To find out if this activity was really helpful, I asked one of my co-workers to conduct an ex-

periment. The children were instructed to hold their mouths open or to immobilize their tongues with their teeth while they wrote. In these circumstances, unable to articulate the words, the children made six times as many spelling mistakes!

It turns out that a separate area of the brain cortex, in the central (kinesthetic) region of the left hemisphere, controls the articulation of speech sounds. People with lesions in this area confuse the sound of *b* with that of *m* (both made with similar tongue and lip movements) and often cannot distinguish between *d, e, n* and *l*. A Russian with such a lesion may write *ston* ("groan") instead of *stol* ("table") and *khadat* (meaningless) instead of *khalat* ("dressing gown").

After evaluation of the speech sounds and recognition of the word, the next step toward writing the word is the coding of the sound units (phonemes) into the units of writing (letters). We find that this step calls into play still other parts of the brain cortex, in the visual and spatial zones. Patients with lesions in these zones (in the occipital and parietal lobes) have a perfectly normal ability to analyze speech sounds, but they show marked difficulty in recognizing and forming written letters. They find it difficult to visualize the required structure of a letter, to grasp the spatial relations among the parts of the letter and to put the parts together to form the whole.

The mental process for writing a word entails still another specialization: putting the letters in the proper sequence to form the word. Lashley discovered many years ago that sequential analysis

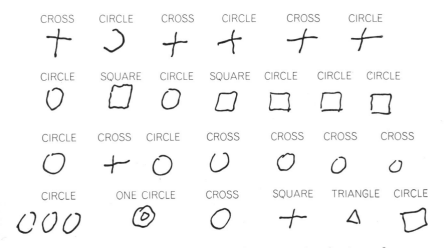

LESIONS OF FRONTAL LOBES interfere with the programming of actions and cause errors such as repetition. On each line of the illustration are drawings made by patients; printed words show what they were asked to draw. The first, second and fourth patient had tumors of the left frontal lobe; the third patient had an abscess of the right frontal lobe.

involved a zone of the brain different from that employed for spatial analysis. In the course of our extensive studies we have located the region responsible for sequential analysis in the anterior region of the left hemisphere. Lesions in the prefrontal region disturb the ability to carry out rhythmic movements of the body, and they also give patients difficulty in writing letters in the correct order. Such patients transpose letters, are unable to proceed serially from one let-

ter to another and often replace the required letter with a meaningless stereotype. If the lesion is located deep in the brain where it interrupts connections between the basal ganglia and the cortex, the patient becomes incapable of writing words at all; he may merely repeat fragments of letters. Yet such a patient, with the higher parts of the cortex undamaged, can recognize phonemes and letters perfectly well.

Finally, there is an overall require-

ment for writing that involves the apparatuses of the third block of the brain as a whole. This is the matter of writing not merely letters or words but expressing thoughts and ideas. When the third block is damaged by severe lesions of the frontal lobes, the patient becomes unable to express his thoughts either orally or in writing. I shall never forget a letter written to the noted Russian neurosurgeon N. N. Burdenko by a woman with a severe lesion of the left frontal lobe. "Dear Professor," she wrote, "I want to tell you that I want to tell you that I want to tell you..." and so on for page after page!

The analysis of the writing process is just one of the tracers we have used in our psychological exploration of the functional organization of the brain. Over the past three decades investigators in our laboratory and our clinical associates have carried out similar analyses of the brain systems involved in perception, bodily movements, performance of planned actions, memorization and problem-solving. All these studies have demonstrated that detailed investigation of the nature of a behavioral disturbance can indeed guide one to the location of the causative lesion in the brain.

Factor Analyses

Obviously the neuropsychological approach provides a valuable means of dissecting mental processes as well as diagnosing illness. It is enabling us to search out the details of the brain's normal operations and capacities. A generation ago L. L. Thurstone of the University of Chicago and C. E. Spearman of the University of London learned some of the details by the statistical technique of factor analysis based on batteries of tests administered to great numbers of subjects. With the neuropsychological technique we can now make factor analyses in individual subjects. When a particular factor is incapacitated by a brain lesion, all the complex behavior processes that involve the factor are disturbed and all others remain normal. We find, for example, that an injury in the left temporal lobe causes the patient to have serious difficulty in analyzing speech sounds, in repeating verbal sounds, in naming objects and in writing, but the person retains normal capacities in spatial orientation and in handling simple computations. On the other hand, a lesion in the left parietooccipital region that destroys spatial organization does not affect the patient's fluency of speech or sense of rhythm.

Sorting out the various factors and

DISRUPTION OF HEARING in patients with bullet wounds in the left hemisphere of the cerebral cortex is charted. Affected areas of the brain are numbered, and the correspondingly numbered bars show the percent of patients who had difficulty recognizing sounds.

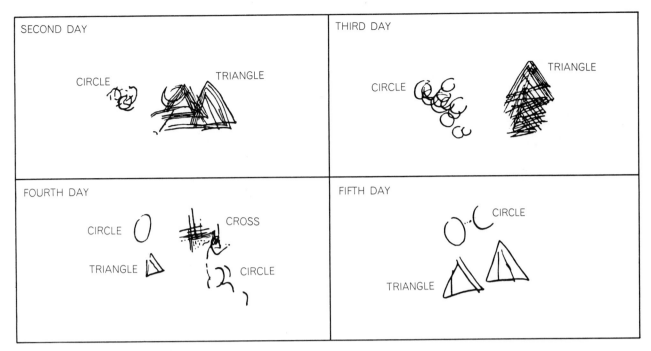

INFLUENCE OF PREMOTOR REGION on the organization of movement appears in drawings made by a patient after surgery for removal of a meningioma, which is a tumor arising from the meninges, from the left premotor region. On each of the days represented in the illustration the patient was asked to draw simple figures such as those shown here. Performance improved steadily.

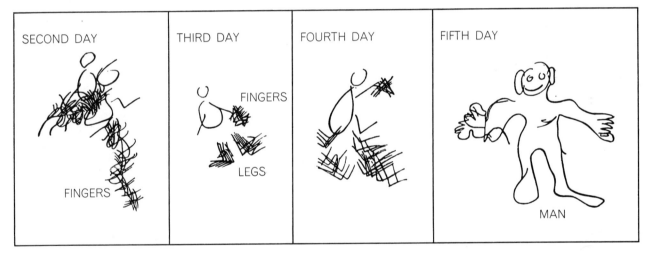

DRAWINGS OF A MAN were attempted by the same patient during the postoperative period. At first he drew a head and body, represented by the circles at top center in the drawing at left. Then he drew a second man, whose head is to the right of the first man's body. Then he made a series of stereotyped pen strokes. The ones that trail off at lower right in the first drawing were made on moving paper. On successive days the patient's work improved. Difficulty in stopping a movement often appears in premotor lesions.

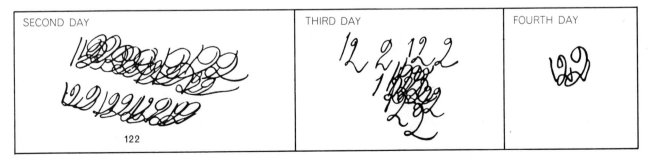

WRITING OF NUMBERS was attempted by the same patient on the second, third and fourth day after the operation. As in the other cases the patient at first showed a tendency to repeat part of the task, but the repetition diminished on the following days.

(OKHO = OKNO)
(WINDOW)

(ИВАН = IVAN)

WRITING ABERRATION was shown by a patient with a tumor in the deep part of the brain's left premotor zone. He was asked to write the Russian words for window and Ivan, which are printed in Russian and in English transliteration below each example. Arrows show repetition or fragments.

analyze phonemes leaves musical hearing undisturbed. I observed an outstanding Russian composer who suffered a hemorrhage in the left temporal lobe that deprived him of the ability to understand speech, yet he went on creating wonderful symphonies!

On the other hand, behavioral processes that seem to have nothing in common may actually be related through dependence on a particular brain factor. What can there be in common between the capacities for orientation in space, for doing computations and for dealing with complexities in grammar logic? Yet all three of these abilities are affected by the same lesion in the lower part of the left parietal lobe. Why so? A close analysis of the three processes suggests an explanation. Computation and the ability to handle language structure depend, like orientation, on the ability to grasp spatial relations. In order to subtract 7 from 31, for example, one first performs the operation $30 - 7 = 23$ and then adds the 1 to this preliminary result. There is a spatial factor here: one indicates unambiguously that the 1 is to be *added* by placing it to the right of the 23. A patient with a lesion disturbing his capacity for spatial organization is unable to cope with the problem because he is at a loss whether to place the 1 to the left or the right—in other words, whether to add it or subtract it.

The same principle applies to understanding complex grammatical constructions. In order to grasp the difference between "father's brother" and "brother's father" or between "summer comes after spring" and "spring comes

after summer," for example, one must make a clear analysis of the quasi-spatial relations between the elements in each expression.

Finally, the neuropsychological approach gives us a new insight into the effects of learning on the brain's processes. There is a well-known story of a patient of the 19th-century English neurologist Sir William Gowers who, after many unsuccessful attempts to repeat the word "no" in response to his instruction, at last burst out: "No, doctor, I can't say 'no.'" We have observed many cases of automatic performances of this kind in brain-injured patients who could not achieve a given task when they thought about it. One was an old lady who was unable to write a single word on instruction, but when she was asked to write a whole sentence quickly (a kinetic skill), she did so without hesitation. Patients who cannot write from dictation are often able to sign their names readily. It appears, therefore, that training or habituation changes the organization of the brain's activity, so that the brain comes to perform accustomed tasks without recourse to the processes of analysis. That is to say, the task may invoke a stereotype based on a network of cortical zones quite different from the one that was called on originally when the performance required the help of the analytical apparatus.

Neuropsychology has put us on a new path in the investigation of how the brain functions, and we can suppose that it is likely to lead the way to substantial changes in the design of psychological research in the future.

their effects, we arrive at some surprising findings. One is that behavioral processes that seem very similar or even identical may not be related to one another at all. For example, it turns out that the mechanism for perception of musical sounds is quite different from that for verbal sounds. A lesion of the left temporal lobe that destroys the ability to

KASHA
(PORRIDGE)

GORA
(MOUNTAIN)

GRIBY
(MUSHROOMS)

ZDOROVIE
(HEALTH)

GASHA
(MEANINGLESS)

KARA
(PENALTY)

KRIBI
(MEANINGLESS)

STOROVE
(MEANINGLESS)

WRITING DISTURBANCES appear in a patient with a lesion of the left temporal area. The patient was writing to dictation; the dictated Russian word, its transliteration and its English meaning are on the top line. The written response of the patient in each case appears below with its transliteration and English meaning in the single instance (*kara*) where the patient wrote a meaningful word.

т m   л l

л l   н n

халат
KHALAT
(SMOCK)

большой
BOLSHOI
(BIG)

ханат
KHANAT
(MEANINGLESS)

Бонишои
BONISHOI
(MEANINGLESS)

хадат
KHADAT
(MEANINGLESS)

Бониш
BONISH
(MEANINGLESS)

ERRORS IN WRITING also were shown by a patient with a lesion of the left parietal area. Again the dictated letter or word appears on the top line; the bottom lines show the written response by the patient. None of the words that the patient wrote were meaningful.

BIBLIOGRAPHIES

I EVOLUTION AND HUMAN BEHAVIOR

1. Tools and Human Evolution

CEREBRAL CORTEX OF MAN. Wilder Penfield and Theodore Rasmussen. Macmillan Company, 1950.

THE EVOLUTION OF MAN, edited by Sol Tax. University of Chicago Press, 1960.

THE EVOLUTION OF MAN'S CAPACITY FOR CULTURE. Arranged by J. N. Spuhler. Wayne State University Press, 1959.

HUMAN ECOLOGY DURING THE PLEISTOCENE AND LATER TIMES IN AFRICA SOUTH OF THE SAHARA. J. Desmond Clark in *Current Anthropology*, Vol. I, pages 307–324; 1960.

2. The Casts of Fossil Hominid Brains

THE EVOLUTION OF THE PRIMATE BRAIN: SOME ASPECTS OF QUANTITATIVE RELATIONSHIPS. R. L. Holloway in *Brain Research*, Vol. 7, pages 121–172; 1968.

AUSTRALOPITHECINE ENDOCASTS, BRAIN EVOLUTION IN THE HOMINOIDEA, AND A MODEL OF HOMINID EVOLUTION. R. L. Holloway in *The Functional and Evolutionary Biology of Primates*, edited by R. Tuttle. Aldine Press, 1972.

EVOLUTION OF PRIMATE BRAINS: A COMPARATIVE ANATOMICAL INVESTIGATION. H. Stephan in *The Functional and Evolutionary Biology of Primates*, edited by R. Tuttle. Aldine Press, 1972.

3. The Present Evolution of Man

EVOLUTION, GENETICS AND MAN. Theodosius Dobzhansky. John Wiley & Sons, Inc., 1955.

MIRROR FOR MAN. Clyde Kluckhohn. McGraw-Hill Book Co., Inc., 1949.

RADIATION, GENES AND MAN. Bruce Wallace and Theodosius Dobzhansky. Henry Holt & Co., Inc., 1959.

II GENETIC AND DEVELOPMENTAL ROOTS OF BEHAVIOR

4. Genetic Dissection of Behavior

BIOLOGY OF DROSOPHILA. Edited by M. Demerec. Hafner Publishing Co., Inc., 1965.

BEHAVIORAL MUTANTS OF DROSOPHILA ISOLATED BY COUNTERCURRENT DISTRIBUTION. Seymour Benzer in *Proceedings of the National Academy of Sciences of the United States of America*, Vol. 58, No. 3, pages 1112–1119; September, 1967.

CLOCK MUTANTS OF DROSOPHILA MELANOGASTER. Ronald J. Konopka and Seymour Benzer in *Proceedings of the National Academy of Sciences of the United States of America*, Vol. 68, No. 9, pages 2112–2116; September, 1971.

MAPPING OF BEHAVIOR IN DROSOPHILA MOSAICS. Yoshiki Hotta and Seymour Benzer in *Nature*, Vol. 240, pages 527–535; December 29, 1972.

5. "Imprinting" in a Natural Laboratory

"IMPRINTING" IN ANIMALS. Eckhard H. Hess in *Scientific American*, Vol. 198, No. 3, pages 81–90; March, 1958.

IMPRINTING IN BIRDS. Eckhard H. Hess in *Science*, Vol. 146, No. 3648, pages 1128–1139; November 27, 1964.

INNATE FACTORS IN IMPRINTING. Eckhard H. Hess and Dorle B. Hess in *Psychonomic Science*, Vol. 14, No. 3, pages 129–130; February 10, 1969.

DEVELOPMENT OF SPECIES IDENTIFICATION IN BIRDS: AN INQUIRY INTO THE PRENATAL DETERMINANTS OF PERCEPTION. Gilbert Gottlieb. University of Chicago Press, 1971.

NATURAL HISTORY OF IMPRINTING. Eckhard H. Hess in *Integrative Events in Life Processes: Annals of the New York Academy of Sciences*, Vol. 193, 1972.

6. The Reproductive Behavior of Ring Doves

CONTROL OF BEHAVIOR CYCLES IN REPRODUCTION. Daniel S. Lehrman in *Social Behavior and Organization among Vertebrates*, edited by William Etkin. The University of Chicago Press, 1964.

HORMONAL REGULATION OF PARENTAL BEHAVIOR IN BIRDS AND INFRAHUMAN MAMMALS. Daniel S. Lehrman in *Sex and Internal Secretions*. Edited by William C. Young. Williams & Wilkins Company, 1961.

INTERACTION OF HORMONAL AND EXPERIENTIAL INFLUENCES ON DEVELOPMENT OF BEHAVIOR. Daniel S. Lehrman in *Roots of Behavior*, edited by E. L. Bliss. Harper & Row, Publishers, 1962.

7. Learning in Newborn Kittens

DEVELOPMENT OF SUCKLING AND RELATED BEHAVIOR IN NEONATE KITTENS. Jay S. Rosenblatt, T. C. Schneirla and Gerald Turkewitz in *Roots of Behavior: Genetics, Instinct, and Socialization in Animal Behavior*, edited by Eugene L. Bliss. Harper & Brothers, 1962.

MATERNAL BEHAVIOR IN THE CAT. T. C. Schneirla, Jay S. Rosenblatt and Ethel Tobach in *Maternal Behavior in Mammals*, edited by Harriet L. Rheingold. John Wiley & Sons, Inc., 1963.

DEVELOPMENT OF HOME ORIENTATION IN NEWLY BORN KITTENS. Jay S. Rosenblatt, Gerald Turkewitz and T. C. Schneirla in *Transactions of the New York Academy of Sciences*, Vol. 31, Series II, No. 3, pages 231–250; March, 1969.

SUCKLING AND HOME ORIENTATION IN THE KITTEN: A COMPARATIVE DEVELOPMENTAL STUDY. Jay S. Rosenblatt in *The Biopsychology of Development*, edited by E. Tobach, L. R. Aronson and E. Shaw. Academic Press, 1971.

III NEURON, SYNAPSE, AND BRAIN ACTIVITY

8. The Nerve Axon

THE CONDUCTION OF THE NERVOUS IMPULSE. A. L. Hodgkin. Liverpool University Press, 1964.

9. The Synapse

EXCITATION AND INHIBITION IN SINGLE NERVE CELLS. Stephen W. Kuffler in *The Harvey Lectures, Series 54*. Academic Press, 1960.

PHYSIOLOGY OF NERVE CELLS. John C. Eccles. Johns Hopkins Press, 1957.

THE PHYSIOLOGY OF SYNAPSES. John Carew Eccles. Academic Press, 1964.

THE TRANSMISSION OF IMPULSES FROM NERVE TO MUSCLE, AND THE SUBCELLULAR UNIT OF SYNAPTIC ACTION. B. Katz in *Proceedings of the Royal Society*, Vol. 155, No. 961, Series B, pages 455–477; April, 1962.

10. The Analysis of Brain Waves

COMPUTER TECHNIQUES IN EEG ANALYSIS. Edited by Mary A. B. Brazier. *Electroencephalography and Clinical Neurophysiology*, Suppl. 20; 1961.

THE ELECTRICAL ACTIVITY OF THE NERVOUS SYSTEM. Mary A. B. Brazier. The Macmillan Co., 1960.

PROCESSING NEUROELECTRIC DATA. Communications Biophysics Group of Research Laboratory of Electronics and William M. Siebert. The Technology Press of the Massachusetts Institute of Technology, 1959.

SOME USES OF COMPUTERS IN EXPERIMENTAL NEUROLOGY. Mary A. B. Brazier in *Experimental Neurology*, Vol. 2, No. 2, pages 123–143; April, 1960.

THE WAKING BRAIN. H. W. Magoun. Charles C. Thomas, Publisher, 1958.

11. The States of Sleep

ASPECTS ANATOMO-FONCTIONNELS DE LA PHYSIOLOGIE DU SOMMEIL. Edited by M. Jouvet. Centre National de la Recherche Scientifique, 1965.

AN ESSAY ON DREAMS: THE ROLE OF PHYSIOLOGY IN UNDERSTANDING THEIR NATURE. W. C. Dement in *New Directions in Psychology: Vol. II*. Holt, Rinehart & Winston, Inc., 1965.

SLEEP AND WAKEFULNESS. Nathaniel Kleitman. The University of Chicago Press, 1963.

SLEEPING AND WAKING. Ian Oswald. American Elsevier Publishing Company, Inc., 1962.

SLEEP MECHANISMS. Edited by K. Akert, C. Bally and J. P. Schadé. American Elsevier Publishing Company, Inc., 1965.

IV CHEMISTRY OF BEHAVIOR AND AWARENESS: TRANSMITTERS, HORMONES, AND DRUGS

12. Neurotransmitters

THE UPTAKE AND STORAGE OF NORADRENALINE IN SYMPATHETIC NERVES. L. L. Iversen. Cambridge University Press, 1967.

BIOGENIC AMINES AND EMOTION. Joseph J. Schildkraut and Seymour S. Kety in Science, Vol. 156, No. 3771, pages 21–30; April 7, 1967.

BIOCHEMISTRY OF CATECHOLAMINES. Perry B. Molinoff and Julius Axelrod in Annual Review of Biochemistry, Vol. 40, pages 465–500; 1971.

NORADRENALINE: FATE AND CONTROL OF ITS BIOSYNTHESIS. Julius Axelrod in Science, Vol. 173, No. 3997, pages 598–606; August 13, 1971.

THE PINEAL GLAND: A NEUROCHEMICAL TRANSDUCER. Julius Axelrod in Science, Vol. 184, No. 4144, pages 1341–1348; 1974.

13. The Hormones of the Hypothalamus

NEURAL CONTROL OF THE PITUITARY GLAND. G. W. Harris. The Williams & Wilkins Company, 1955.

THE HYPOTHALAMUS: PROCEEDINGS OF THE WORKSHOP CONFERENCE ON INTEGRATION OF ENDOCRINE AND NON-ENDOCRINE MECHANISMS IN THE HYPOTHALAMUS. Edited by L. Martini, M. Motta and F. Fraschini. Academic Press, 1970.

CHARACTERIZATION OF OVINE HYPOTHALAMIC HYPOPHYSIOTROPIC TSH-RELEASING FACTOR. Roger Burgus, Thomas F. Dunn, Dominic Desiderio, Darrell N. Ward, Wylie Vale and Roger Guillemin in Nature, Vol. 226, No. 5243, pages 321–325; April 25, 1970.

STRUCTURE OF THE PORCINE LH- AND FSH-RELEASING HORMONE, I: THE PROPOSED AMINO ACID SEQUENCE. H. Matsuo, Y. Baba, R. M. G. Nair, A. Arimura and A. V. Schally in Biochemical and Biophysical Research Communications, Vol. 43, No. 6, pages 1334–1339; June 18, 1971.

SYNTHETIC POLYPEPTIDE ANTAGONISTS OF THE HYPOTHALAMIC LUTEINIZING HORMONE RELEASING FACTOR. Wylie Vale, Geoffrey Grant, Jean Rivier, Michael Monahan, Max Amoss, Richard Blackwell, Roger Burgus and Roger Guillemin in Science, Vol. 176, No. 4037, pages 933–934; May 26, 1972.

SYPTHETIC LUTEINIZING HORMONE-RELEASING FACTOR: A POTENT STIMULATOR OF GONADOTROPIN RELEASE IN MAN. S. S. C. Yen, R. Rebar, G. VandenBerg, F. Naftolin, Y. Ehara, S. Engblom, K. J. Ryan, K. Benirschke, J. Rivier, M. Amoss and R. Guillemin in The Journal of Clinical Endocrinology and Metabolism, Vol. 34, No. 6, pages 1108–1111; June, 1972.

14. Stress and Behavior

ADRENOCORTICAL ACTIVITY AND AVOIDANCE LEARNING AS A FUNCTION OF TIME AFTER AVOIDANCE TRAINING. Seymour Levine and F. Robert Brush in Physiology & Behavior, Vol. 2, No. 4, pages 385–388; October, 1967.

HORMONES AND CONDITIONING. Seymour Levine in Nebraska Symposium on Motivation: 1968, edited by William J. Arnold. University of Nebraska Press, 1968.

EFFECTS OF PEPTIDE HORMONES ON BEHAVIOR. David de Wied in Frontiers in Neuroendocrinology, edited by William F. Ganong and Luciano Martini. Oxford University Press, 1969.

THE NEUROENDOCRINE CONTROL OF PERCEPTION. R. I. Henkin in Perception and Its Disorders: Proceedings of the Association for Research in Nervous Mental Disease, 32, edited by D. Hamburg. The Williams & Wilkins Co., 1970.

15. The Hallucinogenic Drugs

THE CLINICAL PHARMACOLOGY OF THE HALLUCINOGENS. Erik Jacobsen in Clinical Pharmacology and Therapeutics, Vol. 4, No. 4, pages 480–504; July–August, 1963.

LYSERGIC ACID DIETHYLAMIDE (LSD-25) AND EGO FUNCTIONS. G. D. Klee in Archives of General Psychiatry, Vol. 8, No. 5, pages 461–474; May, 1963.

PROLONGED ADVERSE REACTIONS TO LYSERGIC ACID DIETHYLAMIDE. S. Cohen and K. S. Ditman in Archives of General Psychiatry, Vol. 8, No. 5, pages 475–480; May, 1963.

THE PSYCHOTOMIMETIC DRUGS: AN OVERVIEW. Jonathan O. Cole and Martin M. Katz in The Journal of the American Medical Association, Vol. 187, No. 10, pages 758–761; March, 1964.

V SENSORY PROCESSES

16. Three-Pigment Color Vision

THE EYE. Edited by Hugh Davson. Academic Press, 1962.

IN SITU MICROSPECTROPHOTOMETRIC STUDIES ON THE PIGMENTS OF SINGLE RETINAL RODS. Paul A. Liebman in *Biophysical Journal*, Vol. 2, No. 2, Part 1, pages 161–178; March, 1962.

JOURNAL OF THE OPTICAL SOCIETY OF AMERICA, Vol. 53, No. 1; January, 1963.

RETINAL MECHANISMS OF COLOR VISION. E. F. Mac-Nichol, Jr., in *Vision Research*, Vol. 4, No. 1/2, pages 119–133; June, 1964.

17. Contour and Contrast

MACH BANDS: QUANTITATIVE STUDIES ON NEURAL NETWORKS IN THE RETINA. Floyd Ratliff. Holden-Day, Inc., 1965.

LINEAR SYSTEMS ANALYSIS OF THE *LIMULUS* RETINA. Frederick A. Dodge, Robert M. Shapley and Bruce W. Knight in *Behavioral Science*, Vol. 15, No. 1, pages 24–36; January, 1970.

CONTOUR AND CONTRAST. Floyd Ratliff in *Proceedings of the American Philosophical Society*, Vol. 115, No. 2, pages 150–163; April, 1971.

INHIBITORY INTERACTION IN THE RETINA OF *LIMULUS*. H. K. Hartline and F. Ratliff in *Handbook of Sensory Physiology: Vol. VII/Part IB*. Springer-Verlag, in print.

18. The Visual Cortex of the Brain

DISCHARGE PATTERNS AND FUNCTIONAL ORGANIZATION OF MAMMALIAN RETINA. Stephen W. Kuffler in *Journal of Neurophysiology*, Vol. 16, No. 1, pages 37–68; January, 1953.

INTEGRATIVE PROCESSES IN CENTRAL VISUAL PATHWAYS OF THE CAT. David M. Hubel in *Journal of the Optical Society of America*, Vol. 53, No. 1, pages 58–66; January, 1963.

RECEPTIVE FIELDS, BINOCULAR INTERACTION AND FUNCTIONAL ARCHITECTURE IN THE CAT'S VISUAL CORTEX. D. H. Hubel and T. N. Wiesel in *Journal of Physiology*, Vol. 160, No. 1, pages 106–154; January, 1962.

THE VISUAL PATHWAY. Ragnar Granit in *The Eye, Volume II: The Visual Process*, edited by Hugh Davson. Academic Press, 1962.

19. The Neurophysiology of Binocular Vision

THE NEURAL MECHANISM OF BINOCULAR DEPTH DISCRIMINATION. H. B. Barlow, C. Blakemore and J. D. Pettigrew in *Journal of Physiology*, Vol. 193, pages 327–342; 1967.

BINOCULAR INTERACTION ON SINGLE UNITS IN CAT STRIATE CORTEX: SIMULTANEOUS STIMULATION BY SINGLE MOVING SLIT WITH RECEPTIVE FIELDS IN CORRESPONDENCE. J. D. Pettigrew, T. Nikara and P. O. Bishop in *Experimental Brain Research*, Vol. 6, pages 391–410; 1968.

EYE DOMINANCE IN THE VISUAL CORTEX. Colin Blakemore and John D. Pettigrew in *Nature*, Vol. 225, No. 5231, pages 426–429; January 31, 1970.

FOUNDATIONS OF CYCLOPEAN PERCEPTION. Bela Julesz. University of Chicago Press, 1971.

VI MOTOR CONTROL SYSTEMS

20. How We Control the Contraction of Our Muscles

TREATISE ON PHYSIOLOGICAL OPTICS: VOL. III. Herman L. F. Helmholtz. English translation by James P. C. Southall. Dover Publications, Inc., 1962.

POSITION SENSE AND SENSE OF EFFORT. P. A. Merton in *Homeostasis and Feedback Mechanisms*. Symposia of the Society for Experimental Biology, Vol. 18, pages 387–400; 1964.

THE INNERVATION OF MAMMALIAN SKELETAL MUSCLE. D. Barker in *Ciba Foundation Symposium: Myotatic, Kinesthetic and Vestibular Mechanisms*, edited by A. V. S. de Reuck and Julie Knight. Little, Brown and Company, 1967.

SERVO ACTION AND STRETCH REFLEX in HUMAN MUSCLE AND ITS APPARENT DEPENDENCE ON PERIPHERAL SENSATION. C. D. Marsden, P. A. Merton and H. B. Merton in *The Journal of Physiology*, Vol. 216, pages 21–22P; July, 1971.

PROJECTION FROM LOW THRESHOLD MUSCLE AFFERENTS OF HAND AND FOREARM TO AREA 3a OF BABOON'S CORTEX. C. G. Phillips, T. P. S. Powell and M. Wiesendanger in *The Journal of Physiology*, Vol. 217, pages 419–446; September, 1971.

21. Brain Mechanisms in Movement

MOTOR APPARATUS OF THE BABOON'S HAND. C. G. Phillips in *Proceedings of the Royal Society of*

London: B; Vol. 173, No. 1031, pages 141–174; May 20, 1969.

THE BASIS OF MOTOR CONTROL. Ragnar Granit. Academic Press, 1970.

CENTRAL CONTROL OF MOVEMENT. Edited by Edward V. Evarts, Emilio Bizzi, Robert E. Burke, Mahlon DeLong and W. Thomas Thach, Jr., in *Neurosciences Research Program Bulletin,* Vol. 9, No. 1; January, 1971.

22. The Cortex of the Cerebellum

HISTOLOGIE DU SYSTEME NERVEUX DE L'HOMME & DES VERTEBRES: VOL. II. Santiago Ramón y Cajal. A. Maloine, 1911.

THE CEREBELLUM AS A NEURONAL MACHINE. John C. Eccles, Masao Ito and János Szentágothai. Springer-Verlag, 1967.

NEUROBIOLOGY OF CEREBELLAR EVOLUTION AND DEVELOPMENT: PROCEEDINGS OF THE FIRST INTERNATIONAL SYMPOSIUM OF THE INSTITUTE FOR BIOCHEMICAL RESEARCH. Edited by R. Llinás. The American Medical Association, 1969.

CEREBELLAR CORTEX: CYTOLOGY AND ORGANIZATION. Sanford L. Palay and Victoria Chan-Palay. Springer-Verlag, 1974.

EIGHTEENTH BOWDITCH LECTURE: MOTOR ASPECTS OF CEREBELLAR CONTROL. Rodolfo Llinás in *The Physiologist,* Vol. 17, No. 1, pages 19–46; February, 1974.

VII PERCEPTION: SENSORY-MOTOR INTEGRATION

23. The Neural Basis of Visually Guided Behavior

WHAT THE FROG'S EYE TELLS THE FROG'S BRAIN. J. Y. Lettvin, H. R. Maturana, W. S. McCulloch and W. H. Pitts in *Proceedings of the Institute of Radio Engineers,* Vol. 47, No. 11, pages 1940–1951; November, 1959.

A QUANTITATIVE ANALYSIS OF MOVEMENT DETECTING NEURONS IN THE FROG'S RETINA. O.-J. Grüsser, U. Grüsser-Cornehls, D. Finkelstein, V. Henn, M. Patutschnik and E. Butenandt in *Pflüger's Archiv für die gesamte Psysiologie des Menschen und der Tiere,* Vol. 293, pages 100–106; 1967.

NEUROPHYSIOLOGIE DES BEWEGUNGSSEHENS. O.-J. Grüsser and U. Grüsser-Cornehls in *Ergebnisse der Physiologie,* Vol. 61, pages 178–265; 1969.

NEURAL MECHANISMS OF PREY-CATCHING AND AVOIDANCE BEHAVIOR IN THE TOAD (BUFO BUFO L.). J.-P. Ewert in *Subcortical Visual Systems,* edited by D. Ingle. S. Karger, 1970.

LOKALISATION UND IDENTIFIKATION IM VISUELLEN SYSTEM DER WIRBELTIERE. J.-P. Ewert in *Fortschritte der Zoologie,* Vol. 21, pages 307–333; 1973.

24. Eye Movements and Visual Perception

PATTERN RECOGNITION. Edited by Leonard M. Uhr. John Wiley & Sons, Inc., 1966.

CONTEMPORARY THEORY AND RESEARCH IN VISUAL PERCEPTION. Edited by Ralph Norman Haber. Holt, Rinehart & Winston, Inc., 1968.

A THEORY OF VISUAL PATTERN PERCEPTION. David Noton in *IEEE Transactions on Systems Science and Cybernetics,* Vol. SSC-6, No. 4, pages 349–357; October, 1970.

SCANPATHS IN EYE MOVEMENTS DURING PATTERN PERCEPTION. David Noton and Lawrence Stark in *Science,* Vol. 171, No. 3968, pages 308–311; January 22, 1971.

25. Plasticity in Sensory-Motor Systems

MOVEMENT-PRODUCED STIMULATION IN THE DEVELOPMENT OF VISUALLY GUIDED BEHAVIOR. Richard Held and Alan Hein in *Journal of Comparative & Physiological Psychology,* Vol. 56, No. 5, pages 872–876; October, 1963.

NEONATAL DEPRIVATION AND ADULT REARRANGEMENT: COMPLEMENTARY TECHNIQUES FOR ANALYZING PLASTIC SENSORY-MOTOR COORDINATIONS. Richard Held and Joseph Bossom in *The Journal of Comparative and Physiological Psychology,* Vol. 54, No. 1, pages 33–37; February, 1961.

PLASTICITY IN HUMAN SENSORIMOTOR CONTROL. Richard Held and Sanford J. Freedman in *Science,* Vol. 142, No. 3591, pages 455–462; October 25, 1963.

26. Multistability in Perception

THE ANALYSIS OF SENSATIONS AND THE RELATION OF THE PHYSICAL TO THE PSYCHICAL. Ernst Mach. Dover Publications, Inc., 1959.

AMBIGUITY OF FORM: OLD AND NEW. Gerald H. Fisher in *Perception and Psychophysics,* Vol. 4, No. 3, pages 189–192; September, 1968.

TRIANGLES AS AMBIGUOUS FIGURES. Fred Attneave in *The American Journal of Psychology,* Vol. 81, No. 3, pages 447–453; September, 1968.

VIII   LEARNING AND MEMORY

27. Nerve Cells and Behavior

NERVE, MUSCLE, AND SYNAPSE. Bernhard Katz. McGraw-Hill Book Company, 1966.

RESPONSE DECREMENT OF THE FLEXION REFLEX IN THE ACUTE CAT AND TRANSIENT RESTORATION BY STRONG STIMULI. W. A. Spencer, R. F. Thompson and D. R. Neilson, Jr., in *Journal of Neurophysiology*, Vol. 29, No. 2, pages 221–239; March, 1966.

CELLULAR NEUROPHYSIOLOGICAL APPROACHES IN THE STUDY OF LEARNING. Eric R. Kandel and W. Alden Spencer in *Physiological Reviews*, Vol. 48, No. 1, pages 65–134; January, 1968.

ANALYSIS OF RESTRICTED NEURAL NETWORKS. Donald Kennedy, Allen I. Selverston and Michael P. Remler in *Science*, Vol. 164, No. 3887, pages 1488–1496; June 27, 1969.

THE ROLE OF SYNAPTIC PLASTICITY IN THE SHORT-TERM MODIFICATION OF BEHAVIOR. E. R. Kandel, V. Castellucci, H. Pinsker and I. Kupfermann in *Short-Term Processes in Neural Activity and Behavior*, edited by R. A. Hinde and G. Horn. Cambridge University Press, 1970.

28. Brain Changes in Response to Experience

CHEMICAL AND ANATOMICAL PLASTICITY OF BRAIN. Edward L. Bennett, Marian C. Diamond, David Krech and Mark R. Rosenzweig in *Science*, Vol. 146, No. 3644, pages 610–619; October 30, 1964.

EFFECTS OF ENVIRONMENT ON DEVELOPMENT OF BRAIN AND BEHAVIOR. Mark R. Rosenzweig in *Biopsychology of Development*, edited by Ethel Tobach. Academic Press, 1971.

ENVIRONMENTAL INFLUENCES ON BRAIN AND BEHAVIOR OF YEAR-OLD RATS. Walter H. Riege in *Developmental Psychobiology*, Vol. 4, No. 2, pages 157–167; 1971.

QUANTITATIVE SYNAPTIC CHANGES WITH DIFFERENTIAL EXPERIENCE IN RAT BRAIN. Kjeld Møllgaard, Marian C. Diamond, Edward L. Bennett, Mark R. Rosenzweig and Bernice Lindner in *International Journal of Neuroscience*, Vol. 2, No. 2, pages 113–128; August, 1971.

29. Memory and Protein Synthesis

ANTIMETABOLITES AFFECTING PROTEINS OR NUCLEIC ACID SYNTHESIS: PHLEOMYCIN, AN INHIBITOR OF DNA POLYMERASE. Arturo Falaschi and Arthur Kornberg in *Federation Proceedings*, Vol. 23, No. 5, Part I, pages 940–989; September–October, 1964.

CHEMICAL STUDIES ON MEMORY FIXATION IN GOLDFISH. Bernard W. Agranoff, Roger E. Davis and John J. Brink in *Brain Research*, Vol. 1, No. 3, pages 303–309; March–April, 1966.

MEMORY IN MICE AS AFFECTED BY INTRACEREBRAL PUROMYCIN. Josefa B. Flexner, Louis B. Flexner and Eliot Stellar in *Science*, Vol. 141, No. 3575, pages 57–59; July 5, 1963.

30. The Neurophysiology of Remembering

THE PROBLEM OF CEREBRAL ORGANIZATION IN VISION. K. S. Lashley in *Biological Symposia, a Series of Volumes Devoted to Current Symposia in the Field of Biology: Vol. VII, Visual Mechanisms*, edited by Jaques Catell. The Jaques Catell Press, 1942.

IN SEARCH OF THE ENGRAM. K. S. Lashley in *Physiological Mechanisms in Animal Behavior: Symposia of the Society for Experimental Biology, No. 4*. Academic Press, 1950.

TOWARD A SCIENCE OF NEUROPSYCHOLOGY (METHOD AND DATA). Karl H. Pribram in *Current Trends in Psychology and the Behavioral Sciences*. University of Pittsburgh Press, 1954.

THE PHYSIOLOGY OF IMAGINATION. John C. Eccles in *Scientific American*, Vol. 199, No. 3, pages 135–146; September, 1958.

SOME DIMENSIONS OF REMEMBERING: STEPS TOWARD A NEUROPSYCHOLOGICAL MODEL OF MEMORY. Karl H. Pribram in *Macromolecules and Behavior*, edited by John Gaito. Appleton-Century-Crofts, 1966.

IX   COMMUNICATION AND LANGUAGE

31. Animal Communication

MECHANISMS OF ANIMAL BEHAVIOR. P. R. Marler and W. J. Hamilton III. John Wiley & Sons, Inc., 1966.

ANIMAL COMMUNICATION: TECHNIQUES OF STUDY AND RESULTS OF RESEARCH. Edited by T. A. Sebeok. Indiana University Press, 1968.

SEX PHEROMONE SPECIFICITY: TAXONOMIC AND EVOLUTIONARY ASPECTS IN LEPIDOPTERA. Wendell L. Roelofs and Andre Comeau in *Science*, Vol. 165, No. 3891, pages 398–400; July 25, 1969.

THE INSECT SOCIETIES. Edward O. Wilson. The Belknap Press of Harvard University Press, 1971.

LANGUAGE IN CHIMPANZEE? David Premack in *Science*, Vol. 172, No. 3985, pages 802–822; May 21, 1971.

NON-VERBAL COMMUNICATION. Edited by R. A. Hinde. Cambridge University Press, 1972.

32. Teaching Language to an Ape

SYNTACTIC STRUCTURES. Noam Chomsky. Mouton & Co., 1957.

THE GENESIS OF LANGUAGE. Edited by F. Smith and G. A. Miller. The M.I.T. Press, 1966.

BEHAVIOR OF NONHUMAN PRIMATES: VOLS. III–IV. Edited by Fred Stollnitz and Allan M. Schrier. Academic Press, 1971.

LANGUAGE IN CHIMPANZEE? David Premack in *Science*, Vol. 172, No. 3985, pages 808–822; May 21, 1971.

A FIRST LANGUAGE: THE EARLY STAGES. Roger Brown. Harvard University Press, 1973.

33. Language and the Brain

CEREBRAL DOMINANCE AND ITS RELATION TO PSYCHOLOGICAL FUNCTION. O. L. Zangwill. Oliver and Boyd, 1960.

DISCONNEXION SYNDROMES IN ANIMALS AND MAN: PART I. Norman Geschwind in *Brain*, Vol. 88, Part 2, pages 237–294; June, 1965.

DISCONNEXION SYNDROMES IN ANIMALS AND MAN: PART II. Norman Geschwind in *Brain*, Vol. 88, Part 3, pages 585–644; September, 1965.

HUMAN BRAIN: LEFT-RIGHT ASYMMETRIES IN TEMPORAL SPEECH REGION. Norman Geschwind and Walter Levitsky in *Science*, Vol. 161, No. 3837, pages 186–187; July 12, 1968.

TRAUMATIC APHASIA: ITS SYNDROMES, PSYCHOLOGY AND TREATMENT. A. R. Luria. Mouton & Co., 1970.

X ATTENTION, AWARENESS, AND THOUGHT

34. Attention and the Perception of Speech

CONTEXTUAL CUES AND SELECTIVE LISTENING. Anne M. Treisman in *Quarterly Journal of Experimental Psychology*, Vol. 12, No. 4, pages 242–248; November, 1960.

ON THE FUSION OF SOUNDS REACHING DIFFERENT SENSE ORGANS. D. E. Broadbent and Peter Ladefoged in *The Journal of the Acoustical Society of America*, Vol. 29, No. 6, pages 708–710; June, 1957.

PERCEPTION AND COMMUNICATION. D. E. Broadbent. Pergamon Press, Inc., 1958.

THREE AUDITORY THEORIES. J. C. R. Licklider in *Psychology: A Study of a Science*, edited by Sigmund Koch, Vol. 1, pages 41–144. McGraw-Hill Book Company, Inc., 1959.

35. The Asymmetry of the Human Brain

FUNCTIONAL ASYMMETRY OF THE BRAIN IN DICHOTIC LISTENING. Doreen Kimura in *Cortex*, Vol. 3, No. 2, pages 163–178; June, 1967.

SPATIAL LOCALIZATION IN LEFT AND RIGHT VISUAL FIELDS. Doreen Kimura in *Canadian Journal of Psychology*, Vol. 23, No. 6, pages 445–458; December, 1969.

HEMISPHERIC SPECIALIZATION FOR SPEECH PERCEPTION. Michael Studdert-Kennedy and Donald Shankweiler in *The Journal of the Acoustical Society of America*, Vol. 48, No. 2, Part 2, pages 579–594; August, 1970.

RIGHT HEMISPHERE SPECIALIZATION FOR DEPTH PERCEPTION REFLECTED IN VISUAL FIELD DIFFERENCES.

Margaret Durnford and Doreen Kimura in *Nature*, Vol. 231, No. 4302, pages 394–395; June 11, 1971.

36. The Split Brain in Man

CEREBRAL COMMISSUROTOMY. J. E. Bogen, E. D. Fisher and P. J. Vogel in *Journal of the American Medical Association*, Vol. 194, No. 12, pages 1328–1329; December 20, 1965.

CEREBRAL ORGANIZATION AND BEHAVIOR. R. W. Sperry in *Science*, Vol. 133, No. 3466, pages 1749–1757; June 2, 1961.

LANGUAGE AFTER SECTION OF THE CEREBRAL COMMISSURES. M. S. Gazzaniga and R. W. Sperry in *Brain*, Vol. 90, Part 1, pages 131–148; 1967.

MICROELECTRODE ANALYSIS OF TRANSFER OF VISUAL INFORMATION BY THE CORPUS CALLOSUM. G. Berlucchi, M. S. Gazzaniga and G. Rizzolati in *Archives Italiennes de Biologie*, Vol. 105, pages 583–596; 1967.

OBSERVATIONS ON VISUAL PERCEPTION AFTER DISCONNEXION OF THE CEREBRAL HEMISPHERES IN MAN. M. S. Gazzaniga, J. E. Bogen and R. W. Sperry in *Brain*, Vol. 88, Part 2, pages 221–236; 1965.

37. The Functional Organization of the Brain

HIGHER CORTICAL FUNCTIONS IN MAN. A. R. Luria. Basic Books, Inc., 1966.

HUMAN BRAIN AND PSYCHOLOGICAL PROCESSES. A. R. Luria. Harper & Row, Publishers, 1966.

THE CO-ORDINATION AND REGULATION OF MOVEMENTS. N. Bernstein. Pergamon Press, 1967.

TRAUMATIC APHASIA. A. R. Luria. Mouton, 1969.

INDEX